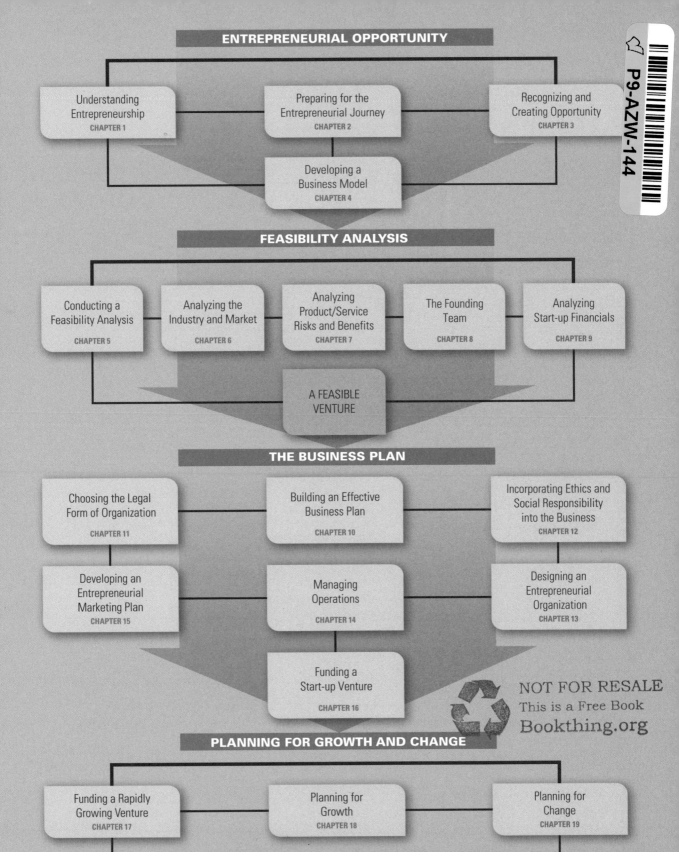

ENTREPRENEURIAL OPPORTUNITY

Understanding Entrepreneurship
CHAPTER 1

Preparing for the Entrepreneurial Journey
CHAPTER 2

Recognizing and Creating Opportunity
CHAPTER 3

Developing a Business Model
CHAPTER 4

FEASIBILITY ANALYSIS

Conducting a Feasibility Analysis
CHAPTER 5

Analyzing the Industry and Market
CHAPTER 6

Analyzing Product/Service Risks and Benefits
CHAPTER 7

The Founding Team
CHAPTER 8

Analyzing Start-up Financials
CHAPTER 9

A FEASIBLE VENTURE

THE BUSINESS PLAN

Choosing the Legal Form of Organization
CHAPTER 11

Building an Effective Business Plan
CHAPTER 10

Incorporating Ethics and Social Responsibility into the Business
CHAPTER 12

Developing an Entrepreneurial Marketing Plan
CHAPTER 15

Managing Operations
CHAPTER 14

Designing an Entrepreneurial Organization
CHAPTER 13

Funding a Start-up Venture
CHAPTER 16

PLANNING FOR GROWTH AND CHANGE

Funding a Rapidly Growing Venture
CHAPTER 17

Planning for Growth
CHAPTER 18

Planning for Change
CHAPTER 19

LAUNCHING
NEW VENTURES

Fifth Edition

LAUNCHING NEW VENTURES

AN ENTREPRENEURIAL APPROACH

Kathleen R. Allen

University of Southern California

Houghton Mifflin Company   Boston   New York

Executive Publisher: *George Hoffman*

Executive Editor, Business and Economics: *Lise Johnson*

Senior Marketing Manager: *Nicole Hamm*

Development Editor: *Suzanna Smith*

Senior Project Editor: *Bob Greiner*

Art and Design Manager: *Jill Haber*

Cover Design Director: *Anthony L. Saizon*

Senior Photo Editor: *Jennifer Meyer Dare*

Senior Composition Buyer: *Chuck Dutton*

New Title Project Manager: *Susan Peltier*

Editorial Associate: *Katilyn Crowley*

Marketing Assistant: *Lauren Foye*

Editorial Production Assistant: *Laura Collins*

Cover Art: © *Werner H. Muller/Peter Arnold Inc.*

Text Credits: **p. 262:** Statement of Mission reproduced with permission of Ben & Jerry's Homemade, Inc.; **p. 263** (eBay): These materials have been reproduced with the permission of eBay Inc. Copyright © eBay Inc. All rights reserved; and (leadertoleader): Reprinted with permission of Leader to Leader Institute; **p. 302:** Reprinted with special permission from "Playbook: Best-Practice Ideas," Business Week Online. Copyright © 2007 The McGraw-Hill Companies; **p. 495:** Chris Chen, Izu Matsuo, Winnie Peng. Reprinted with permission.

Printed in the U.S.A.

Library of Congress Catalog Number: 2007937004

ISBN-10: 0-547-01456-2
ISBN-13: 978-0-547-01456-2

1 2 3 4 5 6 7 8 9 –DOC– 11 10 09 08 07

BRIEF CONTENTS

CONTENTS

All chapters include Learning Objectives, a New Venture Checklist, Issues to Consider, Experiencing Entrepreneurship, and Relevant Case Studies.

Part Four Planning for Growth and Change   361

Appendix   495

PREFACE

Before writing the preface for this book, I looked back at the first edition, which came out in 1995, and thought about how the field of entrepreneurship has changed since then. In 1995, I wrote about the global economy and the information superhighway, a term for the Internet that has since disappeared. I said that large corporations were looking for ways to think and act small and that being customer driven was the name of the game. I wrote about change and passion, and being world class. Thirteen years and four editions later, those of us in this field are still writing and talking about the global marketplace, the Internet, and how we can all be more entrepreneurial—only the terms have changed a bit, and we as a business community now have a lot more experience in all three areas. We have seen trade barriers fall and the Internet bring our farthest international competitors, customers, and partners right to our doorstep. We have observed big companies break up into smaller, more entrepreneurial companies and watched with great interest as the pendulum swung back to a time of mergers, acquisitions, and multinational conglomerates, which characterize the business environment today. In the thirteen years that I have been writing *Launching New Ventures,* we have witnessed the meteoric rise of the Internet as a commercial vehicle that has captured the imagination of entrepreneurs and investors alike. We have seen the resiliency of the Internet as it rose from the ashes of the dot com bust in the spring of 2000, a bit bruised but so much wiser for the journey. Today the Internet is truly a frontier of opportunity for entrepreneurs.

Even with more knowledge about how to operate effectively in the global market, more knowledge and skills in building successful companies with extraordinary valuations, and more knowledge about how to innovate, we still have so much more to learn. And that is perhaps why so many of us enjoy the field of entrepreneurship, because it is messy, chaotic, and in a constant state of change. We are continually challenged to revise our ideas—what we knew to be true—in the face of almost daily changes in the countless variables that affect the launch and growth of a new business.

Launching New Ventures, Fifth Edition, represents the most current thought, ideas, and practices in the field of entrepreneurship. In fact, ever since its first edition, *Launching New Ventures* has endeavored to extend the boundaries of what we know about entrepreneurship.

Content, Organization, and Unique Coverage

Launching New Ventures is organized around the process of creating a new venture, from the recognition of an opportunity to the launch of the business. It is designed to help the reader organize and plan for venture creation by mentally (and sometimes physically) engaging in the various activities that entrepreneurs typically undertake. This book has never sought to be all things to all people. It has a very specific focus on pre-launch activities—those things that entrepreneurs do to prepare to launch a business and secure the first customer. Post-launch operations and growth are the subject of *Growing and Managing a Small Business*. Because the book focuses on the pre-launch phase of venture creation, it explores activities, such as opportunity creation and feasibility analysis, in more depth than the average book on entrepreneurship. The book also takes a distinctly entrepreneurial view of new businesses as opposed to a small business perspective. We believe that in a complex, global world, any new business owner, no matter whether that owner's business is the next Google or a small restaurant, needs to think like an entrepreneur. He or she needs to be opportunity-focused, innovative, growth-oriented, and constantly looking for new ways to create and capture value for customers.

Part One introduces the foundations of entrepreneurship and entrepreneurial opportunity that are important to understanding the decisions that entrepreneurs make, the environment in which they make those decisions, and the tasks they must undertake before launching a new company. In Chapter 1, students will learn the nature of entrepreneurial ventures and how they are distinct from other types of businesses as well as the role of entrepreneurship in the economy. Chapter 2 dispels many myths about entrepreneurs and helps readers understand the characteristics and behaviors that work for and against entrepreneurs. Students will also learn the entrepreneurial mindset that is so critical for a successful new business. Chapter 3 introduces the subject of opportunity and how entrepreneurs recognize and create opportunities for themselves. Part One closes with Chapter 4, "Developing a Business Model," where readers will learn how to define and develop a business concept, position it in the value chain, and evaluate it.

Part Two addresses the heart of entrepreneurial activity, the testing of a new business concept through feasibility analysis. Chapter 5 begins with an overview of feasibility analysis and its critical tools. Chapter 6 is a discussion of how to analyze an industry, which is the environment in which the new business will operate, and follows that with a discussion of the role of the primary customer for a new business and how to conduct market research on the customer to determine first customer and demand. Chapter 7 explores the way entrepreneurs develop products and services; it considers product development, prototyping, and intellectual property. Chapter 8 provides a way to assess the founding team and also discusses how to determine what gaps in experience and expertise may exist in the team and how to compensate for them with such solutions as strategic alliances and independent contractors. Part Two closes with Chapter 9, which discusses the start-up resources that entrepreneurs must gather and how to calculate how much capital will be required to launch the venture and operate it until it achieves a positive cash flow from the revenues it generates.

Part Three focuses on the business plan, which is the document that explains the strategy for executing a feasible business concept and building a company. It begins with Chapter 10, which describes how to move from a feasible concept to a business plan and how to organize and present the plan effectively. Chapter 11 looks at the legal form of the business and discusses the advantages and disadvantages of sole proprietorships, partnerships, and corporate forms. Chapter 12 explores the increasingly important topics of vision, ethics, and social responsibility. The value system of a new business shapes the culture of the business and the image it will have to live up to as it builds its reputation. Students will be challenged to define a vision for a new venture based on the values they believe to be important. They will also gain a greater understanding of the need for ethics and social responsibility in any business. Chapter 13 considers how entrepreneurial businesses are organized, how entrepreneurs determine the best business site, and how they develop their initial human resource capability. Chapter 14 focuses on how products and services are produced and addresses issues related to managing the operations of the business, such as production, quality control, customer service, outsourcing, and managing the supply chain. Chapter 15 deals with the role and implementation of the marketing plan and how to promote new products and services effectively with limited resources. It pays particular attention to the role of new media: social media, search engine marketing, and affiliate programs. The chapter also addresses personal selling and customer relationship management. Chapter 16 considers the entrepreneur's resource strategy, how to construct a resource plan, and how to finance a start-up venture with equity and debt.

Part Four looks at planning for growth and change in the new organization. It begins with Chapter 17, which looks at how to fund a rapidly growing venture, including the cost and process of raising capital, venture capital, and the IPO market. Chapter 18 deals with growth strategies for entrepreneurial ventures, such as strategic innovation, and intensive, integrative, and diversification growth strategies. It also pays particular attention to growing by going global. Chapter 19 discusses how to plan for change and for a successful exit or harvest.

Special Features in the Fifth Edition

The fifth edition contains a variety of features of value to both instructors and students.

▹ *Learning Objectives* highlight the key topics for each of the chapters.

▹ Entrepreneur *Profiles* that begin each chapter provide real-life examples to illustrate the application of chapter concepts and to inspire students.

Smaller-scale examples are also scattered throughout the chapters to maintain the real-life tone of the book.

▶ *"Global Insights" and "Socially Responsible Entrepreneurship" boxed inserts* highlight additional examples, companies, and organizations that have taken a global or a socially responsible approach to entrepreneurship.

▶ *Sidebar* features offer quick tips and interesting anecdotes.

▶ The *New Venture Checklist* serves as a reminder of the tasks that need to be completed at particular stages of the entrepreneurial process.

▶ *Issues to Consider* are questions at the end of each chapter that provoke interesting discussions in class.

▶ *Experiencing Entrepreneurship* is a series of activities at the end of each chapter that give students a chance to learn about entrepreneurship by getting involved in entrepreneurial activities and interacting with entrepreneurs and others in an industry of special interest to the student.

▶ Two new *Case Studies* have been added to the fifth edition to reflect a wider variety of businesses and types of entrepreneurs. The companies and products discussed include Command Audio (commercialization of an invention) and MySpace (the phenomenon of social networking). The cases are followed by discussion questions.

Supplemental Materials

An *Instructor's Resource Manual with Test Items* features suggestions for planning the course; instructional tips; learning objectives; lecture outlines; answers to end-of-chapter questions; a test bank with true/false, multiple-choice, and essay questions; and notes for the instructor's use with the case studies. The test bank is also offered in an electronic, editable, and downloadable format on the HMTesting CD.

The *website* contains resources for both students and instructors. For students it provides links to other useful sites on the web, ACE self-test questions, and examples of feasibility studies and business plans. For instructors it includes sample syllabi, PowerPoint slides for classroom presentation, and downloadable files from the *Instructor's Resource Manual* so that instructors can edit and adapt the material for their particular course needs.

A *video program*, along with a video guide, will be offered to supplement in-class discussions.

Acknowledgments

Many people helped make this fifth edition of *Launching New Ventures* happen—entrepreneurs, university students, professors, and, of course, the publishing staff at Houghton Mifflin. In particular, I would like to thank development editor Suzanna Smith, whose patience and humor got me through a tough production schedule. In addition, appreciation is due to

Susan McLaughlin, development editor, who kept me on the straight and narrow, and to Bob Greiner, senior project editor.

I want to thank the instructors who used the fourth edition and gave me feedback, as well as my students at the Lloyd Greif Center for Entrepreneurial Studies at the University of Southern California, who willingly share their ideas and comments with me. I also want to thank those instructors who provided formal manuscript reviews at various stages of the revision process for this and previous editions:

Donna Albano
Atlantic Cape Community College

Richard Benedetto
Merrimack College

Bruce Dickinson
Southeast Technical Institute

Todd Finkle
University of Akron

Frederick D. Greene
Manhattan College

Jo Hamilton
Franklin University

Timothy Hill
Central Oregon Community College

Lilly Lancaster
*University of South
Carolina–Spartanburg*

Clare Lyons
Hagerstown Community College

Ivan J. Miestchovich, Jr.
University of New Orleans

Eugene Muscat
University of San Francisco

Robert Novota
Lincoln University

Juan A. Seda
Florida Metropolitan University

Charles N. Toftoy
The George Washington University

Barry L. Van Hook
Arizona State University

Joseph S. Anderson
Northern Arizona University

Edward Bewayo
Montclair State University

Janice Feldbauer
Austin Community College

Susan Fox-Wolfgramm
San Francisco State University

Jeffry Haber
Iona College

Steven C. Harper
*University of North Carolina at
Wilmington*

Sandra Honig-Haftel

Tom Lumpkin
University of Illinois at Chicago

Steven Maranville
University of Houston–Downtown

Stephen Mueller
Texas Christian University

Terry Noel
Wichita State University

Fred B. Pugh
*Kirksville College of Osteopathic
Medicine*

Randy Swangard
University of Oregon

Lynn Trzynka
Western Washington University

John Volker
Austin Peay State University

Gene Yelle
SUNY Institute of Technology

Mark Weaver
University of Alabama

Dennis Williams
Pennsylvania College of Technology

David Wilemon
Syracuse University

And finally, I would like to thank my husband, John; and my children, Rob, Jaime (a writer herself), and Greg for their love and support.

K.R.A.

ABOUT THE AUTHOR

Kathleen R. Allen, Ph.D., is a professor in the Lloyd Greif Center for Entrepreneurial Studies in the Marshall School of Business at the University of Southern California, where she is also Director of the Marshall Center for Technology Commercialization, which focuses on helping faculty and students commercialize the technologies they develop at USC. At a national level, Allen is president of N2TEC Institute, whose mission is to bring the wealth creation process to rural regions through technology entrepreneurship. In addition to *Launching New Ventures,* Allen is the author of *Entrepreneurship and Small Business Management,* 4th ed., *Bringing New Technology to Market,* and *Growing and Managing an Entrepreneurial Business,* 2nd ed., as well as numerous trade books. As an entrepreneur, Allen co-founded a real estate development company, a real estate brokerage firm that she eventually sold, and two technology ventures, and she is a director of a company listed on the NYSE. In addition to a Ph.D. with an emphasis in entrepreneurship, Allen holds an M.B.A. and an M.A. in Romance languages.

LAUNCHING
NEW VENTURES

## Part One

ENTREPRENEURIAL OPPORTUNITY

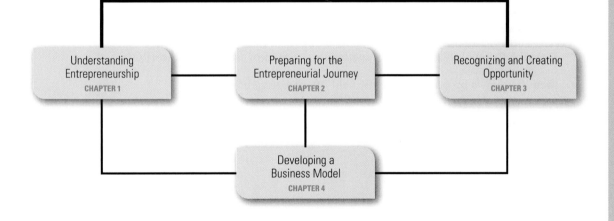

## Chapter 1

UNDERSTANDING ENTREPRENEURSHIP

"We cannot direct the wind, but we can adjust the sails."

—BERTHA CALLOWAY, founder, Great Plains Black Museum

LEARNING OBJECTIVES

▶ Define entrepreneurship.

▶ Explain the role of entrepreneurship in economic growth.

▶ Distinguish entrepreneurial ventures from small businesses in terms of their purpose and goals.

▶ Describe the evolution of entrepreneurship as a field of study since the 1960s.

▶ Identify today's broad trends in the field of entrepreneurship.

Profile 1.1 DAVID CAN STILL BEAT GOLIATH

How do you succeed in a tumultuous industry that can't seem to do anything right and that regularly sues its customers? Meet Mike Boyder and Marc Weinstein, co-founders of Amoeba Music, a three-store California retailer that is the self-proclaimed "largest independent record store on the planet." They have succeeded where industry giants Tower Records (no longer in business), Sam Goody (closed hundreds of stores), and even Target are struggling. They have succeeded despite a recording industry dominated by major labels that no longer produce huge wins. On the afternoon of the 2002 World Series between San Francisco and Anaheim, you could find hundreds of music lovers perusing the racks at the Market Street Megastore, because there they can find the largest collection of music anywhere and an environment that supports their love of music.

In 1992, Boyder and Weinstein opened their first store, a tiny outlet in Berkeley, California, that was jammed to the ceilings with more than 11,000 new and used CDs. In entrepreneurship, timing is usually critical, but these two couldn't have picked a worse time to launch their business. The major record labels were turning out megahits in record numbers. On the retail side of the equation, national chains were quickly acquiring the independents and positioning themselves as giants to take advantage of consumers' love of popular music.

Boyder and Weinstein knew that they had to come up with a very clever strategy to have a chance of surviving in that kind of market. The first part of the strategy was to recognize that independents don't have to be small, so one of the first goals was to outgrow their first location. In 1997, Amoeba moved into its 25,000-square-foot location in San Francisco that houses 250,000 titles. By comparison, Wal-Mart carries on average 350 titles and Tower Records in its heyday carried 60,000 titles, mostly current hits. Diversity and superior merchandising were also important to differentiate Amoeba from the superstores. Amoeba carries an enormously diverse collection of music genres and subgenres and uses every square foot of space for selling merchandise, rather than promoting merchandise as the competitors do. By contrast, the large retail chains tend to push a more homogeneous collection of music on consumers.

The second part of Amoeba's strategy described how customers would view the store not as a music store but rather as a music exchange where they could buy and sell used CDs. This trading concept proved to be a significant piece of their business model and afforded Amoeba margins as high as 70 percent on used CDs (margins are typically 20 percent on new CDs). Whereas the major labels and retailers saw music as a consumable, Amoeba saw it as a commodity for trade with long-term value.

The third component of Amoeba's strategy was to put people first, to make shopping for music a social experience. To make that happen, Amoeba hired people with music and communication skills, people who were obsessed with music. They created an environment exploding with art, live music, and people—and then stood back to watch the show.

The success of a business concept is measured in many ways, but certainly by the more traditional metrics of revenues and growth. In 2005, Amoeba's three-store revenues exceeded $60 million while industry sales fell 7.2 percent. Although they have a successful concept now, Boyder and Weinstein understand that it must continue to evolve as the industry changes. They don't want to make the same mistake that their superstore competitors did. They are now looking at building a website for paid music downloads, and they are launching a record label.

Sources: S. Perman, "Make Your Own Kind of Music," *Business Week Online* (January 30, 2006), http://www.businessweek.com; B. Breen, "What's Selling in America," *Fast Company* (January 2003), p. 86; S. Kang, "CDs a Tough Sell? Music Stores Try Toys," *Wall Street Journal* (June 20, 2003), p. B.1; and N. Wingfield and A.W. Mathews, "Behind the Missing Music: Huge Gaps in Offerings Plague Online Song Sites," *Wall Street Journal* (July 2, 2003), p. D1.

Entrepreneurship is a phenomenon that continues to excite the imagination of students interested in entering careers in which they must adapt to rapidly changing environments, inventors looking for ways to commercialize their discoveries, government leaders attempting to undertake economic development, and CEOs of large firms seeking to remain competitive in a global marketplace. Since the early 1980s, when entrepreneurship was identified as a driver of economic growth, both the term and the field of study have rapidly evolved. From the legendary solo entrepreneur of the 1970s and 1980s to the high-tech entrepreneurial teams and corporate venturers of the 1990s, and the Internet entrepreneurs of 2000 and beyond, entrepreneurs and the entrepreneurial mindset have become ubiquitous and essential elements of this new world.

What is entrepreneurship? Entrepreneurship is a mindset or way of thinking that is opportunity-focused, innovative, and growth-oriented. Although entrepreneurship is most commonly thought of in conjunction with starting a business, the entrepreneurial mindset can be found within large corporations, in socially responsible nonprofit organizations, and anywhere that individuals and teams desire to differentiate themselves from the crowd and apply their passion and drive to executing a business opportunity. Entrepreneurship is also a set of behaviors. Entrepreneurs recognize opportunity, gather the resources required to act on the opportunity, and drive the opportunity to completion. At its core, entrepreneurship is about a novel entry into new or established markets, and about exploiting new or existing products and services.[1]

Entrepreneurship is not the unique domain of any country, gender, race, age, or socioeconomic sector. It can be found in some form in every country, in every age group, and (increasingly) in women as often as in men. The entrepreneurial fever does not distinguish between the rich and the poor; in fact, it touches anyone who has the passion to be self-employed or anyone who is determined to be independent and to take charge of his or her life. The mindset of the entrepreneur can be understood and practiced, and the skills and behaviors of the entrepreneur can be learned and applied. The only characteristic of entrepreneurs that is arguably intrinsic is passion, or the drive to achieve something. Passion cannot be taught or practiced; it simply exists when the right elements come together—for example, when an entrepreneur recognizes a business opportunity and devotes his or her full attention and resources to bringing it to life. Passion is found in successful people in all disciplines—great musicians, artists, writers, scientists, and teachers. Passion is what drives a person to go beyond expectations and to be the best that person can be.

This chapter explores entrepreneurship as a phenomenon and lays the groundwork for the skills and behaviors that form the basis for the remainder of the text.

The Promise of Entrepreneurship

To understand the role that entrepreneurship plays in the economy, it is important to describe the process of entrepreneurship. What exactly happens during the entrepreneurial process? There is no agreement on the components and order of the entrepreneurial process, but, in general, three schools of thought dominate this issue: (1) an integrated input/output model proposed by Morris, Lewis, and Sexton that looks at which variables are put into the process in order to achieve a certain level of entrepreneurship[2]; (2) the career assessment approach, developed by Ronstadt, which proposes that the entrepreneur makes judgments about himself or herself, the new venture, and the environment based on where the entrepreneur is in his or her stage of career[3]; and (3) the new venture creation process, conceived by Gartner, which most closely relates to the approach in this text. Gartner proposes that the entrepreneurial process is affected by three major categories of variables: the individual entrepreneur and what he or she brings to the process; the environment, which consists of all of the external variables that affect the process such as industry, suppliers, and markets; and the organization, which is all the strategic aspects of the new venture such as focus, resources, and strategic partnerships.[4] Figure 1.1 depicts a view of the entrepreneurial process that forms the basis for the topics in this text. Note that the process is not linear, but rather consists of a fluid group of variables that

| FIGURE 1.1 | The Entrepreneurship Process |

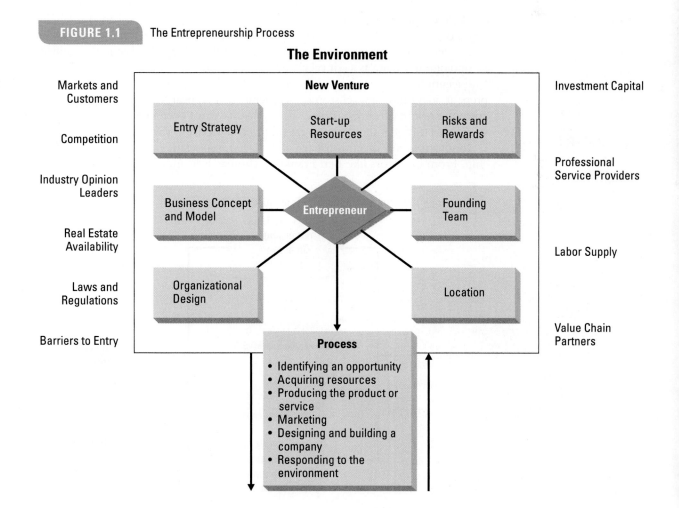

interact with the entrepreneur and his or her team. The entrepreneur then executes the process that results in a new venture. The new venture exists and conducts its business in an environment that includes all the variables that are external to it but that have an important impact on the business and its strategy for launch and growth. Entrepreneurs essentially play two roles—that of the catalyst, initiating and driving the process, and that of a ringmaster in a three-ring (or more) circus, managing the process through all its changes.

As an organic process, entrepreneurship provides many benefits to society. Chief among these benefits are economic growth, new industry formation, and job creation. The following sections offer some insight into these contributions of entrepreneurship.

ECONOMIC GROWTH

Early economists recognized that technology is the primary force behind rising standards of living[5] and that technological innovation would determine the success of many nations in the future. Technological innovation is the engine of growth for the U.S. economy; yet, for a long time economic growth was explained solely in terms of inputs of labor and capital. However, in the 1980s—referred to by many as the Decade of Entrepreneurship—the work of Paul Romer and others identified technological change as a critical element of a growth model that responds to market incentives.[6] Romer asserted that technological change happens when an entrepreneur identifies new customer segments that appear to be emerging, new customer needs, existing customer needs that have not been satisfied, or new ways of manufacturing and distributing products and services.[7] (See Figure 1.2.)

Innovation and invention have also played important roles in entrepreneurship. From inventors like Ben Franklin, Thomas Edison, and Gordon Gould to

FIGURE 1.2   Entrepreneurship and Technological Change

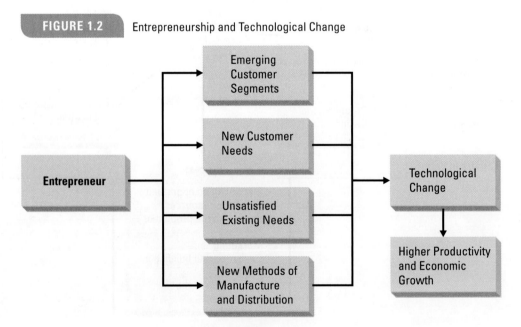

innovators like Bill Gates (Microsoft), Jeff Hawkins (Palm), and Jeff Bezos (Amazon), inventing new technologies and innovating or improving on existing technologies have been key drivers of entrepreneurial opportunity. Platform technologies such as the laser, discovered by Gordon Gould in 1957, serve as fertile ground for start-up ventures that license their technologies and apply them in a number of different ways. Countless examples throughout history illustrate how economic prosperity can result from invention and innovation, even as industries decline.

Technological change has also facilitated globalization and a new form of creative destruction by moving lower-skilled jobs out of the United States to countries where labor costs are substantially less. Although globalization has produced huge economic benefits, it has also resulted in lower costs of information and transportation, allowing for a broader range of goods and services to be traded over greater distances. Today very few markets enjoy freedom from competition in the global arena.[8] For example, where local markets in Florida and California once dominated the market for fresh fruits, today consumers are frequently unaware that much of their fresh produce comes from Chile, New Zealand, and other parts of the world. Even service companies cannot escape the impact of the global economy. India and Pakistan, for example, have become dominant players in the software programming industry by transmitting their services electronically and economically to anywhere in the world.

Economic growth comes about through technological change, investment, and trade, and all interact and are facilitated by entrepreneurship.[9] For instance, an inventor may develop a robotic mechanism for performing routine tasks in the manufacture of printed circuit boards. Implementing the invention requires an investment in plant and equipment, not to mention people. If the new technology is to be sold in another country, trade regulations, tariffs, and international investment or strategic partnerships may be required.

Those who, out of fear, would encourage a more protectionist or closed economy should consider the lessons of history. In the year 1000, China was far more technologically advanced than Western Europe, but then it closed itself off from the rest of the world and resisted change. By 1977, China had become a third-world country, one of the poorest in the world. Today, after reopening its economy, China is growing faster than any modern economy, in part because entrepreneurship has become an integral element of the economy.[10] The bottom line is that entrepreneurship brings about economic growth.

NEW INDUSTRY FORMATION

New industry formation is another important outcome of entrepreneurship and technological change. New industries are born when technological change produces a novel opportunity that an enterprising entrepreneur seizes. Figure 1.3 depicts the general life cycle of an industry relative to gross domestic product (GDP) and the number of firms entering and remaining in the industry at any point in time. In the earliest stages of an industry, a few firms enter. This is a time of rapid innovation and change as young firms struggle to become the industry standard bearers. As these entrepreneurial firms achieve noticeable levels of

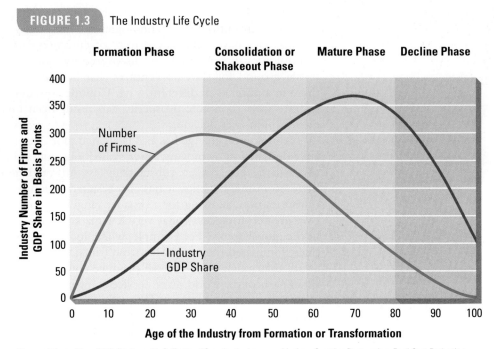

| FIGURE 1.3 | The Industry Life Cycle |

Source: Adapted from M.R. Darby and L.G. Zucker, "Growing by Leaps and Inches: Creative Destruction, Real Cost Reduction, and Inching Up," *Economic Inquiry* (January 2003), pp. 1-19.

success, more and more firms desiring to capitalize on the potential for success enter the industry. As the industry grows, it generally becomes more fragmented as a result of so many firms competing for position. At some point consolidation begins as the stronger firms begin to acquire smaller firms. Eventually, the number of firms in the industry begins to stabilize, and if innovation ceases to occur, the industry output may actually begin to decline. But as the gross domestic product (GDP) curve in Figure 1.3 depicts, the industry as a whole does not decline when the number of firms declines. In fact, the remaining successful companies have achieved economies of scale that make them more productive and efficient, so the industry continues to grow for some time.

In technological industries, the pattern of growth, shakeout, stabilization, and decline can be interrupted at any point by the entry of another disruptive technology. Why are so many more firms created than an industry can support? The answer lies in the uncertainty of not knowing which new firms will be successful in implementing their breakthrough technologies. In the case of incremental innovations, or improvements on existing technologies, research has shown that incumbent firms are generally more successful than new firms; but, with paradigm-shifting technologies, it is anyone's guess who the survivors will be.[11] Take the classic case of the rivalry between VHS and Sony Betamax to establish the standard for videotape recording. Sony was unwilling to license its technology to others, whereas VHS made it easy for people to use its format and develop new applications in niche markets based on it. As a consequence, customers flocked to VHS and made it the standard, even though Betamax was arguably the better technology.

JOB CREATION

Entrepreneurial ventures are responsible for significant job creation. The Small Business Administration (SBA) defines a small business as one with fewer than 500 employees, which by many standards is not very small and includes both high-growth technology ventures and small "mom and pops"—quite a range indeed. Still, businesses classified as small by this SBA definition represent 99.7 percent of all employers and pay more than 45 percent of the total U.S. private payroll. Furthermore, small businesses generate on average 60 to 80 percent of net new jobs annually in the United States. The SBA estimates that in 2005 there were 25.8 million businesses of all forms in the United States.[12]

The most recent data from 2004 indicate that small businesses created 1.9 million net new jobs as compared to 994,667 for large firms.[13] Realistically, however, small business's share of employment generally remains about 50 percent, because as small firms add employees, they eventually become large firms by SBA's definition.

The Nature of Entrepreneurial Start-ups

Entrepreneurial ventures and small businesses are related, but they are not the same in most respects. Both are important economically but each provides different benefits and outcomes. Schumpeter described entrepreneurs as equilibrium disrupters who introduce new products and processes that change the way we do things, while small-business owners typically operate a business to make a living.[14] Examples of small businesses are shops, restaurants, and professional service businesses. They form what has been called the "economic core."[15] It should not be forgotten, however, that most entrepreneurial ventures start small.

In general, entrepreneurial ventures have three primary characteristics. They are

1. Innovative
2. Value-creating
3. Growth-oriented

An entrepreneurial venture brings something new to the marketplace, whether it be a new product or service (the fax machine or an executive leasing service), a new marketing strategy (viral marketing on the Internet), or a new way to deliver products and services to consumers (*The Wall Street Journal Interactive Edition*). An entrepreneurial venture creates new value in a number of ways. Entrepreneurs create new jobs that don't merely draw from existing businesses; and by finding niches in the market, entrepreneurs serve customer needs that are not currently being served. Moreover, entrepreneurs typically have a vision of where they want their businesses to go, and generally that vision is on a regional, national, or (more often) global level.

By contrast, small lifestyle businesses are usually started to generate an income and a lifestyle for the owner or the family. Often referred to as mom-and-pop businesses, they tend to remain relatively small and geographically bound, most often because of a conscious decision on the part of the founder to keep the firm a small, lifestyle business. When Ken Finster started Micro/Sys, now a $4 million electronics manufacturer with 30 employees in Southern California, his goal was simply to provide an income for his family that would allow him to send his children to private schools and eventually college. Doing business in the highly competitive embedded systems industry, he also knew that the only way to survive was to think of his business as a service company that provided customized solutions in small lots, something large manufacturers couldn't afford to do.

Choosing what kind of business to start is very important, because that choice influences all subsequent decisions and determines what kinds of goals the entrepreneur is able to achieve. For example, if the intent is to grow a business to a national level, entrepreneurs will make different decisions along the way than if the intent is to own and operate a thriving restaurant that competes only in the local community. Generally, running a small business requires good management skills on the part of the owner, who must perform all tasks associated with the business as it grows. By contrast, entrepreneurs typically do not have the skills to handle the management aspects of the business and often prefer to hire experts to carry out that function, leaving the entrepreneur and the founding team free to innovate, raise capital, and promote the business. Chapter 2 will address the behavioral characteristics of entrepreneurs.

NEW BUSINESS FORMATION

Entrepreneurs engage in a number of activities in the process of creating a new venture. Although there is no universal agreement on where the process starts and where it ends, one view is that the process starts when one or more people decide to participate in the formation of a new business and devote their time and resources to founding it.[16, 17] Empirical research has found that the process is iterative, nonlinear, and nonsystematic.[18] And although entrepreneurs may go in many directions during the creation process, they typically use identifiable milestones to measure their progress.[19] These milestones include deciding to start a business, researching the concept, preparing for launch, securing the first customer, obtaining the business license, and many other activities that signal that the business is in operation.[20]

The process of new venture formation is depicted in Figure 1.4 and is characterized by four stages and three transitions or decision points. The first transition point occurs when an individual, acting independently or as an employee of a firm, decides to start a business. The nascent entrepreneur is an individual who starts an independent business; the nascent corporate venturer (or nascent intrapreneur) is someone who starts entrepreneurial ventures inside a large corporation. The second transition point comes about during the gestation of a new venture and includes all the start-up processes that lead to the birth of a firm and to the resulting infant firm. These start-up processes include feasibility analysis, business planning, and resource gathering, among other activities. Once the new venture survives start-up, it typically does one of three things: (1) It may grow at a rate higher than normal, (2) it may persist or survive to move into the adolescent (fourth) stage, or (3) it may be abandoned by its founders. Figure 1.4 also

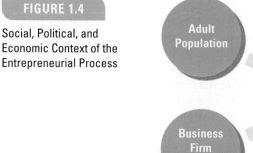

FIGURE 1.4

Social, Political, and Economic Context of the Entrepreneurial Process

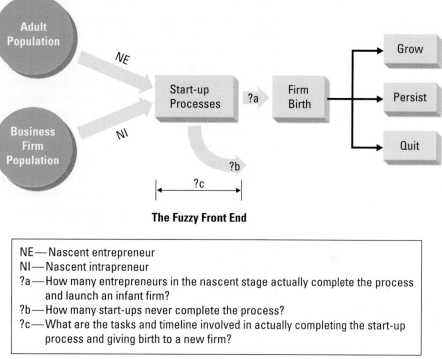

The Fuzzy Front End

NE—Nascent entrepreneur
NI—Nascent intrapreneur
?a—How many entrepreneurs in the nascent stage actually complete the process and launch an infant firm?
?b—How many start-ups never complete the process?
?c—What are the tasks and timeline involved in actually completing the start-up process and giving birth to a new firm?

Source: From Paul D. Reynolds, "National Panel of U.S. Business Start-ups: Background and Methodology," in *Databases for the Study of Entrepreneurship*, edited by J.A. Katz, pp. 153–227. Copyright © 2000, with permission from Elsevier. Modified by *Launching New Ventures* author to reflect the concept of the fuzzy front end and its associated probabilities.

depicts three question marks that represent aspects of the entrepreneurial process about which very little is known. The label ?a stands for the number of nascents that actually complete the process and launch; label ?b, the number that never complete the process; and label ?c stands for the tasks and times to completion.

Borrowing a term from product development, we can call the period of time prior to firm birth the *fuzzy front end*. The fuzzy front end has been modeled in economic terms. Simply put, the amount of investment an individual is willing to make in a new product—or, in this case, in a new venture—is a function of the probability of its success, the value of that success, and the cost of failure $[\text{Inv} = f(\text{PS} + \text{VS} + \text{CF})]$. A change in any one of these values will alter the economics of the bet.[21] In terms of the model in Figure 1.4, the nascent entrepreneur uses the time spent in the fuzzy front end to calculate the probability of success as an entrepreneur, what that success will mean in terms of return on his or her investment of time, money, and effort, and what the risk or cost of failure might be. Those probability estimates are highly subjective. But if the nascent entrepreneur uses the time in the fuzzy front end to gather information about the industry and market, test the business concept through feasibility analysis, and determine the conditions under which he or she is willing to move forward and start the business, much of the subjectivity will be eliminated. Moreover, the risk of start-up will be reduced, and the probability associated with the three outcomes will be more accurate.

It is not entirely clear what actually prompts an individual to become a nascent entrepreneur. Even with the risk assessment and risk mitigation that are part of preparing to launch a new venture, there appears to be no uniform mechanism that consistently results in an individual deciding to put forth the effort to launch a business. One individual may choose to enter the nascent stage despite a high level of risk. Another may choose to reject the nascent phase even under conditions where the perceived risk involved is low. Nascents appear to emerge from the population through both push and pull factors. *Push* is the mechanism that drives an individual to become a nascent entrepreneur because all other opportunities for income appear to be absent or unsatisfactory. *Pull* is the mechanism that attracts an individual to an opportunity and creates a "burning desire" to launch a business and capture a market.

What we do know about business formation is that since 2001, there has been steady growth in the number of new businesses started. In 2005 alone, 671,800 new firms were launched.[22]

BUSINESS FAILURE

The intent to start a business is not enough to make it happen. Many potential entrepreneurs drop out of the process as they move from intention to preparation. And a very high number give up before the new business makes the transition to an established firm.[23]

The Small Business Administration Office of Advocacy reports that two-thirds of new businesses survive at least two years. The survival rate at four years is 44 percent, and these numbers are similar across industries. Survival has been attributed to sufficient capital, having employees, and the entrepreneur's intention in starting the business.[24] (See Table 1.1.)

One body of research views failure as a liability of newness; that is, the firms that are most likely to survive over the long term are those that display superior levels of reliability and accountability in performance, processes, and structure. Because these factors tend to increase with age, failure rates tend to decline with age.[25] Young firms have a higher chance of failure because they have to divert their scarce resources away from the critical operations of the company in order to train employees, develop systems and controls, and establish strategic partnerships. Another body of research sees failure as a liability of adolescence, claiming that start-ups survive in the early years by relying on their original resources, but that as those resources are depleted, the company's chances of failing increase.

TABLE 1.1	Category	2001	2002	2003	2004	2005
Starts and Closures of Employer Firms, 2001–2005	New firms	585,140	569,750	612,296	642,600ᵉ	671,800ᵉ
	Firm closures	553,291	586,890	540,658	544,300ᵉ	544,800ᵉ
	Bankruptcies	40,099	38,540	35,037	34,317	39,201

ᵉEstimate using percentage changes in similar data provided by the U.S. Department of Labor, Employment and Training Administration.

Sources: U.S. Bureau of the Census; Administrative Office of the U.S. Courts; and U.S. Department of Labor, Employment and Training Administration.

Salesforce.com's Culture Is About Philanthropy

It's easy for a big company to write a check, even a very large one, and feel that it has done its corporate duty with respect to social responsibility. But Mark Benioff, founder/CEO of phenomenally successful Salesforce.com, believes that's not enough. Soon after founding what is now the industry leader in on-demand customer relationship management, Benioff formed the Salesforce Foundation, funding it with 1 percent of the company's stock, and then committing to donate 1 percent of profits to the community through product donations and an additional 1 percent of employee working hours to community service. Today more than 85 percent of the company's employees are involved in philanthropy. The mission is to "use Salesforce.com's people, technology and relationships to improve our communities, inspire youth to be more successful, support the world during times of extreme need, and promote compassionate capitalism." (http://www.salesforce.com/foundation) Benioff has even been successful at evangelizing his 1-percent philosophy to his San Francisco Bay Area neighbor, Google.

Source: M. Benioff, "Force for Change," *Inc. Magazine* (November 2006), p. 83.

The vital issue for entrepreneurs is not avoiding failure but minimizing the cost of a possible failure. That comes from starting with a robust business model and testing it in the marketplace prior to starting the business.

A Brief History of the Entrepreneurial Revolution

The term *entrepreneur* has existed for more than 250 years. The United States was founded on the principle of free enterprise, which encouraged entrepreneurs to assume the risk of developing businesses that would make the economy strong. However, it was not until the 1980s that the word *entrepreneur* came into popular use in the United States, and an almost folkloric aura began to grow around men and women who started rapidly growing businesses. These formerly quiet, low-profile people suddenly became legends in their own time, with the appeal and publicity typically associated with movie stars or rock musicians.

Marc Andressen, young entrepreneur and co-founder of Netscape Communications, was responsible for bringing the wealth of information on the Internet to the average person through a user-friendly graphical interface. Under the leadership of Howard Schultz, Starbucks rekindled the love of coffee and turned coffee drinking into an art form. Entrepreneurs such as these shake up the economy. They look for unsatisfied needs and satisfy them. Figure 1.5 summarizes the entrepreneurial evolution that has taken place since the 1960s.

THE DECADES OF ENTREPRENEURSHIP

In the mid-1960s, gigantic companies were the norm. General Motors in the 1960s was so large that it earned as much as the ten biggest companies in Great Britain, France, and West Germany combined.[26] The reason why U.S. companies

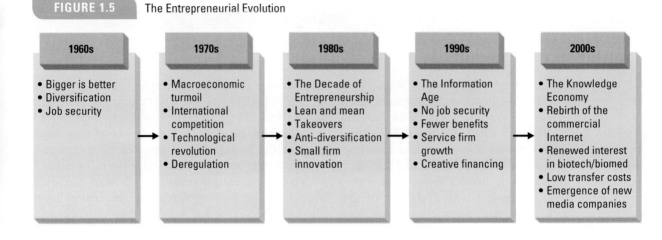

FIGURE 1.5   The Entrepreneurial Evolution

1960s
- Bigger is better
- Diversification
- Job security

1970s
- Macroeconomic turmoil
- International competition
- Technological revolution
- Deregulation

1980s
- The Decade of Entrepreneurship
- Lean and mean
- Takeovers
- Anti-diversification
- Small firm innovation

1990s
- The Information Age
- No job security
- Fewer benefits
- Service firm growth
- Creative financing

2000s
- The Knowledge Economy
- Rebirth of the commercial Internet
- Renewed interest in biotech/biomed
- Low transfer costs
- Emergence of new media companies

enjoyed such unrestricted growth at that time was that they lacked competition from Europe and Japan. Therefore, job security for employees was high, and companies tended to diversify by acquiring other kinds of businesses.

The 1970s saw the beginning of three significant trends that would forever change the face of business: macroeconomic turmoil, international competition, and the technological revolution. A volatile economic climate the likes of which had not been seen since World War II pervaded the 1970s. The Vietnam War economy brought inflation, the dollar was devalued, food prices skyrocketed as a consequence of several agricultural disasters, and the formation of OPEC sent gas prices up 50 percent. Furthermore, by the late 1970s the Federal Reserve had let interest rates rise to a prime of 20 percent. The result was no borrowing, no spending, and a recession that spilled into the 1980s, bringing with it an unemployment rate of 10 percent.[27] To compound the effects of the economy on business, by 1980 one-fifth of all U.S. companies faced foreign competitors that had far more favorable cost structures with much lower labor costs. Imports, particularly in the automobile and machine tools industries, were suddenly taking a significant share of the market from U.S. businesses.

The third event affecting business was the technological revolution brought about by the introduction in 1971 of the Intel microprocessor, the Mits Altair personal computer in 1975, and the Apple II computer in 1977. Microprocessors succeeded in rendering whole categories of products obsolete—such things as mechanical cash registers and adding machines, for example—and effectively antiquated the skills of the people who made them.

Increasing the pressure on business, the government ushered in a new era of business regulation with the Environmental Protection Agency, the Occupational Safety and Health Agency, and the Consumer Product Safety Commission, all of which increased costs to businesses. On the opposite front, deregulation forced planes, trucks, and railroads to compete, and in general big companies no longer had control of the marketplace.

By the early 1980s, business was in terrible shape. The Fortune 500 saw a record 27 percent drop in profits.[28] Large mills and factories were shutting down;

manufacturing employment was declining; and yet, ironically, productivity remained the same or increased. New, smaller manufacturers were still generating jobs—and not only manufacturing jobs, but service jobs as well. How was this possible?

To become competitive, the smaller, more flexible, entrepreneurial manufacturers had hired subcontractors who could perform tasks such as bookkeeping and payroll more efficiently. These service firms developed to support the needs of the product sector, but they inspired the creation of other service firms as well: People who work often need day-care or maid services, so even more jobs were being created.

With the creation of all these jobs, it is no wonder that the 1980s has been called the true Decade of Entrepreneurship by many, including the dean of management science, Peter Drucker, who was not alone in asserting that the United States was rapidly and by necessity becoming an entrepreneurial economy.[29] On the heels of the emergence of Silicon Valley and its legendary entrepreneurs, the mainstream press began to focus on business activities, creating many popular magazines such as *Inc.* and *Entrepreneur.*

Responding to this entrepreneurial drive, big business in the 1980s found it necessary to downsize and reverse the trend of diversification it had promulgated for so long. If big companies were going to compete with the dynamic, innovative smaller firms and fend off the takeover bids so prevalent in the 1980s, they would have to restructure and reorganize for a new way of doing business. This restructuring and reorganizing actually resulted in improved performance, increased profits, and higher stock prices. It also meant, however, that many jobs would no longer exist, employees would receive fewer benefits, and the only "secure" jobs left would be found in civil service.

Toward the end of the 1980s, researchers observed that young entrepreneurial ventures were internationalizing much earlier than expected and at a much smaller size.[30] A significant number of these ventures were in high-tech industries.[31] Large-sample empirical work revealed that directors and managers with significant international experience played a strong role in the internationalization of entrepreneurial ventures at start-up.[32] All these events moved this country toward a period in the 1990s that required the vision, the resources, and the motivation of the entrepreneur to seek new opportunities and create new jobs in a vastly different global environment electronically linked via the Internet. More than perhaps anything else, the 1990s were characterized as the Information Age. The commercial Internet emerged midway through the decade, and suddenly global competition and resources were more readily available than ever before. The Internet made entrepreneurship and the ability to compete alongside large established companies in the same markets a reality. Furthermore, with more and more jobs being shipped overseas, employees learned that job security was no longer a fact of life. U.S. companies quickly discovered that their competitiveness lay in the control of information and new ideas, and clearly the Internet was to play an important role in this new view of the world. The late 1990s brought the "dot com" bubble and the rush of the venture capital community to position itself for what appeared to be a new way of doing business. At the same time, the interest in non-Internet-related technology was waning as investors saw a much quicker return on their investment in the world of e-commerce.

The new millennium ushered in what many refer to as the *knowledge economy*, brought about by increased globalization and the competitive shift to more "knowledge-based economic activity."[33] In the new economy, the primary resource is knowledge rather than raw materials and physical labor.[34] Today, differences in economic performance in regions of the world can largely be explained by the presence or absence of entrepreneurship capital, which is essential to the development of new business models that monetize knowledge. Entrepreneurship capital is characterized by social networks that link entrepreneurs to educational institutions, industries, network brokers, and to resources.[35] California's Silicon Valley and the North Carolina Research Triangle are two examples of environments that have long prospered from knowledge-based economic activity and a high level of entrepreneurial enterprise.

The knowledge economy of the 2000s is also described by low-cost competition from Asia and Central and Eastern Europe that came about when transfer costs were driven down in the telecommunications and computer sectors, making it easier and less expensive to move capital and information.[36] Consequently, most routine tasks in production and manufacturing are now more efficiently accomplished in low-cost locations.

Without a doubt, the 2000s are also influenced by the commercial Internet. In 1998, the media declared that dot com was the business of the future—that it would change the way business is conducted forever. By the spring of 2000, the dot com bubble had burst and funding for dot com ventures virtually disappeared overnight. However, what remained was a distribution channel that had huge potential and merely required good business models to sustain it. Chapter 4 looks at some of these Internet business models. The Internet has also influenced the evolution of the media and entertainment industries with new media companies such as Demand Media, Ripe Digital Entertainment, and EyeSpot pioneering innovative ways to generate revenues from advertising and deliver broadcast quality video and audio to mobile devices.

Renewed interest in non-Internet-related technologies was one of the results of the dot com crash of 2000. A return to solid technologies that could be protected through patents was part of investors' new mantra, and a growing interest in biotech and biomedical devices emerged.

Entrepreneurial Trends

Throughout entrepreneurial history, various trends and patterns of change can be observed. For example, in the 1980s, the solo entrepreneur was prevalent; in the 1990s, team-based entrepreneurship became the norm. In modern times, four major trends have emerged as significant: the increase in female- and minority-owned businesses, social responsibility, the commercial Internet, and globalization.

WOMEN- AND MINORITY-OWNED BUSINESSES

Women now comprise one-third of all entrepreneurial activity globally. In middle-income countries like Venezuela and Thailand where necessity is a dominant motivator of entrepreneurship, women exhibit the highest levels of

Entrepreneurial Activity by
Gender and Country Clusters

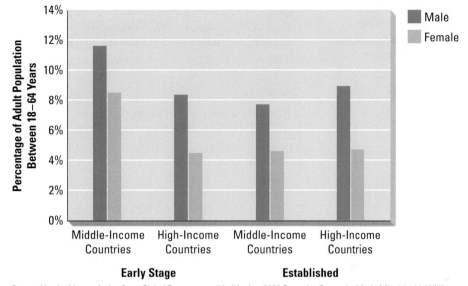

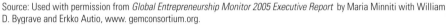

Source: Used with permission from *Global Entrepreneurship Monitor 2005 Executive Report* by Maria Minniti with William D. Bygrave and Erkko Autio, www. gemconsortium.org.

entrepreneurial activity at the early stages; in the high-income countries like Japan and the Netherlands, women exhibit the lowest levels of activity.[37] Figure 1.6 depicts entrepreneurial activity by gender and country cluster.

Small Business Administration data for the United States from 2006 indicate that women owned 6.5 million businesses or 28.2 percent of all non-farm businesses and generated $940.8 billion in revenues. They employed more than 7.1 million workers and produced $173.7 billion in payroll. Three-quarters of these businesses were sole proprietorships with receipts under $50,000, but as is typical of businesses in all sectors, high-growth ventures generated the bulk of revenues and new jobs.[38] The National Women's Business Council, compiling estimates from the U.S. Bureau of the Census, estimates that, as of 2006, majority female-owned firms (where 51 percent of the company is owned by a woman) number 7.7 million, generating $1.1 trillion in sales. Growth in these firms between 1997 and 2006 was twice that of all other U.S. firms.[39]

The size of women-owned businesses is a factor in the impact that they have on the economy. Research has found that the smaller size of women-owned businesses is explained by the different motivations of women to start businesses and by how they define success.[40] Specifically, they tend to redefine how business is done rather than attempt to make a huge impact on the economy. Size differences are also explained by the industries women choose to enter. More than 55 percent of all women-owned businesses are in services, and such businesses tend to be smaller in size.[41]

In 1997, 5.8 percent of all businesses were owned by Hispanic Americans, 4.4 percent by Asian Americans, 4.0 percent by African Americans, and 0.9 percent by American Indians. In 2005, the Office of Advocacy of the SBA reported that minority-owned businesses now account for 15 percent of all U.S. businesses as

TABLE 1.2

Percent of Women-Owned
Business by Ethnicity

White (Non-Hispanic)	Asian American	African American	Hispanic	American Indian and Alaskan Native	Pacific Islander
85.95%	5.25%	8.43%	8.33%	1.23%	0.18%

of 2001. Asian American-owned businesses earned more than 51 percent of all business revenues in the minority-owned sector, with Hispanic Americans following at 31 percent; African Americans at 12 percent; and American Indians at 6 percent.[42] A larger percentage of minority-owned businesses are led by women, as seen in Table 1.2.

Although they constitute a minority, Asian Americans have been very successful as entrepreneurs, owning about one-third of the high-tech firms in Silicon Valley by the early 1990s and 500 companies in the San Gabriel Valley of California by the late 1990s.[43] The highest rate of self-employment is found in the Korean American community; more than one in ten Korean Americans are business owners. Hispanic-owned firms tend to be strong in transportation and construction and were the fastest growing minority group between 1982 and 2002.[44] Among all of the Hispanic groups, Mexican Americans own the largest number of companies. The increasing tide of Hispanic businesses can be attributed to immigrant entrepreneurs who see opportunity where others do not. Rolando Herrera wanted to be a winemaker in Napa, California. To accomplish that goal, he washed dishes, broke rocks, and often slept in his car. He also recognized that the Latino market was untapped when it came to wine, which presented an opportunity for him to capture a niche and satisfy an unmet need. Building on this opportunity, Herrera founded his winery and realized his dream. Today his wine, Mi Sueño, is well-known and was even chosen to be served at President George W. Bush's first state dinner with then Mexican president Vicente Fox.[45]

SOCIAL RESPONSIBILITY

More than at any previous time, we are seeing increasing evidence of social responsibility on the part of entrepreneurs. Social responsibility is about a company's accountability to society, which can range from proactive social programs to rewarding employees for getting involved in community activities. When Mellody Hobson started her Chicago-based investment firm, she made sure that its social mission had equal importance to her now ninety-seven employees. Using her Ariel Community Academy as the basis for teaching Chicago-area children how to invest, she finds that it "allows us to attract like-minded employees who have a sense of community."[46] What used to be only "checkbook philanthropy," responding to a solicitation for donations with money, has now expanded to include the notion of devoting personal time and effort to a nonprofit cause. Social responsibility is the subject of Chapter 12.

THE INTERNET

The Internet will certainly be at the center of many of the major entrepreneurial trends for some time to come. The seismic shift currently underway to move from PC-based broadband Internet to mobile Internet will produce a multitude of new opportunities. It is, in effect, the new client/server model. When one considers that the United States now lags behind China, Japan, Germany, the United Kingdom, Italy, and South Korea in mobile phone to Internet user ratio, this indicates that a lot of room for entrepreneurs exists in the U.S. market. If entrepreneurs simply look at what young people are doing, they will be able to identify at least four major areas for potential innovation: social networking (MySpace.com), mobile content and services (Jamster), social tagging (Flickr), and web-based collaboration, management, and task software (Basecamp). User-generated content has been called the new Web 2.0. The ability of Internet users to post content such as articles, blogs, and reviews, and benefit from revenue sharing with host sites is emerging as public journalism and is becoming increasingly relevant.

In the current decade, the Internet has succeeded in disintermediating aspects of the value chain and in lowering the barriers to entry in some industries. Internet businesses now provide tremendous access to information and personalization as well as an easy way for entrepreneurs to sell goods without the need for a physical location. It has also become the vehicle for next-generation media companies like Demand Media, Facebook, and YouTube that create new and interesting ways to attract advertising dollars and major advertisers who want to do a more effective job of targeting their customers and look to communities of interest to find them. Some are predicting that pay-per-call is not far away. Good marketers understand that one-to-one contact with a customer on the phone is more likely to result in a sale than an Internet ad that a potential customer clicked on. The business models of the Internet are discussed in more depth in Chapter 4.

GLOBALIZATION

Today customers and businesses can find the best products and the best prices anywhere in the world and make purchases more easily through the Internet than by shopping at retail stores or wholesale outlets. Entrepreneurs no longer have the luxury of confining the scope of their businesses to specific geographic regions and expecting to compete only against companies in that region. Today competitors may come from a part of the world that was previously unknown to the entrepreneur. Likewise, entrepreneurs can now compete in global markets almost as easily as they compete in domestic markets. They can move from a U.S. market of 300 million people to a global market of 6.2 billion. In fact, the Small Business Administration reports that 31 percent of all exported goods and services come from businesses with fewer than 100 employees.

Entrepreneurs have looked to global markets to find less expensive ways to produce new products and to locate strategic partners to facilitate their entry into international markets. The Internet has brought the farthest reaches of the world to the entrepreneur's backyard and made it possible to market globally quickly and efficiently.

Looking Ahead: The Organization of the Book

Starting a new venture is a process that begins long before the business ever opens its doors. That process is rarely linear but rather a more iterative—even chaotic—process; however, the entrepreneurial process does have direction and goals. This book is divided into four sections that reflect the entrepreneurial process. Part One focuses on the opportunity. Chapter 1 serves as an introduction to the field of entrepreneurship and the environment in which entrepreneurs start new ventures today. Chapter 2, another foundational chapter, explores the entrepreneurial journey from the entrepreneur's perspective and helps the reader prepare for this journey. At Chapter 3, the process of entrepreneurship begins with the recognition of an opportunity through the development of creativity and problem-solving skills. Chapter 4 covers the development of a business concept and business model.

Part Two (Chapters 5 through 9) explores feasibility analysis in detail by examining the various tests that entrepreneurs use to determine the conditions under which they are willing to move forward with a new business concept.

Once there is a feasible concept, the business plan is the document that explains the execution strategy for the concept. Part Three focuses on the business plan and what it adds to the information gained from the feasibility study. Whereas the feasibility process works from the largest area of study—the industry—inward to a decision, the business planning process begins with the entrepreneur and his or her core values, mission, and goals that form the basis for all the decisions that will be made about the company. The business plan documents the creation of a new company—the business model, operating plan, management plan, marketing plan, financial plan, and contingency plan as well as the funding strategy. Chapters 10 through 16 deal with the development of the business plan.

Any business undergoes growth and change, so Part Four focuses on those issues. Chapters 17 through 19 consider how to fund and grow the business, plan for unexpected changes, and architect a harvest strategy for the entrepreneur and investors.

Entrepreneur skills are key not only to economic independence and success but literally to business survival. The marketplace puts a premium on creativity, initiative, independence, and flexibility. Entrepreneurs who develop those behaviors and display those characteristics will be more likely to succeed.

New Venture Checklist

Have you:

☐ Determined how current trends will affect your search for a business idea?

☐ Decided whether an entrepreneurial venture makes sense for you over a small-business venture?

☐ Examined the history of entrepreneurship to predict what the next decade might look like?

Issues to Consider

1. Define the term *entrepreneurship.*
2. As the mayor of your community, what incentives would you put into place to encourage entrepreneurship?
3. Describe the current environment for entrepreneurship. How does it differ from the environment pre-1980?
4. Which of the entrepreneurial trends discussed in the chapter has had the biggest impact and why?
5. Should all businesses be socially responsible businesses? Should social responsibility be a component of every business?
6. How do entrepreneurial ventures differ from small businesses?

Experiencing Entrepreneurship

1. Interview an entrepreneur in an industry or business that interests you. Focus on how and why this entrepreneur started his or her business. Be sure to include the following:

    a. Contact information

      The entrepreneur's name, address, title, company name, and phone number

    b. Background

      How did you find this person and why did you choose her or him?

      Why is this person an entrepreneur?

      What influenced the entrepreneur to identify and pursue this opportunity?

      How did the entrepreneur's background (family history, prior education, and work experience) affect the opportunity discovered?

    c. Describe the opportunity that the entrepreneur decided to pursue and the process the entrepreneur used to evaluate the opportunity.

      How did the entrepreneur evaluate the opportunity?

      What criteria did the entrepreneur use to decide whether to pursue the opportunity?

      What were the perceived risks of this opportunity and how did the entrepreneur expect to manage them?

    d. What did the entrepreneur do to turn the opportunity into a business?

      Identify specific activities the entrepreneur undertook to develop the opportunity into a business.

      Identify when the entrepreneur did these activities (provide dates: month and year).

      Identify important contacts and individuals who were helpful during the start-up process.

      What major problems did the entrepreneur encounter along the way?

      How were these problems solved?

    e. What advice would the entrepreneur give to someone thinking about pursuing an opportunity?

      Why was this entrepreneur successful?

      Analyze how the factors identified in parts (b), (c) and (d) affected this entrepreneur's success.

2. Visit your local Chamber of Commerce and use an Internet search engine to discover how many of the major entrepreneurial trends discussed in the chapter are reflected in businesses in your community. In a two-page report, discuss your findings.

Relevant Case Studies

Case 1 Overnite Express, p. 438

Case 4 MySpace: The Online Reality Show, p. 458

Case 5 iRobot: Robots for the Home, p. 463

## Chapter 2

PREPARING FOR THE ENTREPRENEURIAL JOURNEY

"Success isn't permanent, and failure isn't fatal."

—MIKE DITKA, professional football coach

LEARNING OBJECTIVES

▶ Dispel myths about entrepreneurs.

▶ Understand the pathways to entrepreneurship.

▶ Prepare to become an entrepreneur.

Profile 2.1 FROM PROFESSOR TO ENTREPRENEUR

Sometimes being a researcher can box you into one thing for the rest of your life—that is, if you let it. Or it can become the launch pad for a whole new career. Corinna Lathan, a thirty-something Ph.D. in neuroscience from MIT, was interested in too many things. While at MIT, she worked at the Center for Space Research, which gave her the opportunity to see firsthand how technology can improve human performance. Upon finishing her Ph.D., she took a job at Catholic University in Washington, DC, where she taught biomedical engineering and explored medical applications of virtual reality and telecommunications technology. Through a friend who worked with disabled children, she became aware of the lack of toys designed for the special needs of these children. She saw an opportunity to apply her skills and experience in a new way, and as a result the idea for CosmoBot was born.

CosmoBot is a small, metallic humanoid that can be programmed to speak to a child or respond to a child's voice. When a child wears a glove and cap embedded with hidden sensors, she can raise her arms to make CosmoBot do the same or can wiggle her head and CosmoBot will do likewise. The robot also records the child's movements so that progress can be tracked and reports can then be sent through the web-based interface so that program adjustments can be made via the Internet as needed.

In 1999, Lathan decided to take a leave of absence from the university to launch her company, AnthroTronix, which would produce CosmoBot. She based the company in College Park, Maryland. After a year working full-time in development mode at the company, she returned to the university, where she was due to get tenure. However, after only a month, she again left the university, this time for good, to devote herself full-time to AnthroTronix.

The company defines itself as follows:

> AnthroTronix provides Research & Development services under contract to government agencies and private sector companies in the defense, space, and healthcare rehabilitation industries. AnthroTronix designs, develops, and tests systems for its clients to optimize human-technology interaction. (http://www.anthrotronix.com/template.php?content=currentprojects)

Lathan had a decision to make. The company could become the best in one tiny area of research or it could develop real-world applications in a variety of areas. Lathan chose the latter. In fact, in addition to learning aids, her company is now working on developing gesture-controlled devices that let soldiers send wireless communications to each other using only hand motions. Her research and development are funded by government grants.

Lathan's work has received a number of awards. In May 2002, Lathan was named one of the world's 100 Top Young Innovators by *Technology Review*, MIT's Magazine of Innovation, and in January 2006, she was named a Young Global Leader by the Forum of Young Global Leaders, an affiliate of the World Economic Forum.

In 2005, AnthroTronix spun off a subsidiary company, AT KidSystems, which commercializes products developed by the parent company. Lathan is continuing to look for new ways to facilitate the interface between humans and technology and build on the platform she has created.

Sources: E. Barker, "Corinna Lathan Has Been Designated a Young Global Leader in 2006" (January 12, 2006), AnthroTronix, http://www.anthrotronix.com/template.php?content=inthenews; "The Prodigal Professor," *Inc. Magazine* (September 2002), http://www.inc.com; AnthroTronix website at http://www.anthrotronix.com; and "Corinna Lathan Named One of the World's Top Young Innovators by *Technology Review*, MIT's Magazine of Innovation" (May 23, 2002).

Entrepreneurship is a personal journey that begins in the mind of the nascent entrepreneur. It is a personal journey because business is fundamentally about people—how they interact, make decisions, plan for the future, deal with conflict, and so on. In fact, all of entrepreneurship can be reduced to people. From the entrepreneur's motivation to start a business to the decisions made about growth, customers, facilities, employees, and the exit from the business, everything comes down to people and the needs of those people. Needs and goals must be satisfied through the start-up of a new venture or entrepreneurs will not have the motivation to continue in their efforts. The new venture must also satisfy the needs of customers or they will not be motivated to buy. Kim Camarella understood this. Through the eyes of her plus-size best friend, she learned about the difficulty that larger young women have finding fashionable apparel. This motivated Camarella to found Kiyonna Klothing, now a successful line of plus-size apparel that is satisfying a real need in the market (http://www.kiyonna.com).

Finding a market need is a vital first step. Market needs are defined by customers who purchase based on product or service benefits. Another essential step in the entrepreneurial journey is assembling the right team, which can often make the difference between success and failure. It is very difficult today to start a new company as a solo entrepreneur, mostly because any single person rarely has all the knowledge and skills required to be successful, so assembling a great team is critical. As part of an enormously successful team, Eric Schmidt stays in the background when it comes to the press about the company he co-founded with his much younger partners Sergey Brin and Larry Page—Google. Brin and Page were the influence for the university culture that is now renowned at Google. This is a team that believes in creating a family in their workplace environment— "it's easier to get a family united behind a cause than a bunch of employees," says Schmidt.[1] In the fast-moving Internet marketplace, having a team with compatible values and a laser focus on the company vision is a sure route to success.

How large to grow the business is very much a personal decision. Entrepreneurs who want to balance work with a personal life may choose to start a business that generates significant revenues but does not require a great deal of people and physical assets to manage. That was the position that Neil Johnston took. After several unsuccessful partnerships that had him doing most of the work, in 2001 he merged his label business with one of his customers' businesses, a solo entrepreneur company that sold bar code labels to libraries. Total investment by the parties to this venture was $383,000, but it added substantially to the company's ability to grow. By 2002, ID Label had made the Inc. 500 list of fastest-growing private companies in the United States, with revenues at about $2.2 million. Johnston was able to reduce his workload and finally live the kind of life he wanted. Johnston is a prime example of an entrepreneur who does not want the type of business that employs many people. He realized early on that in his case more employees would not necessarily equal more profits. Furthermore, the challenges of managing all those employees would involve more stress than he wanted to take on. Instead, he kept the business at a manageable size and secured the balanced life he had always wanted.[2]

The decision about when and how to exit the business is also a very personal one because it is based on the entrepreneur's goals and values. Some entrepreneurs start many ventures in their lives, so they experience the exit multiple times. Others, like Bill Gates of Microsoft or Michael Dell of Dell Computers, stay with their businesses and choose not to exit. And still other entrepreneurs see their exit strategy change in response to unforeseen circumstances. John Lusk co-founded Platinum Concepts Inc. in July 1999 with some of his classmates from the Wharton School of Business at the University of Pennsylvania. Their core product was the MouseDriver, a computer mouse shaped like a golf-club head. Lusk's goal was to build the company up as fast as he could in two years and then sell it to another business. His plan forecasted the company's revenues skyrocketing to $10 million in 6 months. Unfortunately, this did not happen within his predetermined timeframe. It took approximately 18 months to build any sales for the MouseDriver. As a result, Lusk altered his exit strategy, deciding not to sell the company but instead to spend more time diversifying the product line and getting his products into the mass market.[3]

As discussed in Chapter 1, entrepreneurship is a very complex process inspired by and driven by the entrepreneur and his or her co-founders. With the entrepreneur playing such an important role, one would think that there would be a definable profile of a successful entrepreneur. But research has failed to find that stereotypical entrepreneur. There are, in fact, no psychological or sociological characteristics that can predict who will become an entrepreneur or who will succeed as an entrepreneur.[4] This chapter explores the personal journey of entrepreneurship, what it takes to become a successful entrepreneur, and the many ways to approach entrepreneurship throughout a career.

Saying Goodbye to Stereotypes

Given the frequency with which entrepreneurs are discussed in the media, it is not surprising that stereotypes have developed around them. Not all of those stereotypes are flattering and most are simply false. This section attempts to dispel some of the myths surrounding entrepreneurs so that the entrepreneurial journey can begin on a solid, factual foundation.

MYTH 1: ENTREPRENEURS START BUSINESSES SOLELY TO MAKE MONEY

Entrepreneurs start businesses for many reasons, but the number-one reason appears to be their need for independence and to create something new. They don't want to work for someone else; they want to create something they can call their own. Early studies found, and later research confirmed, that entrepreneurs are motivated intrinsically by such things as the desire for independence, the need to be in control of one's destiny, and the satisfaction of being ultimately responsible for the success or failure of the venture.[5] This does not suggest that entrepreneurs don't want to make money; they do. However, the same research found that entrepreneurs are secondarily motivated by extrinsic rewards such as the financial performance of the venture.

MYTH 2: IT TAKES A LOT OF MONEY TO START A BUSINESS

Another false assumption about entrepreneurship is that it takes a lot of money to start a business. Nothing could be further from the truth. Every year *Inc. Magazine* profiles entrepreneurs who started their businesses on $1,000 or less. For example, Lori Bonn Gallagher parlayed her love of travel and of finding unique jewelry into a $2.8-million business. Starting with $1,000 worth of samples of handblown glass jewelry that she discovered in France and a successful selling strategy, Gallagher secured a deal with Nordstrom to begin selling her imported jewelry in the United States. Today her jewelry is designed at her headquarters in Oakland, California, manufactured in Bali, and sold in retail outlets such as Nordstrom, Discovery Store, and Boston's Museum of Fine Arts museum shop.[6] When it comes to the Inc. 500 Fastest Growing Private Companies, the amount of start-up capital is not a predictor of ultimate success.[7] Other factors like the management team and the market being addressed are more important. In fact, some research has determined that it is not specifically the amount of capital the entrepreneur possesses at start-up that is important but rather how many resources (founding team, network of contacts, connections in the value chain, and so forth) the entrepreneur can access and/or control.[8]

MYTH 3: IT TAKES A GREAT IDEA

Jim Collins's research, which was documented in the bestseller *Built to Last,* dispelled the myth that it takes a great idea to start a business. In fact, most of the great businesses that have been successful for at least 50 years—companies such as Walt Disney, Sony, and Merck—didn't start with a great idea. They started with a great team who simply wanted to create an enduring company. In general, venture capitalists say that they will take a great team and a large market opportunity in a fast-growing area over a great idea any day, because it takes a superior team to execute a successful business concept and it takes customers in a fast-growing market to create the return to the investors.[9] Often it's not the idea, but the execution plan that makes the business a success. Howard Schultz did not invent coffee, nor did he invent specialty coffee. Instead, with Starbucks he invented a way for customers to have an experience with coffee, and he made sure they were never far from a Starbucks where they could get their fix. Many great ideas exist, but most never find their way to the marketplace.

MYTH 4: THE BIGGER THE RISK, THE BIGGER THE REWARD

Students of entrepreneurship often hear that risk is correlated with reward—the greater the risk taken, the greater the reward expected. Certainly, it appears that investors hold that point of view. But *risk* is a relative term, and the goal of most entrepreneurs is to reduce the level of risk in any venture. In fact, money people expect entrepreneurs to do what it takes to reduce the risk for them, such as testing the market, writing a business plan, and so forth. And no one expects the business to be worth less because risk was reduced. It is actually to the entrepreneur's advantage to reduce risk for investors so that the entrepreneur can retain more of the equity.

MYTH 5: A BUSINESS PLAN IS REQUIRED FOR SUCCESS

There is no question that lenders, investors, and others want to see a business plan before agreeing to deal with an entrepreneur. They have a lot to lose if the company fails, so they need to satisfy themselves that the entrepreneur knows what she or he is doing. But many entrepreneurs have started highly successful businesses without having a formal plan in place—including recognizable companies such as Pizza Hut and Crate and Barrel that have survived for decades. Other entrepreneurs have put up websites and been "in business" within a day, making money within a couple of weeks. The truth is that research has not agreed on the value of business planning or even on what components of business planning are correlated with success. In the earliest stages of start-up, what may be more important than the business plan itself is spending time and resources testing the market for the feasibility of the business concept in terms of actual sales. Once such feasibility is determined, a business plan helps the entrepreneur work through the building of a company.

MYTH 6: ENTREPRENEURSHIP IS FOR THE YOUNG AND RECKLESS

Many people believe that if they haven't started their first business by the time they are 30, it is too late. They think that the energy, drive, resources, and risk involved are suitable only for the young. But many great businesses have been started by older entrepreneurs who had the passion to do something original. Ray Kroc started McDonald's at age 52, and Colonel Harland Sanders was over 60 when he started Kentucky Fried Chicken. Research supports the conclusion that being older can be an asset when starting a business. The Global Entrepreneurship Monitor Report found that men and women in the 45–64 age bracket are responsible for 36 percent of all the entrepreneurial activity in the United States and for 22 percent of the activity globally. Fifty percent of entrepreneurial activity is accomplished by men and women between the ages of 25 and 44.[10] Entrepreneurship is for anyone, regardless of age, who wants to experience the thrill of building something from scratch and making it a success.

MYTH 7: ENTREPRENEURSHIP CANNOT BE TAUGHT

This myth is a corollary to "Entrepreneurs are born, not made." Both are wrong. There is a lot about entrepreneurship that can be taught, including specific skills and behaviors. People who don't naturally have the skills of a successful entrepreneur can certainly learn and apply them. Management guru Peter Drucker asserted, "The entrepreneurial mystique, it's not magic, it's not mysterious, and it has nothing to do with the genes. It is a discipline. And, like any discipline, it can be learned."[11] Scholarly research over a number of years has supported that claim.[12] What cannot be taught, however, is the passion to achieve. Some have called it the "fire in the belly." And indeed, what motivates someone to leave Harvard University to start a business (like Bill Gates of Microsoft) or to start by driving a garbage truck (like Wayne Huizenga, who founded Waste Management) cannot be learned. It is simply part of a person's makeup as it is in any successful person in any field of endeavor.

Pathways to Entrepreneurship

Entrepreneurs are as varied as the kinds of businesses they start. For every characteristic or behavior that defines one successful entrepreneur, another successful entrepreneur who displays completely different characteristics and behaviors can be found. There are many paths to entrepreneurship, and in the following sections we look at five broad categories: the home-based entrepreneur, the Internet entrepreneur, the serial entrepreneur, the traditional entrepreneur, and the corporate venturer.

THE HOME-BASED ENTREPRENEUR

Home-based businesses comprise over two-thirds of all sole proprietorships, partnerships, and S-corporations in the United States and over 50 percent of all businesses.[13] More than 60 percent of these home-based businesses are in the construction and service sectors. Many of these are hobby businesses, consulting, and freelance type businesses, but many others are entrepreneurial ventures that compete in the same arena as brand name businesses with large facilities. Technology has made it possible to do business from virtually anywhere, so entrepreneurs don't have to work in traditional office spaces to start or run businesses. Moreover, home-based business owners can tap into more resources than ever before from their desktops to locate help for any problem they may be facing, from finding business forms to seeking legal advice to learning how to start and run a business. In addition, U.S. tax laws have become friendlier to home-based business owners, who can take a deduction for their home office space and appropriate business expenses.

Many entrepreneurs with aspirations to grow their businesses start from home to save on overhead and reduce the risk of start-up. Once the concept has proved itself, they often move out to acquire facilities that will support the growth of the company and the addition of employees. Some entrepreneurs choose never to have office space but rather to enjoy the ability to move around and do business from their home, boat, car, or vacation home. With Fortune 500 technologies now available to small businesses at affordable prices, business really can be conducted from anywhere.

THE INTERNET ENTREPRENEUR

The birth of the commercial Internet gave rise to Internet entrepreneurs, who transact all their business with customers, suppliers, strategic partners, and others on the Internet and deal in digital products and services that, for the most part, do not require bricks-and-mortar infrastructure (such as warehousing and physical distribution). Notable exceptions are companies like Amazon and bricks-and-mortar companies like The Gap that use the Internet as another distribution channel.

The Internet has made it possible for those who want to be entrepreneurs to launch a business at relatively low cost. For a few hundred dollars, a market test site can be launched; for a few thousand dollars, an entrepreneur can have a full e-commerce site, something that would have cost hundreds of thousands of dollars less than a decade ago. The Internet has also become an excellent place to "test the waters" with a new business idea. Putting up a simple website to gauge response from potential customers is invaluable and can help a new business get traction quickly. Demand Media, a rapidly growing new media company based in Santa Monica, California, tests new Internet sites by putting up a basic site and monitoring it for a time to see what kind of response they get. When the company tested their deals.com site this way, they received a much larger response than expected, so they quickly developed a full e-commerce site and successfully launched it two weeks later.

THE SERIAL OR PORTFOLIO ENTREPRENEUR

Many entrepreneurs enjoy the pre-launch and start-up phases so much that when those activities are over and running the business takes center stage, they become impatient to move on to the next start-up. The thrill of starting a business keeps them going; they prefer to leave the management issues to someone else. An entrepreneur who starts one business and then moves on to start another is called a *serial entrepreneur*. Often these entrepreneurs start another business that builds on the experience from the first venture or a specific expertise that the entrepreneur possesses or has acquired through a previous venture. An entrepreneur who owns a minority or majority stake in several ventures is called a *portfolio entrepreneur*.[14] Portfolio entrepreneurs tend to create a lot of churn in their portfolios as they seek out new business opportunities that link to their existing businesses. They tend to be constantly on the hunt for new opportunities.[15]

Consummate entrepreneur Wayne Huizenga is a classic serial entrepreneur. He started with a single garbage truck and grew his company truck by truck to become Waste Management Inc., the largest garbage hauler and waste management service in the world. Huizenga then went on to tackle the video rental business with Blockbuster Entertainment and the used-car industry with Auto Nation. However, Huizenga could also be considered a portfolio entrepreneur because he typically owns multiple businesses simultaneously. In addition to the businesses cited, he has also owned numerous professional sports teams.

THE TRADITIONAL ENTREPRENEUR

If there really is such a thing as a "traditional entrepreneur," it would probably be that entrepreneur who starts a bricks-and-mortar business and builds it to a point where the wealth created can be harvested. Traditional entrepreneurs can be found in retail, manufacturing, services, health care, and literally any other industry there is. They start businesses solo or in teams, but what they have in common is a location that is not solely on the Internet, even if they start there. Anthony Arnold reversed the traditional bricks-and-mortar business to Web business path and began his company as an Internet business. Arnold's experience was in Web marketing, and in 1999 he was poised to capture his next big job at Lucent Technologies. While waiting for his employment to start, he and

CyberAngels Protecting Cyberspace

Chat rooms and social network portals attract the young and the young at heart. It is as easy as the click of a mouse button to strike up a conversation with someone anywhere in the world who shares your interests. But it's also easy for criminals to use these sites to prey on unsuspecting young people. One group of socially responsible entrepreneurs saw an opportunity in this problem. Building on their experience with the Guardian Angels, a group that works to keep community streets safe, they started an organization known as CyberAngels, a nonprofit group of volunteers who patrol websites and chat rooms looking for signs of predators. They also work with schools to develop curricula to teach students what to watch out for, and they work with the U.S. Customs' Cyber-Smuggling Unit and the FBI to find and arrest perpetrators. Their Net-Ed division teaches online classes that provide training for parents, teachers, and librarians. They also hold classes for the public in general Internet safety and navigation. Their division Connect-Ed provides Internet safety information to the public through online classes, published materials, and speakers for schools and public libraries.

Source: http://www.cyberangels.org.

his wife launched an Internet consulting firm to sell their Web marketing expertise—nothing unique; there are thousands of them. To demonstrate their credentials to potential clients, they spent $2,000 to build an e-commerce demo for a company they called PremiumKnives.com, because Arnold's hobby was collecting knives. To their surprise, within 3 months they had sold $50,000 worth of knives, while the consulting service languished. In February 2000, the division of Lucent that Arnold was supposed to work for was cut and he was out of a job. Arnold and his wife decided to go for it and expand the growing knife business. They moved the business from the Internet to a bricks-and-mortar site in a historic neighborhood in Omaha and began diversifying into kitchen gadgets and the like. They dubbed their store Premium Home and Garden. But like most entrepreneurs, Arnold envisions things on a grand scale and foresees his company growing to the size of Crate and Barrel or Williams-Sonoma.[16]

THE NONPROFIT ENTREPRENEUR

Today many enterprising people are turning to nonprofit types of ventures to realize their entrepreneurial dreams. Nonprofit, socially responsible businesses typically focus on educational, religious, or charitable goals. They generally seek tax-exempt status so that they can attract donations from companies and individuals who believe in their mission. Contrary to popular belief, nonprofit businesses can make a profit, but that profit must stay within the company rather than be distributed to the owners.

Robert Chambers used the nonprofit organizational structure as a vehicle to help low-income people make better purchasing decisions when it comes to cars. Chambers, a retired engineer in Lebanon, New Hampshire, with five years of auto sales experience, was frustrated by how much low-income people were spending because they didn't understand how car dealerships worked. To solve the problem, he launched Bonnie CLAC (car loans and counseling), which not only guarantees car loans for these people at reasonable rates, but also provides them with training in how to manage their finances.[17] Chapter 11 explores these types of ventures in more depth from a legal perspective.

THE CORPORATE VENTURER

Entrepreneurs can choose to start a new venture from scratch, buy an existing business and build it, or start a venture inside a large existing organization. The choice is a function of the type of business, the opportunity, and the support for such a venture inside the existing organization. For example, when capital markets make it difficult to find funding, entrepreneurs are less likely to start new ventures from scratch. By contrast, they are more likely to start new ventures on their own when the incentives inside large organizations are weak or nonexistent, when the opportunity requires individual effort, and when the normal scale advantages and learning curves do not provide advantages to the large organization.[18] Entrepreneurs also choose the start-up process when industry entry barriers are low, when the environment is more uncertain, and when the opportunity they seek to exploit involves a breakthrough or disruptive technology that will make previous technology obsolete.

Increasingly, large organizations are finding it necessary to provide for entrepreneurial activity to remain competitive. In the 1980s, as they saw themselves lagging behind small, young companies in finding great opportunities, big firms began to look for ways to restructure their organizations to enable creative employees to search for new opportunities the company could exploit. Driven by current markets and rigid financial structures, large firms had to look at new combinations of resources, how to extend the existing capabilities of the company and acquire new capabilities, and how to develop new revenue streams.

Corporate ventures, those entrepreneurial-like ventures inside large companies, are distinct from other types of projects that these firms take on. For one thing, they involve activities that are typically new to the company so the risk of failure is high. There is also a high degree of uncertainty around such projects, so they are often managed separately from the core business activities. Recognizing that it is nearly impossible to re-engineer and redesign an entire organization, many companies have chosen from several options to simulate the entrepreneurial environment required for innovation to occur: the skunk works, intrapreneurship, and acquisition.

The "skunk works®" route (named for Lockheed's unit that developed the Stealth fighter jet) refers to an autonomous group that is given the mandate to find and develop new products for the company that may even be external to the company's core competencies. They typically operate outside the traditional lines of authority in the organization, which makes for a more flexible, fast, and creative work environment.[19] In 2000, IBM made a bold move and tasked one of its best executives, Rod Adkins, with starting a new business that would help IBM apply wireless technology to extend computing beyond the home and office. Within three years, his new venture was generating annual sales of $2.4 billion. EBOs (emerging-business opportunities) is a corporate venturing program at IBM whose goal is to find innovations that will generate more than a billion dollars in annual sales for the company. To counteract the natural tendency of the corporate venturers to want to staff up like a big company, IBM makes them work alone or perhaps with a colleague. They work on a small budget, but they can tap IBM's wealth of expertise.[20]

Other companies try to encourage corporate venturing or entrepreneurship inside the structures of their existing organizations. This approach has been difficult at best to achieve because the bureaucratic structures of most large organizations—deep organizational charts, their inherent avoidance of risk, and strict budgets—all challenge even the most enthusiastic corporate entrepreneur.

For an entrepreneurial mindset to succeed inside a large corporation, the following are required:

▷ *Senior management commitment.* Without the support of senior management, it will be difficult to move any entrepreneurial project forward fast enough and far enough to be successful.

▷ *A champion or several champions.* At various points in the development of the corporate venture, the executive managing the development needs a champion at the highest levels who can open doors and make valuable contacts and who will lend credibility to the enterprise.

▷ *Corporate interoperability.* The environment must encourage collaboration and give the entrepreneur access to the knowledge and resources of all the company's functional areas, while at the same time allowing the entrepreneur a high degree of autonomy.

▷ *Clearly defined stages and metrics.* Entrepreneurial ventures inside large organizations need a timeline with stages at which decisions can be made about whether to proceed and whether additional or different resources are required. They also need a way to measure progress and success that is not based on the corporation's benchmarks but rather on benchmarks appropriate to start-up ventures with limited resources.

▷ *A superior team.* Only the best people should be put in corporate venture situations, because by definition these ventures are riskier than projects based on the company's core skills and products. The new venture team also calls for a champion among the top management who will secure help for the team when the project reaches the inevitable roadblock.

▷ *Spirit of entrepreneurship.* Entrepreneurship is about opportunity—recognizing it, seizing it, and exploiting it—but it's also about failing sometimes. A company that encourages corporate venturing must not penalize its entrepreneurs for failure but must support them as they take what they have learned to a new project.

This book is not intended to address the specific needs of corporate venturers, but recognizing opportunities, conducting feasibility analyses, and business planning are certainly relevant in the corporate environment.

Entrepreneurship as a Career Path: Challenges and Opportunities

Jeff Hawkins, the co-founder of Palm Computing and later Handspring, the successful PDA companies, would argue that entrepreneurship is not a career because "if you're successful at it, you quickly become a business person."[21] In other words, the only people who make a career of entrepreneurship are those who haven't been successful. In some respects, Hawkins was being facetious because he has in fact started more than one business, and Palm, his first, was certainly a successful company. The point is, however, that entrepreneurship is, for the most part, about start-up, about identifying an opportunity and gathering the resources to turn that opportunity into a successful enterprise. Entrepreneurship is not for everyone, no more than any other endeavor is. Table 2.1 presents an overview of the challenges and opportunities that come with choosing entrepreneurship as a career path. When reading the table, it is important to ask if the reader would be able to deal with such a challenge and also if the opportunities of entrepreneurship are meaningful to the reader's life goals.

Readers may come up with even more challenges and opportunities than are presented in the table, but these are the most common. The last challenge listed is "dealing with a sense of isolation and disillusionment." When Susan LaPlante-Dube left her corporate job to start Precision Marketing Group out of her home in Massachusetts, she learned how lonely that could be. "I was used to walking down the hall to bounce ideas off someone. . . ." She had to plan her time to include opportunities to meet with people and to network. The lead-up to the launch of the business is a very exciting time. Everyone wants to see the entrepreneur succeed so encouragement and support are never lacking. But many entrepreneurs are surprised at what running a business is really like. They have

TABLE 2.1

Challenges and Opportunities with the Entrepreneur Career Path

Challenges	Opportunities
Finding the right business opportunity	Creating wealth
Needing to work, often without pay, for long hours	Becoming independent—taking charge of a career
Uncertainty as to when the venture will succeed—high risk	Doing well while doing good through social entrepreneurship
Needing to make major decisions, often that affect other people's lives	Working in a business environment that the entrepreneur creates
Relying on other people for expertise and resources	Doing something the entrepreneur is passionate about
Having no previous experience on which to rely	Making a difference
Facing failure at some point	Creating new jobs
Finding the right people to grow the business	Supporting the community
Raising capital and other resources	
Dealing with a sense of isolation and disillusionment	

no comprehension of how difficult it is, and so often there is a feeling of being overwhelmed. This is one reason starting a business with a team makes sense; the difficulties can be shared.

To succeed at anything requires a higher-than-average amount of self-discipline and perseverance. Entrepreneurs don't give up easily, and they tend to stick doggedly to a concept until something or someone convinces them that it's time to move on to something else. For example, Todd Stennett spoke with more than 450 people before he found the right person to guide him to the perfect model for his now successful laser mapping business, Airborne 1. If entrepreneurs didn't have this tenacity, there would be no great businesses, because every entrepreneur faces doubters and naysayers when a business concept is in its earliest stages. The ability to stick to the task and persevere against all odds is what wins the day for an entrepreneur.

One of the biggest problems that scientists and engineers face when they decide to consider entrepreneurship is the expectation that there should be formulas and right and wrong answers. In short, they expect predictability. People who wish there were no surprises in life and who want an environment that is predictable and stable will find it very difficult to survive in the world of the entrepreneur. One reason why entrepreneurship is such an interesting and exciting field is that it is constantly changing. It is well-known that the greatest, most innovative ideas occur at the edge of chaos when things that don't normally connect are brought together in new ways. Opportunity is rarely found in stable, foreseeable settings, so potential entrepreneurs must learn to embrace change.

Preparing to Become an Entrepreneur

Starting any business, large or small, requires a tremendous amount of time, effort, and resources. Therefore, it usually makes sense to start a business that has the potential to grow large and provide a good return on that investment, rather than spend the same amount of effort on a very small business that yields only a single job. In fact, research supports that notion.[22,23] The probability of success and survival tends to go up with larger businesses or businesses with more potential. Unfortunately, the vast majority of people who start businesses do not think like entrepreneurs. They think like small-business owners, wanting to keep everything under control, to grow slowly, and simply provide a job for the owner. Although there is nothing inherently wrong with looking at business from this perspective, it does, regrettably, expose the entrepreneur to significantly more risk. Because these small businesses do not create new value, innovate, or have a plan for growth, they tend to be undercapitalized, poorly managed, and unable to differentiate themselves from competitors. In a word, they are vulnerable.

How, then, does an entrepreneur increase the chances for success? Through preparation. There are a number of important steps that an individual can take to increase his or her chances of success in entrepreneurship. Figure 2.1 displays these steps, and we discuss them here.

FIGURE 2.1   Steps to Increasing Success as an Entrepreneur

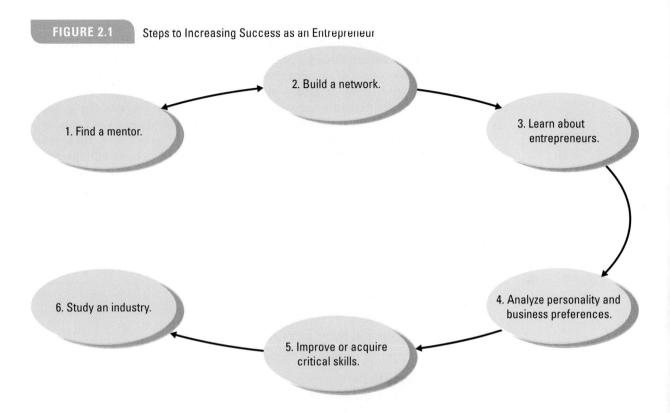

FIND A MENTOR

One very specific task that an entrepreneur can undertake to prepare for success is to find a mentor—that is, someone who is leading the type of life that the entrepreneur envisions for his or her own future and who can be the entrepreneur's guide and sounding board as well as champion and gateway to contacts the entrepreneur would otherwise not been able to meet. Vivek, an Indian entrepreneur, discovered that he had become so passionate about the product side of his computer hardware business that he stopped listening to the good advice he was being given about the need to diversify his product line. It was not until his business was facing failure, something that is viewed very negatively in India, that he sought the guidance and wisdom of a *guruji* or mentor. The mentor helped Vivek understand that it was his own ego that was standing in the way of his success in finding the right path for his business.[24]

BUILD A NETWORK

Networking is the exchange of information and resources among individuals, groups, or organizations whose common goals are to mutually benefit and create value for the members. Research in the field of entrepreneurship has revealed much about the positive effects of networking. For instance, entrepreneurship has been found to be a relational process. Entrepreneurs do not act autonomously but, rather, are "embedded in a social context, channeled and facilitated or constrained and inhibited by people's positions in social networks."[25] These social networks consist of strong and weak ties. *Strong ties* are the entrepreneur's close friends and family members whom he or she knows well, whereas *weak ties* are the entrepreneur's acquaintances and business contacts. In general, acquaintances are not socially involved; that is, entrepreneurs do not generally spend their nonbusiness hours with acquaintances.[26] Nevertheless, these weak ties play an important role in the entrepreneurial process because entrepreneurs typically move forward faster with the help and support of weak ties who are not biased by a prior history with the entrepreneur. Entrepreneurs rely on their weak ties for objective advice. Family and close friends, on the other hand, tend to restrict the entrepreneur's potential because they look at the impact on them of the entrepreneur's business activities.

Effective networks have the following characteristics:

▶ Consistent network growth

▶ Large network size

▶ Network cultivation, interaction, and exchange

▶ Network balance in terms of resources

▶ Legitimacy provided by credible network partners[27]

What this means to the entrepreneur is that building a large network with credible partners and maintaining the connections in that network will be important to the entrepreneur's success. However, how does one achieve a large, but meaningful network? Entrepreneurs accomplish this by connecting with network brokers who serve as gateways to other networks. These brokers, or opinion leaders, exert influence between groups rather than within groups.[28] Figure 2.2 depicts such brokering. The entrepreneur in this example initially has a network of family and friends as well as a network of professional engineers. Outside of these networks, the entrepreneur knows only two people: an angel investor and a production person. However, these two people are well connected into communities with which the entrepreneur has no experience. In effect, they are opinion leaders who serve as the gateways to those new communities and can make the appropriate introductions to provide the entrepreneur with instant credibility within them. Now it is easy to see why the adage "it's who you know" makes sense. Rather than spending an extraordinary amount of time trying to find all the required contacts, it would be more efficient and prudent for the entrepreneur to figure out who is the gateway to the community and endeavor to meet and cultivate that relationship.

Entrepreneurs who successfully use their networks to build their businesses generally are committed to the success of the people in their network, are active listeners, and approach every contact with an open mind.[29] In that way, they derive the maximum value from their network ties. Table 2.2 provides a way to begin to analyze the reader's network. The first row has been filled in to illustrate how to complete the matrix. Networking is discussed in the context of building a start-up team in Chapter 8.

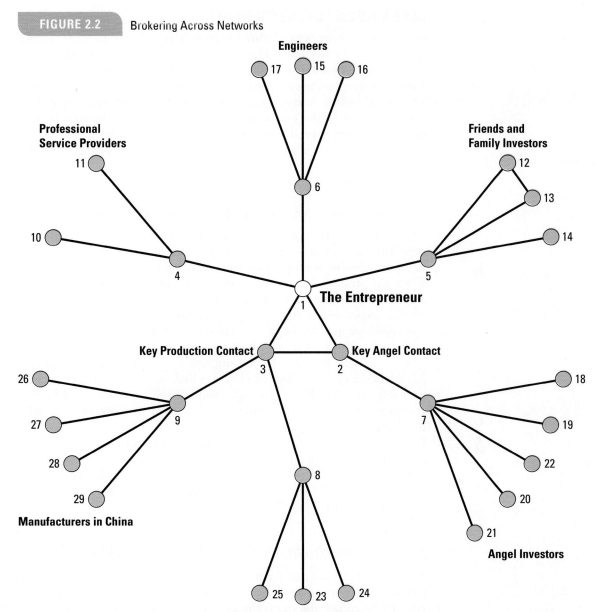

FIGURE 2.2   Brokering Across Networks

Engineers

Professional Service Providers

Friends and Family Investors

The Entrepreneur

Key Production Contact   Key Angel Contact

Manufacturers in China

Angel Investors

Prototype Job Shops in China

TABLE 2.2

Social Network Participants

Name	Weak Tie	Strong Tie	Broker	Source of Help
Tim Burns	X			Business attorney

LEARN ABOUT ENTREPRENEURS

One of the best ways to prepare for entrepreneurship is to learn as much about it as possible by reading magazine articles, books, and newspapers and—most importantly—by talking to entrepreneurs. Some examples of magazines that focus on entrepreneurs are *Fortune Small Business, Inc. Magazine,* and *Entrepreneur.* Studying an industry and looking for trends and patterns of change is an important part of the preparation to become an entrepreneur. These activities increase entrepreneurial knowledge, thereby reducing some of the risk and enhancing the chances of success. They also help the entrepreneur identify opportunities.

IDENTIFY REASONS FOR WANTING TO OWN A BUSINESS

Anyone looking at entrepreneurship solely as a way to make money should understand that there are easier, less risky ways to do so. Recall that most entrepreneurs start businesses for reasons other than money. Although entrepreneurship is still the primary way to create wealth, it happens only when there is a viable and compelling business concept and a team that knows how to execute that concept. Starting a business is a great deal of work, so the reasons for taking on this challenge must grow out of genuine conviction.

An entrepreneur's reasons for wanting to start a business will also affect the type of business that should be launched. For example, if the goal is to own a $100-million company and employ hundreds of people, an entrepreneur would probably not consider starting a consulting business or a small neighborhood restaurant. Similarly, if an entrepreneur wanted to work from home and not have employees, he or she would not start a labor-intensive business like a restaurant, but, given the global reach of the Internet and the fulfillment and logistical support of companies like UPS, it would be possible to build a substantial business in terms of revenues from home. That is the dream of thousands of budding entrepreneurs who sell on eBay and take advantage of PayPal to handle the finances and UPS or FedEx to manage shipping.

ANALYZE PERSONALITY AND BUSINESS PREFERENCES

It is not just the reasons for starting a business that need to be congruent with the actual business started, but the entrepreneur's personality and preferences have to be compatible with the business as well. Although we have dispelled many of the myths surrounding entrepreneurship in this chapter, it is a fact that there are barriers to becoming an entrepreneur that should not be ignored, and many of these barriers relate to the entrepreneur's personality and preferences. Numerous early research studies looked at the issue of what prevents a person from becoming self-employed and have identified a number of factors that negatively affect a person's willingness to take the risk to start a business. In a more recent study, six factors strongly emerged as barriers to people becoming self-employed: (1) lack of confidence, (2) financial needs, (3) start-up logistics, (4) personal or family issues, (5) time constraints, and (6) lack of skills.[30] The

TABLE 2.3

Entrepreneur Personality and
Preferences Questionnaire

		Yes	No
1.	Are you a self-starter?		
2.	Are you able to work for up to a year with no income from the new business?		
3.	Do you stick with a project until it's finished? Or do you frequently abandon a project when you grow tired of it?		
4.	Do you enjoy working with other people on a regular basis?		
5.	Do you enjoy traveling for business purposes?		
6.	Are you comfortable with pressure (i.e., deadlines, fast-paced work environment)?		
7.	Do you enjoy working with people from other countries?		
8.	Are you comfortable hiring people you believe are smarter or more experienced than you are?		
9.	Do you enjoy being in an office at your desk for most of the day?		
10.	Are you comfortable in selling situations?		
11.	Are you comfortable asking for money or other resources?		
12.	Are you comfortable with debt?		
13.	Is security important to you?		
14.	Do you have time to devote to this new business?		
15.	Are you comfortable with unions?		
16.	Are you willing to work in a government-regulated environment?		
17.	Do you have the support of your family to start a business?		

questions in Table 2.3 reflect these factors and others that should be considered as well. The table presents a series of questions that will help entrepreneurs understand more about what they like and dislike about business. Owning a business is a 24/7 occupation, so it is vitally important that entrepreneurs not place themselves in unpleasant situations that will affect their ability to perform at their best. For example, entrepreneurs who have a difficult time with deadlines and pressure would probably not be happy in the world of advertising and promotion.

Launching a new business requires tremendous amounts of time and energy, as well as a great deal of support from family and friends. During the early stages of a new venture, resources are limited and an entrepreneur must wear many hats. This can be immensely stressful, so it is important that an entrepreneur be in good health and optimal physical and emotional condition. It is often said that entrepreneurs start businesses to be in charge of their lives. The reality is that after they start their own business, they might find themselves working more than they ever did for someone else. The major difference is that because they are building something they own, it doesn't feel like the work they are accustomed to; instead, they are bringing to life a new business that reflects *their* goals and values.

It is equally important for potential entrepreneurs to think about the kind of lifestyle they are striving to achieve. Not all businesses support the kind of lifestyle that some entrepreneurs want to lead. Is travel important? Is having a large home and all the things that go with it a requirement? Is achieving a balanced life with plenty of time for family and friends important? If so, starting a business that requires a lot of travel or puts the entrepreneur at the mercy of demanding clients probably won't provide that balanced lifestyle.

Most people spend the majority of the day at their work; therefore, the work environment should be an enjoyable place to be. Entrepreneurs who love the outdoors should probably not start businesses that require them to sit at a desk all day. Entrepreneurs who don't enjoy working with people should probably not start a business that is labor-intensive or involves numerous daily interactions with the public. It is a good idea for a future entrepreneur to take a step back and contemplate his or her ideal work environment. What does this environment look like or "feel" like? What would spending a day in this environment entail?

IMPROVE OR ACQUIRE CRITICAL SKILLS

Because entrepreneurs operate in a world of uncertainty, the ability to analyze a situation, extract the important and ignore the superfluous, compare potential outcomes, and extrapolate from other experiences to the current one is vital. Entrepreneurs also regularly have to weigh options in complex situations. Critical thinking skills can be improved through practice and by observing how others with well-developed skills work through a problem-solving situation. Many colleges and universities offer courses in critical thinking and there are a number of excellent books on the subject.

People who have a difficult time making decisions or who regularly find that they make poor decisions will probably not be successful as entrepreneurs. Making effective decisions is a critical part of the everyday life of an entrepreneur and is a skill that must be developed and exercised carefully. Poor decisions about hiring, business location, investors, and strategic partners can cost a company a great deal of money and prevent it from achieving its goals. Wise decisions, even in times of crisis, can provide an opportunity for growth.

The saying "the devil is in the details" could not be more true in business. Entrepreneurs who proudly claim that they leave the details to others while they focus on the vision are telling the world that they don't participate in the inner workings of their business. Details matter, and although entrepreneurs should not be micromanagers as the business grows, they should be well aware of the status of critical numbers in their business, and they should make their presence known among employees on a regular basis. It is vitally important to the success of the business that an entrepreneur be detail-oriented. Table 2.4 lists some of

TABLE 2.4 Critical Entrepreneurial Skills		
Analysis and critical thinking	Persuasion and negotiation
Opportunity recognition	Written and oral communication
Resource gathering	Leadership and people management
Organizational and time management	Decision making

the skills that entrepreneurs need to hone to be effective at starting and growing their businesses.

Entrepreneurial leaders have a distinct advantage over charismatic or heroic leaders. Being a hero is lonely; there are no peers to confide in or teammates with whom to share the load. Today, more than ever before, entrepreneurs see themselves as part of a team, from the founding of the venture throughout all the various stages in the life of that venture. The days of the gunslinging solo entrepreneur are gone. Today it takes a team to succeed and a leader who can inspire others to motivate and lead as well. Entrepreneurial leadership, like any effective leadership, is a balance of passion and pragmatism. It is the entrepreneur's passion that launches the business and keeps it going through the early days when survival is often in doubt. But a different kind of leadership is often required once the business has survived and has entered a growth mode. A more pragmatic style of leadership that can deliver the right systems and controls to keep the venture on course is not often found in the same person who founded the venture. Unfortunately, in private companies it is often the entrepreneur/founder who is left to decide when it is time for him or her to hand the reins to a different type of leader, and only the rare entrepreneur recognizes when that moment is at hand. Sometimes, however, the entrepreneur remains as the visionary leader of the company but brings on a CEO with professional management skills. This topic is explored in more depth in Chapter 18.

STUDY AN INDUSTRY

One of the best ways to discover an opportunity is to study an industry in depth, perhaps even work in the industry for a time. An industry is a group of companies that are engaged in a similar or related activity; for example, the computer industry consists of all the businesses that provide parts, assembly, manufacturing, and distribution for computers—essentially all of the businesses involved in the value chain for computers. The value chain is comprised of all the businesses involved in the production of a product or service from raw materials through delivery to the final customer and is discussed in more depth in Chapter 4. The best opportunities come from entrepreneurs' experience and knowledge of an industry, a market, or a type of business. Since opportunities are not limited to products and services, studying an industry gives individuals the prospect of identifying opportunity anywhere in the value chain of that industry. A method for analyzing an industry is presented in Chapter 6.

When all is said and done, business is about relationships—with partners, with customers, and with suppliers. Successfully building relationships requires honesty and integrity. It requires giving value and delivering on promises. An entrepreneur's core values are the foundation for the business and are always reflected in the business and in the way customers are treated. Their integrity is something that entrepreneurs guard more carefully than anything else because they cannot afford to taint or lose it. The next chapter explores how entrepreneurs cultivate ideas into business opportunities.

WHEN NEW BUSINESSES GO GLOBAL

Recent research has made a strong case for acceleration in the rate at which companies are internationalizing their business efforts even at the earliest stages. New ventures, which already suffer from the liabilities of size and newness, must now add the risk of entering a foreign market with its unique political, legal, economic, and sociocultural complexities. K.D. Miller's work in this area has provided a framework for managing the risks of internationalization.* Young businesses can increase their chances of international success by (1) imitation, or entering the same countries as others in the industry have; (2) avoidance, or refusing to enter a country where the risk is unacceptably high; (3) flexibility in the design of the company so that it can adapt quickly and effectively when things change; (4) cooperation, or entering into strategic alliances to reduce uncertainty;

and (5) control, or attempting to influence the behavior of others. This last area is most difficult for a new firm, but the possibility of influencing customer behavior exists. For example, in China, entrepreneurs have found funding for mainstream Internet portals such as Sina.com, Netease.com, and Sohu.com because the portal industry is large and demand is great. But entrepreneurs with business concepts that are less mainstream will probably not find a ready market at the outset. Entrepreneurs looking to expand their markets into China (or any other international location) need a very clear strategy, strong financial backing, and an effective team—very much as they do in the United States.

*K.D. Miller, "A Framework for Integrated Risk Management in International Business," *Journal of International Business Studies*, 23 (1992): 311–331.

New Venture Checklist

Have you:

☐ Decided whether or not you have what it takes to be an entrepreneur?

☐ Determined why you want to start a business?

☐ Considered what type of business might be a good fit for you?

Issues to Consider

1. Why do myths emerge around phenomena such as entrepreneurship?
2. How are corporate venturers different from other types of entrepreneurs?
3. What are the steps you should take to prepare yourself for entrepreneurship?
4. What might explain the rise in interest in social or nonprofit entrepreneurship?
5. Why are more ventures started by teams than by solo entrepreneurs?

Experiencing Entrepreneurship

1. Identify an entrepreneur who is leading the kind of personal and business life that you aspire to lead. Interview that person to find out more about how she or he achieved that lifestyle. During the interview, and only if the two of you have developed a rapport, approach the entrepreneur about the possibility of becoming your mentor.

2. Entrepreneurship is a journey, and many people contribute to that journey. Begin a contact portfolio that will contain the names of all the people you meet as you network. Record their contact information, how you met them, and what they contributed to your journey. Strive to meet three to five new contacts a week.

Relevant Case Studies

Case 2 Craigslist, p. 442

Case 7 Linksys, p. 477

Case 8 Finagle a Bagel, p. 481

Chapter 3

RECOGNIZING AND CREATING OPPORTUNITY

"The greater danger for most of us lies not in setting our aim too high and falling short; but in setting our aim too low, and achieving our mark."

—MICHELANGELO

LEARNING OBJECTIVES

▶ Explain the nature of creativity and problem solving.

▶ Identify the challenges to creativity.

▶ Discuss how to remove the roadblocks to creative thought.

▶ Name some sources of new product/service ideas.

44

Profile 3.1 A GENIUS INVENTOR WITH A PASSION FOR LIFE

Dr. Yoshiro Nakamatsu, also known as Dr. NakaMats, is truly the essence of a creative, innovative person. He holds more than 3,218 inventions and 2,300 patents, twice as many as the great American inventor Thomas Edison. And with that he claims to be only halfway to his goal of 6,000 inventions in his lifetime. For example, Nakamatsu is responsible for the floppy disk, which he licensed to IBM (and he does get a royalty on the millions of disks sold every year), the compact disk and disk player, the digital watch, and the water-powered engine. So prolific is he that his offices in Tokyo are located just a short walk from the patent office.

At the tender age of 5, he invented an automatic gravity controller for a model plane that he claims made autopilot possible. The patent on that invention has long since expired, and he earns no royalties from autopilot systems. At the age of 14, he invented a plastic kerosene pump on which he still holds the patent. That device can now be found in any hardware store.

Nakamatsu credits his genius to his parents' constant encouragement to be creative and not focus solely on learning. This is contrary to the traditional Japanese upbringing, where children are typically made to memorize great quantities of information and are not allowed to associate freely until their twenties. These factors, along with his discipline and belief that trying too hard stifles creativity, led to Nakamatsu's stellar career as an inventor.

Nakamatsu believes that successful innovation comes from "freedom of intelligence." By that he means that you have to work with no strings attached. Consequently, Nakamatsu has never sought funding from anyone and uses his own resources to develop and invent. The only licensing of his technologies that he has ever done was to IBM in the 1970s for computer-related patents. He prefers to hold on to his intellectual property and to make his unique products himself.

Nakamatsu has a very idiosyncratic way of generating ideas. He starts the creative process by sitting calmly in a room in his home that he calls the "static room" because it has only natural things in it, much like the meditation gardens in Kyoto, Japan. Here he opens his mind to the creative flow of new ideas—he free-associates, letting his mind go wherever it wants to. He then moves to the "dynamic room," a dark room with the latest audio/video equipment. Here he listens to jazz, easy-listening music, and Beethoven's Fifth Symphony—one of his favorites. In this room, new ideas begin to form. Following a period of time in the dynamic room, he heads for the swimming pool, where he swims underwater for extraordinarily long periods of time. It is underwater that he finishes the process of "soft thinking," or playing with the idea, and becomes ready to move on to the more practical phase of considering how to implement the idea. He even records his ideas under water on a special Plexiglas writing pad.

Nakamatsu, by the way, also swears by the brain food he eats, which he dubbed "Yummy Nutri Brain Food": dried shrimp, seaweed, cheese, yogurt, eel, eggs, beef, and chicken livers! He has consumed only his own food for the past 30 years and lives on 4 hours of sleep a night. He now has 29 guesthouses on his property where "geniuses" of all types spend time. "There is a waiting list of about 100 people who simply want to live here to get inspired by me and my inventions," asserts Nakamatsu. When faced with a choice between the easiest path and the most difficult path, he always chooses the most difficult because there he can find what no one else has found.

Sources: "Twilight Zone: Dr. NakaMats' Inventions," *Pingmag* (October 20, 2006), http://www.pingmag.jp/2006/10/20/twilight-zone-dr-nakamats-inventions; T. Hornyak, "Dr. NakaMats: Japan's Self-Proclaimed Savior," *Japan Inc.* (January 2002); L. Betti, "Yoshiro Nakamatsu: Inventing Genius," *Evolution* (September 15, 2002), http://evolution.skf.com/gb/article.asp?articleID 425; and Linda Naiman and Chic Thompson, "Dr. Yoshiro Nakamatsu," http://www.creativityatwork.com/articlesContent/Nakamats1.html.

What does creativity have to do with entrepreneurship? Everything! Creativity enables entrepreneurs to differentiate their businesses from competitors so that customers will notice them. Creativity is the basis for invention, which is discovering something that did not exist previously, and innovation, which is finding a new way to do something or improving on an existing product or service. Creativity is also fundamental to problem solving. Today, entrepreneurs face a rapidly changing environment brought about in large part by the speed of technological change. The combination of rapid change and the resulting uncertainty about what the future holds presents a fertile ground for new opportunities. Creativity is a critical skill for recognizing or creating opportunity in a dynamic environment and for problem solving, which is necessary to satisfy customer needs.

The American Management Association conducted a survey of 500 CEOs, asking them what companies would have to do to survive in the twenty-first century. The most common answer was "practice creativity and innovation." It seems that the creativity deficit may be the most dangerous threat to businesses today.[1] That is why companies such as 3M, Bell Laboratories, Xerox, and Hallmark practice creativity by looking at ideas that lie on the fringes of their industries, instead of where everyone else is looking. Future opportunities typically lie in the deviations from what is "common practice."

Before going further, it is important to distinguish among four concepts that are critical to this chapter: (1) idea, (2) business opportunity, (3) opportunity recognition, and (4) opportunity creation. Everyone has *ideas,* hundreds of them every day. However, a *business opportunity* is an idea that involves a product, service, or method with commercial potential. To be successful, this idea must create new value for customers and be attached to a viable business model; in other words, there must be a way to make money from the opportunity. In fact, the very act of developing a business concept and successfully testing it in the marketplace with potential customers—a process known as feasibility analysis—is the means by which an idea becomes an opportunity.

Some entrepreneurs use their creativity to improve on what they currently do or on what their competitors are doing. This is the process of *opportunity recognition,* or innovation based on a product or service already in existence. Other entrepreneurs do things that no one else is doing by participating in the process of *opportunity creation,* or "starting from scratch," which involves the invention of technologies, products, and methods that render obsolete those currently in existence.

Some people have an easier time generating ideas than others, but only because they possess better-developed awareness and creativity skills. This is good news, because it means that everyone has the ability to become more creative. The chapter explores how entrepreneurs can hone their natural creativity and problem-solving skills to put themselves in a better position to innovate and recognize or create a business opportunity.

Creativity and Innovation

Entrepreneurship is a creative, not a scientific, process. From the generation of the business idea to development of the marketing plan to management of the growing business, it is creativity in all aspects of the venture that sets the most successful new businesses apart from those that merely survive.

WHAT IS KNOWN ABOUT CREATIVITY

Creativity has been defined from two perspectives: the functionalist and the outcome-based perspectives. The functionalist perspective, which dominates the research literature, asserts that creativity is the production of novel and useful ideas.[2] By contrast, the outcome-based perspective is a more applied approach that defines creativity as the generation of valuable, useful products and services, procedures, and processes.[3] The earliest research on creativity focused on the individual, in much the same way that early research on entrepreneurship focused on the entrepreneur. Researchers looked at personality factors and cognitive skills such as language, thinking processes, and intelligence to attempt to determine the profile of a creative person.[4] Then they examined the context in which people are creative and found that a number of environmental settings are conducive to creativity, among them the absence of constraints or freedom to do as one pleases, the presence of rewards or incentives to encourage creativity, and team effectiveness or the ability of people to collaborate and support each other's efforts.[5]

Invention as a Creative Process

Inventors come in all shapes and sizes, and they approach the invention and creativity process from different perspectives. For example, Claude Shannon, who invented what became the basis for the computer revolution (the encoding of binary digits or bits to define and quantify information), and Gordon Gould, whose inventions covered fundamental laser technology, were domain-specific inventors; that is, they invented primarily within a specific field of knowledge in which they were experts. Contrast that with Dr. Yoshiro Nakamatsu (see opening profile), who invented across many domains. Dr. Behrokh Khoshnevis is another excellent example of an inventor who crosses domains—from machines that cut titanium to create dental crowns to haptics (the ability to manipulate objects in a virtual world) to devices that solve critical problems in oil and gas operations. What differentiates this inventor from many others is that he focuses on solving problems that have a major impact on society.

The common ground among all these inventors is the recognition that the invention process is not formulaic, nor is it linear in nature; however, certain definable patterns and activities can occur in any creative process. These patterns are connection, discovery, invention, and application, as depicted in Figure 3.1.[6] Using the example of Leonardo da Vinci, one of the greatest inventors of all time, is an excellent way to investigate the invention process in more depth.[7]

CONNECTION

A connection occurs when two ideas are brought together using such language devices as metaphor, analogy, symbol, and hypothesis. Da Vinci saw a connection between the branches of trees and the canal system he was designing for the city of Florence, Italy. He verbalized this connection as a metaphor: *canals are tree branches.* It is interesting to note that nature has been the metaphor for

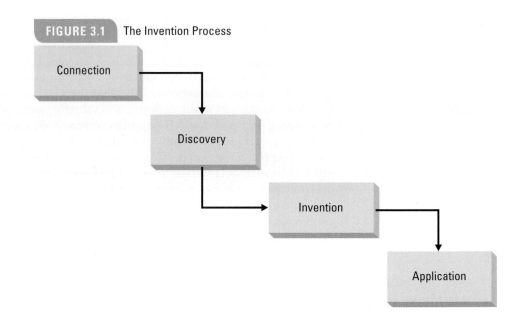

FIGURE 3.1 The Invention Process

many an invention, including Velcro® (inspired by the sticky burr) and the entire field of nanotechnology, which has brought about the development of microscopic machines and processes whose functions are often based on processes found in nature. Similar to how da Vinci recognized the connection between the structure of a canal system and the structure of a tree, the Wright brothers, the inventors of manned flight, observed how buzzards kept their balance during flight and used that information to design a kite glider in 1900 that could carry a pilot.

DISCOVERY

Once a connection has been established, the inventor explores it in depth. Da Vinci did this by drawing tree branches, examining them closely, and conducting a series of experiments with his canal designs to determine if he had drawn the correct conclusion. Through his exhaustive research, he also learned how trees manage the flow of nutrients and water through their systems. This gave him a better understanding of how water might flow through canals and that led to what is often referred to as the "aha" or "eureka" moment: the discovery of something new. To achieve discovery often requires viewing something that already exists from a different perspective as da Vinci did.

INVENTION

Inventions are the product of effort once a discovery has occurred. They usually arise out of needs in the market, but they can be serendipitous as well. An invention is a discovery reduced to practice; that is, a discovery in and of itself cannot benefit society until it is turned into a product of some type. Da Vinci's insight into the inner workings of tree branches helped him in the subsequent development of hydraulic devices to control water levels in canals so a boat could cross under a bridge. Other inventions led to a means to create a waterway from Florence to the sea. It is an unfortunate fact that the vast majority of inventions by independent (noncorporate) inventors never become products that benefit society. There are two principal reasons why this occurs: (1) The cost to bring an invention to market is significant, often beyond the resources of the independent inventor, and (2) often before the inventor can commercialize his invention, a large company can infringe on the patent with impunity. The issues of patents and infringement are discussed in Chapter 7.

APPLICATION

For an invention to be successful it must have applications in the market; that is, there must be specific needs that it can address. Going beyond the initial invention to other applications, da Vinci came up with ideas for mills powered by wind and water. It is interesting that many inventors never see beyond their initial inventions. The four MIT developers of the three-dimensional printing process for rapid prototyping were researchers with no interest in commercializing their invention. It was only when the MIT technology licensing office approached companies in eight different industries that eight possible applications for the technology were discovered, ranging from orthodontics to architectural models to artificial bone. All of these applications emerged from a perceived need in the market.

Challenges to Creativity

Creativity tends to occur naturally if one lets it, but entrepreneurs often unintentionally erect roadblocks that prevent them from following the creative path. Some of these roadblocks are discussed in the following sections.

NO TIME FOR CREATIVITY

Entrepreneurs are often so busy that there is no time to think and contemplate, and this can keep them from exercising their creative skills. In today's world, people are constantly interrupted by mobile devices that overload them with information. Recent research found that most U.S. workers complain that they are under a great deal of pressure in their jobs to get things done quickly. They report difficulty in concentrating on a single task, so workers never feel that they have accomplished anything.[8] When the same study was conducted in 1994, researchers found that 82 percent of respondents claimed to accomplish at least half their planned work for the day, but in the current study that percentage dropped to 50 percent. One of the biggest contributors to lowered productivity is IM, or instant text messages. A 2004 study found that an astounding 90 percent of employees spend at least 90 minutes of their workday sending text messages.[9] Most people rely on routines to keep their lives organized and under control, but relying on routines too heavily also has its downside. It can prevent an individual from taking the time to generate new ideas in response to a changing environment.

It is important for entrepreneurs to set aside some time each day to let their brains free-associate or perhaps to do something creative that is unrelated to work. The simple act of turning off the e-mail notification button or placing IM status in "not available at the moment" can cut down on distractions and open the door to a new idea.

NO CONFIDENCE

"Confidence is the expectation of success."[10] Those who expect to be successful generally are willing to exert the effort, spend the time, and expend the money to achieve it. Rosabeth Moss Kanter believes that confidence is comprised of three elements: accountability, collaboration, and initiative.[11] Accountability is personal responsibility for actions taken and is a component of a person's integrity. Collaboration means working with others and being able to count on each other. Initiative is believing that the actions taken will make a difference. Taking the familiar, easiest, or shortest path usually happens when entrepreneurs lack confidence. They act out of fear of being criticized, and that often keeps them from fully realizing their potential. The need for their ideas to be acceptable or seem rational to others is a significant roadblock for some entrepreneurs. Rationality is not a prerequisite either for innovative ways to seize opportunities or for receiving a patent on an invention! The inventor of patent number 2,608,083 probably thought he was being rational when he invented the Travel Washing Machine, a portable, mobile appliance that is mounted on the wheel of a vehicle and washes the driver's clothes as he or she motors down the road. Unfortunately, the motorist has to jack up the car first to install the device and, for optimum results, cannot travel faster than 25 miles an hour. Ludicrously irrational inventions notwithstanding, many of the products in use every day—the fax machine and the personal computer, to name two—would not have come about if the people who invented them hadn't had the courage to go against the general thinking at the time.

Setting manageable goals that create small wins when they're achieved can help entrepreneurs who lack confidence develop this important attribute. Conducting a feasibility analysis of a new business idea is an excellent way to reduce some of the risk of entrepreneurship and build confidence.

NO CREATIVE SKILLS

All of the aforementioned roadblocks can stifle creativity, but individuals who believe they are not creative are doing themselves the greatest disservice. They are dismissing ideas before even trying them out and, at the very least, setting themselves up for failure. Achieving a state of consciousness that opens the mind to creative thought has been at the root of many religious and philosophical traditions, from India's yogi self-discipline to Asian Zen Buddhism. Anyone can learn to become more creative and develop creative skills. The next section examines some ways to prepare for creative success.

Profile 3.2 ACTOR TURNED ENTREPRENEUR

A number of American actors have become political leaders, so it is not surprising that an actor might also become a successful entrepreneur. Robert Redford, the Sundance Kid, understands the essence of entrepreneurship and its chaotic nature:

> Do you think the world was created by an accountant? No! The universe was created by the combustion of a creative explosion. Fire and chaos started everything. Then order came on top of that.

At the very young age of 24, Redford purchased two acres of land in Utah for $500 and built a log cabin there. From that humble beginning sprang a new industry—the independent film industry or *indie,* an international conglomerate, and a nonprofit institute that produces the renowned Sundance Film Festival. The institute has produced more than 85 feature films in 22 years. So widely recognized is it that 4,000 Blockbuster stores devote an entire shelf to its films. And Redford's Sundance Channel on cable television now has over 16.7 million subscribers.

Redford attributes the success of Sundance to his unwavering belief that growth is a creative process. In his mind, it is the essence of business. The idea for Sundance came from Redford's distaste at seeing studio after studio churn out a continuous stream of formulaic entertainment. In Sundance, he saw the opportunity to build a sanctuary for artists where creative ideas could flourish. Lacking business savvy, he set out to learn, observe, and apply everything he could about business. Unlike many entrepreneurs who compromise their vision to satisfy the demands of investors, Redford refused to do that. The story is told that his partners wanted to build a restaurant adjacent to the ski lift to take advantage of traffic. Redford rejected the idea, however, saying that the restaurant needed its own space so that people could discover it. A huge tree stood in the middle of his proposed site, so he built the restaurant around the tree and called it The Tree Room. It is now one of the finest restaurants in Utah. Not long after that, his partners sold their interests, claiming he was too difficult to work with. According to Redford, it's not just revenue that matters—it's the kind of revenue. And the same might be said of investors.

To foster creativity, Redford keeps the conditions at the institute relatively primitive so that artists must be resourceful and experimental. He is seeking not perfection but originality, process not product. Originality is what makes Sundance different; it has a compelling story and a tribal legend that it fosters through its social and community habits, such as the informal gatherings at the Owl Bar to relive the great moments in Sundance's history and to keep the spirit alive. At the Sundance Institute, innovation is a way of life, not just a business strategy. The design and process of the Institute encourage innovation and creativity. It is a journey without an end.

Sources: S.H. Zades, "Creativity Regained," *Inc. Magazine* (September 2003), http://www.inc.com; and Sundance Institute, http://institute.sundance.org.

Removing the Roadblocks to Creativity

There are a number of things that can be done immediately to remove the roadblocks in the path to more creative thinking. The process starts with preparing an environment that makes it easier to think imaginatively and then moves to some techniques for enhancing creative skills.

DESIGN AN ENVIRONMENT TO STIMULATE CREATIVITY

Great inventors and highly creative companies owe their success to having provided an environment that simulated high levels of innovation. Thomas Edison's greatest invention was arguably not the light bulb but rather the concept of a research and development laboratory that served as an incubator for radical innovation. Likewise, Disneyland was not the greatest invention of the Walt Disney Company. Disney Imagineering, its Edison-like laboratory, is the source of its celebrated ideas.

The environment in which a person works can either stimulate or discourage creativity. For example, suppose a business has a very rigid and hierarchical structure with many layers of management. For this type of environment to be effective, its operations must be standardized so that everyone does things in the same way. That kind of environment is not conducive to thinking "out of the box." Here is another example. Picture an advertising and public relations firm that has to meet many deadlines. A fast-paced environment like this leaves little time for contemplation, which is essential to higher levels of creative thought.

Even in environments like these, however, there are ways to make the setting more conducive to creativity and innovation. Here are a few suggestions:

Minimize distractions. Close the door, shut off the phone, and turn off e-mail to prepare to do some creative thinking.

Devote some time each day to quiet contemplation. Maintaining quiet time on a regular basis trains the mind to shift quickly into the creative mode. It also helps make creative thinking a habit.

Pay attention to the places that inspire the most creative thinking and spend more time there. Individuals who find that they think best outside should arrange their day to spend some time outdoors.

Develop a creative culture so that employees contribute to the company's ability to innovate. For example, Google has been called one of the best companies to work for because it has developed a culture that fosters creativity and invention. That culture is embodied in one of its principles: "you can be serious without a suit."[12]

Mix people up. It is possible to achieve a more stimulating environment by mixing people up—that is, taking them out of their familiar surroundings and putting them in a new setting that forces them to think outside their normal mode. For example, a company might put a technology person in the marketing group for a month and place a marketing person in the technology group. The cultures of the two groups are typically very different, so the marketing person will bring a new perspective to technology issues and the tech person will help the marketing people understand their world. Neville Hockley found that he had to get away from his traditional New York design firm to do his most creative work. So he and his wife took their 41-foot sloop on a trip around the world. Using satellite communications, he was able to do everything he typically does in the office without the distractions of the day-to-day running of the business. This change of environment freed him up to focus on new ideas.

Making a Connection

Try this exercise with a group of friends. It is sure to get you thinking outside the box. Give each person in the group a piece of paper. Then have each person write a noun on his or her paper—any noun. When all of the members have written a noun, everyone then passes his or her paper to the person on the right. Each person will now write an adjective on the paper—any adjective; do not consider the noun when writing it. Then the papers should be passed again to the right. Each person will then write a verb on the paper and pass it to the right. For the final round, each person will write an adverb on the paper. In each case, the word that is written does not have to relate to the previous words on the page.

Then the group should move into the next phase: connecting the words in a relationship so that a potential business opportunity appears. The group should decide on one page only and discard the others. Using the words provided, the group will come up with a business concept that includes product/service, customer, benefit, and distribution.

This exercise is based on the premise that many opportunities are created by going through a process that involves:

- Connecting dissimilar concepts
- Experimentation
- Inventing something new based on connections and experimentation
- Finding applications for the invention/opportunity created

KEEP TRACK OF IDEAS

The creative journey begins with maintaining a journal of one's thoughts and ideas. Many entrepreneurs keep this type of journal with them at all times, even at their bedside at night, to record whatever pops into their heads. They may not be ready to work on a particular idea at that very moment, but they still jot it down so that they can return to it in the future. IDEO, with locations around the world including North America, the United Kingdom, Germany, and Asia, is one of the most successful new product idea companies in the world. One of the reasons for their success is that they stockpile ideas, even those on which they didn't follow through, because these ideas, which can range from glow-in-the-dark fabric to holographic candy, become useful for brainstorming sessions. When they are shared across several IDEO offices through the company's virtual Tech Box, every item, no matter how unusual, has the potential to be the inspiration for the next blockbuster product. The act of putting ideas down on paper reinforces that ideas have value and should be saved. It also serves as motivation for the entrepreneur, who will no doubt see an increase in the number of ideas generated over time.

START WITH THE FAMILIAR

It is a myth that entrepreneurs only build businesses based on concepts that never existed before. Most business concepts derive from existing ideas on which the entrepreneur intends to improve. And most business ideas stem from a problem or opportunity that the entrepreneur sees in his or her immediate environment. The local neighborhood or community is a rich source of opportunity and finding opportunity in things with which the entrepreneur has experience is the most common and effective way to achieve early entrepreneurial success. Howard Schultz, founder of Starbucks, did. He found a new use for coffee as a designer beverage that creates an experience. Johann Gutenberg took two unconnected ideas—the wine press and the coin punch— and came up with the printing press and movable type. The mechanism for the ballpoint pen inspired roll-on deodorant, and playing with a piece of wire while thinking about a debt he had to repay resulted in Walter Hunt's development of the safety pin.

Magazines, newspapers, and the Internet are excellent sources of inspiration for new ideas. Surprisingly, the federal government or state government can also be a great source of new venture ideas. New laws and regulations often require the use of a product or service that didn't previously exist. For example, the establishment of the Occupational Safety and Health Administration (OSHA) provided an opportunity for people who could train businesses in everything from meeting the stringent requirements that OSHA imposed on the workplace to filling out the incredible amount of paperwork associated with those requirements. City ordinances that require certain products, such as glass and plastic, to be recycled have produced many businesses that provide new uses for these materials.

TAKE ADVANTAGE OF A PERSONAL NETWORK

The second most commonly cited source of new venture ideas is business associates. A personal network—a circle of friends, associates, and acquaintances—not only is a rich source of innovative ideas but also opens the mind to new ways of thinking and new possibilities. Contacts within a personal network can help an individual connect ideas that might not have been considered because the individual was relying solely on her or his personal experiences. Contacts can help refine ideas and can direct an individual to resources to assist in testing the business concept. Personal networks arise not by accident but from the concerted effort of entrepreneurs to go out and meet new people on a daily basis.

RETURN TO CHILDHOOD

Many creativity and innovation gurus use toys to get their clients to respond more creatively. Legos and K'NEX are great for stimulating creativity because they start with a simple brick or connector piece, and from there the sky's the limit. Take that one step further and play with children to see unfettered imagination in action. Suspending the adult intellect for awhile and thinking like a

Generating Business Ideas

Here are a few exercises to spark some new ideas. List geographic areas that are not being reached by a particular product or service.

1. _____
2. _____
3. _____

List some market segments (populations) that are underserved.

1. _____
   _____
2. _____
   _____
3. _____
   _____

List a few big or troublesome problems for which the solution could turn into a potential business.

1. _____
2. _____
3. _____

child can stimulate the natural creativity in everyone. Creativity guru Doug Hall, whose famed Eureka! Ranch in Cincinnati, Ohio, has been the birthplace of thousands of new product ideas, uses games and toys to make people more comfortable doing things they've never done before and to come up with ideas that previously they would have dismissed as strange or unworthy. Jose Muñiz was thinking in a childlike fashion when he took a bet from a friend that he could not make a living selling butterflies. He found that releasing scores of butterflies at weddings or other special events was something people were willing to pay for. In 2006, the revenues of his company, Amazing Butterflies, had reached $1 million.[13]

THINK IN OPPOSITES

Great ideas often spring from imagining the opposite of what is normal. For example, think about what can be done with a telephone. A number of years ago, when AT&T was brainstorming some new marketing tactics, the marketing people asked themselves what a telephone is *not*. It's not something that can be eaten, so they came up with a way to eat telephones—chocolate telephones, to be exact, which they sent to their best customers.

Another example can be found in the paradox of recessions. Most people regard recessions, or economic downturns, as negative events, but looking for what is good about a recession is a useful creative exercise. A recession brings about many more needs and problems in which to find opportunity. For example, during a recession, many people lose their jobs and go back to school to retrain themselves for new careers. Educational entrepreneurs know this, so they start private schools offering courses and workshops to people who want to take a new direction in their careers or need retraining after losing a job. Publishers know this as well, so they develop books geared toward retraining and refocusing careers.

Removing the Challenges to Problem Solving

One of the most effective ways entrepreneurs have of finding opportunity is to see a problem and seek a solution. Most people do this out of habit every day; they just don't realize it. They can't find a particular tool they need (say, a hammer), so they substitute something else (the handle of a screwdriver). That's using creative thinking to solve a problem. Todd Smart observed that small, independent towing companies were having a difficult time surviving and getting new customers in a world of big, brand name companies. So he brought many of these little companies together under one umbrella, Absolute Towing and Trucking, based in Los Angeles, California. Absolute Towing and Trucking handles customer acquisition and management activities for the owners so that they could do what they do best—tow vehicles.

In attempting to solve a problem, entrepreneurs make a number of common mistakes that prevent them from defining the problem correctly and then analyzing potential solutions.[14] They often define the problem incorrectly by asking "how can I fix this problem?" when the better question is "what is the source of the problem?" Answering that question opens the door to many more alternatives than are available with the first question. They may take mental shortcuts such as jumping to conclusions, letting personal biases interfere with the process, or relying on intuition. Unfortunately, many of these mental shortcuts are subconscious; that is, we're not aware of them. Entrepreneurs frequently rely on patterns based on previous experience. Sometimes, when a pattern does not actually exist, they develop a mindset about a particular subject that is a consolidation of all their biases about that subject. Finally, they tend to draw conclusions before beginning the analysis or identify the solution before adequately defining the problem and analyzing it.

There are a number of effective ways to overcome these challenges. A few of the more popular strategies include:

▎ Restate the problem so as to uncover the *real* problem. For example, a problem stated as *we need to increase our revenues* appears to be an issue of how to generate more sales, but further investigation might conclude that the *real* problem is *how to better serve the needs of the customer.* If the value proposition for the customer has not been defined correctly, there is no realistic way to increase revenues and solve the problem.

▎ Identify the pros and cons for potential solutions. Then examine the cons and determine whether there is any way to convert those cons to pros. Eliminate

FIGURE 3.2

A Decision Tree Analysis

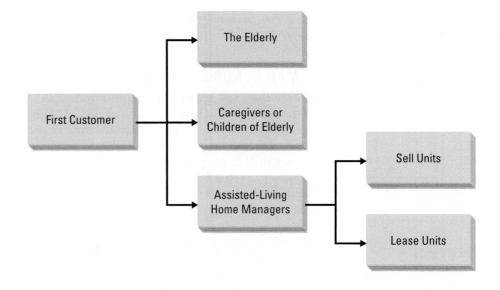

all the cons that can't be fixed. Match them up with the pros and analyze for each option. Then choose the best solution.

▶ Develop a decision tree (like the one shown in Figure 3.2) that reflects all the possible choices to solve the problem and their related outcomes. Notice that the tree branches are mutually exclusive, meaning that only one choice can be made. The branches are also collectively exhaustive; that is, they include all the possible choices. This very simple tree depicts the choices available for an entrepreneur who had developed a videoconferencing system to connect the elderly with their distant family members. The decision to sell to assisted-living managers would generate two additional choices.

Sources of Innovation

Entrepreneurs find inspiration for new ideas that could become new businesses in a variety of places. A few of them are listed in Table 3.1.

In addition to the sources listed in Table 3.1, there are three technology fields of endeavor that will offer plenty of opportunity in the decades to come. Technology

TABLE 3.1

Some Sources of New Product/Service Ideas

Customers (e.g., needs and suggestions for improvements or new products/services)	Unexpected news events (e.g., increased security needs resulting from the 911 attacks)
Newspapers and magazines (source of potential needs in the market)	Trends and patterns of change (e.g., need for privacy protections on the Internet)
Observation (e.g., sitting in a hospital and observing how the staff works)	New government regulation (e.g., Sarbanes–Oxley accounting requirements)
Demographic shifts (e.g., the increase in the Latino population in the United States)	Emerging industries (e.g., private space enterprise)
Small business (e.g., need for logistics support)	Business operations (e.g., new processes that reduce the costs of manufacturing)

affects every industry and every type of business, so some of the opportunities that emerge from these technologies will not be technology based.

HUMAN GENOME PROJECT

Perhaps the most important scientific accomplishment of the last decade was the mapping of the human genome, first announced in June 2000. Mapping the structure of human genes opens the door to therapies targeted to a person's specific genetic makeup and may ultimately make it possible to cure devastating diseases such as cancer. It also makes possible the use of cloning to create duplicate organs to serve the growing transplant segment of the medical industry. The announcement of the mapping of the human genome was greeted with little interest by the general public, who couldn't grasp the significance of something so esoteric and distant in its possibilities. However, despite the current lack of interest on the part of the public, the Human Genome Project will create hundreds of business opportunities. For example, companies like PE Biosystems Group make equipment that genomics companies use to sequence and assemble genes. Entrepreneurs with diagnostic laboratories like BioForce Laboratories, a young entrepreneurial firm, will find new opportunities in gene-based diagnostic tests. Entrepreneurs interested in gene therapy will be able to license new technologies from their inventors and create new applications in the marketplace.

NANOTECHNOLOGY

Nanotechnology is a science that involves matter and processes that occur at the molecular level. (The prefix *nano* stands for one billionth of a metric unit, and 10 nanometers is 1,000 times smaller than the diameter of a human hair.) It is a multidisciplinary field that takes existing science to the nanoscale level. Scientists and engineers are developing molecular machines, such as microscopic-level diagnostic chips that a person can swallow to enable a doctor to track what is happening in that person's body. The ability to create microscopic machines and robots opens the door to thousands of new products and services that never existed before—everything from stain-proof trousers to glass that cleans itself. In the developing world, nanotechnology research is seen as providing possible solutions to the problems of water purification, energy, food production, and medicine and pharmaceuticals.

MOBILE TECHNOLOGY

The ability to communicate without physical connections has opened up many opportunities to provide new products and services. Today, any manager or sales representative equipped with a web-enabled smartphone can check on inventory levels and shipping progress for customers and can send and receive e-mail. And that's only the beginning. Many entrepreneurs interested in this area believe that people will become walking Internet portals with wearable wireless technology. They will be able to extend their senses and become an interface for everything

Entrepreneurs Teaching the Hungry How to Feed Themselves

People who are born to wealth often choose to work in service to humanity. Free from the need to work to survive, they often start nonprofit ventures designed to target a societal problem that hasn't yet been addressed. Doraja Eberle was born into a wealthy Austrian family. Because she was quite rebellious as a child, her family decided that she might learn to appreciate what she had if she were trained in social work and saw how the less fortunate lived. To their surprise, Eberle loved the work. In 1992, during the Bosnian War, Eberle was overcome with compassion for the suffering of the people there. She had met a young soldier in Zagreb who had no arms and no legs, yet he was thankful that he was alive. From that day forward, Eberle knew that she wanted to devote her life to making the lives of others better. She started an organization called Farmers Helping Farmers to provide food and supplies, as well as to build homes for people displaced by war or some other disaster. In 1998, to the surprise of everyone, she moved 900 tons of food from Germany to the starving Bosnians, something that no other aid organization was able to do. Whereas many organizations seeking to provide such aid are mismanaged, bureaucratic, and ineffective, Eberle's entrepreneurial attitude has enabled her to accomplish things once thought impossible. Instead of simply giving people what they need, she provides them with tools, animals, seeds, and the like, thus empowering them to help themselves. Today, Farmers Helping Farmers is helping Kenyan farmers become more self-sufficient by using their organization's volunteers to coordinate projects and raise funding to support their work.

Sources: Craig Hall, "The Train of Hope," in *The Responsible Entrepreneur* (Franklin Lakes, NJ: Career Press, 2001); and Farmers Helping Farmers, http://www.farmershelpingfarmers.ca, accessed January 15, 2007.

they need wherever they go. "Always on, always with you" devices will consider an individual's personal preferences as well as where they are, what they're doing, and whom they're with. With rapid advances in artificial intelligence, processing speeds, and integrated circuitry, the future of mobile devices seems assured.

Opportunity is everywhere, and much of it goes unnoticed. Entrepreneurs who make the effort to become more creative and opportunistic will have an unending supply of new ideas available to play with.

New Venture Checklist

Have you:

☐ Identified the roadblocks that keep you from being creative?

☐ Developed a plan for removing those roadblocks?

☐ Started a file to keep track of business ideas?

Issues to Consider

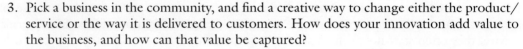

1. Give an example to demonstrate the difference between an idea and an opportunity.
2. Compare the outcome-based approach to creativity with the process approach. Which do you believe is right, and why?
3. Pick a business in the community, and find a creative way to change either the product/service or the way it is delivered to customers. How does your innovation add value to the business, and how can that value be captured?
4. Identify the challenges you face in becoming more creative. What three things will you do to address those challenges?
5. How is invention different from innovation? Which is more common today, and why?

Experiencing Entrepreneurship

1. Spend an afternoon walking around your community or your university or college campus. Don't look for anything in particular. Observe the things that you don't normally pay attention to when you're in a hurry. Watch people—what they do and don't do. At the end of the afternoon, write down all the thoughts that come to you on the basis of your afternoon of observation. Which of these ideas could possibly become a business opportunity and why?

2. Pick one of the sources of new product/service ideas discussed in the section of this chapter that starts on page 57. Using that source, come up with an opportunity that has business potential. Then, using the Internet or talking to people in that industry (always the best approach), develop a brief report that supports the viability of this opportunity.

Relevant Case Studies

## Chapter 4

DEVELOPING A BUSINESS MODEL

"I'd rather have a Class A entrepreneur with a Class B idea than a Class B entrepreneur with a Class A idea."

—GIFFORD PINCHOT III

LEARNING OBJECTIVES

▶ Explain what a business concept is.

▶ Position the concept in the value chain.

▶ Develop an effective distribution strategy.

▶ Build a business model for a new concept.

Profile 4.1 WHY A BUSINESS MODEL MATTERS

It is surprising how many entrepreneurs come up with a great business idea but generate no business model to ensure that they will create and capture value, in other words, make money at what they're proposing to do. In the late 1990s, Marc Fleury was working as a sales engineer at Sun Microsystems when he decided that he wanted to develop an application server, which is a software program that manages the applications for a business. At the time, it seemed very likely that he could find venture capital to fund the effort. Fleury was highly motivated to start his own business, so with a partner, he founded Telkel, Inc., in the fall of 1999. Their business model involved an application hosting business sitting on top of JBoss, the Java application server they had built. They would charge fees to companies for running programs on their server.

To launch the business, they needed funding, but the venture capitalists they approached quickly pointed out that Fleury and his partner had no experience in the hosting business; their expertise was in application development. A more difficult challenge was that their product was ready in the spring of 2000, precisely when the dot com world came crashing down, leaving funders running scared and not interested in tech companies. Unfortunately for Fleury and his partner, whatever money they had gathered quickly ran out, so they closed Telkel, Inc., in November 2000.

Fleury did not let this failure get him down; in fact, he was more determined than ever to start his own business, and he still believed in JBoss. This time, however, he conducted a feasibility analysis before he invested much time and money in the business. He started by examining all the mistakes he had made the first time around and acknowledged that he had to modify his business model to suit the post-2000 environment. Because he couldn't seek venture capital and had used up all his own money, he realized that the business had to make it on its own from the start.

During this period of feasibility analysis, Fleury began receiving e-mails from users of JBoss who wanted to know whether training was available. Without hesitation, Fleury said that it was and then immediately set out to develop a training course. His first course in Atlanta, Georgia, sold out, grossing him $60,000 for the week. While the training opportunity was taking off, customers also began requesting support, consulting, and documentation, and Fleury soon hired programmers to help him take care of that end of the business. This time he had gotten the business model right and achieved his goal of being profitable from day one. In 2006, JBoss Group was acquired by another open source leader, Red Hat, with the goal of driving down the cost of developing and deploying web-enabled applications.

Sources: "Red Hat Signs Definitive Agreement to Acquire JBoss," http://www.redhat.com/about/news/prarchive/2006/jboss.html, accessed April 10, 2006; M. Fleury, "Doing It Wrong, Getting It Right," *Business Week Online* (September 2, 2003), http://www.businessweek.com/print/smallbiz/content/sep2003/sb2003093_8638.htm?sb; http://www.jbossgroup.com; and Business Editors, "JBoss Group Introduces Annual Compensation Plan: JBoss Developers Receive Profit Sharing and Economic Interest Options in JBoss Group LLC," *Business Wire* (March 25, 2003), http://www.findarticles.com/cf_0/m0EIN/2003_March_25/99150218/p1/article.jhtml?term_JBoss_Group.

In today's vibrant, fast-paced business environment, it is easy to get the impression that business concepts are developed on a napkin during dinner and that the business is funded and operating within a few days. But even for Internet businesses, that exciting scenario is a stretch. Just because an entrepreneur builds a business does not mean that customers will come. In reality, a substantial amount of planning must take place and a great deal of effort must be put forth before a company's products or services ever successfully reach the market. That planning includes developing a business concept that meets a real market need and a business model or way to capture value. New technology and business support tools such as overnight shipping and search engines, such as Google and Yahoo!, have produced new business models while making it easier than ever before for entrepreneurs' businesses to appear larger than they are. Edgar Blazona owns ElevateHome, a multinational children's furniture firm that operates out of a small building in the backyard of his home in Berkeley, California. He manufactures the furniture using a factory in Thailand and one in India and oversees production using a document-sharing program, WebEx, that lets Blazona and his factories collaborate on the design of kids' furniture and bedding under the name True Modern. In 2006, after 18 months in operation, the company began earning a profit.[1]

This chapter explains how to develop an effective business concept, position it in the value chain, and develop a business model that creates and captures value for the customer and the business.

Developing a Business Concept

A business concept is a concise description of an opportunity that contains four essential elements: the customer definition; the value proposition (or benefit to the customer); the product/service; and the distribution channel or means of delivering the benefit to the customer. (See Figure 4.1.) The business concept can be thought of as a quick elevator pitch. *Elevator pitch* is a term that has been applied to the idea that entrepreneurs have only a few seconds— the time it takes to ride an elevator up to the twelfth floor—to get an investor (or other interested party) to "buy into" a business concept. A few seconds is not a lot of time, so providing a clear, concise, and compelling statement of the business concept is important. Most people, whether they are potential customers or potential investors, aren't patient enough to give an entrepreneur with an idea more than a few seconds of thought before they decide whether to dismiss it or investigate it further. The next sections will detail the elements of an effective business concept so that entrepreneurs can get beyond the elevator pitch.

THE CUSTOMER DEFINITION

Who is the customer? This vital question is deceptively simple. Many entrepreneurs cannot answer it accurately, because they simply assume that their customer is the user of a product or service they are offering. Although it is more common today than ever before for that to be the case, in many industries it is not. When Jordan NeuroScience first considered who the customer was for its ER-EEG technology designed to remotely monitor the brainwaves of trauma patients in emergency rooms, it immediately thought of the patients, the beneficiaries of the technology whose lives would be saved. But when faced with figuring out how to make money, the company realized that its customers were not

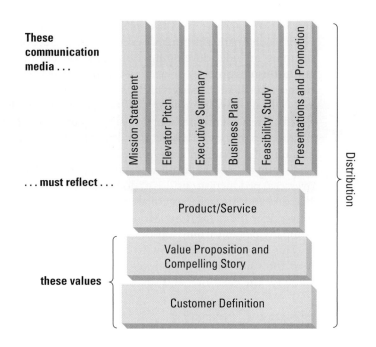

FIGURE 4.1

The Business Concept

the patients, or even the doctors, but rather the hospital administrators who made the purchasing decisions. This revelation changed everything about the business concept and its associated business model. Jordan NeuroScience had to decide what benefit its product was providing to the hospital administrators, which was quite different from the benefit to the patients. Although hospital administrators are interested in obtaining technologies to improve patients' quality of life, they are still primarily focused on increasing revenues and reducing costs.

In general, the customer is the one who pays, so, depending on where the company lies in the value chain, each customer will be different. As an example, consider Figure 4.2, which depicts a value chain, or distribution channel, for a furniture importer. The importer buys from the furniture manufacturer and sells to the furniture retailer; therefore, the retailer is the entrepreneur's customer, and the consumer is the beneficiary or end-user of the product and the customer of the retailer. Now, if the entrepreneur were to decide to sell direct through a catalogue or via the Internet, the consumer would become the direct customer. Clearly, it is important for entrepreneurs to understand both their customers and their end-users. At the very least, they will need to convince their customer—for example, the retailer—that there are plenty of consumers ready to buy.

Defining the customer is a critical part of the business concept, because the customer determines all the other components—what the entrepreneur will offer, what the value proposition is, and how the benefit will be delivered to the customer. A clear and precise customer definition increases the chances that the business concept will meet the customers' needs.

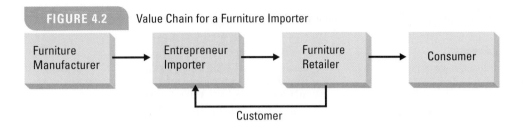

FIGURE 4.2   Value Chain for a Furniture Importer

THE VALUE PROPOSITION AND COMPELLING STORY

The value proposition is the benefit that the customer derives from the product or service; in other words, the reason the customer will buy. It is common for entrepreneurs mistakenly to think that they are identifying the benefits to the customer when in fact they are merely describing features of the product or service. Consider the furniture importer discussed earlier. Claiming that the entrepreneur is providing retailers with unique pieces of furniture from many parts of the world is certainly true, but uniqueness is a feature or characteristic of the furniture, not necessarily a benefit to the customer. In this example, the entrepreneur is offering the retailer/customer the ability to purchase from a single supplier (the importer), who will supply unique pieces of furniture from many parts of the world. In short, the benefits to the customer are convenience and access. In general, benefits are intangibles such as better health, speed, saving time and money, or reliability. Table 4.1 offers an example of the distinction between features and benefits for a different type of business. In this business, the product is premium hay for thoroughbred racehorses. Note that the benefits for the customer and for the end-user or beneficiary are different.

No value proposition is complete without a compelling story that answers several questions. Why should anyone be interested in this concept? What is the pain that is being eased or what problem does this concept solve? In general, if the problem has to be explained, then a real need has not been identified. A simple statement of the problem should elicit a response of "I get that!" or "That makes sense. Why didn't I think of it?" Here is the compelling story for the hay example.

> Imagine spending close to a million dollars on an investment in a horse. This investment has the potential to return millions of dollars to the owner if the horse can make it around the track faster than the competition. If you were the owner, trainer, or breeder of a performance racehorse, wouldn't you be interested in finding a method of ensuring high performance from your animal? C3 will manufacture a premium horse feed product, C3 Performance, in China and sell it to retailers in Singapore/Malaysia, Japan, Hong Kong, and South Korea. Distributors and retailers will benefit from this product by enjoying a consistent revenue stream from a premium product that will offer their customers healthier, better-performing, and more profitable horses.

This statement identifies the challenge for horse owners, trainers, and breeders and the company's solution to the challenge. Discovering a way to improve the

TABLE 4.1	Features Versus Benefits for Premium Horse Feed for Thoroughbred Racehorses	
Features	**Benefit to Retailer**	**Benefit to End-User**
2-foot length for hay	Revenue potential—this feature makes the product more attractive to end-users, leading to higher potential sales and customer loyalty	Cost savings, because less of it is wasted than is wasted with regular hay
Packaged in plastic bags	Cost savings, because it leads to less waste in inventory	Cost savings, because there is less waste in storage
Flash-baked for greater nutrition and to reduce dust and mold spores	Revenue potential, because of cost savings from longer shelf life	Higher revenues and lower costs, by preventing common ailments that impede racing performance
Made with molasses, giving it a good taste for the horse	More reliable revenue potential—this feature leads to more consistent use among horse owners because horses typically do not switch after trying it	Higher revenue—its good taste leads horses to eat this high-nutrition feed, which can improve racing performance

Source: Prepared by Sheryl Sacchitelli, Daniel Wang, and Jason White, MBA class of 2003, University of Southern California.

chances of realizing a huge return on this kind of investment is something that would definitely interest this customer.

THE PRODUCT/SERVICE

Today, most businesses produce both products and services, even if one category dominates. Doing so provides multiple revenue streams, which gives the company a competitive advantage. Definition and design of the product or service stem directly from customer needs and the founding team's core competencies. Therefore, the concept statement should reflect the customer's perspective on the product or service that is being offered. If the product is proprietary, that is, there is intellectual property such as a patent associated with the product, it would be important to include that information in the concept statement because it is a competitive advantage.

THE DISTRIBUTION CHANNEL

The distribution channel element of the business concept answers the question "How do you deliver the benefit to the customer?" Many options exist, but in general, the best option is the one that fulfills the customer's expectations about where and how the product or service should be sold. Most services are delivered direct to the customer, but products often go through channel intermediaries such as distributors and retailers. How to reach customers is a critical decision that is discussed in more detail later in this chapter.

PUTTING THE CONCEPT STATEMENT TOGETHER

Creating a clear and concise concept statement is not difficult, but telling a compelling story can be. For example, consider the creation of artificial nerves called BIONS, being developed at the Alfred Mann Institute for Biomedical Research at the University of Southern California. The purpose of BIONS is to re-animate paralyzed muscles through electrical stimulation. In this case the proposed company, BIONNIX, is studying the treatment of pressure ulcers in patients who are bedridden or in a coma.[2] The company plans to sell to hospitals and nursing homes.

A compelling story consists of a problem and a solution. In this case, the problem is:

> Every year there are 3.5 to 5 million people in the United States suffering from pressure ulcers, and an estimated 60,000 persons die annually from ulcer-related complications. Pressure ulcers represent a common but preventable medical problem encountered by primary-care practitioners providing care to older patients, particularly in hospital and nursing home settings.

This is the problem that must be solved. It must be stated in a way that captures attention and focuses on the "pain" in the market. If the problem must be explained in detail, then the real pain has not been identified. In other words, the problem statement should be simple and clearly understood.

Adding the four-element concept statement or solution produces the following:

> An estimated 60,000 persons die annually from pressure ulcer-related complications. BIONNIX is the leading implantable electrotherapeutic medical device company for hospitals and nursing homes seeking a way to more cost-effectively and conveniently treat pressure ulcers in immobile patients. BIONNIX will manufacture, sell, and support products that provide patients with an effective, easy, and painless solution to pressure ulcers.

Note that in the development of the concept statement, money was not mentioned. Money is usually assumed to be the most necessary component of a successful venture. But although money is important, it is only an enabler; its presence does not confirm that the business concept is feasible. In fact, the dot com bust of spring 2000 proved that a large investment in a business idea will not make it feasible if customer demand and an effective business model are not present. Until customers express interest in what is offered and will pay for it, all the money in the world will not make the venture feasible. However, once the concept is judged feasible, it is time to think about how to fund it.

QUICK-TESTING THE CONCEPT

With a preliminary business concept in hand, it is helpful to do a quick assessment to determine whether a full-blown feasibility study is warranted. Many weak business concepts can be eliminated from further consideration by asking a few simple questions, such as those that follow. Answering these questions does not require any in-depth research. Entrepreneurs can simply rely on their own knowledge and on the advice of people who can provide objective opinions.

1. *Am I really interested in this business opportunity?* If the concept is developed, time and energy will be invested, so it is important that the entrepreneur be passionate about the idea. Many potential entrepreneurs have gone forward with concepts that others suggested, only to discover after they have spent considerable time, effort, and money that their hearts weren't in the business.

If the excitement for the venture idea is not there in the beginning, it is unlikely to magically appear later in the process.

2. *Is anyone else interested?* A business cannot exist without customers or, in many cases, without investors, so it is important for entrepreneurs to determine whether anyone else is interested in the business concept. If the entrepreneur has a good social network of business associates, these people can be tapped to give that preliminary review.

3. *Will people actually pay for what is being offered?* Often when people hear about a new product or service, they express interest—and even excitement. But what are they willing to pay for it? And how much? If they are not willing to pay what it's worth, the idea may need to be revised. New Internet businesses, in particular, suffer from potential customers who believe that they should be able to get most anything online for free. Will the new venture be able to get beyond that perception and develop a viable business model?

4. *Why me?* An entrepreneur must be convinced that he or she is the right person to execute this concept. What unique capabilities and contacts do the entrepreneur and his or her team bring to the venture and will interested stakeholders find those capabilities and contacts valuable?

5. *Why now?* Why is this a good time to launch this business? Why has no one else done this before? Or, if they have, why did they fail (or succeed)? Every launch of a new venture occurs within a window of opportunity that enhances the chances of success. If the launch timing is premature or too late, those chances disappear.

Once these questions have been satisfactorily answered, it's time to progress to the next level: studying the value chain for the new venture. This is the environment in which the business will operate.

The Value Chain and the Concept

The value chain, or distribution channel, is a central component of the business concept. It consists of two parts: (1) upstream activities, those related to the production of a product or service, which may include raw materials, product development, manufacturing, and warehousing; and (2) downstream activities, those associated with selling the product or service such as customer acquisition, sales transactions, and logistics.[3] Today more than ever before, the value chain has the power to make or break a business concept. Three powerful forces are at work changing how value chains operate: the Internet, reduced transaction costs, and disintermediation.

FORCES AFFECTING THE VALUE CHAIN

The Internet was the most disruptive technology to come about in the decade of the 1990s. It has not only affected the way business is transacted but has also reshaped education, entertainment, communication, collaboration, and even social and professional relationships. The Internet has taken on a life of its own and has given Internet businesses a life cycle of their own. Internet years are counted like dog years; that is, an Internet business that is one year old looks and acts like a business that has been around for seven years.[4]

The Internet can be an extremely efficient channel because it is widely available, relatively inexpensive, and relatively fast. Software, because of its digital nature, can be produced, warehoused, shipped, purchased, negotiated, warranted, and financed completely on the Internet with no intermediaries. In fact, software can entirely bypass the warehousing and shipping parts of the channel by permitting customers to download it from the Internet. Yet many businesses that operate on the Internet must rely on offline intermediaries in channels that move tangible products. Apparel, for example, cannot be as effectively produced and distributed like software over the Internet because it requires offline manufacture, warehousing, and shipping. Only marketing, purchasing, and the actual transaction (placing the order and paying) take place on the Internet.

The Internet has helped to reduce transaction costs, in some cases to zero. Consider the example of running out of ink for a printer. Businesses normally keep an inventory of supplies on hand, so someone simply retrieves a new cartridge from the supply room when needed. Although businesses track the inventory of products for sale that are on hand, they often don't consider the cost of carrying supplies on hand. Supplies are carried as a convenience to employees, so they don't have to spend the time to go out and buy them when they run out. Going out to purchase a new cartridge is a cost of using a printer that has been saved.

Of course, this is a very simple example. But extrapolate for a moment to a manufacturer that purchases raw materials from a supplier and must negotiate terms, conditions, and all sorts of legal issues as part of the purchase. These activities carry a much larger transaction cost, and that cost often prompts a manufacturer to vertically integrate—to acquire its supplier, thus bringing all those expensive processes in-house thereby reducing transaction costs.

The Internet has made firms and markets more efficient and hence reduced transaction costs. The office supply company is now linked electronically to the business's supply inventory, so the owner no longer has to think about stocking printer cartridges. The office supply company knows each customer's usage record and restocks just in time, saving time and money. Of course, much greater savings in transaction costs are possible for the manufacturer who must purchase a wide variety of raw materials. It is no wonder that most companies use the Internet to manage their supply and distribution chains.

The Internet has also shortened the value chain by getting rid of nonessential intermediaries in some industries. Most products are part of a distribution channel that includes one or more intermediaries. The function of intermediaries is to reduce the transaction costs for manufacturers in areas that are outside their core competency. They do this by providing value-added services such as warehousing, bundling of products, shipping, and distribution to retail outlets. They are valuable to the manufacturer as long as the cost of using them is less than those services might cost in the open market. And that's where the Internet comes in. The Internet brings buyers and sellers together in a way that makes many of the services of the intermediaries unnecessary. The process is called disintermediation. If a manufacturer can easily sell directly to the customer over the Internet and ship directly from the manufacturing plant, it has reduced its transaction costs and made a higher profit on each transaction.

Distance does not affect the cost for services or products that can be digitized; online businesses are always open; and they can be operated from anywhere in the world. But the critical difference between the Internet as a distribution channel and traditional channels is that the Internet is interactive rather than merely a passive conduit for products. Consequently, it has the ability to create virtual marketplaces like eBay. One interesting effect of the Internet is that it has taken us back to mass marketing and commoditization (competing on price) because it reduces the marketer's ability to differentiate on the basis of other product attributes or service. Unfortunately, the more efficient channels become, the more opportunity for commoditization.

WHAT DEFINES AN EFFECTIVE CHANNEL?

An effective distribution channel has several characteristics, which are discussed briefly in the following sections.

Inventory

At various points along the channel, inventory must be warehoused and ready to be shipped where needed, whether it is raw materials to the manufacturer or finished goods to the consumer. Entrepreneurs need to decide whether they want to hold inventory or outsource that capability to someone else in the channel. Holding the inventory for distribution gives the entrepreneur more control over what happens to products, but warehousing and distribution are competencies that the entrepreneur's team may not have. Companies that focus on distribution functions typically have invested heavily in technology such as RFID (radio frequency identification) to track items throughout the distribution channel, and logistical systems to manage the physical movement of items through the channel. Entrepreneurs generally start without the resources to replicate these functions, so they are frequently outsourced.

Ownership

It is important to distinguish between ownership of the goods and possession of them. As goods move through the channel, ownership typically changes only at the point of purchase, but possession may change at various points. For example, when a fulfillment house agrees to warehouse and ship for a company, it takes possession of the goods but does not purchase them and therefore does not own them. Information, as an intangible product, presents some unique challenges with respect to ownership, and illegitimate channels may even be formed to move the products through the channel. This can be seen, for example, in the pirating of software and music. Entrepreneurs must review all documents relative to the movement of their goods so as to insure that they can identify who is responsible if something is damaged or missing.

Financing and Payment

Credit is an essential element of an effective channel because it smoothes out the fluctuations in cash on hand experienced by purchasers. Methods for collecting payments for purchases have been enhanced by technologies such as PayPal, which enables buyers to send money online from most countries and merchants to manage payments from buyers' bank accounts or credit cards.

Risk Management

The movement of products through channels entails some level of risk for which third-party insurance is required. Examples of such risk are product loss or breakage during shipping, product liability, and failure of the customer to pay for goods. In addition, manufacturers take on responsibility for risk to the customer via warranty programs and after-sale service agreements. It is important that entrepreneurs understand the types of risk present in the channels they choose to use and identify ways to mediate those risks.

Member Power

Effective channels often produce channel members who gain the power to control aspects of the channel. A channel member gains power if (1) other members rely on it for their primary needs, (2) it controls financial resources, (3) it plays a critical role in the value chain, (4) it has no substitute, or (5) it has information that reduces uncertainty. For example, Wal-Mart is well known for employing strong-arm tactics to exact the lowest possible prices from its suppliers. Because it is the world's largest retailer, it is well aware that smaller suppliers cannot afford to lose such a huge customer. Strong retailers can also force manufacturers to adopt new systems, as was the case in the 1980s when retailers forced manufacturers to provide UPC symbols or bar codes on packages so the retailers could scan them for inventory and sales tracking. Today RFID tags are rapidly becoming the current tracking standard.

In an effective channel, strong members include other members in the decision-making process; they share information and often make concessions when a new policy or technology is costly to a member.[5] One excellent example of channel collaboration comes from the apparel industry, where DuPont, a fiber producer; Milliken & Co., a textile mill; Robinson Mfg., an apparel manufacturer; and JC Penney, a retailer, joined forces to identify customer needs and develop a new line of clothing.

DEVELOPING A DISTRIBUTION STRATEGY

Distributors, retailers, and other outlets are one means through which manufacturers and other producers communicate with the customer, so they are very much partners with the organization, particularly in a virtual company.

Their goal is to gather information from the customer so that the manufacturer or producer can revise and improve its offerings. Finding good, loyal outlets is competitively difficult. In fact, distribution, once a mundane, routine occupation, has become the glamour stock of the business world, and "channel surfer" entrepreneurs constantly seek the most productive channel.

The following examples illustrate just a few innovative distribution strategies.

⬤ Snap-on Tools differentiates itself in its market by stocking mobile trucks with its products and sending them to sites where buyers of tools are likely to be.

⬤ Jet Blast Corporation found its most effective distribution channel in TV shopping channels such as Home Shopping Network and QVC for products like the Pro-Jet 2000, which converts ordinary garden hose pressure into high-velocity water flow. For inventors with single products, TV shopping channels offer a means of competing with major companies.

⬤ McAfee Associates produces and distributes security tools, in particular Virus-Scan, a program that detects and destroys computer viruses. Its initial strategy was to post virus "fixes" (instructions) on computer bulletin boards and ask anyone who downloaded its software to pay what they thought it was worth. That strategy made John McAfee $5 million in his first year. The company continues to offer many of its products free in the form of computer downloads. This strategy gets new users to try their products.

Before choosing a distribution strategy, a wise entrepreneur looks at the various distribution channels that similar companies are using. That provides an indication of customer expectations about time and place of delivery. It also helps reveal opportunity gaps—innovative distribution strategies that might allow an entrepreneur to capture a group of customers that is not currently being served. Market research with the customer may also reveal new channels that customers would be willing to try, such as the Internet.

Factors Affecting the Choice of Strategy

In very broad terms, the choice of distribution strategy is a function of desirability (Will customers be happy with it?), feasibility (Can the channel do what the entrepreneur wants it to do?), and profitability (Can the entrepreneur make money using this channel?). A number of factors should be considered when one attempts to determine the most effective distribution strategy. Cost is certainly one factor. It includes all the various expenses related to marketing the product and distributing it to the customer or end-user. Consider the situation of a manufacturer producing a consumer product in the sporting goods industry.

At each stage, the channel member adds value to the product by performing a service that increases the chances of the product's reaching its intended customer. The wholesaler seeks appropriate retail outlets, and the retailer advertises and promotes the product to its customers. The value created permits each channel member to increase the price of the product to the next channel member. For example, the manufacturer charges the wholesaler a price that covers the costs of producing the product, plus an amount for overhead and profit. The wholesaler, in turn, adds an amount to cover the cost of the goods purchased and his or her overhead and profit. The retailer does the same and charges the final price to the customer. That price can typically be four to five times or more what it cost to manufacture the product (labor and materials).

Suppose the manufacturing entrepreneur decides to bypass the wholesaler and sell directly to retailers:

Manufacturer ⟶ Retailer

On the surface it appears that the price to the retailer could be substantially lower, perhaps even the rate at which the manufacturer sold to the wholesaler in the first example. However, there is a flaw in this reasoning. The wholesaler performed a valuable service by making it possible for the manufacturer to focus on producing the product and not incur the cost of maintaining a larger marketing department, a sales force, additional warehouses, and a more complex shipping department. All these activities now become a cost to the manufacturer of doing business with retailers and must be factored into the price charged to the customer (the retailer) and the consumer as well as the decision to choose this distribution channel. This is not to say that it never makes sense for manufacturers to sell direct to retailers. However, it is important for entrepreneurs to consider all the costs, advantages, disadvantages, and consequences of choosing a particular market channel to reach the customer.

Other aspects of starting the new venture can be examined by studying the distribution channel options. For example, the choice of channel affects where the business is located and how products are transported to the customer. Consider the following channel:

Manufacturer ⟶ Retailer

In this instance, it may be advantageous to locate the manufacturing plant near major transportation networks to hold down shipping costs. Now consider the following channel:

Manufacturer ⟶ Wholesaler ⟶ Retailer ⟶ Customer

Here it is not important for the manufacturer to be located conveniently near the retailer. Having a location that minimizes shipping costs to the wholesaler becomes more relevant. Another consideration is the need to be located near raw materials, particularly if they're costly to transport.

Entrepreneurs who are retailers (or wholesalers) look at the distribution channel from both directions. The customer will be reached directly, but looking upstream in the distribution channel, the retailer must also be concerned with finding a good distributor who represents quality manufacturers. The total cost of a distribution channel will directly affect the company's ability to make a profit. Entrepreneurs who manufacture have yet another concern, which is developing an efficient and effective supply chain. Fortunately, today, many third-party logistics companies like FedEx, UPS Supply Chain Solutions, and DHL

the Internet *was* the business model, so they developed businesses that had no compelling reason to exist beyond the fact that they were on the Internet. As a result, they couldn't get customers to patronize their sites. Pets.com, for example, was built on the notion that customers would find it easier to buy dog food online. What they didn't realize was that most customers purchase dog food when they purchase their own food in a grocery store, so making online purchases was actually an inconvenience for them because it required them to make an additional stop on their computer. Funerals.com experienced a similar fate. The founder did not understand that in times of emotional grief, people did not want to turn to their computers for help; they preferred to deal with someone face-to-face.

In the offline world, problems with strategic choices also exist. Entrepreneurs are continually faced with the challenge of maintaining the value of their products and services so that they don't become commodities competing only on price. Avoiding commoditization means following a strategy of continual innovation and searching persistently for new ways to satisfy the changing needs of the customer.

Imperfect Value Creation and Capture Assumptions

One of the biggest challenges for business models is finding a way to make money from the value that has been created. A poor assumption about the value created by a new venture will mean that there are no customers to pay for that value. Similarly, even if there is a reasonable assumption of value created, it may not be the beneficiary of that value who has to pay for it. This is one of the biggest problems for entrepreneurs in the health care industry. An entrepreneur with a new medical device that can save patients' lives is not collecting revenue from the patient who sees the value but rather from the health care provider, whose mission is to contain costs, a completely different value proposition.

Incorrect Assumptions About the Value Chain

Entrepreneurs often assume that the value chain is static, that is, that it will continue with the current players and with the current processes and information flow well into the future. This is a faulty assumption. Core competencies enable a firm to move into new industries and new value chains unrelated to their current products and services. UPS did this when it examined Toshiba's lengthy and inefficient process for repairing laptops that involved shipping to UPS's hub, then to Japan, then back to UPS, then to the customer. UPS cut out all the excess shipping for Toshiba and now repairs their laptops in UPS's facility.[10] UPS's core competency is designing effective and efficient systems, and it took that competency from the logistics industry to the computer industry.

BUILDING A BUSINESS MODEL

Identifying an opportunity is only part of the equation for new venture success. There also has to be a way to make money with this venture. How does the entrepreneur create value for the customer and capture that value so that the business makes a profit? A number of important business decisions associated with the development of a business model can be summarized in a series of questions that should be answered before proceeding further with the model.[11]

1. What are the size and importance of the revenue streams that the business model can generate?
2. What costs most affect the model, and what are their size and importance to the model? In other words, what are the cost drivers for the business?
3. How much capital is required to execute the business model and what is the timing of the cash needs?
4. What are the critical success factors to achieving the goals of the business model?

Using eBay as an example, the highly successful company had a very simple business model. Its infrastructure enabled users to communicate with each other for a reasonable fee.[12] eBay "has no responsibility for goods offered at auction, for collecting buyer's payments, or for shipping."[13] It is merely responsible for making sure these transactions occur. Its revenues come from seller fees; its cost structure includes the online infrastructure, marketing, product development, and general and administrative expenses. Moreover, it takes only a few salaried employees and partners to implement the model.

It is useful to build a business model in stages, as depicted in Figure 4.3.

Stage 1: Identify the Entrepreneur's Position in the Value Chain

The first step in developing a business model is to identify the entrepreneur's place in the value chain. If the entrepreneur's company is a supplier or producer

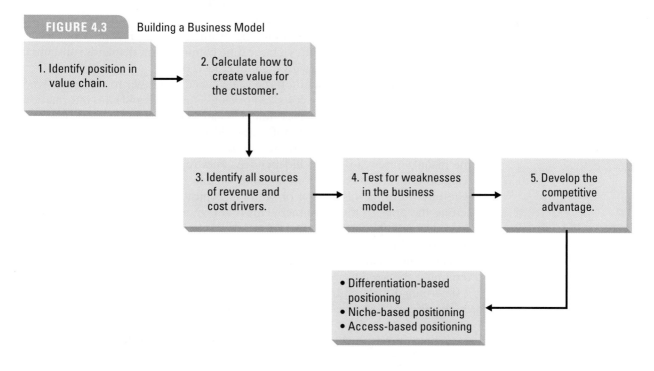

FIGURE 4.3   Building a Business Model

FIGURE 4.4

The Commitment Pyramid

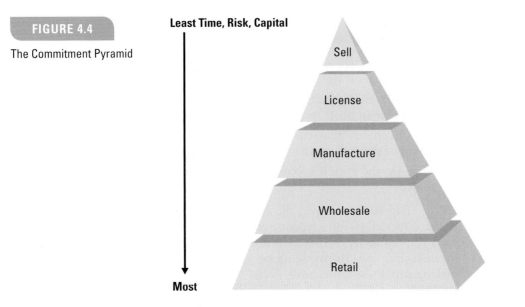

Least Time, Risk, Capital

Sell

License

Manufacture

Wholesale

Retail

Most

of raw materials, it will generally be at the top of the value chain and upstream from manufacturers. Intermediaries, such as distributors and retailers, will be downstream from manufacturers. Where a company is located is normally a function of its capabilities and the desire of the entrepreneur for a particular type of business. Consider Figure 4.4, which depicts a commitment pyramid. In very simple terms, it portrays the relationship between the location of a business in the distribution channel and the time commitment, level of risk, and financial capital required. Selling a business concept takes the least amount of investment and requires the least time commitment from the entrepreneur. Conversely, starting a retail business requires a huge time commitment, demands substantial capital, and generally carries with it a higher level of risk.

Once the business is located on the value chain, it is easier to recognize who pays whom and to determine costs and pricing. Figure 4.5 adds this information to a generic example of a complex indirect channel of distribution. The raw materials producer charges the manufacturer $4 per unit; the manufacturer turns the raw material into product and sells it to the distributor for $6. Alternatively, the manufacturer can use an independent sales representative (sales rep), who will find outlets and receive a commission on sales made. Note that the retailer, who buys from the distributor or sales rep, typically at least doubles its cost in setting the price to the consumer. This is known as keystoning. Also note that as a rule, markups increase as one moves down the channel. This occurs because the cost of doing business increases, as does the risk.

The value chain now illustrates the various markups, which is helpful in determining the lowest price possible for the product. The highest price possible is determined through market research with potential customers. The markups on the original cost reflect profit and overhead for the channel intermediary and are determined by what is typical in the industry. Every product or service has more than one channel option, so it's a good idea to depict distribution options

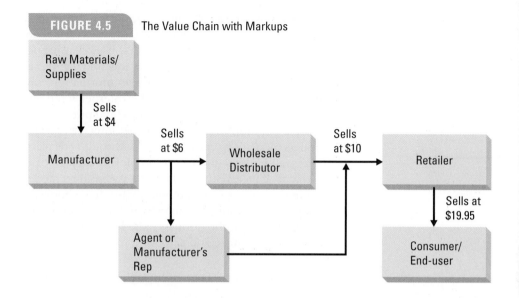

FIGURE 4.5   The Value Chain with Markups

graphically to compare their effectiveness. Graphing the value chain makes it possible to do the following:

▶ Measure the time from manufacturing to customer on the basis of the lead time needed by each channel member.

▶ Determine the ultimate retail price on the basis of the markups required by the intermediaries.

▶ Figure the total costs of marketing the product. For example, manufacturers have to market to distributors, but to support their distributors, they may also market to retailers and even end-users or consumers.

Stage 2: Calculate How to Create Value for the Customer

It is important to determine whether the proposed business model will force customers to change the way they use or find a particular product or service. Will that change benefit customers in a way that they can readily see? For example, many computer users have not switched to the latest Windows operating system because they can't easily see what benefits it offers over the system they are currently using. In other words, the basic functionality has not changed substantially, but the cost to the customer in terms of time and money is too high to warrant switching. It is also important to determine whether the learning curve for the customer will be steep. If customers see that learning to use the new product or service will take some time and require them to change old habits, they will think twice before purchasing.

Stage 3: Identify Revenue Streams and Cost Drivers

One of the most important components of the business model is identifying the revenue streams that will flow from the products and services being offered.

A healthy business model always supports revenue streams from multiple types of customers and multiple products and services. Relying on one revenue stream from one type of customer is dangerous. What happens when the market shifts and that customer goes away? In the mid-1990s, Edmund Publications, the 32-year-old publisher of automotive information, saw the Internet as just another marketing vehicle. Today, the Internet *is* the business. Edmunds's website provides independent ratings, reviews, and pricing data for every make and model of car, in addition to a variety of other interactive features. Edmunds.com's basic business model is to make its money through ads placed by manufacturers, parts dealers, and others in the automobile industry. Books now account for less than 1 percent of its revenues. Changing its business model with the changing times, Edmunds.com now has revenue streams from books, from advertising, and from selling and licensing information to other companies.[14] Equally important are the cost drivers of the business. The business that can keep its costs low enjoys a significant advantage and will bring more dollars to the bottom line.

Stage 4: Test for Weaknesses in the Business Model

It is very important that entrepreneurs consider their business model as a work in progress. Feedback from a variety of sources will help to refine the model and assure its feasibility. Market research can verify the validity of demand forecasts, pricing, and the value of the value proposition to the customer. Testing the feasibility of any outsourcing support is also critical.

Stage 5: Develop the Competitive Strategy

Strategy is very different from a business model because it considers more than the customer; it considers the competition. An effective competitive strategy either differentiates the new venture from existing ventures or creates a niche in the market that other companies are not serving. In short, it describes how the new business will be superior to existing businesses. An individual contemplating the launch of a new business will frequently resort to copying what has succeeded in the past. Hundreds of would-be entrepreneurs attempt every day to emulate successful Internet companies like MySpace and Amazon or successful food services companies like Starbucks and Cheesecake Factory in the offline world without considering why customers would buy from them. A competitive strategy speaks to how a business model is different or unique from the business models of competitors.

SOURCES OF OPPORTUNITY FOR BUSINESS MODELS

Many opportunities exist for finding new and innovative business models. Here are three examples:

1. *Reposition the company on the value chain.* Look for unserved or underserved niches and customer dissatisfaction.
2. *Reinvent the value chain.* Ignore what currently exists and develop a whole new value chain. This is often accomplished by looking at successful value

chains in other industries and extrapolating to the entrepreneur's own value chain.

3. *Redefine value-added.* Don't do things exactly the way everyone else does. If competitors seek out contracts for work from customers and wait for customers to tell them what to do, try learning what customers want in advance, doing the work, and then approaching the customer with a solution.

4. *Redefine distribution.* Find out where the customers are and go there. If the channel contains a lot of intermediaries, consider "selling direct" to save the customer money.

When the Business Model Must Change

It is a fact of business life that business models evolve and sometimes radically change due to circumstances often beyond the control of the entrepreneur. Change can occur in a number of ways.[15]

1. *Change incrementally to expand the existing model geographically, enter new markets, modify pricing, or change product/service lines.* An example would be The Gap, an apparel store that expanded to an Internet business model.

2. *Revitalize an established model to give it new life and stave off competition.* This can be accomplished by introducing new products or services to existing customers as Starbucks did when it began selling CDs of the music it played in its stores.

3. *Take an existing model into new areas.* For example, Amazon.com, known as a highly effective Internet bookseller, began using its successful fulfillment process to market and sell everything from clothing to household goods.

4. *Add new models via acquisition.* For example, a restaurant company might acquire a catering service. Compass Group PLC, a U.K. food services company, acquired catering and vending operations from DAKA International, Inc.

5. *Use existing core competencies to build new business models.* Canadian manufacturer Bombardier originally focused on snowmobiles. Because it sold its products through credit, it developed an expertise in financial services, which enabled the company to move into capital leasing. Its manufacturing expertise was leveraged into large-scale manufacturing for the aircraft industry.

6. *Reinvent the business model.* As a company's products become commodities, it may take an enormous shift in operations, culture, and business model to add new value to the company's offerings. Apple reinvented itself with the introduction of the iPod.

Having taken all of these considerations into account, and armed with a clear and compelling concept and business model, entrepreneurs are ready to conduct an effective feasibility analysis. This analysis begins with an in-depth study of the industry and entry market, which is the focus of the next chapter.

BUSINESS MODELS FOR THE DEVELOPING WORLD

It may surprise many to learn that the "world's 4 billion poor people [are] the largest untapped consumer market on Earth."[16] As a group, they have more buying power than any other, with a total annual income of $1.7 trillion. Fortunately, today many organizations are beginning to address the needs of consumers in the developing world through products and services that meet their very unique requirements. Those organizations that have been successful have been able to transition from a nonprofit business model to a commercial business model.

ApproTEC, now called KickStart (http://www .approtec.org/home), is an East African nonprofit organization that worked with world-famous design company IDEO to develop a water pump that was suited to the needs, budget, and environmental conditions of Kenya. It was designed to employ manufacturing capabilities already available in Kenya; it cost less than $150, could survive the harsh Kenyan environment, and was easy to maintain. More than 24,000 pumps were sold in Tanzania and Kenya.

Approximately 70 percent of those sales were to female entrepreneurs who used the pumps to produce $30 million per year in profits and wages.[17] Success in the form of 33,000 new businesses was due to a compelling value proposition and a way for everyone involved to make money, an important incentive. ApproTEC employed a local supply chain from raw materials to manufacturing and distribution. Its execution plan involved five elements: (1) researching the market for small-business opportunities based on local resources; (2) designing new products and technologies as well as business models; (3) training local manufacturers in the production of the new technologies; (4) promoting the technologies to local entrepreneurs; and (5) monitoring the impact of the program to develop best practices.

Source: H. Chesbrough, S. Ahern, M. Finn, and S. Guerraz, "Business Models for Technology in the Developing World: The Role of Non-Governmental Organizations," *California Management Review,* 48(3) (2006): 54.

New Venture Checklist

Have you:

☐ Developed a clear and concise business concept that contains the product/service, customer, value proposition, and distribution?

☐ Created a compelling story?

☐ Identified your company's place in the value chain?

☐ Done a quick test of the business concept to see whether it is worthy of a feasibility analysis?

☐ Developed a promising business model?

Issues to Consider

1. What is the role of the compelling story in defining the value proposition of the business?
2. Why is it important to identify the real pain in the market that needs to be addressed by the business concept?
3. What is the relevance of identifying where on the value chain the new venture lies?
4. What is the purpose of the business model, and why do business models typically fail?
5. What are the characteristics of an effective business model?

Experiencing Entrepreneurship

1. Define a concept for a new venture using the four components discussed in the chapter: product/service, customer, benefit, and distribution. Conduct a quick test on some potential customers through a focus group or interviews. Did you secure enough information to make a decision to move forward to conduct a feasibility study? Why or why not?

2. Suppose you intend to start a theme restaurant that can be replicated and franchised. Based on an analysis of some existing theme restaurants, what types of revenue streams could this business generate?

Relevant Case Studies

Case 2 Craigslist, p. 442

Case 5 iRobot: Robots for the Home, p. 463

Case 9 Command Audio, p. 485

FEASIBILITY ANALYSIS: TESTING THE BUSINESS CONCEPT

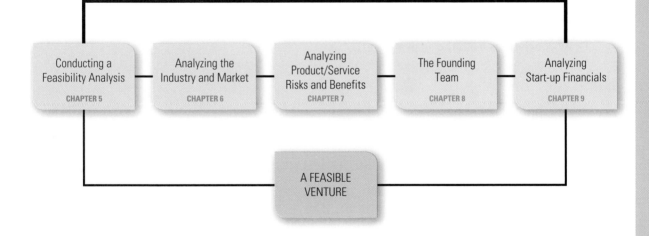

Conducting a Feasibility Analysis — CHAPTER 5

Analyzing the Industry and Market — CHAPTER 6

Analyzing Product/Service Risks and Benefits — CHAPTER 7

The Founding Team — CHAPTER 8

Analyzing Start-up Financials — CHAPTER 9

A FEASIBLE VENTURE

## Chapter 5

CONDUCTING A FEASIBILITY ANALYSIS

"The human mind treats a new idea the way the body treats a strange protein—it rejects it."

—PETER MEDAWAR, Nobel Laureate, for discovery of acquired immunological tolerance

LEARNING OBJECTIVES

▶ Prepare to conduct a feasibility analysis.

▶ Understand the feasibility tests.

▶ Draw conclusions from the analysis.

Profile 5.1 LET YOUR PRODUCT SPEAK FOR YOU

In December 1999, Courtney Hennessey was a 22-year-old junior at Saint Louis University in Missouri. It was winter break just before the holidays, and Courtney decided to indulge her passion for making jewelry. At the local bead shop, she found herself overwhelmed by all the possibilities—beads and crystals in every color and shape imaginable. Before she knew what she was doing, she had spent $400 on her father's credit card. Resolved to pay him back out of revenues from the bracelets she intended to make and sell, she put together some of her original creations and began wearing them around town.

When people saw her jewelry, they immediately wanted to buy it. In fact, she took 20 different samples to her great aunt's wake and left with orders worth $800. As more and more people began to wear her jewelry designs, the customers themselves became advertisements for her new business. Without realizing that she had used a very important technique in business feasibility analysis, Courtney had started her business determining who her customer was, how many of them there were, and what they wanted to buy.

The customer referral marketing strategy eventually led a Neiman Marcus associate to find Courtney and ask her to show her designs. That led to a trunk show and then to sales in upscale boutiques around the United States. To brand her jewelry, she came up with the name Codi, which was the first two letters of her first and middle names, Courtney Diane. She attached a sterling silver heart to every piece of jewelry as a trademark and let her customers sell her jewelry through home parties, much like Tupperware® parties.

Courtney successfully started a business with a product she was passionate about. She tested the feasibility of her concept by letting the customer tell her what to make, and she encouraged customers be her sales staff. She realized that when you have something the customer wants, starting a business is much easier and much more satisfying.

Seven years into her business, Courtney decided that it was time to settle into a retail outlet, Codi The Boutique, in the St. Louis, Missouri, area. She designed it to feature a living-room-like atmosphere similar to what her customers have become accustomed to.

Sources: Codi Jewelry, http://www.codijewelry.com; and C. Hennessey, "The Key Is Happiness," in M. McMyre and N. Amare (eds), *Student Entrepreneurs* (St. Louis, MO: Premium Press America, 2003).

Feasibility analysis is unquestionably one of the most important skills individuals can acquire if they want to become entrepreneurs or use their entrepreneurial mindset inside a large corporation. Opportunities that entrepreneurs identify involve certainty and uncertainty, and the uncertainty aspect is characterized by varying degrees of risk.[1] The degree of risk is revealed by the preparatory research entrepreneurs do in the form of a feasibility analysis. Research has proposed that risk and uncertainty are different concepts as they relate to outcomes. In the case of risk, the distribution of the outcomes in a group of instances is known, often based on past experience.[2] But, in the case of uncertainty, it is impossible to identify a distribution of instances because each opportunity is unique. Since uncertainty and ambiguity are a natural part of the launch of any business, understanding the differences between the market conditions at the development of the business concept and the realities of the market at the time of launch becomes critical.[3] This is accomplished through the use of subjective probability, which argues that in an uncertain situation, there are choices to be made that are based on a subjective prediction of the future.[4] Typically, someone who is naïve about starting a business will be more positive about the potential outcome of an effort, while someone who is experienced in start-ups will be more skeptical about potential success. To more accurately assess a future opportunity, it is vital that entrepreneurs understand their capabilities; the capabilities and intentions of their competition; the needs and desires of customers; and the bargaining power that the entrepreneur has in the value chain.[5] The bottom line is that the more information an entrepreneur acquires during the process of feasibility analysis, the higher the chance that his or her predictions will be close to the mark and uncertainty will be reduced.

The feasibility analysis can be simple or complex depending on the requirements of the business under consideration and the nature of the environment (industry) in which the business will operate. In industries where the environment is dynamic, such as the mobile devices industry, feasibility analysis will require the ability to understand and predict the natural changes that will occur between the time the business is conceived and the time at which it is launched. This is no easy task because it demands that the entrepreneur in such an industry have complete knowledge of all the variables in the equation that might change and what impact those changes might have on the new venture. Industry and market fluctuations affect demand, cash flows, valuation, and even the window of opportunity, and they are very difficult to predict.

By contrast, entrepreneurs with concepts that will launch in more stable industries, like the baked products industry, have an easier time planning for an environment that will likely be the same by the time the business launches.

Accounting for the potential changes in the value of variables considered in the feasibility analysis is typically accomplished by considering a possible range of values along a probability distribution. Probability theory permits the entrepreneur to identify a range of outcomes for various variables involved in the start-up of a business and then assign probabilities to those outcomes. In simple terms, this means looking at a potential change in a forecast in four ways: (1) what is the probability the change will occur, (2) what is the magnitude of the change, (3) what is the impact of the change on the business, and (4) what can be done to mitigate the change. For example, suppose there is a high probability that the estimates for customer demand might be overstated. The probability of this occurring might be 70 percent (based on the entrepreneur's understanding of the market). The magnitude of the impact might be to reduce revenues by 40 percent, which could delay profitability for one year. To mitigate the impact, the entrepreneur needs to plan for additional working capital in the start-up funding requirements. In markets where a lot of information is available, it will be easier to have a high degree of confidence in the robustness of the probabilities assigned to various outcomes.

To make these types of risk assessments, feasibility analysis forces the entrepreneur to conduct serious research, to think critically about the business concept, to answer fundamental questions, and to achieve a high level of confidence about the willingness to move forward with the business or project. Feasibility analysis is an excellent way to reduce the risk of start-up in stages. Figure 5.1 presents a

FIGURE 5.1   The Process of Feasibility Analysis

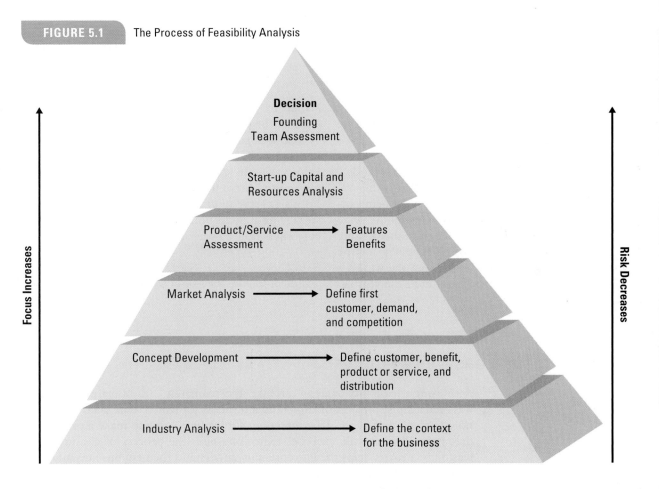

visual depiction of the process of feasibility analysis. At each stage of the process, entrepreneurs are answering questions that enable them to make decisions about whether to move forward with the analysis and ultimately whether to conclude that the concept is feasible. Therefore, as the process moves from industry analysis to team assessment, the questions are answered and the risk of the concept is reduced. Of course, no amount of feasibility analysis can reduce risk to zero. This is because there are also issues related to the operations of a new business that are covered in the business plan that must be addressed. Feasibility analysis is about testing a new business concept, whereas the business plan is about execution—developing a business—its operations, staffing, growth, and financial plans; therefore, a business plan assumes a feasible business. The business plan is discussed in Chapter 10.

Many businesses have launched on the strength of a feasibility analysis alone to get traction and feedback from the market. This is particularly true of Internet-related businesses, where it is relatively easy to create a presence in the market and get quick feedback from customers and end users. The stages of the feasibility process are reviewed later in this chapter, and each stage, along with analytical methods, is discussed in detail in separate chapters of the book.

Socially Responsible Entrepreneurship

Say Hello to a Green Winery

Rutherford, California, is home to the first winery in Napa Valley to be certified as organic. Not only are the grapes that result in the 60,000 cases of Frog's Leap wine sold a year organic, but they are also grown with "water-saving dry farming methods." Until recently, entrepreneur John Williams did not even publicize that fact because in general being organic was not something that was important to wine drinkers. He did it because it leads to higher quality and it's better for the health and longevity of the vineyard and the workers. He also met the winery's energy needs with solar panels and built the visitors'

center to exacting green building standards now used by the construction industry.

The Williams family founded Frog's Leap winery in 1981 beside the Mill Creek in an area known as Frog Farm. It seems that in the early 1900s, frogs were raised there to be sold to gourmet restaurants. Frog's Leap is an example of a business that is both socially and environmentally responsible, even if its customers don't always know it!

Sources: "Talk About Quiet Leadership," *Inc. Magazine* (November 2006), p. 83; Frog's Leap, http://www.frogsleap.com.

Preparing for Feasibility Analysis

A thorough feasibility analysis can take approximately 200 hours of work, but weighed against the cost of launching a business for which there is no market or no effective way to access the market in sufficient volume to make a profit, it is definitely a worthwhile exercise. If nothing else, the process of conducting a feasibility analysis helps the entrepreneur understand the new business and better develop any questions that need to be answered in order to decide whether the conditions are right to move forward. In general, a feasibility analysis is performed to answer the following three broad questions:

1. *Is there a customer or a market of sufficient size to make the concept viable?* No business exists without customers, and even if the entrepreneur can determine that there are customers for a new venture, it will be important to calculate whether there are sufficient customers to make the effort worthwhile. Some market niches are not large enough for an entrepreneur to make a suitable profit once competitors enter the market. Knowing in advance that the market is too small permits the entrepreneur to make adjustments in the concept to broaden the market niche or decide not to go forward with the business before time and money have been wasted.

2. *Do the capital requirements to start, based on estimates of sales and expenses, make sense?* Can this business be started with an amount of capital that the entrepreneur has or will be able to raise? Are there ways to reduce start-up costs through outsourcing or strategic partnering with another company?

3. *Can an appropriate start-up or founding team be assembled to effectively execute the concept?* Recall that in today's complex, global environment, most

successful start-ups involve teams rather than solo entrepreneurs. A team consists of the founders and any required strategic partners, which can be people or other businesses with capabilities that the business needs.

When the feasibility analysis is complete, the entrepreneur should be able to determine whether the conditions are right to go forward with the business concept. If conditions are not favorable, the areas tested, such as industry, market, product, and so forth, will need to be reviewed to discover whether another approach might make the concept viable. For example, suppose an entrepreneur has a concept for a new type of wheelchair that is better suited to disabled people with active lives, for example, those that drive cars or participate in sports. Through the entrepreneur's analysis, she may have determined that the cost to execute the concept (set up a factory, purchase equipment, and so on) is well beyond her means and would probably not be of interest to major investors because this is a niche market that is not rapidly growing. All it may take to make the concept feasible, however, is to consider outsourcing the expensive aspects (such as product development and manufacturing) to an existing company. Immediately, the direct costs are reduced, and the entrepreneur doesn't have to invest in expensive equipment and a manufacturing facility.

The point is that many concepts can achieve feasibility if the right conditions are in place. The real question is whether the entrepreneur is convinced of the concept's feasibility and is confident enough to put the time, money, and effort into its execution. Has the analysis provided the entrepreneur with enough supporting evidence that he or she is willing to take a calculated risk and begin to plan the launch?

For example, one group of entrepreneur hopefuls wanted to capitalize on some interesting photographs of big city icons that one of their members had taken. They decided to transfer those photos to apparel to create a unique product line. Interviews and focus groups with targeted customers revealed that there was not enough interest to sustain a business. Customers did not find the icons that appealing, and the team couldn't charge enough to make a sufficient profit from the effort. So, the team concluded that they should not go forward with the venture.

PRE-FEASIBILITY QUICK LOOK ASSESSMENT

Before undertaking the research associated with a thorough feasibility study, it makes sense to do a quick look at the idea based on what the entrepreneur already knows about the business and industry and based on talking with a few trusted business people. The first step is to draft a description of the business in the manner of the business concept discussed in Chapter 4. This brief description should discuss the problem or pain in the market, the product or service being offered, the first customer, the value proposition for that customer, and the way the value will be delivered to the customer. Here is an example of such a concept statement.

> Aegis will manufacture integrated snowsports apparel that combines fashion, function, and protection to the risk-conscious snowsports participants, enabling feelings of security, freedom, and peace of mind. Targeted direct customers for the line include

specialty snowsports apparel retailers and the end-users will be Generation X and Y, intermediate to advanced snowsports enthusiasts. Products will be shipped directly to retailers who will enjoy high margins and quick product turnover.[6]

Then the industry in which this business will operate should be examined. The industry is the aggregation of all the companies in a value chain that support a common area of business. For example, in the restaurant industry, the value chain consists of sources of food (farms, producers, brokers), sources of supplies, distributors, wholesalers, and so forth. A quick look will reveal the trends in this industry, the opinion leaders, and what impact they have on the industry. Is there room in the industry to enter and grow? Here is a brief industry summary for the concept previously presented.

The snowsports apparel industry is a $1.2 billion industry that is in the midst of significant growth. Given the increased acceptance of the freestyle snowriding popularized by mainstream media in the form of the X Games on ABC/ESPN and the Gravity Games on NBC, the number of snowriders participating in the sport has never been higher. It is a highly fragmented industry and seasonal. Only a few companies have been able to acquire sizable market share. The opinion leaders are companies like Sport Obermeyer and The North Face.

The market is comprised of the customers described in the concept and the competitors for those customers. Knowing who the first customer is and the size of the niche can help to determine if the business can survive and grow to add additional customer niches. At this point, identifying all the possible customers will at least provide a level of confidence that there is potential for growth beyond the original customers.

The primary target market is specialty retail stores catering to Generation X and Y skiers and snowboarders. The market size is about $650 million with over 8,500 retailers in the United States alone. Additional targets include chain retailers that appeal to multiple sports and carry lower-end products.

With the industry context defined and the market identified, the product or service can be described in a way that provides a benefit to the customer. Without being able to solve a problem customers have, it is unlikely that a new product or service will be successful, so the features that describe the product or service should be associated with an intangible benefit to the customer. It is also important to consider any intellectual-property protections that might afford a competitive advantage, such as patents, trademarks, copyrights, and trade secrets. These are discussed in Chapter 7. In the case of a product, the status of development and time to completion are critical factors in predicting when the business concept can become feasible. Of course, at this point, these estimates will be very broad and based on assumptions that may prove incorrect once the entrepreneur does some market research. Here again is an example from the Aegis feasibility study

Initially, the primary focus will be on jackets and pants that offer a proprietary removable, fitted, protective padding layer incorporated into a fashionable shell, as well as integrated knee braces. The focus of protective features will include support and protection for areas of the body identified as being at high risk of injury during participation in snowsports.

The founding or management team is the catalyst that will give the business traction. Examining the capabilities and experience of the team will reveal any gaps that will need to be filled by hiring personnel or outsourcing to an independent contractor or company. Here is the statement about the founding team for Aegis.

> The founding team has experience in the fashion industry and retailing as well as biomedical engineering, with a specialty in tendon and ligament tissue engineering. One of the founders also has experience as an entrepreneur, having founded two web-based companies.

The quick look assessment does not deal with financial projections, because the purpose of this exercise is to weed out concepts that don't meet the market test. Nevertheless, during the quick look, it makes sense to list all the resources that might be needed by a business of this type. Such a list might reveal whether this will be a labor-intensive business, require outsourcing of certain capabilities, or need to be located in a specific geographic region.

> Aegis plans to outsource most of the workflow to third parties and use a trading company to oversee the manufacturing of the product line and shipping to the United States. After the initial roll-out of the product line, a sales team and back office support, including customer service, order fulfillment, and office management, will be required. Aegis will need leased office space for a headquarters. Materials will be sourced through fabric sourcing companies. Design work will be done in-house.

The quick look is an effective way to choose among several business ideas. Rather than spending the time undertaking in-depth feasibility analyses on each of the ideas, a quick look assessment may make it possible to eliminate one or more of the ideas early in the process.

An Overview of the Feasibility Tests

Having accomplished a successful quick look at a new business concept, it is time to do some serious research by consulting existing sources of information and by talking to customers and people in the industry. Table 5.1 provides an overview of the feasibility tests, the questions addressed by each test, and the chapter in this book that discusses in detail that particular aspect of the feasibility analysis and how to accomplish it. Table 5.2 offers an outline to help structure a written feasibility study. An effectively written feasibility study may convince an investor to fund the launch of the business, even without a business plan.

Although feasibility analysis is not a linear process, it often helps to begin at the industry level to understand the context or environment in which the new business will operate including where the industry is in the life cycle, what trends are apparent, whether the industry is growing, and who are the opinion leaders that affect the way the industry operates and determines the entry barriers that entrepreneurs might face. Chapter 6 goes into detail on how to analyze the industry.

Areas to Be Analyzed and Questions to Ask

Business Concept (Chapter 4)

1. Who is the customer?
2. What is the value proposition?
3. What is the product/service being offered?
4. What does the value chain look like?
5. Which distribution channel alternatives are available, and which customers will be served by them?
6. Are there ways to innovate in the distribution channel?
7. What is the business model, or how will the business create and capture value?

Industry and Market/Customer (Chapter 6)

1. What are the demographics, trends, patterns of change, and life-cycle stage of the industry?
2. Are there any barriers to entry? If so, what are they?
3. What is the status of technology and R&D expenditures?
4. What are typical profit margins in the industry?
5. Who are the opinion leaders in the industry and how do they affect the industry?
6. What are distributors, competitors, retailers, and others saying about the industry?
7. What are the demographics of the target market?
8. What is the profile of the first customer? Are there other potential customers?
9. Have you talked with customers?
10. Who are your competitors, and how are you differentiated from them?

Product/Service (Chapter 7)

1. What are the features and benefits of the product or service?
2. What product development tasks must be undertaken, and what is the timeline for completion?
3. Is there potential for intellectual property rights?
4. How is the product or service differentiated from others in the market?

Founding Team (Chapter 8)

1. What experience and expertise does the team have?
2. What are the gaps and how will you fill them?

Financial Needs Assessment (Chapter 9)

1. What are your start-up capital requirements?
2. What are your working capital requirements?
3. What are your fixed cost requirements?
4. How long will it take to achieve a positive cash flow from the revenues generated?
5. What is the break-even point for the business?

Cover for the Feasibility Study

Executive Summary

• Include the most important points from all sections of the feasibility study. Do not exceed two pages.
• Make sure that the first sentence captures the reader's attention and that the first paragraph presents the business concept in a compelling way by emphasizing the need or pain in the market that the business addresses.

Title Page (Name of Company, Feasibility Study, Founding Team Members' Names)

Table of Contents

Feasibility Decision

• The decision regarding the conditions under which the entrepreneur is willing to go forward with the business concept

The Business Concept
- Business concept and compelling story
- The first customer
- The value proposition, or benefit(s), being delivered to the customer
- How the benefit will be delivered (distribution)
- The business model (how the company will create and capture value)
- The potential for growth and spin-offs

Industry/Market Analysis
- Industry analysis
- Target market analysis
- Customer profile
- Niche the entrepreneur is entering
- Competitor analysis and competitive advantages
- Distribution channels (alternatives and risks/benefits)

Founding Team
- Qualifications of founding team
- How critical tasks will be accomplished
- Gap analysis—what is missing and how the needed skills and experience will be acquired (professional advisers, board of directors, independent contractors)

Product/Service Development Plan
- Detailed description and unique features of product/service
- Current status of product development
- Tasks and timeline to completion
- Intellectual-property acquisition (if relevant)
- Plan for prototyping and testing

Financial Plan
- Summary of key points on which financial feasibility is based
- Narrative assumptions or premises for resource needs assessment
- Cash needs assessment (cash-flow statement from start-up to positive cash flow)
- Pro forma income statement (1–3 years) by month or quarter
- Break-even analysis

Timeline to Launch
- Tasks that will need to be accomplished up to the date of launch in order of completion

Bibliography or Endnotes (Footnotes May Be Substituted)

Appendix (A, B, C., etc.)
- Questionnaires, maps, forms, résumés, and so on

The entrepreneur's target market is defined by the customers, those who pay, and the end-users, those who actually use the product or service. The market test is a way to define a profile of the first customer, the one who needs the product/service the most, to learn how large the market is and who the competitors might be. How to analyze a market is the subject of Chapter 6.

Good product/service definition is critical to providing the customer with what he or she wants. During the feasibility analysis, the entrepreneur will assess the features and benefits that customers have expressed are important to them and that will create a market advantage for the company. Determining what it will take in terms of raw materials, production capability, people, and expertise to produce such a product or service will also be important. Whether the product/service can be protected through legal means such as patents and trademarks should be evaluated, as this intellectual property may provide an additional competitive advantage to the new venture. Chapter 7 focuses on these areas.

Evaluating the skills and experience of the founding team is a critical task because without a team that can effectively bring the concept to market, it doesn't matter how exciting the idea is; its chances of success will not be as great without traction. Chapter 8 discusses the evaluation of the start-up team.

The final feasibility test is to calculate how much capital will be required to launch the business and operate it until it achieves a positive cash flow from the revenues generated. This is no easy task. Most entrepreneurs underestimate the expenses associated with operating the business and overestimate their ability to generate sales quickly, not to mention overestimating demand. This subject is treated in Chapter 9.

All of these tests contribute to an entrepreneur's understanding of the proposed new venture and to a decision about the conditions that must be in place for an entrepreneur to feel comfortable moving forward to consider launching the business. If the conditions are right, an entrepreneur can launch the business in a limited way to "test the waters" and then complete a comprehensive business plan to prepare for growth and the possible need for outside capital.

Drawing Conclusions from Feasibility Analysis

Rejecting new ideas is an age-old practice. In the 1940s, von Neumann talked about self-replicating programmable manufacturing architectures, and in the 1960s Feynman revealed that atoms could be arranged in new ways, further supporting the notion that what we know today as nanotechnology was a feasible concept.[7] But most products in common use today—airplanes, automobiles, telephones—were originally thought to be infeasible. Furthermore, even business concepts like eBay and Starbucks were initially considered to be infeasible. So how does an entrepreneur determine whether a new business concept is feasible once all the research is accomplished and the various aspects of the concept tested?

Recall that the process of feasibility analysis is designed to convert an uncertain opportunity to one that has a specific level of risk associated with it. Uncertainty is reduced by acquiring more information and answering the questions that contributed to that uncertainty. At each point in the feasibility process, the entrepreneur is able to make a judgment about whether to proceed with the analysis. For example, if, during the industry analysis, it was discovered that Congress was planning to pass legislation that would render it difficult for the entrepreneur to do business, he or she might consider designing another business opportunity in that industry that would not be affected.

Each step in the analysis provides information about the conditions that are necessary to make the business feasible. The sum total of these conditions should give the entrepreneur a level of confidence about the risk associated with the concept and his or her ability to execute the concept given that risk. But there is another important decision that must be made, perhaps as important as whether or not the business is feasible. And that is whether this business, given the necessary conditions for success, satisfies the personal needs and goals of the entrepreneur. The feasibility analysis should provide an entrepreneur with significantly more information about how this business would work than was available when the concept was conceived. Sometimes, in learning more about the industry and how businesses operate in that industry, an entrepreneur may discover that he or she is not suited to this type of business. Perhaps the initial excitement over the business has waned and in its place is a reality that is no longer attractive to the entrepreneur. Maybe launching this business will be too difficult a task, more difficult than the entrepreneur first thought it would be.

Alternatively, the process of feasibility analysis might make an entrepreneur even more enthusiastic about the business and its potential, enough so that it compensates for any identified risk associated with it. What is generally certain in all of this is that the process of feasibility analysis will definitely help an entrepreneur draw an appropriate conclusion about the business, and therein lies its real value.

New Venture Checklist

Have you:

☐ Identified an opportunity that you would like to pursue?

☐ Conducted a quick look assessment to see if a feasibility study is warranted?

☐ Undertaken a feasibility analysis to understand the risks?

☐ Drawn a conclusion as to whether to move forward with this opportunity?

Issues to Consider

1. Why is feasibility analysis a critical step in the launch of a new venture?
2. What is the purpose of the quick look assessment?
3. What is the difference between uncertainty and risk?
4. What are the areas of analysis in a feasibility study?
5. What conclusions can be drawn from a feasibility analysis?

Experiencing Entrepreneurship

Identify three opportunities to investigate. Ideally, you will find a business idea that interests you and from which you might want to do a feasibility analysis and eventually start a business, although this is not a requirement of the assignment.

You can do the assignment individually or in a group with no more than three people in the group. Following are questions in five categories that are commonly used in this type of assessment: (1) idea statement, (2) industry, (3) market/customer, (4) resource requirements, and (5) intellectual-property issues. Please answer all the questions for each of the three ideas you have chosen. Do not leave any question unanswered. Every question except those marked with an asterisk is to contain a reference to the source of the information, such as a website or an expert whom you contacted. If you contacted an individual, provide his or her name, phone number, and day and time of contact. If your source of information is a website, be sure to provide the exact link and not a general domain name.

QUESTIONS FOR QUICK OPPORTUNITY ASSESSMENT

Be sure that you collect all of the following information on each idea.

Idea Statement

1. What is the business idea?*
2. What is the problem the idea addresses?*

Industry

1. What is the NAICS code for your idea? (See http://www.census.gov/epcd/www/naics.html.) Go to at least 4 digits for the code listing.
2. Provide one finding each for economic, technological, legal, or sociocultural trend (one of each)

that is likely to influence demand for a product based on this idea. If all three ideas come from the same industry, your industry study will suffice for this section—just refer to it.

Market/Customer

Identify at least three markets in more than one industry for each idea:

1. Interview a potential customer in each of these three markets, either in person, by phone, or by e-mail.
2. Brainstorm with others about market ideas.

Resource Requirements

1. What human resources are required to bring this concept to market?
2. For what purposes will financial resources be required to commercialize this idea?

Intellectual-Property Issues

1. What intellectual property could be secured for this idea?
2. How is the product based on the idea you selected differentiated from other products in the market (could be size, convenience, a better method, and so forth)?

Decision

Based on the information you have obtained, provide your conclusions as to the potential for commercialization of each of the three ideas. Then rank order the ideas from most viable to least viable. For the most viable idea, tell whether you will move forward with this idea and justify your go or no go decision. You can complete this task in no more than three single-spaced pages.

Relevant Case Studies

## Chapter 6

ANALYZING THE INDUSTRY AND MARKET

"A moment's insight is sometimes worth a life's experience."

—OLIVER WENDELL HOLMES (1809–1894)

LEARNING OBJECTIVES

- ▌ Explain the industry life cycle.

- ▌ Use frameworks to characterize an industry.

- ▌ Conduct an industry analysis.

- ▌ Characterize the target market and first customer.

- ▌ Gather competitive intelligence.

- ▌ Gather demand data.

Profile 6.1 JOAQUIM SPLICHAL: REALLY COOKING IN A TOUGH INDUSTRY

If you look at a ranked listing of the industries in which venture capital is most likely to be spent, you'll typically find restaurants and food services at the bottom, right next to retail. That's because the restaurant industry is notorious for its high failure rate. Therefore, to succeed in the restaurant business, you have to understand the industry inside out, and you have to find a niche market in which to enter.

Joaquim Splichal came to the United States in 1981 from Spaichingen, a small village in Germany, in his early thirties, having worked in the hotel and culinary businesses from the age of 18. His years in Holland, Switzerland, and France, serving as an apprentice to some of the great chefs, had earned him many culinary awards when he took his first job in the United States as executive chef for the Regency Club in Los Angeles. Later he became part of the launch of the successful Seventh Street Bistro, also in Los Angeles. Then, in 1984, he had his first entrepreneurial opportunity when one of his customers gave him a minority stake in his own restaurant, Max au Triangle. The food he created there was outstanding; but unfortunately, he knew nothing about managing a restaurant, and very soon the restaurant closed. For the next five years, Splichal took consulting jobs until he was ready to try his luck at entrepreneurship again. As a consultant, he learned some important lessons that would ensure the success of his later ventures: "Control the capital investment . . . and make sure you're in the right area to open a restaurant." Splichal had a very clear vision of what he wanted to achieve and what a superior restaurant should be when, in 1989, he opened Patina, an upscale French restaurant in Los Angeles, with an investment of $650,000 from people who believed in him. He also took advantage of the expertise of his wife, Christine, who has an MBA in international management and runs the management and investment end of the business. Joaquim was the visionary, and Christine was the one who executed the concept. This time, their restaurant was a huge success, paying back its investors to the tune of 110 percent in 15 months.

With investors paid, the Splichals now owned 50 percent of the company. But with typical entrepreneurial vision, Joaquim Splichal had determined early on that opening more restaurants was his dream. At Patina, he was the chef and was in the kitchen every night. He wanted to build a company that endured beyond him—that didn't require him to be in the kitchen. Splichal knew that he had no desire to build a brand based on his persona, as his good friend, the renowned chef Wolfgang Puck, had done. He wanted to take a more low-profile approach. In 1992, he had an opportunity to purchase a failed French restaurant in the San Fernando Valley. He turned that site into Pinot Bistro and once again paid back the million dollars in investment capital in less than two years, and retained a 60 percent interest in the restaurant. Splichal's biggest concern with this new restaurant was that he had developed an image for Patina that was upscale and expensive. Pinot was intended to be a different experience: less expensive and not the super-high quality of the original restaurant. Would customers accept the difference? After a short period of confusion, they did and the restaurant succeeded. To achieve his goal of not being at the restaurant all the time, he hired a very talented executive chef who trained all the chefs he would later need in his subsequent restaurants.

Splichal did not take a cookie-cutter approach to his new restaurants; instead, he tried to give each its own unique character. He went on to develop four more restaurants, all rooted in classic French cuisine, but with a touch of California whimsy. Restaurants were not the only undertaking of this multi-talented entrepreneur; however, catering became one of the most important divisions of his ever-growing company. In 1995 he hired a catering manager, who promptly won the right to produce the Emmy Awards dinner that next year. The catering business began earning $1 million a year and by 1999 had reached $6.2 million in revenues.

In 1998, the Splichals consolidated all their holdings under The Patina Group (http://www.patinagroup.com), which made the company more attractive to lenders and investors. When they received a lowball offer from Restaurant Associates (RA), who wanted to expand to the West Coast, the Splichals decided it was time to retain the services of an investment bank. That decision nearly doubled the value of their business, and in 1999, after careful consideration, the Splichals merged the business with RA in a deal said to be worth about $40 million. Joaquim Splichal and his wife Christine still run The Patina Group of restaurants, which has grown to 28 operations and over 4,000 employees. Splichal was named Bon Appétit/Food Network Restaurateur of the Year for 2002. With the huge resources of RA behind them, the Splichals are expanding at a rapid pace, even looking into vineyards in Europe, perhaps to find their next entrepreneurial venture.

Sources: The Patina Restaurant Group, http://www.patinagroup.com (accessed March 4, 2007); Mary Caldwell, "Joachim Splichal: Patina Group Founder Creates New Concepts, from Fine Dining to Bistros, with Elegant Flair," *Nation's Restaurant News* (January 27, 2003); Restaurant Associates, "Joachim Splichal" and "News: The Patina Group Merges," *Nation's Restaurant News* (January 1997), http://www.restaurantassociates.com; and Arthur Lubow, "Recipe for a $40 Million Score," *Inc. Magazine* (October 2000).

Unquestionably, the analysis of the industry in which the business will operate is critical to the feasibility of a new venture. From the broadest perspective, the industry is a grouping of businesses that interact in a common environment as part of a value chain or distribution channel. There is enormous value in knowing an industry well. Ideas for new ventures frequently come from understanding and having experience with an industry. In addition, comprehending how an industry works can help an entrepreneur find strategic partners, customers, venture capital, and strategies for success. A strategic position in a growing, dynamic, healthy industry can go a long way toward ensuring a successful venture. For example, a young, growing industry with many new entrants, like the new media industry spawned by the Internet and user-generated technology such as blogs and video, offers an opportunity to position a business to become a major player in the industry. By contrast, occupying a weak position in a mature industry, such as the PC industry, may sound a death knell for the business before it ever opens its doors. Understanding how an industry operates is fundamental to shaping effective entry and growth strategies.

A market is a grouping of customers that an entrepreneur targets. Identification of the primary market and the first customer is one of the most important tasks to be undertaken during feasibility analysis. What is meant by "first customer"? The customer is the one who pays for the product or service, so the first customer for the entrepreneur generally represents that segment of the marketplace that needs the product or service most—in other words, the customer in the most pain.

Entrepreneurs identify their primary customers by recognizing a need, or pain, in the market. Gus Conrades and his partner Bryan Murphy saw a need for a central online place where people and businesses could purchase auto parts and car-care products. In the highly fragmented auto products market, customers had a difficult time finding what they needed. Conrades and Murphy launched Wrenchead.com to remedy that situation, and they now sell millions of auto parts and brand name accessories around the world to people who love cars and, at the same time, they provide e-commerce business solutions to dealers.

Identifying a pain or need in the market is only the first step. Unfortunately, many entrepreneurs don't place enough emphasis on in-depth market analysis to support the need they have recognized. As a result, they tend to overestimate their market forecasts for demand by as much as 60 percent. And that kind of error can be devastating to a start-up venture. This chapter helps the reader do efficient and effective industry and market research within the constraints of the limited resources available to entrepreneurs.

An Overview of Industry Analysis

Exploring an industry will involve gathering and synthesizing an enormous amount of information as well as talking to people who spend their days working in that industry. Starting with a clear understanding of what an entrepreneur needs to know will increase the chances that the assessment is as accurate as possible.

The data collected should answer the following key questions:

1. *How is the industry described?* Every industry possesses a particular character that may be described as hostile, collaborative, highly competitive, friendly, and so forth. It is also characterized by its demographics, such as size, number of active companies, revenues, and age.

2. *Is the industry growing?* Growth is measured by sales volume, number of employees, units produced, number of new companies entering the industry, and so forth. A growing industry means more opportunities for new ventures to enter and survive. The appropriate growth measure is determined by the type of industry. For example, the food services industry is typically labor intensive, so looking at growth in the number of employees makes sense. On the other hand, the import/export industry is not necessarily labor intensive so growth in the number of employees is not a good measure of overall industry growth.

3. *Where are the opportunities?* Does the industry provide opportunities for new businesses with strategies involving new products and/or processes, innovative distribution, or new marketing strategies? Are there clear examples of new ventures that have succeeded in this industry?

4. *What is the status of any new technology?* How quickly does the industry adopt new technology, and does technology play a significant role in the competitive strategy of firms in the industry?

5. *How much do industry companies spend on research and development?* Expenditures on R&D indicate how important technology is, how rapid the product development cycle is, and whether technology is critical to industry success.

6. *Who are the opinion leaders in the industry?* Which firms dominate the industry and what impact do they have? How do they influence new firm strategy?

Opinion leaders may or may not be a new firm's competitors in its markets depending on how the entrepreneur has defined his or her customers. Nevertheless, opinion leaders will affect the new venture's ability to access the supply chain and distribution channels.

7. *Are there young, successful firms in the industry?* This information will provide an indicator of how formidable the entry barriers are and whether the industry is growing rapidly.

8. *What does the future look like?* What appears likely to happen over the next five years? What are the trends and patterns of change? Entrepreneurs need to prepare their new ventures for success beyond the date of launch.

9. *Are there any threats to the industry?* Is there any chance that new technology will render obsolete either the industry or that segment of the industry in which the entrepreneur is doing business?

10. *What are the typical margins in the industry?* Looking at average gross margins in the industry provides an indication of how much room there is to make mistakes. A gross margin is derived by dividing gross profit by sales. It indicates how much money is left to pay overhead and make a profit. If the industry typically has 2 percent margins or less, as the grocery industry does, making a profit will require selling in large volumes and keeping overhead costs to a minimum. Where margins run at 70 percent or higher, there is a lot more room to play, but generally these industries (such as the software industry) have relatively short product life cycles, so R&D costs are high.

Going into the analysis with a firm grip on which questions need to be answered is the first step. Figuring out where to find this information is the next step.

GATHERING SECONDARY SOURCES OF INDUSTRY INFORMATION

It's generally wise to begin any research by looking at secondary sources of information to gather background data. Today, Google search engine (or Yahoo!, MSN, and others) and Wikipedia.com are great places to get an introduction to the industry and pick up some trends by seeing what is being talked about. Journals, trade magazines, industry analysts, government publications, and annual reports of public corporations—normally available in a university or community library and on the Internet—are also excellent starting points, but they also provide more targeted information and generally from experts. For example, a number of industry analysts offer excellent overviews of most of the major industries. Table 6.1 presents a listing of a few of these analytical resources. Trade magazines provide a good sense of key firms and of the direction the industry may be taking. LexisNexis and STAT-USA are fine sources of industry statistics.

The North American Industry Classification System (NAICS), the classification system that the United States, Canada, and Mexico developed to identify industries and allow for common standards and statistics across North America, is replacing the traditional U.S. Standard Industrial Classification system (SIC).

TABLE 6.1 Resources for Industry Analysis	Business.com Forrester (private—available at some universities) Datamonitor Industry Market Research Gartner (private—available at some universities) Encyclopedia of American Industries Hoover's Online Encyclopedia of Emerging Industries OneSource Encyclopedia of Global Industries Standard & Poor's Industry Surveys

NAICS covers 350 new industries that have never been coded before. Some of these industries reflect high-tech developments such as fiber optic cable manufacturing, satellite communications, and the reproduction of computer software. However, far more of these new categories are not technology-based: bed and breakfast inns, environmental consulting, warehouse clubs, pet supply stores, credit card issuing, diet and weight reduction centers, to name only a few. These codes can be found at http://www.census.gov/epcd/www/naics.html.

NAICS industries are identified by a six-digit code, in contrast to the four-digit SIC code. The longer code accommodates the larger number of sectors and allows more flexibility in designating subsectors. It also provides for additional detail not necessarily appropriate for all three NAICS countries. NAICS is organized in a hierarchical structure much like the existing SIC. The first two digits designate a major economic sector (formerly division), such as agriculture or manufacturing. The third digit designates an economic subsector (formerly major group), such as crop production or apparel manufacturing. The fourth digit designates an industry group, such as grain and oil seed farming or fiber, yarn, and thread mills. The fifth digit designates the NAICS industry, such as wheat farming or broadwoven fabric mills. The international NAICS agreement fixes only the first five digits of the code. The sixth digit is used for industrial classifications in other countries where necessary. With the NAICS code, one can find statistics about size of the industry, sales, number of employees, and so forth.

It is easy to research common industries like consumer goods and technology because they are frequently covered by the government, news sources, brokerage firms, and the financial press. More difficult are small industries, whose data may end up aggregated with a larger industry; new or emerging industries, which are not yet represented in the government classification system; business-to-business industries where information is kept proprietary; and those industries that are not yet perceived to be legitimate industries. However, there are some less direct ways to extrapolate valuable information to guide the feasibility process.

1. *Check the business press.* Often the popular business publications and newspapers will write about an industry before it hits the radar of the more established sources.

2. *Talk to trade associations.* Since these organizations are comprised of industry companies, they tend to collect data that describes that industry. The *Encyclopedia of Associations* is a good way to find such a trade organization. Also consider searching online using the ".org" domain, which is typical of nonprofit organizations.

3. *Consult trade association journals.* These journals are often found online or through services like LexisNexis or Factiva.
4. *Check organizations that list government and agency resources.* For example, Fedstats lists U.S. government sites that contain statistical information, and it can be searched by topic or agency.

THE IMPORTANCE OF PRIMARY INDUSTRY DATA

Secondary research paints a broad picture of the industry, but given the lead time from data gathering to print, it rarely yields the most current information available. Therefore, to access the timeliest information, it is extremely important to gather primary field data on the industry. In other words, entrepreneurs need to talk with people in the industry to validate what they have gathered with their secondary research. Some of the sources to tap are:

Industry observers, who study particular industries and regularly report on them in newspapers or newsletters or through the media.

Suppliers and distributors, who are in an excellent position to comment on the health of the industry in terms of demand for products and services, as well as on the financial strength and market practices of major firms in the industry.

Customers, who can be a clue to satisfaction with the industry and the products or services supplied by firms in the industry.

Employees of key firms in the industry, who are a good source of information about opinion leaders and competitors.

Professionals from service organizations, such as lawyers and accountants, who regularly work with a particular industry.

Trade shows, which give a good indication of who the opinion leaders are and who has the strongest market strategy.

Frameworks for Understanding Industries

Industries do not remain static or stable over time; in fact, they are constantly evolving. Like people, industries and their products move through a life cycle that includes birth, growth, maturity, and ultimately decline. Today, many industry life cycles are accelerating with the corresponding speeding up of their product cycles and many companies have been caught in the inertia of believing that their products would live forever. Like companies, industries decline when the "original story, the founding vision, loses originality and power."[1] When companies in that industry stick to the old strategies while customers move on, the cycle slows and eventually dies. We witnessed the demise of the typewriter industry, and now one wonders if the PC industry is prepared for its eventual collapse. Currently, the newspaper industry is suffering from disruptive change brought about by the Internet and the new consumer-generated media—blogs, Google, online newsletters, eBay, and Monster.com. Despite this powerful competition, the industry is still focusing most of its resources on print media even after making the shift to the Web.[2]

FIGURE 6.1

Industry Life Cycle

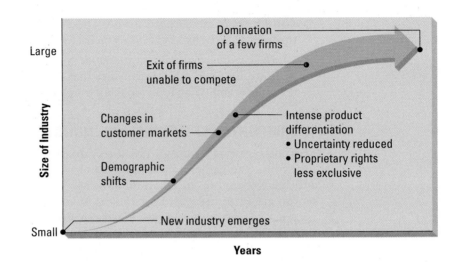

The stages of the industry life cycle are identified by the different kinds of activities occurring at each stage. Figure 6.1 displays this life cycle, and we describe the stages and their strategic implications here.

BIRTH

A new industry emerges, often with the introduction of a disruptive technology, such as the Internet, that displaces previous technology and creates opportunities that didn't exist before. One might argue that the new consumer-generated media (CGM) sector discussed previously is an example of an emerging industry that came about as the result of affordable and accessible production technology via the Internet. Successful examples of early companies in this space are YouTube, MySpace, and Wikipedia. For entrepreneurs contemplating an industry entry at the earliest stage, it truly is the Wild West, with no rules and plenty of opportunities to try anything and everything. With sufficient resources, an entrepreneurial firm can position its technology to potentially become the industry standard; without them, the new venture's strategy will be influenced by the standards set by more dominant players.

GROWTH AND ADAPTATION

Following birth, a new industry typically goes through a volatile and rapid stage of growth as companies and their respective technologies jockey for position and the right to determine industry standards. This is an expensive period for most companies because they need to use extensive resources and develop critical partnerships to establish their position in the industry.

DIFFERENTIATION AND COMPETITION

As more firms enter the industry, intense product differentiation occurs, because the industry's established standards and proprietary rights no longer provide the exclusivity they once did. Entrepreneurial ventures that enter the industry at this point must either identify niches that have not been served or differentiate themselves sufficiently in order to attract enough customers to be successful. One of the biggest threats of this stage is commoditization. It is commonly believed that all products eventually become commodities; however, recent research has learned that this is not always the case. Take, for example, the humble toaster, which has gone through multiple iterations in its product life cycle and is still a prominent fixture in the home appliance industry. Today, the global marketplace in countertop toasting technology is demonstrably driven by differentiation, segmentation, and ongoing technical innovation.[3] When price becomes the most important differentiator, it signals to entrepreneurs that the time for innovation has arrived and that new value must be created.

SHAKEOUT

When competition is the most intense, those companies that are unable to compete leave. The remaining firms then grow more rapidly as they pick up the slack. In fact, it is a curious truism that as the industry goes through its shakeout, the GDP (gross domestic product) actually increases, meaning that firms in the industry become more productive. Nevertheless, although shakeouts may lead to temporary efficiency gains, they also eliminate the possibility of competition and therefore contribute to a social loss from decreased market competition.[4] Entrepreneurial firms will not enter such an industry if they cannot survive the predatory tactics of the dominant players in the industry. The shakeout period moves the industry from an oligopoly, with many companies and high product costs, to a more stable and mature industry with only a few efficient firms. This is the period in the industry when the opinion leaders establish themselves.

MATURITY AND DECLINE

In this stage, the industry reaches a mature state in which several major players dominate. If new research and development in the industry do not produce a resurgence of growth, the industry could face impending decline. At this stage, earnings and sales growth slow and growth prospects decline. Typically, mature industries are described by high-dividend yields and low price-to-earnings ratios, and CEOs of companies in mature industries tend to focus on cost containment. In general, it takes the introduction of disruptive technology to turn a declining industry around. Broad industries like mining, manufacturing, and agriculture are all in decline, although some sectors within those industries have found new life. For example, in Iowa, soy farmers have developed a new soy flour that can substitute for eggs in baked goods with no cholesterol. And miners of mica in South Dakota are finding new applications for their minerals as a result of new technology that can reduce the size of mica granules to the nano level or less than 12 microns in size. Mica, traditionally used as an insulating material in electronics, is now used to dampen sound in automobiles and add shine to cosmetics.

For every industry, these life-cycle stages occur at different times and vary in their duration. The video rental industry presents a classic example of an industry

FIGURE 6.2

Industry Trajectories

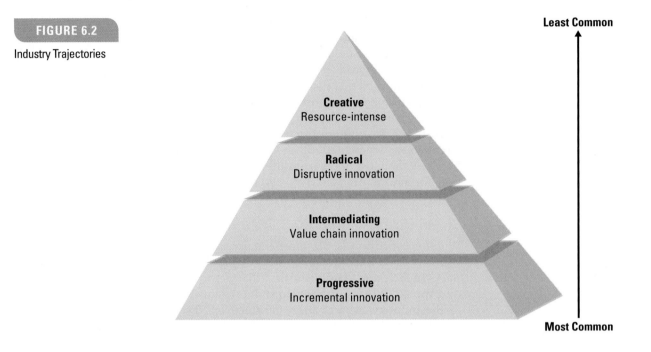

FIGURE 6.2

Industry Trajectories

in transition. In the early stages it was made up of small independent (mom-and-pop) owners. Wayne Huizenga sought to consolidate the industry by developing Blockbuster Video, a video megastore. In just a few years, independents were disappearing in favor of large-volume chain outlets. Then the megastores gave way to video on demand, available over cable television and even the Internet. And then Netflix made DVDs easily available through the mail at an even lower cost and more convenience.

Recent research has identified four major industry trajectories that signal how fast change occurs in a particular industry.[5] Figure 6.2 depicts these trajectories from most common—progressive—to the least common—creative.

Working from the most common type of change in an industry, progressive change takes place as companies in the industry grow geographically and increase profits through innovations in operations, processes, distribution, and technology. Examples are discount retailers like Wal-Mart and airlines like Jet Blue. Intermediating change, by contrast, is industry change that comes about when there are major shifts in the value chain in the form of forward and backward integration, strategic partnerships, and developing new ways to transact business with customers. A good example is the automobile industry, where dealers have moved onto the Internet in an effort to reach more customers and bring down costs.[6]

Radical change occurs in industries when an innovation results in the obsolescence of previous technology and drives old-line companies out of business. The Internet produced such a change for the automobile industry, and the PC drove typewriter manufacturers out of business. Finally, creative change is found in industries where resources turn over frequently and must continually be replaced. Companies in industries like the film production industry tend to undertake multiyear projects to develop new assets for customers (the moviegoers) who constantly seek new forms of entertainment.[7]

It is important to identify which stage of the life cycle an industry is in. Reading the analyses of industry watchers in trade magazines and talking with people who regularly work in that industry are also good ways to learn where an industry is in the life cycle. Using a framework such as Porter's Five Forces, discussed in the next section, will assist the entrepreneur in determining the competitive characteristics of an industry or market as well as the industry's trajectory.

Analyzing an Industry

It is often helpful to put a framework around the concept of an industry to organize all the data collected and to be able to evaluate the industry. Many frameworks have been proposed, and several have been adapted successfully by entrepreneurs. Perhaps the most commonly used competitive framework is Porter's Five Forces. Porter's work has been challenged on several levels, most notably, that a "sixth force," the government or public, should be included and that the attractiveness of an industry cannot be evaluated independent of the resources the company brings to the industry. Keeping these criticisms in mind, Porter's framework still provides an excellent exercise for entrepreneurs as they seek to characterize the industry and markets they will enter.

PORTER'S FIVE FORCES

For years, the work of Michael Porter has provided a way of effectively looking at the structure of an industry and a company's competitive strength and positioning relative to that industry and to the markets it serves. Porter's basic premise is that sustaining high performance levels requires a well-thought-out strategy and implementation plan based on knowledge of the way the industry works and the attractiveness of markets. Porter asserts that there are five forces in any industry that affect the ultimate profit potential of a venture in terms of long-run return on investment.[8] By contrast, such things as economic forces, changes in demand, material shortages, and technology shifts affect short-run profitability. Figure 6.3 depicts the Five Forces framework, which is discussed in more detail in the following sections.

Barriers to Entry

An entrepreneurial venture's success in a given industry or market is affected by the ability of new firms to enter the entrepreneur's market. If the costs are low and few economies of scale exist, then competitors can easily enter and disrupt the entrepreneur's competitive strategy. In some industries and markets, however, barriers to entry are high and will discourage competitors from entering. Note that these factors may also present a challenge for the entrepreneur. These barriers may include the following:

FIGURE 6.3   Porter's Five Forces Framework

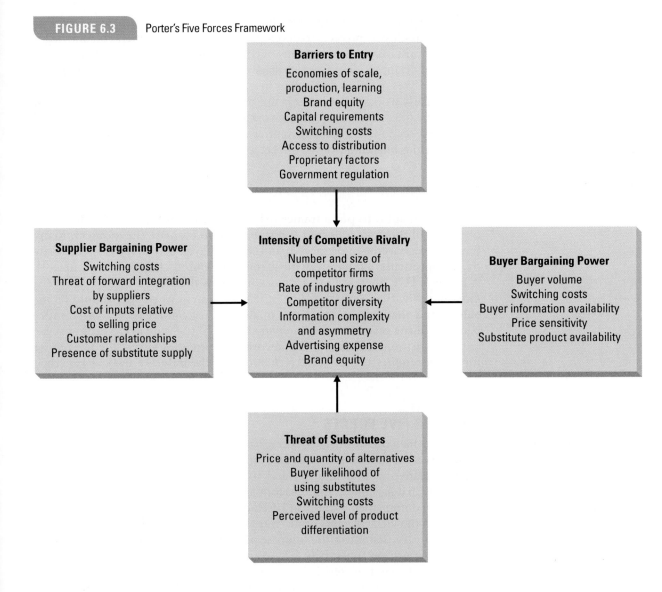

Economies of Scale: Many industries have achieved economies of scale in marketing, production, and distribution. This means that their costs to produce have declined relative to the price of their goods and services. Typically, economies of scale are found in more mature industries. A new venture cannot easily achieve these same economies, so it is forced into a "Catch-22" situation. If it enters the industry on a large scale, it risks retaliation from those established firms in the industry. If it enters on a small scale, it may not be able to compete because its costs are high relative to everyone else's. Another version of this dilemma occurs in an industry in which the major players are vertically integrated; that is, they own their suppliers and/or distribution channels, which effectively locks out the new venture. What most new ventures do when they must compete with companies that have achieved economies of scale is attempt to form alliances with other small firms to share resources and thus compete on a more level playing field. This type of collaboration is occurring more and more often as businesses realize that the industry is too complex for any one company to have all the resources and intellectual property required to control a portion of it. An example of this strategy is the grocery industry, where independent grocers have joined forces to achieve more buying power in their industry.

Brand Loyalty: New entrants to an industry face existing products and services with loyal customers who are not likely to switch easily to something new. A new firm will need to undertake an extensive marketing campaign focused on making the customer aware of the benefits of the new venture's products. The cost of undertaking this strategy can be a significant barrier to entry unless customers are dissatisfied with the competing brands. On the Internet, it has become clear that when incumbents like The Gap and Barnes & Noble set up shop online, they retain the brand presence they have already established in their bricks-and-mortar stores—consequently, they can be profitable immediately. By contrast, it takes a company like Amazon (with the strongest online brand recognition), which had no bricks-and-mortar presence, years to become profitable. In Amazon's case, the primary reason was that it was trying to grow the business into multiple areas—books, DVDs, music, and so forth—simultaneously and that kind of growth is very costly in terms of marketing and inventory.

Capital Requirements: The cost of entering many industries is prohibitive for a new venture. These costs may include up-front advertising, research and development (R&D), and expenditures for plant and equipment. Entrepreneurs often overcome this barrier by outsourcing to or partnering with established companies to leverage their resources and industry intelligence.

Switching Costs for the Buyer: Buyers in most industries don't readily switch from one supplier to another unless there is a compelling reason to do so. Switching costs the buyer money and time. For example, a manufacturing business that has spent a lot of time and money finding the best supplier for the raw materials it needs to produce its product will not easily change suppliers, because that would mean going through the whole process again.

Access to Distribution Channels: The new venture must persuade established distribution channel members to accept its new product or service and must prove that it will be beneficial to distributors to do so. This persuasion process, like any sale, can be costly for a new venture in terms of time, personnel, and travel. One solution for some types of businesses is distributing via the Internet, which is a direct method of reaching the customer.

Proprietary Factors: Barriers to entry also include proprietary technology, products, and processes. Where established firms hold patents on products and processes that the new venture requires, they have the ability either to keep the new venture out of the industry or to make it very expensive to enter. Most favorable location is another form of proprietary barrier. Often entrepreneurs will discover that existing firms in the industry own the most advantageous business sites, forcing the new venture to locate elsewhere, perhaps in a less desirable location. The Internet diminishes such location advantages somewhat, but the ability of customers to find a Web address quickly through the major search engines also becomes a location advantage. Making sure the website is optimized so that the business name comes up near the top of the search list is important.

Government Regulations: The government can limit entry to an industry or market through strict licensing requirements and by limiting access to raw materials via laws or high taxes and to certain locations by means of zoning restrictions. Food products and biochemicals must obtain FDA approval, which is a significant barrier to entry. Isis Pharmaceuticals, a drug development company located in Carlsbad, California, recognizes that any delay in approvals can result in millions of dollars lost. It invested in a local area network for its company and an intranet on the Web; now it can manage its FDA-mandated clinical trials on thousands of patients without losing time. By submitting its required forms electronically, it cuts several months off the FDA's normal 15-month review process.

Threat from Substitutes

A new venture must compete not only with products and services in its own industry but also with logical substitutes that other industries bring to the market. Generally, these substitute products and services accomplish the same basic function in a different way or at a different price. For example, movie theaters regularly compete with other forms of entertainment for the consumer's disposable dollars. The threat from substitute products is more likely to occur where firms in other industries are earning high profits at better prices than can be achieved in the new venture's industry. It is also likely to happen where an incumbent firm has deep resources and technical talent so that it can move quickly into new markets.

Threat from Buyers' Bargaining Power

In industries where buyers (customers) have bargaining power, it is more difficult for a new entrant to gain a foothold and grow. Examples of buyers that have this type of bargaining power include Price/Costco, Barnes & Noble, and Wal-Mart. Buyers like these can force down prices in the industry through volume purchases. This is particularly true where industry products constitute a significant portion of the buyers' requirements—books for Barnes & Noble, toys for Wal-Mart. Under this scenario, the buyer is more likely to be able to achieve the lowest possible price.

The largest buyers also pose a threat of backward integration; that is, they may actually purchase their suppliers, thus better controlling costs and affecting price throughout the industry. The more buyers understand the nature of the industry and the more their products are standardized, the greater the likelihood that these buyers will have significant bargaining power.

Threat from Suppliers' Bargaining Power

In some industries, suppliers exert enormous power through the threat of raising prices or changing the quality of the products that they supply to manufacturers and distributors. If the number of these suppliers is few relative to the size of the industry, or the industry is not the primary customer of the suppliers, that power is magnified. A further threat from suppliers is that they will integrate forward—that is, they will purchase the outlets for their goods and services, thus controlling the prices at which their output is ultimately sold.

Competitive Rivalry Among Existing Firms

The four factors just discussed all work together to create competitive rivalry. In general, a highly competitive market will drive down profits and ultimately the rate of return on investment. To position themselves in a competitive market, firms often resort to price wars and advertising skirmishes. Once one firm decides to make such a strategic move in the market, others will usually follow. The clearest example is the airline industry; when one airline discounts its prices significantly, most of the others immediately follow. The problem with this tactic is that it ultimately hurts everyone in the industry and may even force out some smaller firms because competitive prices drop below costs. Most new ventures can't compete on price and can't afford costly advertising battles to build an image. To compete in a market that is highly competitive, they must instead identify a niche that serves an unmet need for customers and will allow them to enter quietly and gain a foothold. Many entrepreneurs seeking entry into industries such as software, biomedical, biotech, and telecommunications deliberately position themselves to be eventually acquired by the larger rivals rather than trying to compete against them.

Using the Framework to Draw Conclusions

Using the Porter framework to characterize an entrepreneur's industry and target market is just the first step. To be able to use this information to develop a business concept and strategy requires drawing some conclusions based on the information gathered. One way to do this is to start by determining the impact of the variables that describe each of the five forces. The following scale will help to differentiate the direction and strength of the impact.

Threat of new entry or substitution is extremely high and impact will be very negative = ↓↓

Threat of new entry or substitution is high or strong = ↓

Threat of new entry or substitution is moderate = +

No threat = 0

Supplier/buyer power is extremely high and impact will be very negative = ↓↓

Supplier/buyer power is high or strong = ↓

Supplier/buyer power is moderate = +

Supplier/buyer power is not a th it = 0

Once the strength and direction of impact of the various variables is defined, it is important to analyze how this knowledge will affect business strategy. For example, suppose the entrepreneur finds that in the particular industry being considered, competitive rivalry is extremely high and there are few barriers to entry (market entry is not a threat). Suppose also that buyer power is strong, signaling that buyers could exert downward pressure on prices, forcing a commodity pricing situation, and that there appear to be viable substitutes for what the entrepreneur is offering. This scenario is certainly not a very positive one for the entrepreneur who must either figure out a way to change the conditions by perhaps modifying the business concept or ultimately deciding that the business is not feasible under these circumstances.

When making decisions based on the Five Forces, it is important to consider the core competencies and resources that the new venture brings to the equation. For entrepreneurial ventures, an industry has to enable the venture to access the supply chain and distribution channels; however, it does not mean that existing markets must be favorable. Entrepreneurs typically enter with a niche strategy serving an unmet need in the market, so by definition, there will be no competitive rivalry for a time. In the end, the Five Forces Model should be used as one of several tools to aid in the decision making that entrepreneurs must do when judging the feasibility of their new business concepts.

PEST ANALYSIS

In addition to viewing the industry and market through the lens of the Five Forces Model, it may be helpful for an entrepreneur to also conduct a PEST (or STEP) analysis to examine the environment in which the new venture will operate and ensure that the entrepreneur's strategies are aligned with the trajectory of the industry and the markets in which the new business will compete. PEST analysis (Figure 6.4) examines specific aspects of the macro-environment: its social, technological, economic, and political facets. Social factors consist of demographic and cultural aspects of the environment, such as age distribution and health consciousness or attitudes toward the environment. Technological factors include such things as R&D activity and rate of technological change. Economic factors

FIGURE 6.4

PEST Analysis

Political Government, Regulatory, and Legal	**Sociocultural** Demographics and Cultural
Economic Cost of capital, Inflation, Customer purchasing power, Employment rate	**Technological** R&D and Rate of change

Having It All

Imagine an entrepreneurial venture competing against the likes of AT&T and Verizon. Sound impossible? Not at all. Working Assets is a long-distance, wireless, credit card and broadcasting company that was started in 1985 to "build a better world." It donates 1 percent of its revenues to "progressive" nonprofits nominated by its customers. Customers can also round up their bills to the next dollar amount, and the difference is contributed to charity. Working Assets has funded nonprofits such as Greenpeace, Planned Parenthood, Oxfam America, and the Children's Defense Fund. It works with socially responsible companies such as Ben & Jerry's Ice Cream to create joint promotions and is internally consistent in its environmental message. It uses recycled paper for billing and recycled plastic for its calling card. And in an industry that is not known for customer loyalty, Working Assets has a loyal customer base. The company also enhances its customers' ability to speak out on important issues by allowing them to place free calls to decision makers on critical issues of the month. Since its inception, the company has raised $35 million by helping its customers make a difference in the world through philanthropy and political activism, while still succeeding as an entrepreneurial venture.

Sources: http://www.workingassets.com (February 2007); J.G. Dees, J. Emerson, and P. Economy, *Enterprising Nonprofits* (New York: Wiley, 2001), p. 224.

deal with the firm's cost of capital and customers' purchasing power as well as inflation, employment rate, and economic prospects over time. Political factors involve government regulation and the various legal issues that affect the business's operations in addition to the stability of the government and trade agreements. Depending on the needs of the entrepreneurs, the PEST analysis can be extended to include environmental, legal, and ethical factors (STEEPLE).

A PEST analysis should begin with the identification of the macro-environmental factors that apply to the new business and then an examination of the potential impact these factors might have on the business. For example, factors that make it more difficult to do business—high taxes, real estate costs, and labor costs—may cause an entrepreneur to consider a different location for doing business where these items are more favorable. However, these negatives are often found in high-economic-growth regions like major metropolitan areas, so the trade-off is that going to a more favorable location from an economic perspective may not provide the type of skilled labor required for the business operations. The bottom line is that for any new business, a thorough understanding of the context in which the business will operate is essential to success and long-term survivability.

Characterizing the Target Market

Market research for entrepreneurs is very different from the research conducted by large, established companies. In general, entrepreneurial market research is limited by resources, time, and high levels of uncertainty, so the data collected is far from perfect and just enough to give the entrepreneur confidence that he or she should go forward with the new business. The previous discussion of frameworks for analysis of the industry and market also provides an effective way to describe the characteristics of the potential market the entrepreneur wishes to serve. However, it is not until an entrepreneur gets into the field and talks to potential customers and those who deal with potential customers that a clearer understanding of various customer segments and the first or entry customer is revealed. Ashbury Images, a San Francisco-based nonprofit screen printer that serves as a source of transition jobs for the homeless, had always viewed its primary customers as small nonprofits. The problem was that these businesses were not profitable customers for Ashbury. As the company began to analyze its customers in depth, it discovered that its best customers, the ones whose needs were actually being served, were larger corporate clients. These clients understood Ashbury's value proposition: a high-quality product and a social mission. Ashbury has now refocused its efforts to put more emphasis on its best customers.[9]

In the beginning stages of market analysis, the customer definition will be fairly loose and may even change substantially as field research is conducted. It is easy to become overwhelmed by the amount of information available about the target market, so it's important to keep in mind the key questions that should be answered:

What are the potential markets for the product or service?

Of these potential markets, which customers are most likely to purchase the product or service at market introduction? In other words, who is in the most pain?

How much do these customers typically buy, how do they buy, and how do they hear about the product or service?

How often do they buy? What is their buying pattern?

How can the new venture meet these customers' needs?

It is important to remember that for a new company, the goals of market research are to (1) identify and profile the first customer; (2) estimate potential demand from that customer; and (3) identify subsequent customer segments and needs to grow the company.

TARGETING THE FIRST CUSTOMER

Target market research provides some of the most important data that one needs to decide who the first customer is. Recall that the first customer is the one who most needs the benefits of the entrepreneur's product or service. Therefore, the first customer may not be the biggest market, but rather an unserved niche that enables the entrepreneur to enter a market with no direct competition for a time. To narrow the focus of market research and to save time and money, entrepreneurs should consider identifying two to three prototypes of a business that seem to be the most feasible. For any product, for example, the entrepreneur could be a manufacturer, distributor, or a retailer. If the product has patents associated with it, licensing the technology to another company is yet another business opportunity. By narrowing the focus, market research can be more targeted, take less time, and generally be more productive.

TABLE 6.2		
A Four-Step Market Research Process	Assess your information needs.	• How will the data be used? • What data need to be collected? • What methods of analysis will be used? • What are the potential business designs under consideration?
	Research secondary sources first.	• What are the demographics of the customer? • What are the psychographics of the customer (i.e., buying habits)? • How large is the market? • Is the market growing? • Is the market affected by geography? • How can you reach your market? • How do your competitors reach the market? • What market strategies have been successful with these customers?
	Measure the target market with primary research.	• What are the demographics of your customer? • Would they purchase your product or service? Why? • How much would they purchase? • When would they purchase? • How would they like to find the product or service? • What do they like about your competitors' products and services?
	Forecast demand for the product or service.	• What do substitute products/services tell you about demand for your product/service? • What do customers, end-users, and intermediaries predict the demand will be? • Can you do a limited production or test market for your product or service?

The market data the entrepreneur collects is only as good as the research methods used to collect them. To ensure that useful and correct conclusions can be drawn from the data collected, sound research methods must be employed. Table 6.2 depicts a four-step process for ensuring that the right information is gathered and that it is used correctly.

The Internet is a good starting point for gathering secondary data. Many of the traditional resources found in libraries are now available in online versions; for example, U.S. census data can be found at http://www.census.gov. Using census data, entrepreneurs can determine whether the geographic area they have defined for the business is growing or declining, whether its population is aging or getting younger, or whether the available work force is mostly skilled or unskilled, along with many other trends.

Some demographic data (data on age, income, race, occupation, and education) help identify the likelihood that a person will choose to buy a product. Demographic data also make it possible to segment the target market into subgroups that are different from one another. For example, if the target market is retired people over age 65, their buying habits (such as product requirements and quantity or frequency of purchase) may vary by geographic region or by income level.

Finally, census data can be used to arrive at an estimate of how many target customers live within the geographic boundaries of the target market. Then, within any geographic area, those who meet the particular demographic requirements of the product or service can be segmented out.

It is not only consumer markets that are described by demographic data. Business markets can also be described in terms of their size, revenue levels, number of employees, and so forth. Online sources are not the only sources of secondary market data. Most communities have economic development departments or Chambers of Commerce that keep statistics on local population trends and other economic issues. Some communities have Small Business Development Centers (SBDCs), branches of the Small Business Administration that offer a wealth of useful information, as well as services, for small and growing businesses. Other sources were noted in an earlier section—"Resources for Industry Analysis."

EXPLORING THE MARKET WITH PRIMARY DATA

The most important data that entrepreneurs can collect on potential customers are primary data derived from observation, online or in-person surveys, phone surveys, interviews, and informal focus groups. Each data collection technique has advantages and disadvantages, and the decision about which one(s) to use is generally based on time and money. Survey techniques require drawing a representative sample from the population of customers that the entrepreneur is interested in. The sample should be selected with great care, for it will determine the validity of the results. In general, in order to avoid bias, a sample should be random—that is, one in which the entrepreneur has as little control as possible over who participates. Most entrepreneurs, because of limitations of cost and time, use what is called a convenience sample. This means that not everyone in the defined target market has a chance of being chosen to participate. Instead, the entrepreneur may, for example, choose to select the sample from people who happen to be at the airport on a particular day. Clearly, this method will not reach all possible customers at the airport, but if the target customer is typically found at airports, there's a good chance of obtaining at least a representative sample from which results can be derived fairly confidently.

Even if a convenience sample is used, there are ways to ensure the randomness of selection of the participants. Using the airport example, an entrepreneur can decide in advance to survey every fifth person who walks by. Thus the respondents are not chosen on the basis of attractiveness or lack of it—or for any other reason, for that matter. A random-number generator on a computer can select names from a telephone book. Whatever system is employed, the key point is to make an effort not to bias the selection so that the outcomes are more meaningful.

Each of the techniques discussed has advantages and disadvantages associated with it. In general, surveys have a response rate of only about 2 percent, and several follow-ups are usually required to get a sufficient sample. Phone surveys are typically ineffective because in the past few years, people have been bombarded by telemarketers and now resist responding to a telephone survey. With limited resources, entrepreneurs tend to use structured interviews, informal focus groups, and online and immediate-response surveys.

Structured Interviews

Although personal interviews are more costly and time-consuming than surveys, they have many advantages:

They provide more opportunity for clarification and discussion.

The interviewer has an opportunity to observe nonverbal communication and hence assess the veracity of what the interviewee is saying.

The response rate is high.

Interviews permit open-ended questions that can lead to more in-depth information.

They provide an opportunity for the entrepreneur to network and develop valuable contacts in the industry.

Where time and money permit, structured interviews are probably the best source of valuable information from customers, suppliers, distributors, and anyone else who can help the entrepreneur determine who the first customer is.

If interviewing a number of people, it would be important to have some questions in common so that there is a basis for response comparison and useful patterns can be identified. It is critical to prepare for interviews by developing questions that focus on the information required to answer the feasibility questions, and by conducting some background research on the person being interviewed and the company. That way, more insightful questions can be asked rather than wasting the interviewee's time with questions that can be easily answered from material on the company website.

Informal Focus Groups—The Group Interview

One efficient way to gain valuable information and feedback from customers and others is to conduct a focus group, in which a representative sample of potential customers is brought together for a presentation and discussion session. It is often used to elicit feedback on customer needs relative to a potential product or service or to compare products.

It is essential to ensure that the person leading the focus group have some knowledge of group dynamics and be able to keep the group on track. Often these focus group sessions are videotaped so that the entrepreneur can spend more time later analyzing the nuances of what occurred. It is important to get the written permission of attendees before videotaping. In many ways, informal focus groups can prevent an entrepreneur from making the costly error of offering a product or service for which there is little or no interest.

Online and Immediate-Response Surveys

Conducting a survey entails designing a survey instrument, usually a questionnaire that, once filled out, provides the desired information. Questionnaire design is not a simple matter of putting some questions on a piece of paper. There are, in fact, proven methods of constructing questionnaires to help ensure unbiased responses. It is not within the scope of this text to present all the techniques for questionnaire construction; however, a few key points should be remembered:

Keep the questionnaire short, with lots of white space, so that the respondent is not intimidated by the task.

Be careful not to ask leading or biased questions.

Ask easy, simple questions first, progressing gradually to the more complex ones.

Ask demographic questions (questions about age, sex, income, and the like) last, when the respondent's attention may have waned. These questions can be answered very quickly.

The Internet has made it easy for small businesses to collect valuable data without having to enlist the help of costly market research firms.[10] Internet surveys such as SurveyMonkey and ZapSurvey are less expensive than traditional surveys, the response time is greatly reduced, and it's easier to include global respondents seamlessly. Posting surveys on the Internet is a convenient way to conduct research if the primary customer is an Internet user. The survey can be posted in user groups, social networks, sent via e-mail to target customers, or placed on a website (as long as the people who need to respond to the survey have a way of knowing that it's there). Here are a few things to take into account when conducting Internet surveys.[11]

▶ Use color for visual cues to help the respondent move more quickly through the questionnaire.

▶ Include hypertext links to assist the respondent without making the questionnaire any longer.

▶ If using graphics or pictures, remember that respondents will interpret questions based on those graphics.

▶ Don't use drop-down boxes unless absolutely necessary because it slows down the process.

▶ Use open-ended responses boxes such as "other" where it is not possible for the entrepreneur to list all the potential responses.

▶ Don't require a respondent to answer every question before proceeding to the next. It will only cause frustration and the respondent may fail to complete the questionnaire.

▶ Password protect the survey to restrict access and provide a way of uniquely identifying the respondent.

More information about this topic, including examples of question types, can be found at "Online Survey Design Guide," which is a project of the University of Maryland (http://lap.umd.edu/survey_design/index.html).

Some entrepreneurs prefer to conduct their surveys in person at a location where their target customer can be found, for example, a shopping mall if the respondent is a consumer. Alternatively, a trade show is another popular source for these types of surveys. The advantage of this approach is an immediate and more targeted response as well as the opportunity to perhaps delve deeper into a particular response.

Whatever method is chosen, nothing beats feedback from the customer, whether it be at the design stage or as part of an effort to profile the customer and calculate demand.

SEGMENTING THE MARKET WITH A CUSTOMER MATRIX

One useful way to look at various customer segments to determine which should be the primary or first customer is to construct a customer matrix that lays out the benefits, distribution channel, product/service, and potential competition for each of the identified customer segments. The matrix in Table 6.3 highlights three potential customers for Rhino Records, a producer and distributor of music compilations. Once the customer segments are identified, the entrepreneur has to make a choice. Which of these three customers should the entrepreneur go after first? The decision about where to go first is affected by size of the market, customer demand, and resources, but the most important consideration is which customer is most likely to buy. Market research with customers may suggest, for instance, that the quickest early sales will come from music enthusiasts who like to peruse a retail outlet. Note also that, in this example, the different benefits and distribution strategies for each of the three customers actually produce three distinct types of businesses: a retail outlet, a wholesale distributorship, and an Internet business. The type of business the entrepreneur wants to own will then also influence the decision on first customer.

The Customer Profile

Out of the primary research will come a complete profile of the customer, that is, a description of the primary customer, be it a consumer or a business, in great detail. The profile is critically important to the marketing strategy, because it provides information vital to everything from product/service design to distribution channels and the marketing plan to attract the customer. Here is a list of

	Customer	Benefit	Distribution	Competition
TABLE 6.3 Customer Grid for Rhino Records	Baby-boomers	Convenience, economy, and entertainment: Can find compilations of their favorite songs without having to buy multiple one-artist albums.	Retail outlet—direct to the consumer	Amoeba Records Virgin Superstore Barnes & Noble
	Music stores	Access to unique compilations of hard-to-find great hits of the past to satisfy the baby-boomer segment of their market. Will produce high margins and quick turnover.	Wholesale to music store	Sony Atlantic Records Apple iTunes
	Busy professionals	Convenience: Can shop any time of the day or night and have all the information at their fingertips.	Internet business for online purchasing direct to the consumer	Amazon.com Barnes & Noble Apple iTunes Borders Pandora

some of the information that goes into the customer profile, whether that customer be a consumer or a business:

- Age
- Income level
- Education
- Buying habits—when, where, how much
- Where these customers typically find these types of products and services
- How they would like to purchase these products and services

Sandy Gooch is one of the leaders in the health food industry. When she was preparing to open her first organic foods store, she had a complete picture of her target customer: a 45- to 50-year-old professional woman who was well educated, a life-long learner, valued physical fitness, and read labels when she shopped. She would also be a regular shopper who stopped into the store several times a week on her way home from work. Certainly, not everyone who shopped at Mrs. Gooch's was a 45- to 50-year-old professional woman, but that was the customer most likely to purchase when Gooch started the business: her primary customer. Knowing that much about her customer enabled Gooch to tailor her advertising directly to that customer. For instance, Mrs. Gooch's ads always contained a lot of information because she knew her customers wanted to learn something new from each ad. Her success in understanding her customer led to the development of eight stores and an eventual acquisition by Whole Foods, Inc.

If the customer is a business, it can be described in essentially the same way—for example, the first customer is a small to midsized construction company with annual revenues of $5 million that makes purchases quarterly, buys primarily over the Internet, and pays within sixty days. The customer profile will also play an important role in the development of the marketing plan, as we will see in Chapter 15.

Gathering Demand Data

It is no easy task to figure out what the demand for a new product or service might be. Even large, experienced companies have failed at it. (Remember the Apple Newton, the first PDA? Its handwriting recognition capability was poor; customers became frustrated, and demand went to zero.) This chapter focuses on collecting demand data while Chapter 9 discusses how to forecast demand from the data collected.

If entrepreneurs are attempting to give customers what they need, the first thing they must understand is that customers can describe their problems and they can describe what they need to be able to do—their outcomes, but they are typically not effective at describing solutions to their problems.[12] For example, if entrepreneurs ask customers to identify what they like and don't like about the entrepreneur's product or the competitor's product, customers will typically respond in the context of something they know. "I wish this smart phone had a scroll wheel on the right side." Customers are merely providing a missing feature that perhaps a competitor offers. They are responding within the context of what they know. By contrast, if the entrepreneur asks a question that seeks an outcome—"how do you want to use a communication device?" (or better yet, "how do you want to communicate?")—he or she has put no boundaries on the customer. Customers are free to think about how they want to communicate in various scenarios without describing features. With these outcomes understood, the entrepreneur can better design a solution to the customer's problem. More importantly, with this knowledge in hand, the entrepreneur is better prepared to gather demand data.

The question that entrepreneurs do not want to ask is "Would you buy this product?" The simple reason is that in many cases, the respondent will be reluctant to offend the entrepreneur and so will say "yes," knowing full well that they won't be asked to purchase it that day so there is no commitment on their part. A better approach is to identify a problem, confirm that the respondent is experiencing that problem, and then ask if the entrepreneur's solution would interest them. This approach makes it easier for the customer to respond sincerely.

Talking to customers to gauge demand is only the first step. It is also important to discuss demand with industry people such as suppliers and retailers. Getting estimates from three different sources enables the entrepreneur to derive a range of values and then triangulate to a best estimate. More detail about this process is found in Chapter 9.

DRAWING CONCLUSIONS FROM MARKET RESEARCH

Entrepreneurial decision making is more art than science, so the data gathered during the market research process must be analyzed, synthesized, and result in some conclusions about market feasibility. One of the first steps in working toward a conclusion is to organize the data into meaningful categories—customer profile, market demographics, demand indicators, and so forth. This organization makes it possible to more easily analyze the data and seek patterns or trends that might provide vital information. A thorough review of all the data collected may also enable the entrepreneur to develop some sense of whether there are more positive aspects to the market than there are negative aspects. Furthermore, from the review, threats and challenges to the business goals can be identified and opportunities or courses of action that can include potential business models, customers, distribution channels, and business strategies can be taken. It is the entrepreneur's job to interpret all the raw data and turn it into business intelligence. With a complete picture of the market in hand, an entrepreneur will be in an excellent position to draw a conclusion regarding the market feasibility of the new venture.

Gathering Competitive Intelligence

One of the weakest portions of any feasibility analysis or business plan is the competitive analysis. Why do entrepreneurs frequently underestimate the competition? For one thing, their information is generally incomplete because competitors don't reveal their most proprietary strategies and tactics. Entrepreneurs also tend to underestimate what it takes in the way of resources and skills to establish a presence in a market and they don't identify all the roadblocks along the way. That talent comes from experience. Furthermore, it is difficult for entrepreneurs to know what they don't know! The competition generally possesses market share, brand recognition, management experience, customer knowledge, value chain relationships, industry knowledge, and resources. That is a formidable package of competitive strength. By contrast, many entrepreneurs take the naïve view that their concept is so new that they have no competition. Sadly, that is rarely the case. Even a niche strategy, probably the most effective strategy for a start-up, will only leave an entrepreneur competitor-free for a very short time. Add to that the real fact that entrepreneurial start-ups are short on resources and long on commitment and it is easy to see why it would be difficult for a small start-up to respond effectively to a competitor attack.

In assessing the competition, the idea is not to benchmark the new venture against a competitor but rather to find ways to create new value that customers will pay for. To undertake effective competitor research, one has to first determine the target market that the entrepreneur's venture is serving, which was discussed in the previous section.

IDENTIFYING THE COMPETITION

There are generally three types of competitors for a product or service: direct, indirect or substitute, and emerging or potential. Identifying exactly who these companies are, including their strengths, weaknesses, and market strategies, will put the new venture in a better position to be a contender in the market.

The noteworthy research of M.I. Chen[13] on competitor analysis suggested that to correctly assess the competitive market, one must view it from two sides: the supply side, which includes resource capabilities such as R&D and production, and the demand side, which is represented by the customer and the customer's needs. Figure 6.5 depicts this framework and enables a clearer understanding of competitor types based on resources and customers addressed. Direct competitors then are those businesses that serve the same customer needs with the same types of resources, while indirect competitors serve the same customer needs but with different resources as in substitute products or services. Potential competitors are those that are not currently serving the same customer needs but have the resources to move into that space and compete.[14] Therefore, it is important to look outside the immediate industry and market for alternatives. An entrepreneur also needs to look beyond existing competition to emerging competitors. In many industries today, technology and information are changing at such a

FIGURE 6.5

Competitive Framework

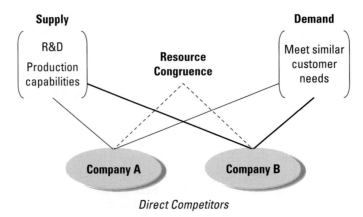

Direct Competitors

rapid pace that the window of opportunity for successfully starting a new venture closes early and fast. Consequently, entrepreneurs must be vigilant in observing new trends and new technology that might portend new competitors.

Sometimes the most threatening aspect of a competitor is not readily visible in the typical facts that are reported, and frequently competitors come from outside the entrepreneur's industry and market. For example, understanding a competitor's core competency helps to determine whether that competency can ever be shifted to the entrepreneur's niche market. Suppose the entrepreneur's business concept is a company that trains unskilled workers for well-paying jobs in industry. The entrepreneur looks at all the competitors in the training industry and decides that he can compete because he has created a unique niche in the market. What the entrepreneur has failed to do is look outside his industry to companies that might have the same core competency and might have the deep resources required to shift to his niche very rapidly. Those companies are not always obvious. For example, one of Marriott's core competencies is training unskilled workers in the language and work skills they need to perform the various jobs in Marriott's hotel chain. It certainly has the resources to take this competency into any niche it desires. Therefore, to make certain that a potential threat like this one is not missed, entrepreneurs should:

▶ Determine what the competitor has to do to be successful in its own core business. Are there any core competencies that it must acquire?

▶ Determine which of the competitor's core competencies are transferable to the entrepreneur's business.

▶ Determine whether the competitor has a competency in the same area as the entrepreneur.

If the competitor is a large company, the entrepreneur may strategically position his company to be eventually acquired, because large companies typically acquire core competencies rather than developing them.

Entrepreneurs also need to distinguish between good competition and bad competition. Good competition comes in the form of companies that are doing what they do very badly; in other words, they aren't making customers happy. Ways to identify good competition include checking complaint levels at the Better Business Bureau, examining the archives of local newspapers for stories about the company, or checking the public records for financial or legal difficulties. It will be relatively easier to succeed against a good competitor than a bad one. Bad competitors are those companies that are doing everything right. Their customers are happy; they add value; and they're prosperous. In this case, identifying a niche that is currently not being served might be the most effective way to enter such a market and begin to build a brand.

FINDING INFORMATION ABOUT COMPETITORS

Collecting information on competitors is one of the most difficult parts of researching a market. It is easy to gain superficial information from the competitor's advertising, website, or facilities; but the less obvious types of information, such as revenues and long-term strategies, are another matter. Information on publicly held competitors can be found in annual reports and other filings required by the Securities and Exchange Commission (SEC). Unfortunately, however, most start-up companies are competing against other private companies that will not be willing to divulge these sensitive data. Data that are important to gather include current market strategies, management style and culture, pricing strategy, customer mix, and promotional mix.

The following are some suggestions on where to look for this information.

▶ Visit competitors' websites or the outlets where their products are sold. Evaluate appearance, number of customers coming and going, what they buy, how much, and how often. Talk to customers and employees.

▶ Buy competitors' products to understand the differences in features and benefits and to learn about how they treat their customers.

▶ Use Internet search engines such as Google.com to read what customers are saying about the company.

▶ Find information on public companies to serve as benchmarks for the industry. Public companies can be investigated through Hoover's Online (http://www.hoovers.com), the U.S. Securities and Exchange Commission (http://www.sec.gov), and One Source (http://www.onesource.com), to name a few.

Studying the industry and market that the new venture will serve is a difficult and time-consuming task, but it is perhaps the most important information an entrepreneur can collect because with it the business context or environment can be understood, and the entrepreneur will learn whether the business will have customers. This is the heart of feasibility analysis and the basis for the business plan.

New Venture Checklist

Have you:

☐ Identified the NAICS code for the industry in which the new venture will operate?

☐ Collected secondary data on the industry?

☐ Conducted field research by interviewing suppliers, distributors, customers, and others?

☐ Developed an industry profile that will indicate whether the industry is growing, who the major competitors are, and what the profit potential is?

☐ Defined the target market and first customer for the product or service?

☐ Determined the most effective method for gathering primary data on the target market in order to generate a customer profile and evidence of demand?

Issues to Consider

ACE

Self-tests

1. Which primary and secondary information will tell you whether the industry is growing and favorable to new entrants?
2. What kinds of information can suppliers and distributors provide?
3. How should a market entry strategy be determined? What factors should be considered?
4. What is the value of defining a market niche?
5. Suppose you are introducing a new type of exercise equipment to the fitness industry. What would your strategy for research with the customer look like?
6. Given the definitions of direct and indirect competitors, provide an example of each for a product of your choosing.

Experiencing Entrepreneurship

1. Choose an industry that interests you. Create a status report using the Internet, LexisNexis or other industry source, current periodicals, and interviews with people in the industry. In your estimation, is this an industry that has a great potential for new business opportunities? If so, where do those opportunities lie? Write your analysis in a two-page report, indicating sources.
2. Pick a product or service, and formulate a plan for researching the customer. Identify what information needs to be collected (secondary and primary) and how to collect it. Justify the plan in a two-page report.

Relevant Case Studies

## Chapter 7

ANALYZING PRODUCT/ SERVICE RISKS AND BENEFITS

"When each thing is unique in itself, there can be no comparison made."

—**D.H. LAWRENCE,** British author

LEARNING OBJECTIVES

▌ Discuss the current trends in product/process development.

▌ Differentiate the way entrepreneurs develop products from the way they develop services.

▌ Describe the product development cycle.

▌ Explain the process of intellectual-property development for patents, trademarks, copyrights, and trade secrets.

Profile 7.1 WHEN PROPRIETARY RIGHTS BITE

Johnny's Selected Seeds has been in business in Winslow, Maine, since 1973. In 1995, when the Internet was just catching the attention of retailers, Rob Johnston, Johnny's CEO, hired a Web developer to build an online site to promote and sell his seeds to gardening enthusiasts and commercial customers. Much to Johnston's surprise, once the site went live his company was hit with a lawsuit for patent infringement by Divine Inc., a Chicago-based software and technology services company that claimed ownership of the shopping-cart technology that Johnny's was using. Divine Inc. wanted a one-time licensing fee of $20,000 or 1 percent of Johnny's Internet sales. Although Johnston didn't believe that the claim would hold up in court, at revenues of $10 million annually he couldn't afford to spend approximately $1 million to defend his rights. In January 2003 he negotiated a settlement with Divine—unfortunately, one month too soon because in late February 2003 Divine Inc. voluntarily filed for bankruptcy protection under Chapter 11 reorganization. An auction in May of that year saw Divine's assets divided by four bidders.

Johnston's case is not unique. Patent filings on fundamental activities associated with online retailing make it difficult for new businesses to operate.

And with the lure of enormous royalties from patents, companies have sprung up whose business model is finding infringers and suing them. PanIP, a San Diego technology development company, has sued 51 companies for activities like having a website that gathers financial data such as credit card information. PanIP claims that it is not in the business of filing lawsuits (called *patent trolling*); it is simply trying to protect its intellectual property. Still, for small business owners, one lawsuit can be a devastating financial blow. To fight back, a group of 15 defendants in the PanIP case banded together to create a joint legal defense, PanIP Group Defense Fund, Inc. Demonstrating the power of cooperation, they were able to force PanIP LLC to terminate its patent infringement lawsuits.

Sources: P. Sayer, "PanIP Drops Patent Litigation Against Small Businesses," *The Industry Standard* (March 30, 2004), http://www.thestandard.com/article.php?story=20040330180701368; Elaine Pofeldt, "Patent (Lawsuits) Pending Small e-Tailers Get Squeezed by Questionable IP Claims," *Fortune Small Business* (March 1, 2003), http://www.fortune.com; Barbara Rose, "Filipowski Not Among Bidders at Divine's Auction," *Chicago Tribune Online* (May 2003), http://www.chicagotribune.com; and Jef Bailey, "How Some Small Firms Are Fighting Off Giants," *Wall Street Journal—Startup Journal* (July 2002), http://www.startupjournal.com.

Putting the customer at the center of the business is a persistent theme throughout this book, particularly when a new product or service is being developed. Every business—large or small, product or service—is involved in product/service development at every stage of its life cycle. Each time a new product or service or an improvement on an existing product or service is introduced, it will have gone through a design and development process. Moreover, because new products and services create assets that need to be protected—called *intellectual property*—it is essential that entrepreneurs understand the process of protecting those assets.

On a sleepless night in 1957, Gordon Gould conceived the idea for the laser. He wrote down all his thoughts, sketched the design and its components, and forecasted future uses. He had a notary witness, sign, and date his notebook in anticipation of applying for intellectual-property protection in the form of a

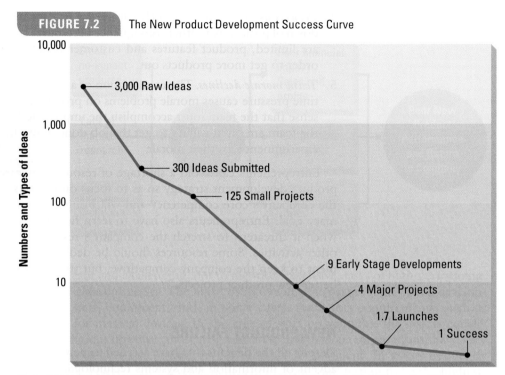

FIGURE 7.2 The New Product Development Success Curve

- 3,000 Raw Ideas
- 300 Ideas Submitted
- 125 Small Projects
- 9 Early Stage Developments
- 4 Major Projects
- 1.7 Launches
- 1 Success

(y-axis: Numbers and Types of Ideas — 10,000, 1,000, 100, 10)

Source: Based on the research of Greg A. Stevens and James Burley in "Piloting the Rocket of Radical Innovation," *Research Technology Management*, March/April 2003. Reprinted with permission.

THE PRODUCT DEVELOPMENT CYCLE

Entrepreneurs who develop products usually go through a process much like that shown in Figure 7.3. The product development cycle consists of a series of tasks leading to introduction of the product in the marketplace. Although it appears to be a linear process, it is actually quite iterative with multiple feedback loops. Because new product success usually requires an ongoing dialogue with the customer, an iterative or sense-and-respond approach to the process is more appropriate.[7] All of the tasks displayed in Figure 7.3 will take place; however, they occur often in parallel or out of order.

Opportunity Recognition: Recall from Chapter 3 that the first stage in the development of a business concept is opportunity recognition: identifying a niche that has not yet been served, detecting a potential improvement in an existing product, or seeing an opportunity for a breakthrough product or process.

Technical Feasibility Analysis: Technical feasibility analysis is simply conducting some preliminary research to determine whether the product or service idea currently exists, whether there is a potential application in a market, whether the product can be produced, how much it will cost to produce the product, and how much time it will take to produce it.

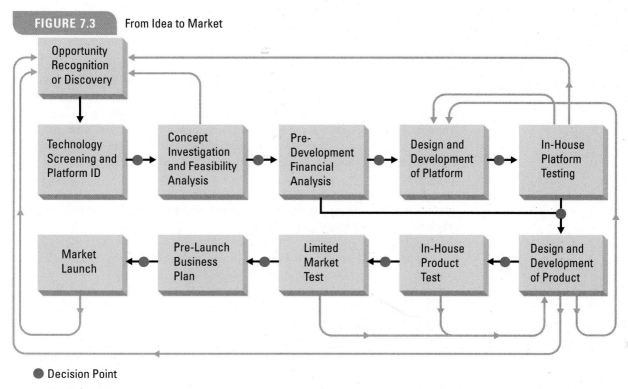

FIGURE 7.3 From Idea to Market

● Decision Point

→ Feedback Loop

Source: From Kathleen R. Allen, *Bringing New Technology to Market*, 1st edition, Copyright © 2003. Reproduced by permission of Pearson Education, Inc., Upper Saddle River, New Jersey.

Design and Development of Platform: The first stages of design preparation go hand in hand with concept investigation, because planners normally need some preliminary working drawings of the product to estimate costs and manufacturing processes. These preliminary drawings are also used to apply for a patent if the product is patentable. The platform is the core product or technology from which other products or applications can be developed. In an ideal situation, the entrepreneur will be working with a platform product that will provide many derivative products and services and their corresponding revenue streams.

Prototype Building and Field Testing: From the initial engineered drawings will come the prototype or model of the product. Often the first prototype does not closely resemble the final product in appearance, but it usually does in function. Physical prototypes are helpful in communicating the form, fit, and function of the device; in providing an example to a vendor for quotation; in facilitating quick changes in a design; and in designing the correct tooling—those devices that hold a product component in place during manufacturing and assembly. Entrepreneurs often use small engineering firms or solo engineers with small job shops and machine shops to complete the prototype. These sources are normally quicker and less expensive than the larger, better-known firms. When seeking an engineer or a model builder, it is important to be cautious and check out their qualifications, experience, and references relative to the task required of them. A major university engineering department is a good source of referrals, as are other engineers.

Businesses that do not manufacture products—service, retail, wholesale, and so forth—still need to design a prototype, but the prototype in this case will not always be physical. Instead it will be a design or flowchart for how the business will provide a service or product to its customer. For example, a restaurant entrepreneur will design the layout of the restaurant and kitchen with an eye to how customers and servers move through the restaurant. The food preparation area will need to be laid out efficiently so that the chef and cooks can work quickly and not have to move great distances to retrieve cooking utensils and food items. Every activity the restaurant undertakes should be prototyped to ensure that there is no duplication of effort and that each task is performed as efficiently and effectively as possible.

Initial Market Tests: With a working prototype of near production quality, it is possible to field-test it with potential users in environments where the product will typically be used. For example, it would be important to put a new construction tool in the hands of construction workers on real jobs in the field. In this way, the company can collect feedback based on actual use in real-life situations. The number of prototypes used in the field-testing stage is normally limited, because the cost per unit is much higher (as much as ten times higher) than it will be when the company is in normal production because the company will not yet be meeting its suppliers' volume levels for discounts. After conducting a small initial test production run in a limited market, the entrepreneur can go back and fine-tune the product to completion and market-ready status. This is also the first opportunity to test the manufacturing and assembly processes and determine accurate costs of production at varying levels of volume.

Product Market Introduction and Ramp-Up: The achievement of a production-quality prototype—one that has specifications that can be replicated in a manufacturing and assembly process—is a major milestone in the product development process, because the company now has a product that can be sold in the marketplace. During the final phases of developing this production-quality product, other aspects of the feasibility analysis have been completed. Now it will be important to consider manufacturing and assembly needs and whether to manufacture in-house or outsource. Table 7.1 provides a checklist for assessing the feasibility of new products.

OUTSOURCING PRODUCT DEVELOPMENT

It is becoming more and more common for entrepreneurs with both large and small companies to outsource all or part of their product development to third parties. The decision is due in large part to today's requirements for fast-paced innovation with shorter windows of opportunity. Most start-up companies don't have the resources to do adequate product development in-house. And there is no reason why it should be done this way when it is possible to reduce risk,

TABLE 7.1	New Product Checklist

	YES	NO	PERHAPS
THE MARKET			
Is there an existing need for this product in the marketplace?	_____	_____	_____
Will I be first in the marketplace with this product?	_____	_____	_____
Can the product be protected through intellectual-property rights?	_____	_____	_____
Can market entry barriers be erected?	_____	_____	_____
SWOT ANALYSIS (STRENGTHS, WEAKNESSES, OPPORTUNITIES, AND THREATS)			
Do the strengths of this product exceed any weaknesses?	_____	_____	_____
Are there various opportunities for commercializing this product?	_____	_____	_____
Do any significant threats exist to the development of this product?	_____	_____	_____
DESIGN/DEVELOPMENT/MANUFACTURING			
Is the product innovative?	_____	_____	_____
Can it be developed quickly to market-ready state?	_____	_____	_____
Can it be easily manufactured?	_____	_____	_____
Do I have the resources to manufacture the product?	_____	_____	_____
Is it more practical to subcontract the manufacturing?	_____	_____	_____
Is there a possibility for spin-off products?	_____	_____	_____
FINANCIAL			
Is the return on this investment sufficient to justify the effort?	_____	_____	_____
Are the development costs within reason?	_____	_____	_____
Will it be possible to minimize the manufacturing investment through outsourcing, while still maintaining quality and control?	_____	_____	_____
Is the money needed to produce the product available?	_____	_____	_____

lower costs, and decrease cycle times by factors of 60–90 percent by outsourcing product development.[8] Outsourcing provides a young firm with a network of expertise that it couldn't afford to hire in-house. Some of the areas of product development that require engineering analysis, design, and expertise and are suitable for outsourcing are component design, materials specifications, machinery to process, ergonomic design, packaging design, assembly drawings and specifications, parts and material sourcing (suppliers), and operator's and owner's manuals.

When using other companies to do part or all of the product development, it is important to understand that these partners work with many other companies, so no single company will be a high priority for them. That's why it's important to plan well in advance and allow extra time for delays that strategic partners might cause in the time-to-market plan. If time-to-market is the most critical factor in a business's success, it may want to consider doing tasks that could delay the process in-house rather than outsourcing them and being dependent on someone else's time schedule. It is also a good idea to help suppliers and original equipment manufacturers (OEMs) understand that the partnership will be a win-win relationship, so they have a vested interest in seeing it succeed. Contracts

Six Elements Critical to Successful Product Realization

Going from an idea to a commercial product is not easy. Here are the top six elements that must be in place to be successful:

1. A multidisciplinary team that works well together

2. Excellent communication skills that help you convey ideas, information, and data both verbally and in written form

3. The ability to design for manufacture effectively by reducing the number of parts needed, developing modular designs, and designing multifunctional parts

4. Computer-aided design systems (CAD) that enable you to design product specifications by creating images and then assigning mass, kinematics, material, geometry, and many other properties to the product

5. Ethical standards of conduct on the part of both the industry and the team

6. Creative thinking that lets the team make new connections and expand the scope of opportunities

Source: Based on a presentation at the 1996 National Design Engineering Conference by three members of the PRP Project: Donovan G. Evans, Hugh R. Mackenzie, and Christian Przirembel, http://www.prosci.com/prp1.htm.

should be drawn up with every consultant, original equipment manufacturer, or vendor with whom the company does business so that there will be no confusion about what is expected and needed. During the process, it is vital to stay in touch with outsourced vendors and to be available to answer questions as they arise.

Intellectual Property

Developing a new product creates an asset that must be protected. If the product is a unique device, a unique process or service, or another type of proprietary item, it may qualify for intellectual-property rights. These are the group of legal rights associated with patents, trademarks, copyrights, and trade secrets. Every business, no matter how small, has intellectual-property rights associated with it: a trademark on the name of the business or a product brand, copyrights on advertising design, patents on a device the entrepreneur has invented, or trade secrets such as the company's customer list.

In the growing knowledge economy, where intellectual assets are often more valuable than physical assets, the recognition and protection of intellectual-property rights are gaining increasing importance. Beginning in the late 1990s, approximately 75 percent of the Fortune 100's market capitalization was based on intellectual property: patents, copyrights, trademarks, and trade secrets.[9] Every entrepreneur needs to understand what those rights are, not only to protect his or her property but also to avoid infringing on the rights of others. Moreover, intellectual-property rights can provide a temporary monopoly, enable the company to establish a standard, and protect its brands. The rest of this section provides an overview of the various rights under intellectual-property law and how they can be used to protect the new venture's inventions and gain a competitive advantage.

PATENTS

If a new venture opportunity relies on a product or device of some sort, it is especially important that the entrepreneur investigate applying for a patent, which is the primary means of protecting an original invention. A patent gives the patent holder the right to defend the patent against others who would attempt to manufacture, use, or sell the invention during the period of the patent. At the end of the patent life, the invention is placed in public domain, which means that anyone can use any aspect of the device the inventor created without paying royalties to the inventor.

The U.S. patent system was designed 200 years ago by Thomas Jefferson. Its purpose was to provide a brief legal monopoly to give the inventor an opportunity to get the invention into the market and recoup development costs before competitors entered the market. Since the first patent was issued in 1790, more than five million U.S. patents have been granted.

Today, although most inventors work in the research departments of large corporations and 80 percent of all patents come from large companies, the basic legal tenets of patent law still protect the interests of the independent inventor. And in cases where large corporations have infringed on those interests, the courts have generally sided with the independent inventor. In a further effort to support the small inventor, the Patent Office created the Office of the Independent Inventor to handle the 20 percent of patents submitted by independent inventors.

Is the Invention Patentable?

Before filing for a patent on an invention that an entrepreneur believes to be unique, he or she should consider the USPTO's four basic criteria that the invention must meet before it can be patented.

The invention must fit into one of the five classes established by Congress:

1. Machine or something with moving parts or circuitry (fax, rocket, photo-copier, laser, electronic circuit)
2. Process or method for producing a useful and tangible result (chemical reaction, method for producing products, business method)
3. Article of manufacture (furniture, transistor, diskette, toy)
4. Composition of matter (gasoline, food additive, drug, genetically altered lifeform)
5. A new use or improvement for one of the above that does not infringe on the patents associated with them

Many inventions can be classified into more than one category. That does not present a problem, however, because the inventor does not have to decide into which category the invention fits. In fact, the Supreme Court of the United States has stated that "anything under the sun that is made by man" falls into the statutory subject matter (*Diamond v. Chakrabarty,* 1980).[10]

With this definition, it may appear that anything can receive a patent, but in fact, there are some exclusions. Laws and phenomena of nature, naturally occurring substances, abstract mathematical formulas, and mere ideas are not eligible to be patented. However, alterations to something found in nature, such as genetically enhanced corn, can be considered for a patent. In *Diamond v. Chakrabarty,* Chakrabarty engineered a bacterium that broke down components of crude oil. No such bacterium existed in nature; thus, the Court ruled that this bacterium was the product of human ingenuity and could be patented.

The invention must have utility; in other words, it must be useful: This is not usually a problem unless the invention is an unsafe drug or something purely "whimsical," although the USPTO has been known to issue patents on some fairly strange inventions, such as a laser beam to motivate cats to exercise (Patent No. 5,443,036, Aug. 22, 1995). However, the utility of the device must be a reality, not merely speculation, and must be described in the patent application.

The invention must not contain prior art; that is, it must be new or novel in some important way: Prior art is knowledge that is publicly available or was published prior to the date of the invention—that is, before the filing of the patent application. This means that an invention can't be patented if it was known or used by others, patented, or described in a printed publication before a patent was applied for. Accordingly, it is important to document everything that is done during the creation of the invention. Also, the invention must not have become public or available for sale more than one year prior to the inventor's filing the patent application. This rule is meant to ensure that the invention is still novel at the time of application. Novelty consists of physical differences, new combinations of components, or new uses. There are two levels of challenge to novelty: statutory and anticipatory. If the invention is published or used in an unconcealed manner either in the United States or in another country, the inventor is statutorily barred from seeking a patent. Furthermore, if the patent is substantially similar to an existing patent, the inventor may not seek a patent because, in this case, the patent was anticipated.

The invention must not be obvious to someone with ordinary skills in the field: This is a tricky criterion, but it has been further explained by the USPTO as meaning that the invention must contain "new and unexpected results." That is, the invention should not be the next logical step for someone knowledgeable in the field. Obviousness is one of the most common reasons why patent applications are rejected.

Obviousness, however, did not keep Ron Lando from securing a patent on his CliC eyeware (http://clicgoggles.com). The "unique" aspect of his eyeware is that instead of hooking over the ears, the glasses wrap around the wearer's head and snap together between the lenses with a tiny but powerful neodymium magnet. The benefit? When you unhook them, they simply drop around the wearer's neck so they don't get lost. Lando knows that he will face copycats—it's a simple product, but he is counting on his brand and his strategy to supplement his patent protection.[11]

If all the requirements for patentability have been met, then the type of patent most appropriate for the invention should be considered. There are three major categories of patents: utility patents, design patents, and business method patents.

Utility Patents

Utility patents are the most common type of patent. They protect the functional part of machines or processes. Some examples are toys, film processing, protective coatings, tools, and cleaning implements. Software qualifies for patent protection if it produces a useful and tangible result. For example, the USPTO will not issue a utility patent on a mathematical formula used in space navigation, but it may on software that translates equations and makes a rocket take off.[12] (Copyrights, discussed in a later section, are commonly used for software programs that don't qualify for a patent.) A utility patent is valid for 20 years from the date of application.

Design Patents

Design patents protect new, original ornamental designs for manufactured articles. A design patent protects only the appearance of an article, not its structure or utilitarian features. The design must be nonfunctional and part of the tangible item for which it is designed. It cannot be hidden or offensive or simulate a well-known or naturally occurring object or person. Some examples of items that can receive design patents are gilding, an item of apparel, and jewelry. Inventors should be aware that although design patents are relatively easy to obtain, they are very hard to protect. It is not difficult to modify a design patent without infringing on the original patent. Design patents are valid for 14 years from date of issuance.

Business Method Patents

The 1990s saw the advent of the business method patent, which arose out of the need of Internet companies to protect their ways of doing business. The rush to patent business methods all started with one click—that is, the single click of a mouse that enables a user to order a book from Amazon.com. That one click tells Amazon to charge the purchase, take the book from its warehouse shelves, and send it to the purchaser. Jeff Bezos, Amazon's founder, thought the concept was so original that he decided to patent it. And in September 1999, the PTO granted him U.S. Patent No. 5,960,411, "method and system for placing a purchase order via a communications network." Bezos followed that success with a lawsuit in U.S. District Court in Seattle for patent infringement against Barnes & Noble (*Amazon.com v. Barnesandnoble.com*,

73F. Supp. 2 1228 [W.D. Wash. 1999]). In December 1999, a federal judge issued an injunction against Barnes & Noble to stop it from using its version of the "One-Click" process, but in February 2001, a federal appeals court over-turned the lower court's ruling because it "raised substantial questions as to the validity" of Amazon.com's patent.[13] Barnes & Noble ended up designing around the Amazon patent with its double-click.[14]

Although the Amazon case opened the floodgates for business method patents, it was actually the ruling in *State Street Bank & Trust Co. v. Signature Financial Group,* 149 F.3d 1360, that first allowed patents for business models in 1998. Priceline.com quickly followed in the wake of Amazon, filing a patent for its reverse-auction process. Since that time, much controversy has surrounded the method patent. *Business method* is actually a generic term to describe a variety of process claims, and as of this writing, the courts have not yet defined what differentiates a business method claim from a process claim. Thus business method claims are treated like any other process claim.[15] On March 29, 2000, the Patent Office issued a statement that the business method patent will cover only fundamentally different ways of doing business and that the embedded process must produce a useful, tangible, and concrete result.[16]

The process for applying for any of these patents is well defined by the USPTO and is discussed in the next section.

THE PATENT PROCESS

Although the USPTO has described the process clearly on its website (http://www.uspto.gov), it is always a good idea to seek the counsel of an intellectual-property attorney when considering a patent. An attorney who specializes in intellectual property can increase the chances of moving successfully through the USPTO application process. The following sections outline that process as an introduction and guide.

File a Disclosure Document

One very important way in which inventors can protect their inventions at the earliest stages of conceptualization is to take advantage of the USPTO's Disclosure Document Program. The purpose of a disclosure document is to serve as evidence of the date of conception of an invention. This statement is crucial if it turns out that two inventors are working on the same idea at the same time. The one who files the disclosure document first has the right to file for a patent. However, filing a disclosure statement does not in any way "diminish the value of the conventional, witnessed, permanently bound, and page-numbered laboratory notebook or notarized records as evidence of conception of an invention."[17] Furthermore, a disclosure document is not a patent application, so the date of its receipt at the USPTO will not be the effective filing date of any patent application an inventor might subsequently file.

The disclosure document contains a detailed description of the invention and its uses and may include sketches and photos such that a person of "ordinary knowledge in the field of the invention" could make and use the invention.[18] The USPTO will keep the document in confidence for two years, and the inventor has that two-year period in which to file a patent application. Even so, the inventor must demonstrate diligence in completing the invention and filing the application to maintain the right to first filing for a patent. Many people are under the mistaken impression that mailing a dated description of the invention to themselves by certified mail is as good as filing a disclosure document. Do not use this tactic because it has no value to the Patent Office.

File a Provisional Patent

A provisional patent is a way for inventors to undertake a first patent filing in the United States at a lower cost than a formal patent application. It is legally more powerful than a disclosure document, allows the inventor to use the term *patent pending,* and is designed to protect the small inventor while he or she speaks with manufacturers about producing the invention. A provisional patent also puts U.S. applicants on par with foreign applicants under the General Agreement on Tariffs and Trade (GATT) Uruguay Round Agreements (see the discussion in the section on foreign patents). The provisional patent does not, however, take the place of a formal patent application, which is discussed in the next section.

The term of the provisional patent is 12 months from the date of filing, and it cannot be extended. This means that the inventor must file a nonprovisional (formal) patent application during that period. The 12-month period does not count toward the 20-year term for a nonprovisional patent. Because the 20-year clock starts with the filing of the formal patent application, the provisional patent effectively extends patent protection by 1 year. The invention disclosure in the provisional patent application should clearly and completely describe the invention so that someone with knowledge of invention could make and use it. If a nonprovisional application is not filed within the 12-month period, the provisional application is considered abandoned, and the entrepreneur loses the ability to claim the nonprovisional date of application as the date of invention.

File a Nonprovisional Patent Application

The nonprovisional patent application is required for any patent, whether or not the entrepreneur previously filed a provisional patent application, and it extends for 20 years from the date of filing. The patent application contains a complete description of the invention, what it does, how it is uniquely different from anything currently existing (including prior art), and its scope. It also includes detailed drawings, explanations, and engineering specifications such that a person of ordinary skill in the same field could build the invention from the information provided.

The claims section of the application specifies the parts of the invention on which the inventor wants patents and must include at least one claim that attests to its novelty, utility, and nonobviousness. The claim serves to define the scope of patent protection; whether the USPTO grants the patent is largely determined by the wording of the claims. The claims must be specific enough to demonstrate the invention's uniqueness but broad enough to make it difficult for others to circumvent the patent—that is, to modify the invention slightly without violating the patent and then duplicate the product.

For example, suppose an entrepreneur attempts to patent a new type of rapid prototyping device. If the patent application defines the invention for use in prototyping of machine components, that would be a narrow definition. Another inventor could conceivably patent the invention for a new use, such as creating artificial bone, for example. That's why it is important to define the claims as broadly as possible to include as many potential applications as can be identified. Drafting a claim is an art, so it's a good idea to hire an intellectual-property attorney to draft the patent application.

Once it has received the application, the USPTO will conduct a search of its patent records for prior art. The Patent Office then contacts the inventor to either accept or deny the application claims and, in the case of denial, gives the inventor a period of time to appeal or modify the claim. It is not uncommon for the original claims to be rejected in their entirety by the USPTO, usually due to the existence of prior art, but often because of lack of nonobviousness. It will then be the job of the inventor's attorney to rewrite the claims and resubmit the revised application for another review.

If and when the Patent Office accepts the modified claims, the invention enters the patent-pending stage; that is, it awaits the issuance of the patent. The inventor may market and sell the product during this period but must clearly label it "patent pending." Most patent applications will be published 18 months after the filing date of the application. This is a much shorter time frame than was previously true. The USPTO maintains all patent applications in the strictest confidence until the patent is issued or the application is published. Once the patent has been issued, the original application and the patent itself become public record.

If the patent examiner rejects the modified claims again, the inventor has the right to appeal to a Board of Patent Appeals within the Patent Office. Failing to find agreement at this point, the inventor may appeal to the U.S. Court of Appeals for the Federal Circuit. This appeals process may take years.

One thing that many inventors fail to realize is that there are maintenance fees on patents to maintain them in force. These fees are paid to the USPTO $3\frac{1}{2}$, $7\frac{1}{2}$, and $11\frac{1}{2}$ years from the date the patent is granted. Failure to pay these fees can result in expiration of the patent. Entrepreneurs should check with the USPTO to determine if their company qualifies for Small Entity Status, which may lower their maintenance fees.

Patent Infringement

Once issued, a patent is a powerful document that gives the holder the right to enforce the patent in federal court. If such a lawsuit is successful, the court may issue an injunction preventing the infringer from making any further use of the invention and award the patent holder a reasonable royalty from the infringer; if the infringer refuses to pay, the patent holder can enjoin or close down the operation of the infringer. Alternatively, the court may mediate an agreement between the parties under which the infringing party will pay royalties to the patent holder in exchange for permission to use the patented invention.

Infringement of patent rights occurs when someone other than the inventor (patent holder) or licensee makes and sells a product that contains every one of the elements of a claim. The Patent Office also protects inventors from infringers who would violate a patent by making small, insignificant changes in the claims. This policy is called the *doctrine of equivalents*. If, for example, an entrepreneur had a patent on a three-legged wooden chair, and the infringer produced and distributed the exact same chair but gave it three metal legs, that person would be violating the entrepreneur's patent under the doctrine of equivalents. Patent infringement actions are costly and difficult to prosecute. Many times, the alleged infringer will defend himself or herself by attempting to prove that the patent is invalid—that is, that the USPTO mistakenly issued the patent. Today, unfortunately, a number of companies regularly challenge their competitors' patents in the courts as a business strategy, as Profile 7.1 illustrates.

FOREIGN PATENTS

It is important to remember that the patent rights granted to an individual in the United States extend only to the borders of the United States. They have no effect in any foreign country. Because every country has different laws regarding intellectual property, patent attorneys face a real challenge when helping their clients apply for or defend foreign patents. Two important differences exist between international and U.S. procedures in the areas of first-to-file and novelty.[19] First, the European Patent Convention (EPC) grants patent rights to the first person to file for the patent, whether or not that person is the original inventor. By contrast, in the United States, only the original inventor has the first right to file an application. It should be noted that the U.S. Congress is considering changing to the European Convention, but for now, first-to-invent is still the rule. Second, in the United States, an inventor can sell an invention up to one year before filing a patent application. That is not true in other countries, where publication of any kind before the date of filing will bar the right to a patent. Furthermore, most countries require that the invention be manufactured in the country within three years of the issuance of the foreign patent. In 1983, the Trilateral Co-operation was established between the European Patent Office (EPO), the Japan Patent Office (JPO), and the USPTO to process patent applications filed worldwide. The Patent Cooperation Treaty (PCT) allows inventors in any nation that signed on to the treaty to file a single international patent application covering all the countries under the treaty. That application is then subjected to an international search to determine the probability of a patent being issued. Subsequent to a positive finding, the applicant can begin to pursue the grant of patents directly from the countries or regions desired.

When considering foreign patents, be sure to consult an intellectual-property attorney who specializes in this area. Because of the high cost and effort involved in obtaining foreign patents, it is important to determine whether a reasonable profit can be made from them. Often, it's more valuable to seek solid strategic alliances in other countries, thus obtaining good distribution channels through which to export products, than to spend the time and money seeking patents in every country in which the entrepreneur will do business. Advice from a knowledgeable attorney can make this decision easier.

Global Insights

SPEEDING TIME-TO-MARKET

For entrepreneurs who resort to bootstrapping product development, outsourcing to the international market has been a survival tactic. Product development is an expensive and time-consuming process, so the ability to find great talent at reasonable prices may mean the difference between getting to market and missing a window of opportunity. Charlotte, North Carolina-based ESP Systems puts the timing of a customer's restaurant meal in the hands of the customer. Using a wireless network and "aesthetically designed devices," customers are able to communicate with the wait staff and control the pace of their meals. ESP's competitive strategy was a first-mover strategy, but U.S. equipment manufacturers were not cooperating. ESP was just not big enough

to grab their attention. So the company found Flextronics, a $16 billion contract manufacturer that had global R&D facilities. Using Flextronic's Shenzhen, China, design facility, ESP was able to cut its start-up costs in half and reduce time-to-market significantly. The talented brains in Shenzhen even figured out a way to triple the square footage that ESP's system could cover. As of January 2007, ESP had 74 restaurants under contract.

Sources: L. Buchanan, "The Thinking Man's Outsourcing," *Inc. Magazine* (May 2006), http://www.inc.com/magazine; ESP Systems, http://www.espsystems.net, accessed March 7, 2007; "Operators Use Wireless Technology to Connect Customers, Employees," *Nation's Restaurant News* (December 11, 2006).

TRADEMARKS

Trademarks have become nearly as popular as patents as intellectual-property assets. A trademark is a symbol, logo, word, sound, color, design, or other device that is used to identify a business or a product in commerce. The term *trademark* is regularly used to refer to both trademarks and service marks, which identify services or intangible activities "performed by one person for the benefit of a person or persons other than himself, either for pay or otherwise."[20] Other, less commonly used types of trademarks can be found at the USPTO website.

Here are some examples of trademarked items:

Logo: McDonald's double arches (http://www.mcdonalds.com)

Slogan: L'Oreal: "Because you're worth it." (http://www.loreal.com)

Container shape: Coca-Cola's classic beverage bottle (http://www.coca-cola.com)

Colors can even be trademarked. In the 1995 Supreme Court case *Qualitex Co. v. Jacobson Products Co.*, 115 S.Ct. 1300 (1995), the Court held that the green-gold color of a dry-cleaning press pad could be trademarked. To do so, the applicant must be able to demonstrate that the color has a secondary meaning—that is, that people associate the color with the product. For example, pink has been associated with insulation, even though the color has nothing to do with the insulation's function. Colors that are functional in nature cannot be trademarked.

A trademark—with certain conditions—has a longer life than a patent. A business has the exclusive right to a trademark for as long as it is actively using it. However, if a trademark becomes part of the generic language, as have *aspirin* and *thermos,* it can no longer be trademarked. Furthermore, a trademark cannot be registered until it is actually in use. The symbol ® means "registered trademark." Before a trademark is registered, the holder of the trademark should file an intent-to-use application with the USPTO and place ™ (or ℠ for services) after the name until the trademark has been registered. This is an important point, because trademarks cannot be stockpiled and then sold to potential users. They must be in use in the market to be protected.

The USPTO does not require a search for potentially conflicting marks prior to filing the application. However, it is probably wise to conduct a search; doing so is not difficult and can save time and effort later. A search can be conducted in the USPTO public search library at http://www.uspto.gov or in a patent and depository library, or a specialist can be hired to conduct the search. In any case, after application the USPTO determines whether the mark may be registered and notifies the entrepreneur. If the USPTO rejects the application, the entrepreneur has six months to respond.

Marks that cannot be trademarked include:

▶ Anything immoral or deceptive

▶ Anything that uses official symbols of the United States or any state or municipality, such as the flag

▶ Anything that uses a person's name or likeness without permission

Trademark Infringement, Counterfeiting, and Dilution

Like patents, trademarks can suffer from infringement, counterfeiting, or misappropriation. Infringement is found if a mark is likely to cause confusion with a trademark already existing in the marketplace. The deliberate copying of a mark (counterfeiting) is subject to civil and criminal penalties.

Trademarks are also subject to dilution, which occurs when the value of the mark is substantially reduced through competition or through the likelihood of confusion from another mark. For example, American Express was able to prove that it suffered dilution when a limousine service used the American Express trademark for its business, even though the two companies were in different industries.[21] In 2006, the Trademark Dilution Revision Act was signed into law to provide relief to owners of famous trademarks whose marks had been tarnished by third-party marks. The act says that the injured party can seek injunctive relief and monetary damages against a third party that adopts a trademark that will cause dilution of the famous mark even though it is a noncompeting use. It is difficult to say what the impact of the legislation will be until there are court rulings.

COPYRIGHTS

It has been said over and over again that we live in an information economy. Certainly, information-based products and services have been growing at a breathless pace, propelled by technology and the Internet. But with the proliferation of digital works comes the difficult task of finding ways to protect all the intellectual property that is being accessed, duplicated, transmitted, and published in digital form. Copyrights are the form of protection that comes into play here.

Copyrights protect original works of authors, composers, screenwriters, and computer programmers. A copyright does not protect the idea itself but only the form in which it appears, which cannot be copied without the express permission of the copyright holder. For example, a computer programmer can copyright the written program for a particular type of word processing software but cannot copyright the idea of word processing. This is why several companies can produce word processing software without violating a copyright. What they really are protecting is the unique programming code of their software. The First Sale Doctrine [Section 106 of the 1976 Copyright Act] grants a copyright owner six rights: reproduction, preparation of derivative works, distribution, public performance, public display, and digital transmission performance.[22] What this means is that the owner can distribute or dispose of only the particular copy that he or she owns.

Under the Copyright Extension Act of 1998, a copyright lasts for the life of the holder plus 70 years, after which the copyrighted material goes into public domain. Works for hire and works published anonymously now have copyrights of 95 years from the date of publication.

The first copyright statute was enacted in 1793, but it has been successfully adapted for over 200 years. The courts have said, "the purpose of the copyright law is to create the most efficient and productive balance between protection (incentive) and dissemination of information, to promote learning, culture, and development."[23] There is no question that copyright law is undergoing its most strenuous test in the information economy. One of the areas of contention is the Doctrine of Fair Use, which has been codified in Section 107 of the copyright law. This section asserts that reproduction of a copyrighted work is "fair" when it is done for purposes such as criticism, comment, news reporting, teaching, scholarship, and research. There is no clear distinction between fair use and infringement; even acknowledging the source may not be sufficient, so the safest course is to secure permission from the original copyright holder.

The Digital Millennium Copyright Act

One of the problems associated with delivering products over the Internet is the ease with which a person can infringe on another's rights. In October 1998, President Clinton signed into law the Digital Millennium Copyright Act (DMCA), which prohibits the falsification, alteration, or removal of copyright management data on digital copies. In other words, it made it a crime to circumvent an encrypted work without authorization. The law also made it illegal to manufacture and distribute products that facilitate the circumvention of encrypted work.

John Lech Johansen was just 15 years old when, out of frustration with his MP3 player, he wrote a "fix it" program and posted it on the Web to help others who were having trouble playing some of their DVDs. Unfortunately, by removing the encryption code with his program, DVDs could now be copied. His ingenuity won him an award from the Electronic Frontier Foundation, a non-profit organization that works to protect digital rights, but it also won him a visit from the Norwegian police in his hometown. He went on to figure out how to play legally acquired songs from distributors other than iTunes on the iPod, something Steven Jobs certainly did not want to happen. This involved circumventing Apple's FairPlay encryption program. According to Johansen, "If you legally acquire music, you need to have the right to manage it on all other devices that you own."[24] But under the First Sale Doctrine, when a digital file is transferred, there is no transfer of ownership. As a result, the First Sale Doctrine does not permit distribution of digital works.[25]

The DMCA does contain a safe harbor clause to protect service providers from monetary damages if they unknowingly infringe on someone's rights, either by transmitting or storing infringing material or by linking users to websites containing infringing material. This law clears the way to licensing intellectual property for a fee over the Internet.

Obtaining Copyright Protection

To qualify for federal copyright protection, the work must be in a fixed and tangible form—that is, someone must be able to see or hear it. Although it is not required by law, to provide notice to a potential infringer and so that a potential violator cannot claim innocence because there was no notice, the notice should use the word *copyright* or the symbol © and should provide the year and the complete name of the person responsible for the work, as in © 2004 Stephen Barry. Though not required, registration at the Copyright Office at the Library of Congress in Washington, DC, is important in order to obtain full protection under the law and to create a document trail.

International Protection

Fortunately, copyright protection laws are fairly consistent across countries because of a number of international copyright treaties, the most important of which is the Berne Convention. Under this treaty, which includes more than 100 nations, a country must give copyright protection to authors who are nationals of any member country for at least the life of the author plus 50 years.

TRADE SECRETS

A trade secret consists of a formula, device, idea, process, pattern, or compilation of information that gives the owner a competitive advantage in the marketplace, is novel in the sense that it is not common knowledge, and is kept in a confidential state. Some examples of trade secrets are the recipe for Mrs. Field's cookies, survey methods used by professional pollsters, customer lists, source codes for computer chips, customer discounts, and inventions for which no patent will be applied.

Many companies, such as Hewlett-Packard (HP), choose not to patent some of their inventions but rather keep them for internal use only as trade secrets. The reason is that once a patent has been issued, anyone can look up the patent on the USPTO website and see how the device is made. Some of HP's inventions are devices and processes used in the manufacture of its computers and peripherals, and they give the firm a significant competitive advantage that it would lose if this information got into the hands of competitors. With the patent in hand, the competitor could build that device and use it to improve its own manufacturing processes. As long as the competitor is not selling the device in the market, it would require a court to decide whether the firm is actually infringing on HP's patent.

There are no legal means under patent and trademark law to protect trade secrets. The only way to protect them is through confidentiality agreements or contracts. An employer might have all employees sign an employment contract that specifically details what is considered trade secret information, both at the time the employee is hired and during his or her tenure as an employee. Then, should a current or former employee use or reveal a specified trade secret, the company can pursue legal remedies, such as an injunction or suing for damages.

This chapter discussed how important it is to an entrepreneur's business strategy to protect the assets created. The key point to remember about intellectual-property rights is that they can't stop someone from infringing on the entrepreneur's rights. What they can do is provide the entrepreneur with offensive rights—that is, the right to sue in a court of law, a long and costly process (remember the story of Gordon Gould at the beginning of this chapter). Consequently, intellectual-property rights should never be the sole competitive advantage a business possesses, but rather one of a bundle of strategies that includes customer relationships and organizational culture.

There are risks and benefits associated with the products and services that entrepreneurs develop. Part of the goal of feasibility analysis is to address those risks and benefits so that informed decisions can be made about whether to go forward with a new business concept.

DRAWING CONCLUSIONS ABOUT THE PRODUCT/SERVICE PLAN

The product/service plan gives the entrepreneur a level of confidence about the ability to actually produce and protect the product or service being offered. The first conclusion to be drawn centers on the issue of whether it is possible to make the product in sufficient quantities to meet a market need. Are there methods of manufacturing available globally that enable the product to be manufactured at a cost that yields a final price the customer is willing to pay? In the case of a service, how large an organization would be required to serve the size of the market identified. Are there efficient ways to deliver the service at a reasonable cost? Being able to patent a product or service affects the product development strategy as well as the market adoption strategy, so this test should answer the question *is a patent a feasible strategy*? Then conclusions should be drawn about any other forms of intellectual property that could become part of the bundle of competitive advantages the entrepreneur is developing. Finally, a timeline for the development of the product or service will prepare the entrepreneur for considering financial requirements.

New Venture Checklist

Have you:

☐ Found ways to incorporate customer input into the design of your products, processes, and services?

☐ Found independent contractors who can build a prototype?

☐ Identified intellectual-property rights appropriate to the business concept?

Issues to Consider

1. How has the environment for product development changed in the last decade, and what does this mean to entrepreneurs starting new businesses?
2. What are the principal reasons why new products fail?
3. Suppose you are going to develop and market a new device for tracking calories consumed during the day. What will your product development strategy be, and why?
4. In what ways should you protect an invention from the time of its earliest conception?

Experiencing Entrepreneurship

1. Visit an entrepreneurial company that is developing new products. What is the company's product development strategy, and how effective is that strategy? What criteria did you use to measure effectiveness? You may need to use outside sources to confirm what the company tells you.

2. Visit the U.S. Patent Office at http://www.uspto.gov. Pick a patented product that interests you and contact the inventor to determine whether the patent has ever been commercialized. If so, in what ways? If not, can the inventor provide a reason? What can you conclude about the potential for this patent?

Relevant Case Studies

## Chapter 8

THE FOUNDING TEAM

"The people who get on in this world are the people who get up and look for the circumstances they want, and, if they can't find them, make them."

—GEORGE BERNARD SHAW

LEARNING OBJECTIVES

▶ Explain how to build a founding team effectively.

▶ Understand how to work with professional advisers.

▶ Discuss when to add a board of directors.

▶ Compare and contrast the pros and cons of outsourcing with independent contractors versus hiring employees.

Profile 8.1 ALL FOR ONE AND ONE FOR ALL

D'Artagnan, Inc. is a specialty food producer, selling 200 prepared products and 700 raw products. With revenues topping $46 million, it sells to high-end retailers and restaurants. But as late as spring 2005, it was anyone's guess whether the company would survive the dissolution of the fiery partnership of its founders, Ariane Daguin and George Faison. This is the story of how a partnership, even of friends, can be torn apart by circumstances.

Daguin and Faison had met in 1979 while students at Columbia University. Daguin was an aficionado of *fois gras* (fattened goose or duck liver), which at the time was only available in Europe. When a New York farmer saw an opportunity to raise ducks for fois gras, Daguin capitalized on the opportunity by distributing the delicacy to upscale chefs in the United States. D'Artagnan was launched in 1985 with Daguin applying her food expertise and Faison running the business operations. The business grew quickly, becoming profitable in its second year. Although things were going well, it was not easy for the partners. Neither was drawing a sufficient salary and both were working long hours, so arguments soon began to break out over everything from business strategy to whether Daguin was spending too much time with her new baby. At one point in 1993, their consultants suggested that they divide the responsibilities of the business: Daguin would take marketing and sales, and Faison would take finance and operations. The positive side of the change was that the partners now had their own space, but the negative was that they were not communicating enough to keep everyone working as a cohesive team.

The tipping point came in 1999 during Christmas week, when the Centers for Disease Control and Prevention found that a number of their food products from a particular factory tested positive for listeria, a highly dangerous bacteria. Understanding the seriousness of the situation, Daguin recalled 70,000 pounds of tainted meat, fired the supplier, and personally called the 3,575 people who had purchased the product. But despite her extraordinary effort, many retailers were still reluctant to purchase products from D'Artagnan and sales dropped precipitously.

In 2001, Daguin made the decision to open a French restaurant in New York City to help rebuild their reputation, promote their products, and reinforce their brand. It was a huge success from the start, but just seven weeks later their dream disintegrated, a victim of the fallout from the September 11 attacks on the World Trade Center. Even when business in the city began to return, they were faced with a boycott of French restaurants brought on when France refused to support the United States in the Iraq War. Daguin was spending all her time trying to save the restaurant while Faison had to run D'Artagnan. Both had to invest more money into the business to save it, but the restaurant would not survive, and they closed it in 2004. In July 2005, Faison surprised Daguin by exercising the shotgun clause in their buy-sell agreement that provided for a price at which he could buy Daguin out of the business. Stunned but ready to fight back, Daguin raised the money to match Faison's price and instead bought him out. With one person in charge, the company eventually got back on track and grew its revenues 18 percent in just over a year from when Faison left the company.

What saved D'Artagnan, despite the dissolution of the partnership, was the buy-sell agreement they had signed to dictate what would happen if one partner left the company and the shotgun clause that had provided for a fair price should the partnership end on a bad note. Had it not been for these agreements, it is doubtful that D'Artagnan would be in business today. Buy-sell agreements are discussed later in the chapter.

Sources: S. Clifford, "Until Death or Some Other Sticky Problem Do Us Part," *Inc. Magazine* (November 2006), pp. 102–110; "D'Artagnan, All for one, Food for all!" Specialty Food Services, http://www.specialtyfoodservices.com/dartagnan.htm, accessed March 9, 2007.

n the past, entrepreneurs in their quest for independence often attempted a new venture as soloists. In this way they could retain sole ownership, make all the key decisions, and not have to share the profits. This approach to starting a business is still common in small lifestyle businesses and among craftspeople and artisans. However, in today's global, complex, and fast-changing environment, most entrepreneurs find it necessary to start their ventures with a team. In fact, a growing body of research supports a team approach to entrepreneurial events.[1] Teams have a much greater chance for success than solo efforts for a variety of reasons:

▶ The intense effort required of a start-up can be shared.

▶ Should any one team member leave, it is less likely to result in the abandonment of the start-up.

▶ With a founding team whose expertise covers major functional areas—marketing, finance, operations—the new venture can proceed further before it will need to hire additional personnel.

▶ A skilled founding team lends credibility to the new venture in the eyes of lenders, investors, and others.

▶ The entrepreneur's ability to analyze information and make decisions is improved because he or she benefits from the varied expertise of the team, and ideas may be viewed from several perspectives.

When the start-up effort is collective, with a team that displays diverse capabilities, the new venture is more likely to be innovative and carve out a unique niche for itself.[2] Yet another body of empirical research has provided evidence that firms founded by heterogeneous teams are generally more successful than those founded by individuals.[3]

Despite the research support for team-based entrepreneurship, there is also evidence to support the role and importance of a lead entrepreneur—that is, a person who displays a higher level of entrepreneurial vision and self-efficacy than other members of the team.[4] Lead entrepreneurs drive the development of new ventures and serve as the guardians of their vision. They have the ability to see what others cannot see and to identify ways to change the marketplace rather than simply recognize an opportunity.

The reality is that entrepreneurs never start businesses all on their own; rather, they are "embedded in a social context, channeled and facilitated, or constrained and inhibited, by their positions in social networks."[5] Successful ventures take advantage of social networks to grow and maintain loyal customers, seek and acquire resources, and eventually sell their companies. For example, building a community or social network was online auction company eBay's goal from the start, and its success in doing so has been one of the most important reasons why eBay has survived where others have failed. Its customers manage the site—rating the quality of trading experiences with buyers and sellers, forming neighborhood watch groups to protect users against fraud and abuse, and providing input to the company on website design. eBay has become the place where people go to network with others who share their interests. eBay's CEO describes eBay as "of the people, by the people, for the people."[6]

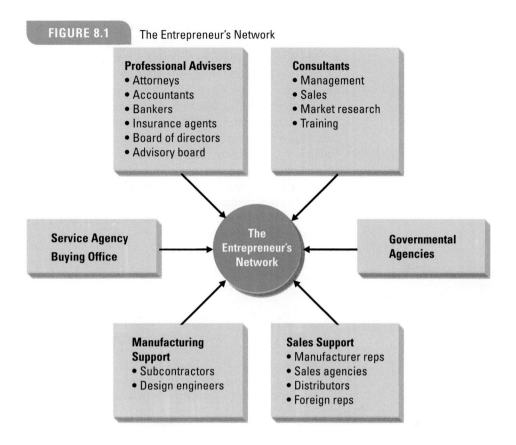

FIGURE 8.1 The Entrepreneur's Network

The extended networks of entrepreneurs are critical to the entire entrepreneurial process.[7] Extended networks consist of "the relations between owners, managers, and employees, and they are structured by patterns of coordination and control."[8] Furthermore, when the entrepreneurial firm interacts with other firms in its industry, it creates additional extended networks. At the hub of this network (or *agile web,* as it is often called) is the founding team that has the vision and dedication to coordinate the efforts of all the partners toward a common goal. See Figure 8.1 for a view of the entrepreneur's network.

Creating the Founding Team

Choosing partners to start a new venture is one of the most critically important tasks that an entrepreneur must undertake. It is a difficult task because it is often not possible to understand a person's character until that person has spent some time working in the company. The stressful environment of a start-up may bring out traits and responses that were not apparent when the person was originally selected. Everyone from investors to bankers to potential customers looks at the founding team of the new venture to determine whether its members have the ability to execute their plans. Thus it is vital to choose partners who have complementary skills and experience and who do not have a history that might be detrimental to the company.

Finding partners with complementary skills means making sure that the team is not overloaded with people who all have the same expertise. A team of three engineers or three finance analysts is generally less attractive than a team with more diverse skills. Research has suggested that teams with diverse skills make better strategic choices that lead to higher performance.[9] In fact, some research has found team heterogeneity to be a significant predictor of long-term performance.[10] In terms of skill sets, heterogeneous teams also tend to handle the complexity of new ventures better than homogeneous teams.[11] Table 8.1 presents five factors that are significant in team composition: (1) homophily, or similarity; (2) functionality, or skill diversity; (3) status expectations, or cultural bias; (4) network constraints, or social contacts; and (5) ecological constraints, or geographic distribution.

TABLE 8.1

Significant Factors for Founding Team Composition

Homophily	The extent to which the characteristics of founding team members, such as gender, race, age, values, and beliefs, are similar.
	The benefit is that a high degree of similarity predisposes the team toward interpersonal attraction, trust, and understanding.
Functionality	The degree of diversity among team members with respect to leadership skills and task expertise.
	Diversity of work experience and occupational background has been found to be linked to functional performance* and to communication and innovation.[†]
Status Expectations	Widely held cultural biases regarding status (such as men having higher status than women) frequently affect the process of task group formation (although, in the case of gender, less so today).
	Those who perceive themselves to be in a higher-status group will tend to choose team members of the same status, however they define that status. Therefore, the entrepreneur who has lower status typically starts a venture as a soloist.
Network Constraint	The ability to choose members of a team is constrained by structural opportunities for social contact. For example, starting a business with only family members makes it more difficult to create a diverse team, because family members tend to be linked by strong ties and are in many respects an undesirably homogeneous group.[‡]
Ecological Constraint	The size of the population of potential team members and their geographic proximity is critical in the formation of founding teams.[§] The likelihood that different team members will associate is a function of their relative proportions in the population and their proximity to each other.[‖]

* K. Eisenhardt and C.B. Schoonhoven (1990). "Organizational Growth: Linking Founding Team, Strategy, Environment, and Growth Among U.S. Semiconductor Ventures, 1978–1988." *Administrative Science Quarterly*, 35: 504–529.
† D. Ancona and D. Caldwell (1992). "Demography and Design: Predictors of New Product Team Performance." *Organization Science*, 3: 321–341.
‡ H.E. Aldrich, A. Elam, and P.R. Reese (1996). "Strong Ties, Weak Ties, and Strangers: Do Women Business Owners Differ from Men in Their Use of Networking to Obtain Assistance?" in S. Birley and I. MacMillan (eds), *Entrepreneurship in a Global Context*. London: Routledge, pp. 1–25.
§ G. Carroll and M. Hannan (2000). *The Demography of Corporations and Industries*. Princeton, NJ: Princeton University Press.
‖ P. Blau (1980). "A Fable About Social Structure." *Social Forces*, 58: 777–788.
Source: Based on Martin Ruef, Howard E. Aldrich, and Nancy M. Carter, "The Structure of Founding Teams: Homophily, Strong Ties, and Isolation Among U.S. Entrepreneurs," *American Sociological Review* (2003), 68(2): 195.

There is also another advantage to forming a team. Because members of an entrepreneurial team often invest not only their time but also their money, the burden of gathering resources is shared. The lead entrepreneur also gains access to the network of contacts of the other members. This vastly increases the information and resources available to the new venture and enables it to grow more rapidly.

Of course, it isn't always possible or necessary to put together the "perfect" team from the start. The right person to fill a particular need may not have been determined, or the right person may be too expensive to bring on board during start-up. In the latter situation, it is important to talk to that person about joining the team at a later date and to keep him or her apprised of the company's progress. Many an aggressive start-up company has eventually wooed an experienced person away from a major corporation.

A BENCHMARK FOR AN EFFECTIVE TEAM

Although there are no perfect founding teams and no fail-safe rules for forming them, effective founding teams tend to display the following characteristics:

▶ The lead entrepreneur and the team share the same vision for the new venture.

▶ The team members are passionate about the business concept and will work as hard as the lead entrepreneur to make it happen.

▶ One or more members of the founding team have experience in the industry in which the venture is being launched.

▶ The team has solid industry contacts with sources of capital.

▶ The team's expertise covers the key functional areas of the business: finance, marketing, and operations.

▶ The team members have good credit ratings; this will be important when the team seeks financing.

▶ The team is free to spend the time a start-up demands and can endure the financial constraints of a typical start-up.

Despite knowing a potential business partner as a friend or colleague for many years, the new venture scenario presents a different set of challenges that may reveal some negatives that were not apparent before. The founding team will need to agree on a number of important issues before launching a business together. One of the most effective ways to determine whether the team has the potential to work together successfully is to individually take a quiz that uncovers each person's values, goals, and expectations. Table 8.2 presents such a quiz. After each team member has taken the quiz independently of the others, the team should review the responses to learn if this team is in the same boat, heading in the same direction. It is not uncommon to find that one or more members of an otherwise cohesive team had different expectations for the outcomes of the business or their role in it. These differences must be discussed and agreed upon before moving further as a team. It will be far more costly in time and money, not to mention friendships, if these differences are ignored and cause problems later when the business is growing.

TABLE 8.2

A Founding Team Quiz

1. What are your core values?
2. What is your goal for this business?
3. What do you see as your role in the business? Why?
4. What roles do you see the other team members playing and why?
5. How should ownership of the business be divided?
6. How should decisions be made?
7. Do you enjoy business travel?
8. What kinds of hours will you keep?
9. What is your preferred mode of communication?
10. What is your credit rating?
11. How do you spend money?
12. What is your lifestyle goal?

SPECIAL ISSUES FOR HIGH-TECH TEAMS

New ventures in the high-tech arena are frequently funded by "angel," or venture capital, and these start-ups face different issues in the formation of their founding teams. Very often, the founding team consists of scientists and engineers with little market or business experience. Investors understand clearly that these kinds of teams are not the most effective for overseeing the rapid and successful execution of the business strategy. A high-tech venture with significant up-front funding and the potential for exponential growth early on requires a professional management team with experience and an excellent track record in the industry. Usually, the investors will help the entrepreneurs locate the right people for the job. Bringing on professional management at start-up ensures that there will be no glitches when rapid growth begins, and it also leaves the creative founders the time they need to continue to develop and improve the product and/or service.

UNIQUE ISSUES SURROUNDING VIRTUAL TEAMS

Technology has made it possible for geographically dispersed teams to form and collaborate through synchronous and/or asynchronous communication media, relieving team members of the need to juggle global and local priorities.[12] Virtual teams are distinctly different from face-to-face teams in both spatial distance and communication. It is not the actual distance that matters but the effect that this distance has on how the team interacts. For example, suppose a start-up team is located in Los Angeles and one team member lives in Pasadena, approximately 10 miles away. The spatial distance is not great, but given traffic and other challenges, the time distance may be 40 minutes or more. Therefore, technologies such as videoconferencing, phone, and e-mail are used to mediate the distance. In addition, appropriate routines keep everyone connected and on track.[13]

Despite any disadvantages caused by distance, virtual teams have several advantages. They enable the entrepreneur to access the most qualified individuals for a particular position, regardless of location, and to create a more flexible organization. This will entail finding partners who will evolve into a coherent, seamless, and well-integrated team.[14] Trust, therefore, is a critical component of an effective virtual team.

Rob Bevis, president of Winspeer International Group Ltd., a Vancouver, Canada–based wine importer, has faced the challenges and advantages of working in a virtual environment. His company extends from Vancouver to Edmonton to Calgary and all roads in between. It is impossible for him to run his business in any other manner. In a rapidly growing global marketplace that is easily accessible via the Internet, an entrepreneur needs to expand into new markets. These new markets may not be geographically local, and therefore may create significant personnel challenges, complicating the task of getting people to work together. In his role as president of Winspeer, Bevis quickly realized that he needed to be able to coordinate the activities of his employees who were scattered throughout western Canada. His needs fell into three areas: (1) tactical collaboration to reach employees at their desks or on the road through e-mail, instant messaging, and cell phone; (2) strategic collaboration that involved information sharing, file sharing, and message boards; and (3) task management using public calendars and checklists. His major concern was that all employees would be able to know what was going on at any given time. This required a central database, a virtual private network (VPN), and a common calendar. Today, with these collaboration tools in place, Bevis and his team can respond quickly to a marketplace that changes daily, and this has reduced costs and increased revenues—in short, it made all the difference for his winning team.[15]

FOUNDING TEAMS FOR INTERNATIONAL VENTURES

Traditionally, entrepreneurs were advised to establish themselves in the domestic market before taking on the enormous challenge of a global market. Increasingly, however, we are seeing more and more firms going international from start-up. And these international start-ups are generally being founded by teams.[16] Research indicates that whether these small firms succeed in the international market depends on the skills and knowledge of the entrepreneurial team.[17] The characteristics found to predict success in international ventures include the extent to which members of the founding team have traveled and/or worked abroad and the number of languages spoken.[18] Experienced founding teams are also more likely to form partnerships to facilitate their entering a foreign market.[19] Because international start-ups are relatively more vulnerable, because their operations are at a distance, they usually seek partnerships to provide financial, political, and cultural resources and the contacts they will need to be successful. The topic of global entrepreneurial ventures is discussed in Chapter 18.

RULES FOR FRIENDS AND FAMILIES

Turning to friends and family members is certainly the easiest and quickest way to find partners to start a new venture, but it may not be the best decision for the business. If a small business has no intentions of seeking outside financing, having a founding team that consists entirely of family members may not be a problem if they are all compatible. But if the plan is to grow the venture significantly, seek outside investors, or potentially do a public offering, a founding team consisting of only family members may not be an attractive asset. Here are some things to think about before making the decision to take on a family member or close friend as a partner in a new venture:

▶ Friends or family members should possess real skills and expertise that the business needs to be successful.

▶ They should have the same work ethic as the entrepreneur. If the entrepreneur is a workaholic and loves it and a family member is a slacker, there will be problems.

▶ If there are family members on the start-up team, there should be outsiders on the advisory board and/or board of directors so that the company will have the benefit of objective input to the business.

▶ The relationship with family and friends should be treated as a business relationship. The responsibilities and duties of all should be clearly spelled out, and everyone should understand how disagreements will be settled. As much as possible, the business should not be brought home at night.

As with any other partnership, it is important to execute buy-sell agreements with family members to minimize inevitable disagreements.

Seeking Professional Advisers

When a new venture is in its infancy, it generally doesn't have the resources to hire in-house professional help such as an attorney or accountant. Instead, it must rely on building relationships with professionals on an "as-needed" basis. These professionals provide information and services not normally within the scope of expertise of most entrepreneurs, and they can play devil's advocate for the entrepreneur, pointing out potential flaws in the business concept. They provide the new venture—and the entrepreneurial team in love with its own concept—a invaluable reality check. There are a number of these professional advisers that entrepreneurs rely on at various times in their venture's life.

ATTORNEYS

There is hardly any aspect of starting a new venture that is not touched by the law. Unfortunately, entrepreneurs who have never had any education in the legal aspects of business often don't recognize that they need legal help until their business gets into trouble. Attorneys are professionals who typically specialize in one area of the law (such as taxes, real estate, business, or intellectual property) and can provide a wealth of support for the new venture. Within their particular area of expertise, attorneys can

▶ Advise the entrepreneur in selecting the correct organizational structure: sole proprietorship, partnership, LLC, or corporation.

▶ Advise about and prepare documents for acquisition of intellectual-property rights and for licensing agreements.

▶ Negotiate and prepare contracts for the entrepreneur, who may be buying, selling, contracting, or leasing.

▶ Advise the entrepreneur on compliance with regulations related to financing and credit.

▶ Keep the entrepreneur apprised of the latest tax reform legislation and help to minimize the venture's tax burden.

▶ Assist the entrepreneur in complying with federal, state, or local laws.

▶ Represent the entrepreneur in any legal actions as advocates.

Choosing a good attorney is a time-consuming but vital task that should be accomplished prior to start-up. Decisions about such things as the legal form of the business or contracts made at inception may affect the venture for years to come—hence the need for good legal advice. To find the best attorney for the situation, entrepreneurs should

▶ Ask accountants, bankers, and other business people to recommend attorneys who are familiar with the challenges facing start-ups, particularly those in the entrepreneur's industry.

▶ Look for an attorney who is willing to listen, has time, and will be flexible about fees while the business is in the start-up phase.

▶ Check out the firm by phone first. One can learn a lot about a law firm by noting who answers the phone and with what tone of voice. If the attorney answers his or her office phone directly, this may be a very small firm with limited resources. Does the person answering the phone sound genuinely interested in being helpful?

▶ Confirm that the attorney carries malpractice insurance.

ACCOUNTANTS

A lawyer is an advocate, but an accountant is bound by rules and ethics that do not permit advocacy. Whereas an attorney is bound to represent his or her client no matter what the client does, an accountant cannot defend a client who does something that violates the accounting industry's Generally Accepted Accounting Principles (GAAP).

Accounting is a fairly complex field that the entrepreneur needs to understand at least at a basic level in order to communicate with accountants, auditors, lenders, bankers, and investors, in addition to internal and external stakeholders. In the beginning, the accountant may set up the company's books and maintain them on a periodic basis, or, as is often the case, the entrepreneur may hire a bookkeeper to perform the day-to-day recording of transactions. The accountant will also set up control systems for operations, as well as payroll. The entrepreneur then goes to the accountant during the tax season. Once the new venture is beyond the start-up phase and is growing consistently, it's a good idea to do an annual audit to determine whether the company's accounting and control procedures are adequate. The auditors may also require a physical inventory. If everything is in order, they will issue a certified statement, which is important should the entrepreneur ever decide to take the company public.

Accountants are also a rich networking source in the entrepreneur's search for additional members of the new venture team. Like attorneys, accountants tend to specialize, so it is wise to find one who is used to working with young, growing businesses. Indeed, the accountant who takes a business through start-up and early growth will probably not be the best person to take care of the company's needs when it reaches the next level of growth. As the financial and record-keeping needs of the business increase and become more complex, the entrepreneur may have to consider a larger firm with expertise in several areas.

BANKERS

There is a saying that all banks are alike until you need a loan. Today this is truer than ever, so having a qualified banker on the advisory team will put the new venture in a better position to seek a line of credit for operating capital or a loan to purchase equipment. The firm's banker should be thought of as a business partner who can be a source of information and networking; help make decisions regarding capital needs; assist in preparing pro forma operations and cash-flow analyses and evaluate projections; and assist in all facets of financing.

To narrow the search for a banker, entrepreneurs should prepare a list of criteria that defines the banking needs of the new venture. They should also talk with other entrepreneurs in the same industry to identify a bank that works well with the type of venture they plan to launch. Another approach is to ask an accountant or attorney to suggest the best bank for a particular type new venture.

When choosing a banker, seek out an officer with a rank of assistant vice president or higher, because these officers are trained to work with new and growing businesses and have enough authority to make decisions quickly. In particular, it is important to ensure that the lending officer can approve loans and lines of credit in the amounts needed. Today many of the largest banks have moved their lending facilities to a central location, so it is difficult to establish a relationship with the person who has responsibility for approving a request. That's why many entrepreneurs seek out community banks that have a vested interest in supporting local businesses.

INSURANCE AGENTS

Many entrepreneurs overlook the value of a relationship with a competent insurance agent, but a growing venture will require several types of insurance:

- Property and casualty
- Medical
- Errors and omissions
- Life (on key managers)
- Workers' compensation
- Directors and officers
- Unemployment

- Auto (on the firm's vehicles)
- Liability (product and personal)
- Bonding

Major insurance firms can handle all types of insurance vehicles, but specialists will be required for certain kinds of protection, such as bonding (which is common in the construction industry to protect against a contractor's not completing a project), product liability insurance, and errors and omissions (which protects the business against liability from unintentional mistakes in advertising). The new venture's insurance needs will change over its life, and a good insurance agent will help the entrepreneur determine the needed coverage at the appropriate times.

Building a Board of Directors

Although the decision to have a board of directors is influenced by the legal form of the business, it is a long-held belief that establishing corporate governance early in the organization of a start-up will enhance the quality of the company as it grows. If a new venture is a corporation, a board of directors is required and is elected by the shareholders. If the business needs venture capital, a board will be necessary, and the venture capitalist will probably demand a seat on it. Boards of directors serve a valuable purpose; if chosen correctly, they provide expertise that fill gaps in the entrepreneur's knowledge. In that capacity they act as advisers. They also assist in establishing corporate strategy and philosophy. They do not have the power to sign contracts or commit the corporation legally; instead, they elect the officers of the corporation, who are responsible for its day-to-day operations. Board members assist with business development, act as arbitrators for dispute resolution, and give credibility to the new company's image.

It is important to distinguish between boards of privately owned corporations and those of publicly owned corporations. In a privately owned corporation, the entrepreneurial team owns all or the majority of the stock, so directors serve at the pleasure of the entrepreneur, who has effective control of the company. On the other hand, directors of publicly traded companies have legitimate power to control the activities of the company and liability for what they do or fail to do. They are elected by the shareholders and represent the shareholders' interests in the company.

Boards can be comprised of inside or outside members or a combination of the two. An inside board member is one who is a founder, employee, family member, or retired manager of the firm, whereas an outside board member is someone with no direct connection to the business. Which type of board member is better is a matter of opinion and circumstance; research has not provided any clear results on this issue. In general, however, outside directors are beneficial for succession planning and for raising capital. They can often bring a fresh point of view to the strategic planning process, along with expertise that the founders may not possess. Insiders have the advantage of complete knowledge about the business; they are generally more available and have demonstrated their effectiveness in the particular positions they occupy in the business. Typically where the entrepreneur/CEO has power to configure the board, the board will be small and comprised primarily of insiders, particularly family members.[20] Often the company chief executive officer (CEO), chief financial officer (CFO), and in-house attorney sit on the board. But there are political ramifications when the board members report to the CEO; insiders may not always be objective and independent. They also may not have the broad expertise from outside the company that is necessary to guide the growth of the business effectively.

Consider carefully whether the new venture requires a working board—that is, one that directs the strategy of the business. Most working boards are used for their expertise, for strategic planning, for auditing the actions of the firm, and for arbitrating differences. These activities are not as crucial in the start-up phase, when the entrepreneurial team is gathering resources and raising capital. However, a board of directors can assist the entrepreneurial team in those functions and can network with key people who can help the new venture. At this juncture, some potential directors will ask to be included on the board so that they can monitor their investment in the company. This is common among large private investors, bankers, and even accountants. To be sure of getting only the best people on the board, entrepreneurs should set standards for membership in advance and should strictly adhere to them.

The size and complexity of the entrepreneur's business, as well as the legal requirements of the state in which the company operates, will determine how many directors serve on the board. There is no research consensus on the relationship between the size of the board and the performance of the company, although some research has found that a large board encourages laziness on the part of some members[21] and thus may undermine the board's ability to initiate strategic actions.[22] Moreover, larger boards tend to develop factions and coalitions that often lead to conflict. The general recommendation is to have no fewer than 5 and no more than 15 board members. In the earliest stages of a new venture, the board will often consist of the founders, though that should quickly change as the company begins to grow and needs to tap the expertise of people who have managed growth in their own companies.

When choosing people to serve on the board of directors, entrepreneurs should consider those who have

- The necessary technical skill related to the business.
- Significant, successful experience in the industry.
- Experience running a company at the level the entrepreneur wants to grow to next.
- Important contacts in the industry.
- Expertise in finance, capital acquisition, and possibly IPOs.
- A personality compatible with the rest of the board.
- Good problem-solving skills.
- Honesty and integrity, to engender a sense of mutual trust.

In addition, it is critically important to choose the right board members for the stage the company is in. Figure 8.2 displays the various stages of a company's growth, the status of the business during that stage, and the type of board

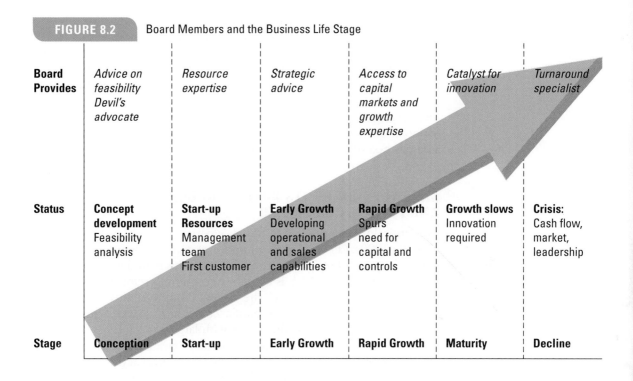

| FIGURE 8.2 | Board Members and the Business Life Stage | | | | |

Board Provides	Advice on feasibility Devil's advocate	Resource expertise	Strategic advice	Access to capital markets and growth expertise	Catalyst for innovation	Turnaround specialist
Status	**Concept development** Feasibility analysis	**Start-up Resources** Management team First customer	**Early Growth** Developing operational and sales capabilities	**Rapid Growth** Spurs need for capital and controls	**Growth slows** Innovation required	**Crisis:** Cash flow, market, leadership
Stage	**Conception**	**Start-up**	**Early Growth**	**Rapid Growth**	**Maturity**	**Decline**

member that may be most appropriate for the needs of the business at that point in time. Entrepreneurs must align their objectives with the venture's stage in its life cycle and then select the board members and advisers so that they are congruent with these objectives.

If the entrepreneurial team is not careful, it may learn too late that a director it has appointed to the board considers the position an appointment for life, much like being appointed to the Supreme Court. To prevent such a misunderstanding, and to bring a fresh point of view to the board, directors should be asked to serve on a rotating basis for a specified period of time.

The board is headed by the chairperson, who, in a new, private venture, is typically the lead entrepreneur. The entrepreneur is also likely to be the president and CEO. The current trend is for the CEO and perhaps the chief operating officer (COO) or chief financial officer (CFO) to be the only inside members on the board. Depending on the type of business, boards normally meet face-to-face an average of five times a year and through teleconferences as necessary. How often the board meets will be largely a function of how active it is at any given time. Directors typically spend about nine to ten days a year on duties related to the business and are usually paid a retainer plus a per-meeting fee. Their expenses are also reimbursed. The compensation can take the form of cash, stock, or other perquisites.

Today it is more difficult to get people to serve as directors because in some cases they can be held personally liable for the actions of the firm, and the frequency with which boards are being sued is increasing. For this reason, potential directors often require that the business carry directors' and officers' (D&O) liability insurance to indemnify them. The expense of this insurance is often prohibitive for a growing company, but it is essential in getting good people to serve. Additional expenses related to the development of a board of directors include meeting rooms, travel, and food. Because of the expense of maintaining a formal board of directors, many entrepreneurs with new ventures maintain a small insider board of directors and rely heavily on their informal advisory board for a more objective perspective.

SARBANES-OXLEY: ITS IMPACT ON BOARDS AND PRIVATE COMPANIES

Two critical themes relative to boards emerged from the accounting scandals of the early 2000s: (1) regulation is important and (2) "boards count."[23] The most important piece of legislation to come out of this period was the Sarbanes-Oxley Act (SOX) of 2002, which is a "public accounting reform and investor protection act" designed to improve the accuracy and reliability of corporate disclosures.[24] Although directed at public companies, private companies are also affected to the extent that they work with large companies as strategic partners or work with lenders and investors.[25] Because these third parties are scrutinizing the corporate governance practices of the companies they deal with more closely, entrepreneurs should consider developing systems and controls that comply with the act's requirements from the beginning of the business.

There are four primary areas of SOX compliance where private companies can focus their efforts and their limited resources at their own pace:

1. Work with more than one accounting firm. Many entrepreneurial and family businesses are using one CPA firm for a certified audit and then one for tax filing and consulting.

2. Establish an audit committee to provide an internal system of checks and balances and oversight. The members can come from the board of directors.

3. Develop a whistleblower policy that provides a way for people to register complaints anonymously without the fear of being fired.

4. Ensure that the board of directors is substantially independent. What this means is that the majority of directors should not be reporting to the CEO or have any business relationship or conflict of interest relative to the company.

Making an effort to comply with these aspects of Sarbanes-Oxley provides many benefits to the entrepreneur launching a new venture. It raises the level of confidence that investors have in the business; it prepares the business so that when an IPO or a public acquisition is imminent, the company has the required systems and controls in place; it makes the company more attractive to potential board members; and it generally makes for a more efficient and effective operation. One professional services company concluded that an IPO or acquisition was in its sights within about three years and its accountant advised the founders that SOX offered a menu of best practices that could make their business more attractive. In addition to adding independent members to their board of directors, they began a systematic review of all their business processes to reveal weaknesses that might be viewed as "deal hair" by investors and buyers. They were able to find redundancies in many of their processes that when eliminated resulted in substantial cost savings for the company and made it more competitive.[26] Entrepreneurs contemplating the launch of a new venture would be well advised to implement SOX best practices from the beginning, which is far less onerous than incorporating them once the company has developed inefficient and potentially damaging processes.

ADVISORY BOARD

The advisory board is an informal panel of experts and other people who are interested in seeing the new venture succeed. They are a useful and less costly alternative to a formal board of directors. Advisory boards can range from those that meet once or twice a year and do not get paid to those that meet more regularly and are provided honoraria of anywhere from $500 to $1,000 per meeting.

Advisory boards are often used when a board of directors is not required or in the start-up phase when the board of directors consists of the founders only. An effective advisory board can provide the new venture with needed expertise without the significant costs and loss of control associated with a board of directors. In a wholly owned or closely held corporation (in which the entrepreneur or team holds all the stock), there really is no distinction between the functions of a board of directors and those of a board of advisers, because in either case, control remains in the hands of the entrepreneurial team. The advisory board is not subject to the same scrutiny as the board of directors, because its actions are not binding on the company.

Entrepreneurs tend to resist the idea of having outside advisers because of the founders' intense desire to be independent and to maintain some secrecy about the business. They also tend to believe that an outsider could never understand the business.[27] Although many business owners may reject a formal board, they risk developing "tunnel vision" unless they consider using an advisory board. An advisory board is a step in the direction of creating a more professional organization that exhibits

1. Shareholder harmony, achieved through shareholder agreements and buy-sell agreements.
2. Effective management that has a vision and goals for the company.
3. Efficient internal communication, achieved through shareholder meetings, advisory board meetings, and management meetings.[28]

MISTAKES TO AVOID WITH TEAMS AND BOARDS

Assembling the extended founding team is a serious undertaking, and failure to put the team together effectively could have severe ramifications for the future of the business. It is important that all team members who are brought on board have the required experience and qualifications as well as the same goals for the business. The same is true of the board of directors. Appointing only friends and family members instead of the most qualified people will not result in the best advice for the entrepreneur. Due to limited resources, many entrepreneurs choose family members or friends to serve as professional advisers, such as an attorney or accountant, but it is often difficult for these advisers to be objective about the business, something that is necessary if the entrepreneur is to receive effective guidance.

One of the biggest mistakes cash-strapped entrepreneurs make is giving team members stock in lieu of salary or fees, for example, in the case of independent contractors. Once a person has stock in the company, it is much more difficult to terminate their position. It makes sense to wait to give stock until an individual has proven his or her worth to the company. Of course, the original founding team will want to split up the stock or ownership in the company, and it will be necessary to keep some stock available to offer to professional management personnel that must be hired. The issue of stock distribution is discussed in Chapter 13.

The Buy-Sell Agreement

A buy-sell agreement is used to prevent an owner from selling his or her interests in the company to an outsider without consent of the other owners and to determine what happens to the business should the owner or one of the partners in a partnership agreement decide to leave the business. A properly written buy-sell agreement will also specify how an owner's interest will be valued. Jay Steinmetz learned the importance of buy-sell agreements the hard way when he started CaptureTech, a reseller of liquidated bar coding equipment in 1997. He brought in his unemployed friend Andy Stern to run the business and agreed to split ownership 50/50 even though the two strongly disagreed on many aspects of the business. One year into the business, the partners were completely at odds, but they had no agreement that spelled out how to deal with the situation. After a disgruntled Stern stole the company laptop, changed the company's locks, and liquidated the joint bank account, he then filed assault charges against Steinmetz. Eventually, everything was resolved by the courts in Steinmetz's favor, but he had to close the business and start over again, this time without a partner. Today his new company, Barcoding, has revenues of over $24 million, employs more than 80 people, and buy-sell agreements are standard practice.[29]

There are two types of buy-sell agreements: a cross-purchase agreement and a stock redemption agreement. In the cross-purchase agreement each owner or shareholder purchases an insurance policy on the other shareholders and is named as the beneficiary on the policies. Proceeds received on the death of a shareholder are not taxable. This approach is complicated if there are several owners. In a stock redemption agreement, by contrast, the corporation owns the insurance policies on the lives of the owners. Upon an owner's death or departure for other reasons, the corporation purchases the owner's interest using the proceeds of the insurance policy. In either case, if an owner leaves the company, the owner is required to sell his or her interest back to the remaining owners.

Socially Responsible Entrepreneurship

Survival of the Fittest

Survival is a skill that is critical to entrepreneurs, and no one understands survival better than Rabbi Arthur Schneier, who lost his father and grandparents to the Nazis when he was six years old. Surviving that ordeal and making it to America, he felt compelled to dedicate his life to public service. Schneier trained to become a rabbi in honor of his grandfather, and in 1962, he became the senior rabbi at Park East Synagogue in New York City. There he was determined to develop a new school dedicated to young children—a type of pre-school, which at the time was a fairly radical vision for Orthodox Jewish life. His entrepreneurial spirit drove him to find the land, raise money, and design the building. By 1966, he had put all the property pieces together, and by 1973 he had finally raised enough money to begin construction. In 1977, his ultimate dream of building a school was realized in an 8-story facility. And today, more than 25 years later, the Park East Day School serves 320 children.

But Schneier didn't stop there. He had a simultaneous dream to end human oppression. He founded the Appeal of Conscience Foundation to fight against social injustices and promote religious freedom in Russia and other countries where people could not freely practice their religious beliefs. Since then he has served presidents, won medals for his contributions to society, and continued to display the best attributes of successful entrepreneurs giving back to their communities.

Sources: C. Hall, "It's All About Freedom," in *The Responsible Entrepreneur* (Franklin Lakes, NJ: Career Press, 2001); and the Appeal of Conscience Foundation, http://www.appealofconscience.org, accessed March 10, 2007.

THE MENTOR BOARD

In addition to an advisory board and a board of directors, entrepreneurs should have a personal board of mentors who serve as a sounding board for ideas and act as coaches to raise their spirits and warn them when they're heading down a wrong path. The members of a personal board are usually role models and people who have businesses and lifestyles like the one the entrepreneur wants to create. Mentors also provide a safe place for entrepreneurs to air their fears and concerns and express their hopes and dreams. Jennifer Lawton benefited from several important career mentors when she founded her Boston-based computer networking consulting firm, Net Daemons Associates in 1999, but she maintains that the lessons that lasted a lifetime came from role models who had nothing to do with her chosen career path. Lawton credits her grandmother and mother with instilling a strong belief system, and her grandfather, a survivor of the Great Depression, with teaching her that laughter is the best medicine.[30] Clearly, it is helpful to have both personal and professional mentors throughout the entrepreneurial journey.

Outsourcing with Independent Contractors

A new business typically does not have the resources to pay for all the management and operational staff that may be necessary to keep it running. In fact, most entrepreneurs avoid hiring employees as long as possible, because employees are the single biggest expense in the business. But how does a new venture survive with as few employees as possible and still grow?

The solution lies in outsourcing, which means using independent contractors to undertake functions that the entrepreneur doesn't want to handle. Independent contractors (ICs) own their own businesses and are hired by the entrepreneur to do a specific job. They are under the control of the entrepreneur only for the results of the work they do, not for the means by which those results are accomplished. The independent contractors that entrepreneurs use on a regular basis include consultants, manufacturers, distributors, and employee leasing firms (note that professional advisers are also independent contractors). The popularity of outsourcing can be seen in the fact that 69 percent of companies outsource their information technology services.[31] The key areas for outsourcing are IT services, business processes, and manufacturing. It is hard for most companies to keep up with changes in technology, and the vendors to which they outsource can provide the same service and better performance at a lower cost. Entrepreneurs seek out independent contractors for their expertise in specific areas. Using an independent contractor means that the new venture doesn't have to supply medical and retirement benefits, provide unemployment insurance, or withhold income and social security tax. These are costly benefits that can amount to more than 32 percent of an employee's base salary. But there are hidden costs to outsourcing whether domestically or globally that entrepreneurs should be aware of:[32]

▶ *The cost of searching for and contracting with an independent contractor.* The best way to reduce this cost is for entrepreneurs to secure referrals from people they know who have had a successful experience with the IC.

▶ *Transferring activities to the IC.* Getting the IC "up to speed" on the business takes time and human resources. Transfer costs can be reduced if entrepreneurs identify up front what they want the IC to handle and lay out a plan for preparing the IC to do the work.

▶ *Managing the independent contractor.* This is one of those cases where experience counts. The first IC contract takes the longest and costs the most. The best IC relationships occur when communication is an ongoing process so that the IC becomes a real part of the business.

▶ *Bringing the activity in-house.* Many companies eventually bring in-house activities that they once outsourced. This may occur because the company has grown to the point where it needs and can afford in-house staff for the activity or because the company wants more control over the activity. One way to reduce the transition cost is to have the person who manages the IC relationship learn enough about the activity to be able to ease the company through the transition.

To reduce the hidden costs of using independent contractors, entrepreneurs should retain in-house critical activities and core competencies that are idiosyncratic or unique to the business. They should also research vendors carefully and seek referrals. Above all, entrepreneurs must work with legal advisers who have experience with independent contractor law to draft binding contracts.

THE IRS AND INDEPENDENT CONTRACTORS

The IRS has very strict rules for the use of independent contractors. The Law of Agency defines the terms *employee* and *independent contractor.* It states, "While an employee acts under the direction and control of the employer, an independent contractor contracts to produce a certain result and has full control over the means and methods that shall be used in producing the result."[33] If an employer doesn't follow the rules regulating classification of workers as independent contractors, they can be considered employees for tax purposes, and the employer can be held liable for all back taxes plus penalties and interest, which can amount to a substantial sum.

To ensure compliance with IRS regulations, entrepreneurs who use independent contractors should

- Consult an attorney.
- Draw up a contract with each independent contractor, specifying that the contractor will not be treated as an employee for state and federal tax purposes.
- Be careful not to indicate the means or methods of accomplishing the work, only the desired result.
- Verify that the independent contractor carries workers' compensation insurance.
- Verify that the independent contractor possesses the necessary licenses.

More specifically, the IRS uses a 20-point test for classifying workers (see Table 8.3). Even if an employer follows all the IRS rules, however, there is no guarantee that the IRS won't challenge its position. Therefore, it is important to document the relationship with an independent contractor through a legal agreement that explicitly demonstrates that the independent contractor owns his or her own business. The IRS can decide that a worker is an employee even if only one of the 20 points is true!

On the positive side, independent contractors can make the very small start-up venture look like an established corporation to anyone on the outside. A large corporation will generally have vice presidents for departments of operations, sales, marketing, and finance. It is possible to replicate these functions by using independent contractors, thereby lowering costs and remaining more flexible. Figure 8.3 depicts how a growing entrepreneurial venture can imitate the strength, stability, and expertise of a much larger, more established company through the use of independent contractors. The concept is called the "virtual company" and will be discussed at length in Chapter 13.

TYPES OF INDEPENDENT CONTRACTORS

Many types of independent contractors operate behind the scenes of the new venture but make a valuable contribution nonetheless. Various independent contractors make up the entrepreneur's extended team. These include constants, professional employer organizations (PEOs), manufacturing support, sales support, and government agencies.

TABLE 8.3

The 20-Point Test for
Independent Contractors

A worker is an employee if he or she

1. Must follow the employer's instructions about how to do the work.
2. Receives training from the employer.
3. Provides services that are integrated into the business.
4. Provides services that must be rendered personally.
5. Cannot hire, supervise, and pay his or her own assistants.
6. Has a continuing relationship with the employer.
7. Must follow set hours of work.
8. Works full-time for an employer.
9. Does the work on the employer's premises.
10. Must do the work in a sequence set by the employer.
11. Must submit regular reports to the employer.
12. Is paid regularly for time worked.
13. Receives reimbursements for expenses.
14. Relies on the tools and materials of the employer.
15. Has no major investment in facilities to perform the service.
16. Cannot make a profit or suffer a loss.
17. Works for one employer at a time.
18. Does not offer his or her services to the general public.
19. Can be fired at will by the employer.
20. May quit work at any time without incurring liability.

FIGURE 8.3   A Virtual Company

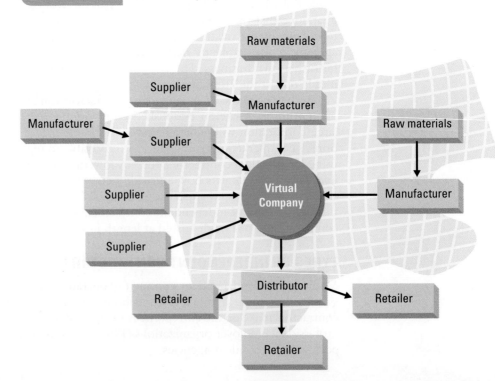

Consultants

The consulting industry is one of the fastest-growing industries in the United States, and it can provide a variety of services for a new venture. Consultants can

▷ Train the sales staff and/or management.

▷ Conduct market research.

▷ Prepare policy manuals.

▷ Solve problems.

▷ Act as temporary key management.

▷ Recommend market strategy.

▷ Design and engineer products.

▷ Design a plant layout and equipment.

▷ Conduct research and development.

▷ Recommend operational and financial controls.

Because they tend to be fairly expensive, consultants are best used for critical one-time advising or problem-solving assignments. In that capacity, they are typically more cost-effective than employees because they are accustomed to working quickly within the constraints of a fixed budget. Consultants are generally paid in one of three ways: monthly retainer, which pays for a specified amount of time per month; hourly rate; or project fee. More recently, consultants have also been known to ask for some form of equity stake in the companies for which they consult. Some entrepreneurs have chosen to go this route when cash is in short supply. However, entrepreneurs should consult an attorney before giving up any equity in their company. It is much harder to dismiss an IC who is a shareholder in the company.

Professional Employer Organization (PEO)

Leasing staff is a way for a new business to enjoy the advantages of major corporations without incurring many of the expenses. A professional employer organization assumes the payroll and human resource functions for the business for a fee that generally ranges from 3 to 5 percent of gross payroll. Each pay period, the new venture pays the PEO a lump sum to cover payroll plus the fee. In addition to payroll processing and taxes, the services they provide include safety and risk management, benefits administration, and human resource management. PEOs and human resource business process outsourcing are growing rapidly as more companies take advantage of their services.

Manufacturing Support

Even those new ventures that involve manufacturing a product can avail themselves of the benefits of independent contractors. Because the cost of building and equipping a new manufacturing plant is immense by any standard, many entrepreneurs choose to contract the work with an established manufacturer domestically or in another country. In fact, it is possible for an entrepreneur who has a new product idea to subcontract the design of the product to an engineering firm, the production of components to various manufacturing firms, the assembly of the product to another firm, and the distribution to yet another.

With the rapid rate of technological innovation, it is difficult for any one company to keep up, so remaining focused and profitable is critical to success. The global market for contract manufacturing increased from $103 billion in 2000 to $231 billion in 2005 and shows no signs of slowing.[34]

Sales Support

Hiring sales staff can be an expensive proposition for any new venture, not only from the standpoint of benefits but also because salespeople must be trained. As new high-growth ventures seek a geographically broad market, even a global one, it is vital to consider enlisting the aid of manufacturer's representatives (reps) and foreign reps who know those markets. Using distributors enables the entrepreneur to reach the target market without having to deal with the complex retail market. In addition, sales agencies can provide the new venture with fully trained salespeople—in much the same manner as temporary services supply clerical help. Some can also provide advertising and public relations.

Governmental Agencies

Many agencies at the federal, state, and local levels offer various services to new ventures. Notable among them are the Small Business Administration, which provides education, loans, and grants to small businesses; the Department of Commerce, which can assist the entrepreneur on issues of trade; and state and local economic development corporations. By taking advantage of the many services available, an entrepreneur can literally start a business from home to reduce start-up capital requirements, yet still operate like a major corporation. This is not to suggest that a company can always avoid hiring employees and still grow. That will depend on the type of business. However, it does suggest that in the start-up phase of a new venture, the use of independent contractors can help ensure that the business survives long enough and generates enough revenues to hire employees.

A carefully conceived founding team, combined with an extended team of expert advisers and outsourced capability providers, can make the uncertain life of a start-up venture much easier.

Drawing Conclusions from the Founding Team Assessment

It is rare for an entrepreneur to conclude that he or she has all the expertise and access to resources that are needed by the new venture. Gaps in the founding team are bound to exist; therefore, it is important to identify them and use the entrepreneur's social network to get recommendations on people who could fill those gaps. A complete team is not necessary to launch a business in its earliest stages. What *is* important is that the entrepreneur identifies the essential participants for the initial launch. This decision is typically based on critical functions that the business will undertake immediately, whether that is a chef and personnel manager for a restaurant so that meals can be designed, produced, and distributed; or a sales manager and international sales partner for an import company so that sales outlets can be secured and the best suppliers located. The most important thing for the entrepreneur to remember is that not everyone involved with the new venture has to be an owner or an employee. Many other options are available.

> ### New Venture Checklist
>
> Have you:
>
> ☐ Identified the members of the founding team or at least the expertise needed to start the venture?
>
> ☐ Determined what expertise is missing from the management team and how you will supply it?
>
> ☐ Begun asking questions about potential professional advisers, such as an attorney or accountant?
>
> ☐ Determined whether you will need a board of directors, an advisory board, or a mentor board?
>
> ☐ Identified at least one type of independent contractor that the new venture could use?

Issues to Consider

business.college.hmco.com/students

1. For what kinds of businesses is starting as a solo entrepreneur sufficient? Are there advantages to starting even these types of businesses with a team?
2. What strategy should an entrepreneur employ when selecting a personal board, an advisory board, or a board of directors?
3. How might the need for an attorney differ for a service business and a high technology company?
4. How can you ensure that you are using independent contractors correctly and in accordance with the law?
5. Suppose you are starting an apparel company where you will design and manufacture a unique line of clothing. What kinds of independent contractors can help you start this venture?

Experiencing Entrepreneurship

1. Interview an entrepreneur who started a venture as a soloist, and then visit an entrepreneurial venture started by a team (two or more people). Based on your interviews, write a two-page report discussing the advantages and disadvantages of each approach.

2. Choose a lawyer, accountant, or banker to interview as a potential professional adviser to your business. What information will you need to secure from him or her to make your decision?

Relevant Case Studies

## Chapter 9

ANALYZING START-UP FINANCIALS

"Finance is the art of passing currency from hand to hand until it finally disappears."

—ROBERT W. SARNOFF, former president of NBC/RCA

LEARNING OBJECTIVES

▷ Demonstrate an understanding of entrepreneurial resource gathering.

▷ Explain how to find the right numbers.

▷ Estimate sales and expenditures for the new venture.

▷ Prepare the pro forma income statement.

▷ Forecast start-up cash needs.

▷ Discuss the role of the balance sheet in the business plan.

Profile 9.1 HOW MUCH DOES IT REALLY TAKE TO REALIZE A DREAM?

What do you do when your dream business appears to be financially beyond your reach? You start getting creative and figure out a way to have what you want. That's precisely what Michael Brill did when, one day in 2002, he decided that he was tired of the high technology work life and wanted to pursue his dream of making wine. Isn't that many people's dream—to own a vineyard in Napa/Sonoma or Italy or France and live the idyllic life of a vintner? The problem is that the wine business requires a significant amount of capital. Brill's research figured the total cost of creating and maintaining the vineyard in Napa at $15 million, and he just didn't have access to that kind of money. Nevertheless, he wasn't about to give up, so he dug up his 625-square-foot lot in the Potrero Hill area of San Francisco and turned it into a tiny vineyard, planting some pinot noir and syrah vines. He also began immersing himself in the winemaking process, reading everything he could get his hands on. Although he remained at his software marketing job during the day, at night and on the weekends, he was a vintner.

Soon he became a curiosity in his neighborhood, and people would stop by and spend the day with him, helping his pick, crush, and process the grapes, so he didn't have to hire any help. But more importantly, the discussions and interest that he gained from his visitors gave him the confidence to start a business that would cater to wine enthusiasts who would typically pay $50 a bottle and up and who wanted to be part of the wine-making process. In 2004, he launched Crushpad as an online company that links vineyards with wine enthusiasts and cuts out the intermediaries.

It provides customers with the opportunity to select a particular grape from a specific vineyard and have those grapes brought to Crushpad's 17,000-square-foot warehouse at the edge of the Mission District, where the grapes would then be developed into a fine wine. The secret to his initial funding was his business model, which had customers fronting the cost of development by paying $6,000 to $9,000 to produce a barrel of wine (about 300 bottles) at a cost to customers that is about 40 to 50 percent of retail. Some customers have grouped together via the Crushpad website to share the cost of a barrel. Customers who love working with the grapes under the guidance of professional winemakers can participate in the process and then either pick up the wine at the headquarters or have it shipped to them. Some of Brill's customers have looked at the experience as an apprenticeship that helped them make a decision about a career change. At least two of his customers have won gold medals in wine competitions, and many of the wines produced can be found in upscale restaurants in San Francisco. Crushpad now has more than 2,000 customers from 35 states and 8 countries. In February 2007, Brill succeeded in finalizing $3.5 million in debt and equity financing to double his production.

Sources: C. Rauber, "Crushpad Custom Winery Completes $3.5M Financing Round, Plans to Expand," *San Francisco Business Times* (February 7, 2007), http://sanfrancisco.bizjournals.com; J.M. O'Brien, "In Vino Profitas," *Fortune* (December 22, 2006), p. 59; W. Reisman, "Michael Brill: Virtual Winemaker Lets Vino Lovers Taste Their Dream," *The Examiner* (April 6, 2007), http://www .examiner.com; and Crushpad, http://www.crushpadwine.com.

Every business requires resources to start and grow. Resource gathering is one area where entrepreneurs demonstrate their unique capabilities to maximize the use of minimal resources, whether in the form of people, equipment, inventory, or cash. Up to this point, feasibility analysis has focused on testing the concept in the market to ensure that there are customers and sufficient demand, and on testing the product or service to gauge whether it can be produced at a cost that leaves room for overhead and profit. With a positive response from the market and a feasible product/service, it now becomes important to consider the financial conditions under which an entrepreneur would be willing to go forward—that is, what types of resources will be needed to start the business and sustain it until it generates a positive cash flow. No matter how many financial tools entrepreneurs use or how many complex analyses they construct, the bottom line for any new venture is cash. Income statements and balance sheets can make a company look good on paper—these are accounting measures—but cash pays the bills and enables the company to grow. A new venture's health is measured by its cash flow.

This chapter examines entrepreneurial finance at start-up and provides a plan for conducting an assessment of resource needs so that entrepreneurs will have a clearer picture of the financial feasibility of the new venture concept and the start-up capital requirements. Once an entrepreneur decides to execute a business concept, a business plan with a full set of pro forma financial statements will be developed.

Identifying Start-up Resource Requirements

Determining what resources are needed, when they are needed, and how to acquire them is a critical piece of the feasibility puzzle. Start-up resources include (1) people, such as the founding team, employees, advisors, and independent contractors; (2) physical assets, such as equipment, inventory, and office or plant space; and (3) financial resources, such as cash, equity, and debt. At start-up the goal is to create a mix of resources that will enable the new venture to start and operate until the revenues of the business produce a positive cash flow, that is, enough cash to cover all the cash outflows without investment capital.

One of the secrets to success in constructing this resource mix is to maintain flexibility by acquiring and owning only those resources that cannot be obtained by any other means because ownership reduces flexibility and mobility, two critical needs of a start-up venture. A dynamic marketplace, coupled with the natural chaos of a start-up venture, requires that a new venture remain lean so that its products, services, and strategies can be tested and modified quickly in response to customers' feedback. Consider the case of the software management entrepreneur who let his ego get the better of him. After signing a long-term lease on prime office space in an expensive section of Los Angeles, he expected customers to be impressed by his success and want to do business with him. Instead, he discovered that his customers wanted to meet at their sites or in restaurants, not in his office. Moreover, his programmers did not require offices; they could work from home. As a result, this entrepreneur soon found himself saddled with expensive overhead that neither his customers nor his employees needed.

Bootstrapping is the term often applied to the minimizing of resources. It simply means that entrepreneurs beg, borrow, or lease resources whenever they can so that they can keep their overhead, or fixed costs, as low as possible. Some bootstrapping techniques will be discussed in Chapter 16 on funding a start-up venture. New venture start-up teams typically have no previous history, no track record with customers, and no evidence of performance, so their resource decision making is based solely on current information and advice from others.[1] Consequently, many new ventures fail because of poor decisions about resources and the management of those resources. To succeed, entrepreneurs must create innovative combinations of resources that will generate a competitive advantage and lead to the creation of wealth.[2] Research has also concluded that innovative entrepreneurial ventures require different types of resources than their small business counterparts.[3]

Figure 9.1 presents a plan for approaching the capital needs assessment for a new venture. The next sections will walk through those steps entrepreneurs need to take to have a clear picture of their resource needs.

CONSTRUCTING A BUSINESS PROCESS MAP

Recall that resources can be divided into six categories: human, social, financial, physical, technological, and organizational. To identify accurately the resources required to start the venture, it's important to understand all the activities and processes in the business—in other words, to know exactly how the business works. This is best accomplished by creating a process map that details how information flows through the business. Having such a map at hand makes it much easier to define the operations, information flow, and resource requirements of the business. To create a process map, take an imaginary tour of the business during a single day, listing all the functions, people, equipment, supplies, and space required to run the business. Begin at the front door of the business and ask the following questions:

1. Who does the work in this business?
2. Where do these people work?
3. What do they need to do the work (equipment, major supplies, space, etc.)?
4. What information is being generated (work orders, invoices, customer lists, etc.)?
5. Where does that information go?

Then begin making lists of tasks, equipment, and people needed to complete a particular process or activity. This information will be useful for figuring expenses for financial projections and for determining what kind of personnel will have to be hired to perform those tasks.

In a packaging solutions business, for example, what is the first thing a customer sees when he or she approaches the site? The sign for the business? A display window? When customers enter, is there a counter attended by someone who will answer their questions? What equipment does that person use to do his or her job? Note that without going beyond the customer's entry through the door of the business, a significant list of resources has already been amassed. The imaginary tour is one of the best ways to begin to detail the processes in the business. Figure 9.2 traces one such imaginary tour of a service business.

FIGURE 9.1   Steps to Assess and Calculate Start-up Capital Requirements

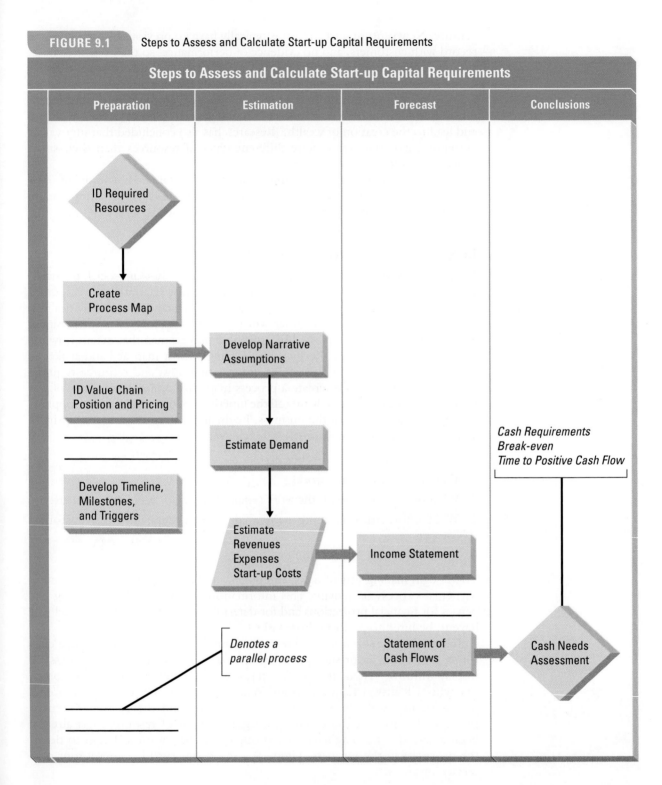

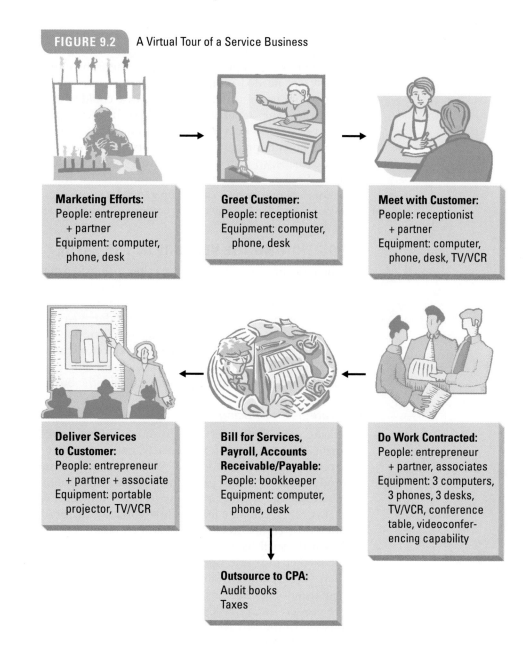

FIGURE 9.2   A Virtual Tour of a Service Business

Marketing Efforts:
People: entrepreneur
+ partner
Equipment: computer,
phone, desk

Greet Customer:
People: receptionist
Equipment: computer,
phone, desk

Meet with Customer:
People: receptionist
+ partner
Equipment: computer,
phone, desk, TV/VCR

**Deliver Services
to Customer:**
People: entrepreneur
+ partner + associate
Equipment: portable
projector, TV/VCR

**Bill for Services,
Payroll, Accounts
Receivable/Payable:**
People: bookkeeper
Equipment: computer,
phone, desk

Do Work Contracted:
People: entrepreneur
+ partner, associates
Equipment: 3 computers,
3 phones, 3 desks,
TV/VCR, conference
table, videoconfer-
encing capability

Outsource to CPA:
Audit books
Taxes

A product business may involve production and assembly processes in addition to packaging and shipping. Alternatively, the entrepreneur may be trying to reduce overhead costs by outsourcing production. In this instance, the outsourced capability could be shown on the graphic outside of the workflow of the new venture because it does not require any resources on the part of the entrepreneur beyond coordination with the company that is managing production. Returning to Figure 9.2, once all the activities of the business have been identified and the people and equipment recorded, the entrepreneur can go back over the map to see whether the people required for various tasks need to be full-time or part-time employees. A preliminary pass through the example might suggest that six people are needed (entrepreneur, partner, receptionist, two associates, bookkeeper) but upon further reflection a case could be made for reducing that number to just the essentials. For example, the entrepreneur and his/her partner might be able to deliver services to the customer in the early stages of the business. The entrepreneur may also outsource bookkeeping on a part-time or as-needed basis, so that would bring the number of full-time employees down to three. Looking at the equipment required is also important. Capital expenditures or equipment expenses can eat up a lot of start-up capital, so it would make sense to consider whether any of this equipment could be leased.

POSITIONING THE VENTURE IN THE VALUE CHAIN

Where the new venture lies in the value chain will determine what its margins are, who its customer is, and how much it can charge for its products and services—in short, what business the entrepreneur is in. In the case of a service business, the task is easy because services are delivered direct to the customer. But the case is much different with a product company. Where the company is positioned determines whether it is a manufacturer or producer, a wholesaler or distributor, or a retailer. Each position has different margins and different ways of pricing. This topic was discussed more fully in Chapter 4, where the business model was addressed.

Strategies for Pricing

Pricing a product or service is as much a part of a marketing strategy as of the financial strategy and, unfortunately, entrepreneurs typically have to price their products and services long before they know the exact costs of producing the product. Pricing is one of the many features associated with a product or service; it becomes the central selling point when the product or service is a commodity—that is, when the only feature differentiating the product or service from those offered by competitors is price. Some examples of commodities are basic food products, such as milk, and most electronics categories that have been in the market for some time, such as desktop computers and printers. Wherever there is competitive rivalry, prices will be driven down. Entrepreneurs can price new technology higher because it offers features and benefits not currently in the market, but it quickly becomes a commodity as competitors introduce their versions of the new technology.

How a product or service is priced is a function of a company's goals. If the goal is to *increase sales or market share*, prices may need to be lowered to raise the volume sold. If the goal is to *maximize cash flow*, raising prices and reducing direct costs and overhead may be the answer. *Maximizing profit* can be accomplished by raising prices, lowering prices and increasing volume, or decreasing overhead. If the goal is to *define an image*, setting a higher price based on higher perceived and/or actual quality is one way of establishing a particular image in a market. To *control demand* when a company doesn't have the resources to meet it may mean temporarily setting prices at a level that discourages sales to a

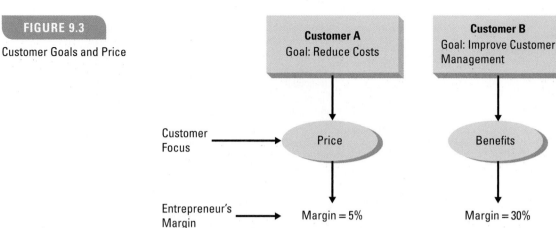

FIGURE 9.3

Customer Goals and Price

Source: Chris Chen, Izu Matsuo, Winnie Peng. Reprinted with permission.

particular degree. This approach also enables the company to recuperate its initial development costs through higher margins. The Internet and search engines like Google have had a major impact on companies' pricing models because it is easy for customers to compare pricing across all competitors. Simple products, those whose price is transparent, or easily identified, are most subject to downward pricing pressure. Complex products (those that are bundled or modular) are more difficult to compare directly across companies, so they typically command a higher price.[4] An example is cell phone rates when they include a fixed monthly fee and a per-minute charge for options.

Customer goals also influence entrepreneurs' pricing strategies. Figure 9.3 depicts two scenarios for an entrepreneur who is offering a customer management software solution. In the first scenario, Customer A's company goal is to keep operational costs low because their own margins are thin. This type of customer focuses on price and makes purchasing decisions accordingly, so consequently the entrepreneur's margins will be small. This is a typical commodity situation. By contrast, the second scenario depicts a customer whose goal is to improve the way they manage their customers; in other words, this customer has a problem that the entrepreneur can solve, so the entrepreneur's margins can be greater because a higher price can be charged. Entrepreneurs must decide which customer to target first so their company can enter the market and survive until it has a chance to grow. To accomplish that, it makes sense to target the customer who is in the most pain—who has a problem that the entrepreneur's product or service can solve. In this way, the entrepreneur can charge a premium and recoup development costs before competition enters the market and causes prices to decline.

Knowing what a pricing strategy is supposed to accomplish in advance of setting a price will ensure compatibility with company goals, both the entrepreneur's company and the customer's company. Table 9.1 presents the most common pricing strategies. For entrepreneurs, a combination of cost-based pricing and demand-based pricing with consideration for a premium based on the novelty of what is being offered can work well. For new products or services with no direct comparison, this approach is often used to arrive at a satisfactory

TABLE 9.1

Common Pricing Strategies at Start-up

Premium Pricing	Uses a high price to reflect a unique product/service and a significant competitive advantage.
Price Skimming	Starts with a high price to capture uniqueness and competitive advantage. Then as new competitors enter the market, drops the price to stay ahead of competition.
Demand-based Pricing	Finding out what customers are willing to pay for the product and pricing it accordingly.
Captive Product Pricing	Where the entrepreneur's product has complements, charge a low price for source product (i.e., a printer) and a premium for consumables (i.e., ink cartridges).
Psychological Pricing	To create a complex pricing structure by combining multiple products and services into one package.
Product Bundle Pricing	In a channel with many intermediaries (distributors, retailers), it is important to ensure that the final price to the consumer or end-user is tolerable, given all the markups along the value chain. That is why it is crucial to compare what the market will bear with the cost of getting a product to market.
Geographical Pricing	Used where there are price variations in different geographical locations where the product is sold.

price. In general, customers recognize several prices for any one product: the standard price, which is the price normally paid for the item; the sale price; the price paid for specials; and the relative price, which is the price of the item compared to the price of a substitute product. For some products, customers may have to add the normal cost of shipping, handling, or installation to their comparison with other like products.

One mistake many entrepreneurs make is to set their prices so that they cover total costs plus a margin the entrepreneur is expecting to achieve. The problem with this approach is that pricing is not designed to cover *total* costs but "to maximize total contribution (i.e., unit price minus unit variable costs)."[5] What this means is that fixed costs (overhead) should not be apportioned within the price because these costs do not come into play when generating additional sales. It is the contribution margin that affects profitability. For example,

Unit price = $49.95

Variable costs (material costs, direct and indirect labor, factory overhead) = $35

Contribution margin = $49.95 − $35.00 = $14.95 or 30%

The contribution margin represents the amount available to pay for fixed costs and provide a profit to the business.

Entrepreneurs need to be aware that every industry has discounts associated with its various products and services. These include such things as cash and quantity discounts. Entrepreneurs should factor these discounts into their pricing models and into their cash needs for the business.

Converging on a Price

There are no formulas that will give a new venture with no track record a solution to the problem of pricing. Furthermore, getting answers from industry will not be an easy task; most companies do not want to talk about pricing because it is the cornerstone of their competitive strategy.[6] However, given the considerations discussed previously and triangulating by taking into account (1) costs, (2) any competitor pricing, and (3) feedback from customers and value chain partners, entrepreneurs can reach a number that can be tested in the market. The importance of understanding customer behavior cannot be stressed enough. If a product is complex and it is difficult for customers to judge quality, they will rely on price as a proxy for quality and therefore choose the higher-priced item. On the other hand, if the product bears a known brand, they might be willing to purchase the lower-priced item.

FIGURING A TIMELINE, MILESTONES, AND TRIGGERS

The next step in preparing to calculate how much capital will be required to launch the business and operate to a positive cash flow is a typical month-by-month timeline for a year in the life of the business. This timeline will note key milestones that the entrepreneur expects to achieve during the year and triggers for change. Figure 9.4 depicts a one-year timeline for a hypothetical product business. Sales of most start-up businesses are not consistent, nor do they take the form of the overconfident "hockey stick," which suggests that sales reach a point where they shoot straight up. The vast majority of new businesses never see that kind of growth. Instead, the first year is typically a series of ups and downs. In the example given, this entrepreneur has managed to secure a major customer in month 5, but it will take until month 8 to see the benefits of that acquisition in terms of sales revenue. Then about month 9, the company needs to plan for a seasonal downswing of revenues. Every company experiences seasonality, which may match the seasons of the year or, as in the case of restaurants, may be a weekly event, with certain days of the week being low revenue days. Understanding the market and when customers purchase is important to determining when the company will experience downswings or upswings in its revenues. Going

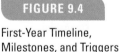

FIGURE 9.4

First-Year Timeline, Milestones, and Triggers

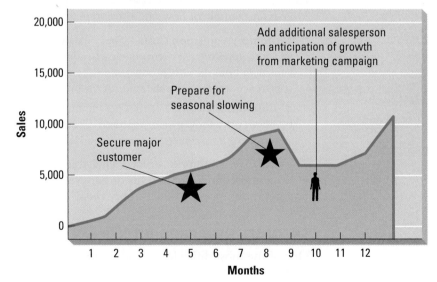

Source: Chris Chen, Izu Matsuo, Winnie Peng. Reprinted with permission.

back to the example, in month 10, the company plans to hire an additional sales-person to prepare for the busy season that begins about month 12 and for which they have prepared a vital marketing campaign. It is important to remember that there is always a lead time with respect to milestones. These lead times are known as triggers that indicate a change in the current revenue pattern. For example, the major customer was a trigger for an upswing in revenues.

Develop Estimates for Financials

Now that the entrepreneur has a good understanding of how his or her business works and what the resource needs are and their timing, it's time to attach some numbers to the timeline and prepare to create the statement of cash flows and the income statement. This will be accomplished by developing some narrative assumptions about those numbers, estimating demand, revenues, expenses, and start-up costs.

START WITH NARRATIVE ASSUMPTIONS

One of the biggest problems that many entrepreneurs have when trying to present a case for the financial feasibility of their business concepts is that they can't justify the numbers they have put into their projections. Unfortunately, the business education courses they may have taken typically haven't prepared them to do this. Although they are wizards at creating spreadsheets with all sorts of what-if scenarios, they are rarely asked to explain where they found the numbers they entered into those spreadsheets. When asked, the response is typically "Well, I did best-case, worst-case, and most-likely-case scenarios and took the average." It is not likely that an investor or banker would accept that explanation.

The most important part of any financial plan is the assumptions on which it is based. Every line item in the cash flow and income statements should be explained. Here is an example of how one entrepreneur explained customer acquisition costs.

> **Customer Acquisition Costs**—The company will sell via a direct sales model, which requires regular client contact. In addition, the product plan calls for launching both the core product and the ancillaries at well-attended industry conferences to maximize the value of the presentations.
>
> a. Customer site visits: 3–4 trips per month beginning Jul 07 @ $800 each
> b. Booth price for Gartner-sponsored data mining conference = $3,000
> c. Travel to/from conference for two attendees—3 conferences, 2 people @ $2.2K each[7]

The narrative assumptions play a vital role in helping to explain the entrepreneur's mindset and establish his or her credibility. Therefore, the first step is to find good numbers and then justify them.

ESTIMATE NEW PRODUCT/SERVICE DEMAND

One of the most difficult tasks facing the entrepreneur is estimating the demand for a new product or service, particularly if that product or service has never existed previously in the marketplace. Much of this difficulty is due to the lack of historical data and to issues of seasonality and price discounts. Because entrepreneurs often overestimate the level of sales they will achieve in the early stages of the company, it is important to triangulate demand from three different points of view: historical analogy with similar products/services; customer feedback, end-user and intermediary feedback; and the entrepreneur's own perspective, gleaned from going into limited production or doing a test market. Calculating total demand is only part of the challenge, because every product or service is subject to adoption patterns and rates. Total demand is never achieved all at once but rather accumulates over time. Understanding the adoption patterns of similar products or services will be critical to forecasting sales revenues over the first couple years. A number of different techniques can help entrepreneurs arrive at a realistic forecast of demand.

Use Historical Analogy or Substitute Products

If the new product is an extension of a previously existing product, it may be possible to extrapolate from the existing product's adoption rate and demand to the new product. For example, the demand and adoption rate for compact disks was derived from the historical demand for cassette tapes and records. The adoption patterns did not match exactly but they certainly landed the entrepreneur in the ballpark. In other cases, it may be possible to turn to another product in the same industry for an indication of demand potential and the rate at which customers will purchase, assuming that the target markets are the same.

Talk to Customers

When attempting to gauge levels of demand, the customer is certainly the prime source of information, but many entrepreneurs fail to ask the right questions so that customers will give them honest answers. Asking "would you buy this product?" or "how much would you pay for this product?" is going about it the wrong way. This approach will overestimate the level of demand because customers have no reason to say no—no one is asking them to write a check, so they have nothing to lose by saying "yes." A better approach is to gauge demand from the customers' responses to the entrepreneur's solution to their problem. In other words, presenting potential customers with a solution in the form of a product or service and then monitoring the feedback and response to it will give the entrepreneur an honest estimate of whether this customer would purchase or not.

For example, suppose that 7 out of 10 potential customers respond positively to the entrepreneur's product. Given that these responses might be optimistic, the entrepreneur should consider reducing the ratio. The amount of reduction is purely arbitrary and is based on how confident the entrepreneur is in the responses received from research with the customer. Suppose the entrepreneur decides to reduce the estimate of demand to 6 out of 10, or 60 percent. Applying this percentage to the size of the niche market that the entrepreneur intends to enter can give a rough estimate of how many total customers might purchase. Then comparing these results with feedback from value chain partners might confirm the numbers or cause the entrepreneur to modify the estimate. Results of research on adoption patterns for similar products or services would then be applied to determine sales on a month-by-month basis.

Interview Prospective End-Users and Intermediaries

No one knows the market better than the men and women who work in it every day. They are typically very astute at predicting trends and patterns of buyer behavior. Spending time in the field talking with intermediaries (distributors or wholesalers, sometimes referred to as "middlemen"), retailers, and the like can provide a fairly good estimate of demand or at least a range that would validate what the entrepreneur found when talking with customers.

Use the Entrepreneur's Knowledge and Experience

The knowledge and experience an entrepreneur brings to the business will be helpful in forecasting sales, particularly if the entrepreneur has worked in the industry in which the business will be operating. However, it is important to remember that the entrepreneur's experience is anecdotal and should always be confirmed by other sources.

Go into Limited Production

The best way, and sometimes the only way, to accurately gauge customer demand is to go into business in a limited way—produce a small number of products and get them into the hands of people to use. If the business is an Internet business, put up a limited website to get feedback. Going into limited production is also an appropriate next step if the other two techniques have produced positive results. Limited testing of a product will not only gauge customer satisfaction, but it may also suggest possible modifications to improve the product. This technique also works for service businesses and is excellent for testing procedures and for gauging the actual time it takes to provide a service, something that is difficult to do when the entrepreneur is not working with an actual customer.

ESTIMATING REVENUES, EXPENSES, AND START-UP COSTS

Estimating revenues, expenses, and start-up costs at the feasibility stage is a daunting task at best for an entrepreneur with a new business concept. At this stage the concept is still fluid, so many of the numbers collected may change when the business plan is complete. Even the numbers in the business plan's pro forma statements will change when the business is in operation and the real world throws unexpected curves at the new venture. There are many reasons why feasibility estimates of sales, expenses, and start-up costs will probably change by the time the business plan is written.

1. If the entrepreneur's business is manufacturing or outsourcing to a manufacturer, it will be nearly impossible to estimate parts and manufacturing costs accurately without a production-quality product in place. For this reason, it is important to get to a physical prototype early, so as to have a better idea of the parts, components, and types of materials that will be needed, as well as what provision to make for labor.

2. For many new product companies, product development may take several months to several years, depending on the nature of the product—and the

Global Insights

BORN GLOBAL

It appears that the old adage about our shrinking planet may be true, at least as it pertains to entrepreneurial ventures. More and more start-ups are "born global." The term *born global* has been used to refer to a firm that has "at least 25 percent international sales within three years of founding" and is operating in some form in multiple countries. This is quite a change from a time when companies went global gradually, in stages. Recent research conducted in Denmark and Australia has uncovered some commonalities among start-ups that are born global. For example, founders don't always have intentions to start an international company, but they typically recognize quite early that the product or service they are offering must compete in a global market. In all cases, the research found that such businesses are started because the founders want the independence of owning their own business. But their products and services dictate the need to go global, whether they are producing expensive furniture in Denmark or developing software for Web design in Australia. The research also revealed that entrepreneurs with international experience are more likely to found born-global companies. Three major factors seem to be driving the born-global phenomenon: (1) the rapid globalization of markets, (2) lower transportation and communication costs, and (3) the increase in the use of strategic alliances to expand capabilities.

Sources: N. Karra and N. Phillips, "Entrepreneurship Goes Global," *Ivey Business Journal* (November/December 2004); P.D. Harveston, B.L. Kedia, and P.S. Davis, "Internationalization of Born Global and Gradual Globalizing Firms: The Impact of the Manager," *Advances in Competitiveness Research,* 8(1) (2000): 92–100; and E.S. Rasmussan, T.K. Madsen, and F. Evangelista, "The Founding of the Born Global Company in Denmark and Australia: Sensemaking and Networking," *Asia Pacific Journal of Marketing and Logistics,* 13(3) (2001): 75–108.

costs for prototyping are always substantially higher than the ultimate production costs will be. Therefore, it is difficult to determine true feasibility from an economic perspective before there is a physical prototype.

3. For service companies, the actual costs to deliver a service must be based initially on information gathered from other companies in the industry. This is tricky to achieve without "inside information"—that is, without knowing someone who works in that type of company. Estimates for the cost of delivery of the service will be more accurate if the service is prototyped under a variety of the most common scenarios. For example, a restaurant owner might want to calculate how long it takes to completely serve a customer, from arrival to departure. The owner needs to look at the number of tables planned, hours of operation, and the number of servers and cooks needed. Peak and slow periods and other aspects of serving customers are also factored in. The more variables that can be accounted for, the better the estimates will be.

4. As entrepreneurs grow in knowledge of their industry, they naturally gather better information because they know whom to talk with and where to find the best industry intelligence. Because getting inside an industry is difficult and time-consuming, many entrepreneurs choose to start ventures in industries with which they're familiar or in which they have experience.

Sales Forecast

The sales forecast should be calculated first because sales affect the expenditures of the business. Using the timeline, milestones, and triggers developed previously, and the demand and adoption rate estimates, the sales revenues can be laid out. Figure 9.5 depicts a 12-month sales forecast for CliqUp, an Internet company (see the feasibility study in the appendix to learn more about the company). The milestones indicated in Figure 9.5 reflect key events for the business that affect the sales forecast. With this type of business, as with many businesses, there are no sales in the first months because of the lead time required to generate a sale. It is also necessary to remember that any increase in sales will be influenced by the following factors:

▶ Growth rates in the market segment of the product or service

▶ The innovations offered that will make the product/service more attractive to the consumer, even at a higher price

▶ The technological innovations employed that enable the entrepreneur to produce the product or service at a lower cost than competitors, thus making it more accessible and enticing to the consumer

Expenses

Once sales have been forecast, predicting expenditures becomes much easier, particularly if expenditures vary with sales, as do the direct costs of producing the product or service. In wholesale businesses, for example, after the sales forecast has been determined, the figures for inventory purchases can be applied as a percentage of sales and forecast from that. Therefore, if inventory cost is 25 percent of sales, one can apply that percentage to sales as they increase to forecast increases in the volume of inventory. Be aware, however, that in some industries, volume discounts on raw materials or inventory may actually reduce costs over time and should be factored into the expenditure forecast. Whether volume discounts will be available is an important piece of information that is gathered during field research.

In manufacturing businesses, forecasting expenditures is a bit more complex because cost of goods sold (COGS) must be derived first. COGS consists of direct labor, cost of materials, and direct factory overhead. Applying COGS as a percentage of sales will probably suffice for purposes of pro forma statements for the feasibility stage. Month-by-month analysis of outcomes and use of a cost accounting model that considers raw materials inventory, work-in-process inventory, finished-goods inventory, total inventory, factory overhead, work-in-process flow in units, and weighted-average cost per unit will give a more accurate estimate as the business grows.

In service businesses, the COGS is equivalent to the time expended to produce and deliver the service. The rate at which the service is billed, say $100 an hour, comprises the actual expenses incurred in providing the service, a contribution to overhead, and a reasonable profit. The actual expenses incurred are equivalent to the cost of goods sold.

The aggregate of all direct and indirect selling expenses and all general and administrative expenses is called SG&A (sales, general, and administrative

FIGURE 9.5   CliqUp Sales Forecast

TIMELINE	Mo 1	Mo 2	Mo 3	Mo 4	Mo 5	Mo 6	Mo 7	Mo 8	Mo 9	Mo 10	Mo 11	Mo 12
MILESTONES	Development	Website Goes Live					Basic Reporting Product Release		First Corporate Customer			
REVENUES												
Number of subscriptions sold	0	0	0	0	0	0	0	0	8	8	8	8
Subscription attrition	0	0	0	0	0	0	0	0	0	0	0	1
Cumulative number of subscriptions	0	0	0	0	0	0	0	0	8	16	23	31
Total Basic Reporting Revenue	0	0	0	0	0	0	0	0	24,000	47,400	70,215	92,460

Basic Reporting

Growth Drivers   **Assumptions**

Overall growth of the blogosphere   Dedicated direct sales team for Basic Reporting product

Number of sales persons   Closing percentage increases as reputation and brand evolve from 20% (year 1) to 27% (year 4)

Number of sales calls   Product release: Jan 2008

Percentage of sales closing   Monthly subscription fee of $3,000 per month – reference penetration pricing

Attrition rates   Product is directed to small-medium-sized businesses

230% growth in blogosphere in 2006 and continued growth into 2011 based on primary research with five corporate marketers using online advertisement and experimenting with interactive/social media.

Source: Chris Chen, Izu Matsuo, and Winnie Peng, *CliqUp Feasibility Study* (April 18, 2007). Reprinted by permission.

expenses). To make the financial statements clearer and more concise, one can use only the totals of SG&A expenses for each month in the financial statements, with a footnote directing the reader to the SG&A breakout statement. Direct selling expenses, which include advertising costs, travel expenses, sales salaries, commissions, and the cost of promotional supplies; and indirect selling expenses, which are not linked to the sale of a specific product, but rather are proportionally distributed to all products sold during a particular period of time (telephone, interest and postal charges), can be handled in the same manner, in a breakout statement, with only totals appearing in the financial statements. General and administrative expenses will include the salaries of non-sales personnel and overhead such as rent, utilities, and equipment expenses. Table 9.2 presents some sample expenditures for various types of businesses. These are not necessarily all-inclusive. The entrepreneur's knowledge of the industry and the business will be important in adding to these lists.

The last item to forecast is taxes: payroll taxes (which include Social Security and Medicare) and federal, state, and local income taxes. The various rates for those taxes and when they must be paid can be found by consulting the IRS website at http://www.irs.gov and any state franchise tax board or local governmental agency. To calculate the business tax liability, a pro forma income statement will need to be developed. This is discussed in the next section.

TABLE 9.2

Sample Expenditures for Various Types of Businesses

Sample Manufacturing or Construction Expenses List

Manager's Salary	Paid Employees' Salaries
Payroll Taxes	Vehicle Lease and Maintenance
Related Travel	Packaging Costs
Supplies	Depreciation on Owned Equipment

Sample Distribution and Warehouse Expenses List

Manager's Salary	Employees' Salaries
Drivers' Salaries	Payroll Taxes
Vehicle Lease and Maintenance	Warehouse Loading Vehicles
Lease/Maintenance	Depreciation on Owned Equipment
Freight Expenses	Supplies

Sample List of Selling Expenses

Sales Manager's Salary	Inside Sales Salaries
Inside Sales Commissions	Telephone Sales Salaries
Telephone Sales Commissions	Field Sales Salaries
Field Sales Commissions	Payroll Taxes for Sales Employees
Sales Vehicles Lease and Maintenance	Sales-Related Travel
Advertising and Promotion	Depreciation on Owned Equipment

Sample List of General, Selling, and Administrative Expenses

Advertising	Rent
Salaries and Wages	Utilities
Office Supplies	Insurance
Office Equipment	Business Taxes
Payroll Taxes	

Start-up Costs

The bulk of expenses in the first year of a new business are probably incurred prior to the business's opening its doors for the first time. The costs of purchasing furniture, equipment, start-up inventory, and supplies can quickly add up to a substantial amount—and that doesn't include deposits for leases and utilities. A manufacturing start-up might also include product development costs, a deposit on the lease for a plant, and raw materials costs. Start-ups with new products typically accrue heavy pre–start-up development costs that include engineering, prototyping, and patent assessment and application. These are one-time expenses to get the business started. In addition, entrepreneurs must remember that employees may need training before the business opens, so that becomes part of the start-up costs as well.

For accounting purposes, some of these initial costs, such as those for equipment, must be depreciated (discounted over a period of time) on the income statement; others, such as organizational and formation expenses, must be amortized, or spread out over time, as start-up costs. It is important to check with a good accountant to learn the correct method for depreciating and amortizing certain start-up expenses. For purposes of determining start-up funding requirements, however, these costs will be treated as a lump sum. Table 9.3 presents the start-up costs for CliqUp. These are incurred during preparation for launch.

In the two financial statements used for feasibility analysis—the statement of cash flows and the income statement—an entrepreneur has two choices: (1) show all start-up costs in a Month 0 column on the spreadsheet and make

TABLE 9.3

CliqUp Start-up Costs

Marketing	
Advertising	700
Marketing General	300
Total Marketing	1,000
Other Expenses	
Office Rent	872
Office Equipment (Furniture, Phone)	3,500
Comm. Exp. and Phone Bills	954
Legal	2,651
Accounting	358
Misc.	2,500
Total Other Expenses	10,835
Human Resources	
Total G&A	26,000
Total Other Personnel for Development	4,200
Total Human Resources	30,200
System Maintenance	6,500
Total	**48,535**

Source: Chris Chen, Izu Matsuo, and Winnie Peng, *CliqUp Feasibility Study* (April 18, 2007). Reprinted by permission.

Month 1 the first month of actual operations, or (2) make Month 1 the first month when expenses were incurred relative to the start-up of the business and then actual operations (post–product development) begin in some month later in the first or second year, depending on the status of product development.

With all the numbers forecast and assumptions prepared, it is time to prepare the two key financial statements that help an entrepreneur determine the capital requirements and financial feasibility of the new venture. It is important to note that the descriptions in the next sections do not substitute for using a qualified CPA to review any financial statements developed by the entrepreneur, particularly those that appear in the business plan. Recall that the principal use of feasibility analysis is to give the entrepreneur a high level of confidence about the conditions under which the new venture could move forward. Although it can be successfully used to seek investment capital, that is not its primary purpose.

Preparing the Pro Forma Income Statement

The income statement, also known as a profit and loss statement, gives information about the projected profit or loss status of the business for a specified period of time. *Profit* and *loss* are accounting terms that refer to how much the business earned or lost after all the expenses were deducted. Figure 9.6 displays an income statement for CliqUp. The income statement is normally the first financial statement prepared so that the business's income tax liability can be calculated. The taxes owed are based on the profit made by the company. Because income taxes vary from state to state, the financial statements presented here are not indicative of tax rates in every state. Furthermore, whether a company pays the taxes or the entrepreneur pays the taxes at his or her personal rate is a function of the type of legal entity chosen for the business. Choice of the legal form of organization, discussed in Chapter 11, is a significant decision made during the development of the business plan.

It is important to note that revenues and expenses are recorded in the income statement when a transaction occurs in the case of sales, or when a debt is incurred in the case of expenses, whether or not money has been received or expended. If a sale occurs in March, for example, it is recorded as a sale in March even if the money is not received until May. In the interim, that money becomes an account receivable.

The first section of the income statement details the revenues coming into the business from a variety of sources, but typically from sales. A product-oriented business will show a cost of goods produced or sold, which is a calculation of all the costs directly related to making the product or purchasing the goods to be sold. Refer to the discussion of cost of goods sold in the previous section. A service business does not typically calculate a COGS. The difference between COGS and revenues is gross profit. This is an important figure because gross profit divided by sales gives the gross margin, a figure often used to describe the room that businesses have to make financial mistakes. For example, suppose a company sees revenues of $500,000 in year 1 and the COGS equals $350,000. Subtracting the COGS from revenues gives a gross profit of $150,000. Then the gross margin is 30 percent

FIGURE 9.6   CliqUp—Pro Forma Income Statement—Year One

	Month 0	Month 1	Month 2	Month 3	Month 4	Month 5	Month 6	Month 7	Month 8	Month 9	Month 10	Month 11	Month 12
REVENUES													
Basic Reporting Revenue	0	0	0	0	0	0	0	0	0	24,000	47,400	70,215	92,460
Ad Hoc Reporting Revenues	0	0	0	0	0	0	0	0	0	0	0	0	0
Premium Reporting Revenue	0	0	0	0	0	0	0	0	0	0	0	0	0
Advertisement Revenue	0	0	0	0	0	0	0	0	0	0	0	0	0
Total Revenues	**0**	**0**	**0**	**0**	**0**	**0**	**0**	**0**	**0**	**24,000**	**47,400**	**70,215**	**92,460**
EXPENSES													
COGS													
Bloggers revenue share	0	0	0	0	0	0	0	0	0	960	1,896	2,809	3,698
Credit card transaction costs	0	0	0	0	0	0	0	0	0	4,320	8,532	12,639	16,643
Sales commission	0	0	0	0	0	0	0	0	0	0	0	0	0
Total COGS	0	0	0	0	0	0	0	0	0	5,280	10,428	15,448	20,341
Gross Profit	**0**	**0**	**0**	**0**	**0**	**0**	**0**	**0**	**0**	**18,720**	**36,972**	**54,768**	**72,119**
SELLING, GENERAL & ADMINSTRATIVE													
Marketing													
Advertising (web)	700	700	700	700	700	700	700	700	700	700	700	700	700
Marketing General	300	300	300	300	300	300	300	300	300	300	300	300	300
Total marketing	**1,000**	**1,000**	**1,000**	**1,000**	**1,000**	**1,000**	**1,000**	**1,000**	**1,000**	**1,000**	**1,000**	**1,000**	**1,000**
Administrative													
R&D	0	0	0	0	0	0	0	0	0	4,800	9,480	14,043	18,492
Office rent	0	872	872	872	872	872	872	872	872	872	872	872	872
Office equipment	0	3,500	-500	0	0	500	500	2,000	0	0	0	0	0
Comm. exp. & phone bills	0	954	954	954	954	954	954	954	954	954	954	954	954
Legal	2,000	651	651	651	651	651	651	651	651	651	651	651	651
Accounting	0	358	358	358	358	358	358	358	358	358	358	358	358
Misc.	2,000	500	500	500	500	500	500	500	500	500	500	500	500
Total other expenses	**4,000**	**6,835**	**2,835**	**3,335**	**3,335**	**3,835**	**3,835**	**5,335**	**3,335**	**8,135**	**12,815**	**17,378**	**21,827**

(continued)

FIGURE 9.6	CliqUp—Pro Forma Income Statement—Year One *(continued)*

	Month 0	Month 1	Month 2	Month 3	Month 4	Month 5	Month 6	Month 7	Month 8	Month 9	Month 10	Month 11	Month 12
Human Resources													
Total G&A	0	26,000	26,000	26,000	26,000	26,000	26,000	26,000	26,000	26,000	26,000	26,000	26,000
Total sales & marketing	0	0	0	0	0	0	5,200	9,100	9,100	9,100	9,100	9,100	9,100
Total systems personnel	0	0	0	0	0	11,700	16,900	23,400	23,400	23,400	23,400	23,400	23,400
Total other personnel	0	4,200	2,600	2,600	2,600	1,000	0	3,000	3,000	3,000	3,000	3,000	3,000
Total human resources	0	30,200	28,600	28,600	28,600	38,700	48,100	61,500	61,500	61,500	61,500	61,500	61,500
TOTAL SG&A	4,000	38,035	32,435	32,935	32,935	43,535	52,935	67,835	65,835	70,635	75,315	79,878	84,327
System maintenance	5,000	1,500	1,500	1,500	1,500	1,500	1,500	2,000	2,000	2,000	2,000	2,000	2,000
EBITDA	-9,000	-39,535	-33,935	-34,435	-34,435	-45,035	-54,435	-69,835	-67,835	-53,915	-40,343	-27,110	-14,208
Depreciation	0	186	186	186	186	186	203	270	270	270	270	270	270
Amortization	0	0	0	0	0	0	0	0	0	0	0	0	0
Total Deprec. & Amortiz.	0	186	186	186	186	186	203	270	270	270	270	270	270
EBIT	-9,000	-39,721	-34,121	-34,621	-34,621	-45,221	-54,638	-70,105	-68,105	-54,185	-40,613	-27,380	-14,478
Total Interest Expense	0	0	0	0	0	0	0	0	0	0	0	0	0
PRE-TAX NET INCOME	-9,000	-39,721	-34,121	-34,621	-34,621	-45,221	-54,638	-70,105	-68,105	-54,185	-40,613	-27,380	-14,478
Cumulative Net Income	-9,000	-48,721	-82,842	-117,464	-152,085	-197,306	-251,944	-322,048	-390,153	-444,337	-484,950	-512,330	-526,808
Income tax 35%	0	0	0	0	0	0	0	0	0	0	0	0	0
NET INCOME AFTER TAX	-9,000	-39,721	-34,121	-34,621	-34,621	-45,221	-54,638	-70,105	-68,105	-54,185	-40,613	-27,380	-14,478

Source: Chris Chen, Izu Matsuo, and Winnie Peng, *CliqUp Feasibility Study* (April 18, 2007). Reprinted by permission.

($150,000/$500,000), which means that out of every dollar the company earns, it has 30 cents left to pay its general, administrative, and selling expenses.

The next major section of the income statement is operating expenses—sales, general, and administrative expenses (SG&A), which details all the expenditures of the business. This is followed by earnings calculations in various forms:

EBITDA: earnings before interest, taxes, depreciation, and amortization are deducted

EBIT: earnings before interest and taxes are deducted

Taxable Income: earnings subject to income tax

Net Income or Net Profit: earnings of the business

Most entrepreneurs project profit and loss out about three years. Going beyond that time frame makes no sense because the farther out the projections go, the less reliable they are. The income statement should contain footnotes for each item to refer the reader to supporting material in the "Notes to Financial Statements" or "Assumptions." Any unusual or one-time major expenses, such as the cost of participating in a trade show, should be explained in a footnote.

The income statement depicts when the new venture will cover its costs and begin to make a profit. However, the expenses of the business are paid not with profit but with cash. Therefore, during feasibility analysis, the most important financial statement is the cash flow statement or cash budget, which is discussed next.

FORECASTING A START-UP'S CASH NEEDS

Developing the cash flow statement is the first step in arriving at start-up cash needs. Figure 9.7 displays a cash flow statement for CliqUp. As in all financial statements, each item on the statement should be footnoted in the "Notes to Financial Statements" to explain what the assumptions were and how the figures were derived. The first section of the statement, cash inflows, records all the inflows of cash into the business *when they are received*. It is important to remember that the cash flow statement records cash inflows and outflows when they occur. Therefore, if a sale is made in March, for example, but payment is not received until April, the sale is counted in April on the statement. Recall that the income statement differs from the cash flow statement in this regard. That is why the cash flow statement is so valuable; it lets the entrepreneur see the patterns of cash inflow to the business when they occur.

The next section records cash outflows or disbursements. The final section of the cash flow statement provides crucial information about the net change in cash flow—in other words, whether the business had a positive or a negative cash flow in that month. Note that in each month, the net cash flow reflects only the cash inflows and outflows for that month, assuming no start-up capital. An additional line, the cumulative cash flow, provides a critical piece of the cash needs assessment, which is the highest cumulative negative cash flow number. This figure ($688,808 in month 18; see the feasibility study in the appendix), plus start-up costs, is the minimum amount the entrepreneur needs to survive until a positive cash flow is generated from the revenues of the business, which occurs in month 25, supposing no investment capital. Because this figure is an

FIGURE 9.7 CliqUp Pro Forma Cash Flow Statement—Year One

	Mo 0	Mo 1	Mo 2	Mo 3	Mo 4	Mo 5	Mo 6	Mo 7	Mo 8	Mo 9	Mo 10	Mo 11	Mo 12
CASH INFLOW													
Basic Reporting Revenue	0	0	0	0	0	0	0	0	0	0	24,000	47,400	70,215
Ad Hoc Reporting Revenues	0	0	0	0	0	0	0	0	0	0	0	0	0
Premium Reporting Revenue	0	0	0	0	0	0	0	0	0	0	0	0	0
Ad Revenue	0	0	0	0	0	0	0	0	0	0	0	0	0
Total Cash Inflow	0	0	0	0	0	0	0	0	0	0	24,000	47,400	70,215
CASH OUTFLOW													
Direct Costs													
COGS - Affiliate blogs revenue share (ad)	0	0	0	0	0	0	0	0	0	0	0	0	0
COGS - Credit card transaction costs (basic)	0	0	0	0	0	0	0	0	0	0	960	1,896	2,809
COGS - Sales commission	0	0	0	0	0	0	0	0	0	0	4,320	8,532	12,639
Total G & A	0	26,000	26,000	26,000	26,000	26,000	26,000	26,000	26,000	26,000	26,000	26,000	26,000
Total sales & marketing	0	0	0	0	0	0	0	5,200	9,100	9,100	9,100	9,100	9,100
Total systems personnel	0	0	0	0	0	0	11,700	16,900	23,400	23,400	23,400	23,400	23,400
Total other personnel	0	4,200	2,600	2,600	2,600	1,000	0	3,000	3,000	3,000	3,000	3,000	3,000
Systems Development/Maintenance	5,000	1,500	1,500	1,500	1,500	1,500	1,500	2,000	2,000	2,000	2,000	2,000	2,000
Total Direct Costs	5,000	31,700	30,100	30,100	30,100	40,200	49,600	63,500	63,500	63,500	68,780	73,928	78,947
Indirect Costs													
Marketing and Promotion	0	1,000	1,000	1,000	1,000	1,000	1,000	1,000	1,000	1,000	1,000	1,000	1,000
R&D	0	0	0	0	0	0	0	0	0	0	4,800	9,480	14,043
Office rent	0	872	872	872	872	872	872	872	872	872	872	872	872
Office equipment ($500 per employee)	0	3,500	-500	0	0	0	0	500	2,000	0	0	0	0
Comm. exp. & phone bills	0	954	954	954	954	954	954	954	954	954	954	954	954
Legal	2,000	651	651	651	651	651	651	651	651	651	651	651	651
Accounting	0	358	358	358	358	358	358	358	358	358	358	358	358
Misc.	2,000	500	500	500	500	500	500	500	500	500	500	500	500
One-time expenses 1	0	0	0	0	0	0	0	1,000	0	0	0	0	0
Computers & software	0	7,000	0	0	0	0	0	0	4,000	0	0	0	0
Income Tax	0	0	0	0	0	0	0	0	0	0	0	0	0
Total Indirect Costs	4,000	7,835	3,835	4,335	4,335	4,835	4,835	4,835	10,335	4,335	9,135	13,815	18,378
Total Cash Outflow	9,000	39,535	33,935	34,435	34,435	45,035	54,435	54,435	73,835	67,835	77,915	87,743	97,325
Inflow-Outflow	-9,000	-39,535	-33,935	-34,435	-34,435	-45,035	-54,435	-54,435	-73,835	-67,835	-53,915	-40,343	-27,110
Cumulative Inflow-Outflow	-9,000	-48,535	-82,470	-116,905	-151,340	-196,375	-250,810	-332,645	-400,480	-454,395	-494,738	-521,848	

Source: Chris Chen, Izu Matsuo, and Winnie Peng, *CliqUp Feasibility Study* (April 18, 2007). Reprinted by permission.

<table>
<tr><td>**TABLE 9.4**</td><td></td><td>**Amount**</td><td>**Assumption**</td></tr>
</table>

	Amount	Assumption
CliqUp Cash Needs Assessment		
Start-Up Expenses		
Marketing	1,000	
G&A	10,835	
Human Resources	30,200	
System Maintenance	6,500	
Total Start-up	**48,535**	
Total Working Capital	**640,273**	Difference between highest negative CF and start-up expenses
Highest Cumulative Negative Cash Flow	**688,808**	Occurs in month 18
Safety Margin	82,470	Based on 3 months of cash expenses
Total Cash Needs	**771,278**	

estimate based on a whole series of estimates, there is a very good chance that it is not entirely accurate, so entrepreneurs typically add a safety margin or contingency factor. The safety margin is an amount of cash that is often based on the sales and collection cycle of the business. If, for example, customers typically pay on a 60-day cycle, it will be important to be able to cover at least 60 days of fixed costs. The business used in this example is typical of most start-up businesses in that it takes time to generate enough sales and other revenues to cover the costs of doing business, but it is important to calculate how much money is needed to start and operate the business to a positive cash flow, so that the entrepreneur can make a wise assessment of how much capital to raise.

Table 9.4 presents a breakout of the start-up capital requirements for CliqUp. Note that the cash needs are separated into types of money: start-up expenses, working capital (the difference between the highest cumulative negative cash flow and the start-up expenses), and the safety margin, which is a contingency amount based on the probability that their estimates might be off. This is important information that the entrepreneur can use when the time comes to fund the business. For example, rather than purchasing equipment, which in some businesses can amount to several thousand dollars, the entrepreneur could choose to lease it and thus reduce start-up expenditures significantly. From this cash needs assessment, it is clear that the entrepreneur will need a minimum of $771,278, including the safety margin, to start and operate this business until it generates a positive cash flow in month 18.

ASSESSING RISK

Many entrepreneurs make the mistake of thinking they have done a complete analysis of their start-up financial requirements because they have generated pages of spreadsheets with numbers that, on the surface, appear to work. And if they have developed assumptions that justify their numbers, it is not irrational on their part to believe their work is done. But this would be a mistake. The true test of financial feasibility is whether the key financial figures are in line with the company's goals and are achievable. What would be the effect on the financials of a change in price, a decline in sales, or unexpected demand? What would be the effect on cash flow if the company grew at a more rapid pace than the predicted percentage a year? What if it grew more slowly? How sensitive to change are the cash flow numbers and net income? And how will the company deal with these changes? Creating scenarios to consider the impact of these kinds of changes is called sensitivity analysis.

At the feasibility stage, it is important to consider the potential changes to the forecasts with the highest probability of occurring and to factor in how the impact of these changes will be dealt with. Analyzing the financial risks and benefits of a new venture is a difficult and challenging exercise, but it must be done so that two fundamental questions can be answered: (1) Do the start-up capital requirements make sense? In other words, is the business financially feasible? and (2) looking at the capital investment and the profit possibilities, is there enough money in this opportunity to make the effort worthwhile?

Unfortunately, many businesses are financially feasible—they can make a profit—but the return on the initial investment is so low that an entrepreneur would be better off putting that investment into real estate or some other vehicle. New businesses take an extraordinary amount of work, which entrepreneurs often fail to put a value on. All too often, the business is running and making a profit, but the entrepreneur is making less than he or she would have made working for someone else. The feasibility stage, when the investment has still been minimal, is the time to look seriously at financial feasibility and quantify the risks and potential benefits. Once the venture has been deemed feasible in all respects, a business plan with a full set of financial statements can be developed. That process will further reduce the uncertainty inherent in the start-up process. In the next section, we look at the financials that typically appear in a business plan.

Looking Ahead to Business Plan Financials

Business plan financials may or may not be based on a business already in operation, and this is important because the financials will differ somewhat if the business has even a short record of performance. For example, many CEOs use a statement of cash flows from operations, which is a bit more complex than the simple cash flow statement used for feasibility analysis. It provides information on changes in the company's cash account through inflows and outflows of cash and cash equivalents associated with the daily operations of the business. Operating cash inflows include sales and accounts receivable that have been collected, whereas nonoperating cash inflows are comprised of loans, investments, or the sale of assets. Cash outflows consist of inventory payments, accounts payable payments, and payments associated with payroll taxes, rent, utilities, and so forth. Nonoperating cash outflows include such items as payments of principal or interest on debt, dividend distribution, and asset purchase. A financially healthy company will see its major source of cash inflows coming from operating sources, such as sales. In preparing this type of cash flow statement, the income statement items are linked with changes from normal operations in the balance sheet from one period to the next. These include sales, cost of sales, and operating expenses. It is not within the scope of this book to go into further detail on this statement.

THE ROLE OF THE BALANCE SHEET

The balance sheet, called a "statement of financial position," is different from the other financial statements in that it looks at the financial health of the business at a single point in time—a given date—whereas the cash flow and income statements review a period of time: month, quarter, or year. The balance sheet is divided into two parts that must balance, that is, be equal to each other based on the following formula:

$$\text{Assets} = \text{Liabilities} + \text{Shareholders' Equity}$$

In small businesses, shareholders' equity is often called "owners' equity." Figure 9.8 depicts a sample quarterly balance sheet for CliqUp for two years. This was done to show the balance sheet at start-up and again when it had retained earnings in the second year.

The first section of the balance sheet includes the assets, which are valued according to their actual costs. A business will have current assets, those that are consumed during the course of an operating year, and fixed assets, which are assets that have long lives, such as equipment. The liabilities side of the balance sheet consists of current liabilities, such as accounts payable, and long-term liabilities, such as debt. The shareholders' equity section will display the value of the shareholders' ownership interest in the company, any additional investment, and retained earnings, which are those business earnings that are not distributed as dividends but retained to grow the company.

Decisions made by the entrepreneur have a direct affect on the balance sheet. For example, an increase in sales typically results in an increase on the asset side of the balance sheet because the entrepreneur has had to increase inventory or purchase equipment to meet demand. Likewise, an entrepreneur's decision to retain earnings for growth will increase the equity portion of the balance sheet. The balance sheet is an important tool for answering questions about the health of the business. For example,

▶ Did debt financing increase or decrease from period to period? It is important to match any changes in debt financing to a particular decision or event.

▶ Did the amounts of accounts receivable and inventory increase or decrease relative to sales in the same period? This is an important measure of how well the business is managing these items.

Examining changes from period to period on the balance sheet is one way to gauge business performance. Ratios are another.

FIGURE 9.8   CliqUp Pro Forma Balance Sheet

| | Year 1 | | | | Year 2 | | | |
	1Q	2Q	3Q	4Q	1Q	2Q	3Q	4Q
ASSETS								
Cash	-122,905	-256,810	-472,115	-607,175	-820,697	-944,058	-744,909	-320,412
Accounts receivable	0	0	24,000	92,460	264,930	536,920	772,512	1,045,939
Inventory	0	0	0	0	0	0	0	0
Prepaid expenses	0	0	0	0	0	0	0	0
Total Current Assets	**-122,905**	**-256,810**	**-448,115**	**-514,716**	**-555,767**	**-407,138**	**27,603**	**725,527**
Property, Plant, Equipment net of depreciation	6,441	6,866	10,058	9,249	17,440	20,632	20,823	25,015
Unamortized developments	0	0	0	0	0	0	0	0
Total Assets	**-116,464**	**-249,944**	**-438,057**	**-505,467**	**-538,327**	**-386,507**	**48,426**	**750,542**
LIABILITIES								
Accounts payable	1,000	2,000	6,280	21,341	111,271	221,186	316,949	429,386
Accrued liabilities	0	0	0	0	0	0	0	0
Total Current Liabilities	**1,000**	**2,000**	**6,280**	**21,341**	**111,271**	**221,186**	**316,949**	**429,386**
Loans payable	0	0	0	0	0	0	0	0
Total Long Term Liabilities	0	0	0	0	0	0	0	0
Total Liabilities	**1,000**	**2,000**	**6,280**	**21,341**	**111,271**	**221,186**	**316,949**	**429,386**
SHAREHOLDERS' EQUITY								
Common stock	0	0	0	0	0	0	0	0
Preferred stock	0	0	0	0	0	0	0	0
Additional paid-in capital (1st round)	0	0	0	0	0	0	0	0
Additional paid-in capital (2nd round)	0	0	0	0	0	0	0	0
Retained earnings	-117,464	-251,944	-444,337	-526,808	-649,598	-607,693	-268,522	321,156
Total Equity	**-117,464**	**-251,944**	**-444,337**	**-526,808**	**-649,598**	**-607,693**	**-268,522**	**321,156**
Total Liabilities & Equity	**-116,464**	**-249,944**	**-438,057**	**-505,467**	**-538,327**	**-386,507**	**48,426**	**750,542**

Source: Chris Chen, Izu Matsuo, and Winnie Peng. *CliqUp Feasibility Study* (April 18, 2007). Reprinted by permission.

USING KEY RATIOS TO GAUGE PROGRESS

Entrepreneurs have a number of ratios that can be used as gauges to analyze a company's performance. Ratios compare items in the financial statements and convert them to relative terms so they can be compared to ratios in other periods or in other companies. It is not within the scope of this text to present all of the possible ratios available, so we discuss here five of the most common ratios used to measure liquidity, debt, and profitability.

▌ *Current ratio:* The current ratio provides information on the company's ability to meet short-term obligations. It is found by

Current ratio = Total current assets/Total current liabilities

The higher the number, the more liquid the company is and the more easily these assets can be converted to cash to pay off short-term obligations.

▌ *Acid test:* This ratio is another way to measure liquidity, but it's tougher to meet because it removes inventory, which may be difficult to convert to cash because of obsolescence. It is found by

Acid test = (Current assets – Inventory)/Current liabilities

This ratio forces the company's assets to stand on their own.

▌ *Profit margin:* This is a profitability ratio that uses net income and net sales from the income statement to give the percentage of each dollar of sales remaining after all costs of normal operations are accounted for. It is found by

Profit margin = Net income/Net sales

The inverse of this percentage (100% – PM) equals the expense ratio, that is, the percentage of each sales dollar accounted for by operating expenses.

▌ *Return on Investment:* This ratio provides a measure of the amount of return on the shareholders' investment based on the earnings of the company. It is found by

Return on investment (ROI) = Net income/Shareholders' equity

▌ *Inventory turnover:* This ratio is a measure of the liquidity of inventory or the number of times it turns over in a year. It is found by

Inventory turnover = Cost of good sold/Average inventory

This ratio helps the entrepreneur judge whether the business has too much capital tied up in inventory.

One other tool that is valuable to know is break-even analysis, which tells an entrepreneur how many units must be sold before the company can achieve a profit or the sales volume required to be profitable. The break-even point is that point at which the total variable and fixed expenses are covered and beyond which the company makes a profit. The formula to calculate break-even is as follows:

$$BEQ = \frac{TFC}{SP - VC \text{ (unit)}}$$

Where

TFC = total fixed costs

SP = selling price

VC = variable cost

As an example, assume that total fixed costs are $300,000; selling price per unit is $95.00; and variable costs per unit are $45.00. Then the number of units that must be produced and sold to break-even is found by

$$B/E = \frac{\$300,000}{\$95 - \$45} = 6,000 \text{ units}$$

Figuring out how much money will be needed to launch and operate a new venture can be a daunting task for any entrepreneur, even one with a finance background, because there are so many unknowns and unknowables. Start-up finances are based on best-guess projections for what the future might look like. That is why the entrepreneur's assumptions are so important; they serve to justify the numbers and provide a rationale for the thought process the entrepreneur followed to reach those numbers. A well-conceived financial plan will go a long way toward ensuring that the business is started with the appropriate amount of capital for the right reasons.

New Venture Checklist

Have you:

☐ Gathered the numbers you need for performing your financial analysis?

☐ Gathered sales forecast data through triangulation?

☐ Prepared a pro forma income statement?

☐ Created a cash flow statement from start-up until a positive cash flow is achieved?

☐ Performed a cash needs assessment to determine how much capital you will need to start the business?

☐ Determined whether this venture is financially feasible?

Issues to Consider

1. What are the types of resources that entrepreneurs need to gather to start a new venture?
2. Why is the cash flow statement the most important statement for the entrepreneur?
3. What are the primary differences between an income statement and a cash flow statement or cash budget?
4. What are some ways to forecast sales effectively for a retail business? For a manufacturer? For a service business?
5. What are the three categories of funds in the cash needs assessment, and how are they used to calculate how much money is needed to start the business?
6. What is the role of the balance sheet in the business plan?
7. How are financial ratios used to gauge the financial health of the business?

Experiencing Entrepreneurship

1. Interview a banker and an accountant about the key financial statements that entrepreneurs need to understand to run their businesses. Ask about the biggest mistakes business owners make in preparing their financial statements. Compare and contrast the responses of the banker and the accountant. Are their views of the financials different? Why? Prepare your responses in a two-page report.

2. Interview an entrepreneur who has been in business no longer than five years to find out how he or she calculated how much money was needed to start the venture. Did it turn out to be enough? Why or why not? In a brief PowerPoint presentation, present what you would have advised the entrepreneur to do differently.

Relevant Case Studies

## Part Three

THE BUSINESS PLAN: BUILDING A COMPANY

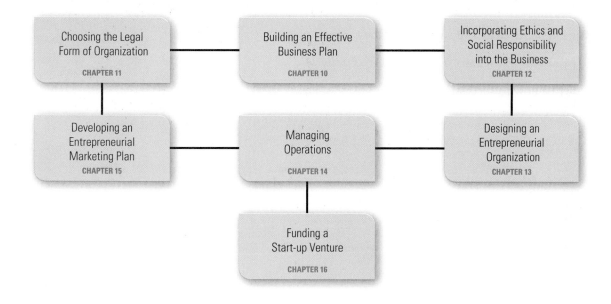

Choosing the Legal Form of Organization
CHAPTER 11

Building an Effective Business Plan
CHAPTER 10

Incorporating Ethics and Social Responsibility into the Business
CHAPTER 12

Developing an Entrepreneurial Marketing Plan
CHAPTER 15

Managing Operations
CHAPTER 14

Designing an Entrepreneurial Organization
CHAPTER 13

Funding a Start-up Venture
CHAPTER 16

BUILDING AN EFFECTIVE BUSINESS PLAN

"When all is said and done, the journey is the reward. There is nothing else."

—Randy Komisar, The Monk and the Riddle

LEARNING OBJECTIVES

▷ Describe how to move from a feasible concept to a business plan.

▷ Discuss the strategy and structure of the business plan.

▷ Explain how to organize a business plan effectively.

▷ Describe how to successfully present a business plan.

Profile 10.1 ANATOMY OF A NEW BUSINESS FAILURE

Stories of great successes can be inspiring, but entrepreneurs often learn much more and avoid fatal mistakes by doing a postmortem on a failed business. A good example of a business that seemed to have everything going for it and yet could not succeed is Future Beef, an Arkansas-based business founded in 2001.

The Opportunity

In today's world where genetic engineering is used to improve the quality, shelf life, and size of the foods we eat, Future Beef saw an opportunity to use genetic data and high-tech equipment to produce enormous amounts of superior meat. That was the company's primary product, but their plan also included providing its workers with the highest wages and benefits in the industry, as well as apartments and day-care centers as an additional benefit. Accomplishing these ambitious goals required a tremendous amount of investor capital. By late 1997, Future Beef had acquired its first round of capital, enough to allow the founders to quit their day jobs and recruit an experienced CEO (H. Russell Cross, former director of the Institute of Food Science and Engineering at Texas A&M) and two financial officers. A deal with grocery giant Safeway included a $15 million infusion of capital, and with the over $200 million total raised, the company was able to begin building plants.

Experience of the Founders

Rod Bowling and Rob Streight were the brains behind Future Beef. Bowling had a Ph.D. in meat and muscle biology from Texas A&M, and he had held the highest positions at some of the biggest plants in the industry. In 1996, frustrated by his inability to implement his innovative ideas inside a very traditional industry, Bowling sought the help of Streight in designing a very different kind of beef-producing company, one that integrated the value chain. Streight's role was to build the business's technology infrastructure.

How the Business Made Money

Not only did Future Beef want to control the entire value chain from the ranch to the packinghouse, but it also wanted to use every bit of the cow to create value-added products and deliver those products through one grocery retailer, Safeway. Unfortunately, at that time prices for cattle that were fed and grown to certain specifications were soft, and the September 11 terrorist attacks followed by a foot-and-mouth disease rumor that drove down the futures market only served to worsen the situation. Future Beef found itself in trouble, with unexpected cost overruns, malfunctioning equipment, and even some lawsuits. It was losing money on every steer because it had purchased its cattle at market high prices and at lower weights than normal. Because Future Beef kept cattle in the grow yards longer than normal to control their nutrition, its holding costs were high. Only one month after it opened its first 450,000-square-foot plant in August 2001, the worst time of the year for any meat packer to source supply, its exclusive retail partner, Safeway, stopped paying on its contract. Safeway accounted for 51 percent of its sales, and it was an exclusive agreement that prevented Future Beef from developing other customers. Future Beef was selling to Safeway at rock-bottom prices, figuring to make up the difference in value-added product sales, but that never happened. Three months later, Future Beef was forced to declare Chapter 11 bankruptcy. Five months after the bankruptcy, it laid off all its workers and, in August 2002, liquidated its holdings. The postmortem revealed that the company was trying to implement too many expensive new systems simultaneously, largely because there was a lot of industry knowledge in the company but unfortunately no real business experience. It appears that the founders were visionaries and not execution people—a fatal flaw in many business plans. More importantly, a business model characterized by high costs and that relies on one customer is a dangerous position to be in.

Epilogue: In May 2003, just nine months after Future Beef closed its operations, the plant resumed cattle slaughter operations as Creekstone Farms Premium Beef. Creekstone Farms was the successful bidder for the plant and equipment at auction. It is estimated that 80 percent of Creekstone's employees are former Future Beef employees. Today Creekstone is a very successful company, leading the charge for beef products free of bovine spongiform encephalopathy (BSE), or "mad cow" disease. In May 2007, Creekstone Farms won a decision in federal court to allow it to test for BSE. The USDA will appeal.

Sources: http://www.creekstonefarmspremiumbeef.com; J. McCuan, "Failure of Genius," *Inc. Magazine* (August 2003); "New Owners of Defunct Future Beef Plant Begin Operations," DodgeGlobe.com, accessed January 15, 2004; and Wes Ishmael, "Why Future Beef Went Under" (November 1, 2002), http://beef-mag.com/mag/beef_why_future_beef/, accessed June 24, 2004.

It is an unfortunate fact that many universities and institutions are perpetuating the myth that entrepreneurs must create business plans before they start businesses. Potential entrepreneurs are spending up to 200 hours of their valuable time in pursuit of the perfect plan to present at a competition or to an investor, only to discover that investors are more impressed by a founding team that has gotten the business up and running, even in a minimal way, to prove the concept.

When Jennifer Lawton started Net Daemons Associates in 1992, she didn't have a plan. At that time the economy was in recession, so as an independent contractor providing computer networking services to companies without in-house staff, she had plenty of business opportunity. She didn't have to prove the market; it was knocking down her door. Not until she had been in business for several years during more competitive times and had fifteen associates did Lawton and her management team realize that it would be easier to concentrate on strategy and explain where the business was going if they had a plan.[1] Given an existing track record, her business plan would be real, not a work of fiction like the plans of many ventures that have yet to start.

Recall that feasibility analysis tests the business concept in the market to determine the conditions under which the entrepreneur is willing to move forward and start the business. Going through the process of feasibility analysis helps the entrepreneur learn about the business and prepare to launch. The business plan depends on a feasible concept that has been market-tested, because the business plan is about building a company and executing that feasible concept.

There is another reason why business plans should be based on reality. The post–dot com era and the crash of technology stocks resulted in a much cooler investment climate. In the wake of many investments that failed, investors are taking a far more conservative approach to both formal and informal investing. There is plenty of investment capital available if entrepreneurs can convey a compelling story and deliver a management team that can execute the plan effectively.

For years, the traditional model of business planning involved carefully crafting a business plan and then sending it out to potential funders for consideration. Of course, much like a slush pile of manuscripts at a publishing house, these business plans sat stacked on the investor's desk, rarely seeing the light of day. Today, submitting a professionally crafted business plan is less important than making it clear what the entrepreneur has accomplished in the way of starting the business.[2] Investors want to see that the venture has customers and a track record, however brief. They want to see that the business model actually works. The new environment for business planning actually makes the case for the importance of the feasibility study to prove the concept and enable the founding team to launch the venture and test it before completing the formal business plan and seeking outside investment capital.

From Feasible Concept to Business Plan

Chapters 1 through 8 dealt with analyzing the feasibility of a new venture concept. Simply stated, feasibility is about the business idea and testing the business concept. The business plan is about the execution strategy that will bring that concept to market. The business plan serves three purposes: (1) It serves as a reality check for the entrepreneur, who will need to think very carefully about all aspects of the operating business; (2) it is a living guide to the business, a complete and comprehensive picture; and (3) it is a statement of intent for interested third parties such as investors, bankers, and strategic partners. Each of these potential stakeholders in the new venture will view the business plan from a different perspective.

INVESTORS' INTERESTS

Anyone investing in a new venture has four principal concerns: rate of growth, return on investment, degree of risk, and protection. Investors are generally betting that the value of their ownership interest in the business will increase over time at a rate greater than that of another type of investment or of a bank account. They want to know how fast the business is projected to grow, when that growth will take place, and what will ensure that the growth actually occurs as predicted. For this reason, they tend to look for market-driven companies rather than product- or technology-driven companies. They expect that predictions will be based on solid evidence in the marketplace and on thorough knowledge of the target market.[3] Investors are naturally concerned about when and how the principal portion of their investment will be repaid and how much gain on that investment will accrue over the time they are invested in the company. The answers to these concerns are largely a function of the structure of the investment deal: whether it involves a limited or general partnership, or preferred or common stock, and so forth. Investors want to understand thoroughly the risks they face in investing in the new venture; principally, they want to know how their original equity will be protected. They expect the entrepreneur to present the potential challenges facing the new venture, along with a plan for mitigating or dealing with them to protect the investors against loss.

Although the business plan is vital to investment decision making, it is not the only piece of information considered. In one survey of 42 venture capitalists, 43 percent claimed to having invested in a venture in the previous three years without the benefit of a business plan.[4] Only 36 percent reported that the business plan was "very important" in their evaluation. And perhaps the most revealing statistic of all was that 96 percent preferred to learn about a potential investment through a referral from someone they trusted. Furthermore, investors found that the primary flaws in most business plans were overly optimistic financial projections, too much hype, poor explanation of the business model, and no demonstration of customer demand.

BANKERS'/LENDERS' INTERESTS

Bankers/lenders are primarily interested in the company's margins and cash flow projections, because they are concerned about how their loans or credit lines to the business will be repaid. The margins indicate how much room there is for error between the cost to produce the product (or deliver the service) and the selling price. If margins are tight and the business has to lower prices to compete, the firm may not be able to pay off its loans as consistently and quickly as the bank would like. Similarly, bankers look at cash flow projections to see whether the business can pay all its expenses and still have money left over at the end of each month. Bankers also look at the qualifications and track record of the management team and may require personal guarantees of the principals. When considering a business plan and an entrepreneur for a loan, lenders have several concerns:

▶ *The amount of money the entrepreneur needs.* Lenders are looking for a specific amount that can be justified with accurate calculations and data.

▶ *The kind of positive impact the loan will have on the business.* Lenders would like to know that the money they are lending is not going to pay off old debt or to pay salaries, but rather will improve the business's financial position, particularly with regard to cash flow.

▶ *The kinds of assets the business has for collateral.* Not all assets are created equal. Some assets have no value outside the business, because they are custom-made or specific to that business and therefore cannot be sold on the open market. Lenders prefer to see industry-standard equipment and facilities that can easily be converted to another use.

▶ *How the business will repay the loan.* Lenders are interested in the earnings potential of the business over the life of the loan, but even more important they want to know that the business generates sufficient cash flow to service the debt. Fixed expenses are fairly easy to predict, but variable expenses—those related to the production of the product or service—present a more difficult problem. In an attempt to avoid any long-term issues, lenders pay close attention to the market research section of the business plan, which highlights the demand for the product/service. They also focus on the marketing plan, which tells them how the entrepreneur intends to reach the customer.

▶ *How the bank will be protected if the business doesn't meet its projections.* Lenders want to know that the entrepreneur has a contingency plan for situations where major assumptions prove to be wrong. They want to ensure that they are paid out of cash flow, not by liquidating the assets of the business, which generally would only give them a small percent of the value of the assets.

▶ *The entrepreneur's stake in the business.* Like investors, lenders feel more confident about lending to a business in which the entrepreneur has a substantial monetary investment. Such an investment reduces the likelihood that the entrepreneur will walk away from the business, leaving the lender stranded.

STRATEGIC PARTNERS

Some entrepreneurs, particularly those who intend to manufacture a product or bring a new drug or medical device to market, choose to form a strategic alliance with a larger company so that they don't have to incur the tremendous costs of purchasing equipment for a manufacturing plant or funding expensive clinical trials required by the FDA (Food and Drug Administration). They may, for example, license another firm to manufacture and assemble the product and supply it to the entrepreneur to market and distribute. Alternatively, an entrepreneur may enter into an agreement with a supplier to provide necessary raw materials in exchange for an equity interest in the start-up venture.

Strategic alliances may take the form of formal partnership agreements with major corporations or may consist simply of an informal agreement such as a large purchase contract. In either case, the larger company that is allying itself with the new venture is usually looking for new products, processes, or technologies that complement its current line of products or services. Accordingly, it will seek a new venture management team that has some previous corporate experience so that the relationship will be smoother. Larger companies are also interested in strategic issues such as the marketing and growth strategies of the new venture. Tim Welu, CEO of Minnesota-based Paisley Consulting, finds that strategic alliances are essential to the success of his business accountability software product. His premiere product, AutoAudit, enables businesses to document internal audit results. Its benefits led to Paisley gaining a Big Five accounting firm as a partner, which gave it distribution to 80 countries. The only problem was that the strategic partner was Arthur Andersen, the accounting firm that went bankrupt as a result of its association with Enron as its auditor. Fortunately, however, many of Andersen's employees went to Ernst & Young, which became Paisley's next strategic partner. Although there are risks associated with partnering with a larger firm, the benefits of broader distribution and access to deeper resources usually make the positives outweigh the negatives.[5]

Knowing in advance what these third parties are looking for will help entrepreneurs address their specific needs in the business plan, enhancing the partnership's ability to achieve the goals of the business.

STARTING THE PROCESS WITH A COMPELLING PITCH

Given the new investor environment discussed previously, it makes sense to begin the process of business planning by preparing an extended version of the classic "elevator pitch." The elevator pitch is a brief but convincing statement of the business concept including the important issues of "why you, why now, how you will change the world." The exercise of putting together a pitch, often with

Socially Responsible Entrepreneurship

The Little Schoolhouse That Could

Gifford Pinchot is best known for his classic 1985 book, *Intrapreneuring: Why You Don't Have to Leave the Corporation to Become an Entrepreneur;* but largely thanks to the influence of his grandfather, who founded the forest service in 1905, Pinchot has become an avid conservationist. In that capacity, he founded the Bainbridge Island Graduate Institute (BGI) near Seattle, Washington, in 2002. There, students are immersed in studies of environmental sustainability and social responsibility in the context of entrepreneurship and innovation.

BGI was launched in just six months with $120,000 of Pinchot's own money. Thereafter, he raised another $300,000 from Ben Cohen (Ben and Jerry's co-founder) and Wayne Silby (founder of the Calvert Fund). He recruited a president and together they worked to gain state authorization to award an MBA. The first class of 18 students enrolled in the fall of 2002. BGI is one of the first graduate schools in the United States to focus on sustainable business,

to "create profit in ways that contribute to taking care of people and the planet." Pinchot is determined to make a mark on society by educating more people in how to be entrepreneurial while also being socially responsible. Today the school also prides itself on teaching its students how to find their "internal compass," which helps them figure out what they really want to do with their lives. Kelly Scott-Hanson, president of Co-Housing Resources, attended one of the entrepreneurial classes, where she learned how to write a business plan and present to local investors. Now her company is doing a better job of investing in projects that return their investment in five years while at the same time doing good for society.

Sources: BGI, http://www.bgiedu.org; "Green Curriculum," *Washington CEO* (January 12, 2006); BGI, http://www.bgiedu.org/index.htm; and E. Winninghoff, "The Little Green Schoolhouse," *Inc. Magazine* (July 2003), http://www.inc.com.

PowerPoint slides, forces the founding team to focus on the critical success factors for the business. In other words, what must be in place for the business to succeed? With a highly focused pitch presentation in hand, it will be easier to develop the full business plan without deviating from the essentials. Later in the chapter, we will address the matter of how to present the business plan effectively in a more formal presentation format. Several fundamental questions about the business must be answered before creating the pitch.

What Need Is Being Served?

Is there really an opportunity here? Support for the answer to this question will come from the market research with potential customers and should demonstrate a growing market for the opportunity that is based on solving a real need that customers have.

Can the Founding Team Serve That Need?

Why is this founding team the best team to execute this concept? Can it be demonstrated that the founding team has the experience and skills required by the various areas of the business? Do the founders have their own money invested in this concept? It is easy to spend other people's money or to consider "sweat" equity as equivalent to cash—but it isn't equivalent in the eyes of investors, who figure that the founding team won't give up easily if they have invested their own money in the deal. Does the team have the passion and the drive to make this business a success? Passion and drive are difficult to measure but are reflected in the level of work that was put into the market research. How many people did the team talk to—industry experts, customers, and so forth?

Why Is Now the Right Time to Launch This Venture?

What makes this concept so valuable right now? If this business is the only one of its kind, why is that so? Has anyone tried this before and failed? If so, why? What makes the current environment right for this venture? Timing is critical in the launch of any new venture, so it is important to explain why *now* is the right time.

What Is This Venture's Competitive Advantage?

No venture can succeed in the long term without a sustainable competitive advantage—not a single competitive advantage, but a bundle of them encompassing every aspect of the business. The pitch needs to address what advantages will enable this venture to create a unique unserved niche and to enter the market and secure customers with little or no competition in the beginning.

Can This Venture Make Money?

Most business plans do not adequately address the business model. How will the business create and capture value that will enable it to make money over the long term? In general, value is created when the business is adequately capitalized and has highly regarded investors, an experienced management team, customers, a unique technology or service, the ability to continually innovate, and a rapidly expanding market.[6] Once the new venture has passed the start-up stage, additional value is created by its position in the market, significant customers, effective operating systems, a strong gross margin, positive cash flow, and a high return on equity.

Because business plans are most often used to raise capital, the questions they answer are frequently of great interest to an investor or lender. How much money is needed to address this opportunity? How will capital be allocated (i.e., to increase sales, to boost profits, or to enhance the value of the company) and at which milestones? How will the business provide a superior return on investment (ROI)? Which exit strategies are possible?

STARTING THE BUSINESS PLANNING PROCESS WITH A WEBSITE

Today when people hear about a new business or a new product or service, the first place they go for more information is the Internet. This makes sense, because the Internet is the perfect place to communicate a new venture's message and to get feedback. However, many new businesses make the mistake of simply slapping up a single page marked "under construction" or "coming soon" until they finish their business plan and start the business. It is far better to wait to put up a website until the entrepreneur has something ready for customers to see. On the Internet, a new business can look as successful and established as any large company for relatively few dollars invested in development of the site. A quick online demonstration can communicate to the visitor what the business does, who its customers are, and what its value proposition is. The site can inform users about the founding team, the company's mission and goals, and disclose to potential investors, customers, and other interested parties how to contact the business.

One word of caution about websites: Proprietary information that is not protected by patents or trademarks should not be put on the site, because companies regularly peruse the Internet for information on their competitors. In fact, entrepreneurs should definitely study the websites of their competitors for important clues about what features they should build into their own sites and how they might improve on what their competitors are doing. As with every promotional or informational piece about the business, differentiation is critical. It is not within the scope of this text to discuss website development. Information on building an effective website is ubiquitous on the Internet and in every bookstore.

The Business Plan: Strategy and Structure

Writing a business plan is a huge undertaking that should be planned in terms of tasks and timeline. If a new venture has already been launched in limited form as suggested in previous sections—via a website or an actual start-up based on a successful feasibility analysis—the writing of the business plan must now be sandwiched among all the day-to-day activities associated with an operating business. Even if a new venture has not yet been launched, an action plan for completing a business plan in a relatively short period of time will help accelerate the process. The following tasks are a guide to the founding team in preparing to write the business plan.

▶ *Identify who is responsible for what.* A lot of updated information must be gathered about industry, market, customer, and costs. Even though all of these data were gathered when the feasibility study was conducted, some time may have elapsed before the writing of the business plan, so it is important to make sure that all information is current. Make a list of everything that must be collected and how it needs to be collected (secondary research, talking to customers, etc.). Decide who will do what and by when it must be accomplished.

▶ *Develop a timeline based on tasks identified.* It is important to be realistic about how much time it will take to complete all the tasks associated with the business plan. The timeline is very likely to be too long, especially if the work is being done on evenings and weekends, so the next job will be to determine whether all of the tasks are critical to the business plan and to prune any that are not.

▶ *Hold the team to the timeline and work diligently to get the plan done.* Once the business plan is complete, it's a good idea to get a trusted third party to review the plan to catch anything the team may have missed.

COMPONENTS OF THE BUSINESS PLAN

All business plans have some major sections in common. The following sections and the outline in Table 10.1 are merely guides. It is important that entrepreneurs customize their business plan to meet their specific needs and the needs of those who will read it.

Executive Summary

The executive summary, the most important part of the business plan, is a stand-alone piece and is the primary means of stimulating an investor, banker, or other interested party to read the full business plan. Typically, the executive summary should be no more than two pages and should contain the most important points from all the sections of the business plan. Figure 10.1 presents an example of what an actual executive summary might look like.

It is vital that the executive summary capture the reader's attention instantly in the first sentence. This is often best accomplished by hitting the reader with a one–two punch: a strong and compelling statement about the pain or need in the market, followed by a clear and concise statement of how the entrepreneur intends to cure that pain. This concept statement spells out the product/service, customer, value proposition, and distribution channel by which the benefit to the customer will be delivered. Recall that the business concept was discussed at length in Chapter 4. The business model should also be emphasized, along with the profitability potential of the company and its potential for growth. Table 10.1 presents an outline of a typical business plan.

Business Concept

The business concept—product/service, customer, value proposition, and distribution—should be stated clearly and concisely. The statement should be followed by some elaboration on each of the components so that the reader will have a clear understanding of the opportunity. The business model—how the business will make money—should be discussed in enough detail to ensure that the reader understands the sources of revenue to the new venture and the sustainability of the business model. The vision and core values for the company should be expressed here because they form the foundation on which the company is built and decisions will be made. Chapter 12 discusses how to arrive at a vision and core values for the business. The business concept section can conclude with a brief discussion of the growth possibilities and any potential for spin-off products and services. Refer to Chapter 4 for a more in-depth discussion of how a business concept is developed.

Founding or Management Team

This section needs to provide evidence that the founding team has the necessary skills and experience to execute the business plan successfully. Everything depends on a great team. Investors typically look at the components of the business plan in the following order of importance: market, team, product/service. If the founding team is lacking in some area of expertise or experience, that gap needs to be closed by a member of the board of directors, by additional managers

TABLE 10.1	Business Plan Outline

Executive Summary

Include the most important points from all sections of the business plan.

Keep the summary to two or three pages max.

Make sure that the first sentence captures the reader's attention and the first paragraph presents the business concept in a compelling way.

Table of Contents

The Business Concept

What is the business?

Who is the customer?

What is the value proposition or benefit(s) being delivered to the customer?

How will the benefit be delivered (distribution)?

What is your differentiation strategy?

What is your business model?

What are the spin-offs from your original products/services, and what is the company's potential for growth?

Founding or Management Team

Qualifications of founding team

How critical tasks will be covered

Gap analysis, or what's missing (professional advisors, board of directors, independent contractors)

Industry/Market Analysis

Industry analysis

Demographics, major players, trends, etc. . .

Target market analysis

Demographics, customer grid or market segmentation, etc. . .

Customer profile (based on primary research)

Competitor analysis and competitive advantages (competitive grid)

Distribution channels (alternatives and risk/benefit)

Entry strategy (initial market penetration, first customer)

Product/Service Development Plan

Detailed description and unique features of product/service

Technology assessment (if applicable)

Plan for prototyping and testing (all businesses require this)

Tasks and timeline to completion of products or service prototype (all businesses)

Acquisition of intellectual property

Operations Plan

Facilities

Business processes

Plan for outsourcing

Manufacturing and distribution

Organization Plan

Philosophy of management and company culture

Legal structure of the company

Organizational chart

Key management

Duties and responsibilities

Marketing Plan

Purpose of marketing plan

Target market

Unique market niche

Business identity

Plan to reach first customer

Financial Plan

Summary of key points and capital requirements

Risk factors and mediation

Break-even analysis and payback period

Narrative assumptions for financial statements

Full set of pro forma financial statements (cash flow, income, balance sheet) for three years

Plan for funding

Growth Plan

Strategy for growth

Resources required

Infrastructure changes

Contingency Plan and Harvest Strategy

Strategies for dealing with deviations from the plan

Strategies for harvesting the wealth created from the business

Timeline to Launch

Graphic: Tasks that will need to be accomplished up to the date of launch of the business in the order of their completion. Also includes milestones of first customer, multiple customer, and multiple products.

Bibliography or Endnotes (footnotes may be substituted)

Appendices (A, B, C, etc.)

Questionnaires, maps, forms, résumés, and the like

FIGURE 10.1

A Sample Executive Summary

Executive Summary

Every day hospitals waste precious resources and are delayed in meeting patient needs due to poor communication between the patient and the care provider. Patient Provider Communications (PPC) specializes in health care communications using hardware and software solutions to provide integrated information technology whereby patients, health care providers, and hospital departments are able to relay information to one another through messaging.

Concept Statement

PPC will revolutionize the methodology of the health care delivery model, enhancing patient provider communications by selling their software-based system to hospitals through established hospital technology providers. The PPC communication system will enable hospitals to address the nursing shortage health care crisis and ever-increasing nursing expenses through efficient workflow operations and collection of communication metrics to guide reallocation of staffing.

The PPC system consists of proprietary software running on a central communications hub, a central display at each nursing station, bedside electronic tablets, as well as pagers issued to staff doctors, nurses, and nurse assistants. The required electronic hardware is all commercially available; however, minor customization may be implemented in later versions of this system.

Value Proposition

Currently, patient communication outflow is through a call light system, which signals nurses with a white light that then beckons nurses to come to the bedside. These communications are not recorded, nor is there a way to predetermine the appropriate staff level to attend to patient requests.

Hospitals will benefit from

- Reduced hospital operating expenses through increased staffing efficiency and utilization and reduction in errors
- Improved patient care through transparent, efficient communications with health care providers and amongst health care providers and departments with timely delivery of care
- Metrics collected on health care communications data and related activities to validate appropriate staffing
- Increased revenues and staffing resources by magnetizing the community, drawing patients and nursing resources to experience higher levels of care

By quantitatively analyzing nursing communication, the PPC system can determine how many nurses and nurse aides are required to fulfill the demands on any given unit. In this manner, administration will be able to more efficiently allocate an expensive resource whose scarcity is a mounting threat to the health care industry today. The nursing staff shortage in the United States has been the driving force behind hospital staff wages growing over 8 percent annually since 2001. Switching one registered nurse with a nurse assistant provides a net savings of $300,000 annually. Currently nursing wages consume 50 to 80 percent of hospital operating expenses. It is estimated that by 2010, more and more hospitals will move into the red due to rising wages for nursing staff.

Management Team

Lance Patak has 16 years of nursing experience with various institutions in southern California, with a majority of his career invested at UCLA Medical Center. He completed his undergraduate degree in nursing with honors and went on to pursue his degree in medicine at the David Geffen School of Medicine at UCLA and masters in business at the Marshall School of Business at USC. Bryan Traughber is currently a graduate fellow in the Clinical Research Center at the National Institutes of Health, working on high-intensity focused ultrasound (HIFU) enhanced drug delivery and gene therapy. Thomas Morphopoulos has 15 years of hardware and software experience in the aerospace and data communications industries.

Industry and Market

The National Institutes of Health (NIH) has recently built a hospital with single patient rooms equipped with bedside tablets that would support the installation of this system. Trials will be conducted at five such institutions, optimizing the academic leadership, feasibility of implementation, innovative culture, and infrastructure already in place to minimize set-up costs. *US News & World Report* has compiled a list

(continued)

of the top 100 most wired hospitals; these institutions would be natural partners for preliminary trials of the PPC system. To increase cooperation with such institutions, Patient Provider Communications will negotiate contracts for continued service in exchange for shared costs, staffing trials, and speed of trial process. This strategy may also increase speed to market by providing an immediate trial to market rollout.

Although the PPC system currently has no direct competitors for this product, several key players in the industry are building service platforms to be used with the patient room tablets. These platforms validate and complement the PPC system, allowing for immediate extendibility. A feasibility analysis has been conducted along with focus groups and individual interviews that examined the institutional need and development of an appropriate technology solution. Two intermediate-sized software technology companies, SeaTec and Orion Health, have already expressed interest in developing and distributing the PPC platform. Either company could sell directly or through one of their alliances, Cardinal Health or McKesson, respectively.

Financials
The base installation will retail for approximately $400,000, which includes nursing station central displays and patient room tablets. Software licensing will begin at $500,000 annually and increase as upgrades demonstrate value-added improvements. Additionally, each bedside tablet will be leased at $200/month; pagers, leased at $20/month with a minimum 1-year service contract valued at $100,000. Based on primary research, initial COGS and service expenses are estimated to be 50 percent of installation and lease revenue, providing average 50 percent gross margin. PPC system pricing is justified by the estimated reduction of at least 1 full-time nurse within each nursing unit at fully loaded cost to the hospital of $350,000 per nurse per year. Capital requirements for development are estimated to be $500,000 and trials would cost an additional $200,000. The development for this system should take approximately 1 year followed by trials the following year. Revenue will begin in year two with the aim to capture a minimum of 50 hospitals followed by growth of 150 percent over the following two years.

Initial capital requirements to develop a beta product by the end of Q2 are projected at $750,000. Initial financing will be in the form of convertible notes. By Q3, the company plans to raise an A Round of $3,000,000 following beta testing prior to launching five hospital trials throughout the United States, targeting key leading institutions. PPC will require additional financing of $3,000,000 during Q1 of year 2 to support up-scaling of sales and marketing staff. PPC will also seek an equity partner with an IT consulting firm, such as Accenx Technologies.

Source: Based on a business plan created by Lance Patak and Thomas Morphopoulous for the USC Business Plan Competition, April 2007.

hired, or by a strategic partner. Chapter 8 explores the building of a founding team. This section also elaborates on the general management plan for the company—how the company will be structured. It includes such things as the philosophy of management and company culture, the legal structure, key management, compensation, and key policies. The issues that need to be addressed in the organization plan are dealt with in Chapter 13.

Industry/Market Analysis
Recall that the industry is the environment in which the new business will operate. This section discusses the nature of the industry including life-cycle stage, defining characteristics, demographics, opinion leaders, and trends and patterns of change. A more detailed discussion of performing an industry analysis is found in Chapter 6. The section also speaks to the markets the entrepreneur will serve. A market is defined by a set of customers; therefore, this section addresses the size of the market, the customer profile, and the level of demand expected. It is arguably the most crucial section of the business plan because it should provide a persuasive argument that there is a market of sufficient size and

TABLE 10.2

Product Development
Milestones

1. Completion of concept and product testing to determine whether there is a market
2. Completion of physical prototype
3. First financing from outside sources (investors and/or bank financing), normally to fund taking the initial prototype to market-ready product
4. Completion of initial plant tests (pilot or beta test): testing the manufacturing capability and producing a run of the product. This is true even if the manufacturing activity is outsourced.
5. Market testing: conducting a limited sale of the product to potential customers to gauge response and refine demand
6. Production start-up for product launch
7. Bellwether sale (first substantial sale to the primary customer)
8. First competitive action in the form of a response to the new product
9. First redesign or redirection in response to the market
10. First significant price change in response to the market

demand to interest the entrepreneur and any investors. An in-depth discussion of market research can be found in Chapter 6.

Product/Service Plan

This section provides more detail about the product or service being offered by the business. A plan for prototyping the product/service and its associated tasks and timeline gives the reader a sense of the timing of product/service development. Block and MacMillan suggest milestone planning, a process that includes ten milestones, or performance points at which the entrepreneur must make choices that will have a significant impact on the success of the company.[7] See Table 10.2 for these milestones. Note that although this table focuses on products, many of these milestones are also appropriate for service development. In addition, if a new technology is being offered, then a technology assessment will be included in this section that describes the nature of the technology, the status of the development, associated costs, and the status of the acquisition of intellectual property such as patents. The product/service plan is detailed in Chapter 7.

Operations or Organization Plan

This section of the business plan contains a detailed description of the business operations, including those processes that the new venture will own and undertake in-house, such as assembly, and those that will be outsourced to a strategic partner, such as manufacturing. A major portion of this section explains how the business will operate, where it will get its raw materials, how a product will be manufactured and/or assembled, and what type and quantity of labor will be required to operate the business. Producing products and services is discussed in detail in Chapter 14. This section also discusses the legal form of organization that the venture will take, whether that be sole proprietorship, partnership, LLC, or corporation. Legal forms are discussed in Chapter 11.

Marketing Plan

The marketing plan is something quite distinct from market analysis. Market analysis gives the entrepreneur the information about the customer and market that will be used to create a marketing plan. The marketing plan, by contrast, is the strategy for communicating the company's message, developing awareness of the product or service and enticing the customer to purchase. The marketing plan includes a discussion of the plan's purpose, the market niche, the business's identity, tools that will be used to reach the customer, a media plan for specific marketing tools, and a marketing budget. The marketing plan is found in Chapter 15.

Financial Plan

The financial plan begins with a summary of the key numbers for the business: time to positive cash flow, break-even, sales volume, and capital requirements to launch the business. In essence, it presents a snapshot of the entrepreneur's predictions for the immediate future of the business. Generally, these forecasts are in the form of a complete set of pro forma financial statements broken out by month in the first year or two, and then annually for the next two to three years. This section demonstrates the financial viability of the venture and indicates the assumptions made by the entrepreneur in doing the forecasts. It is designed to show that all the claims about the product, sales, marketing strategy, and operational strategy can work financially to create a business that can survive and grow over the long term.

The dynamic nature of markets today makes it almost impossible to project out three to five years with any degree of certainty—hence, the need and importance of having detailed financial assumptions that explain the rationale for the numbers. Also important is sensitivity analysis to identify triggers that may change the financial forecasts and affect the business negatively. A complete discussion of the financial plan appears in Chapter 9.

Growth Plan

The growth plan discusses how the entrepreneur plans to take the business from start-up through various stages of growth and outlines the strategy that will be used to ensure that the business continues to grow over its life. This may mean looking at new products and services or acquiring other businesses. It is important that this section reassure an investor or lender that the company has a future. Growth is covered in Chapter 18.

Contingency Plan and Harvest Strategy

The contingency plan is simply a way of recognizing that sometimes, even "the best laid plans" don't work the way they were intended to work. It presents potential risk scenarios, usually dealing with situations such as unexpected high or low growth or changing economic conditions, and then, for each situation, suggests a plan to minimize the impact on the new business. By contrast, the harvest or exit strategy is the plan for capturing the wealth of the business for the entrepreneur and any investors. It typically involves a liquidity event, such as an initial public offering, a merger, or a sale, among other options. The contingency plan and harvest strategy are discussed in Chapter 19.

It is not normally a good idea to discuss deal structure in the business plan. Entrepreneurs rarely value their businesses correctly—typically, they are far too optimistic. Putting such optimistic statements into the business plan only alerts an investor or other interested party that the entrepreneur is naïve. Entrepreneurs who seek investment capital will find that it is a process that evolves over many meetings with potential investors and the ultimate deal structure will be reflected in a term sheet. Deal structure is discussed further in Chapter 17.

Timeline to Launch

The business plan should contain a graphic that depicts the timeline to launch and should include critical milestones that take the business from its current status to first customer, multiple customers, and multiple products.

Appendices

Appendices are the appropriate place to put items that support the entrepreneur's claims in the main body of the report—things like résumés, calculations, surveys, and so forth. A good rule of thumb is not to put in the appendix anything that it is vital for a reader to see. Refer to appendix entries at the points in the body of the report where they are relevant.

Effectively Organizing the Business Plan

The outline discussed previously gives a common structure for the body of the business plan. Although there are no hard and fast rules about all the items to include in a business plan and where to put them, most business plans contain the items shown in Table 10.3.

MISTAKES IN DEVELOPING THE BUSINESS PLAN

Developing an effective business plan involves more than merely inserting information or data into the plan in an organized fashion. A persuasive plan requires that the entrepreneur weave a compelling story with supporting evidence so

TABLE 10.3

Organizing the Business Plan

Cover Page	Professional, attractive, and conveys the nature of the business
	Name of business, address, key contact person, and the words *Business Plan*
	Number the plan and include a confidentiality statement.
Executive Summary	Contains all the critical points from the business plan in two pages
Body of the Plan	Major sections contained in the business plan outline: concept, management team, industry/market, product/service plan, marketing plan, operations plan, financial plan, growth plan, contingency and harvest plan
The Appendices	Supporting documents: financial spreadsheets, assumptions, media plan, résumés of management team, letters of intent, evidence of intellectual property, etc.

that the reader can reasonably conclude that the business is viable. Unfortunately, many entrepreneurs make some common mistakes that could potentially cost them an investor or other interested party. For example, it is not uncommon for entrepreneurs to project rapid growth that requires capabilities beyond those of the founding team, such as rapidly increasing demand, or sales doubling or tripling on an annual basis in the first few years. Entrepreneurs believe this will be very attractive to investors, but what they don't realize is that there is no evidence in the business plan that the founding team can manage and control this type of growth, which can cause great concern on the part of the investors who frequently have seen a business fail during rapid growth because management didn't have the systems in place to deal with it. It is far better to project controlled growth and have a plan for bringing on the necessary personnel when the company is ready for more rapid growth. The other danger in projecting too high a level of success is that doing so increases the chances that the new venture will not be able to live up to the projections; consequently, it is better to project more conservatively and try to exceed those projections.

Another common mistake is the entrepreneur who envisions a three-ring circus but only has one ringleader. Many entrepreneurs pride themselves on being generalists, claiming to have expertise in all the functional areas of the new venture. What they really have is general knowledge of all the functional areas and a real expertise in perhaps only one area. Investors are very nervous about relying on solo entrepreneurs to lead world-class ventures. They much prefer a team of founders with at least one person specializing in each of the functional areas.[8]

Reporting performance that exceeds industry averages in some or all areas of the business is a serious red flag for investors. Although it is possible for a new venture to exceed industry averages in a particular area, it is not likely. Most averages, such as those for receivables turnover, manufacturing costs, and bad debt losses, have come about as a result of economies of scale, which the new venture is not likely to achieve for some time. An entrepreneurial business should report performance measures at or slightly below industry averages, with a credible plan for exceeding those averages at some time in the future.

Entrepreneurs often make the mistake of employing price as a market strategy for a product or service. Using price as a strategy suffers from the same problem as projecting performance above industry averages. It is rarely possible for a new venture with a product or service that currently exists in the marketplace to enter on the basis of a lower price than that of its competitors. Established companies have achieved economies of scale that the new venture usually cannot duplicate; moreover, they can no doubt easily match the price set by a new entrant into the market.

One of the biggest mistakes that entrepreneurs make is not investing capital in their own businesses. Investors are more comfortable investing in a new venture where the entrepreneur has contributed a significant amount of the start-up capital. That signals to the investors a level of commitment necessary to achieve the goals of the company and gives the investors confidence that the entrepreneur will not easily walk away from the venture. Table 10.4 contains a business plan checklist that can be used to help avoid some of these mistakes.

TABLE 10.4 Business Plan Checklist	1. Does the executive summary grab the reader's attention and highlight the major points of the business plan?
	2. Does the business concept section clearly describe the purpose of the business, the customer, the value proposition, and the distribution channel and convey a compelling story?
	3. Do the industry and market analyses support acceptance and demand for the business concept in the marketplace and define a first customer in depth?
	4. Does the management team plan persuade the reader that the team could successfully implement the business concept? Does it assure the reader that an effective infrastructure is in place to facilitate the goals and operations of the company?
	5. Does the product/service plan clearly provide details on the status of the product, the timeline for completion, and the intellectual property that will be acquired?
	6. Does the operations plan prove that the product or service could be produced and distributed efficiently and effectively?
	7. Does the marketing plan successfully demonstrate how the company will create customer awareness in the target market and deliver the benefit to the customer?
	8. Does the financial plan convince the reader that the business model is sustainable—that it will provide a superior return on investment for the investor, and sufficient cash flow to repay loans to potential lenders?
	9. Does the growth plan convince the reader that the company has long-term growth potential and spin-off products and services?
	10. Does the contingency and exit strategy plan convince the reader that the risk associated with this venture can be mediated? Is there an exit strategy in place for investors?

Successfully Presenting the Business Plan

If the entrepreneur is seeking outside investment capital, it is not uncommon to be asked to do a pitch or presentation of the business concept, highlighting the key points of the business plan. Usually this occurs after the potential funders have read the executive summary and perhaps done a cursory reading of the complete business plan. In any case, they feel it is worth their time to hear from the entrepreneur and the founding team to judge whether they measure up to expectations.

The presentation of the business plan should answer the fundamental questions discussed in the section on components of the business plan. The presentation itself should take less than half an hour—usually about 15–20 minutes, though questions and discussion will probably follow. The pitch should catch the audience's attention in the first 30 seconds. This is usually accomplished by conveying the compelling story of the pain or problem in the market and how the new venture will cure or solve the pain. During the pitch, standing without using a podium enables a better command of the situation, enhances rapport with the audience, and makes it easier to use gestures and visual aids. The entrepreneur should feel free to move around (but no pacing), because moving helps reduce stress and livens up the presentation. The entrepreneur should maintain eye contact with everyone and talk to the audience, not over their heads to the back of the room. This technique only works in large auditoriums. Visual aids, such as colorful PowerPoint slides or overheads, keep the presentation on track and focused on key points. The entrepreneur should be careful, however, not to dazzle the audience with too many slides and animations, or listeners may find themselves more interested in the rhythm of the slides' motion than in what the entrepreneur is attempting to convey. The slides should be kept simple (no more than five lines per slide), be big enough to read, and be professional-looking. The technology (overhead projector, PowerPoint projector, or the like) should be tested *before* the presentation to be sure it's working correctly. Typically, the CEO and chief technical person will do the pitch, although other members of the team may be drawn in during the question and answer period. If there is a service or product involved, a live demonstration helps to generate excitement about the concept. Most important, the team should practice the pitch in advance for a small group of friends or colleagues who can critique it. Alternatively, a practice session can be videotaped so that the founding team can critique themselves.

ANSWERING QUESTIONS

When the founding team has successfully made it through the pitch, it has cleared the first hurdle. The second hurdle, however, is harder: answering questions from investors. One thing to remember about investors is that they generally like to ask questions to which they already know the answers; this is a test to see whether the founding team knows what it's talking about. Furthermore, investors often ask questions that either require an impossibly precise answer or are so broad that it's hard to tell what they are looking for. Another type of question typically asked is "What are the implications of . . . ?" With this question, investors are looking for an answer that addresses their needs and concerns relative to the request for capital. Finally, the type of question that poses the most problems for the founding team is the inordinately complex one that contains several underlying assumptions. For example, "If I were to analyze your new venture in terms of its market share before and after this potential investment, how would the market strategy have changed and how much of the budget should be allotted to changing that strategy?"

The first thing an entrepreneur should do when faced with such questions is to ask that the question be repeated, to ensure that she hasn't missed anything or made an incorrect assumption. Alternatively, the entrepreneur can restate the question and confirm that she has understood it correctly. She can then take a few seconds to formulate an answer. With the more complicated question, the entrepreneur may feel comfortable answering only part of it; for example, the entrepreneur may have evidence that could be presented to support a change in market share as a result of the capital infusion. On the other hand, it is critical not to commit the venture to any course of action or any budget amount without having had time to consider it further and gather more facts. Saying this to the investors in response to the question will no doubt gain the entrepreneur a measure of respect for having demonstrated that she doesn't make important decisions precipitously, without considering all the facts.

If investors ask a factual question to which the entrepreneur does not know the answer (usually, such queries are tangential to the business plan and are asked to see how the entrepreneur will respond), the entrepreneur should admit that he doesn't have that answer off the top of his head but will be happy to find it after the meeting is over and get back to the questioner. If the pitch or anything the team has proposed is criticized by investors (a likely possibility), the entrepreneur should be careful not to be defensive or to turn the criticism in any way on the audience.

Preparing and presenting the business plan is the culmination of months of work. The business plan represents the heart and soul of the new venture, and if it has been researched thoroughly and written well, it can enhance the chances of starting a successful high-growth venture. Entrepreneurs should understand, however, that a business plan is not just for those starting new businesses, but for growing companies as well. The business plan enables benchmarking progress toward company goals. It establishes the purpose, values, and goals of the company that will guide its decision making throughout its life. No entrepreneur plans to fail, but many fail to plan and thus end up reacting to situations in the environment instead of proactively dealing with changes.

Undertaking a business plan is certainly a daunting task, but it is an important exercise that helps an entrepreneur understand more clearly every aspect of the new venture and how all the pieces fit together. Even successful entrepreneurs who have started businesses without a written plan have had to write business plans when they needed growth capital or a credit line from the bank. Those starting high-growth global ventures often find that they need outside capital and resources fairly quickly, so a business plan is essential. A sample business plan can be found on the website. Be aware that no business plan is perfect; sample plans merely guides to stimulate discussion about effective and ineffective plans. What works in one type of plan may not work in another. The important thing to remember is that the business plan is a living document that will no doubt undergo numerous changes.

New Venture Checklist

Have you:

☐ Determined the conditions under which you are willing to go forward?

☐ Gathered all the information necessary to complete the business plan?

☐ Determined the focus of the plan and who the potential readers are?

☐ Developed a set of tasks and a timeline for completing the business plan?

☐ Decided on the presentation format for the business plan?

Issues to Consider

1. Why is the business planning process an excellent exercise for any entrepreneur contemplating the start-up of a new venture?
2. What is the difference between a feasibility study and a business plan?
3. Why might it be better to start the business after completing the feasibility study and before completing a business plan?
4. How might the business plan change if the reader were an investor versus a potential management hire?
5. What are three key elements of a successful business plan pitch?

Experiencing Entrepreneurship

1. Interview someone who invests in small businesses about what he or she looks for in a business plan. On the basis of your discussion, what will you need to remember when you write your business plan?

2. Go to http://www.bplans.com and select a business plan to review. Using the guidelines for an effective plan given in this chapter, evaluate the plan in three to five pages. What are its strengths and weaknesses? How can it be improved?

Relevant Case Studies

Case 1 Overnite Express, p. 438
Case 6 The Crowne Inn, p. 467

Case 9 Command Audio, p. 485

## Chapter 11

CHOOSING THE LEGAL FORM OF ORGANIZATION

"It will not injure you to know enough of law to keep out of it."

—The Old Farmer's Almanac (1851)

LEARNING OBJECTIVES

▶ Distinguish between sole proprietorships and partnerships.

▶ Discuss the corporate form and its advantages and disadvantages.

▶ Explain the limited liability company.

▶ Define the nonprofit corporation.

▶ Make a decision about which legal form to use for which purpose.

▶ Discuss how a business entity can evolve from one legal form to another.

Profile 11.1 WHICH FORM IS BEST?

Making a decision about the best legal form for your business is no longer a simple task; there are more choices than ever before. Yet many new business owners are making the decision without adequate expert advice. Mark Kalish is the co-owner and vice president of EnviroTech Coating Systems, Inc., of Eau Claire, Wisconsin. His company paints products ranging from motorcycles to musical instruments using an electrostatic process known as powder coating. In trying to determine which legal form made sense, Kalish and his business partner, John Berthold, focused on three key issues: legal liability, tax ramifications, and cost of creation. Kalish and his partner didn't want (and couldn't afford) the personal liability for any potential losses or problems arising from the operation of the business. This meant that they could not consider the sole proprietor and partnership forms, both of which entail personal liability for the owner.

The next consideration was the owners' desire to minimize tax liability. Corporations have more options in this regard but are also subject to "double taxation"; that is, income is taxed first at the corporate level and again when dividends are distributed. However, Kalish learned that his company might benefit from the limited liability company (LLC) form of organization, which passes profits and losses through to the owner to be taxed at the personal income tax rate. In addition, the losses that businesses typically face in the early years can be used to reduce the owners' personal tax liability. The next issue to consider was the cost of forming and maintaining the chosen form. Kalish learned about the high cost, in time and money, of record keeping and paperwork associated with a corporation, as well as the higher initial costs of incorporating. His conclusion was that the sole proprietorship was the best option in terms of cost, assuming that he had a substantial umbrella insurance policy for protection against liability. But Kalish could not choose that option because he had intentions of growing the business by issuing and selling additional shares of stock. The corporate form makes this relatively easy to do, as does the LLC with its membership interests. He also wanted to ensure that the business survived his death, and both the corporation and the LLC would do that. Kalish finally settled on the corporate form.

Sources: Laura Tiffany, "Choose Your Business Structure," Entrepreneur.com (March 19, 2001); and Envirotech Coating Systems, Inc., http://www.envirotechcoating.com, accessed August 26, 2007.

The choice of legal structure is one of the most important decisions to be made because it will affect every aspect of the business, including tax planning and the cost of maintaining the legal structure. For example, if a business entails any degree of risk, such as product liability, then choosing a legal form that protects the entrepreneur's personal assets from being attached as the result of a lawsuit is just as important as carrying the appropriate insurance. The decision about the legal form of the business should reflect careful consideration about the type of business and the entrepreneur's personal goals for that business, and it should always be made under the guidance of a qualified attorney. In order to make an informed decision about the legal form of the business, it is imperative to understand all the risks and benefits associated with the chosen form. Figure 11.1 depicts an overview of the various legal forms available to entrepreneurs according to the level of risk, with the sole proprietorship carrying the most risk.

FIGURE 11.1

Legal Forms of Organization

Making the Decision About Legal Form

Prior to making the decision on which type of legal form to choose, seven very important questions should be asked.

1. Does the founding team have all the skills needed to run this venture?
2. Do the founders have the capital required to start the business alone or must they raise it through cash or credit?
3. Will the founders be able to run the business and cover living expenses for the first year?
4. Are the founders willing and able to assume personal liability for any claims against the business?
5. Do the founders wish to have complete control over the operations of the business?
6. Do the founders expect to have initial losses or will the business be profitable almost from the beginning?
7. Do the founders expect to sell the business some day?

The answers to these questions will narrow the choices by eliminating legal forms that do not facilitate the achievement of the outcomes in these seven questions, but it is always wise to get the advice of an attorney and/or accountant. For example, if the new venture is expected to have initial losses in the first year due to product development or other large start-up costs (question 6), a form that allows those losses to pass through to be taxed at the owner's personal income rate would be advantageous. Since the company is not yet generating income, the entrepreneur will be able to shelter other personal income from a tax liability. Sole proprietorships, partnerships, S-corporations, and limited liability companies all permit pass-through earnings and losses, but S-corporations and LLCs offer more protection from liability. The next sections review the various legal forms of organization and their advantages and disadvantages.

Sole Proprietorships and Partnerships

All businesses operate under one of four broad legal structures—sole proprietorship, partnership, limited liability company, or corporation. Because the legal structure of a new venture has both legal and tax ramifications for the entrepreneur and any investors, entrepreneurs must carefully consider the advantages and disadvantages of each form. It is also quite possible that a business may decide to change its legal form sometime during its lifetime, usually for financial, tax, or liability reasons. These situations are discussed as each legal form is examined. Table 11.1 presents a summary comparison chart of all the structures.

SOLE PROPRIETORSHIP

More than 76 percent of all businesses in the United States are sole proprietorships, probably because the sole proprietorship is the easiest form to create. For the tax year 2005, there were 21.5 million tax returns that reported sole proprietor income that was non-farm in nature.[1] In a sole proprietorship, the owner is the only person responsible for the activities of the business and, therefore, is the only one to enjoy the profits and suffer the losses.

To operate as a sole proprietor requires very little—only a DBA, and not even that if the entrepreneur uses his or her name as the name for the business. In other words, a sole proprietorship called Jennifer Brooks Corporate Consultants does not require a DBA if the entrepreneur's name is Jennifer Brooks, but a sole proprietorship called Corporate Consultants does. A DBA, or Certificate of Doing Business Under an Assumed Name, can be obtained by filing an application with the appropriate local government agency. The certificate, sometimes referred to as a "fictitious business name statement," ensures that this is the only business in the area (usually a county) that is using the name the entrepreneur has chosen and provides a public record of business ownership for liability purposes.

Advantages of a Sole Proprietorship

A sole proprietorship has several advantages. First, it is easy and inexpensive to create. It gives the owner 100 percent of the company and 100 percent of the profits and losses. It also gives the owner complete authority to make decisions about the direction of the business. In addition, the income from the business is taxed only once, at the owner's personal income tax rate, and there are no major reporting requirements such as those imposed on corporations.

Disadvantages

There are, however, some distinct disadvantages that deserve serious consideration. The sole proprietor has unlimited liability for all claims against the business; that is, any debts incurred or judgments must be paid from the

TABLE 11.1 Comparison of Legal Forms

Issues	Sole Proprietorship	Partnership	Business Form Limited Liability Company	Subchapter S-Corporation	C-Corporation
Number of Owners	One	No limit	No limit. Most states require a minimum of two members.	100 shareholders or fewer	No limit on shareholders
Start-Up Costs	Filing fees for DBA and business license	Filing fees for DBA; attorney fees for partnership agreement	Attorney fees for organization, documents; filing fees	Attorney fees for incorporation; filing fees	Attorney fees for incorporation documents; filing fees
Liability	Owner liable for all claims against business, but with insurance can overcome liability	General partners liable for all claims; limited partners liable only to amount of investment	Members liable as in partnerships	Shareholders liable to amount invested	Shareholders liable to amount invested; officers may be personally liable
Taxation	Pass-through; taxed at individual level	Pass-through; taxed at individual level	Pass-through; taxed at individual level	Pass-through; taxed at individual level	Tax-paying entity; taxed on corporate income
Continuity of Life of Business	Dissolution on the death of the owner	Dissolution on the death or separation of a partner, unless otherwise specified in the agreement; not so in the case of limited partners	Most states allow perpetual existence. Unless otherwise stated in the Articles of Organization, existence terminates on death or withdrawal of any member.	Perpetual existence	Continuity of Life
Transferability of Interest	Owner free to sell; assets transferred to estate upon death with valid will	General partner requires consent of other generals to sell interest; limited partners' ability to transfer is subject to agreement	Permission of majority of members is required for any member to transfer interest	Shareholders free to sell unless restricted by agreement	Shareholders free to sell unless restricted by agreement
Distribution of Profits	Profits go to owner	Profits shared based on partnership agreement	Profits shared based on member agreement	Paid to shareholders as dividends according to agreement and shareholder status	Paid to shareholders as dividends according to agreement and shareholder status
Management Control	Owner has full control	Absent an agreement to the contrary, partners have equal voting rights	Rests with management committee	Rests with the board of directors appointed by the shareholders	Rests with the board of directors appointed by the shareholders

owner's assets. Therefore, the sole proprietor puts at risk his or her home, bank accounts, and any other assets. In today's litigious environment, exposure to lawsuits is substantial. To help mitigate this liability, a sole proprietor should obtain business liability insurance, including "errors and omissions coverage," which protects against unintentional negligence such as disseminating incorrect information in a company advertisement. Another disadvantage is that it is more difficult for a sole proprietorship to raise debt capital, because often the owner's financial statement does not qualify for the amount needed. The sole proprietor usually needs to rely on his or her skills alone to manage the business. Of course, employees with specific skills can be hired to complement those of the owner. Another complication associated with a sole proprietorship is that the business's ability to survive is dependent on the owner; therefore, the death or incapacitation of the owner can be catastrophic for the business.

Often small businesses such as restaurants, boutiques, and consulting businesses are run as sole proprietorships. This is not to say that a high-growth venture cannot be started as a sole proprietorship—many are—but it will in all likelihood not remain a sole proprietorship for long, because the entrepreneur will typically want the protections and prestige that organizing as a corporation affords.

Patti Glick was a nurse by trade but knew that most of all she wanted to balance being a mom and raising her kids with a career that she enjoyed. In her practice as a nurse, Glick discovered that she had great interest in podiatry and realized that for many people, feet were simply an afterthought. Hoping to educate and help people in her Silicon Valley community take better care of their feet, Glick envisioned starting a business that would enable her to be home when her children arrived from school. With the full support of her family, Glick started Foot Nurse (http://www.footnurse.com), a business dedicated to helping people understand foot care, protection, safety, and health. In her first year as a sole proprietor, she conducted 24 paid presentations for major companies such as Cisco and PG&E. Demand grew as companies saw her presentations as an important part of their wellness programs, and in her second year she did 46 presentations. Now she is finding ways to leverage her new-found celebrity with foot-care products and a website. She still prefers the life of a soloist; however, she is now offering in-clinic screenings at the offices of a podiatry group.[2]

PARTNERSHIP

When two or more people agree to share the assets, liabilities, and profits of a business, the legal structure is termed a partnership. The partnership form is an improvement over the sole proprietorship from the standpoint that the business can draw on the skills, knowledge, and financial resources of more than one person. This is an advantage not only in operating the business but also in seeking bank loans. Like the sole proprietorship, however, the partnership requires a DBA when the last names of the partners are not used in naming the business.

Professionals such as lawyers, doctors, and accountants frequently employ this legal structure.

In terms of its treatment of income, expenses, and taxes, a partnership is essentially a sole proprietorship consisting of more than one person. However, where liability is concerned, there is a significant difference. In a partnership, each partner is liable for the obligations that any other partner incurs in the course of doing business. For example, if one partner signs a contract with a supplier in the name of the partnership, the other partners are also bound by the terms of the contract. This is known as the doctrine of ostensible authority. Creditors of an individual partner, on the other hand, can attach only the assets of that individual partner, including his or her interest in the partnership.

Partners also have specific property rights. For example, unless otherwise stated in the partnership agreement, each partner owns and has use of the property acquired by the partnership. Each partner has a right to share in the profits and losses, and each may participate in the management of the partnership. Furthermore, all choices related to elections such as depreciation and accounting method are made at the partnership level and apply to all partners.

Advantages

Partnerships have all the advantages of sole proprietorships plus the added advantage of sharing the risk of doing business. Partnerships enjoy the clout of more than one partner and, therefore, more than one financial statement. Partners can also share ideas, expertise, and decision making. Financially, partnerships enjoy pass-through earnings and losses to the individual partners, to be taxed at their personal tax rates.

Disadvantages

Partnerships also suffer from several disadvantages that entrepreneurs should consider carefully before choosing this form. Partners are personally liable for all business debts and obligations of the partnership, even when individual partners bind the partnership to a contract or other business deal. Unless otherwise stated in the partnership agreement, the partnership dissolves when a partner either leaves or dies. And finally, individual partners can be sued for the full amount of any partnership debt. If that happens, the partner who is sued, and loses, must then sue the other partners to recover their shares of the debt.[3]

Partnership Agreement

Although the law does not require it, it is extremely wise for a partnership to draw up a written partnership agreement, based on the Uniform Partnership Act, that spells out business responsibilities, profit sharing, and transfer of interest. This is advisable because partnerships are inherently fraught with problems that arise from the different personalities and goals of the people involved. A written document executed at the beginning of the partnership will mitigate eventual disagreements and provide for an orderly dissolution should irreconcilable differences arise. Many partnerships have minimized conflict by assigning specific responsibilities to each of the partners and detailing them in the partnership agreement. Additional issues arise when one or more of the partners in a partnership leaves, either voluntarily or through death. To protect the remaining partners, the partnership should have in place a buy-sell agreement and "key-person" life insurance.

A buy-sell agreement is a binding contract between the partners. It contains three primary clauses that govern the following issues:[4]

1. Who is entitled to purchase a departing partner's share of the business? May only another partner do so, or is an outsider permitted to buy in?

2. What events can trigger a buyout? Typically, those events include a death, disability, or other form of incapacity; a divorce; or an offer from the outside to buy the partner out.

3. What price will be paid for the partner's interest?

Having this formula in place from the beginning prevents disagreements and legal battles with the departing partner or with the estate of a deceased partner.

It is unfortunate that many entrepreneurs fail to take the precaution of creating a partnership agreement with a buy-sell clause. The consequences can be critical for the business. For example, say one partner dies, and the partnership, absent a buy-sell agreement, is forced to work with the spouse or a family member of the deceased, who may not be qualified to run the business. Furthermore, with no partnership agreement, one partner can sell his or her interest to a stranger without the consent of the other partners, so it is critically important to have such an agreement.

"Key-person" life insurance is a policy on the life of principal members of the partnership, usually the senior partners. Upon the death of a partner, the insurance proceeds can be used to keep the business going or to buy out the deceased partner's interest under a buy-sell agreement. For more protection from liability than a partnership affords, organizing the business as a corporation or a limited liability company should be considered.

Types of Partnerships

There are two types of partnerships: general and limited. In a general partnership, all the partners assume unlimited personal liability and responsibility for management of the business. In a limited partnership, by contrast, the general partners have unlimited liability, and they seek investors whose liability is limited to their monetary investment; that is, if such a limited partner invests $25,000 in the business, the most he or she can lose if the business fails is $25,000. It is important to note, however, that limited partners have no say in the management of the business. In fact, they are restricted by law from imposing their will on the business. The penalty for participating in the management of the business is the loss of their limited liability status. Other types of partnerships include (1) secret partners, who are active but not publicly known; (2) silent partners, who typically provide capital but do not actively participate in the management of the business; and (3) dormant partners, who are generally not known publicly and are not active, but still share in the profits and losses of the partnership.

Global Insights

CHINA ESPOUSING NEW FORMS OF BUSINESS OWNERSHIP

Since the 1970s, the Chinese economy has experienced exceptional growth, despite the fact that its transition from a centrally directed to an open market economy has been relatively slow. China made a conscious decision to reform its state-owned enterprises gradually at the same time as it encouraged the development and growth of other forms of ownership, such as private, cooperative, and joint ventures. Today much of the success that China has experienced in the marketplace has been due to the rapid growth of entrepreneurial firms that were privately owned and market-driven. In China there are four types of entrepreneurial ventures: (1) state-owned businesses; (2) stock companies, which are businesses that were previously state-owned but now a major percentage of ownership shares are held by private individuals; (3) private enterprises; and (4) foreign-owned ventures, which can be wholly owned by a foreign company or as a joint venture with a Chinese firm.

To continue its annual growth rate of approximately 9 percent, obstacles that the government has placed in the path of entrepreneurial ventures will need to be removed. These enterprises must be free to make production and business decisions, to set prices, market products, purchase materials, export and import, make investments, form partnerships, and set wages and bonuses, among many other activities common in a free enterprise system. In addition, the government must encourage foreign investment and increase the availability of low-cost borrowing and venture capital.

There is a long road ahead for China to become an efficient market economy where private ownership in the form of entrepreneurial firms drives technological change and economic growth and productivity. But the potential for positive effects domestically—and for the rest of the world—is there.

Source: V. Hu, "The Chinese Economic Reform and Chinese Entrepreneurship," *Jornada d'Economia caixaManresa l'esperit emprenedor* (2005), http://unpan1.un.org/intradoc/groups/public/documents/APCITY/UNPAN023535.pdf; and A.M. Zapalska and W. Edwards, "Chinese Entrepreneurship in a Cultural and Economic Perspective," *Journal of Small Business Management,* 39(3) (2001): 286.

Any partnership should have an agreement to describe the structure of the partnership, who is entitled to what, and what happens if the partners disagree or leave the partnership. Table 11.2 presents some of the critical issues that should be addressed in the agreement. Because this is a legally binding contract, it should be reviewed by a qualified attorney.

TABLE 11.2	Critical Issues to Address with an Attorney Present
Structuring an Effective Partnership Agreement	• The legal name of the partnership • The nature of the business • The duration of the partnership • Contributions of the partners • Sales, loans, and leases to the partnership • Withdrawals and salaries • Responsibility and authority of the partners • Dissolution of the partnership • Arbitration

Corporation

Only about 20 percent of all U.S. businesses are corporations, but they account for 87 percent of all sales transactions. A corporation is different from the preceding two forms in that it is a legal entity in and of itself. The U.S. Supreme Court has defined the corporation as "an artificial being, invisible, intangible, and existing only in contemplation of the law." It is chartered or registered by a state and can survive the death of the owner(s) or their separation from the business. Therefore, it can sue, be sued, acquire and sell real property, and lend money. The owners of the corporation are its shareholders, who invest capital in the corporation in exchange for shares of ownership. Like limited partners, shareholders are not liable for the debts of the corporation and can lose only the money they have invested.

Most new businesses form what is known as a closely held corporation; that is, the corporate stock is owned privately by a few individuals and is not traded publicly on a securities exchange such as the New York Stock Exchange. This chapter will focus on such private corporations. The issue of "going public" typically arises after the business is established and the entrepreneur wants to raise substantial capital for growth by issuing stock (shares of ownership in the corporation) through an initial public offering (IPO). The IPO and public corporations in general are the subject of Chapter 17.

A corporation is created by filing a certificate of incorporation with the state in which the company will do business and issue stock. This is called a domestic corporation. A foreign corporation, by contrast, is one that is chartered in a state other than in the one in which it will do business. A corporation requires the establishment of a board of directors, which meets periodically to make strategic policy decisions for the business. The regular documentation of these meetings is crucial to maintaining the corporation's limited liability status. The board also hires the officers who will run the business on a day-to-day basis.

There are two corporate forms from which to choose: the C-corporation and the S-corporation. Their purpose and advantages and disadvantages are discussed in the next sections.

C-CORPORATION

It would be difficult to claim that the Pennsylvania Railroad Corporation of the 1950s resembles in any way the General Electric Corporation of today, let alone the Business.com Corporation operating on the Internet. Even the most traditional of legal forms—the corporation—has evolved over time. Yet it remains the most commonly chosen legal structure for a growing company that seeks outside capital in the form of equity or debt.

Advantages

The C-corporation offers several important advantages. It enjoys limited liability in that its owners are liable for its debts and obligations only to the limit of their investment. The only exception to this protection is payroll taxes that may have been withheld from employees' paychecks but not paid to the Internal Revenue Service. Capital can be raised through the sale of stock up to the amount authorized in the corporate charter; however, the sale of stock is heavily regulated by federal and state governments. A corporation can create different classes of stock to meet the various needs of its investors. For example, it may issue nonvoting preferred stock to conservative investors who, in the event that the corporation must liquidate its assets, will be first in line to recoup their investment. Common stock is more risky, because its holders are paid only after the preferred stockholders. Common stockholders are, however, entitled to vote at shareholders' meetings and to divide the profits remaining after the preferred holders are paid their dividends, assuming that these profits are not retained by the corporation to fund growth.

Ownership in a corporation is easily transferred. This is at once an advantage and a disadvantage, because entrepreneurs will want to be careful, particularly in the start-up phase, to ensure that stock does not land in the hands of undesirable parties such as competitors. This problem is normally handled through a buy-sell clause in the shareholder's agreement that states that stock must first be offered to the corporation at a specified price before being offered to someone outside the corporation. Most entrepreneurs restrict the sale of their stock so that they can control who holds an ownership interest in the company.

Because it is a legal entity, the corporation can enter into contracts, sue, and be sued without the signature of the owners. In a start-up or young company, however, bankers, creditors, and the like generally require that majority shareholders or officers personally guarantee loans to ensure that the lender is protected against the potential failure of the corporation by having the ability to pursue the assets of the owners. Personal guarantees should be avoided wherever possible, but the reality is that a young corporation has few assets, so its owners may not be able to avoid having to personally guarantee loans.

Corporations typically enjoy more status and deference in business circles than do other legal forms, principally because they are a legal entity that cannot be destroyed by the death of one—or even all—of the principal shareholders. Moreover, to enter the public equity markets, a business must be incorporated, so it will be subjected to greater scrutiny from governmental agencies. The reason for this scrutiny is the fact that the assets of the corporation are separate from the assets of the individual owner/shareholders. Therefore, the owners may take risks that they wouldn't take with their personal assets. Corporations can also take advantage of the benefits of retirement funds, Keogh and defined-contribution plans, profit-sharing arrangements, and stock option plans for their employees. These fringe benefits are deductible to the corporation as expenses and not taxable to the employee. Finally, the entrepreneur can hold certain assets (such as real estate) in his or her own name, lease the use of the assets to the corporation, and collect a lease fee.

Disadvantages

Corporations do, however, have disadvantages that must be carefully considered. They are certainly more complex to organize, are subject to more governmental regulation, and cost more to create than sole proprietorships or partnerships. Although it is possible to incorporate without the aid of an attorney, doing so is not recommended. In too many cases, businesses have failed or endured significant financial hardship because they did not incorporate properly at the start of the business or did not maintain the corporation according to the legal requirements.

A more cumbersome disadvantage derives from the fact that the corporation is literally a person for tax purposes. Consequently, if it makes a profit, it must pay a tax, whether or not those profits were distributed as dividends to the shareholders. And, unlike partners or sole proprietors, shareholders of C-corporations do not receive the pass-through benefit of losses (the S-corporation does enjoy these benefits). In a C-corporation if losses can't be applied in the year they are incurred, they must be saved and applied against future profits. Accordingly, C-corporations pay taxes on the profits they earn, and their owners (shareholders) pay taxes on the dividends they receive; hence, the drawback of "double taxation." It is principally for this reason that many entrepreneurs who operate alone or with a partner do not employ this form. However, if an entrepreneur draws a salary from the corporation, that salary is expensed by the corporation, effectively reducing the company's net income subject to taxes. The entrepreneur will then be taxed at his or her personal income tax rate.

By creating a corporation and issuing stock, the entrepreneur is giving up a measure of control to the board of directors. Realistically however, in privately held corporations, the entrepreneur largely determines who will be on the board and will certainly seek people who support his or her vision. Entrepreneurs who seek outside venture funding in the very early stages of their venture where the risk is highest may find that they have to give up the majority of the stock to the investors. The choice is either to hang on to the equity and watch the business stall because funding can't be secured or to give up control so that the founder can own a smaller piece of something successful. It is not always necessary, however, that the founder retain 51 percent of the stock to maintain effective control. As long as the founder's skills and vision are vital to the success of the venture, and as long as the shareholders share that vision, the founder will have effective control of the organization, no matter how much stock she or he has given up. With a corporate form, unlike the sole proprietorship or partnership, the entrepreneur is accountable principally to the shareholders and secondarily to anyone else. If the corporation is privately held, the board usually serves at the pleasure of the entrepreneur, who is accountable to himself or herself and to any investors.

A corporation must endeavor in all ways to act as an entity separate from its owners. It must keep personal finances completely separate from corporate finances, hold directors' meetings, maintain minutes, and not take on any financial liability without having sufficient resources to back it up. Failing to do any of these things can result in what is known as "piercing the corporate veil," which leaves the officers and owners open to personal liability.

Where to Incorporate

Apart from legal considerations, where to incorporate is also an important issue. It is normally advantageous to incorporate in the state in which the entrepreneur intends to locate the business, so that it will not be under the regulatory powers of two states (the state in which it is incorporated and the state in which it must file an application to do business as an out-of-state corporation). Normally, however, a corporation will not have to qualify as a "foreign" corporation doing business in another state if it is simply holding directors'/shareholders' meetings in the state, or holding bank accounts, using independent contractors, or marketing to potential customers whose transactions will be completed in the corporation's home state. It has often been said that incorporating in Delaware is wise because it has a large body of case law that makes it easier for a company to plan to avoid lawsuits, and Delaware's Chancery Court, which oversees corporate law, is reputed to be one of the finest in the United States. If neither seeking venture capital nor doing a substantial amount of business in Delaware is a goal of the company, however, the cost and hassle of qualifying in another state as well may outweigh the benefits of incorporating in Delaware. Entrepreneurs should also consider the favorableness of the tax laws governing corporations in the state chosen. Some states, such as California, levy a required, minimum annual corporate income tax, whether the business has a taxable income or not.

S-CORPORATION

An S-corporation, unlike the C-corporation, is not a tax-paying entity. It is merely a financial vehicle that passes the profits and losses of the corporation to the shareholders. It is treated much like a sole proprietorship or a partnership in the sense that if the business earns a profit, that profit becomes the income of the owners/shareholders, and it is the owners who pay the tax on that profit at their individual tax rates. In this way, it avoids the double taxation found in the C-corporate structure. Approximately six states tax S-corporations like regular corporations, so it is important to check with the tax division of the state in which the entrepreneur will do business to find out if a tax will be imposed. S-corporation shareholders are not required to pay self-employment taxes (Social Security and Medicare), which can amount to more than 15 percent of income. In recent times, the S-corporation has largely been replaced by the limited liability company (LLC), which is a more flexible form.

Some of the key rules for election of the S-corporation option include the following: The S-corporation may have no more than 100 shareholders. These shareholders must be U.S. citizens or residents (partnerships and corporations cannot be shareholders). Profits and losses must be allocated in proportion to each shareholder's interest. An S-corporation shareholder may not deduct losses in an amount greater than the original investment. In addition, it is always wise to check with an attorney to make certain that the election of S-corporation status is valid. If a C-corporation elects to become an S-corporation and then reverts to C-corporation status, it cannot re-elect S-corporation status for five years.

Advantages

The S-corporation permits business losses to be passed through and taxed at the owner's personal tax rate. This offers a significant benefit to people who need to offset income from other sources. The businesses that benefit most from an S-corporation structure are those that don't have a need to retain earnings. In an S-corporation, if the entrepreneur decides to retain, say, $100,000 of profit to later invest in new equipment, the company must still pay taxes on that profit as though it had been distributed. The S-corporation is a valuable financial tool when personal tax rates are significantly lower than corporate rates. However, as top personal rates increase, a C-corporation might be preferable at higher profit levels. For some small businesses, however, the S-corporation may still be less costly in the long run because it avoids double taxation of income. A good tax attorney or certified public accountant (CPA) should advise the entrepreneur on the best course of action. Ventures that typically benefit from S-corporation status include service businesses with low capital asset requirements, real estate investment firms during times when property values are increasing, and start-ups that are projecting a loss in the early years.

Disadvantages

Entrepreneurs should probably not elect the S-corporation option if they want to retain earnings for expansion or diversification, or if there are significant passive losses from investments such as real estate. This is because unless the business has regular positive cash flow, it could face a situation in which profit is passed through to the owners to be taxed at their personal rate, but the firm has generated insufficient cash to pay those taxes, so they must come out of the pockets of the shareholders. Furthermore, although most deductions and expenses are allowed, S-corporations cannot take advantage of deductions based on medical reimbursements or health insurance plans.

PROFESSIONAL CORPORATIONS

Some state laws permit certain professionals, such as health care professionals, engineers, accountants, and lawyers, to form corporations called professional service corporations. Anyone who holds shares in the corporation must be licensed to provide the service it offers. The limited liability company (LLC) structure is also available to professionals, but in a special form known as a professional limited liability company (PLLC). Under this form, the member is liable only for his or her own malpractice, not that of other members. Some states also offer the limited liability partnership (LLP), which protects the owner from the malpractice claims of its partners but not from other partnership debts.

Limited Liability Company

The limited liability company (LLC), like the S-corporation, enjoys the pass-through tax benefits of partnerships in addition to the limited liability of a C-corporation. It is, however, far more flexible in its treatment of certain ownership issues. Only privately held companies can become LLCs, and they must be formed in accordance with very strict guidelines. LLC statutes vary from state to state, so in addition to meeting the partnership requirements of the Internal Revenue Code, applicants must file with the state in which they intend to do business and follow its requirements as well.

An LLC is formed by filing articles of organization, which resemble articles of incorporation. Today an LLC can be formed with only one person in every state that allows this form except for Massachusetts and the District of Columbia, which require two people. The owners of an LLC are called members, and their shares of ownership are known as interests. The members can undertake the management of the company or hire other people to manage it. Managers, officers, and members are not personally liable for the company's debts or liabilities, except when they have personally guaranteed these debts or liabilities. The members create an "operating agreement," which is very similar to a partnership agreement that spells out rights and obligations of the members.

ADVANTAGES

Most LLCs will be organized for tax purposes like partnerships, so that income tax benefits and liabilities will pass through to the members. In New York and California, however, the LLCs will also be subject to state franchise taxes or fees. Under the Internal Revenue Code, an LLC exhibits all four characteristics of a corporation—limited liability, continuity of life, centralized management, and free transferability of interests—and can still be treated as a partnership for tax purposes without fear of being reclassified as a corporation. This enhances the attractiveness of the LLC, already the most rapidly growing legal form.

The LLC is often thought of as a combination of a limited partnership and an S-corporation. However, there are differences. In a limited partnership, one or more people (the general partners) agree to assume personal liability for the actions of the partnership, whereas the limited partners may not take part in the management of the partnership without losing their limited liability status. In an LLC, by contrast, a member does not have to forfeit the right to participate in the management of the organization in order to retain his or her limited liability status. Moreover, in an LLC, unlike in an S-corporation, there are no limitations on the number of members or on their status. Corporations, pension plans, and nonresident aliens can be members. Also, whereas S-corporations can't own 80 percent or more of the stock of another corporation, an LLC may actually possess wholly owned subsidiary corporations. LLCs are not limited to one class of stock, and in some ways they receive more favorable tax treatment. For example, unlike an S-corporation shareholder, the LLC member can deduct losses in amounts that reflect the member's allocable share of the debt of the company. If at a later date the entrepreneur decides to go public, the LLC can become a C-corporation by transferring the LLC assets to the new corporation. It is, however, a bit more difficult to go in the other direction, and capital gains tax must be paid on the appreciation.

DISADVANTAGES

Clearly, the LLC offers more flexibility than other forms, but it does have a few disadvantages that should be considered. In contrast to the creation of a partnership or sole proprietorship, a filing fee must be paid when the LLC is formed. It is probably not a good form to choose if there will be a large number of members, because it will be difficult to reach consensus among the owners, who might also be the managers of the LLC. It is not a separate tax-paying entity. Earnings and losses are passed through to the members to be taxed at their individual tax rate, so members must make quarterly estimated tax payments to the IRS. If all the members do not elect to actively manage the LLC, the LLC ownership interests may be treated like securities by the state and the Securities and Exchange Commission (SEC). This means that if the company does not qualify for an exemption (most small LLCs do), it must register the sale of its member interests with the SEC.

LLCs are becoming a popular vehicle for companies that may have global investors because the S-corporation does not permit foreign ownership. An attorney should be consulted to find out whether this form is available in a particular state. One ambitious entrepreneur knew that she wanted her furniture-importing business to be global in all respects. She even intended to bring in investors from among her business acquaintances around the world, because that would help her find the important contacts she needed to be successful. As an importer, she needed liability protection but did not want the high tax rates she would have with a corporation. Friends had told her that the S-corporation would solve the tax problem, but her attorney advised her to consider the LLC as her choice of legal form because it would allow her to have foreign investors.

The Nonprofit Corporation

It is not outside the realm of possibility for a nonprofit corporation to be a high-growth, world-class company; however, it is not generally started with that goal in mind. A nonprofit corporation is a corporation established for charitable, public (scientific, literary, or educational), or religious purposes, or for mutual benefit (such as trade associations, tennis clubs), as recognized by federal and state laws. Some additional examples of nonprofits are child-care centers, schools, religious organizations, hospitals, museums, shelters, and community health care facilities. Like the C-corporation, the nonprofit corporation is a legal entity and offers its shareholders and officers the benefit of limited liability. There is a common misconception that nonprofit corporations are not allowed to make a profit. As long as the business is not set up to benefit a single person and is organized for a nonprofit purpose, it can still make a profit on which it is not taxed if it has also met the IRS test for tax-exempt status. However, income derived from for-profit activities is subject to income tax.

There are two distinct hurdles that a business must overcome if it wants to operate as a nonprofit corporation and enjoy tax-exempt status: The first is to meet the state requirements for being designated a nonprofit corporation and operating as such in a given state. The second is to meet the federal and state requirements for exemption from paying taxes [IRS 501(c)(3)] by forming a corporation that falls within the IRS's narrowly defined categories.

ADVANTAGES

Nonprofit organizations offer many advantages to entrepreneurs seeking to be socially responsible or just to start a business doing something they love that helps others. The nonprofit with tax-exempt status is attractive to corporate donors, who can deduct their donations as a business expense. The nonprofit can seek cash and in-kind contributions of equipment, supplies, and personnel. It can apply for grants from government agencies and private foundations. The nonprofit may qualify for tax-exempt status, which means that it is free from paying taxes on income generated from nonprofit activities.

DISADVANTAGES

There are a few disadvantages to a nonprofit organization. For example, profits earned by the corporation cannot be distributed as dividends, and corporate money cannot be contributed to political campaigns or used to engage in lobbying. In forming the nonprofit corporation, the entrepreneur gives up proprietary interest in the corporation and dedicates all the assets and resources of the corporation to tax-exempt activities. If a nonprofit corporation is ever dissolved, its assets must be distributed to another tax-exempt organization. Finally, the nonprofit cannot make substantial profits from unrelated activities, and it must pay taxes on the profits it does make.

It is not uncommon for tax-exempt organizations to engage in activities that generate unrelated business income (UBI)—that is, income that is not related to the nonprofit's exempt purpose. For example, if a research institute were to operate a café on a regular basis, this would be considered a UBI activity. The institute would have to report it to the IRS and pay taxes on the income. If and when their UBI activities start to become significant, nonprofits often establish for-profit entities to run their UBI activities to protect the tax-exempt status of the parent organization.

Musical theatre companies are not the first type of company one thinks of when looking for examples of nonprofit organizations, but James Blackman had no doubt that this was the form of choice for the Civic Light Opera of South Bay Cities in California, one of the leading musical theatre companies on the West Coast. The nonprofit form would allow Blackman to receive donations from corporations and grants from foundations to support his efforts in the community with the physically challenged. It would also allow him to sell tickets to performances and make a profit, as long as that profit was not distributed but remained in the company. More important, he would meet the requirements for tax exemption, and that would enable him to keep more money in the business to help it grow.

Choosing the Right Legal Form at Each Milestone

Having a strategic plan in place for the venture enables the entrepreneur to choose a legal form that won't have to be changed or one that can easily be shifted to when the time is right. For example, suppose an entrepreneur plans to offer shares of stock in the company at some point in the future to raise additional capital. To accomplish that, the company will need to become a corporation or LLC, so if it began as a sole proprietorship, it would need to file incorporation or LLC papers in the state in which it would be doing business. Consider the following example of a married entrepreneur, Cheryl Kastner.

Kastner's spouse is a highly paid executive for a major corporation, making it possible for her to devote herself full-time to developing a tech product she has been designing for some time. Kastner decides to set up a small business with a shop near their home. She is not worried about medical insurance because she is already covered by her spouse's company. However, she needs to limit liability, because they have acquired a number of valuable assets, such as their house and cars, and don't want those to be in danger should things go badly. She realizes that in any business dealing with products, some liability issues might crop up and she wants to make sure they're covered. She also wants to ensure that she and her husband are protected from personal liability for things that happen at the business.

At start-up, it is typical to experience losses as equipment is purchased, and prototypes are built and tested in the market. Once the product is launched, there probably will be continuing losses from promoting the business, finding space outside the home to lease, and hiring new employees. Kastner has big plans for her business; in fact, within a year of introducing the product, she expects to need venture capital to be able to grow as fast as the market demands. She also sees an IPO in the future that will be the liquidity event when investors need to cash out. Given these circumstances, she will consider which organization form is best at each milestone.

During product development, before the business is actually launched, it often doesn't make sense to use a more formal form such as a corporation, especially in a state where the entrepreneur has to pay minimum state franchise taxes. A simple sole proprietorship or partnership (if there's more than one person involved) will suffice. At this stage, the liability to family assets is small. But the minute Kastner's business grows out of the home environment and takes on the responsibilities of a lease and employees, she must consider either being heavily insured or moving to a legal form with limited liability. Kastner plans to move the business to a leased location and hire employees. Since there would still be losses from product development and she would want to use them to shelter other income, she is also advised to consider either the S-corporation or the LLC, depending on the degree of flexibility she needs. She is also advised by her attorney that at the point at which she decides to seek venture capital and/or an IPO, she will need to convert to a C-corporation.

It is clear from this example that the legal form of an organization is not a static decision, but rather one based on the needs of the company at the time of formation and into the future. Choosing the legal structure of the new venture is one of the most important decisions an entrepreneur can make, because it affects the tax strategy of the company for years to come. The correct selection depends on the type of venture the entrepreneur is starting, the profits the venture generates, the personal tax bracket of the entrepreneur, the assets used by the business, the risk factors in the business, its potential for growth, and state laws. Again, particularly in the case of corporations and LLCs, it is important that an attorney who specializes in this area review the documents to ensure that all the rules have been followed and that the entrepreneur will receive all of the benefits to which the business is entitled.

New Venture Checklist

Have you:

☐ Answered the questions on page 231 before considering which legal form to choose?

☐ Consulted with an appropriately qualified attorney to determine the best form to meet your business goals?

☐ Completed the necessary agreements for the legal form you have chosen (partnership agreement, articles of incorporation, and so forth)?

☐ Met the test for tax exemptions under IRC 501(c)(3) if you are founding a nonprofit corporation?

☐ Met with a qualified attorney to determine what other legal issues might arise with your particular type of business?

Issues to Consider

business.college.hmco.com/students

1. Assuming that you were running a successful consulting practice as a sole proprietorship, what would induce you to change the legal form to a corporation?
2. Why would you choose an LLC form over a partnership or an S-corporation?
3. What kinds of businesses are well suited to the nonprofit legal structure?
4. What key factors determine the strategic plan for the legal organization of the business?

Experiencing Entrepreneurship

1. Employing this text and additional research on the Internet, acquire a basic understanding of the different legal forms of organization. Then, using a business that you are considering launching, discuss your initial strategic plan for the business with a qualified attorney to get his or her advice about the best form to use for that type of business. Write a two-page summary of your findings to justify the choice of legal form.

2. Visit an entrepreneur whose business is set up as a partnership. How do the partners describe the experience of setting up the business? How have they divided the duties and responsibilities? What key issues have they covered in their partnership agreement? Summarize your findings in a two- or three-page paper.

Relevant Case Studies

## Chapter 12

INCORPORATING ETHICS AND SOCIAL RESPONSIBILITY INTO THE BUSINESS

". . . An ethic is not an ethic, and a value not a value without some sacrifice to it. Something given up, something not taken, something not gained."

—JEROME KOHLBERG, JR., Kohlberg Kravis Roberts & Co., May 18, 1987

LEARNING OBJECTIVES

▶ Explain the role of ethics in entrepreneurship.

▶ Discuss how entrepreneurs can demonstrate social responsibility.

▶ Describe how an entrepreneur's vision and values contribute to the culture of the new venture.

▶ Discuss the relationship of core values to success.

Profile 12.1 PROMOTING WOMEN ENTREPRENEURS IN BANGLADESH

It is fairly commonplace for women to have financial power in developed countries, but it's the last thing you might expect to find in a third-world country like Bangladesh. Nevertheless, thanks largely to one man's entrepreneurial genius, women are now gaining financial power in this impoverished country. In the 1980s, Muhammad Yunus, a Bangladeshi banker/economist, decided that traditional economic development programs would not bring about economic improvement fast enough in his home country of Bangladesh. A Fulbright scholar in classical economics, Yunus studied the challenges that the poorest people faced in attempting to secure capital to start even the smallest of businesses. They had no collateral and were generally illiterate, so he concluded that a traditional banking model was not appropriate for them. Instead, he began to work on a business model based on the concept of social collateral. He called it his "peer lending" model, wherein small groups of borrowers in the same village would take responsibility for repaying the loans of anyone in the group.

Founded in 1983, the Grameen Bank began lending to the poorest of the poor on a group liability basis with no collateral. Borrowers repay the loans in small weekly installments over one year. Because of peer pressure from the group to repay, the collection rate is about 98 percent, far higher than for traditional banking institutions. But what is most unusual about this entrepreneurial bank is that 95 percent of its borrowers are women. Traditionally, Bangladeshi women have had no employment opportunities and thus have lived far below the poverty line. With no other options, the women are inclined to try the Grameen loan system, which enables them to start micro-businesses such as making bamboo stools, weaving floor mats, and raising poultry. Borrowers are also required to save some of their money against potential natural disasters or sickness, which teaches them responsibility. From Grameen Bank's point of view, the return to them is infinite because, for example, a $100 donation to the nonprofit bank can be lent and repaid over and over again. The Grameen Foundation accepts donations, and the bank administers the loans. From the point of view of the Bangladeshi society, it has helped to create an entrepreneurial culture and raised the standard of living for those who have participated. The bank is owned by the borrowers, 97 percent of whom are women.

Yunus built on the success of the micro credit effort by making mobile phone ownership possible as a business opportunity to Bangladeshis. Women have purchased phones and then provided services to other villagers who can't afford to own their own phones, creating new businesses and inter-village trade. Grameen Phone is a subsidiary of Grameen Bank and now has well over 100,000 subscribers. Today communication between villages across Bangladesh is growing and is succeeding in reducing the gap between rich and poor. In 2006, Yanus and the Grameen Bank were jointly awarded the Nobel Peace Prize.

Sources: "The Nobel Peace Prize 2006," http://www.nobelprize.org; "Motley Fool Selects Grameen Foundation USA for 2002 Foolanthropy Charity Drive," *PR Newswire* (December 3, 2002); "From Small Acorns," http://www.findarticles.com, August 2000; and Abu Wahid, "The Grameen Bank and Women in Bangladesh," *Challenge* (September–October 1999).

Never have entrepreneurial businesses needed ethics policies more than they do today. The lessons of Enron, Worldcom, and many other companies that resorted to unscrupulous tactics to create phantom company wealth should serve as a potent reminder to entrepreneurs that ethics in business practices is vital to business survival. In a dynamic, global marketplace that places a premium on speed and quick returns, shareholder value is often considered more important than basic human values. The pressure to achieve unachievable goals and survive in such a chaotic environment causes stress; and when people suffer stress, they don't always make wise decisions. Moreover, the global economy, made more accessible than ever through the Internet, has juxtaposed U.S. businesses with cultures that may define morality in terms of very different contexts, values, and codes of ethics. Yes, it's a challenging environment, but those entrepreneurs who understand their value systems and create a code of ethics for their businesses can successfully maneuver through these challenges without forsaking their principles.

This chapter looks at three key issues for entrepreneurial companies, issues that will become increasingly important as companies interact more frequently in the global marketplace: vision and values, ethics, and social responsibility. Profile 12.1 on Grameen Bank clearly demonstrates that every industry is looking for ways to reinvent itself and become more socially responsible. The chapter closes with a discussion of the components of success and how to make sure that a company's success is congruent with its vision and values.

Ethics

Ethics, or the moral code by which we live and conduct business—essentially the concept of right and wrong—derives from the cultural, social, political, and ethnic norms with which we were raised as children. People don't often pause to reflect on their value system; instead, they merely act instinctively on the basis of it. It's only when they are faced with a dilemma that raises moral or ethical issues that they may consciously ask themselves what is the correct thing to do. Many people believe that if they follow the Golden Rule, the Judeo/Christian ethic that says "Do unto others as you would have them do unto you," they're safe from ethical dilemmas. Unfortunately, most ethical dilemmas in the business environment are complex and subject to "gray areas" that are troubling when one attempts to apply an ethical principle. One Oregon construction company hired a subcontractor to do a $15,000 concrete job. That particular subcontractor did not have solid bookkeeping practices and never submitted an invoice to the construction company for the work it did. The construction company could have kept quiet, but instead it sent the subcontractor a copy of the plans, specifications, and names of workers on the job, and told the subcontractor how much to bill it. The gray area here is the decision point—whether to notify the subcontractor of its failure to invoice. The construction company demonstrated its ethical values by contacting the subcontractor to ask for the invoice.

Another ethical decision had to be made by a marketing company that received two checks from a client for the same $50,000 project. There was no way the client would have easily discovered it, yet the marketing firm immediately sent the second check back. These kinds of ethical dilemmas occur every day in business. Although these two entrepreneurs did what they believed to be ethically correct, not everyone operates under the same standards of ethics. The employee who steals notepads, pens, and computer CDs because "the employer won't miss them," the executive who abuses his or her expense account, and the business owner who evades taxes by not reporting employee income demonstrate their lack of clear ethical standards. This kind of behavior is accepted too widely and costs entrepreneurs both time and money.

Entrepreneurs face special problems when it comes to ethical issues. Their small companies generally are more informal and often lack systems and controls. They often don't have the time or resources to focus on ethics during their attempts to keep their businesses alive, and they often take for granted that everyone in their organization and everyone with whom they do business shares their values. This is a mistake, because unethical behavior left undetected can contaminate a business for as long as it exists. Another very practical reason why small firms should pay attention to the ethics of employees concerns their ability to defend themselves against criminal action in a court of law. The U.S. Sentencing Commission's guidelines assert that an effective ethics program can serve to protect a company from criminal penalties, or at least in lessening their impact, if an employee violates federal law.[1]

Recent research has identified four categories of ethical decision making that entrepreneurs face on a daily basis: (1) individual values, such as integrity and honesty, (2) organization values concerning employee well-being, (3) customer satisfaction, as reflected in the value provided to the customer, and (4) external accountability, or how the company relates to the community and the environment. This research determined that entrepreneurs do not differ in their ethical values from general societal norms.[2] We will take a more in-depth look at ethical dilemmas in business from the traditional perspective of issues related to conflicts of interest, survival tactics, stakeholder pressure, and pushing the legal limit.

CONFLICTS OF INTEREST

Conflict of interest is one of the most universal problems in business today. A conflict of interest occurs when a person's private or personal interests clash with his or her professional obligations such that an independent observer might reasonably question whether the individual's professional actions or decisions are influenced by personal gain, financial or otherwise. For example, a company may want to continue an important manufacturing process that provides many jobs and profit, even when the community claims that this same process is not good for the environment. Business owners have vested interests in many areas of their lives: careers, a business, family, community, and their investments, to name just a few. It is rare for all these interests to be in complete harmony with one another.

Conflict of interest has also found its way into Internet commerce. Today an online company can use its website to gather information about customers, profile them, and send the right message to the customer at the right moment. Through "cookie" technology, a company can track customers' movements online. Over time, the company will have compiled an enormous amount of data that it can use to better target its marketing messages. A company that uses cookie technology will usually offer a notice of privacy to its customers, promising not to sell the information it gathers to other companies. Unfortunately, many an Internet company has gone back on its promise to protect customers' privacy in the interest of making easy money. When Internet ad company DoubleClick (DCLK) was exposed for matching online and offline databases (essentially matching cookie data to real names, addresses, and phone numbers), it was hit with a Federal Trade

Commission inquiry, investigations by the states of New York and Michigan, six lawsuits, and a lot of bad press.[3] The Electronic Privacy Information Center (EPIC) wants to require companies to obtain customer consent before creating a profile. Proponents of profiling claim that advertising is the "lifeblood" of the Internet and that if it is too heavily regulated, content may no longer be free. This conflict of interest is one that will not go away for a long time because there is so much potential marketing benefit in consumer profiling.

SURVIVAL TACTICS

Many are the stories of entrepreneurs who did whatever it took to survive, even violating their own standards. Survival is the area where most people's ethics really face a test. It's easy to be ethical when things are going your way, but what about the entrepreneur who is facing bankruptcy or can't make payroll? What do that entrepreneur's ethics look like at that point? Small firms, especially in the early years, are vulnerable to setbacks that would not significantly affect a large organization. The loss of a major customer or supplier could put a small business out of business. In these types of life-or-death situations, a small business owner's commitment to ethical practices can force the company to make some difficult decisions. Again, the importance of sticking to an ethical code is critical, because what an entrepreneur does today out of desperation will follow him for the rest of his business career.

One entrepreneur learned the hard way that one can't assume that everyone operates with the same value system and ethical code. This entrepreneur owns two successful bed and breakfast inns and, believing that she had reached the point where she could afford to cut back the time she spent managing them, she decided to rely on her general manager to run them while she took a two-year break to relax and travel; she even got married. She had the utmost confidence in her managers with whom she had been working for some time, but she continued to check in with them while she was on her self-imposed sabbatical. About 18 months into her retreat, she began to learn of problems at the B&Bs from the head housekeeper— reports of dishonesty on the part of the front-desk people, paying employees in cash, and not keeping records of guests' stays. In the end, the entrepreneur did an audit and discovered, to her dismay, that she was losing about $50,000 a year to theft. After firing her general manager, she returned to the B&Bs full-time, only to discover that the losses were much higher than expected. Not only did she not have solid procedures in place, but she also didn't have an effective way to monitor what was going on. Her general manager had actually been teaching employees how to cheat the company.[4] It is important to have high ethical standards in business, but it is also important to put procedures in place that make it difficult for employees to act in an unethical manner. Having more than one person sign checks and making sure that each person matches the check to an invoice or purchase order is one way to put a lid on those who might take more than they deserve.

STAKEHOLDER PRESSURE

There are many stakeholders in a business, and they all want what is owed them when it's owed them. Stakeholders include any person or organization that has an interest in seeing the company succeed—investors, shareholders, suppliers, customers, and employees, to name a few. Every business, no matter how small, has stakeholders. One area of research has focused on what the business ought to do in terms of the "ends it pursues and the means it utilizes."[5] For many entrepreneurs, there are times when managing the demands of stakeholders becomes a real juggling act. For example, to grow the company to the next level, an entrepreneur may decide to consider an IPO. Once that issue is raised, the entrepreneur will find lots of stakeholders pressuring him to move forward, even when he is not sure it's the best thing to do. These stakeholders include investment bankers who get a fee for doing the deal, business partners who may be able to cash out of some of their holdings in the company, and lawyers who want the additional business. All these stakeholders want to be served, but research has revealed that the most healthy outcome is for the entrepreneur to hold to his or her code of ethics and base decisions on it, not on the personal agendas of stakeholders who may not have the best interests of the company at heart.

PUSHING THE LEGAL LIMIT

Some entrepreneurs look for ways to bend the law as much as possible without actually breaking it. Entrepreneurs who regularly play too close to the edge of legality eventually get caught, and the price is often their businesses and their reputations. Ethical entrepreneurs don't play those games, but they're always on the alert for companies that might use quasi-legal practices against them to gain an edge in the market. These types of tactics must be dealt with decisively. For example, a large water-meter repair company that operated within the law was attacked by a competitor in collusion with a newspaper reporter. The competitor accused the company of bribing public officials. It was a false accusation, clearly unethical, but perhaps not illegal. It caused the innocent utility company a great many problems and cost it a lot of money defending itself, but the company had no choice because its reputation was at stake.

LEARNING FROM REAL-LIFE DILEMMAS

There is no better way to understand the role of ethics in any business than to encounter real-world dilemmas and determine how they might be resolved. Here are some examples of real-life ethical dilemmas. Think about how they might be resolved.

1. A struggling Internet company is not producing revenues at the rate originally projected. At the same time, the burn rate (the rate at which cash is spent) is increasing as the company continually seeks new customers. The site claims to protect the privacy of visitors who purchase its products and services, and this is something the company takes pride in. However, the entrepreneur is concerned that if she doesn't find a quick source of income, the company may not survive. The entrepreneur learns that she can sell customer information lists to companies that will pay a lot of money for them. She has also heard that if she starts tracking which websites her customers visit, she can sell that information to major advertising firms for use in targeted advertising, another source of revenue. These tactics will violate customers' privacy,

but if she doesn't do something quickly, she may have no business to offer them. What should she do?

2. One of a company's best customers has asked for a specific product. After telling the customer the price, the company learns from the customer that a competitor is selling the same item at the company's cost. It is well known that this competitor engages in unethical business practices. Should the company tell its customer about the competitor's practices or let the customer purchase where he can get the best price?

3. An employee confides to an entrepreneur that another employee is planning to leave the company in two months to start her own company as a competitor. Armed with this knowledge, the entrepreneur is tempted to fire this employee immediately, but she is in the middle of a major project that is critical to the company, and it will be completed within two weeks. What should the entrepreneur do?

4. A company has hired an engineering design firm as an independent contractor to design and build an e-commerce site. It paid a large portion of the fee, $25,000, up front to begin the work. The owner assures the company that the work is on schedule to be completed on time, but as of a week before the due date, the company has yet to see any designs. A meeting is scheduled at the engineer's office to check on the status of the project. While waiting at the office, the entrepreneur overhears employees talking about the impending closure of the business. She also hears that the programmer assigned to the project has not been paid and there is no money to pay him. The owner of the engineering firm says nothing about this during the meeting and instead assures the entrepreneur that the project will be completed as planned. The entrepreneur suspects that he is not being truthful and worries that if the business closes and she has not received the designs and software for the project, her company will be out $25,000 and will have to file a lawsuit. Should the entrepreneur talk to the programmer and reveal what she has heard? Should she confront the owner? Should she approach his disgruntled employees to find a way to gather the data she needs to win a lawsuit?

5. A company is about to begin doing business in another country where it is well known that paying cash to officials makes business transactions move more quickly. The entrepreneur knows that paying bribes is illegal in the United States, the home base for the business, but this contract will ensure that the company establishes a foothold in the global market before its competitors do. What should the entrepreneur do?

These are all difficult choices when the very survival of the business is at stake. Small businesses are as guilty as multinational corporations when it comes to ethical missteps. Paying personal expenses out of business funds and writing them off, not reporting all cash receipts, cheating customers on price, using misleading advertising, failing to pay bills on time, and lying to customers, employees, and suppliers are all examples of poor ethics. Aristotle, the Greek philosopher, said that courage is the first of the human virtues because without it, the others are not possible. How we make these difficult and courageous choices is the subject of the next section.

Socially Responsible Entrepreneurship

Room to Read

Social entrepreneurs are on a mission. Their ventures often start as the result of an unusual experience that inspires them or simply as a passion to change the world. John Wood knew that being an executive at Microsoft was not going to be his life's work. He was successful, financially secure, and reasonably happy, but there was something missing, and he needed to get away from the rat race to find it. Wood found what was to be his life's mission while on a trek through the Himalayas. He discovered that in the villages of Nepal there were no libraries, and the schools had no books. He sent out an e-mail to his friends back in the United States, telling about his adventure and the need for books. The next morning, his inbox was filled with 100 messages from people wanting to know how they could help. That told him that he could do this. After many bumps in the road (which he recounts in his book, *Leaving Microsoft to Change the World*), in 2000 he made the decision to leave Microsoft and launch Room to Read as a nonprofit organization. Today his organization has established more than 3,600 libraries in the developing world and improved the lives of more than 1.2 million children.

Source: John Wood, *Leaving Microsoft to Change the World* (New York: HarperCollins, 2006); and http://www.roomtoread.org.

THE IMPORTANCE OF DEVELOPING A CODE OF ETHICS

Most of the research on ethics has been conducted in large organizations, so we have very little information about ethics in small businesses. Some research has suggested that entrepreneurs are subject to compulsive behavior such as the need to be right and the need for an instant response. This tendency to make decisions under circumstances with there is little time for reflection and no one to advise can lead to ethical problems.[6] Recent research notes that entrepreneurs have a "distinctive world-view" that is comprised of a "mosaic of virtue ethics, deontology, utilitarianism, and meta-ethical perspectives."[7] What this means is that it is impossible to stereotype entrepreneurs when it comes to decision making in ethical dilemmas.

The ethical behavior of employees is very much influenced by the code of ethics of the company.[8] When a code of ethics is spelled out and written down, people in the organization take it more seriously. Thus it would seem to be important for a business owner to develop a formal code of ethics for the business. After all, the best way to handle ethical dilemmas is to have in place a mechanism for avoiding them to begin with.

The Process of Developing a Code of Ethics

The process of developing a code of ethics begins with a company's self-examination to identify values held by individuals and alert everyone to inconsistencies in how people deal with particular issues. For a new company, this means getting the founding team together to discuss how certain issues should be dealt with. For a larger company, forming a committee to oversee the process may be appropriate.

The Josephson Institute of Ethics developed a list of ethical values that should be considered in any code of ethics,[9] and Table 12.1 presents a worksheet for

TABLE 12.1

Character Counts Inventory

Michael Josephson, President of the Josephson Institute for Ethics, believes that entrepreneurs should consider how they incorporate the six pillars of character in their business and in their relationships with employees and others. List what you do to display each trait in your business environment.

Trustworthiness
Example: I always do what I say I will do.

_____

_____

_____

Respect
Example: I am courteous to everyone I meet.

_____

_____

_____

Responsibility
Example: I do not blame others for my failures.

_____

_____

_____

Fairness
Example: I consider all the relevant facts carefully before making judgments.

_____

_____

_____

Caring
Example: I forgive the mistakes of my employees and guide them to do better.

_____

_____

_____

Citizenship
Example: I give my employees time off from work to do service in the community.

_____

_____

_____

Source: Based on Character Counts! National Office, http://www.josephsoninstitute.org.

employing these values to gauge how to respond in a particular ethical dilemma.

Trustworthiness: loyalty, honesty, integrity

Respect: privacy, dignity, courtesy

Responsibility: accountability, pursuit of excellence

Caring: compassion, kindness, giving, consideration

Justice and fairness: impartiality, consistency, equity, due process, equality

Civic virtue and citizenship: abiding by laws, community service, protection of environment

A code of ethics should also outline behaviors that would allow the business to display these characteristics. This can be accomplished by using a Kantian[10] approach and asking four questions about any ethical decision to be made:[11]

1. Will the actions taken result in the "greatest good for all parties involved"?

2. Will the actions respect the rights of all parties?

3. Are the actions just? Will anyone be hurt by the actions?

4. Would I be proud if my actions were announced in my local newspaper?

The last question, in particular, gets to the heart of how one determines what is ethical in any situation, and most people can immediately and intuitively answer it.

CHARACTERISTICS OF AN EFFECTIVE CODE

The most effective code of ethics will have the following characteristics. The code and its associated policies will be clear and easy to understand. Details about special situations that need further explanation will be included (for example, political factors in particular countries). In cases where employee judgment may be required, descriptions and examples will make it easier for the employee to make the decision.

Entrepreneurs should make sure that all employees are aware of and understand the code as well as the values and culture of the company. The following are some guidelines for ensuring that the code of ethics is implemented and maintained over time.

1. Entrepreneurs should model the behavior expected of others in the company. In some companies, the ethical behavior exhibited by managers and employees in tough situations can become legendary—a part of the company culture that people remember and speak about with pride over and over again.

2. Employees should be educated about ethics through workshops that put employees in hypothetical situations. For example, "What would you do if you found out that your best customer was harassing your administrative assistant?"

An Ethical Dilemma

Superior Machine Works had developed a new type of generator that was environmentally friendly and could be controlled from a distance. Superior's research had determined that the market was quite large and had the potential to be very profitable. Superior was marketing two models: a small, lightweight version for people who would use it to power small tools, and a bigger, heavier version used generally as backup power for an office or home, in addition to supplying power for a variety of electrical tools. The smaller version retailed for $895, and the larger version sold for $1,500. The larger version had a patented noise reduction feature that significantly reduced the sound the machine produced. Studies on similar equipment had shown that over a long period of time, the noise level of the small machine could actually produce hearing loss in the user.

At the same time, Superior's main competitor was also developing a generator very much like Superior's small version, and that company was also aware of the noise problem and the potential for deafness over time. Still, it was going ahead with the product. Superior was faced with a real dilemma. If it didn't move quickly to get its smaller version to market, it would lose its first-mover advantage to its competitor. At the same time, did Superior want to market a product that was known to cause deafness over time? If it marketed only the larger machine, it would quickly lose market share to its competitor's smaller, lighter machine. If Superior could not introduce a successful product quickly, it would have to lay off many of its workers. Considering the downward trend in its current sales, the company might fail if it couldn't introduce its product quickly.

1. What options does Superior have and what are the consequences of each?
2. What should Superior do and why?

3. Entrepreneurs should demonstrate commitment to the ethics program by mentioning it on a regular basis and providing examples of appropriate behavior that employees display during the course of their work.

The code of ethics should be shared with customers so that they understand the company's commitment and are assured of its integrity. A clear channel for reporting and dealing with unethical behavior should exist, and there should be a means of rewarding ethical behavior through recognition, bonuses, raises, and so forth. Examples of Codes of Ethics can be found at http://Yourcodeofethics.com.

There is no way to avoid the ethical problems that business brings. But developing a strong ethical code and enlisting the cooperation of everyone in the business will go a long way toward making those challenges easier to deal with.

Social Responsibility

Today it's not enough to have a successful business and make a profit. The business must hold itself to a higher standard of social responsibility by giving something back to the community or communities in which it does business and, through them, to society as a whole. Social responsibility is operating a business in a way that exceeds the ethical, legal, commercial, and public expectations that society has of business. This means obeying the law, respecting the environment, and being mindful of the impact the business has on its stakeholders, the industry, and the community in general. Socially responsible entrepreneurs, then, are distinct from other entrepreneurs in a number of ways. First and foremost, they start their businesses with a social mission, and they are faced with different challenges as they seek the resources to fund and sustain the business.[12] Their rewards derive not only from profits but also from the social value they create by being change agents for the betterment of society. There are many types of social ventures serving a variety of purposes. For example, Rubicon Programs, Inc., based in Richmond, California, provides job training for people who typically cannot find jobs. It does this through its several ventures, including a bakery, home care, and a buildings and grounds maintenance business.[13] Another example is The Nature Conservancy, which is a global organization based in Arlington, Virginia. With a mission of preserving plants, animals, and natural communities, it operates the largest private system of nature sanctuaries in the world.[14] The benefits to businesses that seek to become socially responsible are many. They include improved financial performance, reduced operating costs by cutting waste and inefficiencies, enhanced brand image and reputation, increased sales and customer loyalty, increased productivity and quality, increased ability to attract and retain employees, and reduced regulatory oversight.

Some business owners have chosen to define their businesses publicly as "socially responsible businesses." Unfortunately, when their goals are too ambitious, their businesses do not always succeed. In 1989, Ben & Jerry's co-founder Ben Cohen launched Community Products Inc. (CPI), whose purpose was to save the rainforest and contribute to a number of worthy causes by donating an astronomical 60 percent of its profits to these causes. But things didn't turn out the way Cohen intended. The idea was to import nuts for the company's ice cream products (namely, Rainforest Crunch) from the local economies in the region of the rainforests. This vision was newsworthy, so Ben & Jerry's received a lot of free publicity, helping to generate revenues of $3 million within the first year.

CPI then partnered with Cultural Survival Enterprises, a nonprofit organization dedicated to finding markets for products from developing countries, but soon found that this organization's goals were not compatible with CPI's. Cultural Survival was charging high prices for its nuts and was not controlling quality. The products received from Cultural Survival contained a number of foreign substances—everything from glass and rocks to insects. Then there were CPI's operating problems, poor working conditions, and constraints on its ability to pay workers because of the requirement that 60 percent of its profits had to go to charity.

By 1993, CPI was losing money and the glow on the "save the rainforest" vision was merely a glimmer. By 1997, the company was in bankruptcy. Although Ben Cohen's goal was certainly lofty, it was highly unlikely that one corporation could do what entire nations had been unable to accomplish. In other words, for all practical purposes, CPI was setting itself up for failure. Furthermore, because a company such as this puts its social goals into all its publicity and advertising, it is held to impossibly high standards by the public and the media, who are ready and willing to remind it of its failure to achieve its goals. Although CPI gave away half a million dollars to save the rainforest, it ultimately crashed, leaving its creditors hanging.[15]

Stories like this should never discourage a company from being socially responsible. But they should warn entrepreneurs of the importance of choosing a mission that is achievable. Paul Brainerd founded a company, the Brainerd Foundation, in Seattle, Washington, for the purpose of helping entrepreneurs "give back" strategically. He suggests that entrepreneurs follow two rules:

1. Don't wait until later in life to begin giving back. Start when the business is young and giving can become part of the culture.
2. Don't go for something huge. Start at the grassroots level, where help is needed the most.

There are three categories of ventures that engage in social entrepreneurship.[16] For-profit ventures in the private sector can have a socially oriented purpose, such as the Body Shop and Ben & Jerry's, whose mission is to respect the environment and to innovate ways to improve quality of life. Social entrepreneurship ventures in the nonprofit sector are conceived with a social purpose in mind and are not constrained by the need to make and distribute a profit. Rubicon Programs and the Grameen Bank are two such ventures. Social entrepreneurship in the public sector includes governmental agencies like the Small Business Administration and community organizations like the Castleford Community Learning Centre of West Yorkshire in the United Kingdom, which works with adults with learning disorders.[17]

EFFECTIVE WAYS TO BECOME SOCIALLY RESPONSIBLE

A company does not have to be a large, multimillion-dollar firm to begin to give something back to society. Even a very small company can have an impact on its community if it does a few things by way of preparation. First, the company needs to set goals. What does it want to achieve with its social responsibility efforts? It should pick a single cause to focus on, rather than trying to support many different causes, and consider partnering with a nonprofit organization.

The nonprofit contributes its expertise in the social issue, while the entrepreneurial company contributes its expertise and the time of its employees to the nonprofit. Next, it is vital that everyone in the organization get involved. There really is strength in numbers. In addition to getting employees involved, the company should also get its customers involved. With goals in place and a cause that fits the company's core values, the new venture can do a number of things to establish positive relationships in the community. Here are just a few of them.

▶ *Donate products, services, or revenues.* Any company can donate the products or services the company produces. However, Laura Scher takes it one step further and donates a portion of the revenues of her company, Working Assets—a provider of long-distance, credit card, and wireless services—to nonprofit organizations to encourage "ordinary people to become activists." Since her company was founded in 1985, it has donated over $47 million.

▶ *Donate expertise.* Room to Read (see the "Socially Responsible Entrepreneurship" box) donated its expertise in raising funding and starting libraries to teach students in Sri Lanka how to raise funding to rebuild the schools lost in the tsunami of 2004. They raised more than $400,000 and inspired a new student-led initiative to provide Room to Read programs around the world.

▶ *Contribute to the community.* Many entrepreneurs have found cost-effective ways to give back to their communities without breaking the bank. In fact, they have made social responsibility a regular part of their businesses. For example, one enterprising bagel store adopts a local nonprofit organization for a year. Customers vote for their favorite charity, and the winning choice receives a cash donation, bagels, meeting space, and a place to advertise its services in the store. They also get volunteer help from the bagel employees, who do their good deeds on company time.

Another entrepreneur shares the benefits of his success with his community by providing ski trips for underprivileged children, food drives for the hungry, highway cleanups, and the Easter Seals poster-child campaign, among many other things. There are numerous ways to demonstrate social responsibility through a business. It doesn't have to cost much time or money to make a significant difference as long as efforts are focused where they will count the most.

Vision and Values

Every great company begins with the entrepreneur's vision of what that company will become. Just as top professional athletes envision every play of an upcoming game before they ever set foot on the playing field, so do entrepreneurs envision the kind of company they want to build. The company's "true north" acts like a beacon, guiding it in the right direction. Although it is possible for a company to be successful without a vision, it is difficult, if not impossible, to become a *great* company without a vision. Researchers Jim Collins and Jerry Porras, authors of *Built to Last: Successful Habits of Visionary Companies* and *Good to Great,* back up this assertion.[18] Collins and Porras found that the number-one company in every industry it studied outperformed its number-two competitor by a significant amount in terms of revenues, profits, and return on investment. The primary reason was that each number-one company had a strong vision comprised of core values that it regarded as inviolable. Vision is made up of core values, purpose, and mission. The following sections on these three topics are based on the work of Collins and Porras.

CORE VALUES

Core values are the fundamental beliefs that a company holds about what is important in business and life in general. They are based on the personal values and beliefs of the founder; therefore, they are not something that can be created or invented for the company out of thin air. A company's core values tell the world who it is and what it stands for. Because they are so fundamental to the existence of a company, core values rarely change over time, and they endure beyond the tenure of the founder. For example, Ben & Jerry's core values from their website are as follows (http://www.benjerry.com/our_company/our_mission):

> We strive to create economic opportunities for those who have been denied them and to advance new models of economic justice that are sustainable and replicable. We strive to minimize our negative impact on the environment.

> We support sustainable and safe methods of food production that reduce environmental degradation, maintain the productivity of the land over time, and support the economic viability of family farms and rural communities.

> We seek and support nonviolent ways to achieve peace and justice.

> We strive to show a deep respect for human beings inside and outside our company and for the communities in which they live.

One way to test whether a value (for example, "The customer is always right") is a core value or not is to ask whether it would ever be relinquished if there were a penalty for holding it. If a company is willing to let go of the value, then it is not a core value.

PURPOSE

Purpose is the company's fundamental reason to be in business. It is the answer to the question "Why does the business exist?" It is not necessarily a unique characteristic of the business; in fact, more than one business may share the same purpose. What is crucial is that the purpose be authentic; that is, the company must mean what it says. "We are in the business of helping people" might be the purpose of a socially responsible business. Jordan Neuroscience, a company that provides patented brain nets to monitor a patient's brainwaves in the emergency room, is in the business of "saving brains." A properly conceived purpose will be broad, enduring, and inspiring, and it will allow the company to grow and diversify.[19]

MISSION

A company's mission is what brings everyone together to achieve a common objective and is closely related to the company's purpose. According to Collins and Porras, a mission is a "Big Hairy Audacious Goal" (BHAG), designed to stimulate progress. All companies have goals, but a mission, or BHAG, is a daunting challenge, an overriding objective that mobilizes everyone to achieve it. The natural metaphor for a mission is mountain climbing. The mission is *to scale Mt. Everest,* a major challenge to be sure. To get there, however, will require smaller goals, such as *reaching base camp in one week.* The smaller wins motivate the team to achieve the more bold and compelling mission.

A company's mission is communicated through a mission statement. A mission statement precisely identifies the environment in which the company operates and communicates the company's fundamental philosophy.[20] Peter Drucker asserted that a company's mission should "fit on a t-shirt."[21] The best mission statements are simple, precise, and use clear words.

Here are three examples of mission statements:

Establish Starbucks as the premier purveyor of the finest coffee in the world while maintaining our uncompromising principles while we grow. (Source: http://www.starbucks.com/aboutus/environment.asp)

eBay pioneers communities built on commerce, sustained by trust, and inspired by opportunity. (Source: http://pages.ebay.com/aboutebay/thecompany/companyoverview.html)

Leader to Leader Institute: To strengthen the leadership of the social sector. (Source: http://www.leadertoleader.org/about/index.html)

The mission statement should convey what the company wants to be remembered for; therefore, in writing a mission statement, it is important to gather the thoughts of everyone in the organization. The initial drafts should be evaluated against a set of criteria and should explain why the organization exists, indicate what the company wants to be remembered for, and be sufficiently broad in its scope. It should not prescribe means but should provide direction for doing the right things. Finally, the mission statement should address the company's opportunities, match the company's competence, and inspire the company's commitment.

Figure 12.1 presents a broad view of the components of a complete vision and their relationship to each other. To review, the vision for the company stems from the founder's core value system. It becomes the guideline for all the decisions made by the company as it grows and operates. The company then needs a compelling mission that is congruent with its core values—a BHAG to propel

FIGURE 12.1

The Components of Vision

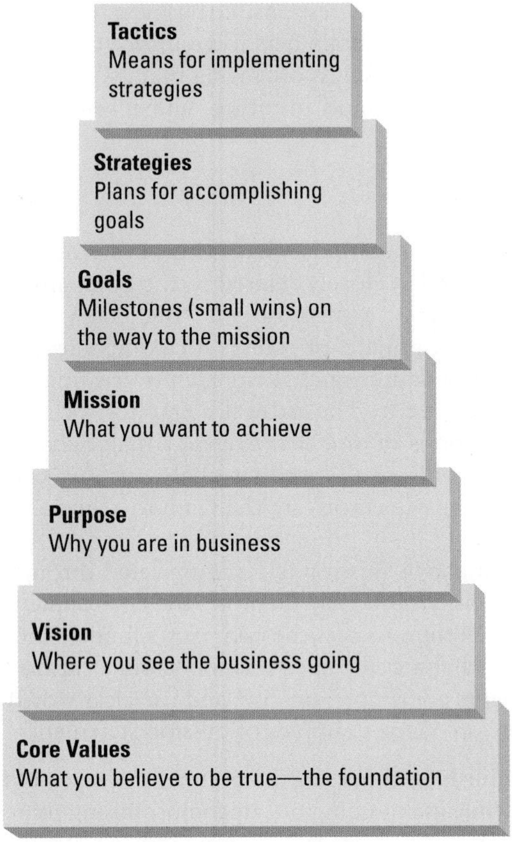

Tactics
Means for implementing strategies

Strategies
Plans for accomplishing goals

Goals
Milestones (small wins) on the way to the mission

Mission
What you want to achieve

Purpose
Why you are in business

Vision
Where you see the business going

Core Values
What you believe to be true—the foundation

it forward—and goals or operating objectives, which are milestones along the way to achieving the mission.

STRATEGIES AND TACTICS

Once goals have been set, strategies should be developed. These are the plans for achieving those goals and, ultimately, accomplishing the mission. Tactics, which are the means to execute the strategies, should also be put in place. An example will make these points clearer. Suppose a company's mission is to be number one in its industry. Two goals or milestones it might set to help it accomplish the mission might be (1) to create an Internet presence and (2) to achieve brand recognition. Strategies for achieving these goals might include building a website to meet goal 1 and developing a marketing campaign to build the brand, goal 2. Then there must be a variety of tactics, or ways to implement the strategies. For example, to implement the strategy of building a website, a company might employ the following tactics: determine the purpose and focus of the website, hire a Web designer and developer, purchase a server, and plan the content.

Merely setting a goal is not enough. A plan for achieving the goal must be in place, and that is the role of strategy. But even strategy is not enough to achieve a company's goals; tactics, or action plans, will also be required.

Core Values and Success

Why are we talking about success in a chapter on ethics and social responsibility? Because an entrepreneur's personal definition of success—what it means to be successful—is really a function of the core values and vision that an entrepreneur has for his or her life. A business's success is easily measured in terms of total revenues, earnings, return on investment, and so forth, but entrepreneurs don't typically measure their personal success solely in these terms. In fact, research has shown that the personal rewards that motivate entrepreneurs to start businesses are independence and freedom.[22] Entrepreneurs tend to be goal-oriented, so being one's own boss, being in control of one's destiny, and having ultimate control of the success of the venture are reasons for going into business. They measure their personal success by their achievement of those goals.

For Sue Szymczak of Safeway Sling in Milwaukee, success is "being happy with what you're doing and feeling as though you're accomplishing something." Muhammad Yanus (see opening profile) takes his belief in social responsibility to the company level and judges his success based on how many people he has helped to achieve economic independence.

CONSTANTS OF SUCCESS

No matter how success is defined, there are some constants that seem to permeate everyone's definition. These constants are purpose, failure, a sense of satisfaction with what was accomplished, and having to pay for, or earn, success.

▶ *Purpose.* To feel successful, entrepreneurs need to know that what they are doing is taking them in the direction of a goal they wish to achieve. True success is a journey, not a destination—even the achievement of a goal will be just a step on the way to the achievement of yet another goal.

▶ *Failure.* The second constant is that life has its ups and downs. Failure is the other half of success, and most entrepreneurs have experienced several failures of one sort or another along the way. Still, they typically do not fear failure, because they know intuitively that those who obsessively avoid failure are doomed to mediocrity. To avoid failing, one has to virtually retreat from life, to never try anything that has any risk attached to it. Most entrepreneurs are calculated risk-takers, so they make sure that every time they come up to bat they give it their best; then, win or lose, they strive to learn from the experience and go on. Entrepreneurs are generally optimists who believe that failure is a normal part of the entrepreneurial process.

▶ *Sense of satisfaction with work.* The most successful entrepreneurs are doing what they love, so their satisfaction level is usually very high. Does satisfaction with the work result in success, or does success bring satisfaction? Probably a little of both, so it's important to know what kinds of tasks and activities will return satisfaction in business.

▶ *No free lunch*. Success rarely comes without work. Entrepreneurs do not have the luxury of a nine-to-five workday; they are usually married to their businesses twenty-four hours a day. It is not just the number of hours of work that distinguishes entrepreneurs, of course, but also the way they use their time. Entrepreneurs make productive use of odd moments in their day—while they're driving, on hold on the telephone, in the shower, or walking to a meeting. Because they love what they're doing, it doesn't feel like work, and that's probably why, wherever entrepreneurs are, they're always working on their businesses in one way or another.

Firm core values and ethics plus a socially responsible business can lead to the kind of success that is meaningful to most entrepreneurs: satisfaction in creating something and seeing it thrive. Today, more than ever before, the world is watching the way entrepreneurs run their businesses, so it is more critical than ever to design a new business on the basis of sound values and ethical practices.

New Venture Checklist

Have you:

☐ Identified the core values held by the founding team?

☐ Developed a code of ethics for the business?

☐ Listed possible ways in which your business can be socially responsible?

☐ Defined what success means to you?

Issues to Consider

business.college.hmco.com/students

ACE
Self-tests

1. Do you believe that your code of ethics should remain firm in any situation? Why or why not?
2. Suppose you are doing business in a country where paying fees (bribes) to get through the process more quickly is standard practice. In the United States, bribery is against the law. How will you deal with this conflict in ethical standards when you're doing business in that country?
3. In addition to the suggestions given in the chapter, name two ways in which your company can demonstrate its social responsibility.
4. Would you require your employees to give back to the community as part of their work contract with your company? Why or why not? If yes, how could you implement this policy?
5. How do you define your personal success? How can your definition be applied to your business?

Experiencing Entrepreneurship

1. Choose an industry that interests you and interview a manufacturer, a distributor, and a retailer about the code of ethics in that industry. In a two-page report discuss whether the industry has ethical problems. If so, what are they and how are people responding? If not, how have they been avoided?

2. Choose two companies in different industries. Interview a manager in each company about its code of ethics and its stance on ethical standards. In a two-page paper, compare these managers' answers and account for any basic differences.

Relevant Case Studies

Case 2 Craigslist, p. 442

Case 6 The Crowne Inn, p. 467

Case 8 Finagle a Bagel, p. 481

## Chapter 13

DESIGNING AN ENTREPRENEURIAL ORGANIZATION

"Until someone has a small business, they have no comprehension of how hard it is. People who start businesses from scratch, if they survive, are the toughest people on the face of the earth."

—SUE SZYMCZAK, Safeway Sling

LEARNING OBJECTIVES

▶ Describe how businesses are organized.

▶ Explain how to identify the appropriate business site.

▶ Discuss the critical issues related to organizing people.

Profile 13.1 YOU WON'T FIND THIS FENDER ON A CAR

If your company and its products achieve the enviable position of being the leading brand in the industry, be prepared for an uproar if you ever make major changes. Fender Musical Instruments can attest to that. Its clients, who range from Bruce Springsteen to Eric Clapton and Travis Tritt, love their Fender guitars because "they're as close to perfection as anything gets." And that has been true for fifty years. Actually, in the 1950s Leo Fender revolutionized the music industry and soon set the standard when he introduced his solid-body electric guitars—the Telecaster and the Stratocaster—to the music industry in a market niche.

In the late 1970s, however, a recession hit, interest rates soared, and Fender's famous quality began a precipitous slide. William Schultz, then an executive for CBS, organized a buyout and in 1985 acquired the name and distribution, taking the company private. At that point Fender was manufacturing only 12 guitars a day because musicians were enthralled by music synthesizers. Schultz, however, was not one to go down in defeat easily. He implemented a total quality management plan to increase productivity, reduce expenses, and give customers exactly what they wanted. More recently, he also implemented an SAP enterprise-level management system to integrate his supply chain as well as other aspects of the business, such as financials, manufacturing, sales, and distribution. These moves made Fender profitable every year from 1985 on. Fender now produces more than 335,000 guitars annually, all presold. Schultz's plan revisited the organization of his business and focused on five areas that needed improvement:

1. *The management team.* Schultz put together a group of people who had musical backgrounds and were as passionate about Fender as he was. As a team, they would carry out the vision.
2. *Location.* He moved the guitar factory from Orange County, California, eastward to less pricey Corona in Riverside County. This enabled the company to focus its resources on production and quality.
3. *Quality.* Schultz invested in state-of-the-art woodworking machines so that the quality of the guitars would be consistent. He also trained every worker in quality control procedures and efficiency, and incorporated inspecting for quality into the manufacturing process, so that every guitar would be defect-free.
4. *Customization.* Schultz created a separate custom shop to meet the needs of customers requesting guitars designed and hand-built to their exact specifications. These customers have a wait of up to one year and pay between $1,500 and $50,000.
5. *Core competency.* One of the outstanding things Schultz did was return Fender to what it had been doing best when it was the industry leader in the late 1950s and 1960s. To win back loyal customers, he reissued some of the original designs and updated 1940s low-tech vacuum-tube amps that were preferred by professional musicians.

Today, Fender Musical Instruments has come of age and is creating the best guitars in the industry; blending science, music, and computer technology; and reducing time-to-market and material costs. Fender partnered with the Experience Music Project (EMP), Seattle's interactive music museum, to create regional and national educational programming. One example of this educational programming is a guitar lease/loan program, which is dedicated to serving underprivileged music students who might not have access to guitars or guitar lessons. Students can learn to play in exchange for giving back to the community by volunteering their time at music-related events. In 2004, Fender acquired Tacoma Guitar, the company that makes guitars for the legendary Bob Dylan, to gain acoustic guitar manufacturing capability and diversify its product line.

This company has successfully reinvented itself. The lesson for entrepreneurs is to maintain the vision at all costs, make sure that employees hold the vision as well, choose the business location carefully, focus on what you do best, and do it the best way you can.

Sources: "Fender Buys Company That Makes Bob Dylan's Guitars," *The New York Times* (October 14, 2004); "Fender Musical Instruments Corp. Partners with Experience Music Project," *Business Wire* (August 28, 2002); Bob Spitz, "And on the Lead Guitar . . . ," *Sky* (August 1996), p. 55; and http://www.fender.com, accessed August 27, 2007.

Organizational design is a critical component of any business plan because it represents the infrastructure, processes, and systems by which the business will move from idea to reality. Therefore, it is important to consider how to organize the business effectively, innovatively, and profitably and in a way that reflects the culture of the organization. Superior organizational design begins with an understanding of how the business works—how information flows through the business. This understanding is critical to making decisions about business location, number of employees, management expertise required, and technology needed to facilitate business goals.

Three broad components make up the entrepreneurial organization: formal processes, people, and culture. Formal processes include the planning system, control mechanisms, compensation and reward policies, and other processes that make the organization run more efficiently and effectively. These processes are not independent but, rather, are linked to all functions of the organization that require them. For example, quality control mechanisms are not solely the purview of a single department, but flow from product development through manufacturing, to distribution, and throughout all the support functions needed to get a product to the customer.

Team building is a common phenomenon in entrepreneurial ventures. People who work in entrepreneurial companies must have team-building skills as well as the ability to make decisions and implement them with very little input from top management or the CEO. In new ventures those teams often consist of independent contractors whose skills are "rented" on an as-needed basis. Out of team building comes informal networks that create flexibility and speed up operations. They also facilitate management of personal issues not easily handled through policies and structure.

Culture is the glue that binds people, processes, and structure. Culture is fundamentally the personality of the organization—the reflection of the company's vision and goals. It forms the basis for all the activities that the company undertakes. It is also the view of the company that customers see. An effective company culture enhances customer relationships, reduces employee turnover, and serves as a formidable competitive advantage for a company.

This chapter focuses on strategies for organizing the business and its many processes, finding a superior location, and putting together a team or work force that will implement the company's processes. Operations related to the production of goods and services are discussed in Chapter 14.

Organization: Understanding the Way the Business Works

There probably is no single best organizational structure for all types of ventures in all situations. Rather, the entrepreneur must find the best fit, given the existing contextual factors (environment, technology, market), design factors (strategy and models), and structural factors (complexity, formalization).[1] A misalignment or misfit among these factors could result in an organizational structure that does not suit the particular market the company wishes to serve. For example, if a firm chose a low-cost strategy to compete but did not implement tight control systems, minimize overhead, and focus on achieving economies of scale, it would probably not succeed.

Firms in different industries tend to also differ in their administrative mechanisms and structures. Several studies have found that the design of the organizational structure—how business activities are grouped, divided, and coordinated—is a critical factor in business performance and that a growing entrepreneurial firm must continually modify its structure to meet the demands of growth.[2] These findings reinforce the argument presented in Chapter 6 on the importance of conducting thorough industry and market analyses to understand the external conditions that will affect the business.

Ambiguity is a significant force in most entrepreneurial ventures. It derives from conflicting constituencies with different goals and needs, and from lack of immediate control over the external environment and resources. As a result, ambiguity often manifests itself in pressures on the new business for legitimacy and commitment.[3] Legitimacy is validation of the business by external constituencies such as suppliers, customers, distributors, and others in the value chain, while commitment is the binding of an individual to the goals of the business. Commitment and legitimacy are interdependent; in particular, legitimacy cannot exist without commitment. The success of an entrepreneurial organization is a function of its ability to secure commitment and legitimacy while operating in an ambiguous context. Suppliers and others in the value chain expect the firm to demonstrate legitimacy through formalized systems and controls, something that entrepreneurial ventures in the earliest stages typically don't have because the dynamic environment in which they operate predisposes them to develop structures that are flexible and loosely defined with informal and minimal management systems.[4]

Information systems technology has facilitated various kinds of organizational structures that enable new businesses to compete more effectively in rapidly changing environments.[5] For example, the move from centralized structures to more decentralized or distributed structures is highly compatible with the mindset of the entrepreneur. Today, companies are increasingly operating at a global level and involving multiple partners on different continents working together. This more distributed form of organization requires new ways to coordinate activities, manage documents, and communicate. Companies are typically distributed on four levels: (1) geographically, whether it be locally or across continents; (2) organizationally by department or project group; (3) temporally by time zone; and (4) by stakeholder groups, which can include such stakeholders as customers, project managers, sales staff, and so forth.[6] Software companies are classic examples of distributed organizations where developers may be located in India, designers in Pakistan, corporate management and sales in the United States, and users around the globe. Despite geographic and organizational distances, the team must find a way to interact effectively to produce the best products and services it can. This is often accomplished through collaborative online work environments and videoconferencing.

Because of limited resources and a creative and opportunistic mindset, entrepreneurs are naturals at improvisation—they are the jazz musicians of the business world—and can find ways to work around even the most rigid structure of a traditional business model. Because entrepreneurial organizations reflect a fine balance between structure and chaos, clarity and ambiguity, they must be innovative and creative. In this type of environment, entrepreneurs can give free rein to new ideas and create space to allow them to grow. They can retain internally what the company does best—its core competencies—and outsource the rest of the activities for which it doesn't have expertise. Limited resources also demand that entrepreneurs look for ways to keep overhead (non–revenue-producing plant and equipment) to a minimum, while spending precious capital on revenue-generating areas of the business like marketing and sales.

IDENTIFYING BUSINESS PROCESSES

One of the most eye-opening experiences an entrepreneur can have is identifying all the processes (activities, tasks, etc.) that occur in the business. Even more revealing of how the business works is a process map or flowchart that traces how information flows through the business. Recall that in Chapter 9, a process flowchart was developed to understand the capital and other resource requirements of the start-up. Designing the operations and organization of the business is not always within the entrepreneur's competence. Nevertheless, considering how the business will operate is crucial to figuring out how many people to hire, how much equipment to purchase, and what kind of facility will be needed. To create such a map of the business processes, take an imaginary tour of the business during a single day, listing all the tasks, people, equipment, supplies, and space required to run the business. Understanding how the business works makes it easier to determine whether to employ a traditional organizational structure or a virtual enterprise structure, which is a more distributed structure.

THE VIRTUAL ENTERPRISE: GETTING TRACTION QUICKLY

In the early 1990s, the virtual organization was a relatively new concept and certainly had yet to benefit from the Internet, which didn't affect the business sector in any significant way until 1995. The term *virtual enterprise* was borrowed from the science of virtual reality, which enables a person to become an integral part of a computer-generated, three-dimensional world. In business, a "virtual enterprise" has much the same purpose. The entrepreneur builds a company that to the rest of the world looks like any other company, but it is a business without walls where the entrepreneur does not incur the risk of acquiring employees, costly equipment, and enormous overhead. A virtual company makes it possible to

FIGURE 13.1	The Virtual Entrepreneurial Organization

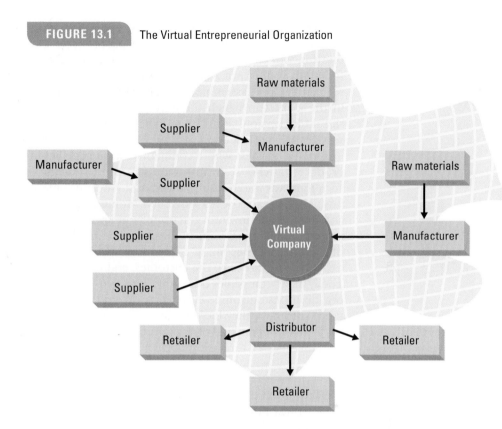

operate the business from practically anywhere—a home, car, or vacation cabin. Research defines the virtual corporation as "a temporary network of independent companies, suppliers, customers, even erstwhile rivals—linked by information technology to share skills, cost, and access to one another's markets."[7] The goal of the virtual enterprise is to deliver to the customer the highest-quality product at the lowest possible cost in a timely manner. To do this requires the participation and management of the entire distribution channel, from producer to customer, through a series of strategic alliances. Once the goal is achieved or a predetermined period of time is met, the virtual organization dissolves itself.[8] Figure 13.1 depicts the network created by a virtual organization. In many cases, the entrepreneurial venture grows to the point where it can afford to buy out its suppliers and/or distributors, giving the company more control over quality and delivery. This strategy is known as vertical integration. Today, in a global business environment, that same goal can also be accomplished through strategic partnerships with other companies in the value chain, which is discussed in the next section.

Outsourcing in a Virtual World

Today it is much more difficult for a new venture to achieve total in-house control of its value chain. The global marketplace is more complex, time-to-market has decreased, and it is difficult for any one company to have the broad expertise necessary to master all the functions of the distribution channel. Today a growing company is more likely to increase its flexibility by choosing one function to concentrate on—its core competency—and subcontracting functions it does not want to handle. The general rule is that if the resources to manufacture, assemble, and distribute the product already exist efficiently in the market in which the entrepreneur wishes to do business, the process should be outsourced. The specific issues related to producing products and services are discussed in Chapter 14.

Often a business whose competitive advantage lies in proprietary rights to its product will choose to maintain control of strategic functions and outsource such things as warehousing, transportation, and some aspects of marketing. Any business may choose to outsource administrative functions such as payroll, accounting, and inventory management and may even lease its employees from an employee-leasing company while operating the company in the virtual world of the Internet. Becoming a virtual company lets the new venture be more innovative, stay closer to the customer, and respond more rapidly to the market. Today many companies outsource aspects of their business processes, but virtual organizations outsource everything except their core management function. To their customers, they look like any other company, but behind the public image lies a very different kind of organization—one where the entrepreneur is basically a ringmaster in a three-ring circus.

Forming a Network of Strategic Alliances

Another way in which virtual companies become more flexible and responsive is by forming strategic alliances, or teams of businesses, to share resources and reduce costs. These alliances are more than sources of capability for the entrepreneurial venture; they are the glue that holds the venture together. Strategic alliances are more like true partnerships. They may purchase major equipment jointly or share the costs of research and development and of training. Particularly in the area of R&D, it is very difficult for any one small company to manage the expense alone. Networking and business alliances enable smaller businesses to bid successfully against large companies. They offer the convenience and savings of access to one source for everything, shared quality standards, and coordination of vendors. The key to managing a small business alliance successfully is being willing to share internal information such as manufacturing processes, quality control practices, and product information for the good of all.

Building a virtual company and dealing with strategic alliances is not without problems. For the entrepreneurial team that wants to maintain control of every aspect of the growing venture, it is frustrating to have to give up some of that control to other companies. Getting virtual partners to meet entrepreneurs' demands for quality, timeliness, and efficiency can also be a long and difficult process. Consequently, it is important that the entrepreneur and the virtual partner come to written agreement on their duties and responsibilities and that they both enjoy the benefits of the relationship. Virtual organizations do have some challenges, namely, higher administrative costs, potential organizational culture differences among the partners, and ethical issues.[9] Many entrepreneurs

BEWARE OF SURPRISES: THE DOWNSIDE OF DOING BUSINESS IN CHINA

Harry Tsao and his partner Talmadge O'Neill were not newcomers to e-commerce. Having founded CouponMountain.com, a place where visitors to the site could find good deals on just about anything, and in 2001, MeziMedia, which became the leading independent online publisher of search, shopping, and content websites globally, they were ready to launch Smarter.com, which would enable users to compare prices and reviews on everything from services to electronics. To accomplish this, they needed top programmers at inexpensive prices—the logical choice was China, since Tsao's parents lived in Shanghai and he was familiar with the business culture there—or so he thought. Tsao set up shop in Shanghai and immediately saved $4,000 per employee over his costs in the United States. Things were looking good, but it wasn't long before he learned that in China employee turnover is very high because everyone is taking one job while they're looking for a better one. He also learned that perks were the norm in China, so he began subsidizing lavish lunches daily; he hired a coach to train employees in things like time management; and he created a budget for fun activities like karaoke outings. He found that Chinese employees did not respond in the same manner as their American counterparts. To get feedback from employees, he had to pull it out of them—the Chinese were unwilling to volunteer their opinions, even when they had them. Learning how to deal with his employees delayed the launch of the company to 2004. Soon after launch, however, he hired two Chinese managers, who also had business experience in the United States and Canada, to run the Shanghai office, figuring that they could more effectively motivate and retain employees than he could. This move also reduced his travel to China to once a quarter, which enabled him to spend more time with his family. Under new management, in time, his employees began showing some initiative and even took leadership roles in developing a new product for the company.

Today Tsao has more than 125 employees in Shanghai and still has the two Chinese managers, who have managed to achieve 80 percent employee retention. The parent company, MeziMedia, hit $40 million in revenues in 2006 and now has offices in Japan as well. According to Tsao, "You've just got to trust your local team and let them do their own thing."

Sources: M. Tsai, "Shanghai Surprises: The Perils of Opening an Office in China," *Inc. Magazine* (March 2007), p. 47; http://www.51job.com, accessed April 14, 2007; and M. Henricks, "Stop the Clock!" *Entrepreneur Magazine*, (June 2006), http://www.entrepreneur.com/magazine/entrepreneur/2006/june/160228.html.

have found that the benefits of virtual partners far outweigh the problems and that the virtual corporation is the most efficient and effective way to give the venture traction. However, there are management issues unique to this type of business, and they must be thoroughly understood. The next section describes what these management challenges are and how to solve them.

Keeping Virtual Employees and Strategic Partners Linked

One of the important challenges that virtual organizations face is keeping everyone connected and in touch even though they are geographically separated. A virtual company may be a great way to keep overhead down and flexibility up, but it is no substitute for human contact and face-to-face communication. Even in a virtual environment, it's important to conduct a face-to-face meeting at least once every three to six months and arrange for employees and partners in specific geographic regions to meet regularly in between company-wide meetings. It is also important to create a discussion area on the company's intranet and to encourage everyone to share important information and discussion points. A regular conference call should be set up once a week to stay in touch, and it's a good idea to investigate video-conferencing. There are companies (Kinko's is one) that rent video time to companies and individuals.

With virtual companies growing by leaps and bounds, online companies have sprung up to provide services and products that these businesses may need. Here are some examples:

Management team: Many websites aggregate independent professionals and help small businesses find experienced financial management on a limited budget.

Marketing: At several online sites, a company can accomplish its public relations, marketing, direct mail, and even market research for far less than it would cost to hire a marketing firm.

Supply chain management: Online companies will do everything from order management to assembly, configuration, packaging, and e-commerce fulfillment and collaboration.

Virtual meetings: Some companies—IBM is one—are holding meetings in cyberspace through a virtual world known as "Second Life" (http://www.secondlife.com). Users (called residents) create avatars (animated characters) to represent themselves and through which they communicate via text messaging, IM, or voice. However, proprietary issues are not discussed because the servers supporting Second Life reside at another company, Linden Labs.

Location: Finding the Appropriate Business Site

If the new venture cannot be operated as a virtual organization, a significant part of the organizing process is finding an appropriate physical site for doing business. Most people are familiar with the three key factors for determining value in home sites: "location, location, location." Similarly, the location of the business has a serious impact on its success. Location determines who will see the business, how easily customers can find it and access it (Is the business at ground-floor level and easily seen? Or is it out of sight in a multistory building?), and whether or not they will want to access it (Is the neighborhood safe? Is parking available?). Even businesses such as manufacturing, where the customer doesn't come to the site, benefit from a location near major sources of transportation. Because many business owners view their business site as permanent, selecting the best site becomes a crucial decision that will need to be justified to investors, lenders, and others. Site decisions generally begin at a macro level, considering first the state or region of the country, next the city, and then the parcel on which the facility will be located.

CHOOSING THE REGION, STATE, AND COMMUNITY

Locating a site for a new business normally begins with identifying the area of the country that seems best suited to the type of business being started. "Best suited" may mean that firms in a particular industry tend to congregate in a particular region, such as the high-tech firms that gravitate to Route 128 in Massachusetts or to the Silicon Valley in California. For some businesses, "best suited" may mean that a state is offering special financial and other incentives for businesses to locate there. In other cases, "best suited" means being located near major suppliers. Often an entrepreneur starts a business in a particular region because that's where he or she happens to live. This may be fine during the incubation period, but soon, what the area contributes to the potential success of the business over the long term must be considered.

The economic base of a region or community is simply the major source of income for the area. Communities are viewed as primarily industrial, agricultural, or service-oriented. In general, industrial communities export more goods than they import. For example, suppose the community's principal income is derived from farming and the associated products that it ships to other communities. This activity brings money into the community. Now suppose the citizens of the community must travel to another community to do major shopping. This activity takes money out of the community. An important thing to learn about any community being considered as the home base for the business is whether the money brought in from farming exceeds the money that leaves through shopping. If it does, the community appears to have a growing economic base, which is a favorable factor for new businesses. Entrepreneurs can learn more about the economic base of any community by contacting the state or regional economic development agency in the area. These organizations exist to bring new business into the region, so they have to stay on top of what is going on. They can provide all the statistics on the economic health of the region, as well as estimate the cost of doing business there. Another helpful site is the U.S. Department of Commerce website (http://www.doc.gov).

Most community governments are faced with cash needs that go well beyond the tax tolerance level of their citizens; consequently, they work diligently with economic development agencies to attract new businesses—and the accompanying tax revenues—into the community. One of the ways they attract businesses is by offering incentives such as lower taxes, cheaper land, and employee training programs. Some communities have enterprise zones, which give the businesses that locate in them favorable tax treatment from the state, on the basis of the number of jobs created, as well as lower land costs and rental rates. They also expedite permit processes and help in any way they can to make the move easier. It is important, however, to be wary of communities that offer up-front cash in compensation for the community's lack of up-to-date infrastructure. The community may be hiding a high corporate tax rate or some other disincentive that could hurt the new business's chances of success. In general, the larger the incentives, the more exacting the entrepreneur's homework must be.

DEMOGRAPHICS

In addition to studying the economic base and the community's attitude toward new business, entrepreneurs should carefully examine the population base. Is it growing or shrinking? Is it aging or getting younger? Is it culturally diverse? The level and quantity of disposable income in the community will indicate whether there is enough money to purchase what a new company is offering, and the skill level of workers in the community will need to meet the needs of the new venture.

Demographic information is usually based on the U.S. census, which tracks changes in population size and characteristics. The United States is divided into Standard Metropolitan Statistical Areas (SMSAs), which are geographic areas that include a major metropolitan area such as Los Angeles or Houston. These are further divided into census tracts, which contain approximately 4,000–5,000 people, and into neighborhood blocks. With this information, it is possible to determine, for example, whether the city in which an entrepreneur wants to locate a new software development firm has enough people with sufficient technical and educational skills to support it. Population data also indicate the number of people available to work. Demographic data are easily obtained from the economic development agency, the public library, the Internet, or the post office, which tracks populations by zip code.

CHOOSING A RETAIL SITE

With a retail business, the entrepreneur is dealing directly with the consumer, so naturally, one of the first considerations is locating near consumers. Because a retail business is unlikely to survive if not enough consumers have access to the business, it is imperative to locate where there are suitable concentrations of consumers. Understanding a trade area is one way to calculate the potential demand from consumers. The trade area is the region from which the entrepreneur expects to draw customers. The type of business will largely determine the size of the trade area. For example, if a business sells general merchandise that can be found almost anywhere, the trade area is much smaller; customers will not travel great distances to purchase common goods. Yet a specialty outlet— for example, a clothing boutique with unusual apparel—may draw people from other communities as well.

Once the location within the community is identified, the trade area can be calculated. With a map of the community, the business site is identified; then, the point of a compass can be placed on the proposed site and a circle can be drawn whose radius represents the distance people are willing to drive to reach the site. Within the circle is the trade area, which can now be studied in more detail. Using a census tract map, census tracts can be identified within the trade area, and the number of people who reside within the boundaries of the

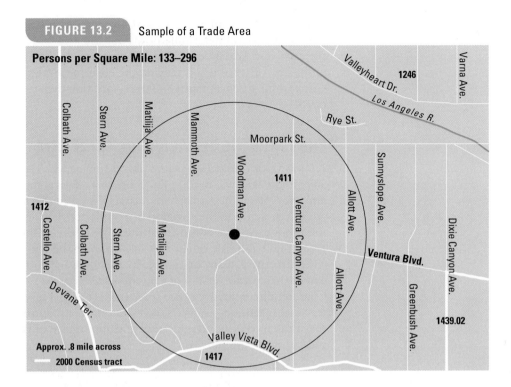

FIGURE 13.2   Sample of a Trade Area

trade area can be calculated (see Figure 13.2). The demographic information will also describe these people in terms of level of education, income level, average number of children, and so forth.

Once the trade area is established, the competition can also be identified. One way to do this is to drive or walk through the area (assuming it is not too large) and spot competing businesses. Note their size and number, and gauge how busy they are at various times of the day by observing their parking lots or actually entering the business. If competitors are located in shopping malls or strip centers, look for clusters of stores that are similar to the new venture and have low vacancy rates. Then look at the stores near the proposed site to check for compatibility. Often, locating near a competitor is a wise choice because it encourages comparison shopping, which is a good thing if the entrepreneur's business has a competitive advantage. Observe the character of the area. Does it appear to be successful and well maintained? Remember that the character of the area will have an important impact on the business.

It is important to identify the routes customers might take to reach a proposed site: highways, streets, and public transportation routes. If a site is difficult to locate and hard to reach, potential customers will not expend the effort to find it. The parking situation should also be checked. Most communities require provision of a sufficient amount of parking space for new construction, through either parking lots or garages; however, in some older areas, street parking is the only available option. If parking is hard to find or too expensive, customers will avoid going to that business. A foot and car traffic count for the proposed site will determine how busy the area is. Remember, retail businesses typically rely heavily on traffic for customers. A traffic count is easily accomplished by observing and tallying the customers going by and into the business. City planning departments and transportation departments maintain auto traffic counts for major arterials in the city.

CHOOSING THE SERVICE/WHOLESALE SITE

If a service or wholesale business has customers who come to the place of business, an entrepreneur will need to find a site that offers some of the same attributes that a retailer looks for. Accessibility, attractiveness, and a trade area of sufficient size are all key factors in the selection of a site. There is no need to choose from among the more expensive commercial sites, because customer expectations are not as great for a wholesale outlet that sells to the public, for example. Customers who patronize these types of businesses usually want to save money, so they don't expect the upscale version of a business site. Some service businesses, on the other hand, require attractive office space that is easily accessible. These are usually professional businesses—lawyers, accountants, consultants, and so forth. The image they present through the location and appearance of their offices is crucial to the success of the business.

CHOOSING THE MANUFACTURING SITE

For the manufacturer, the location choices narrow significantly. Communities have zoning laws that limit manufacturing companies to certain designated areas away from residential, retail, and office commercial sites to reduce the chance of noise, odor, and pollutants affecting citizens. Often these areas are known as industrial parks, and they are usually equipped with electrical power and sewage plants appropriate to manufacturing. By locating in one of these parks, the new business may also benefit from the presence of other manufacturing nearby, which may offer opportunities for networking and sharing resources.

Another common location for manufacturing is within enterprise zones, which are public–private partnerships designed to bring jobs to inner cities, downtown areas, and rural areas suffering from the shift of jobs and population to the suburbs. The draw for businesses is tax incentives, regulatory relief, and employee training programs. Empowerment zones in any state can be found by going to the U.S. Housing and Urban Development Agency website (http://www.hud.gov). Entrepreneurs seeking manufacturing sites are concerned with four key factors: access to suppliers, cost of labor, access to transportation, and cost of utilities. These factors may not be weighted equally. Depending on the type of manufacturer, one or more factors may have greater importance in evaluating a site.

Manufacturers and processors usually try to locate within a reasonable distance of their major suppliers to cut shipping time and save transportation costs. Thus a company that processes food attempts to set up business near the growing fields, so that the food is as fresh as possible when it arrives at the processing plant. Similarly, a manufacturer that uses steel as one of its main raw materials might want to locate in the same region of the country as the steel mills to save the high costs of trucking heavy steel great distances.

Today many manufacturers choose a location on the basis of the cost of labor, rather than proximity to suppliers, because labor is generally the single greatest cost in the production of goods. Wages and laws related to workers, such as workers' compensation, vary from state to state—and sometimes from city to city. For example, California laws and cost of living tend to make it a more expensive place to hire employees than, say, Missouri. Some labor-intensive businesses have found that the only way they can compete is by putting plants in Mexico or China, where labor costs are a fraction of those in the United States, and where laborers are not protected by as many laws. The bottom line is that the entrepreneur must carefully weigh the cost of labor when considering a particular location for a manufacturing plant.

Most manufacturers prefer to locate near major transportation networks: railways, major highways, airports, and ports of call. The reasoning is obvious: The greater the distance between the plant and a major transportation network, the higher the cost to the company and, ultimately, to the customer. Also, the more transportation people who handle the product, the greater the cost. Thus, in terms of simple economics, to remain competitive, manufacturers must conduct a cost-benefit analysis on any proposal to locate away from a major transportation network. Higher transportation costs will result in a smaller profit margin for the company or in higher costs for the customers. Either way, the company loses.

Utility rates vary from state to state, and usually from city to city within a given state. If the new venture is heavily dependent on electricity, gas, or coal, this factor could be a significant variable in the cost of producing a product and therefore should be carefully examined.

Land and location are only part of the equation. If the site contains an existing building, the question becomes whether to lease or to buy. If the site is bare land, building a facility is the only option. Because the facility accounts for a significant portion of a new venture's start-up costs, it is important to consider these scenarios in more detail. See Table 13.1 for an overview of the broad criteria for the lease-build-buy decision and some of the important questions to ask.

ALTERNATIVES TO CONVENTIONAL FACILITIES

Today business owners have a variety of alternatives to conventional business locations. These alternatives lower the cost of overhead and make it easier for a business to change its mind should the location not work out. We'll consider four of these alternative sites: incubators, shared space, mobile locations, and temporary tenant agreements.

Some entrepreneurs find it helpful to start their new venture's life in a business incubator, which has the same purpose as an incubator for an infant—to create a controlled environment that will enhance the chances that the business will survive the start-up phase. Private and state-sponsored incubators can be found in nearly every region of the country for almost any type of business. Incubators offer space at a lower-than-market rate to several businesses, which

TABLE 13.1		The Lease-Build-Buy Decision		

Stage of Business	Lease	Build	Buy	Temporary Space
Questions to Ask	1. Also ask the "buy" questions. 2. Do you need to conserve capital for growth? 3. Do you expect the company to grow rapidly and need to move? 4. Can you include clauses that permit the option to renew the lease? 5. Can you remodel to suit your needs? 6. Which type of lease works best for the business: gross, net, or percentage? Do you have a choice?	1. Do you have the time to build? 2. Is it important to show an asset on your balance sheet? 3. Are your facility needs unique? 4. Do you intend to remain in the facility for a long time?	1. Is the building of sufficient size to meet future needs? 2. Is there sufficient parking? 3. Is there space for customers, storage, inventory, offices, and restrooms? 4. Curbside appeal and compatibility with surroundings? 5. Sufficient lighting fixtures and outlets, and power to run equipment?	1. Do you need to keep overhead costs very low? 2. Are you willing to share space? 3. Is your product or service suitable to a mobile location such as a kiosk or pushcart? 4. Do you need to test the product on customers in a real situation before committing to a building? 5. Do you have a product that can be demonstrated?
Start-up	A short-term lease gives the business the option to move and to gauge its long-term requirements.	At start-up, use this approach only when there is no facility available to meet the needs of the business. It requires large amounts of capital and time.	Not recommended at start-up unless it is the only option and the company is sufficiently capitalized.	Excellent for testing new products, services, and locations on customers. Low overhead.
Rapid Growth	A short-term lease will enable the business to move to larger facilities to meet growing demand without tying up a lot of precious capital.	Resist building during rapid growth as it will use up limited cash needed for growth. It is also a time-consuming process, and time is precious during rapid growth.	Rapid growth is not the time to buy a facility unless the company has received, from investors, a large infusion of cash that more than meets its operational needs.	During rapid growth, temporary locations make sense. This approach keeps the overhead low so that more cash can be directed toward satisfying demand.
Stable Growth	If the location is appropriate to the growth needs of the company, a long-term lease will provide more stability in cash flows.	With stable growth and positive cash flow, the company can afford to spend the time, effort, and capital to build a facility that specifically meets its needs.	Buying a building that allows for expansion is appropriate when company growth stabilizes and the company has a loyal customer base. It is also appropriate when the company needs to show a sizable asset on its balance sheet. If the company subsequently needs cash for a new period of growth, it can sell the building to an investor and lease it back, providing an instant infusion of capital.	Temporary space will typically be used to test new products and services before making a commitment.

may then share common support functions, such as receptionist, copy machine, and conference room. The incubator may even offer business courses and training to help new entrepreneurs with the myriad details involved in running the business. After about three to five years, depending on the incubator, the young business is helped to move into its own site elsewhere in the community.

Some incubators cater only to high-tech firms or to service firms. Others, such as the Entrepreneur Partnership Program at the Mall of America in Bloomington, Minnesota, help entrepreneurs determine whether their retail or service businesses are suited to the demands of a major mall. This particular program helps the entrepreneur formulate a business plan and open a store. It also provides such incentives as waiving the costs of improving the store space and consulting in marketing and operations. When considering an incubator, it is imperative to look at its track record and make sure it provides critical higher-order needs, such as a network of contacts, access to expertise and capital, professional resources, and access to customers.

Another choice is to locate the company within the facilities of a larger company. As the largest of the chain stores continue to downsize, opportunities to take excess space arise. A variation on this theme is to lease a location that has enough space to sublet to a complementary business. For example, a copy service might lease excess space to a new computer graphics company or one that is seeking a new location. A shared arrangement is an effective way to secure the best location at a reasonable price.

One of the more interesting ways to introduce new businesses and new products/services to the marketplace is through the use of pushcarts and kiosks. Pushcarts and their more fixed alternative, the kiosk (a small booth), also enable a company to expand so that they have many new locations without the high overhead of a conventional retail storefront. Mobile locations like these are often found in airports, malls, and other areas where consumers gather.

Some landlords have found that, rather than sitting on an empty space until the new tenant moves in, they can rent the space on a temporary basis so that their cash flow is not interrupted. In fact, the concept of the temporary tenant has grown so rapidly that there are now leasing agents who specialize in that area. The most successful of these temporary tenants possess the following characteristics that seem to draw customers to them: personalized merchandise, opportunities to sample the product, products that can be demonstrated, and products that can be used for entertaining the customers. For the temporary concept to work, significant foot traffic and high customer turnover are required. This is an excellent alternative for retail businesses that want to test a location before making a major commitment. Whichever choice is made, the location and type of facility need to be compatible with the business and its strategic goals.

People: Organizing Start-up Human Resources

At no time is the entrepreneur's role as leader of the organization more critical or more vulnerable than in the first year of the business. If the entrepreneur is not able to gain traction and build momentum to propel the new venture forward, the new business will remain in a constant state of struggle.

To build an effective organization, the entrepreneur must avoid some common leadership traps:[10]

◗ Isolating himself or herself from the rest of the start-up team and failing to keep the lines of communication open

◗ Always having the one "right" answer instead of looking for the best solution

◗ Keeping people on board who are not up to the needs of the company

◗ Taking on too much too soon

◗ Setting unrealistic expectations based on inadequate information

◗ Not building support

The organization of the business processes and the business location are critical aspects of the management and operational plan, but it is people who implement those processes and use the company facility on a daily basis. The roles and responsibilities of people in the organization are typically depicted in an organizational chart. See Figure 13.3 to compare the traditional organizational chart, which tends to have layers or a hierarchy, with the distinctive virtual entrepreneurial start-up depicted in Figure 13.1. The entrepreneur and the founding team often perform all the functions when the business is just starting, and much of the work is accomplished through an informal organization or network of relationships. Informal networks of people consist of those who tend to gravitate toward each other in an effort to accomplish tasks in a more efficient and effective manner than may be dictated by the organizational chart. These networks form the "shadow" organizational structure that often brings the business through an unexpected crisis, an impossible deadline, or a formidable impasse. They are social links that constitute the real power base in the organization.

FIGURE 13.3 Traditional Line and Staff Organizational Chart for a Simple Manufacturing Plant

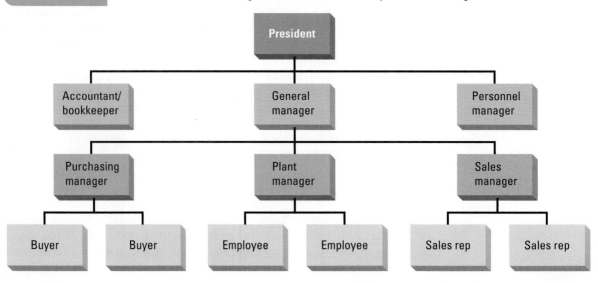

Metaphorically speaking, the organizational chart is the skeleton of the body, while the informal networks are the arteries and veins that push information and activity throughout the organization—in other words, they are the lifeblood of the organization.

Entrepreneurs seem to recognize intuitively the value of informal networks in the organizational structure, and often the most successful new ventures adopt a team-based approach with a flatter structure. The lead entrepreneur is the driving force for the entrepreneurial team, which normally consists of people with expertise in at least one of the three functional areas of a new venture: marketing, operations, and finance. The organization consists of interactive, integrated teams. In the new venture, these are rarely "departments" in the traditional sense, but rather functions, tasks, or activities. What is the explanation for this? For one thing, entrepreneurs are usually too creative and flexible to be bound by the strictures of a formal organizational structure. They are more comfortable bringing together resources and people as a team and making decisions on the spot without having to go through layers of management. Another reason is that new, growing ventures must be able to adapt quickly as they muscle their way into the market. Uncertainty and instability are a way of life for young ventures, and a rigid, formalized, bureaucratic structure would unduly burden a new venture both financially and operationally.

What makes the entrepreneur's situation unique is that—at least when the venture is in the start-up phase or the initial growing phase and capital resources are limited—the team the entrepreneur develops will probably include several people from outside the organization: independent contractors. For example, an entrepreneur may decide to subcontract the manufacturing of a product to an established company. The subcontractor will then, of necessity, become a part of that company's team in the production of the product. Marketing, sales, operations, and finance people must also be able to work with the manufacturing subcontractor to ensure that the goals of the new venture are met with the timeliness and level of quality desired. This requires the team to have skills not normally learned in school, skills such as diplomacy in the management of intra- and inter-team relationships, problem-solving skills, and the ability to take responsibility for innovative changes on the spot, often without direct approval.

HIRING THE RIGHT PEOPLE

Today, with more and more employees suing their bosses for wrongful discharge, sexual harassment, and racial/gender/age discrimination, it is increasingly important that an entrepreneur understand how to hire. Hiring is not a simple matter of placing a help-wanted ad in the newspaper, receiving résumés, and then holding interviews to select the best candidate. The bulk of the work of hiring comes before the person is actually needed.

Part of organizing the business is determining what positions are needed for the required tasks of the business. This is a wise practice, because employees are generally the largest expense of the business and therefore should be hired only when necessary. Nevertheless, it is important to develop job descriptions to prepare for the eventuality of hiring employees. Typically, when entrepreneurs (and managers) develop job descriptions, they focus entirely on the duties and responsibilities of a particular job. Although this is important, it is equally important to develop behavioral profiles of these jobs. Even though a job candidate may have the education and experience required by the job description and may display some of the behavioral traits necessary for success in the position, the candidate's personality and values may not fit in well with the culture of the organization. This is an important distinction, because education and experience can be acquired and behaviors can in most cases be taught, but the right values—which enable compatibility with the company culture—must already be present. In today's business environment, a company's culture is a competitive advantage, so hiring people whose attitudes and values are consistent with it becomes a most important goal in hiring.

The first and best place to look for an employee is among current employees, subcontractors, or professional advisers. Referrals from trusted people who know the business have a greater likelihood of yielding a successful hire. Even during start-up, it is important to be constantly on the lookout for good people who might come on board as the business grows. Executive search firms are good sources for management positions, and online resources have become an effective starting place for hiring, particularly with technically oriented positions. Companies such as Monster.com (http://www.monster.com), Guru.com (http://www.guru.com), and Craigslist (http://www.craigslist.com) are places where qualified people post their résumés, and it's easy for an employer to search for the particular skills required. But to save time and avoid interviewing the wrong people, it's always wise to follow up with references before calling the candidate in for an interview.

Most entrepreneurs dread interviewing job candidates, primarily because they don't know what to say and don't understand that their questions should be designed to reveal the individual's personality and behavior—how he or she might react in certain situations. This can be accomplished in part by asking open-ended questions, questions that call for more than "yes–no" answers. For example, ask, "What is your greatest strength?" or "How would you handle the following hypothetical situation?" While the person is answering the questions, be careful to note the nonverbal communication being expressed through body language.

Entrepreneurs must be aware that certain questions should never be asked in an interview situation because they are illegal and leave the entrepreneur open to potential lawsuits. Under the laws administered by the Equal Employment Opportunity Commission (EEOC), before the point of hire a person may *not* be asked about religion or religious background, nation of origin, living arrangements or lifestyle choices, plans for pregnancy, age (to avoid discrimination against people over 40 or under 21), criminal arrest record ("Have you ever been convicted of a crime?" may be asked), or military record.

Human Resource Leasing

Entrepreneurs who are not ready to hire permanent employees or who need to remain flexible because the business environment is volatile and unpredictable may want to consider leasing employees or employing temporary services. A leased employee is not legally the entrepreneur's employee but is, rather, the employee of the lessor organization. That firm is responsible for all employment taxes and benefits. The entrepreneur simply receives a bill for the person's services. Employee leasing is a rapidly growing industry now known as the professional employer organization (PEO) industry (http://www.peo.com/peo). More and more business owners are finding it advantageous to have a third party manage their human resources. In effect, the PEO becomes a co-employer, taking on the responsibility of payroll, taxes, benefits, workers' compensation insurance, labor law compliance, and risk management. Elizabeth Bradt is an accomplished veterinarian, but like many professional service providers, she did not have the skills or the patience to handle human resource issues, such as hiring interviews, regulatory compliance, and benefits. She couldn't offer the types of benefits that large employers offer, such as 401(k) plans and dental insurance. As a result, her business, All Creatures Veterinary Hospital in Salem, Massachusetts, lost half its employees in the first year. Bradt had not realized how much she would have to deal with when it came to hiring and supporting her staff. To solve the problem, she made Integrated Staffing, a professional employer organization, the legal employer of her staff. The PEO gave her peace of mind and provided her employees with benefits that she alone could not have provided. As a result, in 2006, she had zero turnover.[11]

MANAGING EMPLOYEE RISK

Risk management is a set of policies and their associated decision-making processes that reduce or eliminate risks associated with having employees. For example, one entrepreneurial service company with 120 employees was suffering from a high turnover rate of new hires during the first 90 days of employment. Although the company's overall turnover rate was in line with the industry average, its turnover rate for new hires was about double that of its competitors. This turnover was costing the company more than $10,000 per employee. This was a significant financial risk for the company and raised its cost of doing business substantially. To solve the problem and reduce the risk, they realized that they needed to implement some new procedures, so the company improved its interviewing skills and instituted an orientation program for new employees.

Financial risks are one type of employee risk. In Chapter 11 the legal issues related to the formation of the business were discussed, but the law affects every aspect of business operations as well, especially the way employees are treated. The federal government and state governments have enacted a number of laws and regulations to protect employees from unhygienic or dangerous work environments, discrimination during hiring, and payment of substandard wages. One of the critical tasks of the person in charge of human resources is to make certain that the business is obeying all the laws and regulations to which it is subject. Failure to do so could result in severe penalties for the business and its owners. It is not within the scope of this text to address these laws in depth; however, Table 13.2 presents some of the major employment laws that affect small businesses. More information can be found on the Internet and through the federal and stage agencies associated with these laws.

TABLE 13.2	Law	Type of Business It Applies to
Important Employment Laws	**Age Discrimination in Employment Act** Prohibits discrimination against people age 40 to 70, including discrimination in advertising for jobs	All companies with 20 or more employees
	Americans with Disabilities Act Prohibits discrimination on the basis of disability	All companies with 15 or more employees
	Civil Rights Act Guarantees the rights of all citizens to freedom from discrimination on the basis of race, religion, color, national origin, and sex	All companies with 15 or more employees
	Equal Pay Act Requires equal pay for equal work	All companies with 15 or more employees
	Family and Medical Leave Act Provides for up to 12 weeks of unpaid leave for employees who are dealing with family issues	Companies with 50 or more employees
	Immigration Reform and Control Act and the Immigration Act of 1990 Designed to prevent undocumented aliens from working in the United States. Companies must complete an Employment Eligibility Verification Form (I-9) for each employee.	All companies of any size
	National Labor Relations Act and Taft-Hartley Act Requires employers to bargain in good faith with union representatives and forbids unfair labor practices by unions	All companies of any size
	Occupational Safety and Health Act (OSHA) Designed to ensure safety and health in the work environment	All companies of any size
	Title VII of the Civil Rights Act The original was amended to include discrimination against pregnant women; people with AIDS, cancer, or physical and mental disabilities; and people who are recovering from, or being treated for, substance abuse. Victims of discrimination may sue for punitive damages and back pay.	Companies with 15 or more employees for 20 weeks in the current or preceding year
	Workers' Compensation Each state has enacted a law to compensate employees for medical costs and lost wages due to job-related injuries.	Requirements vary by state

PLANNING FOR OWNERSHIP AND COMPENSATION

Two of the most perplexing management issues faced by an entrepreneur heading a new corporation are how much of the company to sell to potential stockholders and how much to pay key managers. Whatever route is ultimately chosen, it should reflect the goals of the company and reward the contributions of the participants. There is a tendency on the part of small, privately held companies to use minority shares as an incentive to entice investors and to pay key managers, primarily because new companies do not have the cash flow to provide attractive compensation packages. The prevailing wisdom is that providing stock in the new company will increase commitment, cause management to be more cost-conscious, reduce cash outlay for salaries, and induce loyalty to the company in the long term. But studies have found that this is not always the case.[12] More often than not, the person who has been given stock in good faith will ultimately leave the company, possibly taking the stock with her or him (absent an agreement prohibiting this), and this action creates the potential for future harm to the business. During the dot com craze of the late 1990s and into 2000, stock options were the most attractive benefit to potential employees, and many candidates would forgo large salaries in favor of more stock options. But after the dot com crash in April 2000 and the subsequent decline in valuation of technology stocks in general, stock options took second place to salaries in the minds of many employees.

In the initial growth stage of a new venture, it is difficult to determine with any degree of accuracy what long-term role a particular person may play in the organization. As a consequence of their limited resources, entrepreneurs typically are not able to attract the best people to take the company beyond the start-up phase, so they often hire a person with lesser qualifications for little salary plus a minority ownership in the company. In this scenario, the entrepreneur is literally betting on the potential contribution of this person—and it is a gamble that frequently doesn't pay off. Later, when the company can afford to hire the person it needs, it will have to deal with a minority shareholder who has developed territorial "rights." Therefore, when minority ownership is an important issue to a potential employee, it is imperative to make clear to that person exactly what it means. There are few legal and managerial rights associated with a minority position; thus, for all practical purposes, minority ownership is simply the unmarketable right to appreciated stock value that has no defined payoff period and certainly no guarantee of value. Using a stock-vesting agreement is one way to make sure that only stock that has been earned will be distributed. With a stock-vesting agreement, stock purchased by the team is placed in escrow and released over a three- to five-year period. A buyback provision in the stockholders agreement is another way to ensure that stock remains in the company even if a member of the team leaves in the early days of the new venture.

Giving someone ownership rights in the company is a serious decision that should receive very careful consideration. There are several things to contemplate before taking on an equity partner, be it an investor or key manager. For example, anyone brought in as an investor/shareholder or partner with the entrepreneur does not have to be an equal partner. An investor can hold whatever share of stock is warranted on the basis of what that partner will contribute to the business. In general, one should never bring someone in as a partner/investor if that person can be hired to provide the same service, no matter how urgent the situation. The most advantageous way to hire someone for a new venture is to hire the person as an independent contractor. In addition, the company should not be locked into future compensation promises such as stock options, and cash for bonuses should be used whenever possible. It is important that the company be established as the founder's before any partners are taken on—unless, of course, the company has been founded by a team. Finally, employees should typically work for the company at least two years before they are given stock or stock options.

Founder's Stock

Founder's stock (144 stock) is stock issued to the first shareholders of the corporation or assigned to key managers as part of a compensation package. The payoff on this stock comes when the company experiences a liquidity event such as an IPO or an acquisition by another company. Assuming that the company is successful, founder's stock at issuance is valued at probably the lowest it will ever be, relative to an investor's stock value. Consequently, a tax problem can arise when private investors provide seed capital to the new venture. Often the value of the stock the investors hold makes it very obvious that the founder's stock was a bargain and that its price did not represent the true value of the stock. According to Internal Revenue Code (IRC) §83, the amount of the difference between the founder's price and the investor's price is taxable as compensation income. One way to avoid this problem is to issue common stock to founders and key managers and to issue convertible preferred stock to investors. The preference upon liquidation should be high enough to cover the book value of the corporation, so the common stockholders would receive nothing. This action would effectively decrease the value of the common stock so that it would no longer appear to be a bargain for tax purposes and subject the founders to an immediate tax liability.

Founder's stock is restricted, and the SEC rules (Rule 144) state that the restriction refers to stock that has not been registered with the SEC (private placement) and stock owned by the controlling officers and shareholders of the company (those with at least 10 percent ownership). If a stockholder has owned the stock for at least three years and public information about the company exists, Rule 144 can be avoided in the sale of the stock. If the stockholder has held the stock for less than three years, the rules must be strictly complied with. It is not the intent of this chapter to discuss the details of Rule 144. Suffice it to say that the rule is complex and that the appropriate attorney or tax specialist should be consulted.

ISSUING STOCK WHEN THE COMPANY IS CAPITALIZED

The number of shares authorized when a corporation is formed is purely arbitrary. Suppose a new venture, NewCorp, authorizes one million shares of stock. This means that NewCorp has one million shares available to be issued to potential stockholders. If each share of stock is valued at $1 and $100,000 is capitalized, the company will have 100,000 issued shares; if each share is valued at $10, the company will have 10,000 issued shares. The value placed on each share is arbitrary. For psychological reasons, however, it is customary to value a share at $1, so a shareholder who contributes $10,000 to the business can say that he or she owns 10,000 shares of stock (as opposed to 1,000 shares at

$10/share). In short, the number of shares issued depends on the initial capitalization and the price per share.

Now suppose that the founder of NewCorp initially contributes $250,000 in cash and $300,000 in assets (equipment, furniture, etc.) to fund the company. At $1 a share, the company issues the founder 550,000 shares of stock; this constitutes a 100 percent interest in the company, because only 550,000 shares have been issued. At a later date, the company issues 29,000 additional shares at $5 a share to an investor. This minority shareholder has therefore contributed $145,000 (29,000 shares at $5/share) to the company and owns a 5 percent (29,000/579,000) interest in the company (that is, 29,000 of the 579,000 shares of stock that have been issued). The investor will require that the current value or future additional income of the company be sufficient to justify the increase in price per share. As additional shares are issued, the original investor's percentage ownership in the company declines or is diluted. However, the founder's shares will not go below 55 percent (550,000/1,000,000) unless the company authorizes additional shares and issues a portion or all of those additional shares.

The type of stock issued is common stock, which is a basic ownership interest in the company. This means that holders of common stock share in both the successes and the failures of the business and benefit through dividends and the appreciating value of the company. Once common stock is issued, a company can then issue preferred stock, whose holders are paid first if the company is liquidated. Preferred stockholders must accept a fixed dividend amount, no matter how much profit the company makes. Recall that if the company were a sub-chapter S-corporation, it could issue only one class of stock.

ALTERNATIVES TO EQUITY INCENTIVES

There are other ways to compensate key managers that do not require the founder to give up equity in the company. The following are a few of these alternatives. In choosing among them, consider the advice of an accountant, who can recommend the most appropriate structure for the business.

Deferred Compensation Plans

In a deferred compensation plan, the entrepreneur can specify that awards and bonuses be linked to profits and performance of both the individual and the company, with the lion's share depending on the individual's performance. The employee does not pay taxes on this award until it is actually paid out at some specified date.

Bonus Plans

With a bonus plan, a series of goals are set by the company with input from the employee, and as the employee reaches each goal, the bonus is given. This method is often used with sales personnel and others who have a direct impact on the profitability of the company. The key to success with bonus plans is to specify measurable objectives.

Capital Appreciation Rights

Capital appreciation rights give employees the right to participate in the profits of the company at a specified percentage, even though they are not full shareholders with voting rights. Capital appreciation rights, or "phantom stock," provide long-term compensation incentives whose value is based on the increase in the value of the business. The phantom stock will look, act, and reward like real stock, but it will have no voting rights and will limit the employee's obligation should the business fail. Typically, the employee has to be with the company for a period of three to five years to be considered vested in capital appreciation rights, but otherwise employees do not have to pay for these rights.

Profit-Sharing Plans

Profit-sharing plans are distinct from the previously discussed plans in that they are subject to the ERISA rules for employee retirement programs. These plans must include all employees, without regard to individual contribution to profit or performance. They are different from pensions in that owners are not required to contribute in any year and employees are not "entitled" to them.

Organizing business processes, location, and people is an important and difficult task that requires thought and planning. Decisions made in the earliest stages of the new venture can seriously—and often negatively—affect the new firm's ability to grow and be successful in the future. This chapter highlighted many critical organizational considerations and offered suggestions for addressing them. However, it is important to consult with people who specialize in these functions to be sure that the right decisions are made.

New Venture Checklist

Have you:

☐ Identified the processes and information flow in your business?

☐ Identified ways to operate like a virtual enterprise or at least to outsource some aspects of the business?

☐ Located a site for the business?

☐ Decided whether to lease, buy, or build the facility?

☐ Determined the personnel required to run the business at start-up and over the next three to five years?

☐ Created job profiles for positions in the business?

☐ Determined the ownership and compensation requirements of the business? Formulated a plan to find the best candidates for positions in the company?

Issues to Consider

1. What are the advantages and the disadvantages of a virtual company?
2. What is the purpose of the imaginary tour of the business?
3. Which factors important in choosing a retail site would not be relevant to a manufacturing site—and vice versa?
4. What are the advantages and disadvantages of using stock as compensation and incentives?
5. How can the entrepreneur improve the chances of choosing the best job candidate?
6. List three alternatives to equity incentives for key managers.

Experiencing Entrepreneurship

1. Choose an industry in which you have an interest. Find a business in that industry, arrange to visit the site and talk with key personnel, and do a flowchart of the business processes that reflects what you learned about it on your visit. Did you find any inefficiencies that if corrected could improve the process flow?

2. Interview an entrepreneur about his or her hiring practices. How successful have those practices been in getting and retaining good employees?

Relevant Case Studies

Case 6 The Crowne Inn, p. 467
Case 7 Linksys, p. 477

Case 8 Finagle a Bagel, p. 481

## Chapter 14

MANAGING OPERATIONS

"One way to increase productivity is to do whatever we are doing now, but faster. . . . There is a second way. We can change the nature of the work we do, not how fast we do it."

—ANDREW S. GROVE, CEO, Intel Corporation

LEARNING OBJECTIVES

▮ Identify the components of the production process.

▮ Discuss how to manage quality.

▮ Explain how outsourcing can benefit an entrepreneurial venture.

▮ Understand key issues in supply chain management.

Profile 14.1 CAPITALIZING ON GE'S LEAVINGS

Imagine generating $40 million in revenues from someone else's garbage. That's exactly what Thomas Mackie and Paul Reckwerdt did when, in 1997, GE Medical, which had been funding their research, decided that it wouldn't amount to a substantial business. Mackie and Reckwerdt were working on a machine that would make a radiation beam lock onto a tumor so that a doctor could clearly see it and, at the same time, zap it with radiation with amazing accuracy. GE Medical had been providing the duo with approximately $700,000 annually, so losing that funding was a major crisis. But since both men had lost close relatives to cancer, they were not about to give up. Using $1.5 million that they had received for selling a medical software program, they launched TomoTherapy to develop and market the Hi-Art, a combination CT scan and radiation gun. They received FDA approval in 2002 and in 2003 began installing eight of the $3.2-million machines.

Yet as positive as that was, there was danger on the horizon. Large medical device companies such as Siemens Medical Solutions and Varian Medical Systems had also recognized the opportunity and were hastening to bring their own versions of the Hi-Art to market. It is not easy for a small, entrepreneurial company spun out from a university lab to compete with the manufacturing and marketing resources of a public company. But Mackie and Reckwerdt are innovators who are able to look at a problem from hundreds of angles. They also knew that they didn't possess the business smarts to compete in the volatile medical device industry. So they brought on John Barni, a 28-year veteran of Marconi Medical, who was experienced in both manufacturing and marketing. Still, the road ahead may be rocky. Despite patents on aspects of its machine, TomoTherapy can't prevent competitors from building machines that also combine high-quality imaging with radiation treatment. Varian and Elektra are both introducing machines that compete directly with TomoTherapy, but Barni is convinced that Tomo can preserve its advantage by constantly innovating at a faster pace than its much larger competitors. As of 2007, TomoTherapy Inc. has more than 100 clinical partners in more than 15 countries. In February 2007, the company filed for a proposed initial public offering.

Sources: TomoTherapy, http://www.tomotherapy.com, accessed April 22, 2007; J. Martin, "Finding Gold in GE's Garbage," *Fortune Small Business* (April 25, 2004), http://www.fortune.com; and "TomoTherapy Inc. Gains FDA 510(k) Clearance for New Radiation Therapy System," eReleases, http://www.ereleases.com/pr/2002-02-01b.html, accessed July 20, 2004.

In today's competitive environment, operations management has become a critical success factor for any business. Operations management covers activities and processes such as new product development, purchasing, inventory, production, manufacturing, distribution, and logistics that are necessary to produce and distribute products and services. The manner in which operations are managed is dependent on the type of organization, whether that be retail, wholesale, manufacturing, or service. The ability to innovate in the operations of the business can be a superior competitive advantage for any entrepreneurial company. Operational innovation is not merely improving the performance of existing operations but rather "fundamentally changing how [the] work gets accomplished."[1] This means finding new ways to fill customer orders, create new products and services, and deal with customer service. Wal-Mart is the largest company in the world because of operational innovation. Its cross-docking strategy for moving goods from the supplier directly to its trucks going to the various Wal-Mart stores has resulted in substantially lower operating costs that it has passed on to its customers in the form of lower prices. Other companies known for operational innovations include Toyota, Dell, and Progressive Insurance.

Very few business owners think about the cost of operations until their products and services have become commoditized—that is, they find themselves competing on price rather than on value. It is only then that they begin to look for ways to improve operations and cut costs to maintain or improve their profit margins. Entrepreneurs with start-up ventures have an advantage in this regard, because they can more easily implement process innovations without having to overcome the challenge of existing structures. In this chapter we look at the major areas of operations that entrepreneurs need to understand and which areas offer opportunities for both process innovation and operational excellence.

Producing Products and Services

In simple terms, production is about managing the flow of material and information from raw materials to finished goods.[2] Think of manufacturing equipment as hardware, and of the people and information needed to run the machines as software, and it's easy to see why it's possible for two companies to have the same equipment and yet produce significantly different products. The difference lies in the software driving the machinery—in other words, information and people.

Many high-growth ventures market innovative new products. The operational plan for the business consists of a fairly complex product development analysis that includes prototyping, production processes, supply chain, and inventory control mechanisms. The depth of analysis is a function of the type of product offered, the technological newness of the product, and the number of different ways the product can be produced. The more complex the product, the deeper the analysis needs to be.

Building a complex production system while the company is in start-up or even later when it is rapidly growing is a recipe for disaster. Not having a reliable fulfillment process in place prior to launch has cost many a company customer loyalty and significant revenues because the company was unable to produce and deliver products to customers in a timely fashion. Once lost, that customer base is nearly impossible to regain in time to fend off competing firms and save the company from failure. As noted in Chapter 13, the virtual enterprise, consisting of strategic alliances among all links in the value chain, is one way to achieve control of the entire process from raw materials to distribution, while still keeping the firm small and flexible enough to meet changing needs and demands. This model is similar to the Japanese *keiretsu* in the automobile industry, which links banks, suppliers, electronics firms, and auto companies through a series of cross-ownerships. The U.S. model leaves ownership in the hands of the individual owners but links the organizations into a virtual entity that acts as a team with a common goal. Wal-Mart is probably the best example of this type of partnership and integration in the United States. It has established point-of-sale linkups with its suppliers and has given its manufacturers the responsibility for handling inventory. The ultimate goal is to construct one organization with a common purpose that encompasses the entire supply chain from raw materials supplier to retailer, with each link along the chain performing the task that it does best. Establishing this type of network takes time. A start-up company can't expect to achieve quickly the level of integration and control that a Wal-Mart has taken years to accomplish. Instead, start-up companies need to build relationships slowly, beginning with key independent contractors to whom they may be outsourcing some tasks.

One of the best ways to understand how the production process touches customers and affects the bottom line is to follow an order through the company and document where the order flow gets bogged down, is duplicated, or is hindered in some manner. Any slowdown or duplication of effort means higher production costs and slower response to the customer. Consider a market research firm that provides customized reports to companies to enable them to judge their markets for new products and services. This is an example of what would typically be called a service firm, yet note that this service firm produces a product—a market research report. Now suppose that in the process of gathering the research and analyzing it, there is no plan for who should do a particular aspect of the research. Duplication of effort could easily occur, and it's possible that something important, such as an emerging competitor, might be overlooked. Both duplication of effort and the need to go back and cover something that has been overlooked are costly and delay the production process, potentially causing the company to miss a customer deadline.

TECHNOLOGY'S ROLE IN PRODUCTION

Technology has made an enormous difference in the ability of manufacturers to be more productive and flexible, better manage their supply chains, and achieve the highest levels of quality. For example, for any product or project, it's important to track all the components, raw materials (parts), or data that are required to produce a particular product or service. Some items to track include

- The costs to purchase from the supplier and inspect for quality
- The length of time raw materials or supplies sit in the company's inventory before they are used in the production process
- How many people handle the parts or data before they become part of the product or project
- How many set-ups (adjustments of machinery to do a particular task) before the product can be assembled
- How much time a product or project spends in production
- How many times errors occur during the process
- How effective the delivery process is.

Each one of these points in the process can be a source of delay and cost for the company, so the production process needs to make each one as efficient and effective as possible. Bar coding and RFID technology have made this job much easier. Bar codes placed on inventory items contain all of the information about the product. By scanning with remote RFID readers or handheld bar code readers, it is possible to capture production information without entering it manually into a computer, saving time and decreasing the opportunity for errors.

Computer-generated manufacturing is another way that production processes have improved through technology. Today it is possible to program a machine to produce exactly the part needed quickly and more accurately in terms of specifications and tolerances than could be accomplished using traditional, noncomputerized methods. And because the machines are computers, it's easy to track the progress of any product as it moves through production and assembly.

Electronic data interchange, or EDI, enables the movement of complex graphical data between remote sites in real time. EDI is critical for manufacturers that outsource some capabilities to other companies whether domestic or offshore. It also connects manufacturers with their distributors and retailers so that when stock at those outlets needs to be replenished, the manufacturer is notified automatically.

The Production Process

The production process—as depicted in Figure 14.1—consists of a series of inputs, such as raw materials, labor, and machinery, which are then transformed into new products and services. Each component of the process must be managed, measured, and tested for efficiency and effectiveness. In general, manufacturing and production firms are organized as product-focused or process-focused organizations. Product- or project-focused organizations normally are highly decentralized or distributed so that they can respond better to market demands. Each product or project group acts essentially as a separate company or profit center. This type of organization is well suited to products or projects that don't require huge economies of scale or capital-intensive technologies. Process-focused organizations, on the other hand, are common among manufacturers with capital-intensive processes (such as those in the semiconductor industry) and among service companies (such as advertising firms). These organizations are highly centralized in order to control all the functions of the organization.

The primary functions of the product process include (1) purchasing, (2) materials management and production scheduling, (3) production, (4) quality control, and (5) maintenance. Each is discussed in the following sections.

FIGURE 14.1

The Production Process

Inputs
Raw materials
Labor
Machinery
Facility

Transformation
Materials management
Production scheduling
Manufacturing
Assembly
Quality control
Packaging

**New Products
and Services**

PURCHASING

Locating vendors to provide raw materials or goods for resale is not difficult, but finding the best vendors is another matter entirely. The issue of vendor relationships has become increasingly important in markets that demand that companies reduce costs and maintain effective relationships. Research has found that these vendor relationships reflect factors such as trust or commitment,[3] uncertainty and dependence, and the effect of these on performance.[4]

Furthermore, buyers and sellers are connected in an increasing number of ways: through information sharing that improves the quality of the product produced or brings about new product development; operational linkages such as computerized inventory, order replenishment systems, and just-in-time delivery; legal bonds such as binding contractual agreements; cooperative norms; and relationship adaptations wherein vendors modify their products to meet the needs of the customer.

Given the importance of the vendor–customer relationship, should a company buy from one vendor or from more than one? Obviously, if a single vendor cannot supply all the company's needs, that decision is made. However, there are several advantages to using a single vendor where possible. First, a single vendor will probably offer more individual attention and better service. Second, orders will be consolidated, so a discount based on quantity purchased may be possible. On the other hand, the principal disadvantage of using just one vendor is that if that vendor suffers a catastrophe (recall the earlier example of Phillips), it may be difficult or impossible to find an alternative source in a short time. To guard against this contingency, it is wise for a company to use one supplier for about 70 to 80 percent of its needs and one or more additional suppliers for the rest.

When considering a specific vendor as a source, entrepreneurs should ask several questions. Can the vendor deliver enough of what is needed *when* it's needed? What is the cost of transportation using a particular vendor? If the vendor is located far away, costs will be higher and it may be more difficult to get the service required. What services is the vendor offering? For example, how often will sales representatives call? Is the vendor knowledgeable about the product line? What are the vendor's maintenance and return policies?

It is also important to "shop around," compare vendors' prices, and check for trade discounts and quantity discounts that may make a particular vendor's deal more enticing. Computer technology has made materials planning more of a science than ever before. Information systems can now provide a purchaser with detailed feedback on supplier performance, reliability of delivery, and quality control results. Comparing results across suppliers provides more leverage when it's time to renegotiate the annual contracts with suppliers.

MATERIALS MANAGEMENT AND PRODUCTION SCHEDULING

Any business that purchases raw materials or parts for production of goods for resale must carefully consider the quality, quantity, and timing of those purchases. Quality goods are those that meet specific needs. Quality varies considerably among vendors, so if a company has established certain quality standards for its products, it must find vendors who will consistently supply that precise level of quality, because customers will expect it. The quantity of raw materials or parts that are purchased is a function of (1) demand by the customer, (2) manufacturing capability, and (3) a company's storage capability; consequently, timing of purchases is very important. Purchases must be planned so that capital and warehouse space are not tied up any longer than necessary. Because materials account for approximately 50 percent of total production cost, it is crucial to balance these three factors carefully.

Inventory Requirements

Today, businesses that hold inventories of raw materials or goods for resale have found that they must reduce these inventories significantly to remain competitive. Instead of purchasing large quantities and receiving them on a monthly basis, businesses are purchasing daily or weekly in an effort to avoid costly inventories. Of course, some inventory of finished goods must be maintained to meet delivery deadlines; therefore, a delicate balance must be achieved among goods coming into the business, work in progress, and goods leaving the business to be sold.

In the past, inventories were built up on the basis of the state of the economy or in reaction to problems in an inventory control system. If times were good, producers increased stocks of inventory to meet expected demand. Then, when the economy slowed, they usually had shelves of leftover stock. Reductions in inventory succeeded in exposing typical problems: equipment imbalances, paperwork backlogs, excessively long set-ups, vendor problems, and problems with purchase lead time. Newer systems, such as just-in-time (JIT), help manufacturers and producers maintain better control of their inventories by eliminating production and inventory problems and then reducing inventory to only that which is needed. The just-in-time system of materials and inventory management is fundamentally different from other inventory systems. Originating in Japan in the 1970s, JIT rapidly took hold in the United States. The philosophy behind JIT is to produce the minimum number of units in the smallest possible quantities at the latest possible time. A well-devised and implemented JIT system can do many things, such as increase direct and indirect labor productivity, increase equipment capacity, reduce manufacturing lead time, reduce the cost of failure, reduce the cost of purchased materials, reduce inventories, and reduce space requirements. In essence, the goal of JIT is to eliminate waste in the manufacturing process. Consequently, to implement JIT, it is necessary to look beyond mere inventory to all other aspects of the manufacturing process as well. Starting with the last operation, which is usually meeting the customer requirements, work backward through the manufacturing process. Customer demand determines how many products are produced. The number of products to be produced determines the production capability requirements, which in turn determine the amount of raw materials needed. In general, a JIT firm maintains an inventory no larger than is needed to support one day of production. To do this, it has to have the cooperation of its suppliers and its distributors, and it must impose severe penalties for not being on time—that is, for being either too early or late. This stringent requirement reduces the number of suppliers a JIT firm typically deals with. JIT also requires strict quality control, because with minimal inventories there is no excess inventory to cover rejects.

A traditional factory is laid out by functional department, usually based on a particular process or technology. The result is that products are produced in batches. This is the antithesis of JIT, which specifies that the plant be laid out by product. With JIT, the equipment is positioned in the order in which it is used to produce a particular product or family of related products. It is also important to plan production in such as way as to produce only enough to meet demand. For example, consider a situation in which a company expects to sell a total of 100 units of product in the next month. Then

100/20 work days = 5 units a day

5/8 work hours = .63 unit per hour

or 1 unit every hour and a half

This calculation must be reworked approximately every month as demand changes.

One way suppliers are meeting the needs of a company using JIT is by involving independent contractors specializing in "time-sensitive" deliveries. For example, one company has installed two-way satellite communication on its trucks so that shipments can be tracked in real time. Other businesses, such as UPS, help businesses that need to ship to retailers. They stock merchandise in their warehouses, process orders, make deliveries, and handle billing. In that way, retailers don't incur the costs associated with maintaining a backup supply of items. Avoiding too much inventory is a trend that is expected to continue for the next decade. However, working effectively requires careful coordination and cooperation of all members of the supply chain.

Logistics

Logistics is the management and control of the flow of goods and resources from the source of production to the marketplace. Every business is affected by logistics to some degree, even service businesses that rely on logistics to receive their supplies. Logistics is a fundamental part of supply chain management and can make the difference between success and failure, profit and loss in a growing company. South West Trading (http://soysilk.com) had the pleasant problem of more demand for its yarns made from bamboo, corn, and soy fibers than it could handle. The problem was not with its manufacturing operation in China, which churned out 800 metric tons of yarn every month, but rather with the logistics of getting the yarn from China to the warehouse in Phoenix, Arizona. Because founder Jonelle Raffing was concerned about meeting the needs of her customers, she maintained a $1 million excess inventory, which increased her operating costs. She was unable to combine orders from different factories into one container so she incurred a charge of $1,000 to $2,000 for each separate shipment. She also paid a customs agent $17,000 a year to move the products through the various ports. In all, her annual logistics costs amounted to over $100,000.[5] Raffing was able to solve her problem by turning to UPS and its Shanghai facility, which combines orders into one container, handles the paperwork, and delivers the products all the way to Phoenix, Arizona. Raffing's logistical problems are not solely because her business is small; even multinational companies experience them.

Small companies that sell to large discount retailers like Wal-Mart are subject to strict requirements for packing, shipping, and tagging for RFID tracking. Most small companies don't have the people resources to meet these requirements so they outsource to third-party logistics providers who can move packages by air, land, and sea from the factory to the customer without stopping at the entrepreneur's business. Although a majority of the major logistics providers service large companies, today many of those providers have begun offering services to entrepreneurs. Among the most aggressive is UPS Supply Chain Solutions, which uses its own aircraft to handle shipping of products that meet the weight requirement and do not need to go by sea. For heavier products, Seattle-based Expeditors provides services. Global logistics is discussed in more detail in Chapter 18.

Production Scheduling

The lifeblood of any business is its production function. Decisions made about production directly affect output level, product quality, and costs. Planning for production, therefore, is critical to manufacturing efficiency and effectiveness. Most manufacturers and producers begin by scheduling—that is, by identifying and describing each activity that must be completed to produce the product and indicating the amount of time it takes to complete each activity. Two methods traditionally used in the scheduling process are Gantt Charts and PERT Diagrams.

Gantt Charts are a way to depict the tasks to be performed and the time required for each. Consider Figure 14.2. The tasks to be completed (in this case, filling customer orders) are listed in the first column, and the time to completion is traced in horizontal rows. Note that the solid line represents the plan for completion, whereas the dashed line depicts where the product is in the process. Gantt Charts work best for simple projects that are independent of each other.

FIGURE 14.2 Gantt Chart

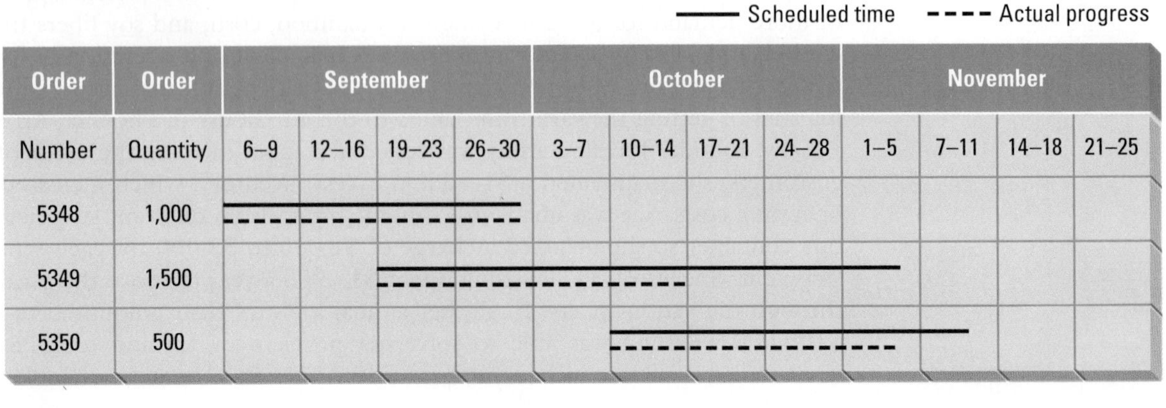

——— Scheduled time   ‑ ‑ ‑ ‑ Actual progress

Order	Order	September				October				November			
Number	Quantity	6–9	12–16	19–23	26–30	3–7	10–14	17–21	24–28	1–5	7–11	14–18	21–25
5348	1,000												
5349	1,500												
5350	500												

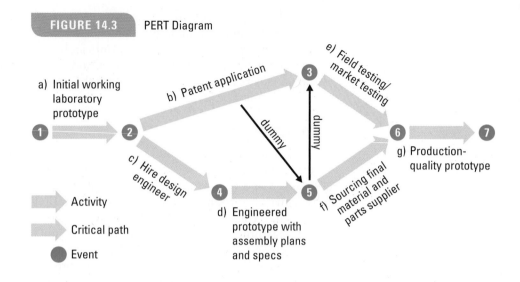

FIGURE 14.3 PERT Diagram

a) Initial working laboratory prototype

b) Patent application

c) Hire design engineer

d) Engineered prototype with assembly plans and specs

e) Field testing/ market testing

f) Sourcing final material and parts supplier

g) Production-quality prototype

dummy

dummy

Activity

Critical path

Event

PERT is an acronym for Program Evaluation and Review Technique. This method is helpful when the production being scheduled is more complex and is subject to the interdependence of several activities going on either simultaneously or in sequence. In other words, some tasks cannot be started until others have been completed. To begin, the major activities involved in producing the product must be identified and arranged in the order in which they will occur. Any activities that must occur in sequence should be identified—that is, cases where one activity cannot occur until another is finished.

A pictorial network that describes the process is then constructed. The time to complete each activity is estimated and noted on the chart. This is usually done three times, and the answers are given as most optimistic, most likely, and most pessimistic. The statistics of analyzing the network are beyond the scope of this book, but the process consists essentially of (1) identifying the critical path, which is the longest path and is important because a delay in any of the activities along the critical path can delay the entire project; (2) computing slack time on all events and activities (the difference between latest and earliest times); and (3) calculating the probability of completion within the time allotted. The numbered nodes on Figure 14.3 refer to the start and completion points for each event. The dummy line was placed in the diagram to account for the completion of event *e*'s being preceded by events *b* and *d*. Both must be completed before event *g* can start. There are several popular software products on the market, such Microsoft Project, that can help entrepreneurs schedule their production capacity. Like any new technique, it takes time to learn the PERT system, but it is time well spent. Tracking production from the outset of the business permits more realistic strategic decisions about growth and expansion.

Identifying all the tasks in the production process makes it easier to determine what equipment and supplies are needed for completing the tasks. If, for example, the equipment necessary to produce the product is beyond the company's start-up resources, it may be time to consider outsourcing part or all of production to a manufacturer that has excess capacity with the needed equipment. This topic is discussed in a later section in this chapter. After the production tasks have been identified, a preliminary layout of the plant can be undertaken to estimate floor space requirements for production, offices, and services. It may be beneficial to consult an expert in plant layout to ensure that the layout makes the most efficient use of available space.

PRODUCTION

Production is the actual manufacturing and assembly of the product. Today manufacturers tend to produce one unit at a time serially in manufacturing cells—also called flexible manufacturing cells (FMCs) or work cells. What that means is that the product moves from raw materials through a series of tasks and processes in a continuous flow to complete the product while remaining inside the manufacturing cell. The benefits of cell manufacturing are reduced lead times, improved costs, quality, and timing in addition to giving employees more involvement in the production of the entire product rather than simply one component of a product. This means that workers need to be cross-trained in all the required tasks to produce the product, but it also means that when a worker is out sick, another is there to immediately fill the gap.

QUALITY

Quality control is the process of reconciling product or project output with the standards set for that product or project. More specifically, it is "an effective system for integrating the quality-development, quality-maintenance, and quality-improvement efforts of the various groups in an organization so as to enable marketing, engineering, production, and service at the most economical levels, which allow for full customer satisfaction."[6] In this sense, quality does not necessarily mean "best"; rather, it means "best for certain customer requirements," which consist of the features and benefits of the product or service and its selling price.[7] Today thousands of manufacturers and producers have embraced the philosophy of quality first but have focused principally on equipment and processes rather than on the human element. Both must be considered in order for total quality control to permeate every aspect of the organization. Over the past twenty years, manufacturers have invested heavily in quality improvements. Concepts such as lean manufacturing and Six Sigma have helped companies lower production costs, produce less scrap, allow fewer defects, and reduce warranty expense.[8]

Producing products for the medical industry is particularly difficult because quality is not simply a desired outcome, but an essential one and is regulated by the FDA. When Corinna Lathan decided to produce devices to help disabled children get the full benefit from their physical therapy exercises, she knew her products had to be perfect. Therapeutic devices are costly—nearly ten times the price of a high-tech toy for able-bodied children. Lathan, a Ph.D. in neuroscience and a professor of biomedical engineering, recognized that although she had the ability to take the product through the primitive prototype phase, she needed a major partner to get the product to the projected $2 billion market. To cut the retail price of her JesterBot to $100 *and* ensure consistent quality, she worked on a licensing agreement with Toytech Creations to mass-produce the robot for her.[9]

Quality is a strategic issue that is designed to bring about business profitability and positive cash flow. Effective total quality programs result in customer satisfaction, lower operating costs, and better utilization of company resources. There are three major processes in any company that must be aligned if quality is going to be the outcome. They are management processes, business processes, and support processes.[10] Management processes are the source of strategic direction and organizational governance, so they usually affect or shape all the other processes of the business. Business processes are "mission-critical" processes and generally relate to the core competencies of the company, such as manufacturing, distribution, and product development. The business processes are critical because they are typically viewed by the customer and include marketing, fulfillment, and service. Support processes are common functions in any business; these include payroll and human resources management and are viewed by the internal stakeholders of the company—the employees.

Testing for Quality

One way manufacturers and producers control quality is through a regular inspection process that takes place during several stages of the production process. Often, primarily to reduce cost, a random sample of products or project outcomes is chosen for the inspection. This method catches potential defects early in the process, before the products become finished goods. Whether each item produced is checked or a random sampling is conducted depends on what is being produced, on its cost, and on whether the inspection process will destroy the item. For example, when a company is producing an expensive piece of machinery, it may be prudent to subject each item to the inspection process, because the cost of inspection is more than offset by the price of the item. But compare the situation when a food is being produced. Once such a product is inspected, it cannot be sold, so it is not feasible to inspect more than a representative random sample of each batch.

Today, technology has made it possible to error-proof processes using sensors, thereby eliminating traditional quality checks and guaranteeing that what is being produced meets the customer's specifications. Entrepreneurs who want to achieve total quality will probably set a no-defect goal for product manufacturing. Pelco Inc., a leader in the video surveillance industry, has designed quality control into every process in its company. Any worker can stop production for a defect, so by the time the product reaches the end of the production line, it is defect-free. Pelco would rather take the time to look for errors before the product reaches the customer than have the customer find defects. Contrast this approach with that of the software industry, which regularly launches products with "bugs" that they expect their customers to find and report.

Six Sigma

Six Sigma is a quality initiative that Motorola introduced in the 1980s. The program identifies quality levels that predict the likelihood that defects will occur—the higher the level, the lower the probability of a defect. Six Sigma relies on statistical tools and specific processes to achieve the measurable goals of fewer defects, increased productivity, reduced waste, and superior products and processes.[11] Although large companies like GE and Allied Signal are widely known for their Six Sigma programs, small companies like Technically, Inc., a Boston-area provider of contract laboratory services and manufacturing to the chemical industry, have also benefited from the program. Technically, Inc.'s founder, Debra Saez, left Dupont to start the company in 1985 and brought with her the Six Sigma skills that are now a hallmark of her company's rigorous approach to refining industrial processes. For example, the statistical technique ANOVA, or analysis of variance, is used to optimize weak processes so that they can be performed with less labor and raw materials and in about half the time.[12]

Quality Circles

Quality circles are groups of employees who regularly work together on some aspect of the production process. They meet several times a month, usually with the help of an outside facilitator, to discuss problems and ideas related to their work environment. They often come up with new solutions to problems, and these solutions are often put into effect, thus improving the efficiency and effectiveness of the manufacturing process and the product as well. Quality circles give employees a vested interest in what they are producing; consequently, they are more likely to pay close attention to improving the way their task is completed.

The real success or failure of the quality control effort is dependent on the human element in the process: customers, employees, and management. Quality begins with satisfying the needs of the customers, and that cannot be accomplished unless those needs and requirements are communicated to managers and employees. An entrepreneur with a new venture has a unique opportunity to create a philosophy of quality from the very birth of the business, in the way the business is run and in the employees hired. The new venture has the advantage of creating new habits and patterns of behavior instead of having to change old ones.

ISO 9000

In an increasingly global market, it is not surprising that the need for international quality standards has arisen. ISO 9000, developed by the International Organization for Standardization, a nongovernmental organization based in Geneva, Switzerland, is a series of international quality standards and certification that makes it easier for a product to enter the export market. Adopted by thousands of companies in over 157 countries, the standards apply to both manufacturing and service businesses and certify quality control procedures. The purpose of ISO is to provide a single set of standards that everyone internationally agrees on. To meet ISO standards, a company must develop a quality management system, a process that starts with a gap analysis—comparing where the company is now with the ISO requirements.

Many quality programs exist to help companies better meet the needs of their customers. Table 14.1 lists several of them.

TABLE 14.1 Quality Management Programs	Benchmarking	Involves the use of criteria or standards that can be used to compare one company with another to better understand organizational performance
	Continuous Improvement	A program that focuses on undertaking incremental improvements in processes to increase customer satisfaction
	Failure Mode and Effects Analysis	A way to identify and rank potential equipment and process failures
	ISO 9000	An internationally recognized quality standard with a certification process
	Total Quality Improvement	A set of management practices designed to meet customer requirements through process measurement and controls
	Six Sigma	A data-driven approach to eliminating defects with a goal of 3.4 defects per million

MAINTENANCE

As a manufacturing process, maintenance refers to taking care of plant and equipment used in the production of goods. Maintenance is an actual cost of producing a product and can often amount to a substantial financial investment. No matter how much care is taken to maintain equipment, at some point it will break down, causing potential loss of sales from the manufacturing downtime. Part of planning for manufacturing is making sure that there are backup systems in place so downtime is minimized. Probably the best strategy is preventative maintenance where equipment is regularly checked and fixed before a major breakdown occurs. This strategy enables the manufacturer to control when the downtime occurs and plan for it to be at a slower production time.

Managing the Supply Chain

The Internet has been a valuable tool for streamlining distribution and supply channels in many industries, and even small, growing businesses can take advantage of its power. For example, suppose a company is sourcing parts for a product it is building; that is, it is trying to find out where to find the best parts at the best prices. Before the Internet, it could have taken months of phone calls and faxes to find the best vendors. Now this new company can quickly compare vendors and products online in the same way that large companies do. But an increasingly complex and global environment where outsourcing, offshoring, and insourcing are common activities has moved supply chain management (SCM) to a mission-critical position for most companies.[13] At the same time, global competitiveness has forced most companies to do more with fewer resources. Because effective supply chain performance is now critical to a company's success, entrepreneurs must have ways to measure that performance, especially in terms of customer satisfaction. Entrepreneurs must have a clear understanding of what is important to their customers—what is the level of service they are expecting and what performance level are they willing to pay a premium for. For example, one company judged its performance by the percentage of orders received in any one day that were filled on time. This metric indicated that the company was performing at over 98 percent effectiveness. However, when the company tracked how long it took for the customer to receive the order from the time they placed it, their

Global Insights

EMERGING PLAYERS IN OUTSOURCING

Although China and India are the acknowledged leaders in the outsourcing world, other countries are scrambling to enter the race and reap the rewards of partnering with developed countries. Three recent additions to the race include Russia, Nicaragua, and Botswana. After visiting places like India to learn how they set up call centers, fulfillment operations, and support services, these countries have developed economic reforms that will make them more attractive to the outsourcers. Some of these improvements include major infrastructure like highways, airports, and telecommunications systems. But infrastructure is not enough to lure outsourcing companies away from China and India; they must be able to provide reliable, trained workers who speak English.

Nicaragua has completed an infrastructure that supports the call centers designed to serve Spanish-speaking customers in North and South America. Nicaragua benefits from being in the same time zone as the United States, which is very appealing to companies such as IBM and Russell Athletic that use them. Botswana, the South African nation, is considered to be the most advanced and politically stable nation in sub-Saharan Africa. It has decided to make training of its workers an incentive for outsourcing companies by paying the companies $2 for every $1 the company spends in training the Botswanan workers for call centers or other outsourced work. Despite Russia's supply of highly trained engineers and scientists, this country did not focus on outsourcing until recently. Now it is in the process of building technoparks to support companies that provide IT services and software programming contract work and offering favorable tax incentives to the outsourcers.

Source: D. Harman, "Outsourcing Gets Closer to Home," *USA Today* (November 7, 2005), http://www.usatoday.com/money/companies/management/2005-11-07-nearsourcing-usat_x.htm; "Up-and-Comers in the Outsourcing Race," Special Report: Outsourcing, *BusinessWeek Online*, http://www.businessweek.com/magazine/content/06_05/b3969423.htm, accessed April 22, 2007; and "Profiting from Contact Center Outsourcing in Botswana," *Datamonitor*, http://datamonitor-market-research.com, accessed April 22, 2007.

performance level dropped dramatically. In examining what was causing the delay, the company found that their system for tracking orders was often sending orders to the wrong distribution center. The goal in supply chain management is to provide the exact service the customer wants at minimal cost. In SCM terms, it's the *efficient frontier* and it's not easy to achieve. To do so, entrepreneurs need to use current technology that provides superior data analysis, ensure that warehouses and distribution centers are efficiently located, and look at every aspect of the supply chain to see if there are ways to reduce costs.

Globalization and an increasing level of outsourcing and offshoring have also made supply chains more vulnerable than ever before. Take the example of the problem Nokia and Ericsson, the cellular telephone companies, faced when the Philips manufacturing plant in Albuquerque, New Mexico, was destroyed by fire. This plant was the source of their radio frequency chips (RFC). The two companies responded very differently and their responses highlight the importance of flexibility in supply chain management. Nokia immediately redesigned its RFCs so that its secondary suppliers in Japan and the United States could begin manufacturing them and then it got Philips to dedicate capability in its other plants to making these RFCs. Ericsson, by contrast, was slower to respond, actually not noticing the interruption in the supply chain until their orders stopped arriving. It had also relied exclusively on the New Mexico plant for its RFCs. Ericsson's loss for that year was $1.7 billion.[14] This example clearly indicates the importance of maintaining awareness of what is going on in the supply chain, whether the suppliers are domestic or global. In the next sections we look at some of the critical activities of the supply chain that entrepreneurs need to understand.

Warranting the Product

Entrepreneurs who subscribe to total quality management will probably wish to provide warranties with products and services, both in order to protect their companies from potential liability and to demonstrate that they stand behind what they produce and the work that they do. Today, product/service warranties have also become a competitive marketing tool.

A number of decisions must be made about warranties. Although the length of the warranty depends on industry standards, the components of the product, or what aspects of the service to cover, depend on the situation. Some components may come from other manufacturers who have their own warranties. In this case, it is important to have use of that component on the product certified by the original equipment manufacturers (OEM) so that the warranty isn't inadvertently invalidated. Then, if a warranted component from that manufacturer becomes defective, it can be returned to the OEM. However, it is probably good business practice to have customers return the product directly to the entrepreneur's company or its distributors for service, repair, or exchange under the warranty, which covers the whole product. Warranties on services cover satisfaction with work completed. For example, a company may conduct ISO 9000 certification workshops for companies and may warrant that if a client's company attends the workshops and implements the suggestions, it will receive certification. If, for some reason, the client does not receive certification, there is no way to "return" a workshop in the way that a product could be returned, but the entrepreneur can offer the client a fact-finding audit to discover what went wrong or can simply refund the client's money (a less satisfactory solution for the client).

The product/process scope should also be considered. Will the warranty cover one or all products in a line or will there be separate warranties? Generally, for services, a warranty covers the service as a whole, unless there are products involved as well. In addition to the product scope, the market scope is a factor. Will the same warranty apply in all markets? This will depend on local laws. Another consideration involves the conditions of the warranty that the customer must fulfill. Is there anything the customer must do to keep the warranty in force, such as servicing or replacing disposable parts? These conditions should not include registering the product via a postcard. Today a product is covered by warranty from the moment it is purchased, whether or not the purchaser returns a postcard stating when and where it was purchased and answering a short, informational questionnaire. What many companies now do is offer update notification and potential discounts on future products in exchange for the information the postcard solicits or the option to register online.

Yet another consideration is who executes the warranty. The entrepreneur must decide who will handle warranty claims (manufacturer, dealers, distributors, the entrepreneur's company), recognizing that customers do not like to mail products back to the manufacturer. It is also necessary to decide how the public will be educated about the warranty. What are the plans for advertising and promotion relative to the warranty? Finally, the policies for refunds and returns, and who will pay shipping and handling costs, need to be considered. A return policy is a function of the entrepreneur's philosophy about doing business. A customer-oriented company is likely to offer a generous return policy and pay for the cost of returns.

The manufacturer who provides a warranty incurs a cost, but that cost must be weighed against the potential loss of business if no warranty is provided. In the case of a new business with a new product or service, it is difficult to anticipate the number of problems that might occur as the product or service gets into the marketplace. Careful and adequate field-testing prior to market entry will go a long way toward eliminating many potential problems and the possibility of a recall (in the case of a product), which is very costly for any firm, let alone a growing new business. Remember the recall of Firestone tires a few years ago and the disastrous financial and public relations impact it had on Firestone and its customer, Ford Motor Company.

Outsourcing to Reduce Costs

Calculation of the up-front investment in plant, office, and equipment, coupled with the high per-unit cost of production, has convinced many entrepreneurs to outsource manufacturing to an established manufacturing firm, particularly one overseas, where labor costs are much less. Some products that consist of off-the-shelf components from original equipment manufacturers (OEMs) can give the entrepreneur the option to set up an assembly operation, which is far less costly than a manufacturing plant. In any case, the process of outlining all the costs of setting up a product company is invaluable in making the final decisions about how the business will operate.

Entrepreneurs who wish to manufacture products have many options today. It is still possible, in many industries, to manufacture domestically and to compete successfully if processes are refined and quality is built into every step. If it is too costly to do all the manufacturing in-house, outsourcing non-core capabilities is one possibility; another is outsourcing everything and playing the role of coordinator until the company is producing a healthy cash flow.

MANUFACTURING OVERSEAS

In some industries, particularly labor-intensive ones, the only way to achieve competitive costs is to manufacture in a country where labor costs are low; Mexico, India, and China are examples. Entrepreneurs should look at what other firms in their industry are doing. Barry-Wehmiller Cos., a St. Louis–based holding company that acquired Paper Converting Machine Company in an industry consolidation strategy and laid off half the company's workforce, was able to turn the company around by sending some of its design work to an engineer center in Chennai, India. Now its U.S. and Indian designers can collaborate 24/7, reducing development costs and speeding service to customers.[15] Tiny Crimson Consulting Group now competes with the likes of market research firms McKinsey and Bain by outsourcing its research to companies in China, the Czech Republic, and South Africa. However, outsourcing is not always the wisest choice. One Tampa, Florida, manufacturing company moved some of its manufacturing operations to China several years ago and achieved real cost savings by doing so. Today, however, it is re-evaluating that decision for several of its products. These products are too heavy to ship by air, and shipping by sea is costly because the company loses the advantage it has in schedule flexibility. Schedule flexibility is an example of an opportunity cost—that is, forgoing an important competitive advantage in order to save on production costs.

The truth is that many companies have not been able to leverage the benefits of outsourcing to create real impact in their companies in the areas of pricing at a premium, entering new markets, and creating entry barriers for competition.[16] That is why entrepreneurs need to work backwards from customer needs and align their workflows appropriately. Not all products are appropriate for offshore manufacturing. For example, a business that uses expensive equipment to produce its products may not achieve enough cost savings to overcome the problems associated with offshore manufacturing, such as difficulties in communication and degradation in quality control. By contrast, a manual-labor-intensive business such as apparel manufacture can often achieve significant cost savings by moving overseas.

The weight of the product is also a factor in the decision whether to manufacture overseas. Heavy products with large "footprints" must be shipped by sea, which typically takes four to six weeks. That represents an inventory issue for the entrepreneur and added cost for the customer. Some entrepreneurs have calculated that it takes a 15 to 20 percent cost savings to justify manufacturing offshore and to balance the added costs of freight, customs, security, logistics, and inventory carrying cost. It is also important to remember that customers are not always looking for the lowest price; rather, they're looking for the highest quality at a competitive price. If products are innovative and meet the specific needs of target customers, a company may be able to manufacture domestically in a successful way. Table 14.2 suggests some important considerations that entrepreneurs should look at before deciding to leap offshore.

TABLE 14.2

Issues in Going Offshore

1. Go offshore when all efforts to boost efficiency and innovation at home have been tried. Don't do it just because everyone else is doing it.

2. Consider whether to set up a captive operation (the entrepreneur owns it) or to contract with a local specialist.

3. Management and employees must both believe in going offshore and must be in the loop during transition.

4. Don't do it if management does not have the time and willingness to put a lot of effort into the process. Savings are in direct proportion to the effort exerted to train and prepare offshore workers in the company's processes.

5. Entrepreneurs must be willing to treat their outsourcing partners as equals, not as subservient workers, and make them part of the project design process.

6. The supply chain needs to be flexible to avoid disruption, particularly through natural and man-made disasters.

Source: "Playbook: Best-Practice Ideas," *BusinessWeek Online*, http://www.businessweek.com/magazine/toc/06_05/B39690605outsourcing.htm, accessed April 22, 2007.

LESSONS FROM OUTSOURCING OVERSEAS

Whether entrepreneurs are looking to ship manufacturing overseas or outsource their back office functions to firms in China and India, successful outsourcers point to several critical lessons they have learned from the experience.[17]

1. It is important to start small and gradually build the overseas capability because there will always be problems in the beginning that will slow the process. The most common problem is a technical workforce that doesn't understand the industry in which the entrepreneur is doing business.

2. Communicating by e-mail and fax is not enough. Most projects require a company expert who can guide the technical workers in person.

3. Often it is best to use a combination of an offshore captive operation and a local contract firm to supplement critical needs. In this way the entrepreneur has more control over outcomes.

4. Outsourced staff typically have a high turnover rate because the average age is 25 and they are constantly looking to move up. Therefore, it is important that the entrepreneur create a culture that encourages the staff to stay with the business long-term.

5. It is important to outsource only those tasks that have a high probability of going smoothly and making the customer happy. Problematic projects are better handled domestically.

Operations is not the glamorous side of an entrepreneurial business, but it *is* a critical aspect of any business because it is increasingly becoming a source of opportunities for innovation that will give a growing company a competitive edge.

New Venture Checklist

Have you:

☐ Outlined the production process for your business?

☐ Found suppliers for your materials and supply requirements?

☐ Determined how inventory will be handled?

☐ Developed quality control measures?

☐ Itemized and calculated your production costs?

☐ Determined warranty service requirements?

☐ Identified a third-party logistics provider?

Issues to Consider

1. Why is it important to consider your manufacturing plan in the earliest stages of a new venture?
2. What are three factors that an entrepreneur must take into consideration when choosing vendors to meet materials requirements?
3. Suppose you had a new advertising firm. How could you use just-in-time scheduling to create more efficiencies in your operations?
4. What are some of the key factors that must be considered when setting up a quality control system?
5. Characterize the critical aspects of an effective supply chain for any business.

Experiencing Entrepreneurship

1. Visit a manufacturing facility that is using technology to facilitate its processes. Develop a flowchart of the manufacturing process. Can you see any ways to improve the process?
2. Interview an entrepreneur with a product company about his or her views on quality. How is this entrepreneur implementing quality control in his or her organization?
3. Choose a young company that has a global supply chain. Develop a process flowchart depicting the supply chain and analyze it for efficiency and flexibility based on information provided in the chapter.

Relevant Case Studies

## Chapter 15

DEVELOPING AN ENTREPRENEURIAL MARKETING PLAN

"Don't forget that it [your product or service] is not differentiated until the customer understands the difference."

—TOM PETERS, Thriving on Chaos

LEARNING OBJECTIVES

▎ Discuss the role of the product adoption/diffusion curve for marketing strategy.

▎ Explain how to create an effective marketing plan.

▎ Discuss the forms of advertising and promotion that entrepreneurs can tap.

▎ Describe the role of publicity.

▎ Explain how entrepreneurs can employ new media to their advantage.

▎ Discuss the role of personal selling in a marketing strategy.

Profile 15.1 SIX APART: FUELING THE BLOGGING PHENOMENON

Ben and Mena Trott were active bloggers long before there was a software platform that made blogging the media phenomenon it is today. In fact, Ben developed their first blog software so that Mena could more easily publish a blog in which she described her daily life. She soon noticed that others began reading the blog, especially other bloggers, and that signaled a trend that might mean opportunity. In 2001, Ben and Mena founded their San Francisco–based software company, Six Apart. Ben had designed a blogware product called Movable Type for corporate accounts like Boeing and General Motors. In 2003, they acquired $10 million in venture capital funds, which enabled the hiring of additional employees, the acquisition of a French Web publishing company—the first of several acquisitions they would make—and the launch of TypePad, a blog hosting service for personal bloggers. The associated software, which they posted for sale on their website, became a popular download for bloggers looking for more user-friendly solutions to their current blog software. By 2005, industry analysts were predicting that the number of bloggers would balloon to 62.5 million by 2007. Things were going well and the company was enjoying significant revenues from its corporate licenses and download subscriptions. But the market began to change quickly. Wordpress, an open-source competitor, was achieving 85,000 free downloads a month, and a new rival, social networking, was gaining an enormous amount of press with the sale of MySpace to NewsCorp for $580 million.

Ben and Mena wondered if it was time for their company to enter the social networking space. They began to conduct some research on the market and decided that the only way to compete was to find a niche that was not being served by the major players. Mena believed that the niche they should target was adults who were essentially alienated from the youth culture of MySpace. In June 2006, they released their new Web 2.0 blogging platform called Vox that featured an easy-to-use interface with photo- and video-sharing capabilities from partners like Flickr, YouTube, and Amazon.com. The target audience for its marketing plan was older adults, such as Mena's mother, who wanted an easy way to communicate with their personal networks. The two lined up advertisers and online partners for affiliate marketing. By the end of the year, Six Apart's Vox platform had over 200,000 registered users.

For now the plan is to grow the company slowly, so they don't suffer the fate of many of their counterparts who have crashed trying to accomplish too much, too soon. They also know that technology development is moving quickly and making obsolete what seems viable today. Ben and Mena continue to focus on how they can build their brand and a sustainable company in the face of change.

Sources: Vox, http://www.sixapart.com/vox; and P. Cliff, "Case Study: Six Apart Feared It Was Missing Out on the Next Big Thing—Social Networks," *Inc. Magazine* (March 2007), p. 61.

Marketing includes all the strategies, tactics, and techniques used to raise customer awareness; to promote a product, service, or business; and to build long-term customer relationships. Marketing can be thought of as a bundle of intangible benefits a company is providing to its customers, and these benefits reflect the company's core values. Traditionally, marketing has been described in terms of the "5 P's"—people, the customer; product, what is being offered to the customer; price, what the customer is willing to pay; place, the channels through which the customer can find the product or service; and promotion, the strategies for creating awareness and reaching the customer. Most entrepreneurs understand that a business cannot exist without customers, so pushing a marketing strategy on potential customers—a very costly approach—does not make sense to entrepreneurs, who typically have limited resources in the early stages of their ventures. Rather, they prefer to invest in building relationships with customers and designing their products or services with the customers' needs in mind. In that way, much of the "selling" that would otherwise have to be done has been taken care of by giving customers what they want, when they want it, and in the way they want it.

Marketing in times of global change means that traditional methods may no longer work, and indeed, given unique products and services with much shorter competitive lives and the impact of Internet search capability on price transparency, price dispersion, market entry, and product variety, the challenge is to rise above the crowd and build a competitive brand that is sustainable.[1,2] Unfortunately, too many entrepreneurs underestimate the strength of their competitors, discount the impact of the global market, and develop products for a broad market rather than a specific and unique niche market. This chapter focuses on marketing for a changing environment—an approach predicated on the need to reinvent, to acquire technological competence, to employ new media techniques through the Internet, and to build relationships with customers, strategic partners, and even competitors.

Who would have thought that just a decade ago we were talking about the importance of moving away from mass marketing strategies toward an innovative one-to-one relationship marketing approach based on the concept of mass customization, and today we're back to talking about marketing to millions. Because entrepreneurs can now reach millions of potential customers for very little cost via the Internet, a new and potentially disruptive paradigm is emerging—that of the "long tail." Chris Anderson, in his best-selling book, *The Long Tail,* adopted the term "the long tail" to describe a probabilistic statistical phenomenon (also known as power laws and Pareto distributions) where niche markets, when aggregated, account for a significant portion of total sales in some consumer sectors.[3] Figure 15.1 depicts a hypothetical long-tail distribution that could describe record sales, book sales, or anything else that is typically sold through brick-and-mortar retail outlets. The vertical axis represents the number of unit sales while the horizontal axis depicts the ranking of those sales from most popular item to least popular. As is the case in many consumer markets, a very tiny percentage of all sales do really well while the vast majority of items in a particular category, like books, sell very few or none. In the traditional retail world, this matters because of the problem of limited shelf space. Barnes and Noble carries multiple volumes of only the top sellers and maybe one of each of those books not listed on the *New York Times* Bestseller list; the rest have to be ordered by special request from the customer. In general, they carry about 100,000 titles. But Barnes and Noble's online store carries everything the customer wants including the most obscure books for the tiniest niche markets. In other words, they believe in the theory that there is someone out there somewhere who will buy any book that was ever written. Using Amazon statistics as

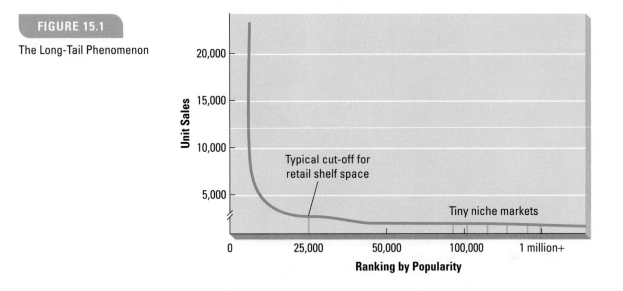

FIGURE 15.1

The Long-Tail Phenomenon

an example, one quarter of all Amazon's book sales come from books that are not included in the top 100,000 bestselling titles, and it is growing. Furthermore, when you consider that most Internet businesses today are aggregators of niche markets (eBay is a good example), the concept of the long tail has huge implications for marketing, and this is good news for entrepreneurs who are accustomed to operating in the niche world.

The intent of this chapter is not to review marketing fundamentals, which are best left to textbooks focused on this subject or to excellent websites like http://www.marketingprofs.com where professionals gather to discuss the subject. The purpose is to explore marketing from an entrepreneurial perspective in an age of new media and look at how to create a marketing plan that will enable a new company to develop a successful brand and build long-term relationships with its customers. This chapter builds on the feasibility analysis and market research strategies and tactics discussed in Chapter 6. The market/customer information gathered during market research can now be applied to the business plan in the form of a marketing plan.

The Product Adoption/Diffusion Curve

Understanding how customers adopt new products is critical to any marketing strategy because it lets entrepreneurs plan for which customer segment to target first and the rate at which sales can occur. The adoption/diffusion curve was developed at the Agricultural Extension Service at Iowa State College in 1957 to monitor patterns of hybrid seed corn adoption by farmers. What they learned was explained in a book, *Diffusion of Innovation,* written by Evert Rogers six years later. It grouped customers into categories based on how quickly they adopted a new product, ranging from those that adopted immediately to those that were the last to adopt.[4] Critics of Rogers's model claim that it is simplistic and doesn't

FIGURE 15.2

New Product Adoption/
Diffusion Curve

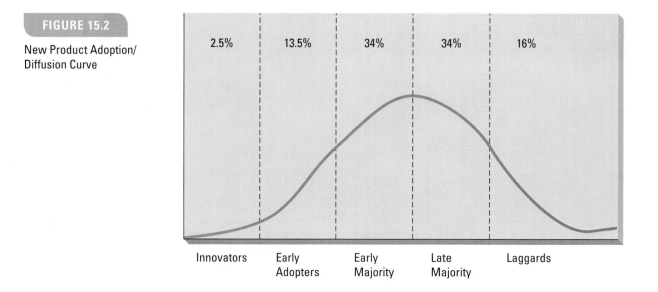

take into account the evolution of the product in terms of improvements as it moves from the first customers to the last customer. Another criticism is that disruptive technologies, those that make previous technology in the area obsolete, tend to follow a different diffusion pattern than the one Rogers described; this pattern will be explained later in the chapter. Despite these challenges, the adoption/diffusion curve is still employed to explain customer adoption behavior. Figure 15.2 presents a depiction of the new product adoption/diffusion curve. What the agricultural agency found over time was that not all farmers would adopt new technology at the same time; only those most comfortable with new methods would adopt in the earliest stages. Everyone else would wait to see what the outcome of the first trials would be before taking on the risk. The innovators are these first adopters; they are a very small customer base that is always interested in trying the latest, greatest thing. These innovators, who are typically younger in age, represent the gatekeepers, the group that is instrumental in deciding whether a new product will go forward to ultimately achieve mass adoption. The early adopters, by contrast, are called the visionaries. They are eager to adopt new products to solve problems and create a competitive advantage for themselves. An optimistic group, they usually have money to spend, and they only require that the product be able to solve about 80 percent of their problem. However, they are not good reference points for the mass market because they tend to understand the need for the product better, and they don't expect productivity improvements and ease of use like the early majority does.

The early majority comprises the customers who tend to wait until a new product is proven and plenty of people are using it. They need to know that a product actually works before they adopt it because they don't want to make bad decisions. They tend to watch the early adopters to see how they fare before leaping into a purchase. The late majority tends to be an older group who typically buys only proven products with good price points. This group waits for

The Technology Adoption/
Diffusion Curve

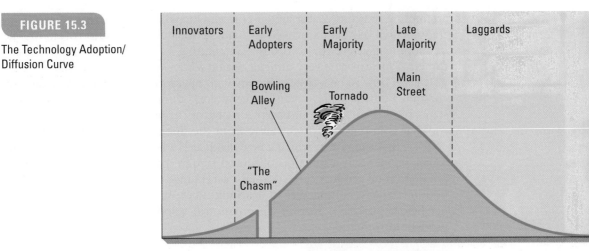

Technology Adoption Process

the price to come down, which means that for the entrepreneur the product has become a commodity. The final group is the laggards, who tend to only purchase the product if they absolutely have to; in other words, they are skeptical that the product is necessary to solve their problem at any price. For the entrepreneur, this group will likely be the least profitable.

For technology products, the adoption/diffusion cycle has a twist. Figure 15.3 presents a modification of the adoption/diffusion curve showing what Geoffrey Moore has called the "chasm."[5] The chasm is a period when the early adopters have been exhausted and the technology stops selling. The reason is that only the innovators and the early adopters had an interest in the technology, while the rest of the potential market was not experiencing any "pain" or problem that the technology would solve. Moore believes that to cross the chasm, the customer has to have a compelling reason to buy. For the entrepreneur, this means identifying niche markets where the technology can produce an application that solves a real problem. For example, GPS (global positioning satellite) technology was available long before there was an actual pain in the market that it could alleviate. When GPS began to be used in luxury automobiles, early-adopter customers liked that it could help them find where they needed to go. Eventually, as the price came down and the technology became more user-friendly, it was adopted by the early majority in less expensive automobiles. It is still in the process of "crossing the chasm."

Moore suggests that to cross the chasm, entrepreneurs must find multiple niche market applications that get the technology into many different customer sectors (called the Bowling Alley). Once a critical mass of niches is acquired, there may be a flashpoint where the market *en masse* adopts the technology. That throws the technology into what Moore calls a "tornado," with year-over-year growth of 100 percent or more and where the most important job of the entrepreneur is to focus on producing and distributing the product. Customer demand is not an issue, because there is more demand than the company can manage. That is why having good systems and controls in place prior to attempting to achieve a tornado is critical. Once the tornado has passed, the entrepreneurial venture has arrived at "main street," which is a period of aftermarket development where the company is attempting to sell more to its current customers. This can be a very difficult period for a young venture because it must now learn how to be a large company with operational excellence. Crossing the chasm is a critical achievement for technology companies that want to set a new standard in the industry and keep competitors from doing the same.

What is important to take away from the discussion of adoption/diffusion cycles is that the rate at which a new product is adopted across the various customer segments is a function of several factors that include perceived benefit, price and total product costs, usability, acceptance of promotional efforts, distribution intensity, switching costs, learning curve, and the ability to test the product before purchase. Not all customers will respond the same way to a new product introduction.

The Marketing Plan

For any company, an effective marketing strategy begins with a marketing plan. The marketing plan for an entrepreneurial company is a living guide to how the company plans to build customer relationships over its life in order to fulfill the mission statement in the business plan. It details the strategies and tactics that will create awareness on the part of the customer and build a brand and a loyal customer base. Furthermore, the marketing plan provides a consistent message to the customer and creates an opportunity for the entrepreneur to make a sale. Marketing plans are written at many points in the life of a business. The original business plan will contain a marketing plan for introducing the company and its products and services to the marketplace. Later a marketing plan may be used to introduce new products and services and/or to grow the business, perhaps in a new direction.

A few important steps taken before the actual writing of the marketing plan ensure that the plan is on target and is one the company can live with for a long time. Living with a plan for a long time may sound inconsistent with an entrepreneur's need to remain flexible and adapt to change in the marketplace, but one of the biggest problems with most marketing plans is that they are not followed long enough to achieve the desired results. Typically, when business owners do not see immediate results from their marketing effort, they decide that it must not be working—so they change it and start the cycle all over again. Changing the plan on impulse is the wrong thing to do. It takes time to make customers aware of a product or service. Furthermore, it takes time for a particular marketing strategy to take hold and secure trust on the part of the customer. For example, from the first time a customer sees an ad to the point at which the customer actually buys the product, weeks or even months may pass. In fact, on average, the customer will see an ad 15 to 20 times before actually purchasing the product. Therefore, just like a successful stock market investor, an entrepreneur must think of the marketing plan as an investment in the future of the business and must remember that any investment takes time to mature. Reaping the benefits of a well-structured marketing plan requires persistence and unwavering dedication until the plan has an opportunity to perform.

A company's mission and core values will set the tone for the marketing plan and inform the initial steps in writing the plan. First, the approach to the market, or the bridge between strategy and execution, must be defined. The approach to the market includes such things as the message, differentiation tactics, channel strategies, and performance goals. Choosing the wrong approach can result in customers not understanding the benefits being provided. Choosing the same approach for all customers will ensure that not everyone will be satisfied. Selecting an approach is based on a thorough understanding of customers—what they need, when they need it, and where they want to find it. That understanding should have been acquired during the market research phase of the feasibility analysis. Next, it is important to identify a niche that the entrepreneur can dominate. Typically, this is a segment of the market that is not being served. To capture customers, entrepreneurs need to create value; consequently, the concept of value creation has been a central aspect of marketing activity.[6] It is the principal way that entrepreneurs differentiate themselves[7] and is essential for customer satisfaction.[8] Customer value has been defined as "a customer's perceived preference for, and evaluation of, those product attributes, attribute performances, and consequences arising from use that facilitates (or blocks) achieving the customer's goals and purposes in use situations."[9] More simply, it is seen as the intangible benefits such as quality, worth, and utility that customers receive from the product as measured against what they paid for it.[10] Recall the discussion of the development of the business concept in Chapter 4. Intangible benefits that customers appreciate include such things as access, saving money, saving time, convenience, health, and so forth.

Once the value proposition has been defined, it's time to develop the marketing message or pitch, which is based on presenting a solution to the problem the customer is experiencing in such a way as to highlight the benefits or value. This is followed by a list of all the marketing options or means to communicate that message. To begin to understand which options should be considered, it is important to talk to other business owners, customers, and suppliers and to read books and articles on marketing strategies for entrepreneurs such as those found at MarketingProfs.com. This process will generate a list of possibilities to consider, which may range from sponsoring a business conference to advertising in a national trade publication. Determining which strategies are the most effective, or even feasible, can be left for later. It is important for the entrepreneur to think like a customer and imagine the business from the customer's point of view. What would entice a customer to enter that store, buy that product, or avail himself or herself of that service? An entrepreneur should study the competition and take a look at competing businesses to determine what makes them successful or unsuccessful. What marketing strategies do competitors seem to employ, and are they effective? What improvements could be made on what competitors are doing? Finally, an entrepreneur must analyze the marketing options and rank them by first eliminating those that either don't meet the needs of the target market or simply are not feasible at the time (usually for budgetary reasons). A ranking of the top ten choices should suffice.

Once the methods to reach the customer have been determined, sales and marketing goals need to be established. These goals should follow the SMART rule; they must be sensible, measurable, achievable, realistic, and time specific.[11]

Measurable means that there must be financial metrics associated with the goals, such as gross profit, sales revenue, and amount of sales per salesperson, as well as customer acquisition costs and number of customers acquired. These metrics are discussed further in a later section.

Many experienced marketers suggest that the first step in creating the marketing plan is to condense all the ideas about marketing strategy into a single paragraph. Impossible? Not at all. Crafting a single well-written paragraph forces an entrepreneur to focus carefully on the central point of the overall marketing strategy. This paragraph should include the purpose of the marketing plan (*What will the marketing plan accomplish?*), the benefits of the product/service (*How will the product/ service help the customer or satisfy a need?*), the target market (*Who is the primary buyer or first customer?*), the market niche (*Where does the concept fit in the industry or market? How does the company differentiate itself?*), the marketing tactics to be used (*What specific marketing tools will be employed?*), the company's convictions and identity (*How will the customers define the company?*), and the percentage of sales that the marketing budget will represent (*How much money will be allocated to the marketing plan?*). Here is an example of an effective one-paragraph statement of the marketing plan for a product/service business.

> TradePartners enables qualified importers and exporters from a variety of countries to find trading partners through an Internet-based, business-to-business network. The purpose of the marketing plan is to create awareness and name recognition for TradePartners in the market space. The target customer or first customer is the small exporter who needs to find buyers for excess inventory in another country; the secondary customer is the importer who wants to find new sources for products to import to the U.S. Customers will enjoy the benefits of reduced time and risk in finding new customers or suppliers. TradePartners has defined a niche targeting small companies that want access to the same opportunities as large companies worldwide. Customers will view TradePartners as a professional, innovative, and customer-focused company. Initial marketing tactics include personal selling at industry events, strategic alliances with complementary companies, and providing free workshops on import/export. TradePartners will spend an average of 40 percent of sales to implement the marketing strategy in the initial stages.

Every marketing plan incorporates the traditional 5 P's of marketing: people, product, price, place, and promotion, which are discussed in any marketing text. Once these aspects of the plan have been addressed, it is time to consider the creative aspects, such as the advertising and promotional goals, and to develop a media plan that details what media will be used, when they will be used, and how much they will cost. The next section outlines the major issues that should be addressed in the marketing plan. Refer also to the business plan outline in Chapter 10 for additional items that should be included in the marketing plan.

Launch Objectives and Milestones

Launch objectives are the key goals for the marketing campaign. What needs to be accomplished, and how does the company intend to do it? For a start-up venture, two important objectives are (1) to create awareness for the company and its brand, and (2) to reach target customers to produce sales. Objectives need to be matched to a timeline for achieving them. Marking on a timeline the major milestones for advertising, promotional events, and trade shows gives some direction to the marketing plan.

Brand Strategy

Brand building is a critical part of any marketing strategy, but what is a brand? The American Marketing Association defines the term as a "name, term, design, symbol, or any other feature that identifies one seller's good or service as distinct" from other sellers. This definition is distinguished from "brand image," which is how the customer perceives the brand.[12] Brand strategy is "a set of decisions about the brand's positioning in a marketplace."[13] These decisions can include developing the brand concept (BMW's "the ultimate driving machine"), building brand extensions to take the brand into new product areas, licensing the brand to third parties to expand the opportunities, or co-branding with another company, such as Godiva chocolate did when it partnered with SlimFast to co-brand a new diet drink. "Brand equity," another often-used term, conveys the effectiveness of the brand in the market, often in terms of financial metrics such as return on marketing costs. These metrics are important because entrepreneurs are typically dealing with limited resources and they want to ensure that the dollars they spend will produce the results they want.

Building brand equity requires that customers form an emotional attachment to the brand. To accomplish that, everything associated with the entrepreneur's company—products, services, signage, location, and so forth—must convey the overall value message that the entrepreneur wants to project. So, if the company is in the educational software business with a focus on children, for example, it may need to create a brand image that suggests expertise, integrity, fun, perhaps a sense of adventure, and trust. The company's location, color scheme, product packaging, and advertising must all be aligned in a consistent message. Customers should have no doubt about what the brand stands for because that clarity and consistency serve to engender trust on the part of the customer.

To ensure that a new brand and the branding strategies used to build the brand image have a chance of achieving a high level of brand equity, an entrepreneur should test the brand against the following three questions:[14]

1. Is everyone in the company in agreement as to what the brand stands for?

2. Is there consistency between the brand image the company is projecting and the perceptions of customers?

3. Do customers describe the brand in ways that could inspire loyalty and evangelism?

Strategic Alignment

Strategies deal with the needs of the market and what is being offered to satisfy those needs. Tactics are the media, channels, and delivery mechanisms used to reach the customer and create brand awareness. To be effective, goals, strategies, and tactics must be in alignment. If an entrepreneur's goal is to emphasize reliability and customer satisfaction, for example, the marketing plan should spell out strategies and tactics for achieving that goal. Some examples might be customer feedback mechanisms and training in the use of the products. Because the brand is such a critical part of any company's success, overall company strategy should be informed by the branding strategy; that includes pricing, distribution, sales, and any activity or process in the company that touches the customer. Everything the company does must be consistent in the message it sends.

Assessing Effectiveness

Measuring the effectiveness of marketing efforts is critical to avoid wasting precious company resources. For example, matching sales forecasts to specific marketing tactics and assigning a specific person responsible for measuring the outcome is important to assessing the effectiveness of the marketing plan. Another way in which entrepreneurs measure success in a marketing effort is to ask customers how they heard about the company or the product/service. Tracking specific marketing efforts, advertising, and promotion, and matching specific performance outcomes to each effort is critical to understanding where to focus resources. It is not within the scope of this text to go into detail on marketing metrics, but Figure 15.4 provides some key performance indicators that should help entrepreneurs understand how successful they are in acquiring customers, maintaining customers, and building brand equity. It is important to note that entrepreneurs should also consider any additional metrics that might be appropriate to their specific business.

FIGURE 15.4

Marketing Metrics for Entrepreneurs

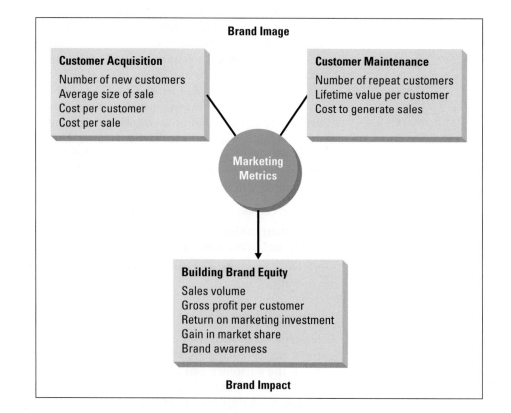

Socially Responsible Entrepreneurship

A Turnaround That Worked

Guests of the Evergreen Lodge in Groveland, California, near the famed Yosemite National Park might be surprised to learn that the owners do not have the typical lodge-owner profile. Lee Zimmerman left a marketing executive position with a restaurant chain and Brian Anderluh was an Internet executive with an online greeting card company. In 2000, they decided that they wanted to start a business where they could help kids who came from disadvantaged backgrounds. The idea for the opportunity came from San Francisco Bay Area Juma Ventures, a nonprofit that provides jobs and services to low-income youth. They found and purchased a family-run guest lodge that needed some renovation. Raising $10 million through loans and equity investments, they added 50 new cabins and a number of community meeting areas. In 2002, they started their internship program,

paying six disadvantaged youths $7.50 to $8.50 an hour to work at the lodge, learn a trade, and live in a supportive community. To mentor the recruits, they teamed each with a staff member and had regular meetings to make sure things were going well. The company has been able to leverage the publicity they have received from their unique story. As of this writing, 40 youths have successfully completed the program and most have secured full-time positions. "Our Youth Program is central to what we do at the Evergreen, and we are proud to have a 'double-bottom line' enterprise with both a business and a social mission."

Sources: Evergreen Lodge, http://www.evergreenlodge.com/youthprogram.html, accessed April 28, 2007; and A. Field, "The Resort That Serves Its Staff," *Fortune Small Business* (December 2006/January 2007), p. 73.

Advertising and Promotion

Advertising and promotion are both used to create awareness for the company's products and services and influence customers to buy, but they are not interchangeable terms because they have different objectives. Advertising generally focuses on non-price benefits and targets end-users. It can also have some influence on the channels of distribution through which the customer will seek the product or service. In that sense, advertising is employed to pull the product through the distribution channel—called a pull strategy. By contrast, promotion tends to be more price-focused or incentive-focused and therefore is usually considered a push strategy. Table 15.1 depicts a matrix of factors that affect whether a push or a pull strategy should be used and under what conditions.

For many entrepreneurs, putting a great deal of money into advertising and promotion doesn't make sense. They simply don't have the resources and budgets of a Starbucks, so their money is better spent on more effective ways of reaching very specific customers. After starting Boston Chicken in 1988, a venture that required a lot of expensive TV advertising, George Naddaff decided that his next business, KnowFat, a franchiser of health food restaurants and fitness shops, would take a more targeted and less expensive approach. With the help of Zoom Media & Marketing, he created a series of small billboards and

TABLE 15.1	Factors to Consider	Use Advertising (Pull)	Use Promotion (Push)
Push or Pull Strategy?	Price sensitivity	Not effective	Effective
	Brand loyalty	High loyalty	Low loyalty
	Need for information	High need	Low need
	Risk—switching costs, learning curve	High risk for customer	Low risk for customer
	Product life cycle stage	Growing or mature	New product or declining product
	Market status	High market share	Low market share
	Purchasing pattern	Predictable	Unpredictable
	Contribution to profit	Above average	Below average
	Differentiation	Strong differentiation	Little differentiation

displayed them in fitness gyms that were located within walking distance of his six Boston restaurants. "I was looking for a way to deliver rifle shots, not buckshots," he claims.[15] Although return on marketing investment is not easy to track with this type of advertising, he has seen the lines at his restaurants get longer, particularly at dinnertime.

Entrepreneurs approach marketing from a point of view distinctly different from that of the traditional marketer. Although they may employ some of the same techniques as a large corporate marketer, they also take advantage of many other marketing opportunities that the corporate marketer may ignore. Jay Conrad Levinson has called the entrepreneurial marketing approach *guerrilla marketing,* an alternative to traditional, expensive marketing tactics.[16] Because entrepreneurs don't have the time or money for elaborate, high-profile marketing strategies, they essentially mimic what the big companies do, but they do it for much less money, in more creative ways, and for a shorter period of time. Guerrilla marketing is a do-it-yourself approach to marketing for entrepreneurs. There are many ways to promote a company and its products and services effectively. The next sections consider a variety of entrepreneurial marketing tactics.

Traditional advertising—a pull strategy—consists of print and broadcast media. It is not the purpose of this book to provide all the information entrepreneurs need to use each medium presented, but only to create awareness of how and when each is used. Table 15.2 presents some of the traditional print and broadcast media options available to the entrepreneur with some hints for how to use them most effectively. Internet advertising and promotion will be the subject of a later section.

Publicity Is King

Publicity and word-of-mouth (referrals) are two of the most effective entrepreneurial marketing tools around because they don't cost the company any money. What they do require is a compelling story that will attract attention. If the business or product is newsworthy, there are several ways to get some publicity. Writing to a newspaper, magazine, or online reporter or editor to captivate him or her with

| TABLE 15.2 | Traditional Media Comparison Chart | | |

Media	Advantages	Disadvantages	Hints
Print Media			
Newspapers	Broad coverage in a selected geographic area Flexibility and speed in bringing to print and modifying Generates sales quickly Costs relatively little	May reach more than target market Difficult to attract reader attention Short life	Look for specialized newspapers for better targeting Include a coupon or 800 number Locate ad on right-hand page above the fold
Magazines	Can target special interests More credible than newspapers	Expensive to design, produce, and place	Look for regional editions Use a media-buying service Use color effectively Check on "remnant space," leftover space that must be filled before magazine goes to print
Direct marketing (direct mail, mail order, coupons, telemarketing)	Lets you close the sale when the advertising takes place Coverage of wide geographic area Targets specific customers More sales with fewer dollars More information provided Highest response rate	Not all products suitable Need consumable products for repeat orders Response rate on new catalogs is very low, about 2%	Create a personalized mailing list and database from responses Use several repeat mailings to increase the response rate Entice customers to open the envelope
Yellow pages	Good in the early stages for awareness Good for retail/service	Relatively expensive Targets only local market	Create ad that stands out on the page
Signs	Inexpensive Encourage impulse buying	Outlive their usefulness fairly quickly	Don't leave sale signs in windows too long; people will no longer see them
Broadcast Media			
Radio	Good for local or regional advertising	Can't be a one-shot ad, must do several	Advertise on more than one station to saturate market Sponsor a national radio program Provide the station with finished recorded commercials Stick to 30-second ads with music
Television	Second most popular form of advertising People can see and hear about product/service Can target at national, regional, or local level	Very expensive for both production and on-air time Must be repeated frequently	Time based on GRP (gross rating points). Range is $5-$500 per GRP. Use only if you can purchase 150 GRPs per month for three months. Seek help of media-buying service
Cable TV shopping	Good for new customer products Targets the consumer Good products sell out in minutes	Not a long-term strategy Good only for products between $15 and $50 Product must be demonstrable	Call network for vendor information kit Contact buyer for your product category Be prepared to fill an initial order of between 1,000 and 5,000 units

(continued)

TABLE 15.2	Traditional Media Comparison Chart (*continued*)		
Media	**Advantages**	**Disadvantages**	**Hints**
Infomercial	Good for consumer items that can't be explained quickly	Very expensive to produce Hit rate is about 10%	Most profitable times are late nights, mornings, and Saturday and Sunday during the day Test time slots and markets to confirm effectiveness
Miscellaneous			
Affinity items (T-shirts, caps, mugs)	Good for grabbing consumer's attention	Value varies significantly with type of business and product or service	Every company should make use of affinity items to create free publicity
Searchlights, Couponing, In-store demonstrations, Videotapes, Free seminars	Effective, yet inexpensive, way to showcase the company		

an idea and then following up with a phone call often works. Whenever possible, it's a good idea to get to know people in the media on a first-name basis. Taking a reporter to lunch before there is a need for free publicity will help to cement a relationship that can be accessed when the time is right. When it comes time to seek publicity, an entrepreneur who already has a contact can simply issue a press release answering the who, what, where, when, and why of the business.

It is also important to understand that seasonality affects publicity just like it does sales in the business. New stories or product introductions receive the most notice when they are placed near an event that normally gets a lot of attention like a presidential election or tax season. Summertime is when many journalists are looking for interesting stories because not much is happening. When contacting the press, a good approach is to include a press kit containing the press release, bios, and photos of the key people in the story, any necessary background information, and copies of any other articles written about the company. The idea is to make it as easy as possible for the reporter to write or tell the story. The media are always looking for news and appreciate the effort to give them something newsworthy. When an article is written about the business, reprints can be used in future advertising and brochures, and thus the company gains even more value for the effort.

Constructing an Effective Press Release

Although some have argued that the traditional press release is dead in the age of new media, the fact is that it is alive and well. Press releases are certainly important for investor relations and they help to tell the ongoing story of a company. An effective news release should contain the date, the name of the person to contact for more information, and a phone number; the release date (for immediate release or for release after a certain date); an appropriate, descriptive headline; the release information typed double-spaced with wide margins; the who, what, where, when, and why at the very beginning of the press release; a photo, if appropriate; and a note explaining briefly why the release was sent.

There are also several publishing services that can be used to gather and distribute information about the business. For example, PR Newswire is the leading source for press releases on companies (http://www.prnewswire.com).

GETTING CUSTOMER REFERRALS

The best customers are those acquired through referrals from current satisfied customers. Unfortunately, most entrepreneurs don't understand how to get customers to refer others to their business and become their company evangelists. It is important to begin by getting critical information that will clarify customers' motivations for buying and referring. Talking with current customers who have provided referrals is an excellent way to find out what they really like about the company, how they describe it to others, and what they value most about it. Specific ways to gather this information include taking a customer to lunch at least once a week and encouraging him or her to do the talking. Another approach is doing a global Internet search on a search engine like Google to find out what is being said about the company. Companies frequently don't know that some customers set up personal websites to either praise or criticize a company they have strong feelings about. Other options include having a qualified third party conduct in-depth interviews with customers, administering an open-ended online survey that's easy to complete, and hosting an online discussion. Finally, another great way to gather customer feedback is to create a customer advisory board to advise the company on everything from what products to carry to how best to market them.[17]

WHEN IT MAKES SENSE TO GIVE IT AWAY

Although it seems contrary to what is taught in business schools, more and more entrepreneurs are using the tactic that Netscape and Microsoft used when they gave their browsers away in order to grow their markets rapidly. Giving customers something for nothing makes sense in an environment where it's hard to get the customer's attention. But it is important to know whether giving something away will help the business or simply cost money that it can't afford to lose. Entrepreneurs should consider giving away information, consulting, or samples of a product when the customer is likely to return; when the cost for each additional item is low and margins are high; when customers need to try the product or service in order to risk the money to buy it, especially if it's unproven technology (consider offering the product or service to a well-known customer who will testify to his or her satisfaction with it); or when samples of the product or service can be offered at a large event such as a conference or trade show. On the other hand, it's important not to give away a service such as financial expertise that relies on credibility, because doing so may cause customers to question its quality. Similarly, expensive items and commodity items, which customers buy on the basis of price, should not be given away, especially when the probability of retaining those customers is low.

Internet Marketing and New Media

Predictions are that Internet advertising will be a $26 billion market in 2009.[18] In fact, Google plans to sell video advertising and eventually transfer that Internet advertising to television. Industry experts see traditional media boundaries disappearing while information floods markets, producing commodity pricing. Information erupting from a multitude of sources and not controlled by any one organization has the potential to overwhelm decision makers or at the very least distract them or prevent them from making effective decisions. Moreover, with everyone having access to the means to produce highly targeted messages to reach customer niches, the competitive advantage of Internet marketing disappears. With video and content production technology now priced within the reach of individuals and small businesses, the barriers to content creation have been breached so that anyone can produce a broadcast-quality commercial or magazine-quality advertisement and distribute it to a very targeted audience. Customers, who are being deluged with these targeted ads, however, have become jaded and can now use the same technologies the marketers use to opt out of receiving promotions and advertising. Customers also find themselves with the power to control when, where, and how they view ads. These and other media trends discussed later in this section present huge challenges to entrepreneurs but also new opportunities for those seeking to market their products and services. Any marketing strategy should be anticipated, personal, and relevant. Potential customers don't want to be surprised by marketing tactics. They want to know that marketing is about them, and they want to know that it's about things they're interested in. The reason why most online marketing campaigns (and offline ones, as well) are unsuccessful is that they are unanticipated, impersonal, and irrelevant. Today entrepreneurs must find ways to give their customers more control over the purchase experience and engage them using new media tools, a topic for discussion in the next section.

In addition, there must be an effective way to measure advertising performance that is interactive, capable of being updated quickly, and minimally intrusive, so that customers don't opt out. There is a misconception that advertising on the Internet is cheap and/or free. Actually, any method of acquiring new customers on the Internet carries an acquisition cost that can often be quite high. In 2001, AOL claimed to spend about $90 to acquire a customer.[19] It could justify that cost only because the company was selling a subscription, so it was building a relationship with the customer for the long term. By contrast, online payments provider PayPal grew from 10,000 users in early 2000 to more than 10.6 million users in September 2001. During that same period they kept a careful eye on their customer acquisition costs, which they succeeded in dropping from $3.29 per customer to 13 cents per customer. The ability to keep customer acquisition costs low is a primary reason why PayPal was the first successful initial public offering by an Internet company following the dot com crash.[20]

SOCIAL MEDIA

Viral marketing emerged as a direct result of the Internet's ability to replicate and distribute information quickly and efficiently. Its offline counterparts are "word-of-mouth" and "network marketing." Even though the term *viral marketing* has negative connotations, it is widely used to describe a marketing strategy that entices customers to pass on the marketing message to others. For example, Hotmail.com, the highly successful free e-mail service, provides its users with free e-mail addresses but carefully includes a tagline on each message the user sends: "Get your private, free e-mail at www.hotmail.com." Hotmail is hoping that when users send messages to friends, they will sign up as well, taking its services to an ever-widening audience. If the strategy is well developed, the viral marketing message will spread rapidly, bringing in many more users. Hotmail will be able to translate the increased usage into higher advertising revenues.

Another example is Adobe Acrobat. Adobe, the successful software company, gives away its proprietary software that lets people share documents across multiple platforms in a form called PDF, which retains the original formatting and can't be manipulated. Adobe puts a link in the document that sends the person to the Adobe website to download the required Adobe Reader. That gives Adobe an opportunity to let the user know about its other software products available for sale. The strategy has been so successful that Adobe is now the de facto standard for sending corporate documents.

Today, social media tools have taken the concept of viral marketing to a new level. Social media tools include blogs, podcasts, vodcasts, RSS Readers, and wikis. Each has a specific purpose and each is more or less effective depending on what the entrepreneur is attempting to promote and to whom.

▶ dotTV enables entrepreneurs to create their own online TV channel or network.

▶ Blogs and e-newsletters are generally a way for an entrepreneur to communicate the expertise of his or her company or opinions on relevant issues of the day. In the case of blogs, the communication is typically bi-directional so that customers can respond or add to the discussion.

▶ Podcasts and vodcasts are ways to bring the human element into communications with customers by adding voice and video. They are often used for "how to" information on new products or to provide advice.

▶ RSS Readers (Really Simple Syndication) provide a way to find out what others are saying about the entrepreneur's company by enabling the entrepreneur to subscribe to blogs and podcasts. RSS is also used to add targeted news, blogs, or podcasts to the entrepreneur's website, usually by using an RSS aggregator, a software that locates all the news of interest to the entrepreneur.

▶ Wikis are editable websites that let multiple users create content and then edit it. Typically they provide information, such as the most popular wiki, Wikipedia, does.

▌ MySpace and YouTube are social networking portals that are good for reaching a broad market, particularly if the target demographic is young consumers who are interested in new types of advertising that can't be found on traditional broadcast TV.

Although there is no single best way to craft a viral strategy using new media, most successful marketers

▌ *Provide free products and services.* Good marketers know that "free" is the most powerful word in any language, and online marketers know that if they generate enough "eyeballs" through a viral marketing campaign, somewhere down the road, they will also achieve their desired level of revenues.

▌ *Make it easy to pass on the message.* There is nothing easier than clicking on a button and forwarding an e-mail to someone. For example, online magazines have made it easy to forward an article to someone by simply clicking on a button that brings up an e-mail message into which the person's address is entered.

▌ *Make sure that the mail server can handle the traffic.* There is nothing worse than starting a viral campaign that ultimately annihilates its host. Remember that viral marketing spreads a message extremely rapidly, so plan ahead for additional server capacity.

▌ *Take advantage of existing social networks.* Just as in the offline world, people in cyberspace create networks of people and information that they tap into regularly. Place an interesting message into one of those networks, and its diffusion is accelerated exponentially.

▌ *Use other people's websites.* Find compatible websites and arrange to place a message on them. In that way, the company is tapping into another network and increasing the scope of its own.

SEARCH ENGINE MARKETING

Search engine marketing (SEM) is simply a set of tools for increasing the level of visibility of a website when customers search. Visibility is critical for businesses that sell products and services online or generate leads from their websites. Today, branding a company online means that entrepreneurs must be aware of their company's positioning in the Google search engine. Although there are a number of search engines available, when customers hear about a company, they immediately Google the name. Therefore, it is critical to have a website that conveys what the entrepreneur wants the customer to learn about the company. Optimizing a site with appropriate keywords can help customers find a company much faster, but it is important to note that the major search engines like Google have very specific rules regarding how keywords are used. Failing to follow those rules could get a website "Google-sacked," which means that the site is not assigned a PageRank (used for parsing sites) and therefore simply disappears from a user's search. It is wise to get referrals for third-party optimization specialists because there are many such companies that do not deliver what they promise.

A number of new terms have emerged out of keyword search marketing, and they represent ways to capture value for an advertiser and measure how effective that advertising is. They also serve as a means for an entrepreneur to create revenue streams on their site. Here are a few of them.

▶ *Conversion rate:* The number of customers who take a particular action such as register on the site, subscribe to a newsletter, download software, or purchase a product.

▶ *Cost-per-action:* A payment model where the advertiser pays based on some manner of conversion such as a sale or site registration. In this model, the entrepreneur, or publisher, is taking the risk because they receive a commission based on leads generated.

▶ *Cost-per-click:* The cost of a paid click-through.

▶ *Cost-per-impression:* Cost per 1,000 advertising impressions, with an impression being a single instance of an online advertisement being displayed. This form of advertising is not dependent on a click-through type of activity.

▶ *Pay per lead:* A model where payment is based on qualified leads.

AFFILIATE PROGRAMS

One way to increase the traffic on a website is to use affiliate programs, which are basically strategic partnerships with other companies that offer complementary products and services. Banner exchange programs are one example of an affiliate program. The banner company posts the entrepreneur's banner on other compatible Internet sites. Costs may be associated with posting a banner, or it may be possible to negotiate a barter exchange if the company's website is compatible with the website on which it wants to place a banner. Getting a banner on a website may be the easiest part of the challenge. Convincing people to click through and buy a product or service is quite another thing. There are many effective ways to attract customers to a website. These include assuring them that their private information will not be sold; giving them something free to entice them to discover more; offering them more, beyond the free information, that they will have to pay for; using electronic gift certificates as a way of getting customers to try products or services; providing a toll-free number for people who need to hear a human voice to overcome resistance; and offering to accept payment for items in as many ways as possible: credit cards, checks, debit cards, and so on.

Lobster Gram, the creation of Chicago-based Dan Zawacki, who sends out fresh lobsters through overnight mail services, relies on 2,000 affiliate sites to generate 6 percent of its online sales. To set up the program, Zawacki paid a one-time fee of $1,800 plus a 13 percent commission on every sale to affiliate marketer Commission Junction, which found and negotiated the appropriate affiliates for Lobster Gram. In addition to the affiliate program, Zawacki spends money on radio ads to drive customers directly to his site without going through an affiliate. However, because affiliate marketing works, many customers hit the affiliate's site first, which generates a commission for Commission Junction that Zawacki must pay on top of his regular marketing costs. Nevertheless, according to Zawacki, his customer acquisition costs have actually gone down as a direct result of affiliate marketing.[21] Like everything else, it's important to get a recommendation from a satisfied user of an affiliate marketing program. Banner ads on affiliate sites should never be the primary source of advertising for any company; rather, they should be one tool in an arsenal of tools designed to create awareness and give customers a reason to think of the brand the next time they want to purchase something.

PRIVACY ISSUES

Although companies have collected consumer information for years and used it to target customers and sell more products and services, the advent of e-commerce has made consumers more aware of privacy issues. When Jane Consumer goes online to purchase a handmade doll for her collection, she soon finds that she is inundated with advertisements for gifts, collectibles, and anything else remotely related to her doll collection. This is the power of the Internet at work, as it magnifies anything done in the offline world. The retailer who sold her the doll collected demographic and contact information about her and then probably also sold her e-mail address and other information to catalog companies and others looking to target the same customer. Amazon.com ran afoul of the Federal Trade Commission (FTC), which claimed that the company's practices were deceptive. Amazon did not make it clear to customers that it was selling their information to other companies. In fact, an FTC survey estimates that 97 percent of all e-commerce websites collect information that is personally identifiable. Therefore, companies must now do more to ensure that their customers' privacy is respected. Customer-focused companies inform their customers how the information collected will be used. The most successful companies maintain policies against selling customer information. Other firms seek seals of approval from online auditing companies such as TrustE and PricewaterhouseCoopers LLP, but these audits can cost up to tens of thousands of dollars. The best practice is to get a customer's permission before using his or her information for any purpose. Any effective marketing strategy, whether online or offline, should target the appropriate customers and address their specific needs, including their need for privacy.

Personal Selling

Traditional selling techniques don't always meet the needs of today's customers, who expect a quality product at a fair price with good service. Today, a business distinguishes itself in the marketplace by identifying and meeting specific customer needs. Therefore, even if an entrepreneur is selling a commodity, he or she needs to figure out some way to add value to the product, and one way is through personal selling. A good example of a company that adds value to a product is a small manufacturer of molded plastic parts in Massachusetts. Its largest account is a major acoustic speaker manufacturer, also in Massachusetts. The speaker company asked the plastics company to assign a full-time salesperson to its plant, which would help it eliminate some of the costs of buyers and planners and, at the same time, enable the plastics plant to concentrate on service rather than on trying to acquire new accounts. As a result, the plastics company's sales have increased nearly 40 percent per year.

Becoming a value-added company by tailoring products to meet customers' needs requires that everyone in the company become service-oriented, a time-consuming task that necessitates training and educating employees. It also demands an opportunity mindset, rather than a selling mindset. It is a lengthier process, but the returns are potentially greater. Working more closely with customers can translate into reduced selling and marketing costs.

IMPROVING PERSONAL SELLING SKILLS

Personal selling is an important talent that entrepreneurs often possess and continue to hone throughout their careers. To improve upon personal selling skills, entrepreneurs should do some research before attempting to sell, whether it's their product, their company, or themselves. It is important to learn what customers want from the sale and give them what they want. The following are some suggestions:

- The first meeting with the customer is typically designed to gather as much information as possible about the customer's needs and build credibility with the customer before trying to sell anything.

- Next, the entrepreneur must position the company as a solution provider in the mind of the customer, making sure to grab the customer's interest immediately. Whenever possible, the customer should be able to actually use the product in order to understand and appreciate it. During demonstrations and conversations, the entrepreneur should stand in front of the customer, not to the side, paying close attention to the customer's facial expressions as the benefits are being explained. The major benefits of the product or service should be explained to facilitate speedy decision making.

- If the customer declines the offer, the entrepreneur should maintain a sense of composure, then inquire why, and follow up by repeating the value the company is providing.

- As a final touch, the entrepreneur could invite the prospect to contact two existing customers and ask them about their experiencing working with the entrepreneur.

Selling at Trade Shows and Exhibits

For entrepreneurs in many industries—electronics, industrial equipment, and gift items, for example—trade shows, fairs, and exhibits are a primary way to expose their products and do some personal selling. Attending trade shows is an effective way to find out who the competitors are and what marketing techniques they are using. A trade show is one of the best places to meet and negotiate with sales representatives and to gather contact information for a mailing list. But the primary reason to display products at a trade show is to eventually sell more product. To accomplish this, entrepreneurs should consider renting booth space and hiring a display designer to produce a quality display booth that will attract attention. Visiting several trade shows before setting up a booth will clarify what works and what doesn't. It may also be possible to work out a deal with a company that has compatible products to share a booth and combine resources. Entrepreneurs should save the expensive brochures to hand out to potential customers who actually come to the booth and provide their business cards. It is important to have enough knowledgeable, personable people in the booth at all times so that potential customers are not kept waiting to talk with someone. Another good idea is to offer something free at the booth, such as a sample or a raffle. Finally, it is vital to follow up with letters to anyone whose business card was collected and to call all serious prospects.

MANAGING CUSTOMER RELATIONSHIPS (CRM)

One of the most rapidly growing areas of marketing is customer relationship management, or CRM. Customer relationship management (CRM) is a combination of technology, training, and business strategy that results in a system for gathering and using information on current and prospective customers, with the goal of increasing profitability. This critical component of any successful marketing strategy has long been a mainstay of large corporations, but until only a few years ago it was too costly for smaller companies. Today, however, affordable database software with sample templates makes it easy to set up a CRM system in a relatively short period of time. A good CRM system can generate better sales leads, allow rapid responses to changing customer needs, and ensure that all employees who need customer information have it when they need it in the form they need. A well-constructed CRM system contains the names, addresses, and attributes of people who are likely to purchase what the company has to offer. It will help the entrepreneur define a trading area, reach new customers in the marketplace, select specific target audiences, and survey current customers.

CRM is not merely a way to reach customers by mail more easily. Today, retaining and maintaining current customers is more important than spending money to find new customers. It has been reported that 65 percent of a company's business comes from current customers. In fact, it costs five to ten times more to go after a new customer than to serve an existing one. Furthermore, with good customer profiles, an entrepreneur can match demographic information about current customers with demographic data in the geographic area of interest to find prospects more effectively. Information contained in the database can be used in advertising, sales promotion, public relations, direct mail, and personal selling.

CRM is really an overall approach to doing business, an approach that requires the total commitment of everyone in the organization. As in any marketing effort, the payoff to this approach takes time, and many frustrated entrepreneurs give up before seeing the results of their efforts. To achieve satisfied, life-long customers, a learning environment must be developed where customer and company learn from each other with the goal of achieving a mutually beneficial life-long relationship.

There is another benefit to building relationships with customers. If a problem occurs, a customer who has a relationship with the company won't automatically shift their loyalty to a competitor. Often their loyalty is actually *strengthened* when a problem-solving session with the company results in a satisfying conclusion. All too often, however, customers have had negative experiences with companies, where the problem has not been resolved satisfactorily. In those situations, the customer never forgets. Today, customers have a multitude of platforms from which to publicize their grievances, and one problem aired on national television can cause a public relations nightmare from which the company may never recover. A case in point was the Cunard cruise line's public relations disaster during the launch of its expensive 2001 Christmas cruise on the renovated Queen Elizabeth II. Despite a ship full of builders still working to complete construction, management decided to sail the ship. Apparently Cunard believed the customers would overlook the mess! They did not and complained bitterly. This is clearly not the way to build long-term customer relationships.

Perhaps the most important benefit of establishing lifelong customer relationships is that over time, the full value of customers is revealed. Customers are no longer viewed as a series of transactions but as bona fide, contributing members of the team who bring value to the bottom line. The more the company learns from its customers, the better the company becomes, and the more difficult it will be for a competitor to attract these customers.

Identifying and Rewarding the Best Customers

It is not uncommon for a company to find that as few as 24 percent of its customers account for 95 percent of its revenues. Those 24 percent are the customers the company needs to know well and to keep happy, because these are the customers who will readily try new products and services and refer the company to others. After a company has been in business for a while, it becomes easier to identify the most valuable customers. One way to do this is to calculate the lifetime customer value as a series of transactions over the life of the relationship. A statistical method for doing this calculates the present value of future purchases, using an appropriate discount rate and period of time for the relationship. Add to that the value of customer referrals, and subtract the cost of maintaining the relationship (advertising, promotions, letters, questionnaires, 800 numbers). The result will be the customer's lifetime value.

Complaint Marketing

A dissatisfied customer will probably tell at least nine other people about the problem he or she faced with a company. (And those nine people will tell their friends as well!) It's easy to see how quickly even one unhappy customer can damage a company's reputation. Consequently, complaints should be viewed as opportunities for continual improvement. Making it easy for a customer to register a complaint and carry on a dialogue with a human being who listens and attempts to understand is an important way to learn from the customer. Nothing is more frustrating than to have to leave a complaint on a voice mail message. Some companies have used bulletin board type services on the Internet to let customers communicate complaints, but this method, though effective, attracts more complaints than any other method. Companies using these methods have found, in fact, that this system works almost too well, because customers feel free to vent their frustrations more angrily online than when they are hearing a soothing, caring voice at the other end of a phone line. Moreover, because anyone with access to the Internet can read the angry messages, a strong complaint can build momentum and create more problems than necessary.

One way to stem complaints at the source is to provide satisfaction surveys at every point of contact with the customer so that problems can be coped with quickly, at the outset, before the customer becomes so angry that resolution and satisfaction are nearly impossible. Effective handling of complaints can be accomplished by understanding that the customer is a human being and should be treated as such—never as a number or as someone without a name or feelings. The customer should be allowed to explain the complaint completely, without interruption. Extending this courtesy acknowledges that the complaint is important and worthy of attention. Customers should always be asked the most important question: "What is one thing we can do to make this better?" A customer's anger should be defused by sincerely taking his or her side on the issue; then the customer should be moved from a problem focus to a solution focus. Finally, the customer should be contacted one week after the complaint to find out whether he or she is still satisfied with the solution and to express the company's desire for a continued relationship.

The most important message that can be sent to customers through a company's marketing effort is that the customer is the most important part of the organization and the company will do whatever it takes to keep good customers satisfied. While it's certainly true that a young, growing company needs to build a customer base by continually adding new customers, it will reap the greatest returns from investing in the customers it currently has.

New Venture Checklist

Have you:

☐ Analyzed the marketing options and ranked them?

☐ Written a clear, concise, one-paragraph statement of the marketing plan?

☐ Developed an advertising, publicity, and promotion strategy?

☐ Discovered your business's compelling story?

☐ Created some innovative ways to promote your business online?

Issues to Consider

1. What are the differences between an entrepreneurial marketing strategy and a large corporation's marketing strategy?
2. Is it important to stick with your marketing plan even if it isn't returning immediate results? Why or why not?
3. What role should new media play in your marketing strategy?
4. What are the critical factors that should be considered in building a brand?
5. How can personal selling be used to build long-term customer relationships?

Experiencing Entrepreneurship

1. Compare and contrast the marketing strategies of two companies in the same industry in terms of the points in the marketing plan on page 322.
2. Find an Internet company that interests you. Contact the entrepreneur or the person in charge of implementing their marketing strategy to discuss their plan for building a brand. Are they undertaking any of the strategies or tactics discussed in this chapter? What is working and what is not? Present your findings in a brief PowerPoint presentation.

Relevant Case Studies

## Chapter 16

FUNDING A START-UP VENTURE

"Money is the seed of money, and the first guinea is sometimes more difficult to acquire than the second million."

—Jean Jacques Rousseau

LEARNING OBJECTIVES

▷ Develop a resource strategy.

▷ Characterize the nature of start-up finance.

▷ Explain funding with equity.

▷ Discuss how to finance with debt.

Profile 16.1 NOTHING HAPPENS UNTIL SOMEONE SELLS SOMETHING

Greg Gianforte's motto "Nothing happens until someone sells something" is the essence of what he believes bootstrapping is—focusing entirely on the customer to figure out whether you have a business that will work. With bootstrapping, if you fail, all you've lost is time, according to Gianforte. At the age of 33, after selling a successful venture for over $10 million, Gianforte moved to Bozeman, Montana, to raise a family. But it wasn't long before he had the urge to start another business. It was 1997, and an Internet software business seemed to make sense. By searching the Internet, he learned that there was no one helping companies respond to e-mail from their customers. To determine whether he could "sell" his fantasy product that didn't yet exist, he began cold-calling companies, talking to them about whether a product like this might be useful if it were available within 90 days. If they said no, he would ask why and then build their response into his product design as long as he could do it within the 90 days he had specified. It took Gianforte only a couple of weeks of cold calls to learn exactly what his potential customers wanted. Then he spent two months developing a rough prototype that potential customers could test and report back to him the features they still needed. Because he wasn't incurring any overhead working out of his house, he decided to give the product away just to get people using it. Within three months he was able to price his RightNow software at a very low license fee. By early 1998, he was bringing in revenues of $30,000 a month and was ready to hire his first

three employees, all of them for sales positions. He didn't create sales materials but, rather, prepared a demonstration website built by students at Montana State University that showed customers how their websites would work with the RightNow software loaded.

In late 1998, Gianforte hired his first technical person, which represented his first investment in real overhead. Nevertheless, he stayed in bootstrap mode until he was confident that he understood the business model. By that time, he also had several large competitors, so it was the right moment to seek some outside funding to open offices in Dallas, London, and Sydney, Australia. He knew he could have grown with internal cash flows, but it would have taken a lot longer.

Gianforte is perhaps an extreme example of a bootstrapper. He housed his business in his home, then in a room at the back of a real estate agency, and then in a former elementary school. It was only when he began to hire experienced managers that he decided it was time to think about the company's image. But he stands by bootstrapping, and although RightNow is now public on the NASDAQ (RNOW) with 1,800 companies as customers, he still makes sure that money is spent to *make* money not just to spend money.

Sources: RightNow, http://www.rightnow.com, accessed May 2, 2007; E. Barker, "Start with Nothing," *Inc. Magazine* (February 2002), http://www.inc.com; RightNow Technologies, http://www.rightnow.com; and M. Middlewood, "RightNow Technologies Jumps on the IPO Bandwagon," *TechNews World*, http://www.technewsworld.com/story/33730.html.

"How can I fund my new business?" Probably no question is more on the minds of entrepreneurs with new venture ideas, and it's no wonder when they hear about huge transactions like Google's acquisition of YouTube for $1.65 billion in a stock-for-stock transaction October 9, 2006. Money seems to be the topic that always draws a crowd, whether it's for a university course on venture capital investment or a conference hosted by Donald Trump teaching investor wannabes how to become rich in real estate.

Budding entrepreneurs suppose that if they have enough money they can make any business concept a success. Unfortunately, that reasoning is faulty. In fact, throwing money at a bad idea won't change it into a good idea; it just delays the inevitable failure. Putting a lot of money into the hands of an inept team is like throwing it away. Moreover, a team that has more money than it needs often makes poor decisions because there's plenty of money to pay for mistakes. The truth is that it is much more challenging (and rewarding) to figure out how to launch without outside capital than it is to raise money. In addition to placing too much value on money as a critical success factor, inexperienced entrepreneurs typically identify venture capital as their first and primary source of funding at start-up, but this mistake springs from a misconception about the needs of start-up ventures, the requirements of venture capitalists, and the nature of financial markets. In general, most start-up ventures do not meet the criteria that venture capitalists use to define high-growth, high-return companies. The reality is that money is only one of the resources needed to start a successful business, and it may not even be the most important resource at start-up.

Funding a new venture is a time-consuming and difficult process made more challenging by the issue of information asymmetry; that is, entrepreneurs have more information about themselves and their ventures than do the people from whom they seek funding.[1] In other words, the value proposition may be very clear to the entrepreneur but if it can't successfully be conveyed to a potential investor, that value is lost. How does an entrepreneur improve his or her chances of securing venture funding from sources available at start-up? Research points to the importance of the entrepreneur's social network and reputation in increasing the chances of securing funding. But that is only the beginning. This chapter will look at sources of financing for start-up companies in order to prepare entrepreneurs to secure the right funding from the right source at the appropriate time. Not all of the sources and strategies discussed in this chapter will be suitable for every business, but it's important to understand all the options in order to make wiser choices.

Resource Strategy

The resources necessary to launch a new venture fall into four broad categories: human capital, social capital, physical capital, and financial capital. Although this chapter focuses on financial capital, it is important to understand its role relative to the other resources. All of these resources have significant implications for the survival and growth of a venture. Determining which activities will require which resources and in what quantities is part of putting together a carefully conceived financial plan. Creating a unique bundle of resources that is rare, valuable, and inimitable becomes a core competency for the business as well as a competitive advantage.[2] The primary resource is the entrepreneur, who brings his or her experience, expertise, personal resources, and vision to the new venture. Many entrepreneurs find themselves in a position much like that of Jeff Hawkins, who founded Palm Computing in 1992. A highly regarded neurobiologist, Hawkins had developed a handwriting algorithm on which he received a patent. He had his reputation and the patent, but no money, no business plan, and no know-how to start a business.[3] Using his social (reputational) capital and his technical skills, he was able to raise $2 million from two venture capitalists whom he had met through one of his work associations. Then he executed a deal with Tandy Computer Corporation, his former employer, for that firm to invest $300,000, sit on the board of directors, and have nonexclusive distribution rights to his new products and cross-license technology.[4] With these pieces in place, he was able to recruit the engineers he needed and an experienced executive to fill the role of president and CEO. Starting with only his social capital and his technical expertise, Hawkins was able to build the beginnings of a complex bundle of resources. Years later, when Hawkins left Palm to start Handspring, he started off with a strong resource base of personal money, a core management team, supplier relationships, customer know-how, and superior technical skills. This time, he was able to launch without the aid of outside investors.

The work of Brush and associates[5] suggests a process for constructing a resource base that will support the development of the business. It consists of five steps:

1. Identify and specify required resources at various milestones in the company's growth: human, social, financial, physical, technological, and organizational.

2. Identify potential suppliers of those resources. Finding the best resources is a long and time-consuming process, so it is important to do this before the venture is launched.

3. Assess the entrepreneur's ability to attract resources. To attract the right resources, entrepreneurs must be out in the industry and market, talking to people and building relationships, so that when a particular resource is needed, the relationship that will produce it is already there.

4. Combine resources to create new, unique resources. One example is using financial resources to acquire rare human capital with unique technical skills.

5. Transform individual resources into organizational resources. Most resources are initially individual resources, usually the founder's. If the entrepreneur can transform these into organizational resources, they can become a core competency and competitive advantage for the company.

START WITH A PLAN

Knowing whom to tap for start-up capital is only half the battle. The other half is having a strategic plan for funding the start-up and growth of the company with the right kind of money from the right sources at the right milestones. Entrepreneurs should raise only what is actually needed, not whatever is possible in the prevailing economic environment. At the same time, planning carefully will avoid the need to seek financing too often, which can be costly both in time and money. It is important at the outset to approach the search for money armed with accurate information. The fact is that relatively few investment sources for start-up companies exist outside of the three F's: friends, family, and fools. When the Kirchhoff Innovation Framework (see Figure 16.1) is used to explain what types of money are available to what types of businesses, it quickly becomes apparent that venture capitalists are interested primarily in "superstar" ventures.[6] *Glamorous firms,* from which the superstars emerge, are firms that grow as a result of high rates of innovation. They tend to attract a lot of media attention and to be based

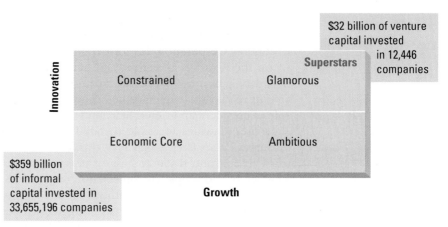

Source: Used with permission from Global Entrepreneurship Monitor 2003 Executive Report by Paul D. Reynold, William D. Bygrave, Erkko Autio, and others, www.gemconsortium.org.

on technology products and processes. eBay is one such firm. *Economic core firms* are generally low-innovation, low-growth companies and epitomize the vast majority of all businesses in the United States. This group also includes those firms that are small temporarily and that will move to other categories as they grow. For example, Wal-Mart founder Sam Walton's first store, Gibson Discount Store, was a typical rural store in the economic core category until he developed the business model that would grow the store into what it is today. Growth in *ambitious firms* is usually based on simple innovations. Dell Computer innovated in distributing and servicing microcomputers through direct mail. *Constrained firms* over time produce most of the glamorous firms. Firms in the constrained category generally have high rates of innovation but are inhibited by limited resources, including the inability to attract the capital or personnel required for growth.

As Figure 16.1 explains, $32 billion of venture capital was invested in 12,446 superstar companies in 2002. But a staggering $359 billion of informal capital was invested in over 33 million businesses in the other categories.[7] Thus the informal markets offer a higher probability of success in the search for funding.

Looking at the informal capital market a little more closely reveals that even in a much broader market, there are limitations. Figure 16.2 depicts the breakdown of informal investment according to where it's placed. Clearly, the majority of informal investment goes to family members and friends, and only about 14 percent is invested in colleagues at work and strangers. This means that it is important for entrepreneurs to elevate their status from strangers to friends to increase their chances of getting funded. How do they do this? By networking and developing relationships before it's time to seek funding.

In general, 77 percent of informal investors want their payback within two to five years. This represents a much shorter timeframe than was historically demanded by informal investors. Furthermore, the Global Entrepreneurship Monitor (GEM) found that most informal investors are male, of high net worth, and well educated and that they are four times more likely than others to have been entrepreneurs themselves. Therefore, this research suggests that, apart from the entrepreneur's personal investment and that of friends and family

FIGURE 16.2

Where Is Informal Capital Invested?

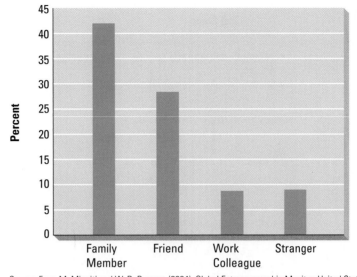

Source: From M. Minniti and W. D. Bygrave (2004). Global Entrepreneurship Monitor: United States 2003 Executive Report. Babson College and the Kauffman Foundation, www.gemconsortium.org. Reprinted with permission.

members, the entrepreneur should be seeking investment capital from former entrepreneurs with a high net worth.

CONSIDER GROWTH STAGES

The starting point for planning is identifying the stages of growth that a business will experience. Every business is different, but in general, each will reach certain milestones that suggest the time has come to grow to the next level. Figure 16.3 indicates the typical funding stages. In the first phase, start-up funds are required. These will normally come from the founders and other sources of "friendly money." Once the company is up and running and has achieved success in a small market, it's time to grow the company to reach a wider audience.

By the second phase, the business is requiring capital to grow on the basis of a proven concept. In fact, customer demand may call for the company to grow, but it may be unable to grow rapidly enough solely using internal cash flows. The company may need outside capital from a private investor, venture capitalist (VC), or debt source. Taking on outside investment capital requires that the entrepreneur plan for some kind of liquidity event so that investors can cash out of the business and receive a return on their investment. That liquidity event may be in the form of an initial public offering (IPO) or an acquisition.

The third phase calls for a different type of money, termed *mezzanine financing* or *bridge financing,* to provide the entrepreneur with the funds the company needs to get through an initial public offering in which millions of dollars may be raised. This phase of rapid growth can come relatively early in the venture's life cycle or very late depending on the type of business and the industry in which it operates. For some businesses, particularly lifestyle businesses, rapid growth may never be part of their evolution. They may instead enjoy slow, steady growth. If a business survives over the long term, it will probably reach a mature phase in

Stages of Financing for Ventures

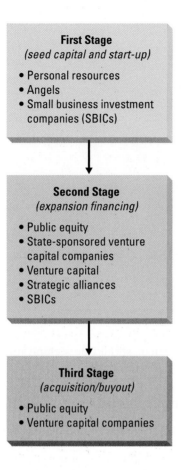

which it ideally maintains a stable revenue stream with a loyal customer base. In today's dynamic environment, however, stability is rarely an enduring state. To continue to be profitable, a mature business must punctuate its equilibrium with new products and services and new markets so that it can remain competitive.

What is clear from this discussion is that there are different types of money for different stages of the venture. In general, each milestone a business achieves creates more value for the company and enables it to seek greater amounts of capital in the form of equity or debt. The issue of growth capital is taken up in Chapter 17.

THE UNIQUE ISSUES OF HIGH-TECH VENTURES

High-tech ventures that introduce breakthrough or disruptive technologies, such as a new drug, device, or process that changes the way we do things, tend to follow a pattern discussed in the works of Geoffrey Moore.[8] Recall that this adoption/ diffusion curve was discussed at length in Chapter 15. Early seed funding supports a long period of product development. Often this early-stage money comes from government grants or foundations. It is a rare venture capital firm that will invest during the earliest product development phase of a high-tech venture, because the risk is too high. The time from idea generation through product development and

THINK SMALL TO GROW BIG IN ISTANBUL

In 2003, Būlent Celebi had just left his Silicon Valley CEO position with Ubicom, a microprocessor company. He had dreams of starting a global business in his native Turkey, but with a twist—it would operate like an American company. The company, AirTies, would manufacture wireless routers in Asia using American chips and sell into developing countries where broadband was still emerging. Celebi figured that in Istanbul he could bootstrap the operation and take advantage of the many new incentives being offered by the Turkish government as a component of its bid to become part of the European Union. For example, his company does not have to pay corporate income tax for ten years because it developed a product inside one of the many "technoparks" set up by the Turkish government as economic zones. However, there were some negatives to Celebi's plan. Turkey is still trying to overcome problems with bribery and corruption, and it suffers from oppressive regulations that make it difficult to launch a business there. Celebi deals with the red tape, but he refuses to pay bribes, so things sometimes take longer. For example, at one point he had $400,000 worth of inventory that remained in customs for six months because he didn't bribe the officials. Nevertheless, for AirTies, Istanbul was ideally located to sell into Europe, Africa, and the Middle East, so with $300,000 that he raised from Silicon Valley investors, Celebi and his family made the decision to change their life and settle in Istanbul. Immediately he began laying the groundwork for an American-style culture in his company; he encouraged his employees to take initiative and to set their own goals and deadlines, and he hired as many Turkish citizens who had been educated in the United States as possible. However, when he and his employees went outside the office, they did business Turkish style. By 2006, his company was enjoying $24 million in revenues, and he was having a positive impact on the creation of an entrepreneurial environment in Turkey. As a successful R&D company entrepreneur, something that is rarely found in Turkey, Celebi has become somewhat of a celebrity and can now influence the decisions of high-profile government officials through his many discussions with them.

Sources: AirTies, http://www.airties.com; S. Clifford, "Fully Committed," *Inc. Magazine* (April 2007).

market testing is often referred to as the "valley of death," because the failure rate is high due to the lack of identifiable markets and inadequate product design. It is similar to the "chasm" referred to by Moore where a new technology languishes because no practical or useful applications have been found. Once the technology approaches market readiness, however, it moves into a phase known as the "early adopter" stage wherein technically oriented users, who regularly purchase leading-edge technology, begin to use it. At this point, the company will require marketing dollars to create awareness on the part of potential customers and enough demand to capture sufficient niches in the market to develop critical mass. A critical mass of users in a variety of niches can shift the product into what Moore refers to as the "tornado," a period of mass adoption of the new technology wherein it has the potential to become the standard in the industry. High technology ventures have longer development times but generally move through the product and business evolution cycle much more rapidly than other types of businesses.

Funding Start-ups

Most start-up ventures begin with a patchwork of funding sources that include credit cards, savings, friends, family members, borrowing, and bartering or trading products and services. The term *bootstrapping* refers to techniques for getting by on as few resources as possible and using other people's resources whenever feasible. It involves begging, borrowing, or leasing everything needed to start a venture and is the antithesis of the "big-money model" espoused by many when they talk about entrepreneurial ventures.[9] More often than not, bootstrapping is a model for starting a business without money—or at least without any money beyond that provided by the entrepreneur's personal resources.

The capital structure of start-up ventures depends heavily on the entrepreneur's personal resources: savings, credit cards, mortgages, stock market accounts, vendor credit, customer financing, and loans. A 2005 PricewaterhouseCoopers survey of the fastest growing private companies found that the number of these companies seeking to fund growth through bank loans has increased 568 percent since 1999. Still, most firms, about 32 percent of those surveyed, seek nontraditional means of financing growth.[10] Jeanne Battaglia-Dillon, founder of Managed Care Network, rented out part of the family's house to college students to get the capital to launch her venture.[11] Dean Soll, president of Sub-Zero Constructors, used frequent-flier miles to purchase a first-class ticket to Atlanta, where, with a "think big, act big" attitude, he managed to secure a $1 million contract with a client from a previous job.[12] These entrepreneurs are the rule, not the exception; typically, personal resources are the most reliable, and sometimes the only, source of start-up funding. This is because new ventures suffer from the liability of newness.[13] By definition they have no track record, so all their estimates of sales and profits are pure speculation. An enormous number of new ventures fail, so the risk for an outside investor is usually high. Many new ventures have no proprietary rights that would give them a competitive advantage and a temporary monopoly in the market they enter. The founders often do not have a significant track record of success. And too many new ventures are "me too" versions of something that already exists, so they have no competitive advantages. Consequently, pre-launch preparation in the form of feasibility analysis and business planning is critical to optimizing the firm's use of the options available at start-up. Poor planning can result in less than advantageous financial choices and a poor return on investment.

Although there are thousands of ways entrepreneurs can bootstrap, the following are some of the most common and tried-and-true methods.

Get Traction as Quickly as Possible

Getting traction, or getting into business in some form, is a step that many entrepreneurs overlook, yet it is one of the most important steps entrepreneurs can take if they want to build credibility so they can eventually raise outside capital. Getting traction means launching the business in the quickest manner possible to start getting real feedback from customers and to test the business model. This may mean putting up a website, opening a kiosk location, or putting product in an existing store on consignment to test the retail potential for a new product. Potential investors, and that includes friendly money, will be much more predisposed to consider an investment if they can see the business in operation and drawing customers.

Hire as Few Employees as Possible

Hiring as few employees as possible runs counter to the economic development efforts of most communities that are looking at job creation, but the goal of the entrepreneur at start-up is survival. Typically, the greatest single expense a business has is its payroll (including taxes and benefits). Subcontracting work to other firms domestically or offshore, using temporary help or PEOs, and hiring independent contractors can keep the number of employees and their associated costs down. However, it is important to follow IRS regulations carefully. One California company, a maker of heart catheters, found out the hard way that failing to follow the rules can cost the company a lot. Several of this company's "independent contractors" were working 40 hours a week exclusively for the high-tech company and were being paid by the hour, all of which suggested to the IRS that they were really employees. This misclassification cost the company $25,000 in penalties and interest. The rules for using independent contractors and leasing employees were discussed in Chapter 8.

Lease or Share Everything

At some point, virtually all new ventures need to acquire equipment, furnishings, and facilities. By leasing rather than purchasing major equipment and facilities, entrepreneurs can avoid tying up precious capital at a time when it is badly needed to keep the venture afloat. With a lease, there usually is no down payment, and the payments are spread over time. A word of caution, however. Be careful about leasing new, rapidly changing technology for long periods of time to avoid saddling the company with obsolete equipment. Some entrepreneurs have shared space with established companies not only to save money on overhead but also to give their fledgling ventures the aura of a successful, established company.

Other People's Money

Another key to bootstrapping success is getting customers to pay quickly and suppliers to allow more time for payment. To accomplish this, entrepreneurs must be willing to continually manage receivables. Sometimes that means walking an invoice through the channels of a major corporation in person or locating the individual who can adjust the computer code that determines when a government agency pays its bills.

Suppliers are an important asset of the business and should be taken care of. Establishing a good relationship with major suppliers can result in more favorable payment terms. After all, the supplier has an interest in seeing the new venture succeed as well. Often a young company can't get sufficient credit from one

TABLE 16.1

Some Great Bootstrapping
Techniques

Use student interns, who will often work free just to get the experience.	Surf the Internet for a wealth of information on anything related to your business.
Barter for media time.	Seek referrals from loyal customers.
Don't hire employees until you absolutely have to.	Use independent contractors whenever possible.
Seek ways to motivate employees without money.	Seek vendor credit.
Manage receivables weekly.	Get customers involved in the business.
Leverage purchasing discounts.	Keep operating expenses as low as possible.
Put resources into things that make money rather than use money.	Use e-mail; it's essentially free.
Work from home as long as possible.	Network to find complementary resources that can be shared or leveraged.

supplier, so it is a good idea to seek smaller amounts of credit from several reputable suppliers. In this way, the firm can establish its creditworthiness, and when it qualifies for a larger credit line, the entrepreneur will know which supplier is the best source. Where possible, it's preferable to sell wholesale rather than retail. Dealing with wholesale distributors makes life easier because they are the experts at working with customers. They have already set up the consumer and industrial channels needed to expand a company's markets. Nevertheless, using a wholesaler (the entrepreneur's customer) does not alleviate the entrepreneur of the responsibility for understanding the needs of the end-user—the wholesaler's customer. No one knows the product better than the entrepreneur, and the relationship with a wholesaler must be a coordinated team effort. More bootstrapping techniques can be found in Table 16.1.

Bootstrapping Ethics

No discussion of bootstrapping would be complete without dealing with the ethical issues that arise whenever bootstrapping tactics are employed to enable a new venture to survive at start-up. When entrepreneurs bootstrap, by definition they are making a new venture appear much more successful than it is to gain credibility in the market. But they must be careful not to cultivate that image at all costs, because those costs can be too great. Lying to survive by misrepresenting who the entrepreneur is or by misrepresenting how long the company has been in business is not an acceptable business practice. Intuit, a very successful software manufacturer, spent several start-up years bootstrapping, during which time it became clear to the company that earning the customer's trust is essential to long-term success. It had been a common practice in the software industry to use promotional schemes to load dealers with excess product in the belief that the dealer would then push that product to get rid of it before taking on a competitor's product. Intuit refused to participate in this behavior scheme and unfailingly communicated honestly its expectations for sales to the dealers. Thus, the dealers were not burdened with excess inventory, and Intuit kept its manufacturing facilities operating on an even keel rather than experiencing costly boom-and-bust cycles.

Funding with Equity

When someone invests money in a venture, it is normally done to gain an ownership share in the business. This ownership share is termed *equity*. It is distinguished from debt in that equity investors put their capital at risk; usually, there is no guaranteed return and no absolute protection against loss. For this reason, most entrepreneurs with start-up ventures seek investment capital from people they know who believe in them. There are a variety of sources of equity financing, including informal capital, such as personal resources, "angels," private placement, and formal sources such as venture capital. This chapter focuses on informal capital.

FRIENDS AND FAMILY

Entrepreneurs need to think very carefully about accepting money in the form of loans or equity investment from family members and friends. This type of money is often called the most expensive money around because the entrepreneur pays for it for the rest of his or her life. Chris Baggott knows that all too well. In 1992, he quit his job and bought a local dry-cleaning business, eventually building it into a seven-store chain. To fund the business, Baggott borrowed $45,000 from his father-in-law, who also co-signed on a $600,000 bank loan. Things were going well until the "business casual" trend happened, and people stopped wearing suits and clothes that needed dry cleaning. The unfortunate end to the story was that Baggott had to sell the business, pay his debts, and live with the very uncomfortable knowledge that his father-in-law had lost tens of thousands of dollars on the deal.[14] Because of the difficulties associated with equity investments from friends and family, many entrepreneurs prefer debt, because it is cheaper and lets the entrepreneur retain control of the business. Debt is discussed in a later section. However, at times, friendly money is the only money available. In that case, it is important to treat the deal as a business deal and put everything in writing so there is no question about who gets what and what happens if there's a disagreement or the business fails.

PRIVATE INVESTORS—ANGELS

The most popular follow-up source of capital for new ventures is private investors, typically people the entrepreneur knows or has met through business acquaintances. These investors, who are called "angels", are part of the informal risk-capital market, the largest pool of risk capital in the United States. They can't be found in a phone book, and they don't advertise. In fact, their intentions as investors are often well hidden until they decide to make themselves known. They do, however, have several definable characteristics. Angels normally invest between $10,000 and $500,000 and usually focus on first-stage financing—that is, start-up funding or funding of firms younger than five years. They are generally well educated, are often entrepreneurs themselves, and tend to invest within a relatively short distance from home, because they like to be actively involved in their investment. They tend to prefer technology ventures, manufacturing, energy and resources, and service businesses. Retail ventures are less desirable because of their inordinately high rate of failure, but angels with restaurant experience can often be found. They typically look to reap the rewards of their investment within three to seven years, but the risk/reward ratio is a function of the age of the firm at the time of investment. Angels may want to earn as much as ten times their original investment if the venture is a start-up, and as much as five times their investment if the venture has been up and running for a couple of years. They find their deals principally through referrals from business associates and tend to make investment decisions more quickly than other sources of capital. Their requirements in terms of documentation, business plan, and due diligence may be lower than venture capitalists, but they are still onerous.

Today, many angels have joined forces to create larger pools of capital. These "bands" of angels have strict rules about how much their members must invest each year and how much time they must spend in exercising due diligence over other members' deals. In some cases, these angel groups look and act like professional venture capitalists. As venture capital pools have grown in size to the point where the deals they engage in are much larger, angels have stepped in to take the deals formerly funded by VCs. The largest angel network in the United States is the Tech Coast Angels, which spans the area from Santa Barbara to San Diego and has hundreds of members. They fund start-ups and early-stage ventures, primarily in high-tech areas like life sciences and information systems, but more recently, they are funding retail and other types of ventures that have high growth potential. Since they organized in 2000, they have funded 128 companies with $85 million of member capital. In addition, they have partnered with venture capital firms to attract an additional $850 million in those 128 ventures.[15]

In general, angels are an excellent source of seed or start-up capital. The secret to finding these elusive investors is networking—getting involved in the business community and speaking with those who regularly come into contact with sources of private capital: lawyers, bankers, accountants, and other businesspeople. Developing these contacts takes time, so it is important not to wait until the capital is needed before beginning to look for them. Of course, taking on an investor will mean giving up some of the ownership of the company. Therefore, it is probably wise to plan at the outset for a way to let the investor exit. Including a buyout provision with a no-fault separation agreement in the investment contract will ensure that the entrepreneur doesn't have to wait for a criminal act such as fraud to end the relationship. Structuring the buyout to be paid out of earnings over time will avoid jeopardizing the financial health of the business. Above all, it is vital to avoid using personal assets as collateral to protect an angel's investment.

The bottom line on an angel investment is that the angel is investing in the entrepreneur, and it's a very personal investment. Angels often want to experience again the excitement of starting a new venture, but they want to do it vicariously through the entrepreneur. That is why they often fund young entrepreneurs with a lot of enthusiasm, a great idea, and the energy to make it happen. They want to be involved and to mentor the entrepreneur. Like the venture capitalist, they would like to make money, but the real payback is in doing good and helping a novice entrepreneur get his or her start.

PRIVATE PLACEMENT

Private placement is a way of raising capital from private investors by selling securities in a private corporation or partnership. Securities include common stock, preferred stock, notes, bonds, debentures, voting-trust certificates, certificates of deposit, warrants, options, subscription rights, limited partnership shares, and undivided oil or gas interests. Private placement provides many benefits over venture capital. Typically investors are willing to stay in longer and accept a lower return on investment. It costs less than either a public offering or venture capital and the money can often be raised more quickly. The best type of business for private placement is one that is seeking some growth funding, but start-ups that have proven their concept and have a first customer may also be able to tap this source.

The investors solicited via a private placement memorandum must be aware of the rules of private placement, which are stated in the Securities and Exchange Commission's Regulation D. Regulation D was designed to simplify the private offering process and enable the entrepreneur to seek funding from private investors who meet the rule's requirements. Doing a private placement memorandum requires first completing a business plan and a prospectus detailing the risks of the investment. Just as in the drafting of any complex legal document, it is crucial that the entrepreneur consult an attorney well versed in the preparation of the private placement memorandum and in the disclosure of information about the company and its principals. Problems don't usually arise if the business is successful; however, if the venture fails and the investors uncover a security violation, the entrepreneur and other principal equity holders may lose their protection under the corporate shield and become personally liable in the event of a lawsuit. Security violations have been dealt with severely by the courts, and there is no statute of limitations on the filing of such a suit.

Private placement is a less costly, less time-consuming process than a public offering, and many states now offer standardized, easy-to-fill-out disclosure statements and offering documents. However, entrepreneurs should never undertake a private placement offering without the guidance of a qualified attorney. The advantages of a private offering are many. The growing venture is not required to have a great many assets or credit references, which it would need for bank financing, nor does it need a lengthy track record. The entrepreneurs also don't have to file with the Securities and Exchange Commission (SEC). They do, however, have to qualify under the rules of Regulation D, which makes it easier and less expensive for smaller companies to sell stock. Not all states recognize the exemptions under Regulation D in their "Blue Sky" laws (laws that protect investors from fraud), so the issuer of a private placement memorandum may have to register with the state.

The burden is on the issuer to document that the exemption from registration requirements has been met. Therefore, the "sophistication" of all offerees should be examined closely, and the reasons why they qualify should be carefully documented. A sophisticated investor is one who has a net worth of at least $2.5 million, earns $250,000 per year, and has taken investment risk in the past. The issuer should number each private placement memorandum and keep a record of who has looked at the memorandum or discussed the offering with the issuer. The memorandum should include a qualifying statement that the contents must not be copied or disclosed to anyone other than the offeree. If an offeree becomes an investor, the issuer should document when and where the offeree examined the books and records of the company. When the offering is complete, the issuer should place in the offering log a memo stating that only those persons listed in the log have been approached about the offering.

Even if the offering qualifies as exempt from registration, it is still subject to the antifraud and civil liability provisions of federal securities laws and state Blue Sky securities laws. Many states have adopted the Small Corporate Offering Registration Form, also called SCOR U-7, which makes the registration process much simpler by providing 50 fill-in-the-blank questions that ask for the basic financial, management, and marketing information for the company. A lawyer should be consulted, because some of the adopting states restrict who can use Form SCOR U-7.

Within the structure of the corporate private placement, the entrepreneur can sell preferred and common stock, convertible debentures (debt that can be converted to equity), and debt securities with warrants (similar to convertible debentures). Recall that preferred stock has dividend and liquidation preference over common stock, in addition to anti-dilution protection and other rights as may be specified in a stockholder agreement. Common stock, on the other hand, carries voting rights and preserves the right of the corporation to elect S-corporation status. Convertible debentures are secured or unsecured debt instruments that can be converted to equity at a later date as specified in the agreement. In its debenture form, however, this instrument provides for a fixed rate of return (interest), which can be used as a tax deduction. Debt securities with warrants give the holder the right to purchase stock at a fixed price for a specified term. Purchasing common stock under this instrument does not invalidate the preferred position of the debt holder as creditor.

STRATEGIC ALLIANCES

A partnership with another business—whether formal or informal—is a strategic alliance. Through strategic alliances, entrepreneurs can structure deals with suppliers or customers that will help reduce expenditures for marketing, raw materials, or research and development (R&D). Reducing expenditures increases cash flow, providing capital that wouldn't otherwise have been available. One type of strategic alliance is the R&D limited partnership. This vehicle is useful for entrepreneurs starting high-tech ventures that carry significant risk due to the expense of research and development. The limited partnership contracts with the new venture to provide the funding for the R&D to develop a market technology that will ultimately be profitable to the partnership. This is advantageous for both the limited partner and the new venture. Limited partners are able to deduct their investment in the R&D contract and enjoy the tax advantages of losses in the early years on their personal tax returns; they also share in any future profits. In the R&D limited partnership, the new venture acts as a general partner to develop the technology and then structures a license agreement with the R&D partner whereby the venture can use the technology to develop other products. Often the limited partnership's interest becomes stock in a new corporation formed to commercialize the new technology.

An alternative to this arrangement is an agreement to pay royalties to the partnership. Yet another vehicle is the formation of a joint venture, which enables the entrepreneur to purchase the joint venture interest after a specific period of time or when the company reaches a certain volume in sales. As in the private placement, it is important to work through an attorney. The new venture may incur significant costs in creating the partnership, a process that could take up to a year. In addition, giving up sole ownership of the technology may be too high a price to pay if the partnership does not survive. Strategic alliances are discussed further in Chapter 17, where growing a company is considered.

SMALL BUSINESS INVESTMENT COMPANIES

Small business investment companies (SBICs) are actually privately managed venture capital firms licensed by the Small Business Administration. They receive financing at very favorable rates, in partnership with the federal government, to invest in small and growing businesses through equity (generally preferred stock or debt with warrants) and long-term debt. Companies that qualify for SBIC financing must have a net worth under $18 million and average after-tax earnings of less than $6 million during the previous two years. In addition, at least 51 percent of assets and employees must reside in the United States. The typical deal involves a loan with options to buy equity, a convertible debenture (debt that can be converted to equity). Preferred stock, which pays the investor back first in the event of a failure, is sometimes used for first-round financing.

GRANTS

The Small Business Innovation Development Act of 1982 was designed to stimulate technological innovation by small businesses in the United States. It requires that all federal agencies with research and development budgets in excess of $100 million give a portion of their budgets to technology-based small businesses in the form of Small Business Innovative Research (SBIR) grants. Small businesses find out about these grants by checking the published solicitations by the agencies to see whether they can qualify by providing what the agency needs. Grants have three phases. Phase I is the concept stage and feasibility phase, which provides $50,000 to $100,000 for an initial feasibility study to determine the scientific and technical merit of the proposed idea. This amount is made available for six months. If results are promising, the company is eligible for Phase II funding. Phase II provides up to an additional $200,000 to $750,000 for two years, for the firm to pursue the innovation and develop a well-defined product or process. Phase III requires the entrepreneur to access private sector funds to commercialize the new technology.

To qualify for an SBIR grant, the company must employ fewer than 500 people, be at least 51 percent independently owned by a U.S. citizen, be technology-based, be organized for profit, and not be dominant in its field. The grant holder must perform two-thirds of the Phase I effort and one-half of the Phase II effort. At least half of the principal investigator's time must be spent working in the small business.

VENTURE CAPITAL INSTITUTES AND NETWORKS

Many areas of the country offer access to venture capital networks through institutes established on the campuses of major universities. The university acts as a conduit through which the entrepreneurs and investors are matched; it neither assumes any liability for nor has any ownership interest in either the new venture or the investor's company. The entrepreneur typically pays a fee, in the range of $200 to $500, and submits a business plan to the institute. The plan is then matched to the needs of private investors in the database who subscribe to the service. If an investor is interested in the business concept, he or she contacts the entrepreneur. In general, venture capital networks are a way for entrepreneurs to gain access to investors whom they may not be able to find through other channels. Furthermore, the investors have chosen to place their names in the database, so they are actively looking for potential investments.

Financing with Debt

When an entrepreneur chooses a debt instrument to finance a portion of start-up expenses, he or she typically provides a business or personal asset as collateral in exchange for a loan bearing a market rate of interest. The asset could be equipment, inventory, real estate, or the entrepreneur's house or car. Although it is best to avoid pledging personal assets as collateral for a loan, it's sometimes unavoidable, because banks generally require first-time entrepreneurs to guarantee loans personally. There are several sources of debt financing.

COMMERCIAL BANKS

Banks are not normally a readily available source of either working capital or seed capital to fund a start-up venture. Banks are highly regulated; their loan portfolios are scrutinized carefully, and they are told in no uncertain terms not to make loans that have any significant degree of risk. Therefore, banks like to see a track record of positive cash flow, because it is out of this cash flow that their loan will be repaid. Unfortunately, new ventures don't *have* a track record, so an unsecured loan is probably not possible. Generally, banks make loans on the basis of what are termed the five C's: character, capacity, capital, collateral, and condition. In the case of the entrepreneur, the first two—character and capacity—become the leading consideration, because the new business's performance estimates are based purely on forecasts. Therefore, the bank will probably consider the entrepreneur's personal history carefully. However difficult, it is important for an entrepreneur with a new venture to establish a lending relationship with a bank. This may mean starting with a very small, secured loan and demonstrating the ability to repay in a timely fashion. Bankers also look more favorably on ventures with hard assets that are readily convertible to cash.

COMMERCIAL FINANCE COMPANIES

As banks have tightened their lending requirements, commercial finance companies have stepped in to fill the gap. Often called "hard asset" lenders, they are able to do this because they are not so heavily regulated, and they base their decisions on the quality of the assets of the business. They do, however, charge more than banks, as much as 5 percent or more over prime, at rates more similar to those charged by credit card companies. Therefore, an entrepreneur must weigh the costs and benefits of taking on such an expensive loan. Of course, in cases where starting the business or not starting it, or surviving in the short term or failing to survive, depends on that loan, the cost may not seem so great.

Factoring, one of the oldest forms of banking, accounts for more than $1 trillion a year in credit. Factoring is a particular type of receivable financing wherein the lender, called the factor, takes ownership of a receivable at a discount and then collects against it. When the U.S. military needed machinery to create the infrastructure in Afghanistan after the invasion, it turned to one of its major contractors, IAP Worldwide Services, which specializes in logistics. But IAP had to purchase the goods the government needed and meet payroll before it would be paid from the order. IAP turned to a factor to get the cash it needed to serve its customer.[16] Factoring has become a popular form of cash management in smaller businesses that sell to big companies. Large companies are notorious for paying extremely slowly, which can wreak havoc with an entrepreneur's cash flow. But a small business that sells to Wal-Mart must be patient with the giant, because that account is probably very important to the entrepreneur. Therefore, the entrepreneur sells some of those receivables to a factor so as to not interrupt its cash flow. Factors know that Wal-Mart will eventually pay, so there is little risk to them of taking on the receivable. In fact, Wal-Mart has helped to grow the factor industry significantly. Entrepreneurs should make sure that any factor they use is a member of the Commercial Finance Association, which is the major trade group for the industry. They should also have an attorney verify the authenticity and background of the factor. In general, taking out a bank loan is less expensive than using a factor.

SMALL BUSINESS ADMINISTRATION LOAN

When a traditional commercial bank loan does not appear to be a viable option, the entrepreneur may want to consider an SBA-guaranteed loan. With an SBA-guaranteed loan, the entrepreneur applies for a loan of up to $2 million from his or her bank, and the SBA guarantees that it will repay up to 75 percent of the loan to the commercial lender (generally a bank) should the business default. This guarantee increases the borrower's chances of getting a loan. A further incentive to banks is that SBA-funded ventures tend to be growth-oriented and have a higher survival rate than other start-ups. Of course, because the government backs these loans, the documentation and paperwork are extensive, and interest rates are usually no different from those paid on a conventional loan.

Entrepreneurs should be aware that it's difficult to secure an SBA loan at start-up. The SBA requires a track record of at least a couple of years before they're willing to step in.

The Small Business Administration also has a program called the micro loan that makes it easier for entrepreneurs with limited access to capital to borrow small amounts (up to $35,000) with the average loan about $13,000. Instead of using banks, as in their guarantee program, the SBA uses nonprofit community development corporations. In addition to the money, they are usually required to participate in business training and technical assistance.

STATE-FUNDED VENTURE FUNDING

Many states provide a range of services to help new and growing ventures. From venture capital funds to tax incentives, states such as Massachusetts, New York, and Oregon are seeing the value of establishing business development programs. New and growing ventures usually receive their funding from the state government, which enables them to seek larger investment amounts from private sources. In states where equity funding is not available, there is typically a loan program aimed at new ventures. In Massachusetts, for example, favorable debt financing is often exchanged for warrants to purchase stock in the new company. Pennsylvania was the first to create a funding program aimed at minority-owned businesses. South Dakota has recently implemented a seed grant program to encourage commercialization of research from its universities.

INCUBATORS

There is no doubt that after the dot com debacle and subsequent drop in the value of technology stocks, the incubators that spawned a rash of Internet businesses fell on hard times. But today incubators are enjoying a resurgence of interest. Incubators are places where start-up ventures can get space and support for the early stages of start-up. They are typically nonprofit organizations designed to help nascent businesses get up and running to improve their chances of survival in the marketplace. See Chapter 13 for some suggestions on what to look for in an incubator.

CUSTOMERS AND SUPPLIERS

Many entrepreneurs neglect to consider one of the largest and most accessible sources of funding—their customers and suppliers. The reason why these two groups are more accessible than many other types of financing is that they are colleagues in the same industry; they understand the entrepreneur's business and have a vested interest in seeing the entrepreneur succeed. Suppliers and customers can grant extended payment terms or offer special terms favorable to the business. In return, the entrepreneur's business can provide such things as faster delivery, price breaks, and other benefits.

Starting a business takes preparation, particularly when outside capital is required. But careful planning and a successful launch can lead to additional sources of funding for growth, the subject of Chapter 17.

New Venture Checklist

Have you:

☐ Considered how many personal resources you have to help fund the new venture?

☐ Determined ways to bootstrap the start-up of the new venture?

☐ Networked to come in contact with potential "angels"?

☐ Identified an attorney who can help structure a private placement agreement if needed?

☐ Investigated the sources of debt financing in the community?

Issues to Consider

1. How does bootstrap financing fit into the strategic plan of a new venture?
2. What is the role of angels as a source of new venture funding?
3. At what stage of venture development do venture capitalists typically become involved, and why?
4. Why are commercial banks not usually a reliable source of new venture financing?
5. What are the benefits of a private offering as compared to a public offering?

Experiencing Entrepreneurship

1. Make a list of all the sources of friendly money, including your personal resources, that you can tap to start a new business. How much start-up money could you reasonably raise?

2. Interview an angel and a banker to learn what his or her expectations are when reviewing business plans for new ventures. In a two-page report, compare their criteria for choosing to fund or not fund the new business.

Relevant Case Studies

Case 1 Overnite Express, p. 438

Case 4 MySpace: The Online Reality Show, p. 458

Case 5 iRobot: Robots for the Home, p. 463

Case 7 Linksys, p. 477

## Part Four

PLANNING FOR GROWTH AND CHANGE

Funding a Rapidly Growing Venture	Planning for Growth	Planning for Change
CHAPTER 17	CHAPTER 18	CHAPTER 19

FUNDING A RAPIDLY GROWING VENTURE

Growth is directly proportionate to promises made: Profit is inversely proportionate to promises kept.

—JOHN PEERS, President, Logical Machine Corporation, 1979

LEARNING OBJECTIVES

▶ Discuss the cost and process of raising capital.

▶ Explain the role of the venture capital market.

▶ Describe the process associated with the initial public offering.

▶ Discuss how to grow with strategic alliances.

▶ Explain ways to value a business.

Profile 17.1 A GROWTH MODEL FOR PONDS

Greg Wittstock may be the only person in the United States to have spent his life in and around ponds and then to have found a way to revolutionize the water garden industry by creating an innovative business model and growth strategy. At the age of twelve, at his Wheaton, Illinois, home, Wittstock built his first pond out of concrete to contain his pet turtles, which had outgrown their aquarium. The pond employed a modified garbage can and cattle trough that served as makeshift pond filters. Unfortunately, the pond leaked and turned green; it eventually sent his turtles scrambling for safer shelter. That first exercise in water gardens became a hobby that turned into a career and a multimillion-dollar business.

Every summer until he reached college age, Wittstock and his father worked on refining and improving their backyard pond, trying different filtration systems, pumps, and construction methods. In the summer of 1990, they thought they had finally built the best pond possible. Wittstock had completed his sophomore year at Ohio State and was working for the summer at a subsidiary of Union Carbide, where his father was an engineer. Wittstock didn't enjoy his job, but what else could he do? And then it hit him. He could start a pond-building business; that was something he knew well and loved doing. For Christmas that year, his parents gave him a wheelbarrow and a shovel, which served as the first investment in his emerging business, Aquascape Designs. Placing ads in the classifieds and leaving business cards at strategic suppliers, Wittstock managed to secure contracts for more than 17 ponds. In the summer of 1992, when a article about his fledging company appeared on the front page of the *Chicago Tribune*'s Tempo section one Sunday, his phone starting ringing off the hook. That one article generated 81 orders, more than he could handle alone.

By that time, Wittstock's father had left Union Carbide and had started a struggling engineering consulting firm. He decided to come on board to help his son manage the demand. With just the two of them doing the work, it was important to create efficiencies immediately so that every order would be filled on schedule. One of these efficiencies was the 20/20 rule—a way to reduce construction time by having all materials at the site before the job began. It was at this time that Wittstock also hired his first employee to implement the one-day pond-building technique without him. But the full potential to grow this business emerged when Wittstock met an Arthur Andersen consultant who helped him understand how to leverage his hands-on knowledge of pond building to reach the broader consumer market. At first Wittstock tried franchising, but when that failed, he decided that instead of selling his knowledge, he would give it away by teaching landscapers how to make money building water gardens.

Over the next few years, as the business grew, Wittstock and his father quarreled about how to run the business. Although they had worked together for ten years, in the end their views of the business differed significantly. Eventually, Wittstock bought out his father for $184,000, and to Wittstock's chagrin, his father became his first real competitor with a company he founded in 1997 called Pond Supplies of America. But Aquascape was on the fast track, and every year from 1995 to 2003, its revenues doubled. In 2003, Aquascape did $45 million in sales. The focus of the company shifted to the design and marketing of pond-building equipment, and Aquascape invested more money in research and development. One of Aquascape's chief competitive advantages is its no-back-orders policy. Parts are always available when a landscaper needs them. Another is its travelling training program, along with its publishing and video division. In March of 1999, Wittstock completed a 57-city tour of sold-out seminars, and although he no longer does the seminars himself, he is often seen attending them and biting his tongue to resist putting in his two cents.

In January of 2003, Aquascape acquired its major competitor, Water Creations. This surprised everyone, because for years Aquascape had denounced this competitor and its products. But the acquisition was strategic. Wittstock wanted to capture the do-it-yourself market that was Water Creations's focus. With ponds and water gardens now being the fastest-growing segment of the lawn and garden industry, Wittstock has room to grow. Today the company has over 130 employees, serves more than 35,000 customers, and has been on the Inc. 500 list three times. The company trains more than 5,000 contractors a year.

Too often, companies try to raise money to grow when what they really need to do is figure out how to operate more efficiently. Wittstock lets his employees know where they stand in the business and what they contribute to its profitability. If an employee wants to make a certain salary, that employee is given the amount in new sales that she or he will have to generate to cover that salary. Wittstock is also adamant about getting estimates right. Often companies will submit a bid to win a contract and never check to see that the contract will actually cover the costs of doing the job. Teaching business financials to landscapers who buy from him is one of the goals of Wittstock's training program. Wittstock's passion for the pond business and his innate understanding of its operations have made it possible for Aquascape to grow substantially. Expectations are that it will outshine its competitors for the foreseeable future.

Sources: D. Dahl, "Big Fish, Small Ponds," *Yahoo Small Business Exchange* (January 22, 2007), http://www.aquascapeinc.com/news/big-fish-small-pond.php; B. Burlingham, "Building a Marketing Juggernaut," *Inc. Magazine* (November 2003), p. 58; AquascapeDesigns, "About Us," http://www.aquascapedesigns.com; and "Aquascape Designs Expands," *Pool & Spa News* (February 28, 2003), http://www.findarticles.com.

The natural by-product of a successful start-up is growth. But growth is costly and often puts an enormous strain on the already sparse resources of the young venture. Typically, to meet significant demand, the new company will need additional capital beyond any internal cash flows. Growth capital, or second-round financing, consists of those funds needed to take the venture out of the start-up phase and move it toward securing a market presence. To the extent that the entrepreneur has met the sales and earnings targets estimated in the start-up business plan, available financing choices increase substantially when growth financing, or second-round financing, is sought. The fact that more choices are available is important because, normally, the amount of money needed to grow a business is significantly greater than that required to start a business. One exception is high-tech companies that incur considerable research and development costs prior to start-up. This type of company may spend millions of dollars and accrue several years of losses before its first sale. It may also go through several rounds of financing and grants before it has something to sell to customers.

Most venture funding today is still going to biotechnology, software, and other high technology ventures, but in general, the best companies in any industry have the easiest time finding capital from any source. Being one of the "best" companies requires having an excellent track record (however short), a sound management team, a potential for high growth, and a plan for investor exit with an excellent rate of return on the money invested. Investors in growth companies typically will not go into a situation where their new money is paying off old debt or where cash flow is poor. They want to know that the infrastructure is in place, sales are increasing, and the growing venture needs capital only to take it to the next stage. This chapter looks at some of the sources of growth capital available to entrepreneurs and how to value a business to prepare for funding.

The Cost and Process of Raising Capital

Make no mistake about it, raising growth capital is a time-consuming and costly process. For this reason, many entrepreneurs choose to grow slowly instead, depending exclusively on internal cash flows to fund growth. They have a basic fear of debt and of giving up, to investors, any control of or equity in the company. Unfortunately, they may act so conservatively that they actually stifle growth. It's important that entrepreneurs understand the nature of raising money so that their expectations will not be unreasonable. The first thing to understand about raising growth capital (or any capital, for that matter) is that it will invariably take at least twice as long as expected before the money is actually in the company's bank account. Consider the task of raising a substantial amount of money—several million dollars, for instance. It can take several months to find the financing, several more months for the potential investor or lender to do "due diligence" and say yes, and then up to six more months to receive the money. In other words, if an entrepreneur doesn't look for funding until it's needed, it will be too late. Moreover, because this search for capital takes an entrepreneur away from the business just when he or she is needed most, it is helpful to use financial advisers who have experience in raising money, and it is vital to have a good management team in place.

The second thing to understand about raising growth capital is that the chosen financial source may not complete the deal, even after months of courting and negotiations. It's essential, therefore, to continue to look for backup investors in case the original investor backs out. If they do complete the deal, second-round investors will often request a buyout of the first-round investors, who typically are friends and family. The rationale is that these early investors have nothing more to contribute to the business and the second-round funders no longer want to deal with them. This can be a very awkward situation, because the second-round funder has nothing to lose by demanding the buyout and can easily walk away from the deal; there are thousands more out there.

IT TAKES MONEY TO MAKE MONEY

It is a fact of life that it takes money to make money. The costs incurred before investor or bank money is received must be paid by the entrepreneur, whereas the costs of maintaining the capital (accounting and legal expenses) can often be paid from the proceeds of the loan or (in the case of investment capital) from the proceeds of a sale or internally generated cash flow. If the business plan and financial statements have been kept up-to-date since the start of the business, a lot of money can be saved during the search for growth capital. When large amounts of capital are sought, however, growth capital funding sources prefer that financials have the approval of a financial consultant or investment banker,

Socially Responsible Entrepreneurship

Investing in Ocean Power

To become a success in ocean power technology, you have to have a lot of patience and wait for just the right moment to launch a serious business and tap the investor market. Back in 1970, George Taylor and his partner Joseph Burns founded a company to design flat-panel liquid-crystal displays and sold it five years later to Fairchild Semiconductor. It was the basis for the technology used in television and computer displays today. Not satisfied to rest on their success, they looked for a technology in the energy arena. After dismissing wind technologies because of the unpredictability of wind, they settled on ocean waves. Taylor, a former surfer, invented a buoy that could convert a wave's up-and-down movement to electricity, which could then be transported via undersea cables to shore to connect with the national power grid. Scientists at Oregon State University predict that approximately 0.2 percent of the ocean's wave energy could satisfy the entire world's need for electricity. Today Taylor is seeing a perfect storm of factors creating the window of opportunity for his technology: high oil prices, climate change, unstable relationships in the Middle East, and a growing interest by investors in environmentally responsible companies.

Taylor has avoided the venture capital route, preferring to seek funding from private investors who have a long-term vision. Two of his first investors were an electrical-components manufacturer and a small Australian energy company. He then took the company public on the London Stock Exchange AIM market (international market for smaller growing companies and with more flexibility in requirements than U.S. stock exchanges) and was able to raise $40 million. His goal is to create an array of 40 buoys that, linked together, could generate clean electricity at rates significantly less than coal-burning plants, which are currently the cheapest form of electricity. However, the U.S. investor market does not appear to be as enthusiastic as the international market as witnessed by Ocean Power Technologies' IPO on NASDAQ in April 2007 (NASDAQ OPTT), which was tepid at best. It appears that the long horizon on this technology is still not attractive to most investors.

Sources: D. Drollette, "Electricity from Wave Power," *Fortune Small Business* (December 2006/January 2007), p. 26; and Ocean Power Technologies, http://www.oceanpowertechnologies.com, accessed May 10, 2007.

someone who regularly works with investors. This person is an expert in preparing loan and investment packages that are attractive to potential funding sources. A CPA will prepare the business's financial statements and work closely with the financial consultant. All these activities result in costs to the entrepreneur. In addition, when equity capital is sought, a prospectus or offering document will be required, and preparing it calls for legal expertise and often has significant printing costs. Then there are the expenses of marketing the offering; such things as advertising, travel, and brochures can become quite costly.

In addition to the up-front costs of seeking growth capital, there are "back-end" costs when an entrepreneur seeks capital by selling securities (shares of stock in the corporation). These costs can include investment banking fees, legal fees, marketing costs, brokerage fees, and various other fees charged by state and federal authorities. The cost of raising equity capital can go as high as 25 percent of the total amount of money sought. Add to that the interest or return on investment paid to the funding source(s), and it's easy to see why it costs money to raise money.

The Venture Capital Market

Private venture capital companies have been the bedrock of many high-growth ventures, particularly in the computer, software, biotechnology, and telecommunications industries. Venture capital is, quite simply, a pool of money managed by professionals. These professionals usually assume the role of general partner and are paid a management fee plus a percentage of the gain from any investments. The venture capital (VC) firm takes an equity position through ownership of stock in the company. It also normally requires a seat on the board of directors and often brings its professional management skills to the new venture in an advisory capacity. Because traditionally venture capitalists rarely invest in start-up ventures outside the high-tech arena, the growth stage of a new venture is where most entrepreneurs consider approaching them. Waiting until this stage is advantageous to the entrepreneur, because using venture capital in the start-up phase can mean giving up significant control. Today, however we are seeing VCs investing in nontechnology-based deals that are located outside their immediate geographic region. The pressure to find great investments for their portfolio investors has caused them to expand the scope of the types of deals they are willing to consider.

The ability to secure classic venture capital funding depends not only on what an entrepreneur brings to the table but also on the status of the venture capital industry. PricewaterhouseCoopers, Thomson Venture Economics, and the National Venture Capital Association have joined forces to track total venture capital investing in the United States. They report that at the historical peak in 2000, the height of the dot com/technology boom, VC investing was at $105 billion. By the end of 2003, that amount had plunged to approximately $20 billion (Figure 17.1). Although that is certainly a drastic decline in investment activity, it is clear from Figure 17.1 that $20 billion invested in 2,904 deals is closer to the historical norm for venture capital investment, so it may be

FIGURE 17.1

Total U.S. Investment in Billions

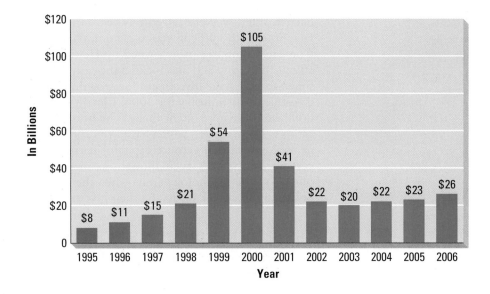

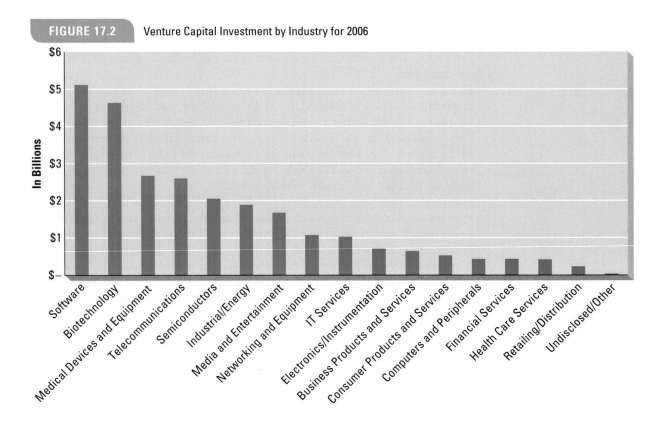

FIGURE 17.2   Venture Capital Investment by Industry for 2006

considered a return to normal from an aberrant period. In 2006, 3,416 U.S. deals received over $25 billion in venture funding.[1] Many would say that the recent trend is a healthy return to investment rates that prevailed before the dot com boom and bust. Fewer deals are being made, but those that are made are likely to fund well-conceived business concepts with solid business models. In fact, historically, difficult economic times have spawned great companies such as Compaq Computer (now owned by Hewlett Packard) in the early 1980s and Palm Computing and Starbucks in the early 1990s. All in all, now is a fairly good time for early-stage investment for growth. Figure 17.2 presents venture capital investments by industry for 2006. Clearly, software and biomedical technology dominated the investment focus. The next biggest category was telecommunications. These results, which have been fairly consistent since 1995, support the general notion that venture capital is narrowly focused on high technology in very specific sectors even though, as mentioned previously, they also invest outside of the technology arena when the business model makes sense and the potential for a quick return on their investment is there.

THE SEQUENCE OF EVENTS IN SECURING VENTURE CAPITAL

To determine whether venture capital is the right type of funding for a growing venture, entrepreneurs must understand the goals and motivations of venture capitalists, for these dictate the potential success or failure of the attempt. VCs

FIGURE 17.3

Funding Stages and Risk

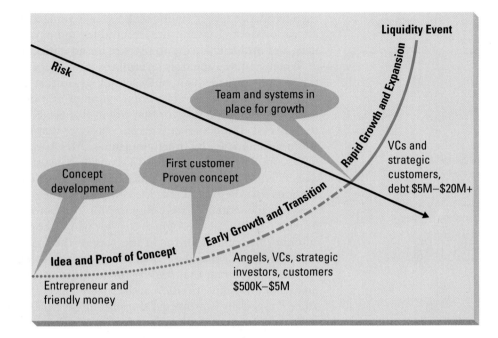

process hundreds of business plans every month, so their first priority is to quickly eliminate those that don't meet their most important criteria. They do this by looking for flaws in the business plan that would suggest that this venture is not a good investment opportunity. This is an important point, because a business plan may present a viable and lucrative investment for the entrepreneur, but if it can't achieve the size and returns that the VC needs to be successful, it will not be deemed a good investment opportunity. VCs are fundamentally risk averse, so it is the entrepreneur's job to reduce risk in the three key areas where VCs find it: management risk, technology risk, and business model risk. A sound business plan demonstrating market research with the customer can help, but proving the concept in the market is even more important. Figure 17.3 depicts the three major stages during which entrepreneurs receive funding: (1) idea and proof of concept stage, which includes start-up and initial survival; (2) early growth and transition; and (3) rapid growth. The first stage, concept development, is the highest-risk stage because uncertainty is at its highest with many questions about the business and the market remaining unanswered until the second stage. VCs rarely invest at this stage even though the returns will be higher because the probability of not achieving those returns is also at its highest. The early growth and transition stage sees the business in operation, having proven the concept and the market, so a significant amount of risk has been reduced. VCs will enter at this stage if the potential to move into rapid growth is imminent. The third stage, rapid growth, is where most VCs invest because this stage is more likely to bring them to the liquidity event they need in three to five years to make the investment worthwhile. Most of the critical questions have been answered, the team has been proven, and now it's a matter of funding rapid growth and preparing the venture for an IPO. At this point, funding is used to finance several stages: scale-up of manufacturing and sales, working capital for expanding inventories, receivables and payables, funding for new products, and bridge financing to prepare for an initial public offering.

When venture capitalists scrutinize a new opportunity, they typically evaluate the market, management, and technology, in that order. Market is usually first because it serves to weed out opportunities that don't have large markets in a fast-growing industry sector that will enable the business to do an IPO in three to five years. If the market is great (year-over-year growth of at least 25 percent and no domination by other companies), the management team does not have to be complete at the time the VC considers investing in the venture. The team does need to have technical skills, industry experience, and a track record that suggests that they could take the company to the next level of growth.[2] In addition to experience, VCs are looking for commitment to the company and to growth because they recognize that growing a company requires an enormous amount of time and effort on the part of the management team.[3] Once they have determined that the management team is solid or that the missing pieces can easily be found, they look at the product to determine whether it enjoys a unique or innovative position in the marketplace. Product uniqueness or "secret sauce," especially if protected through intellectual-property rights, helps create entry barriers in the market, commands higher prices, and adds value to the business. All of these characteristics are important because it is from the consequent appreciation in the value of the business that the VC will derive the required return on investment.

The venture capital firm invests in a growing business through the use of debt and equity instruments to achieve long-term appreciation on the investment within a specified period of time, typically three to five years. By definition, this goal is often different from the goals of the entrepreneur, who usually looks at the business in a much longer frame of reference. The venture capitalist also seeks varying rates of return, depending on the risk involved. An early-stage investment, for example, characteristically demands a higher rate of return, as much as 50 percent or more annual cash-on-cash return, whereas a later-stage investment demands a lower rate of return, perhaps 30 percent annually. Depending on the timeframe for cash-out, the VC will expect capital gains multiples of 5 to 20 times the initial investment. Very simply, as the level of risk increases, so does the demand for a higher rate of return, as depicted in Figure 17.3. This relationship is not surprising. Older, more established companies have a longer track record on which to base predictions about the future, so normal business cycles and sales patterns have been identified, and the company is usually in a better position to respond through experience to a dynamic environment. Consequently, investing in a mature firm does not command the high rate of return that investing in a high-growth start-up does.

Armed with an understanding of what VCs are looking for, an entrepreneur is prepared to begin the search for a company that meets his or her needs. Because the venture capital community is fairly close-knit, at least within regions of the country, it is wise not to "shop" the business plan around looking for the best deal. It is important to do some research on the local venture capital firms to determine whether any specialize in the particular industry or type of business that the entrepreneur is growing. Getting recommendations from attorneys and accountants who regularly deal with business investments is an excellent way to find these VC firms. In fact, the best way to approach venture capitalists is through a referral from someone who knows the VC. Because VC funding is usually later-stage funding, it is likely that entrepreneurs seeking this type of funding have already tapped the angel investor network (see Chapter 16). In fact, new ventures that have successfully navigated through angel investor screenings and mentoring are typically is a more valuable position when they are introduced to the VC firm that can provide them their next round of capital. Angel networks work closely with the VC firms in their region, so they understand their strict requirements and can help prepare the new venture to meet those requirements.

The venture capital firm will no doubt ask for a copy of the entrepreneur's business plan with an executive summary. The executive summary is a screening device—if it can't be immediately determined that the entrepreneurial team's qualifications are outstanding, the product concept innovative, and the projections for growth realistic, the VCs will not bother to read the rest of the business plan. On the other hand, if they like what they see in the plan, they will probably request a meeting to determine whether the management team can deliver what they project. This may or may not call for a formal presentation of the business by the entrepreneur. During this meeting, the initial terms of an agreement may be discussed in a general sense, but it will probably take several meetings before a term sheet is delivered. The term sheet is essentially a letter of intent and it spells out the terms that the VC is prepared to accept. Term sheets are discussed in the next section. If the meeting goes well, the next step is due diligence—that is, the VC firm has its own team of experts check out the entrepreneurial team and the business thoroughly. If after exhaustive due diligence the VCs are still sold on the business, they draw up the term sheet, which signals the start of a negotiation. Entrepreneurs should not expect to receive funding immediately, however. Some venture capitalists wait until they know they have a satisfactory investment before putting out a call to their investors to fund the investment. Others just have a lengthy process for releasing money from the firm. The money is typically released in stages linked to agreed-upon milestones. Also, the venture capital firm will continue to monitor the progress of the new venture and probably will want a seat or several seats on the board of directors, depending on its equity stake in the company, to ensure that it has a say in the direction the new venture takes.

Getting to a Term Sheet

Getting to a term sheet is a sign that the VC firm is serious, but it does not guarantee a "done deal." The term sheet lays out the amount of investment the VC firm is willing to consider and the conditions under which it is willing to consider the funding. The entrepreneur is not required to accept the term sheet as is; it simply represents the start of a negotiating process. At the top of the term sheet will be the actual dollar amount the firm is offering and the form that those funds will take, whether that be common stock, preferred stock, a bond, promissory note, or some combination of the aforementioned. It will also set a price, usually per $1,000 unit of debt or share of stock, which represents the cost basis for investors to get into the deal. The term sheet will also refer to the "post-closing capitalization" or post-money valuation, which is the projected value of the company on the day the terms are agreed upon and accepted by all parties. For example, the VCs might offer $3 million in Series B preferred stock at $.50/share (6 million shares with a post-closing capitalization of $16 million, the VC's estimate of value; see the section on valuation). The VC firm then owns 18.7 percent of the company ($3M divided by $16M). The rest of the term sheet outlines the capital structure for the company and is discussed in the next section.

Capital Structure

It may seem that entrepreneurs are totally at the mercy of venture capitalists when it comes to the negotiation of a deal. That, unfortunately, is true if they enter a negotiation from a weak position, desperately needing the money to keep the business alive. A better approach is to go into the negotiation from a position of strength. True, venture capitalists have hundreds of deals presented to them on a regular basis, but most of those deals are not big hits; in other words, the return on the investment is not worth their effort. VCs are always looking for that one business that will achieve high growth and will return enough on their investment to make up for all the average- or mediocre-performing investments in their portfolio. If entrepreneurs enter a negotiation with a business that has a solid record of growth and performance, they are in a good position to call at least some of the shots.

Any investment deal is comprised of four components:

1. The amount of money to be invested
2. The timing and use of the investment moneys
3. The return on investment to investors
4. The level of risk involved

The way these components are defined will affect the new venture for a long time, not only in constructing its growth strategy but also in formulating an exit strategy for the investors. VCs often want both equity and debt—equity because it gives them an ownership interest in the business, and debt because they will be repaid more quickly. Consequently, they tend to want redeemable preferred stock or debentures so that if the company does well, they can convert to common stock, usually at a 1:1 ratio at the investor's option. Alternatively, if the company does poorly or fails, they will be the first to be repaid their investment. In another scenario, the VCs may want a combination of debentures (debt) and warrants, which enables them to purchase common stock at a nominal rate later on. If this strategy is implemented correctly, they may be able to get their entire investment back when the debt portion is repaid and still enjoy the appreciation in the value of the business as stockholders.

There are several other provisions that venture capitalists often request to protect their investment. One is an antidilution provision, which ensures that the selling of stock at a later date will not decrease the economic value of the venture capitalist's investment. In other words, the price of stock sold at a later date must be equal to or greater than the price at which the venture capitalist could buy the common stock on a conversion from a warrant or debenture. In addition, to guard against having paid too much for an interest in the company, the VC may request a forfeiture provision. This means that if the company does not achieve its projected performance goals, the founders may be required to give up some of their stock to the VC as a penalty. The forfeited stock increases the VC's equity in the company and may even be given to new management that the VC brings on board to steer the company in a new direction. Entrepreneurs should never accept these terms unless they are confident of their abilities and commitment to the venture. One way to mitigate this situation is for the entrepreneur to request stock bonuses as a reward for meeting or exceeding performance projections.

Venture capital is certainly an important source of funding for an entrepreneur with a high-growth venture. It is, however, only one source, and with the advice of experts, entrepreneurs should consider all other possible avenues. Clearly, the best choice is one that gives the new venture the chance to reach its potential and the investors or financial backers an excellent return on investment.

The Initial Public Offering (IPO)

Undertaking the initial public offering, or "going public," is the goal of many companies because it is an exciting way to raise large amounts of money for growth that probably couldn't be raised from other sources. However, deciding whether to do a public offering is difficult at best, because doing so sets in motion a series of events that will change the business and the relationship of the entrepreneur to that business forever. Moreover, returning to private status once the company has been a public company is an almost insurmountable task. An initial public offering (IPO) is just a more complex version of a private offering, in which the founders and equity shareholders of the company agree to sell a portion of the company (via previously unissued stocks and bonds) to the public by filing with the Securities and Exchange Commission and listing their stock on one of the stock exchanges. All the proceeds of the IPO go to the company in a primary offering. If the owners of the company subsequently sell their shares of stock, the proceeds go to the owners in what is termed a secondary distribution. Often the two events occur in combination, but an offering is far less attractive when a large percentage of the proceeds is destined for the owners, because that clearly signals a lack of commitment on the part of the owners to the future success of the business. For IPOs market timing is critical because not every year or portion of a year is favorable for an IPO. Research suggests that the value of the stock at the time of issuance is an important determinant in the ultimate decision to issue stock.[4] The bottom line is that an IPO is never a sure thing, either for the entrepreneur or the investor. Recall what happened to Vonage, the voice-over-IP company, which debuted on the New York Stock Exchange on May 24, 2006, and within the first seven days lost approximately 30 percent of its value, precipitating a class-action lawsuit claiming that shareholders were misled.[5] This is not an uncommon occurrence, however, because historically IPOs have underperformed the broader market. One exception in recent times was the class of 2004, which performed better than any group of IPOs since 1999, with the first day jump averaging 11 percent and total return to shareholders of 34 percent on 216 companies.[6]

Recently, many smaller companies that have not found the U.S. IPO market very inviting have looked to the European and Asian markets to find money. These markets have less stringent capitalization requirements and reporting rules and investors there are eagerly looking for technology companies in which to invest.[7] With small valuations of $10 to $60 million, these companies are very attractive to Japanese investors, for example, who typically only see later-stage Japanese companies on the Nikkei exchange. They would prefer to get in at an earlier stage where there is greater potential for larger gains. The trend of companies looking for money in foreign markets will only increase due to the global economy and the relative ease with which these markets can be tapped.

ADVANTAGES AND DISADVANTAGES OF GOING PUBLIC

The principal advantage of a public offering is that it provides the offering company with a tremendous source of interest-free capital for growth and expansion, paying off debt, or product development. With the IPO comes the future option of additional offerings once the company is well known and has a positive track record. A public company has more prestige and clout in the marketplace, so it becomes easier to form alliances and negotiate deals with suppliers, customers, and creditors. In addition, restricted stock and stock options can be used to attract new employees and reward existing employees. It is also easier for the founders to harvest the rewards of their efforts by selling off a portion of their stock or borrowing against it. In fact, research reveals that the median ownership percentage of officers and directors in public companies actually declines in the decade following an IPO, from about 68 percent to 18 percent.[8]

There are, however, some serious disadvantages to public offerings. Since 1980, more than 9,000 companies have completed initial public offerings, raising a total of $450 billion, but recent research conducted by Peristiani and Hong for the Federal Reserve Bank of New York found that in the two-decade period from 1980 to 2000, there was a dramatic decline in the pre-IPO financial condition of issuers, as well as a significant rise in the failure rate of issuers after the offering.[9] In general, those firms that undertook an IPO with negative earnings (many such cases occurred in the later part of the 1990s) were three times more likely to be dropped from a stock exchange than their profitable counterparts. In fact, 2001 saw an unprecedented 3.8 percent of all publicly traded stocks dropped from the major stock exchanges.[10] A public offering is a very expensive process. Whereas a private offering can cost about $100,000, a public offering can run well over $300,000, a figure that does not include a 7 to 10 percent commission to the underwriter, which compensates the investment bank that sells the securities. An IPO failure can be a financial disaster for a young company. One way to prevent such a disaster is to ask for stop-loss statements from lawyers, accountants, consultants, and investment bankers. The stop-loss statement is essentially a promise not to charge the full fee if the offering fails.

In addition to the expense, going public is enormously time-consuming. Entrepreneurs report that they spend the better part of every week on issues related to the offering over a four- to six-month period.[11] Part of this time is devoted to learning about the process, which is much more complex than this chapter can express. One way many entrepreneurs deal with the knowledge gap about the process is by spending the year prior to the offering preparing for it by talking with others who have gone through the process, reading, and putting together the team that will see the company through it. Another way to speed up the process is to start running the private corporation like a public corporation from the beginning—that is, doing audited financial statements and keeping good records.

A public offering means that everything the company does or has becomes public information subject to the scrutiny of anyone interested in the company. A shift in company control makes the CEO of a public company responsible primarily to the shareholders and only secondarily to anyone else. The entrepreneur/CEO, who before the offering probably owned the lion's share of the stock, may no longer have a controlling portion of the outstanding stock (if he or she agreed to an offering that resulted in the loss of control), and the stock that he or she does own can lose value if the company's value on the stock exchange drops, an event that can occur through no fault of the company's performance. Macroeconomic conditions, such as world events and domestic economic policy, can adversely (or positively) affect a company's stock, regardless of what the company does.

Public companies are also subject to the stringent disclosure rules under the Sarbanes-Oxley Act. This act was passed in response to accounting scandals that started with Enron Corp. and to improve the accuracy and reliability of corporate disclosures. Sarbanes-Oxley covers such issues as establishing a public company accounting oversight board, auditor independence, corporate responsibility, and enhanced financial disclosure.[12] The cost of compliance with Sarbanes-Oxley is high, averaging about $3.7 million annually for larger companies.[13]

Finally, a public company faces intense pressure to perform in the short term. An entrepreneur in a wholly owned corporation can afford the luxury of long-term goals and controlled growth, but the CEO of a public company is pressured by shareholders and analysts to show almost immediate gains in revenues and earnings that will translate into higher stock prices and dividends to the stockholders.

THE PUBLIC OFFERING PROCESS

There are several steps in the IPO process, as depicted in Figure 17.4. The first is to choose an underwriter, or investment banker, which is the firm that sells the securities and guides the corporation through the IPO process. Often called "the beauty contest," investment banking firms parade before the company's board of directors proclaiming their strengths after which the entrepreneur chooses one or more to co-manage the IPO. Some of the most prestigious investment banking firms handle only well-established companies because they believe that smaller companies will not attract sufficient attention among major

FIGURE 17.4

The IPO Process Simplified

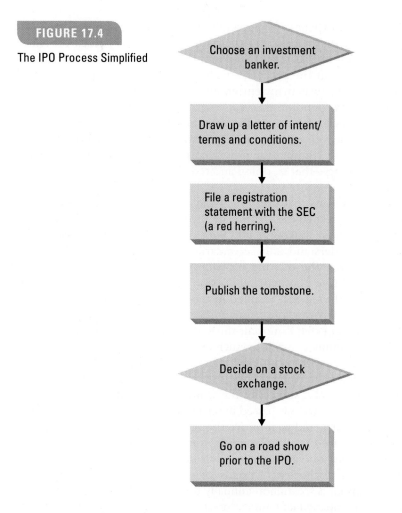

institutional investors. Getting a referral to a competent investment banking firm is a first step in the process. Investment banks underwrite the IPO based on either a firm commitment or a best efforts basis. Best effort suggests that this will not be a strong IPO and should serve as a warning to investors. A commitment, by contrast, means that the investment bank will purchase shares at a discount (typically 7 percent) and resell them at full price to institutional investors primarily, but also to individuals.[14]

The importance of investigating the reputation and track record of any underwriter cannot be overemphasized. Investment banking has become a very competitive industry, and the lure of large fees from IPOs has attracted some firms of questionable character. The entrepreneur should also examine the investment mix of the bank. Some underwriters focus solely on institutional investors; others, on retail customers or private investors. It is often useful to have a mix of shareholders; private investors tend to be less fickle than institutional investors, so their presence contributes more stability to the stock price in the market. The investment bank should also be able to support the IPO after the offering by giving financial advice, aid in buying and selling stock, and assistance in creating and maintaining interest in the stock over the long term.

Once chosen, the underwriter draws up a letter of intent, which outlines the terms and conditions of the agreement between the underwriter and the entrepreneur/selling stockholder. It normally specifies a price range for the stock, which is a tricky issue at best. Typically, underwriters estimate the price at which the stock will be sold by using a price/earnings multiple that is common for companies within the same industry as the IPO. That multiple is then applied to the IPO's earnings per share. This is only a rough estimate; the actual going-out price will not be determined until the night before the offering. If the entrepreneur is unhappy with the final price, the only choice is to cancel the offering, an action that is highly unattractive after months of work and expense.

A registration statement must be filed with the SEC. This document is known as a "red herring," or prospectus, because it discusses all the potential risks of investing in the IPO. This prospectus is given to anyone interested in investing in the IPO. It is a critical document because the SEC will render a decision on the IPO based on this statement. After filing the registration statement, an advertisement called a "tombstone" announces the offering in the financial press. The prospectus is valid for nine months; after that, the information becomes outdated and cannot be used without officially amending the registration statement. Another major decision is where to list the offering—that is, on which exchange. In the past, smaller IPOs automatically listed on the American Stock Exchange (AMEX) or the National Association of Securities Dealers Automated Quotation (NASDAQ) because they couldn't meet the qualifications of the New York Stock Exchange (NYSE). Today, with technology companies such as Amazon.com and Qualcomm listed on NASDAQ, it is the fastest-growing exchange in the nation. NASDAQ operates differently from the other exchanges. The NYSE and AMEX are auction markets with securities traded on the floor of the exchange, enabling investors to trade directly with one another. NASDAQ, by contrast, is a floorless exchange that trades on the National Market System through a network of broker–dealers from respected securities firms that compete for orders. In addition to these three, there are regional exchanges (such as the Boston stock exchange) that are less costly alternatives for a small, growing company.

The high point of the IPO process is the road show, generally a two-week whirlwind tour of all the major institutional investors by the entrepreneur and the IPO team to market the offering. This is done so that once the registration statement has met all the SEC requirements and the stock has been priced, the offering can be sold virtually in a day, before its value has a chance to fluctuate in the market. The coming-out price determines the amount of proceeds to the IPO company, but those holding stock prior to the IPO often see the value of their stock increase substantially immediately after the IPO. The final price is typically agreed upon by the company and its underwriters the day before the offering. In some cases, IPOs reach the final stage only to be withdrawn at the last minute. After the dot com bust, many companies had to pull their plans for an initial public offering because institutional investors were backing away from the public markets. More recently, in August 2006, The Go Daddy Group Inc., a prominent Internet domain registrar, pulled its IPO filing after the SEC had declared it a go. CEO/founder Bob Parsons explained that there were three reasons for the decision: (1) IPO market conditions were not favorable due to volatile global conditions such as the Iraq War, rising oil prices, and poor performance by tech stocks in general; (2) the quiet period (required from the time a filing is made until one month after the stock is available in the market) posed a significant problem for the CEO, who had a regular radio show that would have to be discontinued; and (3) the company really didn't have to go public because the sole investor was Bob Parsons. At the start of the process, it looked like a good thing to do, but by the time the IPO was to occur, the environment had changed.[15] An entrepreneur who is considering doing an IPO should look at the condition of the market and very carefully weigh the pros and cons of becoming a public company at that time.

AN EASIER IPO

Despite the value of being a public company in terms of accessing large amounts of capital relatively easily, it is still beyond the reach of many small companies. Martin Lightsey's company, Specialty Blades, a medical and industrial blade manufacturer with 100 shareholders and $6 million in annual sales, was faced with shareholders who wanted to cash in some of their earnings. Lightsey learned of a little-known exemption in the SEC regulations that permitted an intrastate offering so that Lightsey could sell stock to Virginia residents without having to register with the SEC. Intrastate offerings give entrepreneurs the right to create small local stock exchanges through investment banking firms with shareholders in a single state. Not all businesses can apply, however; the requirements are that the company hold less than $10 million in assets and have fewer than 500 shareholders.[16] The company must also earn more than half of its revenue from operations within the state in which it filed. The reason that not too many offerings of this type have occurred is because of the strict residency requirements. If even a single share of stock is sold to a nonresident or traded to someone in another state within nine months of the offering, the entire offering will be declared void and the entrepreneur will have to buy back all the stock. For Lightsey, the offering has worked out well; in fact, over a period of seven years, he has done two more offerings and his company now has a market capitalization of $33.9 million.

Growing Via Strategic Alliances

Strategic alliances with larger companies are also an excellent source of growth capital for young companies. A strategic alliance is defined as "a close collaborative relationship between two or more firms with the intent of accomplishing mutually compatible goals that would be difficult for each to accomplish alone."[17] Sometimes the partnership results in major financial and equity investments in the growing venture. Such was the case for United Parcel Service of America, which acquired Mail Boxes Etc. (MBE) for $191 million in 2001 after that company had become the industry leader. Growing companies that link with established companies usually get a better deal than they would have gotten from a venture capitalist. In addition, they derive some associated benefits that give them more credibility in the marketplace. Recent research suggests that in a global economy a significant portion of entrepreneurial success is the result of the ability to access formal and informal business networks.[18] In particular, ventures with new inventions but no expertise in commercialization and no social capital are more inclined to seek out partnerships, particularly for manufacturing and distribution.[19] Furthermore, where the environment is characterized by high levels of uncertainty, small businesses use a network of partners as a hedge against the risks associated with this type of environment.[20] The large investing partner is looking for a return of the cost of capital and, in general, for a return of at least 10 percent on the investment.

Strategic alliances are every bit as tricky as partnerships, so the potential partner must be evaluated carefully, and due diligence must be conducted on the company to make sure that it is everything it claims to be. The entrepreneur should examine the potential partner's business practices, talk to its customers and value chain members, and make sure that this company will make the entrepreneur's company look good. It is also crucial not to focus on one potential partner but, instead, to consider several before making a final decision. It probably is wise not to form a partnership that makes one of the partners (usually the smaller company) too heavily dependent on the other for a substantial portion of its revenue-generating capability. This is a dangerous position to be in and can spell disaster if the partnership dissolves for any reason. For the partnership to work best, the benefits should flow in both directions; that is, both partners should derive cost savings and/or revenue enhancement from the relationship. Strategic partnerships are a natural offshoot of a global economy that has been flattened by the Internet. Entrepreneurs should view these partnerships as one effective alternative to grow their ventures.

Valuing the Business

A key component of any financial strategy is determining the value of the company, because a realistic value figure is needed no matter which avenue is taken to raise growth capital. However, valuation of early-stage private companies is typically a very subjective process fraught with the challenge of predicting future earnings in a highly uncertain environment. Moreover, the already difficult task of valuation is exacerbated by the fact that most of the valuable assets that companies hold are intangible. That is, they consist of patents, knowledge, and people instead of plant and equipment.[21] Calculating value is fundamentally challenging because *value* is a subjective term with many meanings. In fact, at least six different definitions of value are in common use. They can be summarized as follows:

Fair market value—the price at which a willing seller would sell and a willing buyer would buy in an arm's-length transaction. By this definition, every sale would ultimately constitute a fair market value sale.

Intrinsic value—the perceived value arrived at by interpreting balance sheet and income statements through the use of ratios, discounting cash flow projections, and calculating liquidated asset value.

Investment value—the worth of the business to an investor based on his or her individual requirements in terms of risk, return, tax benefits, and so forth.

Going-concern value—the current financial status of the business as measured by financial statements, debt load, and economic environmental factors (such as government regulation) that may affect its long-term continuation.

Liquidation value—the amount that could be recovered by selling off all the company's assets.

Book value—an accounting measure of value that reflects the difference between total assets and total liability. It is essentially equivalent to shareholders' or owners' equity.

In today's economy, those who finance ventures also use some new, non-financial yardsticks to measure value. These include

- The experience level of the management team
- The innovative level of the firm's distribution channels
- The nature of the company's relationships in the industry and with customers
- The company's ability to be fast and flexible
- The company's amount and kind of intellectual property

In January 2007, *Inc. Magazine* conducted a study of private business valuation to learn which types of businesses command a premium against their earnings when they're sold. What they found was that companies doing business in the life sciences, energy, financial services, and technology sectors commanded high sales multiples with median sales prices of $100 million, while day-care centers, plumbers, and retailers produced very modest multiples, with median sales prices of $100,000. The most valuable types of companies were garnering 16:1 ratios of their sale price to their annual revenue while the discount zone businesses commanded 8:10 ratios and worse.[22]

The following sections examine some financial measures for business valuation. The first thing to know about valuation is that nearly all techniques rely on the analysis of the future market for the company's products. This is why neither book value nor liquidation value is a satisfactory method, except to establish a residual value to use in a discounted cash flow method. Further, with more businesses—and more new businesses—relying on intangible assets, book value does not make sense. Market multiples such as price/earnings (P/E) ratios are often used by venture capitalists, but their use is speculative because they are based on public companies in the industry and on the bet that the new company will go public in three to five years. The discounted cash flow (DCF) method is probably the technique most commonly used to account for the going-concern value of a business, but it has problems as well. In the following sections, we look at several of the more commonly used methods for applying a value to a business. In general, a combination of methods will help the entrepreneur arrive at a range of possible values.

COMPARABLES

Comparables are a common way to get a fix on the value of a new venture. Comparable companies are those that have similar value characteristics to the new venture, such as risk, rate of growth, capital structure, and the size and timing of cash flows.[23] The most challenging aspect of using comparables is the ability to find actual valuation numbers on other privately held firms to use as comparables. When numbers are found, they may not be accurate or the assumptions used to make the valuation may not be known. To successfully use comparables, nonfinancial measures also need to be used to gauge the value of the new venture. For example, a technology firm can be assessed based on the number of patents it holds and compared against other similar firms in that manner. Simply comparing a new venture to a public company is specious at best because the shares of a private company do not have the marketability of public stock, so an arbitrary discount rate must be applied. In general, comparables should be used only to validate or support findings arrived at by more appropriate means.

MULTIPLE OF EARNINGS

A multiple of earnings is frequently used to value publicly owned companies because the technique is simple and direct. The first step is to figure normal earnings and then capitalize them at some rate of return or at a multiple of earnings. The rate of return or multiple used is based on assumptions about the company's risk level and projected future earnings, so the greater the potential earnings, the higher the multiple will be. Similarly, the greater the risk, the lower the multiple. Table 17.1 presents some information used to calculate the value of a hypothetical company.

A variation of this method, which typically results in a higher valuation, is multiplying a year's worth of after-tax earnings by an industry average multiple based on the P/E ratio of public companies in the industry. This method must be used with care. To say that a young private company with earnings of $250,000 in an industry where the average P/E is 12 should be valued at $3 million is probably overstating the case. It has been suggested that public firms have a premium value of about 25–35 percent over closely held companies because they are more highly regarded by the financial community. It is also important to remember that public companies are subjected to greater scrutiny than private companies, so any P/E multiple that is used should be discounted to reflect that premium.[24] Even with discounting, the variation in the ways in which a company can calculate earnings and the difficulty in finding a public

TABLE 17.1		
Using Multiples to Calculate Value	Net income plus depreciation	$ 2,425,000
	Earnings multiple	6X
	Company value including long-term debt	$17,953,410
	Less outstanding debt	1,500,000
	Company value	$16,453,410

company that is comparable make multiple of earnings a dubious measure for purposes of valuation. Nevertheless, many venture capital firms use one or another version of industry multiples.

DISCOUNTING CASH FLOWS

If valuing the business by its potential earning power is the goal, the most common measure—and the one that gives the most accurate results (assuming forecasts are correct)—is discounted future cash flows, because only cash or cash equivalents are used in the calculations. The method is called discounted cash flow analysis, or capitalization of future cash flows to the present value. This simply means calculating how much an investor would pay today to have a cash flow stream of X dollars for X number of years into the future.

There are four components of the DCF that must be addressed:

1. *The assumptions.* Assumptions define the model for conducting the business and take into account sales, R&D, manufacturing costs, selling costs, and general and administrative costs. These should be benchmarked against the growth of other successful companies in the industry.

2. *Forecast period.* Typically, the forecast period is three to five years and reflects the length of time that investors intend to have a stake in the venture.

3. *Terminal value.* Terminal value is the going-concern value at the end of the projection period, assuming that the company will continue in operation into the foreseeable future (in perpetuity). It may be thought of as a perpetuity, which assumes no growth and constant earnings (annual payment divided by the cost of money), or as a growth in perpetuity, which estimates a growth rate and profitability. The estimate of terminal value is significant because most of the company's value in the early stages lies in the terminal value. The terminal value is found by the following formula:

$$TV_t = [CF_t * (1 + g)] / (r - g)$$

where t is time, r is the discount rate, and g is the growth rate in perpetuity. Although price/earnings ratios and market-to-book value multiples are sometimes used to calculate terminal value, they are simply shortcuts so the outcomes produced from using them are frequently suspect.[25]

4. *Discount rate.* The discount rate determines the present value of the projected cash flows and is, in reality, the expected rate of return for the investor.

For this analysis, pro forma cash flow statements for the business are used and a forecast period is determined. (Refer to Chapter 9 for a discussion of pro forma cash flows and methods for forecasting sales and expenses.) The length and nature of business cycles in the industry must be understood to decide whether the forecast period goes from trough to trough or from peak to peak. In other words, the forecast period must include at least one complete business cycle in order to give a fair representation of the effect of that cycle on cash flow (see Figure 17.5).

Once the forecast period has been defined and the cash flow projections prepared, a discount rate must be chosen. This is not a purely arbitrary exercise.

FIGURE 17.5

Business Cycles and the
Forecast Period

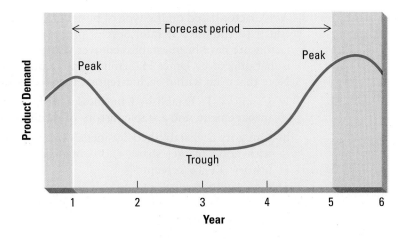

The buyer's or investor's point of view must be considered, and that viewpoint
will often include the opportunity cost of investing in or buying this business.
Table 17.2 lists the main categories of factors that influence the discount rate
and examples of each. It should be observed that these factors are highly subjective and difficult to quantify; yet, they must be considered when making a decision about how to discount the cash flow projections based on risk. In general,
three broad factors should be considered.

1. The rate achievable in a risk-free investment such as U.S. Treasury notes over
    a comparable time period. For example, for a five-year forecast, the current
    rate on a five-year note is appropriate.

TABLE 17.2

Risk Adjustment Factors

Factor Categories	Factors That Affect Risk
External Environmental Factors	Economic expectations
	Current status of the economy
	Current status of the industry
	Trends in the industry
	Competitive environment
Firm Factors	Expectations for the success of the business
	Current financial condition
	Competitive position
	Business size and type
	Management team quality
	Reliability of financial forecasts
Investment Factors	Amount of capital to be invested
	Risk of this investment relative to others
	Probability of a liquidity event
	Amount of management team support required
	Expectations for capital appreciation

Source: J.H. Schilt (1991), http://www.nacva.com/FTT_PDF/Chapter5+.pdf, p. 51.

2. A risk factor based on the type of business and the industry, which should be added to the interest rate. Several precedents for determining what these factors are have been established over years of study. One accepted standard is that offered by James H. Schilt[26] in the form of five categories of business. Note that even within each category, there is room for degrees of risk.

    a. Category 1: Established businesses with good market share, excellent management, and a stable history of earnings: 6–10 percent

    b. Category 2: Established businesses in more competitive industries, still with good market share, excellent management, and a stable earnings history: 11–15 percent

    c. Category 3: Growing businesses in very competitive industries, with little capital investment, an average management team, and a stable earnings history: 16–20 percent

    d. Category 4: Small businesses dependent on the entrepreneur or larger businesses in very volatile industries; also the lack of a predictable earnings picture: 21–25 percent

    e. Category 5: Small service businesses operating as sole proprietorships: 26–30 percent

    It is important to note that the risk premium chosen from this list is then added to the risk-free rate, producing the risk-adjusted capitalization rate that is used to discount the projected cash flow stream.[27]

3. The life expectancy of the business. Discounting is typically based on this factor. The example in Table 17.3 illustrates this valuation method. Assuming that the current rate on a ten-year Treasury note is 6 percent and that the business is a Category 2 business with a 14 percent risk factor, the adjusted discount rate becomes 20 percent. Using a calculator or a present value table, one can calculate the present value of the five-year cash flow stream. The hypothetical business in this example will generate $1,575,000 of positive cash flow over five years. Hence, a buyer would be willing to pay $875,700 today for that business, given the discount rate.

TABLE 17.3

One Method for Discounting Cash Flows

Assume:

6%	risk-free rate
+14%	risk factor (Category 2 business)
20%	discount rate

Discount the Cash Flow

End of Year	Cash Flow ($000)	Factor (20%)	Present Value
1	200	.8333	166.7
2	250	.6944	173.6
3	300	.5787	173.6
4	375	.4823	180.9
5	450	.4019	180.9
Totals	$1,575		$875.7

It is possible to estimate different cash flow scenarios based on best-case, most-likely case, and worst-case assumptions, which will provide a range of values for the business. Then a probability can be assigned to each scenario based on the likelihood that the scenario will occur, and the discounted cash flow can be multiplied by that probability to arrive at an adjusted present value. Once a mathematical estimate of value has been achieved, other factors will come into play that are difficult to put into the equation and are more rightly points of negotiation. All the projections used in the valuation of the business are based on assumptions, and the buyer/investor is likely to question them and perhaps to discount the value of the business even further.

Another factor affecting the final valuation is the degree of legitimate control the owner has over the business. This is typically measured by the amount of stock the owner holds. Buying out an owner who holds the majority of the stock is more valuable than buying out one who does not hold a majority interest. A company in which the entrepreneur can control the majority of the stock is more valuable than one in which the entrepreneur holds only a minority interest. Finally, marketability of the company and intangibles such as a loyal customer list, intellectual property, and the like create additional value. The "real" value or market value of the business will ultimately be determined through negotiation with investors, lenders, or underwriters. However, doing the calculations just discussed provides an excellent point of departure for those negotiations.

THE REAL OPTIONS MODEL

Where an investor has the ability to make decisions about whether to invest now or at some milestone in the future, whether to invest for a particular outcome from many possible outcomes or not, or decide not to go forward with a deal, discounted cash flow models do not accurately measure the value of the company involved in the investment decision. Furthermore, given that VCs typically fund a company in stages based on achieving performance milestones, it makes more sense to use an option-pricing technique that is derived from financial options applied to securities, currencies, and commodities. In a new venture, this technique is applied to the entrepreneur's options under changing circumstances.[28] They are called real options, as opposed to options used with financial instruments, because they refer to tangible choices such as—in the case of a new venture—investing in research and development of a new technology. The investor calculates the probability that specific events will occur and how they will affect the investment in a new venture. Recall that investors are always attempting to reduce their risk, so a real options method enables them to consider the best time to invest for the least risk. For example, suppose that an investor is looking at a company that requires a $10,000 investment today to generate revenues from one of three projected revenue scenarios in the next year. Discounted to today's dollars, those projected revenues could turn out to be $15,000, $12,000, or $5,000 and so the net present value of the investment would be $5,000, 2,000, or –$5,000. Traditional discounted cash flow analysis often yields a negative net present value for many scenarios, and the potential investor who relied on it would decide not to invest in the new venture. However, if the investor were allowed to delay his investment one year, he would gain additional information and may be able to avoid the scenario of investing when the revenues are negative $5,000. In other words, the investor would have reduced his risk to $5,000 and $2,000 because the risk of the third scenario (−$5,000) is now zero. Under a real options approach, the question is whether the future earnings of the company are greater than the cost to grow the business to the level where it can achieve those earnings. In other words, is the return on investment greater than the cost of the investment. Using real options as a valuation method is more complicated than can be presented here, and it is not yet in common use within the private equity community despite its benefits for early-stage investments.

THE VENTURE CAPITAL MODEL

Often employed in the private equity arena to value investments with negative cash flows and earnings but with future promise, the VC firm determines what return on investment is required during the holding period it desires. It then applies a P/E ratio or multiple of earnings to the estimated future value of the venture at the end of that period, which is equivalent to its terminal value. The terminal value is then discounted based on the targeted rate of return the investor is seeking.

$$\text{Discounted TV} = \text{TV} / (1 + \text{Target Return})^{\#years}$$

Percentage ownership is then calculated using the following formula:

Required Ownership Percent = Investment Amount / Discounted Terminal Value

For example, suppose a company required an investment of $5 million over three years. Considering the high risk of an early-stage venture, the VC wants a 50 percent return on the initial investment and forecasts that the company's after-tax earnings in the third year will be $10 million. The investor sets the P/E ratio at 8 on the basis of comparables in the public market and multiplies that times the $10 million to get the terminal value in year three. Using the formulas shown previously, the investor would expect to receive a 21 percent ownership stake in the company assuming no additional capital was raised during that time that might dilute the VC's interest:

Discounted TV = ($10M × 8) / (1 + .50)³ = $23.7 million

Required Percent of Ownership = $5M/$23.7M = 21%

Valuation is by its very nature an incremental process of bringing together key pieces of information that give some insight into the health and future of the business. In all discussions of value, the entrepreneur should be clear about whose definition of value is being used. In general, what a willing buyer and seller can agree on under normal market conditions is the real value of the company at a particular point in time. With a new venture, there are many financing options. However, creating a capital structure that works depends in large part on creativity and persistence in securing, at the right price, the capital needed to launch the venture successfully. Growing a venture requires substantial resources, but if the company has established a healthy track record and has good potential for growth, the number of resources available to the business increases substantially. Preparing for growth is the subject of Chapter 18.

> ## New Venture Checklist
>
> Have you:
>
> ☐ Determined how much growth capital will be needed?
>
> ☐ Developed a strategy for seeking growth capital?
>
> ☐ Considered whether and, if so, when to proceed with an IPO?
>
> ☐ Established a value for the business?

Issues to Consider

1. At what stage of venture development do venture capitalists typically become involved, and why?
2. For what kind of business would soliciting private venture capital be a logical financial strategy for growth? Why?
3. How can strategic alliances be used to help grow the business?
4. What are some things that an entrepreneur should do to prepare for a public offering before the year of "going public"?
5. In approaching a venture capitalist, how can the entrepreneurial team deal from a position of strength?
6. What are the key components in valuing a new or growing venture?

Experiencing Entrepreneurship

1. Interview a partner in a venture capital firm. Ask the partner to describe a recent investment that the firm completed. What were the critical factors that made the firm decide to invest? Discuss your findings in a two-page report.

2. Locate a business that was recently sold or had an initial public offering. Talk to a principal and, if possible, to the buyer or investment banker to learn what was considered when they valued the company. How much of the decision on valuation was based on negotiation and nonmonetary factors?

Relevant Case Studies

## Chapter 18

PLANNING FOR GROWTH

"No great thing is created suddenly."

—EPICTETUS, c. 60–120, Roman Stoic philosopher

LEARNING OBJECTIVES

▪ Explore strategic innovation as a growth strategy.

▪ Discuss intensive growth strategies—growing within the current market.

▪ Explain integrative growth strategies—growing within the industry.

▪ Examine diversification growth strategies—growing outside the industry.

▪ Consider growing by going global.

Profile 18.1 ONE ENTREPRENEUR'S MISERY IS ANOTHER'S OPPORTUNITY

In 1996, with no money and no connections, Vikas Goel, a citizen of India by birth, arrived in Singapore to look for his future. He distributed hundreds of résumés and eventually secured a sales coordinator position with an IT distribution company. But his real future came just four years later when he launched a company he called eSys Technologies, whose purpose was to distribute IT components. Unfortunately, his timing was off, because 2000 was the year of the dot com meltdown and the technology crash, and it was also a time of huge declines in the demand for IT components. But rather than seeing the cup as being half full, Goel saw it as being half empty, believing that what might be a disaster for one entrepreneur could be an opportunity for another—namely, himself. So, undaunted, he launched the company with only one employee and a part-time worker. By the early 2000s, the IT industry had become, for the most part, a commodity industry where lean operations and lean margins in the neighborhood of 3 percent were the norm. Goel knew that to succeed or even survive in this industry he would have to innovate strategically and change the way the IT distribution game was played by cutting costs in every area of his business.

He started by centralizing his business processes at one facility where overhead costs were low but access to skilled labor was high—his native India. Then he connected all of his other offices to that facility via teleconferencing and VoIP (Internet telephony). He then developed a centralized enterprise resource planning system to monitor all his facilities through the Internet and to integrate his manufacturing plants with his supply chain so that he could achieve faster delivery times than anyone else in the industry. Perhaps one of his greatest innovations was his financing model for growing the business. He had quickly deduced that supplier credit (extending the time eSys had to pay its vendors) was free money. But to secure supplier credit, he needed to demonstrate his credibility and the ability of his company to perform. He did this by purchasing insurance on whatever he owed his vendors and making them the beneficiaries. The cost of doing this was equivalent to about 2 percent annual interest, far less than other sources of capital. By 2005, eSys held $250 million in vendor credit and $150 million in short-term bank debt, with no long-term debt. Using this form of financing, he was able to acquire 12 distressed companies worldwide and make them profitable. Today eSys has distribution hubs in Los Angeles, Dubai, New Delhi, Singapore, and Amsterdam; credit insurance in Germany and Switzerland; IT services in India; and financial management in Singapore, the country that has the lowest tax rate in the world. Its sales exceed $2 billion and the company has 112 offices in 33 countries—all of this accomplished without bringing in outside investment.

Sources: J. Stack and B. Burlingham, "My Awakening," *Inc. Magazine* (April 2007): p. 93; eSys Global, http://www.esys .com; "IT Component Distribution Major eSys Technologies Has Charted a Rs 1,000 Crore Investment Plan for India," *India Daily* (July 30, 2005); and R. Jones, "eSys Eyes IPO and Adds Plant," *Gitex Times* (October 4, 2004), http://www .gtextimes.com.

Expansion is a natural by-product of a successful start-up. Growth helps a new business secure or maintain its competitive advantage and establish a firm foothold in the market. It is the result of a strong vision on the part of the entrepreneur and the founding team that guides decision making and ensures that the company stays on course and meets its goals. Some entrepreneurs shy away from growth because they are afraid of losing control. That fear is not unfounded; many businesses falter during rapid growth because of the enormous demands placed on the company's resources. Furthermore, it is unlikely that a business can consistently grow over its life without ever faltering. It is, in fact, a myth that great companies grow indefinitely.[1] Of the original Forbes 100 list of most powerful companies in 1917, only 18 companies remained in the top 100 by 1987, and 61 had ceased to exist. Of the remaining group, only General Electric Co. and Eastman Kodak Co. outperformed the S&P 500's 7.5 percent average return over the 70-year period, and they surpassed it by only 0.3 percent.[2] A pretty dismal record overall, but it is similar to the record of companies that have fallen off the New York Stock Exchange and the NASDAQ since their inception. The truth is that all companies have periods in which they appear to stall, but the larger a company gets the more its growth rate slows.[3] What this means to the entrepreneur is that sustaining double-digit growth over the long term is probably not possible. But with solid planning in place before growth occurs, many of the pitfalls of rapid growth can be avoided, and growth can continue for a longer time than would otherwise be possible.

The Inc. 500 companies are representative of rapidly growing private ventures, and the statistics about them reveal some interesting patterns. According to *Inc. Magazine's* annual survey for 2006, the highest rates of growth were sustained in environmental services and consumer products. The top five growth companies were in the following industries: energy, computers and electronics, health care, telecommunications, and business services. Figure 18.1 displays some interesting characteristics about the 2006 Inc. 500.

FIGURE 18.1

Characteristics of the 2006 Inc. 500 Rapidly Growing Private Companies

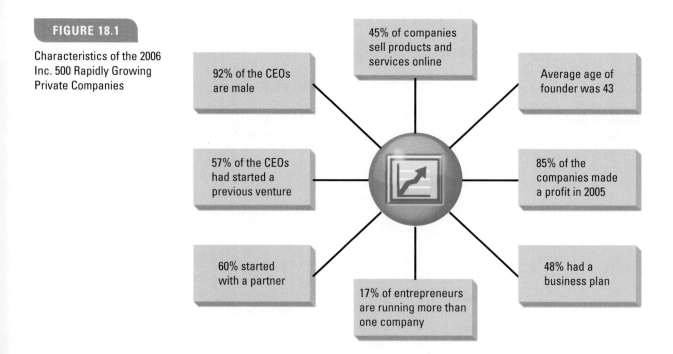

45% of companies sell products and services online

92% of the CEOs are male

Average age of founder was 43

57% of the CEOs had started a previous venture

85% of the companies made a profit in 2005

60% started with a partner

17% of entrepreneurs are running more than one company

48% had a business plan

High-growth companies stand out from the crowd because they display some very distinct characteristics. Typically, they are first in a niche market that they created and in which they soon become the leaders. They are often better at what they do than their competitors, leaner in their operations, and unique in what they offer. Being first in the market with a new product or service, if executed effectively, is one of the strongest competitive advantages. It provides a chance to establish brand recognition so that customers immediately think of the company when they contemplate a particular product or service. This enables entrepreneurial ventures to set the standards for those who follow. This was certainly the strategy of Samuel Adams in the microbrewed beer industry, Amazon.com in the online book industry, and Microsoft in the operations and applications software industry. By combining a pioneering strategy with innovative processes, leaner operations, and a unique, innovative product or service, companies can create formidable barriers to competition. But being number two or three in a market can also be a winning strategy, primarily because pioneers usually haven't perfected the product or service, so the number two or three entrepreneur can learn from number one's mistakes and better serve the customer's needs.

To Grow or Not to Grow

Some entrepreneurs make a conscious choice to control growth even in the face of extraordinary market demand. This is not to say that growth is slowed to single digits. Instead, an entrepreneur may choose to maintain a stable growth rate of 35 to 45 percent per year rather than subject the young venture to a roller-coaster ride in the triple digits. In general, entrepreneurs who restrain growth do so because they are in business for the long term; in other words, they're not in a hurry to harvest their newly created wealth by selling the business or doing a public offering. They also typically don't like to take on a lot of debt or give up equity to grow. Consequently, they don't advertise heavily, and they don't aggressively seek new customers beyond their capabilities. They also diversify their product or service line from the beginning to make themselves independent of problems that may face their customers or their industries. By offering a diversified product/service line, they maintain multiple streams of revenue that protect them from the loss of any one customer or market.

It is intoxicating for an entrepreneur with a new venture to realize that potential demand for its product or service is enormous and that the company could grow well beyond industry averages. But "hyper-growth" has destroyed many companies that did not have the capacity, skills, people, or systems in place to meet demand. Recall the holiday season of 1999, when all the new Internet retail businesses, such as eToys, were unprepared for demand. With inadequate or nonexistent fulfillment systems in place and no plan for handling returns, these companies did not survive. More recently, the failure of American Home Mortgage Investment, a victim of the subprime mortgage collapse of 2007, suggests that even traditional businesses that grow too fast without having a plan in place to deal with the inevitable economic downturns will collapse. The growth phase of a new business can be one of the most exciting times for an entrepreneur.

However, if an entrepreneur has not prepared for growth with a coherent plan and a budget to match, it can be disastrous.

How, then, does an entrepreneur decide whether to grow or not to grow? In many cases, it may not be the entrepreneur's decision at all; demand for the product or service may compel the entrepreneur to keep up, or, by contrast, the market may not be big enough to enable a company to grow. Normally, by the time a company has reached a point where it is poised to grow to the next level, it will have a few employees and, of course, the founding team. To take that next step, some benchmarks for successful growth should be considered. Successful growth requires leadership. When entrepreneurs start businesses, they are involved in every one of the business's activities, but as the company begins to grow, they find it necessary to delegate tasks to others. The more they delegate, the more they realize that their job has suddenly changed. Now they are not needed to do the fundamental tasks of the business; they are needed to lead the business—to make sure that the vision becomes reality. Everyone looks to the entrepreneur to ensure that the company survives. Because leadership involves guiding the company and its people to achieve the company's goals, an entrepreneur must have the ability to inspire people to action to accomplish those goals. Employees must be given opportunities to learn and grow. A company can't successfully grow and change if its people don't grow and change with it. Employees should be encouraged to stretch beyond what they knew when they were hired in the early days of the company, to learn more aspects of the business, and to offer input into how the business is run.

Everyone in the organization must be responsible and accountable for the success of the company. Everyone should understand what he or she contributes to the financial success of the company, and everyone should have a stake in that financial success. Rapid growth requires teamwork, and for teams to operate effectively, they must be given responsibility and accountability for what they do. There are times, however, when saying no to growth makes sense for a business. For example, Bishop Partners' managers learned early on to say no to clients who pulled their small executive search firm away from its core values and mission. Even though the company was growing quickly, Susan Bishop, its founder, noticed that its profit margin remained low and that, even as it took on more clients, the company's earnings remained flat. Bishop pulled her team together and started asking questions. To her amazement, she discovered that everyone had a different vision of the company and where it was going. No wonder they had problems defining the right customer for the company. Once Bishop conveyed her vision to the employees, they worked together to define those customers and say no to those who didn't match their model. In the end, the company grew faster and remained healthy with a more focused strategy.

To comprehend the role of growth in a company's evolution, it is important to understand the factors that affect growth: market factors and management factors.

MARKET FACTORS THAT AFFECT GROWTH

The degree of growth and the rate at which a new venture grows are dependent on market strategy. If the niche market that a company is entering is by nature small and relatively stable in terms of growth, it will of course be more difficult to achieve the spectacular growth and size of the most rapidly growing companies. On the other hand, if the product or service can expand to a global market, growth and size are more likely to be attained.

Entering a market dominated by large companies is not in and of itself an automatic deterrent to growth. A small, well-organized company is often able to produce its product or service at a very competitive price while maintaining high quality standards, because it doesn't have the enormous overhead and management salaries of the larger companies. Moreover, if an industry is an old, established one, a firm entering with an innovative product in a niche market in that industry can experience rapid rates of growth. In some industries, such as the wireless industry, innovation is a given, so merely offering an innovative product is not enough. In highly innovative industries such as this, the key to rapid growth is the ability to design and produce a product more quickly than competitors do. By contrast, in an industry that is stable and offers commodity products and services, entering with an innovative product or process will provide a significant competitive advantage.

Intellectual-property rights, like patents, copyrights, trademarks, and trade secrets, offer a competitive advantage to a new venture because they provide a grace period in which to introduce the product or service before anyone else can copy it. However, relying on proprietary rights alone is not wise. It is important to have a comprehensive marketing plan that enables the new business to secure a strong foothold in the market before someone attempts to reproduce the product and compete with it. True, an owner of intellectual property has the right to take someone who infringes on those proprietary rights to court, but the typical small company can ill afford this time-consuming and costly process when it needs all its excess capital for growth. See Chapter 7 for a more in-depth discussion of intellectual property.

Some industries are by their very nature volatile; that is, it is difficult to predict what will happen for any length of time and with any degree of accuracy. The computer industry in the 1980s was such an industry; it has lately become somewhat more predictable as leading players have emerged. The emerging nanotechnology industry, however, is very volatile at this time. Consequently, there are opportunities for extraordinary growth of new ventures in the industry and, at the same time, a higher risk of failure. A new entry into such an industry needs to maintain a constant awareness of potential government regulations, directions the industry is taking, and emerging competitors.

Some industries, simply by virtue of their size and maturity, are difficult for a new venture to enter and impossible to penetrate with sufficient market share to make a profit. Other industries prohibit new entries because the cost of participating (plant and equipment, fees, and/or compliance with regulations) is so high. Yet in the right industry, a new venture can erect barriers of its own to slow down the entry of competing companies. Patent rights on products, designs, or processes, for example, can effectively erect a temporary barrier to permit a window of opportunity to gain market share.

MANAGEMENT FACTORS THAT AFFECT GROWTH

Along with market factors, management factors also influence a company's growth. When the new company has survived and is successful, even as a small business, there is a tendency to believe that it must be doing everything right and should continue in the same manner. That is a fatal error on the part of many entrepreneurs who don't recognize that change is a by-product of success. Many times it isn't until the venture is in crisis that an entrepreneur realizes the time has come to make a transition to professional management, a step that requires of the entrepreneur a fundamental change in attitudes and behaviors.[4] Rapid growth requires skills different from start-up skills. In the beginning of a new venture, the entrepreneur has more time to take part in and even control all aspects of the business. But when rapid growth begins to occur, systems must be in place to handle the increased demand without sacrificing quality and service. Unless an entrepreneur is able to bring in key professional management with experience in high-growth companies, chances are good that growth will falter, the window of opportunity will be lost, and the business may even fail. Many entrepreneurs have found that at some point in the business's growth, they must step down and allow experienced management to take over. However, growing the business does not have to mean that the entrepreneurial spirit is lost, only that the entrepreneur must become very creative about maintaining that sense of smallness and flexibility while growing. Subcontracting some aspects of the business is one way to keep the number of employees down and retain team spirit. Developing self-managing teams is another way.

Re-evaluation of key metrics is another significant factor for growth. The research of McGrath and MacMillan[5] has uncovered some critical metrics that should not be overlooked. Most businesses are selling a unit of something, whether it be hours of time or boxes of widgets, and those units have some typical metrics associated with them that enable an entrepreneur to determine whether the business is doing well: inventory turnover, working capital ratios, average gross margins, and so forth. Sometimes, simply changing the business unit so that it more closely represents the value customers want is enough to make a significant difference in the business. For example, Cemex, a Mexican cement company, decided to change how it charged customers for cement. Traditionally, cement had been sold by the cubic yard, but over time the company found that what customers really valued was delivery—anytime, any place. On balance, concrete is a commodity product, so customers were not going to pay a premium for it. Cemex decided that its ability to grow depended on finding a way to create new value, so it focused on delivery and decided to become the FedEx of cement companies, delivering cement in a just-in-time fashion. With that change, it became the third largest concrete business in the world.[6] McGrath and MacMillan further suggest eight strategies for growth in addition to the traditional methods discussed in the remainder of the chapter. These strategies are found in Table 18.1.

STAGES OF GROWTH IN A NEW VENTURE

Rates and stages of growth in a new venture vary by industry and business type; however, there appear to be some common issues that arise during growth that suggest areas of strategic, administrative, and managerial problems.

TABLE 18.1

Profit Driver Strategies

1. Change the business unit.	Align the way you bill customers with what they value most.
2. Improve productivity by an order of magnitude.	Use the latest technology to create efficiencies that competitors do not have.
3. Increase the speed at which cash flow is captured.	Make it easy for customers to pay quickly.
4. Increase asset utilization.	Reduce the number of assets the business requires to operate.
5. Find ways to help customers improve their performance.	Study where customers can improve their workflow and find ways to contribute to that improvement.
6. Find ways to help customers save time.	Make the company's customer processes as easy and effortless as possible.
7. Help improve customers' cash flow.	Demonstrate how what the company does improves the customer's bottom line.
8. Help customers improve their asset utilization.	Know the customer's balance sheet and find ways to help the customer remove hard assets from its balance sheet.

Source: Based on the work of R. Gunther McGrath and I.C. MacMillan, "MarketBusting: Strategies for Exceptional Business Growth," *Harvard Business Review* (March 2005), p. 4.

The importance of knowing when these issues will surface cannot be overstated, for it should be part of the entrepreneur's well-orchestrated plan to anticipate events and requirements before they occur. Research results suggest that organizations progress sequentially through major stages in their life and development.[7] Still other studies have noted that at each stage of development, the business faces a unique set of problems.[8] For example, the start-up stage is characterized by marketing and financial problems, whereas the growth phase is associated with strategic, administrative, and managerial problems. The stages of growth (see Figure 18.2) can be described as four phases through which the business must pass. (1) Start-up is characterized by concerns about capital, customers, and distribution; (2) initial growth, by concerns about cash

FIGURE 18.2

Stages of Growth

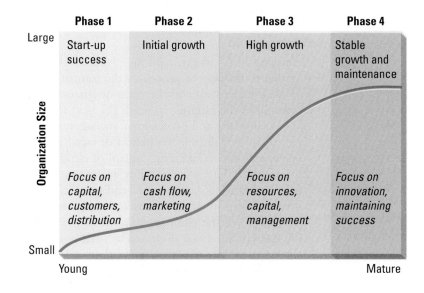

flow and marketing; (3) rapid growth, by concerns about resources, capital, and management; and (4) stable growth, by concerns about innovation and maintaining success.

Start-up Success

During start-up, the first stage, the entrepreneur's main concerns are to ensure sufficient start-up capital, seek customers, and design a way to deliver the product or service. At this point, the entrepreneur is a jack-of-all-trades, doing everything that needs to be done to get the business up and running. This includes securing suppliers, distributors, facilities, equipment, and labor. The very complexity of start-up is one reason why many new ventures fail. Complexity also suggests that a team-based venture is better equipped to achieve a successful launch than a solo effort. If the company survives to achieve a positive cash flow from the revenues it generates, it is in a good position to grow and expand its market. If, however, revenues generated fail to cover company expenses, it will not be possible to grow without seeking outside capital in the form of equity or debt.

Initial Growth

If a new venture makes it through the first phase, it enters the second level of activity with a viable business that has enough customers to keep it running on the revenues it generates. Now the entrepreneur's concerns become more focused on the issue of cash flow. Can the business generate sufficient cash flow to pay all its expenses and at the same time support the growth of the company? At this point, the venture is usually relatively small, there are few employees, and the entrepreneur is still playing an integral role. This is a crucial stage, for the decisions made here will determine whether the business will remain small or move into a period of rapid growth, which entails some significant changes in organization and strategy. The entrepreneur and the team need to decide whether they are going to grow the business to a much larger revenue level or remain stable yet profitable.

Rapid Growth

If the decision is to grow, all the resources of the business have to be gathered together to finance the growth of the company. This is a very risky stage because growth is expensive, and there are no guarantees that the entrepreneur will be successful in the attempt to reach the next level. Planning and control systems must be in place and professional management hired because there will be no time to do that during the period of rapid growth. The problems during this stage center on maintaining control of rapid growth. They are solved by delegating control and accountability at various levels; failure is usually due to uncontrolled growth, lack of cash, and insufficient management expertise to deal with the situation. If growth is accomplished, it is at this stage that entrepreneurs often sell the company at a substantial profit. It is also at this stage that some entrepreneurs are displaced by their boards of directors, investors, or creditors because the skills that made them so important at start-up are not the same skills the company needs to grow to the next level. As a result, many entrepreneurial ventures reach their pinnacle of growth with a management team entirely different from the one that founded the company. To the extent that the entrepreneur is a vital part of the vision of the company and can identify an appropriate new role in the now larger company, he or she will remain the primary driver of the business. Bill Gates, Microsoft's co-founder, is one example of an entrepreneur who stayed at the helm and took his company from start-up to global corporate giant. Only in the past several years has he stepped out of the CEO position in favor of one of the founding team members, Steve Ballmer.

Stable Growth and Maintenance

Once the business has successfully passed through the phase of rapid growth and is able to effectively manage the financial gains of growth, it has reached Phase 4, stable growth and maintenance of market share. Here the business, which is usually large at this point, can remain in a fairly stable condition as long as it continues to be innovative, competitive, and flexible. If it does not, sooner or later it will begin to lose market share and could ultimately fail or become a much smaller business. High-tech companies seem to be an exception to traditional growth patterns. Because they typically start with solid venture capital funding and a strong management team (dictated by the venture capitalists), they move out of Phases 1 and 2 very rapidly. During Phases 3 and 4, if the structure is effective and their technology is adopted in the mainstream market, they can become hugely successful. If, on the other hand, the structure is weak and the technology is not readily adopted, they can fail quickly.

PROBLEMS WITH GROWTH

It is a sad fact that many entrepreneurial ventures that start with great concepts and experience early success eventually hit a wall. Growth stalls and the firm flounders. Studies have found that among all the factors affecting growth, the most critical in a slowdown or failure appears to be inability to understand and respond to the business's environment.[9] That is, the entrepreneur did not recognize the opportunities and challenges developing outside the company and their potential to harm it. For example, in its first 8 years, one manufacturer's representative firm with 30 highly trained salespeople grew to $20 million in sales and came to dominate its midwestern market. But at the 8-year point, the firm stopped growing and sales hit a plateau. Its founder thought the problem was an internal one, sales effectiveness. What really happened, however, was that the firm's competitors had changed their marketing and distribution strategies. One competitor had moved into direct sales; another developed a strong telemarketing capability. The effect of these changes was to depress the sales of the entrepreneur's company in a matter of just months. This entrepreneur had failed to recognize the changes in the environment and respond rapidly to them. What this suggests is that entrepreneurs must continually scan their environment and assess it for changes and emerging competitors. They must also plan for growth and hire for growth. Most important, growth must become part of the company culture. Table 18.2 provides a framework for planning the growth of a business.

<table>
<tr><td rowspan="2">**TABLE 18.2**

A Framework for Growth</td><td>**Strategies**</td><td>**Tactics**</td></tr>
<tr><td>Scan and assess the environment.</td><td>1. Analyze the environment.
  a. Is the customer base growing or shrinking? Why?
  b. How are competitors doing?
  c. Is the market growing?
  d. How does your company compare technologically with others in the industry?
2. Do a SWOT analysis (strengths, weaknesses, opportunities, threats).</td></tr>
<tr><td></td><td>Plan the growth strategy.</td><td>3. Determine the problem to be solved. Where is the pain?
4. Brainstorm solutions.
  a. Don't limit yourself to what you know and have done in the past.
  b. Think about how you can innovate strategically.
  c. Choose two or three solutions to test.
5. Set a major goal for significant change in the organization.
6. Set smaller, achievable goals that will put you on the path to achieve the major goal.
7. Dedicate resources (funding and staff) toward the achievement of these goals.</td></tr>
<tr><td></td><td>Hire for growth.</td><td>8. Put someone in charge of the growth plan.
9. Bring in key professional management with experience in growing companies.
10. Provide education and training for employees to prepare them for growth and change.</td></tr>
<tr><td></td><td>Create a growth culture.</td><td>11. Involve everyone in the organization in the growth plan.
12. Reward achievement of interim goals.</td></tr>
<tr><td></td><td>Build a strategy advisory board.</td><td>13. Invite key people from the industry who can keep you apprised of changes.
14. Make industry partners and customers part of the planning process.
15. Invite more outsiders than insiders onto the advisory board.</td></tr>
</table>

Growth Strategies

Today we can identify at least five general categories of growth strategies: (1) *strategic innovation strategies* change the game in an industry or market; (2) *intensive growth strategies* exploit opportunity in the current market; (3) *integrative growth strategies* take advantage of growth within the industry as a whole; (4) *diversification strategies* exploit opportunities outside the current market or industry; and (5) *global strategies* take the business into the international arena. See Figure 18.3 for an overview of these strategies.

STRATEGIC INNOVATION—CHANGING THE GAME

When upstart company Amazon began selling books online, it changed the playing field and disrupted the rules for retailers in general. When Ryanair began offering no-frills, low-cost airline service that bypassed the major airline hubs in 1991, it changed the game for the major airlines in Europe and eventually in the

FIGURE 18.3 Growth Strategies for Entrepreneurs

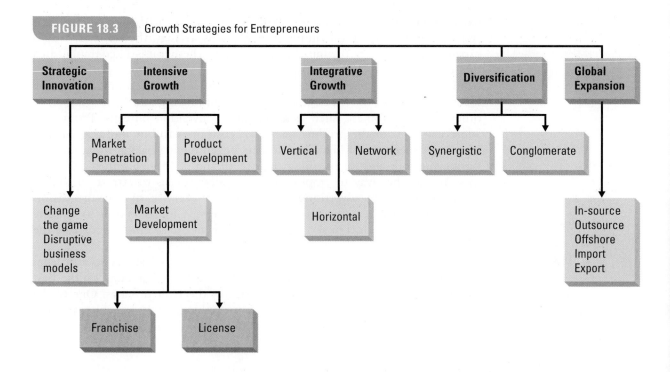

United States. And when First Direct in the United Kingdom introduced telephone banking in 1989, PC banking in 1996, and online banking in 1997, it forced traditional banking institutions to change their centuries-old business model.[10] The reason that small businesses can succeed with an innovation strategy is that new concepts are not generally attractive to established companies in the early stages because (1) they break the mold, which would mean significant change for the large company and possibly pull the company from its core competency; (2) the early markets are generally small with low margins; and (3) large companies typically wait to see how the new model fares in the market and then they either change their model or attempt to acquire the entrepreneur's company.

INTENSIVE GROWTH STRATEGIES—GROWING WITHIN THE CURRENT MARKET

Intensive growth strategies focus on exploiting the current market fully—that is, expanding the market share to the greatest extent possible. This is accomplished by increasing the volume of sales to current customers and the number of customers in the target market. There are generally three methods for implementing an intensive growth strategy: market penetration, market development, and product development.

With market penetration, an entrepreneur attempts to increase sales by using more effective marketing strategies within the current target market. This is a common growth strategy for new ventures because it enables entrepreneurs to work in familiar territory and grow their businesses while they're getting their systems and controls firmly in place. Under this strategy, the company would expand gradually from the initial target market, whether it is a geographic area or a customer base. For example, the initial target market for a portable electronic travel guide might be travel agencies. Efforts and resources would be focused on getting those customers solidified and then gradually moving on to other target customers, such as hotels and convention bureaus. Promoting additional uses for the product persuades customers to buy more, as Arm & Hammer experienced when its customers began buying baking soda not only for cooking but also for brushing their teeth and deodorizing their refrigerators. Yet another way to employ market penetration is to attract customers from competitors by advertising product qualities, service, or price that distinguishes the entrepreneur's product from others. A fourth way is to educate nonusers of the product or service about its benefits, in an effort to increase the customer base.

Market development consists of taking the product or service to a broader geographic area. For example, a company that has been marketing on the East Coast may decide to expand across the rest of the United States. One of the most popular ways to expand a market geographically is to franchise, because this approach is generally less costly than setting up a national distribution system. The next section explores franchising in more detail.

Franchising

Franchising enables a business to grow quickly into several geographic markets at once. The franchiser sells to the franchisee the right to do business under a particular name; the right to a product, process, or service; training and assistance in setting up the business; and ongoing marketing and quality control support once the business is established. The franchisee pays a fee and a royalty on sales, typically 3–8 percent. For this fee, the franchisee may get

- A product or service that has a proven market,
- Trade names and/or trademarks,
- A patented design, process, or formula,
- An accounting and financial control system,
- A marketing plan, and/or
- The benefit of volume purchasing and advertising.

Franchises generally come in three types: dealerships, service franchises, and product franchises. Dealerships enable manufacturers to distribute products without having to do the day-to-day work of retailing. Dealers benefit from combined marketing strength but are often required to meet quotas. Service franchises provide customers with services such as tax preparation, temporary employees, payroll preparation, and real estate services. Often the business is already in operation independently before it applies to become a franchise member. The most popular type of franchise is one that offers a product, a brand name, and an operating model. Examples include Great Harvest Bread

Company and Golf USA. Although it is a popular vehicle for growth, franchising a business is not without its risks. It is much like creating a whole new business, because the entrepreneur (franchiser) must carefully document all processes and procedures in a manual that will be used to train the franchisees. Potential franchisees need to be scrutinized to ensure that they are qualified to assume the responsibilities of operating a franchise. Moreover, the cost of preparing a business to franchise is considerable and includes legal, accounting, consulting, and training expenses. Then, too, it may take as long as three to five years to show a profit.

The risk to franchisees who may have purchased the franchise as an entry into business ownership is also great. Franchisees typically pay the franchiser 2–10 percent of gross sales in monthly royalties and marketing fees, which means that it is a tremendous challenge for the franchisees to control costs and achieve a return on their investment. One reason why some franchises fail is that they are typically found in retail industries, primarily eating and drinking establishments, which have a pattern of high risk and low return. However, other types of franchises in the recent past have been successful. For example, Minuteman Press International, Inc. has grown into one of the top full-service printing franchises, with over 900 locations. And Snap-on Tools, now a public company with over $700 million in net sales, is the leading global developer, manufacturer, and marketer of tool and equipment solutions.

Although the Small Business Administration found that only 5 percent of franchises fail as compared to 30 percent of non-franchise businesses,[11] bankruptcy of the parent company, the franchiser, should be a concern for potential franchisees; it is not uncommon. In the past decade, dozens of franchises, including 7-Eleven, NutriSystem, American Speedy Printing, Church's Chicken, and Day's Inn, have experienced Chapter 11 bankruptcy. Most have emerged intact, but not without some harm to the franchisees. During the bankruptcy, the franchisees are left in limbo, without support or information, wondering whether they'll have a viable business when it's all done. The association of the franchisee with the bankrupt parent is also likely to have a negative effect, because customers assume that if the parent has financial problems, so does the offspring. Furthermore, most franchisees have invested their life's savings in their businesses. Under the arbitration clauses in most franchise agreements, franchisees don't have the option of going to court to recoup their losses. Even if the company comes out of Chapter 11, its image is tarnished. It will have to cut back somewhere, and savvy consumers know this to be true. There are several reasons why franchises might fail; they include ineffective systems, bad location, lack of sufficient marketing, too much competition, and insufficient start-up capital.

Not all businesses should use franchising as a means for growth. A successful franchise system will need to have the following characteristics:

▶ A successful prototype store (or preferably stores) with proven profitability and a good reputation so that the potential franchisee will begin with instant recognition;

▶ A registered trademark and a consistent image and appearance for all outlets;

▶ A business that can be systematized and easily replicated many times;

▶ A product that can be sold in a variety of geographic regions;

▶ Adequate funding, because establishing a successful franchise program can cost upwards of $150,000;

▶ A well-documented prospectus that spells out the franchisee's rights, responsibilities, and risks;

▶ An operations manual that details every aspect of running the business;

▶ A training and support system for franchisees, both before they start the business and ongoing after start-up;

▶ And site selection criteria and architectural standards.

Some examples of successful franchises that can be studied as models include McDonald's (fast food), Curves for Women (fitness), Supercuts (salon), and Jackson Hewitt Tax Service.

Developing a franchise program requires the assistance of an attorney and an accountant, both of whose advice should be carefully considered before undertaking the effort. One of the things that will be developed with the aid of an attorney is a franchise agreement. This document is often 40–60 pages in length and deals with a variety of legal issues. The franchise agreement should include the following:

▶ Rules by which the franchisor and franchisee will have to abide during the term of the franchise

▶ The term of the agreement (a franchise is like a lease where the franchisee is merely renting the business for the period of the franchise)

▶ Renewal provisions that include when notice must be given that the franchisee wishes to renew the agreement and what fees are to be paid

▶ First right of refusal or option to take on additional franchises offered by the franchisor

▶ Costs associated with purchasing the franchise (these may include an up-front fee, regular meeting expenses, and a percentage of the gross revenues to cover marketing and promotion costs)

▶ Rules related to the premises on which the franchise will be located (the franchisor may pay some of the costs of renovation and will often lease the property and grant a sublease to the franchisee)

▶ The stock of goods and materials needed to open the business and maintain a proper level of inventory

▶ Intellectual-property rights and who owns them

▶ Whether the contract gives the franchisee the right to sell the franchise

▶ How the franchise agreement can be terminated and what to do in case of disputes

It should be very clear why it's important to engage an attorney when structuring a franchise offering!

Licensing

Like franchising, licensing is a way to grow a company without investing large amounts of capital in plant, equipment, and employees. A license agreement is a grant to someone else to use the company's intellectual property and exploit it in the marketplace by manufacturing, distributing, or using it to create a new product. For example, a company may have developed a new patented process for taking rust off machinery. That process could be licensed to other companies to use on their equipment in return for paying a royalty back to the company. Conversely, an entrepreneur may have an idea for a new line of promotional products and want to license a famous name and likeness to use on them, to make them more attractive to consumers. This would entail seeking a license agreement from the owner of the trademarked name and likeness to use it commercially. An example is seeking a license from the Walt Disney Company to use Mickey Mouse on a line of products.

But licensing is much more than this, and entrepreneurs need to understand fully the value of intellectual property and how it can provide income in a variety of different ways. For the purposes of this discussion, anything that can be patented, copyrighted, or trademarked, and anything that is a trade secret, has the potential to be licensed. Many entrepreneurs don't realize that frequently in the conduct of their business, they gather valuable data on customers, markets, methods, and processes, but rarely do they package that data as intellectual property for sale. Restaurant Technologies, based in Eagan, Minnesota, is a supplier of cooking oil to restaurant and fast-food chains and grocery stores. To better understand when a customer needed to be restocked, the company installed sensors that tracked oil usage. Over time, the company realized that it had amassed valuable data—intellectual property—that its customers might appreciate having. Using password-protected websites for each customer, it began posting the information. Then the company sold solutions to the customer to fix problems their telemetry had detected; in this way, the company was helping its customers become more efficient.[12] If a company has intellectual property that someone else might pay to use or commercialize in some way, certain steps should be taken to ensure that both parties to the transaction win. Licensor and licensee depend very much on each other for the success of the agreement, so the outcomes must be worthwhile at both ends of the deal.

The following are steps that licensors should take to ensure a successful transaction:

Step 1: Decide exactly what will be licensed. The license agreement can be for a product, the design for a product, a process, the right to market and distribute, the right to manufacture, or the right to use the licensed product in the production of yet another product. It will also be important to decide whether the licensee may only license the product as is or may modify it.

Step 2: Understand and define the benefits the buyer (licensee) will receive from the transaction. Why should the licensee license from the company? What makes the product, process, or right covered by the license unique and valuable? The licensee should be convinced that dealing with the licensor offers many advantages and will be much more profitable than dealing with someone else.

Step 3: Conduct thorough market research to make certain that the potential customer base is sufficient to ensure a good profit from the effort. Of course, the licensee will also have done market research, particularly if he or she approaches a company with a proposal for a licensing agreement. But the latter situation is typical only with intellectual property that is well recognized in the marketplace—characters, for instance (Batman, Harry Potter). A company with a new intellectual property that is unproven in the marketplace may need to seek out licensing agreements to get the product commercialized.

Step 4: Conduct due diligence on potential licensees. It's important to make certain that any potential licensee has the resources to fulfill the terms and conditions of the license agreement, can properly commercialize the intellectual property, and has a sound reputation in the market. A license agreement is essentially a partnership, and choosing partners carefully is vital.

Step 5: Determine the value of the license agreement. The value of a license agreement is determined by several factors: (1) the economic life of the intellectual property—that is, how long it will remain viable as a marketable product, process, or right; (2) the potential that someone could design around the intellectual property and compete directly; (3) the potential for government legislation or regulation that could damage the marketability of the IP; (4) any changes in market conditions that could render the IP valueless. Once the monetary value of the license has been calculated on the basis of these four factors, the license becomes negotiable. Generally, the licensor wants some money up front, as a sign of good faith, and then a running royalty for the life of the license agreement. The amount of this royalty will vary by industry and by how much the licensee must invest in terms of plant, equipment, and marketing to commercialize the license.

Step 6: Create a license agreement. With the help of an attorney who specializes in licenses, draw up a license agreement or contract that defines the terms and conditions of the agreement between licensor and licensee.

PRODUCT DEVELOPMENT

The third way to exploit the current market is to develop new products and services for existing customers or offer new versions of existing products. That is the tactic employed by software companies, which are constantly updating software with new versions their customers must buy if they want to enjoy all the latest features. Savvy businesses get their best ideas for new products from their customers. These new ideas usually come in one of two forms: incremental changes in existing products or totally new products. Incremental products often come about serendipitously when engineers, sales personnel, and management spend time out in the marketplace with customers, learning more about their needs. Bringing all these team members together on a weekly basis to discuss ideas helps the business zero in quickly on those incremental products based on needs that are possible within the current operating structure and budget. The advantage of incremental products is that, because they are based on existing products, they can usually be designed and manufactured quite rapidly, and the marketing costs are less because customers are already familiar with the core product.

Brand-new or breakthrough products, on the other hand, have a much longer product development cycle and are therefore more costly to undertake. Breakthrough products cannot be planned for; instead, they usually come about through brainstorming, exercises in creativity, and problem-solving sessions. In other words, if an entrepreneur creates a business environment that encourages creative, "off-the-wall" thinking, the chances are greater that his or her company will eventually come up with breakthrough products. The breakthrough environment, of out necessity, has no budget or time constraints and does not run on a schedule. Offering a combination of incremental and breakthrough products is probably the most effective approach. The speed and cost efficiency of the incremental products keep cash flowing into the business to help fund the more costly breakthrough products.

Integrative Growth Strategies—Growing Within the Industry

There are many opportunities for entrepreneurs to pursue integrative growth strategies—to grow their ventures through acquisition. Acquisition is in many respects less about the financial ability of the entrepreneur to purchase another company and more about the ability to negotiate a good deal. With several research studies reporting that upwards of 75 percent of all acquisitions damage shareholder value, it is clear that this approach to growth must be taken very carefully.[13] In general, successful acquisitions target opportunities that integrate well with the core business, that can be implemented quickly, and that ensure the continuation of smooth operating processes.[14] Traditionally, when entrepreneurs have wanted to grow their businesses within their industries, they have looked to vertical and horizontal integration strategies, but now that it is important to run leaner operations, they have been looking, more often than not, to a modular or network strategy. This section examines all three strategies—vertical, horizontal, and modular.

VERTICAL INTEGRATION STRATEGIES

An entrepreneurial venture can grow by moving backward or forward within the distribution channel. This is called *vertical integration*. With a backward strategy, either the company gains control of some or all of its suppliers or it becomes its own supplier by starting another business from scratch or acquiring an existing supplier that has a successful operation. This is a common strategy for businesses that have instituted a just-in-time inventory control system. By acquiring the core supplier(s), an entrepreneur can streamline the production process and cut costs. With a forward strategy, the company attempts to control the distribution of its products by either selling directly to the customer (that is, acquiring a retail outlet) or acquiring the distributors of its products. This strategy gives the business more control over how its products are marketed. Surface Technology, Inc. (STI) is a Trenton, New Jersey–based nickel-plating shop working in a very competitive business. To continue to grow, STI had to find broader uses for its customers' parts, so it talked to customers to find out exactly what the various processes are that their parts go through before coming to STI for coating, and then where they go after leaving the STI plant. For example, STI found that before certain steel parts came to its shop, they were hardened in a process conducted by another vendor. STI saw a value in developing its own trademarked process and eliminating one vendor from the customer's process. A side benefit was that quality for the customer went up because STI now controlled how the two processes worked together. Similarly, STI developed downstream processes so that eventually it became more of a one-stop shop for the customer.[15]

HORIZONTAL INTEGRATION STRATEGIES

Another way to grow the business within the current industry is to buy up competitors or start a competing business (sell the same product under another label). This is *horizontal integration.* For example, an entrepreneur who owns a chain of sporting goods outlets could purchase a business that has complementary products, such as a batting cage business, so that customers can buy their bats, balls, helmets, and the like from the retail store and use them at the batting cage. Another example of growing horizontally is agreeing to manufacture a product under a different label. This strategy has been used frequently in the major-appliance and grocery industries. Whirlpool, for example, produced the Sears Kenmore washers and dryers for years. Likewise, many major food producers put their brand name food items into packaging labeled with the name of a major grocery store.

MODULAR OR NETWORK STRATEGIES

Another way for a company to grow within an industry is for the entrepreneur to focus on what he or she does best and let others do the rest. If the core activities of the business include designing and developing new products for the consumer market, other companies can make the parts, assemble the products, and market and deliver them. In essence, the entrepreneur's company and its core activities become the hub of the wheel, with the best suppliers and distributors as the spokes. This *modular strategy,* or *network strategy,* helps the business grow more rapidly, keep unit costs down, and turn out new products more quickly. In addition, the capital saved by not having to invest in fixed assets can be directed to those activities that provide a competitive advantage. The electronics and apparel industries used this growth strategy long before it became trendy. Today many other industries are beginning to see the advantages of a modular approach. Even service businesses can benefit from outsourcing functions such as accounting, payroll, and data processing, which require costly labor.

Outsourcing noncore functions to strategic partners can often help a company get products to market faster and in greater quantities, while at the same time spreading risk and delivering the capabilities of a much larger company without the expense. Finding key capabilities that will help the venture grow more rapidly is another use of outsourcing. The cost to the entrepreneur is perhaps the same as that of performing the task in-house, but the company acquires access to key processes and expertise that will speed its growth.

One study found that firms that used "transformational outsourcing" (outsourcing to facilitate rapid change, launch new strategies, and radically change the

Global Insights

SURFING IN CHINA?

Picture the finest shopping street in Shanghai, the equivalent of Fifth Avenue in New York. Now picture a Quiksilver Boardriders Club positioned between an Adidas outlet and a Starbucks. Surfing in China? What was Quiksilver, the successful Huntington Beach, California, surf, snowboard, and skateboard apparel store, thinking? Well, it was thinking about numbers; there are more teenagers in China than there are people in the United States. That presents a very attractive market for a company whose primary customers are teenagers. Quiksilver's CEO Robert McKnight is confident that patience in this market will pay off. Of the three primary sports that Quiksilver targets, skateboarding appears to be the best one with which to enter the Chinese market.

Quiksilver already had three stores in Hong Kong when it found a partner in Glorious Sun Enterprises, a Shanghai retailer who guided McKnight to open the first Shanghai store at 9:30 a.m. on February 27, 2004. This time and day were the most auspicious according to *feng shui*. Quiksilver used local celebrities to wear its clothing and educate consumers. Educating customers when there is no readily apparent need to satisfy is entering a market the hard way. Quiksilver had to create excitement and play on young people's love of having something new that no one else has. Despite the challenge that China presented for these board fanatics, the founders were steadfast in their belief that "there must be waves somewhere."

Sources: L. Earnest, "Catching a Wave of New Consumers," *Los Angeles Times Business Section* (May 16, 2004); and http://www.quiksilver.com.cn/QuiksilverEn/Index.aspx, accessed May 7, 2007.

scope of the company) achieved dramatic results.[16] An example is TiVo, the personal video recorder company founded in 1997. To achieve its goal of becoming the standard in the industry, it had to bring on strategic partners who had competencies that the new company did not have so that it could quickly make a market impact. TiVo brought on board manufacturing and marketing partners such as Sony Corp. and Royal Philips Electronics. But being the first mover is no walk in the park. It is appearing unlikely that TiVo will ever be able to dominate the market against the deep pockets of cable operators and companies like DIRECTV, owned by News Corp. Without question, however, TiVo could not have built its brand as quickly as it did without outsourcing. Nevertheless, only about 6.5 percent of U.S. households have digital video recorders, and TiVo is now looking at surviving by becoming the improved interface for cable DVR boxes.[17]

As with anything else, there are some drawbacks to outsourcing. If most functions are outsourced, it becomes difficult to develop any kind of corporate culture that will bind workers together and make them loyal to the company. When "employees" are no longer employees, they may find it easier to leave on a moment's notice. They also will tend to be less committed to the company's goals because they don't see a long-term role for themselves. These problems also apply to suppliers and distributors to whom an entrepreneur may outsource a capability. They must understand how they can also benefit from this relationship. That way, when the business begins to grow rapidly, they will be willing to ramp up to meet demand.

Diversification Growth Strategies—Growing Outside the Industry

When entrepreneurs expand their businesses by investing in or acquiring products or businesses outside their core competencies and industries, they are employing a diversification growth strategy. Generally, but not always, this strategy is used when the entrepreneur has exhausted all growth strategies within the current market and industry and now wants to make use of excess capacity or spare resources, adapt to the needs of customers, or change the direction of the company because of impending changes in the market or economy. One way to diversify is to use a synergistic strategy in which the entrepreneur attempts to locate new products or businesses that are technologically complementary. For example, a food processor may acquire a restaurant chain that can serve as a showcase for the food. Another way to diversify is to acquire products or services unrelated to the company's core products or services. For example, a manufacturer of bicycle helmets may acquire an apparel manufacturer to make clothing with the company logo on it to sell to helmet customers. A final strategy for diversifying, conglomerate diversification, entails acquiring businesses that are not related in any way to what the company is currently doing. An entrepreneur might use this strategy to gain control of a related function of doing business—for example, purchasing the building in which the business is housed and then leasing out excess space to other businesses to produce additional income and gain a depreciable asset. Many entrepreneurs whose work causes them to travel extensively find it advantageous to acquire a travel agency to reduce costs and provide greater convenience.

No matter where a business is located, there are ways to diversify in order to grow the business. Daffodil Harris started a tiny laundry business out of her boat in Admiralty Bay off a seven-square-mile island called Bequia near the Grenadines. She would travel from yacht to yacht picking up soiled clothing and returning it washed, dried, and folded. People loved the service. But Harris was not satisfied to be a one-person business. By 1999, she had grown the business into a multidivisional conglomerate that included a desalination plant, a marine service to rent moorings and dinghies and repair sails and equipment, a Chinese restaurant, and a grocery store. All of these businesses came out of asking customers what they wanted and then adding that product or service to her diversified offering. Today, Harris employs 23 workers for her multidivisional company, "Daffodil Marine Service."[18]

A diversification strategy for growth is not something to undertake without careful consideration of all the factors and potential outcomes, and this is particularly true of acquisition. Entrepreneurs can find consultants who are experts in mergers and acquisitions to help smooth the path financially and operationally, but it is extremely difficult to predict with any degree of confidence how the cultures of the two businesses will merge. Acquisitions and mergers cannot be successful on the basis of financial and operational synergy alone. Organizational styles and the individual personalities of key managers all come into play when an acquisition or a merger takes place. As a result, the human side of the two businesses must be analyzed and a plan developed for merging two potentially distinct cultures into one that can work effectively.

Many researchers have attempted to determine the most effective growth strategy for a new venture. In general, it has been found that horizontal integration, vertical integration, and synergistic diversification have been more successful than unrelated diversification. This is true whether the entrepreneur acquires an existing company or starts another company to achieve the goal. That is not to say that unrelated diversification should never be chosen as a growth strategy. If the potential gains are extraordinarily high, the risk may be worth taking. It is also generally true that an acquired business has a better chance of success than a brand-new venture, for the obvious reason that it usually has already passed the crucial start-up and survival stages and is more likely to be poised to grow.

Growing by Going Global

Today the question for a growth-oriented company is not "Should we go global?" but "When should we go global?" There are many reasons why entrepreneurs must consider the global market even as early as the development of their original business plan. Some entrepreneurs will launch companies that are born global. The term *born global* usually denotes a company that generates at least 25 percent of its sales in the first three years from the international marketplace and that derives a competitive advantage from outsourcing and selling in several countries.[19] Entrepreneurs who attend world trade shows know that their strongest competition may as easily come from a country in the Pacific Rim as from the company next door. Entrepreneurs also know they may have to rely on other countries for supplies, parts, and even fabrication to keep costs down and remain competitive. The United States, huge market though it is, represents less than half the total global market.[20]

Furthermore, with increasing competition and saturated markets in some industries, looking to global markets can add a new dimension to an entrepreneur's business. Many entrepreneurs have found new applications for their products in other countries or complementary products that help increase the sales of their products domestically. Although a global strategy should be contemplated in any business planning, a new venture may not be able to export until it is somewhat established and is offering a high-quality product or service at a competitive price. Nevertheless, more and more "global start-ups"—an example is Logitech, the Swiss manufacturer of computer mouses—take a global strategy from their very inception. Researchers have found that the number of global start-ups appears to be growing.[21] Oviatt and McDougall studied a dozen global start-ups and followed them over time. Four failed, for a variety of reasons, but those that failed tended to exhibit fewer of the "success characteristics" that Oviatt and McDougall found in those that survived. These success characteristics include

1. A global vision from the start
2. Internationally experienced managers
3. Strong international business networks

4. Preemptive technology

5. A unique intangible asset, such as know-how

6. Closely linked product or service extensions (The company derives new and innovative products and services from its core technology.)

7. A closely coordinated organization on a worldwide basis[22]

However, going global is also a risky proposition. Building a customer base and a distribution network is difficult in the domestic market; it is a colossal challenge in foreign markets. Moreover, financing is more difficult in global markets because of currency fluctuations, communication problems, and regulations that vary from country to country, to name just a few. Many small entrepreneurial companies have made their first foray into the global marketplace via a single order from a potential customer in another country. If that one transaction goes smoothly, the entrepreneur may forge ahead under the mistaken impression that doing business in another country is easy. One small computer component business learned that lesson the hard way. The company shipped a $10,000 replacement component to a customer in France. Six months later the naïve entrepreneur was billed $2,500 for value-added tax, something he knew nothing about. He had no choice but to absorb the loss.

Exporting is a long-term commitment that may not pay off for some time. In the meantime, it may be necessary to adapt the product or service somewhat to meet the requirements of the importing country and develop good relationships with agents in the country. If the entrepreneur is dealing in consumer products, it's a good idea to target countries that have disposable income and like U.S. products. If, however, the entrepreneur is dealing in basic or industrial products, it might be wise to look to developing countries that need equipment and services for building infrastructures and systems. One example is Mexico, which is taking on the enormous task of building bridges and roads as it positions itself as a major player in the world market. Figure 18.4 presents a strategy for beginning to build a global network of resources that can be tapped when the time is right. Savvy entrepreneurs understand that they can't simply land in a country and immediately do business. It takes time to establish relationships and build trust before a sale can be made. Developing a network of resources such as those depicted in Figure 18.4 will help the entrepreneur get to the right people who can make things happen.[23]

FINDING THE BEST GLOBAL MARKET

Finding the best market for a product or service can be a daunting task, but consulting certain sources of information can make the job easier. A good place to start is the *International Trade Statistics Yearbook of the United States*, which is available in any major library or online at http://unstats.un.org/unsd/trade/default.htm. With the United Nations Standard Industrial Trade Classification (SITC) codes found in this reference book, it is possible to locate information about international demand for a product or service in specific countries. The SITC system is a way of classifying commodities used in international trade. Entrepreneurs should also be familiar with the Harmonized

FIGURE 18.4

Building a Global Resource
Network

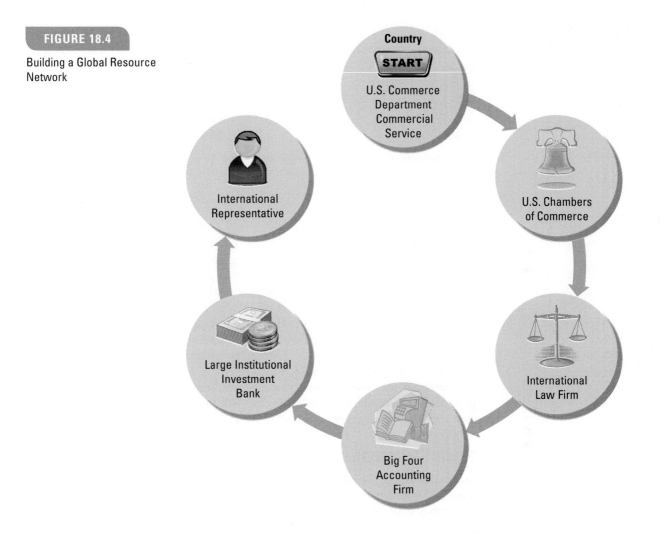

System (HS) of classification, which is a ten-digit system that puts the United States "in harmony" with most of the world in terms of commodity-tracking systems. If an international shipment exceeds $2,500, it must have an HS number for documentation. The district office and the Washington, DC, office of the International Trade Administration are also excellent sources, as is the Department of Commerce (DOC). The commerce department's online database links all the DOC International Trade Administration offices and provides a wealth of valuable research information.

Inc. Magazine researched the world to find the countries that would provide the greatest opportunity for entrepreneurs based on annual GDP and incentives.[24] Not surprisingly, the research found that one of the fastest growing countries, providing entrepreneurs the best chance of flourishing, was China. But other countries growing equally rapidly were Afghanistan, Angola, Azerbaijan (the fastest growing country at 26 percent), Estonia, and Latvia—probably

TABLE 18.3		
Easiest Countries in Which to Do Business	Australia	Japan
	Canada	Norway
	Denmark	Singapore, Malaysia
	Finland	Sweden
	Hong Kong	Switzerland
	Iceland	United Kingdom
	Ireland	United States

Source: Based on data collected by *Inc. Magazine* from the World Bank, the World Economic Forum in Davos, the Global Entrepreneurship Monitor consortium, and the Heritage Foundation's Index of Economic Freedom.

not at the top of most entrepreneurs' lists. Table 18.3 lists the countries in which it is easiest to do business.

The successful launch of a program of global growth should include a marketing plan and a budget directed toward that goal. It is also important to bring onto the team someone who has international management experience or export experience. Depending on the budget, a consultant who specializes in this area can be hired. It is also a good idea to attend foreign trade shows to learn how businesses in countries of interest conduct business, who the major players are, and who the competition is. Entrepreneurs seeking to do business in politically closed countries like China, South Korea, and Pakistan must be vigilant to the potential for political instability and the impact that could have on their business. Entrepreneurs should develop risk-management practices and make sure they have a solid "in-country" network.

EXPORT FINANCING

To make a sale in the global market, a company needs funds to purchase the raw materials or inventory to fill the order. Unfortunately, many entrepreneurs assume that if they have a large enough order, getting financing to fill the order will be no problem. Nothing could be further from the truth. Export lenders, like traditional lending sources, want to know that the entrepreneur has a sound business plan and the resources to fill the orders. Entrepreneurs who want to export can look for capital from several sources, including bank financing, internal cash flow from the business, venture capital or private investor capital, and prepayment, down payment, or progress payments from the foreign company placing the order. A commercial bank is more interested in lending money to a small exporter if the entrepreneur has secured a guarantee of payment from a governmental agency such as the Export-Import Bank of the United States, because such a guarantee limits the risk undertaken by the commercial bank. It is very similar to an SBA loan guarantee. Asking buyers to pay a deposit up-front, enough to cover the purchase of raw materials, can also be a real asset to a young company with limited cash flow.

Another financial issue that plagues companies doing business overseas is currency fluctuation. In a very short time frame, as little as a couple months, currency in a country can move up or down 5 to 10 percent, which is challenging for entrepreneurs who don't have margins that can withstand that kind of volatility. An international bank can help an entrepreneur find ways to mitigate the risk of currency fluctuation. For example, an entrepreneur may be able to take advantage of a forward contract that will lock in the price at which the foreign currency will be converted to U.S. dollars. Some entrepreneurs choose to use local banks and collect and spend the money they earn in the country in which they earn it to avoid having to convert it.

FOREIGN AGENTS, DISTRIBUTORS, AND TRADING COMPANIES

Every country has a number of sales representatives, agents, and distributors who specialize in importing U.S. goods. It is possible to find one agent who can handle an entire country or region, but if a country has several economic centers, it may be more effective to have a different agent for each center. Sales representatives work on commission; they do not buy and hold products. Consequently, the entrepreneur is still responsible for collecting receivables, which, particularly when one is dealing with a foreign country, can be costly and time-consuming.

Using agents is a way to circumvent this problem. Agents purchase a product at a discount (generally very large) off list and then sell it and handle collections themselves. They solve the problem of cultural differences and the related difficulties inherent in these transactions. Of course, using an agent means losing control over what happens to the product once it leaves the entrepreneur's hands. The entrepreneur has no say over what the agent actually charges customers in his or her own country. If the agent charges too much in an effort to make more money for himself or herself, the entrepreneur may lose a customer.

Entrepreneurs who are just starting to export or are exporting to areas not large enough to warrant an agent should consider putting an ad in U.S. trade journals that showcase U.S. products internationally. For products an entrepreneur is manufacturing, it may be possible to find a manufacturer in the international region being targeted that will let the entrepreneur sell his or her products through its company, thus providing instant recognition in the foreign country. Ultimately, that manufacturer could also become a source of financing for the entrepreneur's company. Another option is to use an export trading company (ETC) that specializes in certain countries or regions where it has established a network of sales representatives. ETCs often specialize in certain types of products. What typically happens is that a sales representative may report to the ETC that a particular country is interested in a certain product. The ETC then locates a manufacturer, buys the product, and sells it in the foreign country. Trading companies are a particularly popular vehicle when a company is dealing with Japan.

Choosing an Intermediary

Before deciding on an intermediary to handle the exporting of products, entrepreneurs should undertake some due diligence. Specifically, they should check the intermediary's current listing of products to see whether there is a good match, understand the competition and question whether the intermediary also handles these competitors, and find out whether the intermediary has enough representatives in the foreign country to handle the market. They should also look at the sales volume of the intermediary, which should show a rather consistent level of growth. And they should make sure the intermediary has sufficient warehouse space and up-to-date communication systems, examine the intermediary's marketing plan, and make sure the intermediary can handle servicing of the product.

Once a decision has been made, an agreement detailing the terms and conditions of the relationship should be drafted. This is very much like a partnership agreement, so it is important to consult an attorney who specializes in overseas contracts. The most important thing to remember about the contract is that it must be based on performance, so that if the intermediary is not moving enough product, the contract can be terminated. It is best to negotiate a one- or two-year contract with an option to renew should performance goals be met. This will probably not please the intermediary, because most want a five- to ten-year contract, but it is in the best interests of the entrepreneur to avoid a longer-term contract until the intermediary proves that he or she is loyal and can perform. Other issues should be addressed in the agreement. Retaining the ability to use another distributor is important. An entrepreneur should negotiate for a nonexclusive contract to have some flexibility and control over distribution. Another issue concerns the specific products the agent or distributor will represent. As the company grows, an entrepreneur may add or develop additional products and may not want this agent to sell those products. Specific geographic territories for which the agent or distributor will be responsible should be outlined, as well as the specific duties and responsibilities of the agent or distributor. Finally, the agreement should include a statement of agreed-upon sales quotas and should indicate the jurisdiction in which any dispute would be litigated. This will protect an entrepreneur from having to go to a foreign country to handle a dispute.

Choosing a Freight Forwarder

The job of the freight forwarder is to handle all aspects of delivering the product to the customer. The method by which a product is shipped has a significant impact on the product's cost or on the price to the customer, depending on how the deal is structured, so the choice of a freight forwarder should be carefully considered. Filling shipping containers to capacity is crucial to reducing costs. Freight forwarders can present shipping documents to a bank for collection. They can also prepare the shipping documents, which include a bill of lading (the contract between the shipper and the carrier) and an exporter declaration form detailing the contents of the shipment. The entrepreneur, however, is responsible for knowing whether any items being shipped require special licenses or certificates, as in the case of hazardous materials and certain food substances.

Growth can be an exciting time. And although a company's growth rate won't resemble a hockey stick for long (if ever), strong growth can be sustained over time if entrepreneurs plan for it and keep scanning the horizon for changes.

> ### New Venture Checklist
>
> Have you:
>
> ☐ Identified market factors that may affect the growth of the business?
>
> ☐ Determined which growth strategy is most appropriate?
>
> ☐ Identified potential international markets for the product or service?
>
> ☐ Developed a plan for globalization of the company at some point in the future?

Issues to Consider

1. What are four characteristics of high-growth companies?
2. How can both market and management factors affect the growth of a new venture?
3. What questions should you ask at each level of the new venture's growth?
4. What advantages do intensive growth strategies have over integrative and diversification strategies?
5. Why is it important to start a growth-oriented business with a plan for globalization from the beginning?
6. How do foreign agents, distributors, and export trading companies differ in the services they provide?

Experiencing Entrepreneurship

1. Visit an export center in your area and talk to a Department of Commerce trade specialist who can advise you on how to become prepared to export. What did you learn that you hadn't learned from reading this text?

2. Interview an entrepreneur whose new venture is in its early stages, and question him or her about the growth strategy for the business. Can you identify the type of strategy being used?

Relevant Case Studies

## Chapter 19

PLANNING FOR CHANGE

"We know not yet what we have done, still less what we are doing. Wait till evening and other parts of our day's work will shine than we had thought at noon, and we shall discover the real purport of our toil."

—HENRY DAVID THOREAU

LEARNING OBJECTIVES

▸ Discuss how entrepreneurs should prepare for contingencies.

▸ Explain the purpose of a harvest plan.

▸ Describe the role of bankruptcy in business failure.

Profile 19.1 TAKING RISK IN UNCERTAIN TIMES

Ron Perry was faced with what appeared to be a golden opportunity whose downside was the potential loss of $1 million, but whose upside was at least 10 times that amount. His Montana power company, Commercial Energy, had been approached by a railroad that was trying to reduce its electricity prices by generating energy at much lower cost from diesel locomotives that were not in service. The deal was that Perry's company would put up $1 million, which would pay half the cost of retrofitting the locomotives. Commercial Energy would also handle sales and the scheduling of power transmission to customers.

This was a highly risky venture from the standpoint that using trains to generate power was basically unheard of. Moreover, the energy market was extremely unstable, with "land mines" everywhere. Nevertheless, Perry could identify three reasons why this might be a good investment. If the venture succeeded, he would have a 50 percent share in the profits. He would also develop a closer relationship with his most important customer, and he would have an opportunity to begin producing his own power, a long-term goal of his company. Understanding the nature of his industry well, Perry was a fanatic about risk management. As part of the due diligence he conducted in the course of making this investment decision, he used Crystal Ball, a software product that predicts the probability that various energy-price scenarios will occur. He supplied the computer model with every variable he could imagine and created thousands of alternative scenarios involving possible fluctuations in the price of electricity and diesel fuel. Then he had the program calculate three things: (1) the likelihood that those prices would move in opposite directions, (2) the potential customer demand, and (3) the contract prices. He discovered that the greatest probability was that his company would earn $2 million to $3 million in six months.

If opportunities depended only on business models and did not include the human element, Perry would have been correct in deciding to move forward with the investment. He clearly understood the industry and knew what he stood to lose; he also knew that he could withstand the loss. But problems emerged when neighbors complained about having a diesel conversion plant near their homes. The neighbors' complaints attracted local environmental groups, who managed to attract *NBC Nightly News*, and soon the railroad began to backpedal on the deal. Finally, when the Federal Energy Regulatory Commission capped electricity prices at $100 a megawatt, both parties realized that the profits they predicted would not materialize. When the deal fell apart, Perry lost about half his investment. He was philosophical about the loss, calling it a reversible risk. Risks are not all equal in their severity. The important question is whether, if the deal fails, the company will recover. In Perry's case, he knew it would. He had examined the opportunity under many different assumptions, so his decision to go forward was a good one given the information he had at the time. In 2003, Commercial Energy ranked 147 on the Inc. 500 list of fastest growing private companies; it was the second year in a row that the company had made the list with a growth rate of 1,105 percent and revenues topping $17 million. Today it is acquiring companies to support growth in Montana and California.

Sources: Commercial Energy of Montana, http://www .commercialenergy.net, accessed May 9, 2007; and L. Buchanan, "How to Take Risks in a Time of Anxiety," *Inc. Magazine* (May 2003), http://www.inc.com.

Change is a certainty that every entrepreneur can count on. There is no way to avoid it in today's global environment; therefore, entrepreneurs must be ready and willing to adapt to new conditions, new threats, and new opportunities. Many entrepreneurs have started a business with a vision and a plan for where that business would go but found that things changed along the way. Forces beyond the control of the entrepreneur pushed the venture in new directions, and a new set of plans had to be constructed. Consider the highly volatile technology market during the first two years of the new millennium. How many entrepreneurs who had developed business plans for new e-commerce ventures and were seeking capital in early 2000 knew that their window of opportunity to secure those investments was about to close? In April of that year, the stock market plummeted, foreshadowing an enormous shake-out in the dot com world and the end of "money for nothing." In a matter of months, hundreds of potential new e-commerce ventures failed to make it to the marketplace because they had no backup plan in place. Some would argue that the signs were there all along, but the easy availability of venture capital inspired the notion that all an entrepreneur needed was a great idea that could scale out to a huge market. In any case, most entrepreneurs were not prepared for the change and had no contingency plans in place.

Business owners everywhere knew that the war in Iraq was coming in the early 2000s and that they would have to operate their companies during what might be a protracted period of high uncertainty. No one knew what the impact of the war would be, so for a time, businesses held off on plans to expand. They stopped hiring, and their sales slowed while the economy sputtered under a constant barrage of news from the front. But those businesses that had stayed in touch with the economy, had diversified, and had made contingency plans did not feel the impact nearly as much as their less prepared counterparts. Sam Brown, the CEO of Knight & Carver, a San Diego yacht builder, recognized that his business involved discretionary purchases and customers who, in down times, would simply stop buying yachts. His business couldn't afford to wait until times changed, so it made sense to diversify into activities that didn't experience the same kind of response to a down economy. As early as 1997, Knight & Carver had begun exploring the alternative-energy business with the goal of using their expertise in composite materials to build wind turbine blades. The demand was great, and this new venture provided a strong additional stream of revenue for the company. When the war began, Brown was uncertain of how much of a toll it would take on his business, but because about 70 percent of his business came from repair work, he was relieved to find that customers were still taking care of repairs on their vessels, particularly since they weren't buying new ones. By 2005, the wind turbine business was booming.[1] Brown is an example of a business owner who knows the value of contingency planning. In the absence of planning, entrepreneurs find themselves in a reactionary mode, dealing from a position of weakness.

One of the events for which entrepreneurs often fail to plan is the harvest or exit from the business. Knowing in what manner the entrepreneur wants to realize the benefits of having created a successful business guides decision making throughout the life of the business. Moreover, if an entrepreneur has taken investment capital during the growth of the business, the investors will be looking for an exit strategy that involves some type of liquidity event. This chapter looks at contingency planning, alternatives for harvesting the wealth of the venture, and alternatives to consider if the venture should fail.

Preparing for Contingencies

By compelling entrepreneurs to consider risks that their business faces and multiple outcomes and possibilities as a result of that risk, contingency plans help a growing business deal with downturns and upturns in the economy, new regulations, changes in customer tastes and preferences, and many other events that regularly—and often without much warning—disrupt the equilibrium of the firm. The 2001 recession pointed out how many businesses fail to understand business cycles. Recessions in general are actually quite normal in the U.S. economy, but the 2001 recession displayed distinct characteristics resulting from the fact that it occurred in the middle of an industrial revolution.[2] American icons such as Bethlehem Steel, Burlington, Kmart, and United Airlines all faced bankruptcies. However, recessions do not happen overnight. There are signs, even within specific industries, that signal a slowdown. Since the government began compiling indices on the economy after World War II, some consistent trends have emerged. For example, the Leading Index of Economic Indicators, which consists of such items as the Producer Price Index, the Consumer Confidence Index, and the Manufacturers' Orders for Durable Goods, typically declines for 9 months prior to the onset of a recession. The coincident-lagging index, which is a ratio of the coincident index (employment, personal income, industrial production) to the lagging index (consumer price index, interest rates, unemployment), declines for 13 months prior to the onset of a recession. Recognizing the signs of recession before they affect a business gives the entrepreneur a chance to prepare in many ways, including maintaining a higher degree of liquidity. In recessionary times, it is more difficult to raise capital from either bankers or private sources, so liquidity opens up opportunities that become available only during recessions. For example, an entrepreneur may be able to purchase a building that in good economic times was beyond reach, or he or she may be able to negotiate more favorable terms from suppliers just to keep the business moving forward.

An effective contingency plan will answer several important questions:

1. In the event of a problem, which suppliers would be willing to extend the entrepreneur's repayment time and for how much?

2. What nonessential assets does the business have that can be turned into cash quickly?

3. Is there additional investment capital that could be tapped?

4. Does the business have customers who might be willing to prepay or purchase earlier than planned?

5. Has a good relationship with a banker and accountant been established? How can they help the business get through the crunch?

After answering these questions, entrepreneurs can (1) identify the potential risks associated with their venture, (2) calculate the probability that those

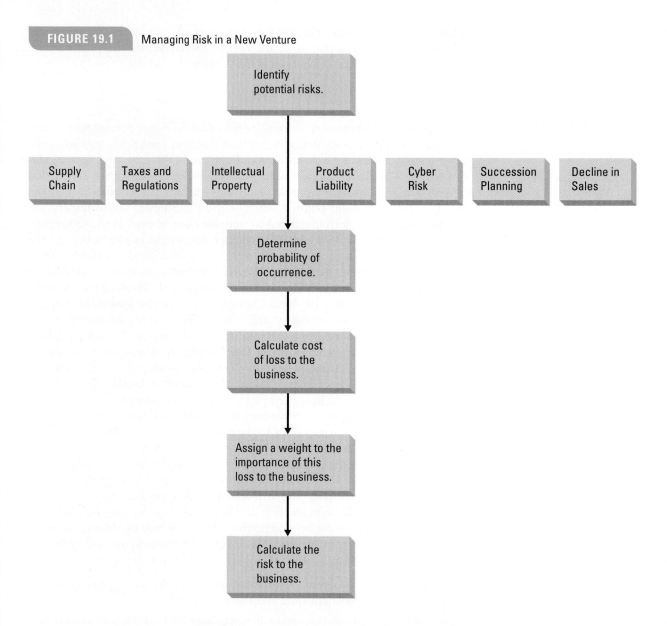

FIGURE 19.1   Managing Risk in a New Venture

identified risks will in fact occur, (3) assign a level of importance to the losses, and (4) calculate the overall loss risk.[3] In the next section we consider some of the major categories of risk that entrepreneurs face. Figure 19.1 summarizes the process for addressing risk.

IDENTIFYING POTENTIAL RISKS

Risk is a fact of business life, and a company's exposure to risk increases as the venture grows. Understanding where the risk lies allows the entrepreneur to respond effectively through process improvement strategies and buffer strategies.

Socially Responsible Entrepreneurship

The Social Venture Network

What happens when a group of visionary leaders comes together to make a difference in the world of entrepreneurship and investment? What happens is a nonprofit network, the Social Venture Network (SVN), whose mission is to promote "models and leadership for socially and environmentally sustainable business." SVN has created a community of practice that provides information and community forums to empower their members to achieve the vision collectively. Founded in 1987, SVN's membership stands at over 420 business leaders, investors, and nonprofit leaders who are dedicated to making the business world a better place. One of SVN's passionate members is Judy Wicks, founder of the White Dog Café in Philadelphia. Serving a clientele that includes the University of Pennsylvania, Wicks's café is a hot spot for promoting social causes in addition to providing locally grown organic foods. In a tough industry where margins are in the 3 percent range, Wicks is posting margins of 7.4 percent. Once a year, the White Dog offers eco tours to visit a family farm or a water treatment facility. On Monday nights, traditionally a slow night in the industry, the restaurant hosts a celebrity lecture series, featuring speakers such as Eric Schlosser, author of *Fast Food Nation*. Wicks provides her employees a living wage, health benefits, paid vacation, and other benefits not normally found in the restaurant world. Like the other businesses that are associated with SVN, White Dog is an excellent example of the triple bottom line: profit, people, and planet. Find out more about SVN at http://www.svn.org

Process improvement strategies involve reducing the probability that the risk will occur by forming strategic alliances with strong partners[4] or by developing backup suppliers and better communication with suppliers.[5] However, even with process improvement strategies in place, it is impossible to eliminate risk completely. *Buffer strategies* are used to protect a company against potential risk that can't be prevented. Maintaining sufficient inventory and alternative sources of supply are two types of buffer strategies.

Supply Chain Risks

The common practice of outsourcing the upstream activities of the business—raw materials, manufacturing, assembly, inventory—presents advantages and risks to the entrepreneur. The advantages of outsourcing include the sharing of risk, expertise, and resources, but the risks are many and significant. The financial health of the supplier is critical to the stability of the entrepreneur's business. When a supplier faces financial hardships and cannot provide supplies, raw materials, and so forth in a timely manner and the entrepreneur has no backup, the results can be loss of customers and, in some cases, the failure of the entrepreneur's business. Supplier capacity constraints are another source of risk for an entrepreneur. When demand fluctuates or increases precipitously, suppliers may not be able to ramp up quickly enough to meet the demand.[6] Quality-related risks and the inability of suppliers to keep up with technological change can have ramifications throughout the entire value chain, including raising the cost of producing a product.[7] Changes in customer needs can affect product design and, by extension, the types and quantities of supplies needed. When suppliers are unable to make required changes in product design, entrepreneurs incur a risk. Finally, risks in the form of disasters—floods, fire, earthquakes—can disrupt supply chains and affect an entrepreneur's ability to manufacture and distribute products.

Taxes and Regulations

During the life of every business, new laws, regulations, and rules will be enacted, and frequently there is no way to prepare for them. Government regulations and regulatory paperwork are severe problems for growing ventures, and the cost of compliance is rising to the point where entrepreneurs are looking for ways to avoid coming under the purview of some of these regulations. For example, the Family Leave Act now has a threshold firm size of 50 employees, which means that very small businesses are now faced with the possible protracted absence of an employee who cannot easily be replaced. As a result, many small businesses fight to stay below that important number.

The cost of employing an individual is becoming so prohibitive that many companies are solving the problem by subcontracting work and leasing employees. The U.S Department of Labor reports that employers' costs for employee compensation averaged $27.54 an hour in December 2006.[8] Of this cost, 30.1 percent was attributed to employee benefits, which include such things as paid vacations, holidays, sick leave, and other leave; supplemental pay (overtime and premium pay for work in addition to the regular work schedule, such as weekends and holidays); insurance benefits (life, health, short-term disability, and long-term disability insurance); retirement and savings benefits; and legally required benefits (Social Security, Medicare, federal and state unemployment insurance, and workers' compensation). Benefits, as a percentage of total compensation, have increased every year since 2001. It is no wonder that many business owners prefer to work with independent contractors. However, the government is cracking down on businesses that incorrectly categorize people as independent contractors, so IRS rules must be carefully followed. (See Chapter 8.)

Intellectual Piracy

For all the benefits of globalization, one of the biggest negatives has been intellectual piracy. The U.S. Chamber of Commerce reports that piracy costs the United States alone more than $250 billion annually and 750,000 lost jobs every year.[9] The industries that suffer the most seem to be the software and pharmaceutical industries. Although piracy cannot be completely stopped, small companies can fight back by investigating suppliers and manufacturers before doing business with them, contractually requiring their foreign partners to submit to international binding arbitration so the entrepreneur won't have to navigate the local courts of a country, and registering all trademarks in whatever country the company is doing business in.

Product Liability

The chances are fairly good that any company that manufactures products will face a product liability suit at some point. More and more of the risk of product-related injuries has been shifted to manufacturers, creating a legal minefield that could prove disastrous to a growing company. Even if a company carefully designs and manufactures a product and covers it with warnings and detailed instructions, that company may still be vulnerable if misuse of the product results in injury. For a company to be legally liable, the product must be defective and an injury must have occurred. But in a litigious society, those requirements don't stop people from initiating lawsuits even when there are no grounds. Most product liability insurance covers the costs of defense, personal injury, or property damage, but not lost sales and the cost of product redesign. Moreover, if the insurance company must pay on a claim, the entrepreneur's premiums will no doubt increase.

A growing company must plan for potential litigation from the very inception of the business. One proven method is to establish a formal safety panel that includes people from all the major functional areas of the business. During the start-up phase, that panel may consist of only the entrepreneur and one or two outside advisers with experience in the area. It is the job of the panel to review safety requirements on a regular basis, establish new ones when necessary, and document any injuries or claims made against the product. Prior to product introduction in the marketplace, the panel should see that careful records are maintained of all decisions regarding final product design, testing, and evaluation procedures. Advertising of the product should contain no exaggerated claims or implied promises that may give customers the impression that the company is claiming more safety features than the product actually possesses. Implied promises can be used against the entrepreneur in a court of law.

Early in the operation of the business, it is important to identify a qualified attorney familiar with the industry to handle any potential product liability claims. This attorney should handle the first case that confronts the business. Thereafter, if other suits arise in various parts of the country, the entrepreneur can save money by hiring a "local attorney" in the jurisdiction of the claim. Then the primary attorney should brief the local attorney on the precedent-setting cases related to the claim and assist while the local attorney carries the case to court. In this way, the entrepreneur does not have to send the primary attorney on the road, incurring significant travel and time expenses.

Cyber Risk

One of the more recent and insidious risks a company that is doing business online faces is cyber risk: hacker attacks that could bring the business network down, phishing attacks (acquiring sensitive information such as user names and passwords), spybots, and the ever-present viruses and worms. In 2006, the CSI/FBI Computer Crime and Security Survey found that 29 percent of all U.S. companies have now secured insurance policies to manage Internet risks, an increase of 25 percent over 2005.[10] However, these policies are often difficult to understand and contain so many exclusions that one company figured the price was close to what it would cost to do what they could to reduce their cyber risk on their own. However, entrepreneurs with companies that rely heavily on Internet-based systems will want to get advice about securing a policy that protects the company against liability for security breaches, crisis management (notifying customers about the theft of information), business interruption, and the cost associated with restoring information that has been corrupted.

Succession Planning

No company can count on keeping the same management team over the life of the business—or even after the start-up phase. The demand for top-notch management personnel (particularly in some industries, such as high-tech) means that other companies will constantly be trying to woo the best people away from the best firms. Losing a CEO in times of high turnover is not uncommon. In 2006 alone, 15 percent of the world's largest companies changed their CEOs,[11] including public giants such as Hewlett-Packard and AOL/TimeWarner as well as private companies like BioMicro Systems. But key employees are often lost for other unpredictable reasons like death or illness. In fact, some estimates suggest that the chances of losing a key executive to death are significantly greater than losing a business to fire.

Robin Gregory and Michael Williamson didn't lose the CEO of their successful financial software firm, Bolosystems, but they were about to lose employees because the co-CEOs were unable to move the company to the next level. After much searching, they found an industry veteran who had a track record of taking a company from $5 million to $20 million and who could install the right systems and controls they would need to grow. It wasn't an easy decision to give up the reins, but it was the best decision for the company that has now grown from $2.2 million in 2004 to $12.3 million in revenue in 2006. Free now from the demands of running the company, the two are focusing on product development, a good part of the reason the company was able to grow.[12] Succession planning—identifying people who can take over key company positions in an emergency—is an important part of contingency planning. Ideally that person or persons will come from within the company, but in the case of a growing entrepreneurial company that has been operating in a "lean and mean" mode, promoting from within may not be possible, so outsiders must be found. To prepare for the possible loss of a key employee, it is a good idea to purchase "key-person insurance," which will cover the cost of suddenly having to replace someone. Bringing in a consultant to guide the management team in succession planning is a valuable exercise for any growing venture. Often consultants are hired temporarily to take over a vacant position for a specified period, during which they train a permanent successor. Another solution is to cross-train people in key positions so that someone can step in, at least for the short term, in the event of an emergency. Cross-training is generally an integral part of a team-based approach to organizational management.

Succession Planning in Family-Owned Businesses

Entrepreneurs who head family-owned companies face special problems because they tend to look to a son, daughter, or other family member to succeed them. Succession in a family-owned business will not happen unless it is planned for, however. In fact, over half of family-owned businesses don't continue into the second generation.[13] This is partly because the owner must deal not only with business issues related to succession—ownership, management, strategic planning—but also with the unexpected, such as a death and relationship issues with family members, a much more difficult task. Succession planning tends to expose family issues that may have been kept in the background but have been building over time. For example, the daughter who the entrepreneur assumed would take over the business may have no interest in doing so but may never have told her entrepreneur father. Or, a child may believe himself or herself capable of simply stepping into a managerial role with no previous experience. If an entrepreneur has created a plan for succession, a problem like this may be solved by making it a requirement that a child or potential successor work for another company for several years to gain some business savvy and to decide whether he or she wants to take over the family business. Robert Bradford is CEO of the Center for Simplified Strategic Planning in Ann Arbor, Michigan. He believes that it is important to think about succession planning very early in the growth of the business, because finding the right person to succeed the entrepreneur parent in the business is not an easy task.[14] CEOs act as visionaries and also play functional roles, balancing finance, marketing, and operations. A person whom an entrepreneur has chosen to succeed him or her must be given the time to understand the role; it's not something that will happen overnight. Bradford planned for succession by assessing his current human resources and also the company's ability to evaluate a potential candidate. He wrote his own job description and then began looking at people inside his firm for signs of leadership skills. Once he had narrowed the field to a few potential candidates, he asked them to do a self-assessment. Then he compared the gaps between the skills they believed they had and his own job description. In fact, Bradford did this himself before he succeeded his father in the business.

To start the process of succession planning, all the active family members should participate on a committee to explore the options. Some of the questions to examine are the following:

▶ Is the next generation being sufficiently prepared to take over the business when the time comes?

▶ What is the second generation's expectation for the future of the business, and is it congruent with the company's vision?

▶ What skills and experience does the second generation need to acquire?

▶ What would the ideal succession plan look like?

Then, with the help of an attorney, buy-sell agreements should be developed to ensure that heirs receive a fair price for their interest in the business upon a partner's death and to protect against irreparable damage in the event of a shareholder's permanent disability by outlining provisions for buying out the disabled partner's interest. An estate planning professional can help evaluate the impact of any changes in the business on the entrepreneur's personal assets. Given that most privately owned businesses in the United States are family-owned businesses, this succession planning strategy is useful for any business that wants to be prepared for the loss or retirement of its leader.

Decline in Sales

When sales decline and positive cash flow starts looking like a memory, entrepreneurs often go into a period of denial. They start paying their suppliers more slowly to preserve cash, they lay people off, they stop answering the phone, and they insulate themselves against the demands of their creditors. Their panic frequently causes them to make poor decisions about how to spend the precious cash they do have. They figure that if they can just hold on long enough, things will turn around. Unfortunately, this attitude only makes the problem worse, effectively propelling the business toward its ultimate demise. How can an entrepreneur lose touch with the business and the market so much that he or she puts the business at risk? What often happens is that entrepreneurs get so wrapped up in the day-to-day operations of the business that they don't have time to contemplate the "big picture" or stay in tune with their customers. Consequently, all too often they don't see a potential crisis coming until it's too late. Beloit Corp., a manufacturer of paper mill machinery, went out of business in 2001 and the ripple affect on small businesses in Beloit, Wisconsin, was enormous. Barker Rockford, a hydraulic systems manufacturer, had depended on Beloit for 75 percent of its sales revenues. When Beloit closed, their company dropped from 51 employees to 11. In an effort to turn around the company, Pierce Barker III, the company's vice president, took an innovative approach to create customers. With two partners he founded ProStuff, which invented a new kind of starting gate for the BMX bike-racing industry. Now Barker Rockford manufactures the gates for ProStuff, which sells them worldwide with high margins. Today both companies are doing well.[15]

When sales decline, lowering prices isn't necessarily the solution. If the company's customers understand the value of the product or service, any such sudden discounting will confuse them. When there is a decline in sales, it is especially important to look at all possible sources, not just the economy. The entrepreneur may have been lax about checking the credit status of customers and distributors, or the inventory turnover rate may have changed. He or she may have failed to notice an emerging competitor offering a product or service more in line with current tastes and preferences. When a growing business first notices a dip in sales, it is time to find the cause and make the necessary changes. This will be easier if the business has a contingency plan in place. If, however, those changes cannot be made in time to forestall a cash flow problem, it is time to consult a debt negotiation company, a crisis management consultant, or a bankruptcy attorney who is willing to work through the problem without going to court. These experts can help an entrepreneur work with creditors until the problem is resolved. To prepare the best defense against a cash flow crisis, entrepreneurs must remain committed to producing exceptional-quality products; controlling the cost of overhead, particularly where that overhead does not contribute directly to revenue generation (expensive cars, travel, excessive commissions); controlling production costs through subcontracting and being frugal about facilities; making liquidity and positive cash flow the prime directive, so that the company can ride out temporary periods of declining demand; and having a contingency plan in place.

CALCULATING THE PROBABILITY THAT THE RISK WILL OCCUR

It is extremely difficult to calculate the probability that a given risk will occur with any degree of accuracy. Consequently, any cost-benefit analysis conducted will probably contain flaws and may even cause the company to decide that the cost of protecting itself is nearly equal to the cost of the loss.[16] Nonetheless, it is important to gauge, based on industry and customer knowledge, the chance that a particular risk will occur and what the impact of that occurrence will be on the company. For example, an entrepreneur might want to know how many widgets to order for the summer season. He knows he can sell 50 in a day and that he makes a profit of $10 each. The average number of days in the season is 95. Thus he multiplies 4,750 widgets times $10 to get the average profit for the season. He has just committed a common error that Sam Savage, a consulting professor at Stanford University, has called the "flaw of averages."[17] The problem with averages is that they mask risk. Savage claims that average inputs don't always produce average outputs. For example, if a lower-than-average demand produces lower-than-average revenues, then a higher-than-average demand is not possible because the company would have made only enough product to satisfy an average demand. This kind of error is quickly exposed when doing probability modeling such as Monte Carlo simulation, which models behaviors under multiple uncertainties within a specified period. It is often used in the insurance industry to model accident risk. Working with this type of modeling software is an effective way to get a feel for the risk inherent in any business. Understanding the magnitude of a potential loss is important in deciding where to devote limited resources to protecting against a particular loss. Assigning a level of significance is again an arbitrary exercise, because the weight given to any risk impact is based on the company's goals, core competencies, and focus.

The overall risk of loss is simply the product of the probability of occurrence times the cost of the impact to the business times the level of significance:

$$\text{Risk of Loss} = (P \times C \times S)$$

For example, suppose an entrepreneur determines that there is a 40 percent chance that she will lose a key manager to a competitor. The financial cost of that loss is the cost of doing a search for a new manager, which she estimates at $10,000 (this does not include the nonfinancial costs, such as loss of tacit knowledge). She assigns a weight of 80 percent, on a scale of 1 percent to 100 percent, to reflect the importance of this risk. Thus, the overall risk of loss is approximately

$$\text{Risk of Loss} = (\$10,000 \times 0.40 \times 0.80) = \$3,200$$

If this calculation is done for all the identified risks, it will be easier to decide on which risks to concentrate efforts and focus resources.

The Harvest Plan

Many first-time entrepreneurs have questioned the need for an exit plan, or harvest plan, because they are more concerned with launching the business and making it a success than with thinking about how they're going to get out. But even though some entrepreneurs stay with their new ventures for the long term, the majority enjoys the challenge of start-up and the excitement of growth and abhors the custodial role of managing a stable, mature company. Consequently, exiting the business does not necessarily mean exiting the role of entrepreneur. It may in fact mean taking the financial rewards of having grown a successful business and investing them in a new venture. And there are serial entrepreneurs who do that very thing over and over again throughout their lives, starting businesses and then selling them or letting others run them. Whether or not an entrepreneur intends to exit a business at any point, there should be a plan for harvesting the rewards of having started the business in the first place. There is another important reason why a harvest plan is essential. Many entrepreneurs take investor capital at some point in the growth of their companies, and investors require a liquidity event so that they can exit the business with their principal and any return on investment they have accrued.

Entrepreneurs need to think of their companies as part of an ongoing career path. So says Jerome Katz, professor of management at St. Louis University. He has been studying the career paths of entrepreneurs and finds that there are four major types:

1. *Growth entrepreneurs.* These are entrepreneurs who measure their success by the size of their company. They tend not to have an exit plan because they're always striving for bigger, better, faster.

2. *Habitual entrepreneurs.* These are people who love to start businesses and may start and run several at once. They are probably even less likely to have an exit plan because there are always new opportunities out there.

3. *Harvest entrepreneurs.* These entrepreneurs start and build a venture for the purpose of selling it. Some of these owners will start, build, and harvest many companies during a career.

4. *Spiral, or helical, entrepreneurs.* Women entrepreneurs often fall into this category. These entrepreneurs are driven by what is going on in their personal lives, so their entrepreneurial tendencies emerge in spurts. At times they may appear oblivious to the business as they deal with family issues.

Katz believes it is never too early to begin to think about an endgame strategy, so that the exit will be graceful rather than "feet first."[18] The following paragraphs examine several methods by which an entrepreneur can achieve a rewarding harvest.

SELLING THE BUSINESS

Selling the business outright to another company or to an individual may be the goal if an entrepreneur is ready to move on to something else and wants to be financially and mentally free to do so. Unfortunately, however, selling a business is a life-changing event because for several years, the entrepreneur has probably devoted the majority of his or her time and attention to growing the business, and it played an important role in structuring the entrepreneur's life. Although the market may be good for selling the particular type of business an entrepreneur owns, he or she may not be ready to "retire" or may not have identified what to do next. Consequently, after the business has been sold, its owner may experience a sense of loss, much like what accompanies the death of a loved one; without preparation, emotional stress could be the consequence. Therefore, planning for this enormous change will be vital.

The best way to sell a business is for entrepreneurs to know almost from the beginning that selling is what they eventually want to do, so that they will make decisions for the business that will place it in the best position for a sale several years later. For one thing, the business will need audited financial statements that lend the business forecasts more credibility. The tax strategy will not be to minimize taxes by showing low profits but, rather, to show actual profits and pay the taxes on them, because that will provide a higher valuation for the business. Throughout the time that the entrepreneur owns the business, its expenses and activity should be kept totally separate from the owner's personal expenses. It will also be important to plan for the amount of time it will take to sell the business and wait to sell until the right window of opportunity has opened.

Smaller businesses for sale often use the services of business brokers; however, a high-growth venture is more likely to employ the services of an investment banking firm that has experience with the industry. Investment banks normally want a retainer to ensure the seriousness of the commitment to sell, but that retainer will be applied against the final fee on the sale, which could average about 5 percent of the purchase price. It is recommended, however, that a third party with no vested interest in the sale be enlisted to judge the fair market value of the business. This "appraiser" can also prepare financial projections based on the history of the company and the appraiser's independent market research. When a business is sold, the entrepreneur does not have to sell all the assets. For example, the building could be held out of the sale and leased back to the business purchaser, with the original owner staying on as landlord.

While the potential purchaser is conducting due diligence on the entrepreneur and the business, the entrepreneur needs to do the same with the purchaser. The purchasing firm or individual should be thoroughly checked out against a list of criteria the entrepreneur has developed. The purchaser should have the resources necessary to continue the growth of the business, be familiar with the industry and with the type of business being purchased, have a good reputation in the industry, and offer skills and contacts that will ensure that the business continues in a positive direction. In order to compare one buyer with another fairly, it is often helpful to make a complete list of criteria and then weight them to reflect their relative importance.

CASHING OUT BUT STAYING IN

Sometimes entrepreneurs reach the point where they would like to take the bulk of their investment and gain out of the business but are not yet ready to cut the cord entirely. They may want to continue to run the business or at least retain a minority interest. There are several ways this can be accomplished.

FIGURE 19.2

Restructuring the Business

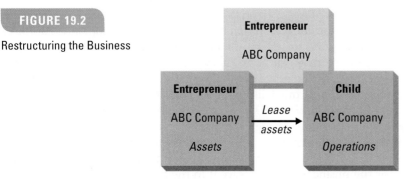

If the company is still privately owned, the remaining shareholders may want to purchase the entrepreneur's stock at current market rates so that control doesn't end up in other hands. In fact, the shareholders' agreement that was drafted when the entrepreneur set up the corporation may have specified that shareholders must offer the stock to the company before offering it to anyone else.

If the company is publicly traded, the task of selling the stock is much simpler; however, if the entrepreneur owns a substantial portion of the issued stock, strict guidelines set out by the SEC must be followed when liquidating the shareholders' interests. If the company had a successful IPO, founders' stock will have increased substantially in value, which presents a tax liability that should not be ignored. That is why many entrepreneurs in such situations cash out only what they need to support whatever goals they have. This strategy, of course, is based on the presumption that the company stock will continue its upward trend for the foreseeable future.

Entrepreneurs who want to cash out a significant portion of their investment and turn over the reins to a son, daughter, or other individual can do so by splitting the business into two firms, with the entrepreneur owning the firm that has all the assets (plant, equipment, vehicles) and the other person owning the operating aspect of the business while leasing the assets from the entrepreneur's company. See Figure 19.2.

A Phased Sale

Some entrepreneurs want to soften the emotional blow of selling the business, not to mention softening the tax consequences, by agreeing with the buyer—an individual or another firm—to sell in two phases. During the first phase, the entrepreneur sells a percentage of the company but remains in control of operations and can continue to grow the company to the point at which the buyer has agreed to complete the purchase. This approach gives the entrepreneur the ability to cash out a portion of his or her investment and still manage the business for an agreed-upon time, during which the new owner will probably be learning the business and phasing in. In the second phase, the business is sold at a prearranged price, usually a multiple of earnings.

This approach is fairly complex and should always be guided by an attorney experienced in acquisitions and buy-sell agreements. The buy-sell agreement, which spells out the terms of the purchase, specifies the amount of control the new owner can exert over the business before the sale has been completed and the amount of proprietary information that will be shared with the buyer between Phases 1 and 2.

In recent times, the consolidation play has become a way for many small business owners to realize the wealth they have created in their businesses. This is how it works. A large, established company finds a fragmented industry with a lot of mom-and-pop–type businesses. The consolidator buys them up and puts them under one umbrella to create economies of scale in the industry. The local management team often stays in power, while the parent company begins to build a national brand presence. The payoff for the entrepreneur comes when the consolidator takes the company public and buys out all the independent owners. It is important to conduct due diligence on any consolidator, because one's ability to cash out will be a function of the consolidator's ability to grow the company and take it public.

Dealing with Failure: Bankruptcy

Death is certainly part of any business life cycle, and, therefore, some entrepreneurs must exit their businesses through liquidation. For whatever reasons, the business could not manage a down sales cycle, find new sources of revenue, pay its obligations, or secure capital to float the business until conditions improved. Certainly no entrepreneur starts a high-growth venture with liquidation in mind as the exit strategy, but sometimes the forces working against the business are so great that the entrepreneur must have an exit vehicle so he or she can move on to do something else. What forces a corporation into bankruptcy is difficult to pinpoint. The immediately precipitating cause is the failure to pay debt; however, myriad other events contributed to that cause. They include a lack of understanding of economic and business cycles, excessive debt, surplus overhead, shifts in demand, excessive expenses, poor dividend policies, union problems, supplier problems, and poor financial management. Of course, the common denominator for all these factors is poor management.

Not all businesses can file for bankruptcy protection, however. Those that are exempt include savings and loan associations, banks, insurance companies, and foreign companies. Furthermore, a bankruptcy filing cannot occur where the intent has been to defraud, and a company may file only once every six years. The Bankruptcy Reform Act of 1978 and Public Law 95–958 provide for more than just liquidation of the business, so that businesses owners might be able to save their businesses through a process of restructuring. Therefore, it is important to have a clear understanding of the bankruptcy mechanisms available if the entrepreneur is faced with financial adversity. The bankruptcy code consists of several chapters, but two chapters are relevant to an entrepreneurial business: Chapter 7 discusses liquidation, and Chapter 11 is about reorganization of businesses.

CHAPTER 11

Chapter 11 reorganization under the bankruptcy code is really not a bankruptcy in the commonly used sense of the word. It is simply a reorganization of the finances of the business so that it can continue to operate and begin to pay its debts. Only in the case where the creditors believe the management is unable to carry out the terms of the reorganization plan is a trustee appointed to run the company until the debt has been repaid. Otherwise, the entrepreneur remains in control of the business while in a Chapter 11 position. If the entrepreneur has aggregate noncontingent liquidated secured and unsecured debts that do not exceed $2 million (11 U.S.C. Sec. §101 [51C]), then she or he qualifies to be considered a small business owner, which puts the case on a fast track and doesn't require a creditors' committee. After filing for reorganization, the entrepreneur and the creditors must meet within 30 days to discuss the status and organization of the business. The court then appoints a committee, which usually consists of the seven largest unsecured creditors, to develop a plan for the business with the entrepreneur. That plan must be submitted within 120 days, and acceptance of the plan must come within 60 days of submittal. Of the total number of creditors affected by the plan, representing at least two-thirds of the total dollar amount, at least one-half must accept the plan. Once the court has approved the reorganization plan, the entrepreneur is relieved of any debts except those specified in the plan.

CHAPTER 7

The filing of a petition under Chapter 7 of the bankruptcy code constitutes an Order for Relief and is usually chosen when the business does not have sufficient resources to pay creditors while continuing to operate. It is essentially the liquidation of the assets of the business and the discharge of most types of debt. The debtor files a petition and several required schedules of assets and liabilities with the bankruptcy court serving the area in which he or she lives. A trustee is appointed to manage the disposition of the business, and a meeting of the creditors is held 20 to 40 days after the petition is filed. The goal of the bankruptcy is to reduce the business to cash and distribute the cash to the creditors where authorized. After exemptions, the monies derived from liquidation go first to secured creditors and then to priority claimants, such as those owed wages, salaries, and contributions to employee benefit plans. Any surplus funds remaining after this distribution go to the entrepreneur. Prior to distribution, the entrepreneur has the right to certain exempt property. If the business is a corporation, those exemptions are minimal. They include interest in any accrued dividends up to a specified maximum; the right to social security benefits, unemployment compensation, public assistance, veterans' benefits, and disability benefits; and the right to stock bonuses, pensions, profit sharing, or a similar plan. Lest it seem as though the entrepreneur is at the mercy of the creditors in a bankruptcy situation, it should be made clear that in either type of bankruptcy petition, Chapter 7 or Chapter 11, the business owner has a great deal of power and control over the process. This power comes from the natural desire of the creditors for a quick and equitable resolution to the problem and from the protections inherent in the bankruptcy law. Often the creditors are better served by negotiating a restructuring of debt while the company is still operating and prior to Chapter 7 liquidation, where they are likely to receive a lesser portion of what is owed them, if anything. There are, however, certain things the entrepreneur will not be permitted to do within a certain period of time before the filing of a bankruptcy petition. These prohibited acts include hiding assets or liabilities, giving preferential treatment to certain creditors up to 90 days prior to the filing of the petition, and making any potentially fraudulent conveyances up to one year prior to the filing. Also the court may nullify any of these transactions during the bankruptcy proceedings.

Entrepreneurs can take advantage of a vehicle under Chapter 11 known as a "prepackaged bankruptcy." It requires an entrepreneur to present the creditors and equity owners with a reorganization plan before the bankruptcy filing actually goes to court. If an entrepreneur can achieve the required number of votes agreeing to the plan (more than half the total creditors and two-thirds within each class of creditors), the prepackaged plan can then go forward expeditiously. This process generally takes just four to nine months to complete, rather than the typical nine months to two years. An entrepreneur gains an obvious advantage from using this approach. Under the traditional Chapter 11 process, the creditors and everyone else learn of the company's problems only at the filing. With a prepackaged plan, by contrast, an approved plan is already in place at the point at which the public becomes aware of the problem, and the creditors thus may experience a greater sense of confidence in the entrepreneur. Moreover, the prepackaged plan ties up far less time in legal processes. For this approach to succeed, however, the statement of disclosure about the positive and negative aspects of the business must be carefully constructed to give the creditors all the information they need in order to consider the plan and protect their interests.

Before considering bankruptcy as an option to either exit a troubled business or restructure the business in an effort to survive, entrepreneurs should seek advice from an attorney and/or a specialist in turnarounds in the industry. Turnaround consultants are good at putting an unhealthy business on a diet; setting small, achievable goals; and making sure the business stays on track until its finances are in the black. Even when the business cannot be turned around, a bad situation can still be turned into a more positive one by heeding the following advice:

▶ Entrepreneurs should talk to other entrepreneurs who have been in a similar situation and listen carefully to what they learned.

▶ If the business is going to fail, end the business quickly before it affects an entrepreneur's personal life. The business may have failed, but the entrepreneur did not. A hard deadline should be set for when the business must be profitable or generate a positive cash flow; if it doesn't, the business should be closed. When the numbers don't add up, an entrepreneur should limit the time devoted to making the business work.

▶ Under no circumstances should a business owner commingle personal and business funds or other assets. If an entrepreneur lends money to the corporation, she or he will simply be another creditor in line to receive funds from the bankruptcy. And, in fact, the owner may be required to return any funds received in repayment of the loan during the year prior to filing of the bankruptcy petition.

▶ It is important not to ignore the government. The entrepreneur may risk personal assets and accrue a debt for life if he or she borrows funds from payroll-tax and sales-tax accounts.

▶ The entrepreneur should begin looking for opportunity. It is important not to wallow in failure. Sometimes the best opportunities are found when an entrepreneur is willing to leave a failing business behind.

▶ The entrepreneur should do whatever possible to pay back investors. Although it is true that they took a calculated risk investing in the business, if there is a way to pay them back—even if it takes a long time—they will respect the entrepreneur and be there when that next opportunity comes along.

In the end, for entrepreneurs, knowing how to harvest the wealth the business has created can help in structuring a growth plan that will get the entrepreneur where he or she wants to go. Preparing for the unexpected—contingency planning—will go a long way toward ensuring that the business stays on the path to achieving its goals.

SOME FINAL THOUGHTS

Entrepreneurship as a field of study has been in vogue for more than 30 years. There is hardly a media source today that does not talk about entrepreneurs. In fact, the term is in real danger of becoming a cliché and losing its value because it is used to describe all kinds of ventures, from the small "mom-and-pop" to the Fortune 500 conglomerate. This book has focused on the birth and early growth of innovative, growth-oriented new ventures and has used a classic definition of the term *entrepreneurship:* the discovery, evaluation, and exploitation of opportunities that are innovative, growth oriented, and that create new value. These ventures face unique opportunities and challenges, but their relatively small size and lean structure also make them particularly adaptable to a rapidly changing environment. They are the source of breakthrough innovation, economic growth, and job creation. Entrepreneurial ventures and the entrepreneurs who start them stand out from the crowd—they are the essence of new venture creation. But entrepreneurship is more than just new venture creation; it is a mindset, a set of attitudes, and a skill set that can be learned. Adopting an entrepreneurial mindset is valuable for corporate venturers, small business owners, and those who want to take charge of their lives and differentiate themselves so they can realize their dreams. In that sense, entrepreneurship is for everyone who wants to experience the freedom and independence that come from knowing that opportunities and the resources to make those opportunities a reality are within their grasp.

> New Venture Checklist
>
> Have you:
>
> ☐ Identified the issues that could affect the business at various points in the future?
>
> ☐ Developed a contingency plan for all the various scenarios that may affect the business in the future?
>
> ☐ Determined goals for the business relative to an exit strategy?

Issues to Consider

1. Contingency planning is not foolproof. How can an entrepreneur ensure that the contingency plans he or she has devised will keep the business on the path to its goals?
2. How can the entrepreneur prepare for potential product liability litigation, both to minimize the chance that such lawsuits will be brought and to give the company the best chance of prevailing against a product liability claim?
3. How can an entrepreneur prepare for a potential decline in sales?
4. Suppose an entrepreneur has built a successful business over several years and now has the opportunity to start another business compatible with the current one. How can the entrepreneur leave the original business and yet stay involved in it?
5. If an entrepreneur's business finds itself in trouble, what are the options available to the entrepreneur to attempt to remedy the situation?

Experiencing Entrepreneurship

1. Interview an entrepreneur in an industry of your choice to learn what his or her harvest strategy is. What is this entrepreneur doing to ensure that the harvest strategy will be achieved?

2. Interview a turnaround consultant about some ways to recognize problems that could lead to business failure. From this interview, devise a list of do's and don'ts that will help an entrepreneur avoid business failure.

Relevant Case Studies

CASE STUDIES

OVERNITE EXPRESS

The overnight-delivery parcel industry is an integral part of today's fast-paced economy. As our "instant gratification" society moves forward, the importance of being able to ship and receive documents and packages in a dependable and timely manner can make or break a crucial business deal. The biggest players in this very important industry are United Parcel Service (UPS), Federal Express (FedEx), and the U.S. Postal Service. These companies offer next-day delivery to many parts of the country.

Background

Rob Ukropina graduated from the University of Southern California in 1976. Upon graduation, Ukropina began a two-year stint in the restaurant business working for the Velvet Turtle in a management capacity. In 1977, he turned his focus to the commercial printing industry while getting his feet wet as a salesman at Welsh Graphics in Pasadena. Ukropina spent the next two years at Welsh before going to work for Jeffries Banknotes Company in 1979. Jeffries specialized in financial printing such as prospectuses and stock certificates. It was during this period that he began laying the foundation of his network. Through his sales and managerial duties, Ukropina made numerous contacts with financial institutions and law firms that would serve him well in the future.

In 1983, Ukropina took a position at Pandick Printing, the largest financial printer in the United States.

This case was originally written by Matthew Benson, MBA University of Southern California, as a basis for class discussion rather than to illustrate either effective or ineffective handling of a business situation. It has been updated by Kathleen Allen. Reprinted by permission.

At the age of 30, he became a division president and ran the Orange County division from 1983 to 1989. Although he was successful at his job—his gross income in 1989 was $300,000—Ukropina found himself bored working for a large company and wanted to do something on his own. His first venture was to start a leasing company in which he served as the director of sales, marketing, and operations, while his partner put up the financial backing to support the endeavor. The company leased small equipment to businesses and also financed small businesses. In addition to the leasing company, Ukropina ventured into the publishing business and started his own magazine, *Business for Sale*. The publication served as an *Auto Trader* of sorts for buying and selling small businesses.

In order to give his businesses the best possible chance to survive, Ukropina did not draw a salary for himself from 1989 to 1992. Everything he made he reinvested into the business. Unfortunately, due to many external factors (i.e., recession and a nonsupportive partner), Ukropina watched his net worth fall from $1.6 million in 1989 to zero in 1992. His family moved from their spacious 3,000-square-foot home in Newport Beach to a 1,000-square-foot apartment. In 1991, his wife went back to work to help the family afford food and clothing (her entrepreneurial success in later years is equally impressive, but that is another story).

The Opportunity

There was little question that Ukropina would eventually run his own company again. He had been brought up in an entrepreneurial family, with his parents owning their own company. In addition to his own family, his in-laws were prominent entrepreneurs in the fields of engineering and real estate. Their influence would eventually entice his wife, Joyce, to start a successful company in advertising. Once he hit rock bottom in 1992, Ukropina decided to explore opportunities that he had uncovered in his past. Throughout Ukropina's career in the printing business, he had had to deal with trying to make his bottom-line cost numbers by dealing with distribution. While at Pandick, Ukropina was quoted in the February 1999 issue of *Traffic World:*

> It was a 24-hour, seven-day-a-week business where 25% of our bills came from distribution costs. To get documents printed and delivered for public offerings on time, the company would routinely spend $30,000 for pick-ups after 5 p.m. and some $5 million a year on Next Flight Out courier services. We're talking about spending $1,100 per five-pound package to deliver documents nationwide, because what's $1,100 when you have a $110 million public offering that needs to be filed on time with the Securities and Exchange Commission?

He believed he could drastically cut those expenses if Pandick distributed on a regional, rather than strictly national, pattern. Ukropina's entire motivation was based on providing superior and less-costly service to his customers. He determined that UPS and FedEx did not deliver 3 percent of their packages due to sorting or having the wrong address. They also stop pickups at 7:00 p.m., even though many businesses work much later into the evening trying to make deadlines. For many of these businesses, the only alternative is to use a ground messenger at a rate of $1 per mile.

Ukropina saw that there was an opportunity to fill a niche as a regional delivery service that was small enough to make corrections in mid-shipment if there were any logistics problems. If a package had been addressed incorrectly, the driver would be able to call in and get proper directions for the destination. The larger companies would simply take it back to the hub and try to redeliver it the next day. There was definitely an opportunity to compete with the big boys in the terms of flexible pick-up times, quality, and service, something Ukropina took a lot of pride in.

From Opportunity to Business

The first thing that Ukropina did was to put together a five-year business plan in early 1992. Drawing from the experience of his failed leasing company and magazine, he knew that he needed a quality advisory board to help him start the company and invest in his idea. He did not look to load his board with a bunch of buddies but started calling on the business contacts he had made throughout his years in sales. Early members on the advisory board included a CEO of a health care network, an airline executive, and an executive from Peat Marwick.

In order to attract investors, he offered 10 percent of Overnite Express for $150,000 and quickly brought the net worth of the company to $1.1 million. To get his first customers, Ukropina used a network of "friends." He called on all the law firms that he had done printing for in the past and explained what he was doing. He asked them if he could put an Overnite Express drop box in their offices and promised unparalleled service if they would use it. Because they had known Ukropina for his service in the printing business, many of them agreed to take a chance on him. With no established delivery system in place, Overnite would pick up the packages in the drop boxes and subcontract a route courier service to deliver them to their destinations in an area that extended from Santa Barbara to the Mexican border. Ukropina claimed to have many a sleepless night in the beginning and kept his fingers crossed, praying that there would not be any problems. Luckily, everything went well and Overnite was able to start delivering on its own.

Nine months into the venture, Overnite Express had exhausted the original capital investment, and Ukropina took on a partner, Doug Schneider. Together they managed to raise another $400,000 and in a year acquired another $100,000 through SBA financing. Also, through his trials and tribulations, Ukropina never allowed his credit to be adversely affected. In year three of business operations, Overnite Express secured a $300,000 receivable line of credit.

As Ukropina had learned from his other jobs, the only way to maintain a high level of quality is to ensure that the people who work for you are happy and enjoy what they do. He used his entrepreneur philosophy in putting together an incentive plan that would allow him to keep good employees from becoming complacent, or worse, leaving the company. Everyone in the company, including Ukropina, is paid a permanently fixed salary. In addition to that, everyone is paid a percentage of the gross profits, along with an incentivised bonus structure that is based on the number of packages delivered and the time they are delivered. For example, a driver can make more money by delivering the majority of his packages before 9:00 a.m. than he can if he delivers them by 11:00 a.m.; he makes even less if packages are delivered by 4:00 p.m. Thus, everyone in the company is an entrepreneur in his or her own right. Ukropina attributes the fact that very few, if any, employees ever leave to the entrepreneur spirit that thrives throughout the company.

Growing the Company

For 15 years, Overnite Express has flourished in the regional Southern California market in which it operates. After constant pressure from clients to expand its delivery area to include Northern California, Ukropina performed a feasibility study to establish the profitability of such a venture. It turned out that many of Overnite's existing clients would choose a national courier if they had more than one package going out and did not know whether Overnite delivered north of Bakersfield. Regardless of cost, it was less trouble to make one call instead of two. As Ukropina was quoted in the April 20, 2000, issue of *Orange County Metro:*

> Many of our customers ship most of their packages inside California. By expanding, we have made it easier for the customer. If it is easier for the customer it is a good business decision. . . . Now they don't have to think, since I have one package going to San Diego and another going to San Jose, I guess I will use FedEx for both. Now they can use us for both. Now it's simple—if you are shipping inside California, use Overnite Express.

Ukropina expected to get 28 percent more business by moving into Northern California and, at the same time, expand the Southern California business by 30 percent. In May 2000, he borrowed $200,000 to finance the expansion and estimated the break-even point to be approximately six months. To his pleasure, and his surprise, the venture broke even in 60 days. Not only did Overnite Express get more packages from Northern California, but it also starting getting more shipping deals from existing customers because they could define the delivery area more clearly—it was an easier decision to just stick with Overnite for all their express needs. Still, developing the northern region went slowly because Overnite did not enjoy the brand recognition that it had in Southern California.

Ukropina continued to expand the company's sales and marketing efforts. He acquired two airplanes to help service the Northern California region. Oakland is now the Northern California hub, while Irvine is the Southern California hub. It is surprising, but 99 percent of Overnite's clients are previous FedEx users, generally in the professions: lawyers, advertising, and title companies. Its competitors are California Overnite, based in Phoenix, and Golden State, based in Alameda, California. Despite serious competition, Overnite has the highest average tariff in the industry, at $14.25, because of the quality of its service. Early on, Ukropina recognized the importance of investing in technology to remain competitive. Overnite's tracking technology sends an e-mail confirmation of delivery to both the sender and the recipient. Its computer lets Overnite know whether a package is in danger of not making it on time to the customer. If the driver has not recorded the delivery 10 minutes before it is due, a message is sent to headquarters and the client is called. In the overnight industry, the primary reason for delays is a minor address discrepancy. It is also the primary reason why packages never get delivered. FedEx and UPS have delivery completion rates of about 97 percent; Overnite Express's completion rate is 99.9 percent because they take the time to figure out what is wrong. Its on-time rate is 99.2 percent, comparable or better than FedEx and UPS. Not bad for a company that ships one million pieces a year and makes 5,000 deliveries a day with 1,000 drop boxes and 110 delivery vehicles.

From 1998 to the present, the company has been growing at 25 to 30 percent a year, due to a high level of client referral and excellent customer care. Ukropina has added more sales and marketing staff and is doing more direct mail. He is now looking at expanding the company's scope.

The Future

When asked what he felt his future held, Ukropina had to take a minute to answer. Then he had to qualify his answer by categorizing his future in terms of Overnite Express, his career, and his family. The growth strategy for Overnite Express is simple. He wants it to grow only in terms of being able to provide the greatest service to his clients. If the business warrants, the company will expand its operations as much as needed to maintain the current level of excellence. However, because of the niche that he enjoys and because his is the only delivery company that can boast 100 percent delivery rates while servicing only the state of California, he does not foresee the company expanding to a national level. As Ukropina likes to say, "We plan to stay humble and continue to operate below the radar screen of UPS and FedEx. The reality is that we have to offer better service here in California in order to compete with FedEx and UPS." Nevertheless, by 2007, he had expanded the business into Arizona, Nevada, and Mexico, with more than 1,200 drop boxes.

To date, Overnite Express has been in the express guaranteed-overnight service delivering primarily documents, but it is faced with a challenge going forward. As business moves rapidly toward a dependence on electronic data, document shipping will likely slow. Therefore, Ukropina is looking at ground product services with smaller packages and reliance on trucks. To give his company a competitive advantage in that market, in 2003, he built a $6 million, 50,000-square-foot building, which serves as the main sorting facility. There he and his team developed the first "humanless" sorting system. A conveyor belt separates packages, scans and weighs them, and sends them to their ultimate delivery route. During the process, if a package falls off the belt or gets misplaced, the system stops and alerts the operator. This innovation has increased Overnite's throughput four times over. It was cost-effective the first day and eliminated the need for ten hand sorters. Curiously, industry giant FedEx still sorts packages by hand. Ukropina did not suffer the drop in cash flow faced by many entrepreneurs when expanding their businesses. The savings from the new sorting system and from ownership of the building helped to maintain cash flows on an even keel.

Overnite is merely a blip on the radar screen of UPS, which enjoys more than $75 billion in sales annually, and Ukropina likes that. He is able to provide service in a niche market where the larger companies do not feel the need to compete. As for his career, Ukropina considers himself a "builder" rather than a "maintainer." As long as the challenges are present to keep him motivated, he will stay with Overnite. The minute he feels that the company has grown to its potential, he will gladly step aside and move on to a new endeavor. So he must also position himself and the company for the time when he might take on a new challenge. There are many ways to exit a business either in part or completely. Ukropina wonders how he should prepare for that eventuality.

Discussion Questions

1. How did Ukropina obtain his first customer and what did that tell him about his business?
2. What is Overnite's competitive advantage in an industry dominated by companies like Federal Express?
3. With the obvious move toward more electronic data transfer, what new sources of revenues should Ukropina consider developing?
4. Is it a wise decision to limit the company to California? Why, or why not?
5. What is Ukropina's growth strategy?

CRAIGSLIST: IT'S ABOUT HELPING OTHERS

Craig Newmark would have fit in perfectly in the 1980s Generation X movie *Revenge of the Nerds,* which is about a group of super bright, but socially inept, young college students who succeed despite being constantly ridiculed by the stereotypical popular set—the football players and cheerleaders. Newmark grew up a nerd and is proud to still be considered a nerd today at 51 years of age. An introvert who describes himself as "academically intelligent and . . . socially retarded," Newmark has surprised everyone with the enormous success of his very hip website Craigslist.org. It's the place where a 24-year-old law student like Kit-Ling Mui, living in West Covina, California, can find an apartment, sell her parents' car, adopt a cat, and even meet her boyfriend. But Craigslist can do more. When 67-year-old Leonard Becker needed a kidney transplant, he decided not to wait for his number to come up on a donor list. Instead, he posted his need on Craigslist, and soon an office manager from nearby Albany, New York, responded, offering her kidney and saving his life.

In fact, the site has become a phenomenon with more than 5 million postings per month. Nielsen/NetRatings reports that Craigslist is ranked in the Top 20 of all U.S. portals, up there with Yahoo!, MSN, and AOL. By itself, this would be surprising, but when you add to it the fact that Craigslist has no sales force, does no advertising, and is visually as sterile as you can make a website, it is a stunning success. Forrester Research calls Craigslist the "most efficient job recruiting site" available, outranking multimillion-dollar companies like Monster.com and Careerbuilder.com.

The Early Years

Newmark grew up in a working-class family in Morristown, New Jersey. After losing his father to lung cancer when he was 13 years old, Newmark and his younger brother were raised by their mother, who was a bookkeeper. At age 18, he entered Case Western Reserve University in Cleveland, Ohio, where he earned bachelor's and master's degrees in computer science. Following a 17-year stint at IBM as a software programmer, he went to work in computer security at Charles Schwab in 1993, and the rest, as they say, is history. While at Schwab, he met Darek Milewski, who introduced him to the Web, which at that time was in its earliest stages. Newmark immediately saw the potential for people to communicate.

In 1995, he left Schwab to become an independent contractor to companies like Sun Microsystems and Bank of America. At that time, there were a lot of people looking for technology jobs, so Newmark began sending e-mails to the people he knew in the area to advise them of art and technology parties at a local art house, the Anon Salon. The e-mails' scope included tidbits about San Francisco culture, and recipients began adding their acquaintances to the e-mail list. By the middle of 1995, Newmark's e-mail distribution list had grown to more than 240 members. It was soon time to post the newsletter on the newly emerging Internet. At first he planned to call the site "San Francisco Events," but because his devoted followers had dubbed it "Craig's List," he decided to use that instead.

The Company Philosophy and Business Model

Located in San Francisco's Inner Sunset neighborhood among coffee shops and restaurants, Craigslist is basically, according to Newmark, a classified ads business. Craigslist makes money from one revenue source. Employers pay $75 a month to list job openings on the site in San Francisco ($25 per ad in New York, Los Angeles, San Diego, Boston, Seattle, and Washington, DC) while users pay nothing. For those employers who subscribe, Craigslist has been a win-win. In particular, casting directors for reality TV shows love the site and often are able to staff an entire production from the respondents to the job offerings on Craigslist. That revenue source supports a staff of 24 as of 2007.

Despite the mundane nature of the business, people who use Craigslist feel connected, and so it has become much more than just a classified ads site. Craigslist is a for-profit business that keeps its financial information private. In 2004, *Fortune* magazine reported that the company generates about $7 million a year, with Newmark taking a salary in the $200,000 range. By 2007, Craigslist watchers were estimating that the company was generating $10 to $12 million in annual revenue. Newmark will not comment on these reports but does reveal that his income allows him to contribute to more than 50 charitable and nonprofit organizations in the San Francisco area. Newmark's philosophy revolves around what he calls "nerd values," which are making "enough for a comfortable living, at which point you do something fun like changing the world." According to Newmark, the only way to change the world is to do the "mundane stuff everyday." His company is about helping people, and his business model is a testament to that belief.

This social responsibility ethic carries over into his personal life as well. He lives in a small flat in a 1908 Edwardian-style building near his office; when he first moved in, it did not have Internet access. He installed a wireless access point on the roof of this building to provide not only his own wireless Internet access needs but those of the entire neighborhood as well. Newmark also serves on the boards of several nonprofit organizations and sponsors many activities for writers. In 2000, the company formed Craigslist Foundation, which provides knowledge, resources, and the visibility they need to raise capital. For example, the foundation sponsors a wish list for teachers that serves as a conduit for them to get their wishes fulfilled by local businesses.

The Growth of Craigslist

Newmark could have easily chosen the route of other Internet businesses by taking one of the many buyout options that have come his way, which would have made him a multimillionaire. But it's not about the money for Newmark; it's about giving someone a break. Therefore, Craigslist has grown, for the most part, by word of mouth, users who wanted others to know that Craigslist was the best resource around. As of November 2006, it was serving more than 450 cities in 50 countries and was the 7th ranked site on the Internet in the United States. Even the technology that supports Craigslist reflects Newmark's "nerd values." The company runs open-source software on generic PC servers using such open-source brands as Linux, Apache, qMail, and Squid cache. Also, true to his philosophy, Newmark even turned down an offer by Microsoft Sidewalk to run banner ads on his site, something that would have brought a lot of money to the company.

Newmark spends about 40 hours a week dealing with issues related to the site—scams, community problems, and anything else that customers toss his way. Since he's an engineer, customer service is not what he's most comfortable doing, so he's determined to spend time on it. In fact, he is actually obsessed with customer service. His mantra is "ask for feedback, read all feedback and summarize, do something in response, and repeat."

Recognizing that he was not the right person to lead the organization as it grew (most entrepreneurs are not), Newmark promoted Jim Buckmaster from his position as CTO and lead programmer to CEO. Both firmly believe that the source of innovation and change in their company must be customers and employees. Craigslist has grown to the point where it is now getting the attention of major newspapers that see it as a threat to their classifieds. Craigslist is pulling recruitment dollars from them with its simple text postings, while the newspapers, along with on-line competitors like Monster.com, continue to add features that make their sites more complex and harder to sort through. Newmark's keep-it-simple philosophy seems to be working—so well, in fact, that The Washington Post Company and Knight Ridder invested in a social networking site, Tribe.net, that includes listings much like those on Craigslist. So far, however, most social networks are not making money while the noncommercial Craigslist is, and without doing any advertising. What makes Craigslist a success is the culture of trust it has built; when something goes wrong, the company fixes it. Time will tell if these competitors survive. According to Newmark, they are not usually around for the long term. They are usually built to attract a lot of traffic and then get sold. In addition, their lack of community service is apparent to users. Because Newmark believes in "putting the *free* in free markets," *Inc. Magazine* voted him one of the 26 most fascinating entrepreneurs. Craigslist's success is often attributed to three factors: (1) their culture of trust, which is achieved by regularly responding to user e-mails, not making site changes without consulting users, not focusing on the money, and employing users to filter inappropriate or miscategorized content; (2) emphasizing the social aspects of the site; and (3) creating a site that's easy to use.

In 2004, reverse-auction giant eBay acquired 25 percent of Craigslist from a trusted stakeholder who was an employee. As a minority stakeholder, eBay will have limited ability to affect the direction of the company. However, this is not the first attempt by Silicon Valley companies to court Craigslist, primarily because of the success of its online classified-advertising market. eBay has made it clear that it will not attempt to change the mission of Craigslist. Many in the industry wonder how long Newmark can hold out before selling out for potentially a billion dollars or more. Will the lure of riches sway the nerd away from his mission?

Sources: "26 Most Fascinating Entrepreneurs." *Inc. Magazine* (2005), http://www.inc.com; Wingfield, N. (August 13, 2004). "eBay Buys Stake in Craigslist." *Wall Street Journal*, http://www.wsj.com; Davidson, I. (June 13, 2004). "The Craigslist Phenomenon." *Los Angeles Times Magazine;* Glaser, M. (June 3, 2004). "Nerd Values Help Propel Tiny Craigslist into Classifieds Threat." *USC Annenberg Online Journalism Review*, http://ojr.org/ojr/business; Mara, J. (August 21, 2000). "List Man—Craig Newmark—Founder of Craigslist.org." *Brandweek,* http://www.findarticles .com; King, C., (October 8, 2003),"Craig Newmark: Geek Chic? Screw It, I'm a Nerd." Sun Developer Network, http://developers.sun.com/toolkits/articles/ Newmark.html, accessed July 5, 2004.

Discussion Questions

1. What was the innovation behind the Craigslist concept?
2. What are Craigslist's competitive advantages?
3. Evaluate the challenges facing Craigslist as it grows globally. How can it overcome those challenges?
4. If you were Craig Newmark, would you sell the company? Why or why not?

A-1 LANES AND THE CURRENCY CRISIS OF THE EAST ASIAN TIGERS

On July 2, 1997, Rick Baker, the president and founder of A-1 Lanes (a manufacturer and an international supplier of wood and synthetic bowling lanes) was having his morning coffee when he was devastated to learn that Thailand had devalued its currency, the baht, by 11 percent. Baker had an uneasy feeling that there would be a domino effect across all countries in Asia because their economies were interrelated. If that happened, Baker wondered, how would it affect the future of his company?

Baker realized that the company faced several critical issues. First, 80 percent of A-1's sales were derived from countries in and around the Asian Pacific Rim. Second, the company had more than $1 million in accounts receivable from this region. Third, in 1996 the company had taken out a loan for $500,000 on a new manufacturing facility to capitalize on the popularity and growth of bowling centers in Korea, China, and Taiwan.

The combination of these issues in conjunction with the cutthroat competition within the bowling equipment industry placed Baker in a position to make a critical decision about the future of his company.

This case was written by Phil E. Stetz, Lavoy Moore Entrepreneurship Professor, Dept. of Management, Marketing, and International Business; Todd A. Finkle, Director, Fitzgerald Institute for Entrepreneurial Studies, The University of Akron; Larry R. O'Neil, Dept. of Management, Marketing, and International Business; Stephen F. Austin State University, Nelson Rusche College of Business, Nacogdoches, Texas 75962, (936) 468-4103. Please direct all correspondence to Dr. Phil Stetz at pstetz@sfasu.edu. This case is intended to stimulate class discussion rather than to illustrate the effective or ineffective handling of a managerial situation. The company, names, events, and financials are all real. Copyright © 2006 All Rights Reserved for Phil Stetz. Reprinted with permission.

He had narrowed his decision to three options: (1) liquidate his company, (2) sell the company, or (3) stay in business and try to weather the impending storm.

Company Background

In 1985, Baker and two investors founded A-1 Lanes in a chicken house and barn in Rusk, Texas. The company's main products were high-grade wood and technologically advanced synthetic bowling lanes for domestic and international markets. According to Baker, "The key to our success is the quality of the wood and the advanced synthetic design of our bowling lanes, supported with responsive service, operational efficiencies, and proven accomplishments at penetrating international markets."

Although the company began with high expectations, A-1 Lanes quickly discovered that locally owned bowling centers across the United States did not have the financial resources to replace existing lanes. Instead, owners would simply sand the lanes. To complicate matters, competitors within the industry developed a synthetic overlay for existing lanes. For example, Brunswick developed a cost-effective way of refurbishing worn and damaged wood lanes that prolonged their service life by as much as 10 years. Rather than tearing out and replacing existing lanes, bowling centers could sand them down and overlay the wood with a synthetic resin, thereby restoring the old lanes to industry standards.

Because of the weakened demand for wood replacement of bowling lanes, A-1 began to concentrate on new bowling lane sales in international markets. According to Baker, "We pursued international markets because the margins were better, receivables were more reliable, and the additional volume meant a healthier bottom line." As a result, A-1 grew and moved operations into a vacant 34,000-square-foot metal building in 1987.

In the same year, A-1 Lanes began to establish relationships with distributors in other parts of the world (e.g., Mendes, a Canadian marketer of bowling lanes). In 1988, Baker and his investors forged a partnership with a company called Dacos, an established distributor of bowling equipment and accessories that was based in Europe and Korea. With a source for U.S.-manufactured lanes, Dacos could offer a complete turnkey package to bowling center owners and developers all over the world. In turn, the arrangement enabled A-1 to compete directly with the largest firms in the industry, Brunswick and American Machine Foundry (AMF). It also gave A-1 an advantage over smaller competitors in the United States because those firms lacked similar distribution channels and presence in Europe and Asia.

The Bowling Industry

When they found pins in a child's tomb, archeologists discovered that bowling dates back to ancient Egypt. The sport expanded into Europe in the early 1900s, but its popularity in the United States did not thrive until after World War II. In the 1950s, television embraced bowling, and the automatic pin spotter was invented. The game grew dramatically in the United States and eventually peaked in the 1960s. New markets emerged in Australia and Mexico, as well as in other Latin American countries. By the mid-1970s, the bowling boom had spread into Japan. Russia followed suit by opening its first bowling center in 1976. Interest in bowling also grew in China. The bowling boom spread into Thailand and the Asian Pacific regions during the early 1990s.

By the 1990s, bowling supported two main industries. One was the ownership and operation of bowling centers; the other was the manufacture of bowling equipment used in bowling centers or by bowlers. These manufactured items included automatic pin spotters, computerized automatic scoring systems, wood and synthetic bowling lanes, lane maintenance systems, masking panes, ball returns, seating, bumper bowling systems, replacement and maintenance parts, and operating supplies such as spare parts, pins, lane oils, bowling balls, bowling shoes, and other bowling accessories.

In 1996, estimates were that more than 100 million people in more than 90 countries bowled at least one game a year and that bowlers in the United States spent approximately $4 billion annually on lane fees, equipment and supplies, uniforms, and food and beverage purchased within bowling centers.[1] More than 53 million Americans patronized the country's bowling centers every year, making tenpin bowling the number one indoor participation sport in the United States.[2]

The Bowling Industry in the United States

During bowling's peak years in the 1960s and early 1970s, bowling centers were being constructed almost overnight across the country. During the early- to mid-1970s, white American blue-collar workers (the primary clientele of the bowling industry) moved to the suburbs, away from the city neighborhoods where most of the bowling centers had been built. Bowling began to open facilities in the suburbs while maintaining their existing centers in the cities. This strategy was not successful due to the lifestyle changes of the blue-collar workers.[3] They were simply less interested in bowling than they had been.[4]

As a result, the new suburban bowling centers were not as successful, while existing bowling centers in the cities became only marginally profitable. The number of bowling centers gradually declined, but the number of lanes increased due to the construction of large new centers and the remodeling of surviving ones.[5] Exhibit 1 shows the historical relationship between the number of centers, lanes, and population in the United States.[6]

[1]Chuck Pezzano. "The Push Is On for Olympic Status." *The Record* (New Jersey), Sports (January 7, 1996), p. S17.

[2]"AMF Bowling Looks to Equity Markets. Going Public." *The IPO Reporter* (September 1, 1997). Securities Data Publishing.

[3]Cindy Stooksbury. "Bowling Boasts Lengthy History as Popular Pastime." *Amusement Business* (May 1998), p. 20.

[4]"Bowling Centers." *Encyclopedia of American Industries* (2001), p. 2.

[5]Nancy King. "Bowling Must Learn by Its Mistakes." *The Ledger* (Lakeland, Florida), Sports (July 20, 1997), p. C2.

[6]From A-1 Lanes company literature.

EXHIBIT 1

U.S. Bowling Centers,
1955–1995

				Population	
Year	Centers	Lanes	Lanes per Center	Total (000)	Per Center
1955	7,062	60,648	8.6	165,275	23,403
1965	11,363	165,601	14.5	193,460	17,025
1975	8,974	144,829	16.1	215,973	24,046
1985	8,629	159,394	18.5	237,950	27,575
1995	7,331	144,187	19.7	262,755	35,841

Source: A-1 Lanes company literature.

EXHIBIT 2

Operators of U.S. Bowling
Centers in 1997

Operator	Number of Bowling Centers	Percent of Total
AMF	370	6.3
Brunswick	111	1.9
Bowl America	23	0.4
Active West	16	0.3
Mark Voight	16	0.3
Bowl New England	15	0.2
Subtotal:	551	9.4
Single-Center and Small-Chain operators	5,302	90.6
Total	5,853	100.0%

Source: AMF Bowling Worldwide Inc. (1997). Annual Report: 10(k), period ending December 31.
Accession #: 0000916641-98-000297.

In response to the decreasing popularity of bowling, many bowling operators started differentiating their image by renovating their alleys into entertainment centers in the early 1990s.[7] Their strategy was to market to families with children and teenagers by offering child care, video games, laser lights, light-weight neon-glowing bowling balls, and fog machines. They also devised bumper bowling, in which gutters are filled with plastic tubes to keep the balls on the lane. This strategy proved to be profitable and operators were able to restore their revenues to the levels of the 1960s.[8]

Many analysts thought operators had created a "double-edged sword" by pampering one market segment and alienating another. The upgraded facilities with flashy, loud, and modern atmospheres were the opposite of the dark, quiet, smoky lanes to which league bowlers were accustomed. Evidence indicated that league bowlers, a steady source of revenue for bowling centers, further dwindled due to these changes.[9] A league bowler commented, "The centers have all of these great gimmicks and are giving financial breaks to families and people that really do not bowl that much. Meanwhile, they're raising the prices for league bowlers, the true loyal customers, and driving them away."[10]

The U.S. bowling center industry (see Exhibit 2) was highly fragmented. The top eight operators, including AMF, accounted for less than 10 percent of U.S. bowling centers. The two largest, AMF and Brunswick Corporation ("Brunswick") owned approximately 370 and 111 U.S. bowling centers,

[7]Sandy Hansell. Overview of the Bowling Industry, http://www.ltfun.com/documents/hansell_article.pdf, accessed January 7, 2006.

[8]Marla Matzer. "Bowling for Dollars." *Brandweek* (August 1996), p. 18.

[9]Sandy Hansell. "A Double-Edged Sword." *International Bowling Industry* (July 1998), p. 37.

[10]Ian P. Murphy. "Bowling Industry Rolls Out Unified Marketing Plan." *Sports Marketing* (January 1997), p. 2.

EXHIBIT 3	Major Competitors in the Bowling Equipment Industry in 1997

Company Name	Product Line	Total Employees	Estimated Sales ($M)	Headquarters
Brunswick Corp.	Bowling equipment[a]	1,000	$350.0	Lake Forest, IL
AMF	Bowling equipment[a]	635	$250.0	Richmond, VA
Heddon Bowling Corporation	Synthetic lanes	50	$ 40.0	Tampa, FL
Hodge Lumber Company	Wood lanes	40	$ 30.0	New Knoxville, OH
Mendes	Synthetic lanes	40	$ 30.0	Quebec City, Canada
Murrey International	Synthetic lanes	35	$ 30.0	Los Angeles, CA
A-1 Lanes	Wood and synthetic lanes	35	$ 12.5	Rusk, TX

[a]Equipment includes bowling lanes, automatic pinsetters, ball returns, computerized scoring equipment, business systems, and other industrial equipment and supplies sold to bowling centers in addition to resale products, such as bowling balls, bags, shoes, and other bowlers' aids, sold primarily through pro shops.
Source: From A-1 Lanes; 1997 company estimates.

respectively.[11] Four medium-sized chains together accounted for 70 bowling centers. Over 5,300 bowling centers were owned by single-center and small-chain operators, which typically owned four or fewer centers.

By 1997, the U.S. bowling center industry was considered mature and was characterized by a continual contraction in the number of bowling centers. Nevertheless, the decreasing lineage (games per lane per day) was offset by an increasing average price per game and by revenue from ancillary sources. Bowling centers derived their revenues from bowling (60.2%), food and beverage (25.4%),[12] and other sources such as rentals, amusement games, billiards, and pro shops (14.4%).[13]

According to the 1997 Economic Census, 619 establishments existed with 17,109 employees in the hardwood dimension and flooring mills classification (NAICS 321912).[14] However, there were few companies in the bowling lane and equipment supply business (see Exhibit 3).[15] Some of the

competitors manufactured a broad range of products; others produced only a specific line of equipment. All competitors were active in both the domestic and international markets.

Foreign-based competition in the bowling lane manufacturing industry was almost nonexistent due to the lack of key raw materials. For example, lane construction required the use of specific types and grades of maple and pine. The necessary maple is found only in the United States, and the preferred southern yellow pine is found only in the southeastern region of the United States. Furthermore, Asian bowling operators showed little interest in purchasing bowling lanes or other bowling products and accessories manufactured outside the United States. They considered bowling an American sport and the equipment had to be manufactured there.

Bowling in Asia

In the late 1980s, because of the saturation of bowling lane markets in the United States and Europe, Brunswick and AMF began to expand into the Asian Pacific Rim by developing bowling centers throughout the region. The pivotal event that triggered Asian interest was the inclusion of bowling as a trial event in the 1988 Olympics in Seoul, South Korea.[16] After the Olympics, a bowling boom began in East Asia.

[11]AMF Bowling Worldwide Inc. (1997). Annual Report: 10-K, period ending December 31. Accession #: 0000916641-98-000297.

[12]Food and beverage includes bar sales. On average, bar sales would account for 55 percent of these sales.

[13]Op. cit., Ian P. Murphy, 1997.

[14]1997 Economic Census: Bridge Between NAICS and SIC Manufacturing, http://www.census.gov/epcd/ec97brdg/E97B1321 .HTM#321918, accessed August 25, 2004.

[15]From A-1 Lanes 1997 company estimates.

[16]Marc Cooper. "On the Shining Paths of Tenpin." *The Nation*, Vol. 267 (August 10, 1998), p. 35.

EXHIBIT 4

Selected Markets in the
International Bowling
Industry in 1997

Country	Centers	Lanes	Lanes per Center	Population	
				Total (000)	Per Lane
Japan	1,123	32,200	29	125,000	3,900
Korea	1,104	16,300	15	45,350	2,800
Taiwan	370	11,567	31	21,120	1,800
U.K.	210	4,400	21	58,160	12,900

The population per lane is an industry statistic that enables a bowling lane distributor to get an idea of how many customers per lane there are per city or area. This is a better statistic than "bowling centers" because it gives an idea of literally how many people can actually bowl and a good indication of a saturation point for bowling centers in a given area.

Source: From A-1 Lanes company literature.

U.S. bowling exports increased by 27 percent from 1988 through 1993, and sales to China accounted for almost one-third of sales. It was estimated that there were approximately 15,000 lanes in China, and most industry analysts expected this demand to blossom into a market of 100,000+ lanes. With a population of 1.3 billion, 100,000 lanes would amount to approximately one lane per 13,000 people, much lower than the U.S. rate of one lane per 1,800 people. Exhibit 4 estimates the population per lane for selected international markets in 1997.[17]

Asian Cultures

Asian cultures reflected numerous influences. Their business practices differed in many ways from those in the United States. Conducting business in Asia required a long-term perspective through the formulation of strong bonds and ties with potential business partners. Patience was important and connections were crucial. Asia, particularly China, was a gift-giving culture, and the giving of gifts was a means to solidify personal ties.[18]

Many social and cultural demographics helped to explain the popularity of bowling in Asia. Half the Asian population was younger than 25, an optimal age range for introducing the sport to new bowlers.

A bowling enthusiast and Asian market analyst, Mort Luby, Jr., explained bowling's popularity:[19]

Bowling is popular in the Asian market because many young urban people complain there isn't much to do with their leisure time (and increased disposable income). Disco is dead, the nightclubs are intimidating, the bars are full of AIDS, and foreign movies are expensive and largely incomprehensible. There are very few mid-price restaurants. Bowling has filled this recreational void with a vengeance.

Asian Economies

Following the rapid growth in the 1980s of Taiwan, Korea, Singapore, and Hong Kong, the so-called Four Tigers, a new wave of economic growth swept across Asia. This wave was driven primarily by the newly industrializing economies of Malaysia, Thailand, Indonesia, and others. Thailand's growth was especially noticeable. *The Nation*, Bangkok's independent newspaper, predicted that Thailand would become known as the "Fifth Tiger" during the 1990s. The Asian Development Bank predicted that Asia's economy would grow at a pace twice as fast as other world regions. Some suggested that the new millennium would begin with the "Asian Century."[20]

The early 1990s also marked the globalization of financial markets. With slow growth and competitive home markets, private capital flows turned to

---

[17]From A-1 Lanes company literature.

[18]Mort Luby, Jr. "Asia's Malaise Is Only Temporary." *Bowler's Journal International* (January 1998), p. 12. http://www.census .gov/epcd/naics/NAICS32A.HTM#N321918.

[19]Ibid.

[20]"Wave of Growth Sweeping Across Asia." Jiji Press Ticjer Sercie, Jiji Press Ltd. (June 7, 1990).

Short-Term Debt (Percent of
Total External Debt) Thailand

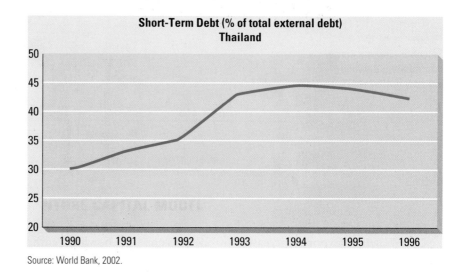

**Short-Term Debt (% of total external debt)
Thailand**

Source: World Bank, 2002.

these emerging markets, which offered higher interest rates and robust economic growth.[21] From 1990
to 1997, capital flows to developing countries rose
more than five-fold. While world trade grew by
about 5 percent annually, private capital flows grew
annually by 30 percent. The most mobile forms of
flow, commercial bank debt and portfolio investments, set the pace,[22] with East Asia absorbing nearly
60 percent of all short-term capital.[23]

Thailand attempted to "become the regional financial hub" for neighboring economies. The government enacted policies in 1993 that allowed some
foreign and local banks to make loans in U.S. dollars
and other currencies through what was called the
Bangkok International Banking Facilities (BIBF).[24]
However, with the Thai government continuing to
maintain high interest rates on baht-denominated
loans to keep inflation in check,[25] the policy was in

reality a conduit by which local Thai companies
could obtain special foreign loans at far lower interest rates than could be borrowed in baht.[26]

For example, in the mid-1990s, an investor could
borrow yen at near 0 percent interest and invest in
Bangkok skyscrapers, where the expected annual
return was 20 percent.[27] With access to low-interest
loans and readily available capital, and high demand,
foreign capital flowed into the region and accounted
for as much as 13 percent of Thailand's GDP, reaching a peak of $25.5 billion in 1995. Nearly 75 per-
cent of these foreign capital inflows were from
international banks in the form of bank loans with
maturities of less than one year. The majority of these
loans were made to Thai banks and finance companies, which in turn made domestic loans of much
longer duration.[28]

The dramatic influx of cheap capital spurred investment in the domestic infrastructure, such as
chemical and steel plants. Developers counted on the
continuation of strong growth. Luxury hotels and
high-rises became plentiful as development companies borrowed and invested at a breakneck pace.[29]

[21]Martin N. Baily, Diana Farrel, and Susan Lund. "The Color of
Hot Money." *Foreign Affairs,* Vol. 79(2) (March/April 2000),
pp. 99–110.

[22]"East Asia: The Road to Recovery." World Bank (1998),
Washington, DC.

[23]WEO cited in "East Asia: The Road to Recovery." World Bank
(1998), Washington, DC.

[24]Bruce Einhorn and Ron Corben. "One Tired Tiger." *Business
Week,* International Edition (March 24, 1997).

[25]"Thailand Finally Lets Its Currency Float." *Wall Street Journal*
(July 3, 1997).

[26]Jathon Sapsford. "Asia's Financial Shock: How It Began, and
What Comes Next." *Wall Street Journal* (November 26, 1997).

[27]Op. cit., World Bank, 1998.

[28]Op. cit., Baily et al., 2000.

[29]Op. cit., Lebourgre, 1997.

The year 1996 marked the beginning of an economic downturn in Thailand.[30] Exports began to stagnate and growth slowed.[31] The Asian Development Bank attributed the decline in exports to several factors, including a slump in the electronic sector, tight monetary policies in other countries, and the appreciation of the U.S. dollar against the Japanese yen.[32]

The appreciation of the U.S. dollar had a serious effect on Thailand's economy because the Thai baht was "pegged" to a basket of currencies with strong ties to the U.S. dollar.[33] As the dollar strengthened, so did the baht. Meanwhile Japanese exports, priced in yen, became more attractive to consumers in the United States.[34] Another disadvantage of letting the baht remain on par with the U.S. dollar was that Thai interest rates were far above U.S. rates, which caused distortion of the real worth of the baht. Nevertheless, the combination of exchange-rate stability and high interest rates continued to attract vast capital inflows.[35]

In light of an economic slowdown and the accumulation of aggressive investment, heavy borrowing, and wasteful use of resources, the International Monetary Fund (IMF), in September 1996, warned that several Southeast Asian economies' "current growth rates may be above their sustainable long-term trends." The report also suggested that a key economic problem confronting the developing countries was how to prevent big foreign-capital inflows from fueling inflation, blowing out their current accounts, and producing a repeat of Mexico's financial market crunch. The report also stated that the rapid growth of spending on real estate—a classic sign of speculative excess—in Indonesia, Malaysia, and Thailand and the appearance of skilled-labor bottlenecks in the region were early signs of overheating.[36] Following the IMF's warning of impending peril, senior Asian central bankers met on November 20, 1996, at the World Economic Forum to discuss how to prevent a "financial crisis from hitting the region."[37]

In the first and second quarters of 1997, Thailand's banks experienced a net $6 billion outflow of foreign investment. Short-term loans were not being renewed by foreign banks. During this time, Baker watched the exchange rate and was confident the Thai government would be able to maintain the value of the baht, therefore preserving the existing dollar/baht pegged exchange rate. However, the Bank of Thailand began to run out of reserves in its attempt to maintain the baht's value. On July 2, 1997, the Thailand government devalued its currency.[38]

Because the Asian Pacific economies were interconnected,[39] there was a high likelihood that this event would affect the currencies of the whole Asian Pacific region.[40] For American bowling manufacturers exporting to East Asia, this was a major concern on three accounts. First, U.S. firms feared that their Asian customers would be unable to pay off their accounts (usually payable in U.S. dollars). Second, a significant devaluation would make U.S. exports substantially more expensive across the entire region. Finally, governments usually raise interest rates in conjunction with any devaluation to assist in the stabilization of their currency. Manufacturers worried that the higher prices of capital equipment and higher interest rates could quash Asian investment in bowling centers (and new bowling equipment) almost overnight, especially if governments acted quickly.

[30]Thailand, http://www.infoplease.com/ipa/A0108034.html.

[31]Catherine Lebourgre. "Thailand: 'Tis an Ill Wind That Blows Nobody Any Good.'" *Banque Paribas Conjoncture* (May 1997).

[32]"Asia-Pacific to Grow at Slower Pace in '97 and '98." Japan Economic News Wire. *Kyodo News Service,* (April 17, 1997).

[33]Henny Sender. "Get a Grip: Can Thailand's Central Bank Handle the Baht Crisis?" *Far Eastern Economic Review,* Vol. 160(13) (March 27, 1997).

[34]"Several European Bourses Float at Lofty Levels: Tokyo Shares Rise Following Pause for Holiday." *Wall Street Journal* (January 17, 1997).

[35]Op. cit., Sender, 1997.

[36]Peter Kandiah. "Malaysia Warned over Possibility of Mexico-Style Crash." *The Nikkei Weekly* (September 30, 1996), http://web.lexis-nexis.com/universe/document, accessed April 23, 2003.

[37]Sheel Kohli. "Bankers Fear Asian 'Mexico' Crisis." *South China Morning Post* (November 21, 1996), http://web.lexis-nexis.com/universe/document, accessed April 10, 2003.

[38]Op. cit., Baily et al., 2000.

[39]Richard Y. C. Wong (1999). "Lessons from the Asian Financial Crisis." *Cato Journal,* Vol. 18(3) (Winter 1999), pp. 391–398.

[40]Alex Brummer (1996). "East Asian Tigers Are Endangered." *The Guardian* (London) (October 16, 1996), http://web.lexisnexis.com/universe/document, accessed April 1, 2003.

A-1's International Expansion

Following the 1988 Olympics, A-1 began shipping lanes to Taiwan. From 1990 to 1992, the company concentrated on developing contacts through Dacos' Asian networks. Increasing sales to Korea and Taiwan more than offset A-1's declining sales to Europe, where the market was saturated. Baker saw a distinctive Asian business mindset: "They were much more aggressive than we are in the West," he said. "They would actually build a bowling alley next to an existing one to drive out a local competitor."

By the end of 1992, Taiwan and South Korea were also reaching a saturation point for new wood bowling lanes; however, China had a growing interest in bowling. AMF and Brunswick had already developed centers in China. A-1 was able to penetrate this market in 1993 and 1994, mainly through its partnership with Dacos. A-1 had developed a synthetic lane called UltraLane, a growingly popular substitute for wood flooring. As a result of this innovation, A-1 Lanes was one of only three companies in the world to supply both wood and synthetic lanes. By 1995, Asia was the company's main market. In 1996, A-1's sales increased to $12.4 million, 33 percent above the previous year.

In 1995–1996, AMF attempted to consolidate the highly fragmented bowling equipment industry by slashing the prices of its capital equipment, especially wood and synthetic flooring. The aggressive move drove down prices and profitability across the industry. A-1 matched AMF's pricing, but its profits suffered substantially.

In spite of the region's problems, Baker and his Asian distributors saw increasing interest in bowling in Singapore and Malaysia. They thought these markets were very promising, and the additional volume could possibly offset the smaller profit per unit and thereby restore net income to its 1995 level. At this time, A-1 had 80 percent of its sales volume in the Asian markets and 20 percent in the U.S. market.

A-1's Situation

As Rick Baker contemplated the changes in the international market, he couldn't help but think about his own firm's viability. A-1's domestic sales were primarily of synthetic overlay systems. He wondered how A-1 could survive an Asian crash and continue to make a profit, or at the very least, generate a positive cash flow. To understand his company's financial health, he began to assess its activities, assets, and capabilities.

A-1 Lanes had become an important player in the international bowling industry within 10 years of its chicken-house origin. In Baker's view, his company strove to provide competitively priced, premium-quality bowling lanes and related equipment to the domestic and international markets and had earned a very favorable industry reputation. Over 30 capital equipment distributors used A-1 as a source for bowling lanes.

Manufacturing Facilities

A-1 was operating at about 60 percent of the capacity of its state-of-the-art plant. The company could expand production quickly to meet the demand in Singapore and Malaysia. More than 160 companies supplied the materials A-1 used to produce its bowling lanes and complementary components and accessories, such as gutters, capping, and return tracks. Rusk, Texas, was an ideal location because of its proximity to southern yellow pine. In Baker's mind, this gave A-1 a distinct advantage over rivals in the northern states due to low inbound costs of lumber and easy access to the mills.

Products and Innovation

Wood lanes were constructed of the highest quality southern yellow pine and hard maple boards, which were routed and milled to specification, and shipped either pre-nailed or loose to be installed by the ultimate buyer. According to Baker:

> The specifications for building wood lanes are very strict concerning the orientation and grain of the wood. Some wood is not appropriate, so there are many rejected boards. To aid in lowering the rejection rate and our costs, we have trained graders in local sawmills to grade lumber for use in our manufacturing process.

Once purchased, the lanes were shipped from the plant and assembled on site by highly skilled carpenters who specialized in the installation of bowling lanes.

EXHIBIT 5	Breakdown of A-1's Sales in 1996

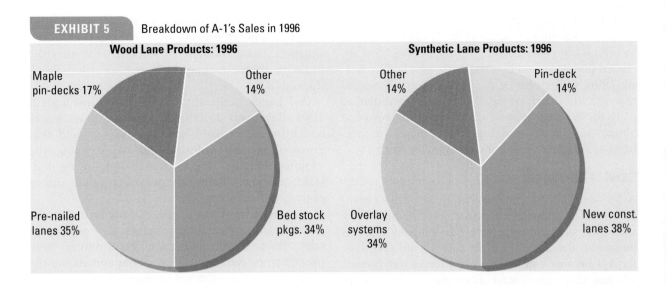

Wood lanes and various derivatives accounted for 58 percent of A-1's revenues in 1996. Each wood lane cost $6,250, including accessories. A breakdown of revenue from the company's various products is shown in Exhibit 5.

To address some of the shortcomings associated with wood lanes, such as marring and gouging (deep etching), synthetic lanes were introduced during the 1980s. However, A-1 did not introduce its first synthetic flooring, UltraLane, until 1992. Baker was especially proud that this innovation had been developed within the company and that the resin could be used not only for the construction of new lanes but also for refurbishing existing wood lanes (overlay system). He elaborated,

> The advantage of UltraLane is its improvement to the approach surface. Our competitors' synthetic flooring used the same product on the approach and the lane. The lane material was not slick enough for the approach. Bowlers' shoes stubbed on the material, and some lawsuits have been filed over injuries. UltraLane's approach has an orange peel texture that is very slick to the bowling shoe and allows it to slide properly.

By 1996, synthetic sales accounted for 42 percent of A-1 Lanes' total revenue, up from 25 percent of total sales in 1994. New synthetic lanes sold by the company were typically shipped in sections, installed on site, and cost $7,000 per lane. Exhibit 5 shows the breakdown of revenue from various synthetic lane products sold by A-1 Lanes.

In addition to UltraLane, Baker and his team continuously developed innovative products to complement or improve their existing products. For instance, A-1 developed a unique "snap on" ball return capping system and engineered changes in lane components that made the system less costly to manufacture. The capping system, made of high-impact plastic, covers (caps) the gutter dividers and ball returns that are positioned alternately between lanes.

Baker believed that continuously improving A-1's products was crucial to being competitive—even to survival. Technological enhancements could alter the entire bowling equipment industry, bringing changes that could accelerate the development of bowling in foreign markets. Baker thought it ironic that the entire industry could be undermined by the recent currency devaluation rather than by a radical innovation.

Marketing

"We need to do little advertising because the coverage of our company in trade publications is very positive due to our quality of products and reputation," Baker said. However, to stay in continual contact with its customers, A-1 bought display space at trade shows and at regional and international meetings of national bowling associations.

A-1's ongoing relationship with Dacos was a "win-win situation," he thought. It allowed Dacos to offer a complete bowling center package that included pinsetters and bowling lanes supplied by A-1. By 1996, 50 percent of A-1's sales were channeled through this partnership. Dacos was formulating plans for developing bowling centers in Malaysia and Singapore, thereby enabling A-1 to be at the forefront of bowling's continuing growth in Asia.

Service and Sales

A-1's sales force was smaller than those of most competitors. The company's top three executives were its sales force and had been with the company since its inception. Baker thought that this was an advantage for A-1 because competitors' sales forces were generally not very experienced. Furthermore, because of the knowledge and experience of its sales team, A-1 was able to provide consistent and reliable service. In Baker's mind, this was especially important because business in Asia was primarily based on relationships.

Being small brought another advantage, he believed. Asians were insulted when larger companies sent middle managers to negotiate deals. Since A-1 was so small, all encounters with the company were with executives. Baker remembered that when he gave his Asian customers his business card and introduced himself as the president of A-1 Lanes, they responded as if he were the president of AMF. When Baker traveled to Asia, he was treated "like royalty."

Performance Metrics

According to Baker, "It is amazing how a small firm in a rural community could sell millions of dollars of product to customers halfway around the world."

Even so, Baker felt helpless in the currency crisis. Feeling a sense of urgency in his company's financial situation, Baker thought, "I wonder what story the financial statements might tell me?" (See Exhibits 6 through 8.)

A-1 Lanes' net profit reached an all-time high in 1995. Baker was sure that his decision to cut prices had hurt the bottom line, but he surmised that everyone in the industry was experiencing the slimmer margins. The real question, he figured, was how long AMF would pursue its price-cutting policy.

Another troublesome aspect of the financials was the increase in operating expenses as a percent of sales. Baker knew that these expenditures were needed to modernize A-1's facilities and enable the firm to meet the expected increase in sales. In fact, A-1 had increased production to bring its finished inventory to 25 percent of projected sales. Baker reasoned that if A-1 were unable to meet demand, customers could easily go elsewhere. The outlay of $554,000 to modernize the plant was financed by a 10 percent note payable over 10 years.

Credit and Currency Risk

Although sales contracts with foreign customers specified payment in U.S. dollars, the fluctuations of foreign currencies against the dollar produced risk for both the customer and A-1. A large appreciation in the U.S. dollar could affect the collectability of foreign accounts receivable. Standard industry practice was to ship to foreign customers only after receipt of full payment in U.S. dollars, or upon presentation of irrevocable letters of credit. However, Baker did make exceptions for long-standing customers that were key

EXHIBIT 6		1996	1995	1994
A-1 Lanes Income Statement, 1994–1996	Sales	$12,359,561	$9,326,649	$7,781,131
	Cost of Goods Sold	9,887,649	6,460,768	6,035,549
	Gross Profit	**2,471,912**	**2,865,881**	**1,745,582**
	Operating Expenses	1,680,900	1,325,557	742,081
	Earnings Before Interest and Taxes	**791,012**	**1,540,324**	**1,003,501**
	Interest Expense	111,340	45,113	70,322
	Income Tax Expense	203,902	447,779	317,281
	Net Income	**$ 475,770**	**$1,047,432**	**$ 615,898**

EXHIBIT 7

A-1 Lanes Balance Sheet, 1994–1996

	1996	1995	1994
Cash	$ 277,603	$ 95,847	$ 73,411
Accounts Receivable	2,101,125	1,416,523	950,180
Inventory	2,050,636	2,418,940	1,571,758
Other Current	84,622	58,752	25,000
Total Current Assets	**4,513,986**	**3,990,062**	**2,620,349**
Fixed Assets	1,121,783	567,877	462,939
Accumulated Depreciation	(496,993)	(301,163)	(258,981)
Net Fixed Assets	624,790	266,714	203,958
TOTAL ASSETS	**$5,138,776**	**$4,256,776**	**$2,824,307**
Accounts Payable	$1,382,526	$1,440,354	$1,043,776
Short-Term Notes Payable	0	0	249,000
Taxes Payable	11,711	271,529	336,905
Other Current Liabilities	38,008	56,083	227,957
Total Current Liabilities	**1,432,245**	**1,767,966**	**1,857,638**
Long-Term Notes Payable	1,289,400	547,449	72,740
Common Stock	15,000	15,000	15,000
Excess of Par	60,000	60,000	60,000
Retained Earnings	2,342,131	1,866,361	818,929
Total Equity	**2,417,131**	**1,941,361**	**893,929**
TOTAL LIABILITIES & EQUITY	**$5,157,776**	**$4,275,776**	**$2,824,307**

EXHIBIT 8

A-1 Lanes Cash Flow Statement, 1994–1996

	1996	1995
Cash Flow from Operating Activities		
Net Income	$475,770	$1,047,432
Depreciation	195,830	42,182
(Increase) Accounts Receivable	(684,602)	(466,343)
Other Current	(25,870)	(33,752)
(Increase) Decrease Inventory	368,304	(847,182)
Increase (Decrease) Accounts Payable	(57,828)	396,578
Taxes Payable	(259,818)	(65,376)
Net Cash from Operating Activities	**11,786**	**73,539**
Purchase of Fixed Assets	**(553,906)**	**(104,938)**
Financial Proceeds		
Decrease Short-Term Notes	0	(249,000)
Increase Long-Term Debt	741,951	474,709
(Decrease) Other Current Liabilities	(18,075)	(171,874)
Total Proceeds (Payments)	**723,876**	**53,835**
Net Change in Cash	**$181,756**	**$ 22,436**

accounts. The exception applied to several major Asian customers, and Baker wondered if this had been a smart business decision. He thought that hedging techniques to reduce A-1's transaction exposure would entail too much work; already, he was too busy growing his business and filling orders. Besides, he had irrevocable letters of credit.

A-1's Future

Although Baker knew he didn't fully understand the story within A-1's financials, he was growing uncomfortable with how the crash in Asian currency markets could affect his company. Should he have monitored the Asian economic environment more closely? Should he have expanded manufacturing operations in 1996? Should he have extended credit to his selected foreign customers? How could he have protected his company?

Baker recalled that his old management professor at college once told him there is a story behind each set of financial statements—especially when you compare your company with the industry averages. Now Baker visited the library and collected the ratios pertaining to his industry. He laid them on a table next to A-1's financial statements (see Exhibit 9). He grabbed an ice cream bar from the freezer and sat down to ponder his next move.

EXHIBIT 9   A-1 Lanes Financial Ratios Versus Industry[1] Averages

	A-1 Lanes			Industry[2]			1996[4] Sales $10–$25 M
	1996	1995	1994	1996	1995	1994	
1. Firm Liquidity							
Current Ratio	3.15	2.26	1.41	1.80	1.70	1.70	1.8
Average Collection Period for Accounts Receivable	62.05	55.44	44.57	NA	NA	NA	NA
2. Operating Profitability							
Operating Income Return on Investment	15.39%	36.19%	35.53%	7.20%	11.10%	9.30%	10.00%
Operating Profit Margin	6.40%	16.52%	12.90%	3.60%	4.63%	4.43%	5.56%
Total Asset Turnover	2.41	2.19	2.76	2.00	2.40	2.10	1.8
Accounts Receivable Turnover	5.88	6.58	8.19	13.00	12.50	12.20	12.9
Inventory Turnover	4.82	2.67	3.84	5.10	6.30	5.90	7.00
Fixed Assets Turnover	19.78	34.97	38.15	7.20	6.60	6.50	6.80
3. Financing Decisions							
Debt Ratio	25.09%	12.86%	2.58%	20.10	20.30%	20.80%	15.6%
Times Interest Earned	7.10	34.14	14.27	3.10	4.50	6.00	14.6
4. Return on Equity							
Return on Equity[3]	32.73%	79.34%	112.26%	17.31%	25.06%	23.13%	18.28%

[1]SIC 2426; NAICS 321918 Manufacturing, Other Millwork (including flooring).

[2]Source: Robert Morris & Associates (1996). *Annual Statement Studies: Financial Ratio Benchmarks*. Philadelphia, PA.

[3]RMA does not report net income (after taxes) nor stockholders' equity. Therefore, a derivative was used—(profit before taxes/net worth) as an indicant for return on equity.

[4]This information is reported for the current year (1996) of firms with sales of $10–$25 million.

Discussion Questions

1. What events and/or trends were occurring in the macro environment that were important to the bowling industry?
2. Using Porter's 5-Forces Model, describe the dynamics of the industry environment.
3. Analyze the financial ratios for the company. Compare them to the industry averages. Is the firm financially healthy? Why or why not?
4. What were the internal strengths and external opportunities for A-1 Lanes? What were the internal weaknesses and external threats?
5. Drawing from the analysis of the firm's strengths and weaknesses, articulate the firm's capabilities and determine the degree to which the firm has a core competency. (Use VIRO and the resource-based views of the firm for the analysis. It is suggested that students list the tangible and intangible resources that might contribute to the firm's strategic capabilities.)
6. What were the major problems facing A-1 Lanes? Is the irrevocable letter of credit the best means by which a firm can protect the collection of its international accounts receivable? Or, as an alternative to letters of credit, how might A-1 Lanes protect its transaction exposure?
7. What should Baker do now? Why?

MYSPACE: THE ONLINE REALITY SHOW

In the fall of 2006, Chris DeWolfe found himself stepping back in time as he stood before a crowd of alums and current students from the Lloyd Greif Center for Entrepreneurial Studies at the Marshall School of Business of the University of Southern California. He was there to receive an award as the Alumni Entrepreneur of the Year for co-founding the second largest site on the Internet, MySpace, the social networking phenomenon. But more than that, he was there to remember his roots and to tell an eager audience of entrepreneur hopefuls what to watch out for. "Technology does not drive demand," he cautioned the students. "MySpace has always taken a sociological viewpoint—How do people do things? What do they like to do? Then the MySpace team figures out how they can enable their users to do what they want." Asked what he would have done differently, DeWolfe doesn't miss a beat—"I would have started it sooner." He would have expanded aggressively and hired more developers in the early days, because "speed to market is important."

DeWolfe was looking back at the launch of the company he co-founded with Tom Anderson from a new position in that fall of 2006. MySpace had recently been acquired by Rupert Murdoch's News Corporation (News Corp) as part of a $580 million package deal for Intermix Media, MySpace's parent company. With the enormous resources of News Corp behind it, MySpace was taking on an astounding number of new projects: a new Google agreement for text ads, a MySpace records label, a VoIP feature so their users could call one another, international sites, and another 20 products in various stages of development in the pipeline. How did MySpace go from launch in late 2003 to online media giant by 2007?

In the Beginning

Chris DeWolfe hails from Portland, Oregon; both parents were teachers. So it was a bit of a break from tradition when he decided to major in business at the University of Washington. Upon graduation he took a job, but two years into it, he began to have some doubts.

> I looked to my left and looked to my right and saw that my colleagues were twenty years older than me, and it was almost like looking into the future. And I was scared because that wasn't something that I wanted to do. I wanted to create my own business; I wanted to do my own thing; I wanted to innovate.

Frustrated, he decided to further his education by getting an MBA. His friends told him that he had to have a plan to get into a good business school. He had to know whether he wanted to be a consultant, an investment banker, or a marketing manager. Again, DeWolfe sidestepped the traditional route—"My plan is, I'm going to figure out a plan when I get there." He was accepted into the Marshall School of Business at the University of Southern California (USC), and for the first year he immersed himself in the Internet, which in 1995 was just beginning to gain some ground as a commercial channel. Netscape and Yahoo! had gone public and things were getting interesting. In the second year of his MBA, he took a class in the Lloyd Greif Center for Entrepreneurial Studies and was hooked. He knew what he wanted to be—an Internet entrepreneur—that was his passion.

After graduation, DeWolfe and three of his USC Marshall friends took jobs at an Internet data-storage company, Xdrive; DeWolfe became the company's head of sales and marketing. It was in that capacity that he met one of his future partners, Tom Anderson, in 2000. Anderson, a frustrated English major at UC Berkeley and then film school major, responded to an ad to earn $20 for testing an Xdrive product. Although Anderson disliked the product immensely, DeWolfe liked him so much that he offered him a full-time job. Xdrive was not a success, however. It was the typical dot com company of the day, raising $120 million and spending it foolishly on parties, excess advertising, and hiring people it didn't need. That experience told DeWolfe that it was time to start his own company, so he and Anderson left the firm (in bankruptcy) in 2001 and launched an Internet direct-marketing firm called Response Base. They sold that business for several million dollars in late 2002 to eUniverse, a holder of multiple Internet assets. Both joined the company, but just six months later, DeWolfe and Anderson were asking themselves, "What's next?"

A Brief History of the Internet

Although the Internet didn't become the focus of consumer attention until about 1995, its history actually dates back to August 1962, when MIT's J.C.R. Licklider began discussing what he called the "galactic network," a "globally interconnected set of computers," which would enable anyone in the network to access data and programs from any site. While serving as the first head of the computer research program at DARPA, he convinced his colleagues of the significance of his concept. By late 1966, MIT researcher Lawrence Roberts had created a plan to build the ARPANET and by 1969, the first node was installed at UCLA. Within a month, two additional nodes were added at UC Santa Barbara and the University of Utah, and by the end of 1969, there were four host computers connected on ARPANET. Nevertheless, it took until October 1972 to demonstrate ARPANET's capability to the public at an international conference and to introduce its newest application, electronic mail.

ARPANET was the first of what would become many networks linked by an open architecture networking called the Internet. In open architecture each network could have its own design and user interface, yet they would all be connected seamlessly to the Internet. The 1980s saw the rapid development of LANs (local area networks), PCs, and workstations, which contributed to the swift expansion of the Internet that was now serving a broad base of researchers and developers.

In 1991, the first user-friendly interface was developed at the University of Minnesota. *Gopher,* as it was named after the university's mascot, quickly expanded to over 10,000 systems around the world while other universities developed enhancements to it, such as a searchable index of gopher menus and a spider that crawled gopher menus to collect links and place them in the index. But it was the development in 1993 of Mosaic, a graphical user interface, by Marc Andreessen and his team at the National Center for Supercomputing Applications that became the catalyst for the commercial Internet as we know it today. With the launch of Delphi, the first national commercial online service that offered Internet access to subscribers in 1992, the commercial Internet could not be stopped. In 1995, the National Science Foundation halted funding of the Internet backbone, and commercial networks like AOL and CompuServe were born.

Until 1998, when Microsoft released Windows 98 with a full-scale browser incorporated, Netscape's browser, which was free, was the most popular browser on the market. At this point, there was no stopping the proliferation of Internet sites as more and more companies tried to find business models that would enable them to make money through this exciting new channel. The highly speculative period between 1995 and 2001 has been called the "dot com bubble," because stock markets saw their value explode to unprecedented levels from the growth in Internet companies and related sectors only to crash in the spring of 2000 because these same companies couldn't deliver business models that made sense or contributed to realistic valuations. The dot com bubble was not a unique event. History has witnessed other booms and busts: radio in the 1920s, transistor electronics in the 1950s, and home computers in the early 1980s. Some of the more notable dot com failures were Webvan, the online grocer; Pets.com; and eToys.com.

Today many pundits question whether we are heading into another dot com bubble—the sequel—with the recent acquisitions of MySpace and YouTube at extremely high valuations. These social networking sites depend a good deal on content that their users create and on their users' ability to build large networks among their friends and associates. There are no fees charged to the users, so the sites rely on advertising revenue and sponsorships and often have no proprietary technology. However, if MySpace is the model for the current Internet venture, then we will see more acquisitions by large corporations instead of IPOs by unprofitable Internet companies.

The Birth of MySpace

Ready to start another business, DeWolfe and Anderson surveyed the Internet landscape and recognized a "perfect storm" of activities that seemed to suggest a space to do something that wasn't being done. In late 2002, the term *social networking* was getting some play due to the emergence of Friendster (a dating site), Tribe (a classifieds and local information guide), and Facebook (social networking for college students). DeWolfe and Anderson noticed that they were receiving a constant stream of requests through their e-mail to join these networks, so they began to do some research and quickly determined that these were niche players without a lot of potential to become huge. The two had bigger plans in mind, specifically a portal that would bring all of the niche functions together and let users do whatever they do offline in a more product way: express themselves, send out invitations, blog, discover music, share photos, and play games. DeWolfe's mantra has always been "once you've done the research, stop strategizing and jump off the cliff." So he and Anderson made the leap to start the company. They pitched the idea to eUniverse and took a seed round of financing for 66 percent of their equity. They also purchased the myspace.com domain name from a data-storage company no longer in existence.

It took three months to build the site, and they launched at the end of 2003. However, the day after launch the site blew up—in other words, it stopped working. DeWolfe quickly consulted with his developer and learned that the system they had built couldn't survive an assault by more than 200 people at the same time. Realizing the mistake that had been made, DeWolfe instructed the developer to build the site to hold millions of people at the same time. Shortly thereafter they were back in business. Growth did not come quickly for this social networking portal; in fact, the company didn't start to see success for at least six to nine months. At first they attracted their users by inviting bands and club owners in Los Angeles to create pages and then invite others to "become their friends." Because the bands and clubs could use MySpace as their promotional platform, they very willingly invited others onto the site. And everyone came, because MySpace allowed them to do and post what they wanted, whereas rival Friendster made sure that its site did not contain anything that didn't fit its core proposition, which at the time was essentially Internet dating. MySpace also succeeded in correcting many of the problems that users had with Friendster, such as speed of access to the site. Giving bands an outlet to let users sample and share songs as well as communicate with the bands was the secret sauce that catalyzed MySpace's growth. By 2004, more than 350,000 bands and solo artists, both unknown and famous, had set up pages on the site and invited their friends to join, creating a viral effect. In September 2004, R.E.M. became the first band from a major record label to stream its latest album on MySpace before its release.

The *New York Times* wrote of MySpace:

> Even with many users in their 20s MySpace has the personality of an online version of a teenager's bedroom, a place where the walls are papered with posters and photographs, the music is loud, and grownups are an alien species.

And that's just what DeWolfe and Anderson intended. Users are able to customize the look of their pages, add personal photographs, and create a network of friends who must receive permission before being added to someone's site. The biggest celebrity on MySpace is co-founder Tom Anderson because it is his face that pops up when a new member registers, so his list of friends was running over 46 million as of

2006. Of the two founders, Anderson, who came out of music and film, is the most gregarious and creative while the quieter DeWolfe manages MySpace's finances and keeps a lower profile. In fact, it was DeWolfe who shielded Anderson from much of the turmoil surrounding the later acquisition of MySpace.

In July 2004, eUniverse changed its name to Intermix Media (IMIX) and brought on a new CEO, Richard Rosenblatt, a successful Internet pioneer who in 1999 had sold his company iMall for $565 million. His challenge was to turn around the struggling company, which had gone through an SEC investigation, had its stock halted from trading for nearly four months, had to restate the first three quarters of fiscal year 2003, had been delisted from NASDAQ, and was being sued by its shareholders in various class-action and derivative lawsuits. All of these problems cost the company a lot of money, so it was soon clear that the company needed more funding to support its rapid growth and that of its fastest growing asset, MySpace. This meant talking to venture capitalists, most of whom didn't understand the MySpace concept, didn't know the management team, and thought they were trying to do too much. But Redpoint Ventures, a Silicon Valley firm, did understand the technology–entertainment mix. In December 2004, they agreed to invest $4 million in Intermix Media, Inc., for one million shares of its common stock and a five-year warrant to purchase 150,000 shares of common stock at $4/share. With the ink on that deal still drying, in February 2005, Redpoint Ventures again invested, this time a total of $11.5 million for a minority stake of 25 percent in the newly formed independent subsidiary of Intermix, MySpace, Inc. As of February 2005, Intermix held a 53 percent equity interest in MySpace, Inc. DeWolfe served as chief executive officer for a three-year term that ended in October 2007.

The Acquisition of Intermix and MySpace

In 2005, a number of large media companies began approaching Richard Rosenblatt, CEO of Intermix and chairman of MySpace, about acquiring Intermix and its three main assets: MySpace, Alena (marketing analytics and e-commerce), and its media network, which consisted of about 30 different websites. At the time, MySpace was supporting approximately 18 million unique visitors and was the fastest growing part of Intermix. DeWolfe was very nervous when News Corp's Rupert Murdoch, the media icon, approached them about an acquisition, because he did not want to risk losing the no-rules culture they were known for and become buried in a huge conservative conglomerate; however, they needed the money to support their blistering growth, and their board approved the sale. In approximately 18 months from the time he had become CEO of Intermix, Rosenblatt had turned the company around and sold it and its highly successful subsidiary MySpace for a premium, $580 million in cash, to News Corp to become part of its Fox Interactive Media, Inc. Rosenblatt remained a consultant to News Corp to help grow the Intermix properties until he launched Demand Media in 2006, raised $220 million in investment capital, and bought back the non-MySpace assets of Intermix Network LLC from News Corp.

Prior to the acquisition, Murdoch had assured DeWolfe and Anderson that he would not interfere with the running of MySpace; however, shortly after the acquisition of Intermix in July 2005, News Corp decided to move MySpace from its laid-back office a block from the beach in Santa Monica to Beverly Hills, where all of News Corp's Internet companies were based. It was at that point that DeWolfe and Anderson first realized that they no longer really owned MySpace. They soon found that other things had changed as well. Decisions took a lot longer now with all the big corporate processes and the culture was not as casual. The upside, though, was that MySpace had significantly more resources at its disposal to launch multiple projects and products simultaneously.

DeWolfe believes that MySpace is at the nascent stage of where it can potentially go. As the number two Internet site in terms of page views, the duo needs to make sure that they continue to listen to the market, not the experts, and not "follow the pack." DeWolfe attributes the success of MySpace to several factors: (1) an experienced management team that had worked together for 8 years; (2) great timing on the launch of the site, with social networking taking off and advertising revenues returning to Internet companies; (3) features on the site that were compelling to their users—they provided a solution that made sense and that users couldn't find on other sites; and (4) the use of influencers from entertainment to drive interest in the site. As long as DeWolfe and Anderson remain with the company, the intent is to make sure that users control the site and users dictate the features that MySpace offers. That philosophy often presents problems, with the less desirable elements of society easily setting up shop in MySpace and preying on other users. "We take safety very seriously and we make huge investments in it," asserts DeWolfe. Monitoring the site while still giving users freedom is a real balancing act, but it has to happen for MySpace to be able to attract national advertisers like Coca-Cola and Procter & Gamble, who will not risk their brands by having them associated with off-color or inappropriate content. These "sponsors" supply significant revenue for a company that depends primarily on ads in its business model. In December 2006, with the resources of News Corp at its disposal, MySpace went mobile on a grand scale with a service that enables Cingular Wireless subscribers to use many of the social networking features of MySpace on their cell phones for a $2.99 per month premium. This was a way to diversify its business model and again meet one of the requested needs of its users.

In the spring of 2007, with their contract end date looming in October, DeWolfe and Anderson were again faced with the question, "What's next?"

Sources: "A Brief History of the Internet." *Internet Society*, http://www.isoc.org, accessed May 29, 2007; Interview with Chris DeWolfe, Alumni Entrepreneur of the Year Event, November 2006, University of Southern California; "Dot-Com Bubble, Part II? Why It's So Hard to Value Social Networking Sites." *Knowledge@wharton*, http:// knowledge.wharton.upenn.edu, accessed October 4, 2006; Sellers, P. (2006). "MySpace Cowboys." *Fortune* (September 4): 67; "Interview with Richard Rosenblatt, Intermix and MySpace." *Socal Tech* (January 30, 2006), http://www.socaltech.com; Williams, A. (August 28, 2005). "Do You MySpace?" *New York Times*, http://www.nytimes.com; Weintraub, J. (July 25, 2005). "A, B, C, D, eUniverse." *DM Confidential*, http://www.adastro.com; "Entry Material Agreement, Other Events, Financial Statements and Exhibits." Form 8-K for Intermix Media, Inc., published February 17, 2005; Exhibit 99.1, eUniverse Issues Open Letter to eUniverse Stockholders, January 7, 2004, http://sec.edgar-online.com.

Discussion Questions

1. How did DeWolfe and Anderson recognize the opportunity for MySpace?
2. What mistakes were made with Xdrive that ultimately made MySpace go more smoothly?
3. How did MySpace differentiate itself from the competition?
4. Should DeWolfe and Anderson have given up so much equity (66%) in the beginning to eUniverse? Was there an alternative strategy available?
5. Evaluate the acquisition of MySpace as part of the Intermix package. Would you have made that decision? Why or why not?

iROBOT: ROBOTS FOR THE HOME

Robots have been around for a long time. Detroit has used robots for four decades to build cars, and manufacturers of all kinds of goods use some form of robotics to achieve efficiencies and productivity. But until iRobot brought its battery-powered vacuum cleaner to the market, no one had successfully used robots in the home as an appliance. The issue was not whether it was possible to use robots in the home, but could they be produced at a price customers would pay. Until the introduction of Roomba, iRobot's intelligent vacuum cleaner, robots for the home cost tens of thousands of dollars. At Roomba's price point of $199, it was now possible for the average consumer to afford to have a robot clean the house. That in itself is an interesting story, but even more interesting is the entrepreneurial journey of Colin Angle and his company, iRobot.

Background

Colin Angle grew up in Schenectady, New York, where he was raised by his mother and stepfather. He and his three stepbrothers all became engineers, but Angle was the inventor/builder of the group. Beginning in his earliest years, he built pinball machines and constructed complex pulley systems in the trees of his back yard. While attending MIT in the 1980s, he was drawn to the innovative work of Rodney Brooks, director of the university's artificial intelligence lab. Brooks was a controversial figure in the robotics field, but he served as the inspiration for what would become some of Angle's most practical inventions. As a student, Angle was part of the group that succeeded in building insect-like robots that could perform simple tasks on reflex. In fact, Angle's creation, Genghis,

appeared on the cover of *Popular Science*. It was clear by then that his future lay in inventions.

The Opportunity

In 1990, Brooks and Angle, who by then had become close working partners with their MIT colleague Helen Greiner, borrowed from their credit cards and used bank debt to found iRobot in a tiny apartment in Somerville, Massachusetts. The goal of the company was to build robots that would affect how people lived their lives. At that time, no one could conceive of a way to bring robots into domestic life in an affordable way, and iRobot was still years away from discovering the one application that would launch it into the consumer market. To stay alive, the company sought government and corporate contracts for new product development. Over the next decade, iRobot designed and built a vast array of products, from nuclear waste detectors to toy robots. Angle and his team believed that diversifying their product development skills would insulate them from the risk of any one customer killing a project, something that happened frequently in their industry. Angle also had no idea which of the many products they developed would be the one that would propel the company into rapid growth, so he did not want to focus the company too narrowly too soon.

Diversification in those first years enabled the company to stockpile a range of patents that would become the basis for the product for which they became most famous. Angle reasoned that he had to make certain that customers did not end up owning technology that his company might need in future product development. For example, in 1992, he sold the rights to the underlying technology on a robot called Grendel to separate it from technology that would be used to take the company in new directions. Prior to this, iRobot did not control the patents for products it developed for large customers, as is typical with smaller businesses. However, after selling the Grendel rights, Angle decided that henceforth the company would retain all rights to the technologies it developed. As it turned out, a cleaning technology that iRobot had developed for Johnson Wax Professional and tiny processors developed for Hasbro, the toy company, were critical components of Roomba.

Shall We Dance?

iRobot had secured two parts of the three components of its growth strategy. It had become a flexible company that could develop products in a broad area, and it had built a strong base of intellectual capital. Now, the only thing missing was a way to bring robots to the domestic market economically, and that was no easy task. Angle had already experienced the agony of defeat on a proposal for Hasbro. In 1996, iRobot had developed a storytelling machine with characters that moved and gestured while they talked. It seemed like this could be the next big toy until they showed Hasbro management what it looked like inside. It was a masterpiece of engineering, but the microprocessors cost $60 each, the flash card cost $400, and the parts all totaled ran about $3,000. Hardly a likely candidate for the next Christmas season! But Angle had learned a lot about the consumer products industry from this experience and what it would take to develop successful products for the toy industry. It was all about cost—saving pennies so that the toy company could meet its competitive price point in the market. iRobot became an exclusive partner to Hasbro, and over the next two years, it proposed dozens of new toy projects, most of which were turned down because they were too expensive to make. Finally, in 2000, iRobot saw one if its creations, My Real Baby, hit the store shelves.

It was, in fact, this new understanding of the consumer products business that inspired the idea for Roomba. Originally, they had considered partnering with a large vacuum cleaner company like Hoover, but one of the reasons a smaller company partners

with a large established company is to take advantage of their access to suppliers. The iRobot team had become experts in sourcing product components efficiently, so they chose to do it on their own.

Developing Roomba

The engineers at iRobot were unaccustomed to building mundane products for domestic use, so to avoid wasting the talents of his most brilliant engineers, Angle created a new division in the company that would design and launch these domestic products. Technologies developed from contract work now found a home in Roomba. For example, the crop circle algorithm it uses came from a technology used to sweep minefields. The company worked its way through 20 iterations of Roomba, bringing each version home to spouses and relatives to test. One thing was clear: this device had to be easy to use. In general, consumers won't tolerate a steep learning curve, so iRobot's engineers pictured something as simple as a large button labeled "clean." In fact, they ended up with a button that provided a choice of "S," "M," or "L," for small, medium, or large (denoting the room size). The customer puts Roomba on the floor, turns it on, and presses the size button. Then the robot plays a tune and starts sweeping the floor in ever-widening circles. When it runs into something, it heads off in a different direction. The circle algorithm alternates with a wall-and-furniture-hugging algorithm and straight lines. Sometimes at random it will simply go in one direction until it runs into something. It runs on a nickel-metal-hydride battery that gets recharged on an overnight charger. It also comes with an invisible wall that projects an infrared beam if you need to keep the robot confined to a particular area. It even has three different backup systems to keep it from falling down stairs.

From its experience with Hasbro, iRobot had learned to be extremely stingy on costs, down to the penny; they knew that a price tag of $199 would keep competitors at bay for awhile.

Market Entry

iRobot's shrewd entry strategy saw Roomba hitting the market just in time for the Christmas season through such gift outlets as Sharper Image and

Brookstone. These stores are willing to demonstrate products, something that is critical with a new product. Although Roomba was the first product from iRobot, sales were $15 million in 2002 and soared to $50 million in 2003. This was accomplished on five rounds of venture funding totaling $27.5 million.

iRobot also hired a Boston public relations firm to conduct a media blitz to create customer awareness. Stories appeared in the *Wall Street Journal* and *Time* and on TV shows like *Live with Regis and Kelly*. Women's magazines were another popular media venue. But all advertising is not good advertising. Angle had to be careful that Roomba would not be perceived as a novelty—a toy—but rather as an everyday appliance. Therefore, the company chose not to refer to Roomba as a robot in any of its advertising or promotional materials. Instead it was described as an "intelligent floorvac system." These high-tech engineers left their techie egos at the door and resorted to consumer terms, but the market dictates what companies should do. Once iRobot found out that 60 percent of its customers were naming their Roombas, the company began using the term *robot* on its packaging. Angle realized that once competition entered the market and was able to achieve a lower price point, it would be important to customers to know that their robot vacuum came from a robot company and not a vacuum cleaner company.

The Future

iRobot continues to do contract research. The federal Defense Advanced Research Projects Agency (DARPA) has funded its Robot's Swarm project, where it is working on getting robots to coordinate with each other. Called "PackBots," they are used by bomb squads for unmanned reconnaissance and bomb disposal. By 2006, iRobot had over 900 of these rugged bomb-busters spotting landmines and searching caves in Iraq and Afghanistan. Although weighing only 68 pounds, the robot has an arm that can stretch more than six feet, and it can lift 30-pound objects in its "hand." Angle can see a future for this technology in the home as well. Picture a scenario where robot appliances decide among themselves what should be cleaned first.

But are consumers willing to go that far with domestic robots? Are they willing to give them decision power in the home? That remains to be seen. In November 2005, iRobot's PackBot robots opened trading on the NASDAQ exchange, marking the first ever opening by a robot and the first profits (in 2004) for a company in business for 15 years.

iRobot is now facing an emerging challenge from conventional vacuum manufacturers, who have started teaming with robotics researchers to develop competing machines. The company is rapidly turning out new products based on its core technology to stay ahead of what will surely be fierce competition. In 2005, the year the company went public, it released Scooba, a floor-washing robot. In 2006, a workshop robot designed to pick up small objects such as nuts and bolts was released. And in 2007 the company offered iRobot Create, a hobby robot; Verro, a pool-cleaning robot; and a new line of vacuum robots. But is this enough to grow the company to a level where it can withstand the onslaught of intense competition that is just at hand? With consumer robots accounting for at least half the company's revenues, this is a serious concern for the founders. In 2006 with 371 employees, the company saw revenues of about $189 million and net income of $3.56 million. But competitors like Electrolux and Samsung Electronics are weighing in with resources that total $16 billion and $79 billion, respectively. Is iRobot doing what it needs to do to grow its markets and prevent being commoditized by the competition?

Sources: Ulanoff, L. (May 16, 2007). "Robots Embedded in Warfare and Our Lives." *PC Magazine,* http://www.pcmag.com; Storrs, F. (May 2007). "Heavy Mettle." *Boston Magazine,* http://www.bostonmagazine.com; Jewell, M. (November 10, 2005). "Investors Buy into Consumer Robotics as iRobot Shares Debut." *Associated Press;* Buchanan, L. (July 2003). "Death to Cool." *Inc. Magazine,* http://www.inc.com; "Mechanically Inclined: These Entrepreneurial Robophiles Take Their Business Where No Man Has Gone Before," *Entrepreneur Media, Inc.,* http://www.findarticles.com; Garfinkel, S. (October 9, 2002), "iRobot Roomba," *MIT Technology Review,* http://www.technologyreview.com

Discussion Questions

1. What are the unique challenges facing a new product development company?
2. What role did patents play in iRobot's strategic plan?
3. Evaluate iRobot's approach to the consumer market. Was it effective? Would you have done anything differently?
4. How will iRobot maintain its lead in the consumer market?

THE CROWNE INN: A CLASSIC CASE OF A FAMILY BUSINESS IN TURMOIL

Introduction

It was a clear, cool fall day in late 2000 when Barbara Johnston, a retired nurse, was confronted with one of the biggest challenges of her life. Her son Bruce had entered her dilapidated house, thrown down his keys, and blurted out the following:

> You are all plotting behind my back. You are trying to bankrupt and steal the bar away from me. Well, you can have the keys to my house, car, and the lousy bar. But you will lose your son and two grandchildren forever.
>
> No one wanted the bar. I made the bar what it is today. If I leave, the business will collapse and then you will have nothing. I have already talked to the employees and they will all walk out. After this is over, I am going to disown this whole family. I have had it with all of you!!

Barbara's family was on the verge of being torn apart over the family's largest asset, a bar called The Crowne Inn, located in Kansas City, Missouri. Since the death of her husband Harvey in 1997, Barbara had had problems with Bruce's inability to meet his previously agreed-upon oral agreement to take care of her. On the day of his father's retirement in 1995, Bruce had made an oral agreement to pay off the second mortgage of his parents' house ($23,500), give them $500 in cash per month, and pay their health insurance and medical bills for the rest of their lives. He had made this oral agreement in front of his parents and

This case was written by Todd A. Finkle, Director, Fitzgerald Institute for Entrepreneurial Studies, The University of Akron, as a basis for class discussion. Reprinted by permission.

their attorney, Bobby Free. However, despite repeated warnings from Free, Harvey had refused a formal written contract. As a result of the agreement, Bruce received all of the proceeds from the bar.

After five years, Bruce had not lived up to his agreement with his parents. The family was trying to work out a deal with Bruce's lawyer and accountant to sell him the business. The family's attorney, Bobby Free, devised three possible solutions to the problem: (1) have Bruce pay a lump sum, (2) have Bruce pay a smaller lump sum and $500 per month, or (3) sell the bar outright to an outside party.

Bruce stated that he would pay a lump sum of not more than $60,000 to his mother. The family was unsure whether this was a fair offer. If not, what was a fair offer? Also, was the lump sum method the best way to handle the problem? Furthermore, would Bruce be willing and/or able to pay a higher lump sum? Previously, he had told his older brother Karl that he refused to pay $75,000. He stated that he would be better off going into business with someone else rather than pay $75,000.

The real challenge was solving the family crisis without alienating Bruce and his family. Furthermore, Bruce had only one good relationship with his four brothers—Karl. Barbara was looking to her sons and her attorney for an answer to this complicated, nerve-racking, family crisis.

The Johnston Family

Born in Kansas City in 1934, Barbara Johnston grew up in a lower-middle-class Lutheran family and was a by-product of the Depression. Despite her challenging upbringing, Barbara was a gregarious, warm, friendly, family-oriented woman.

During her junior year in high school, she fell in love with a senior named Harvey Johnston. Harvey married Barbara four years after she graduated from high school. The marriage proved to be very tumultuous, but produced five healthy boys and six grandchildren. Most of the boys had personality characteristics like their father, which included a very high need for independence, an extremely strong work ethic, and an entrepreneurial flair. The oldest son, Karl, a twice-divorced, 47-year-old, was currently married (Caren). Karl was a street-smart, successful entrepreneur who owned a 3M dealership in Seattle, Washington. He had grown the business to over $1.5 million in sales in four years. His salary, not including the profits from the business, was around $85,000 a year.

Her second son, Cal (Jessica), had been married for 22 years. His marriage produced three children: Jason, Jennifer, and Jim. Cal was a religious, optimistic, and successful 45-year-old cardiologist who lived in Kansas City. Of the five brothers, Cal was the most financially successful. His independent medical practice had sales of $1,000,000 with an annual net income of $250,000.

The middle child, Bruce (Sharon), had been married since 1985 and had two children, Albert and Bob. Bruce and Sharon were currently running the family business, The Crowne Inn.

Bruce enjoyed partying with his friends from the bar. Bruce and Sharon worked at the bar and made a combined salary of $84,000 (1999), not including the profits from the bar (see Exhibit 1).

The fourth son, Tyler, was a single (never married), 40-year-old dentist living in Las Vegas, Nevada. He was a hard-working free spirit who enjoyed his freedom and convertibles. His dental practice was very successful, and he made approximately $100,000 a year.

Danny, the last son, was also single (37 years old). He was extremely creative and enjoyed working with his hands. He had just started his own entertainment company that specialized in decorations for holidays and special events.

The Crowne Inn

Harvey and Barbara Johnston were married in 1952. Before their marriage, Johnston's father, Norm, realized that his son needed a profession to support his new wife. Norm approached his 22-year-old son and asked him what profession he wanted to enter. After some thought, Johnston stated that he wanted to start his own bar. The loose, free lifestyle appealed to him.

Before opening the bar, Johnston asked his best friend, Leo Smith, if he wanted to be his partner. Smith had been bartending with Johnston for the past two years and enjoyed it, so he agreed. Smith also had more experience in the bar business, so it was a good match. He was a warm, friendly man who was married and had one daughter.

In 1952, Johnston and Smith took out a $10,000 loan and started a bar called "Leo and Harvey's" in downtown Kansas City. The bar was structured as an S-corporation; both Johnston and Smith owned 50 percent of the stock in the company.

After seven years of moderately successful business, they made a decision to move the business to the northeast part of Kansas City. The downtown area had become increasingly dangerous with an increase in crime and an increase in the number of homeless people. The new location had fewer competitors, less crime, and a better clientele. The partners purchased the land and building and moved

EXHIBIT 1			Bar's Net Income	
	Year	Bruce	Sharon	Pre Tax	Totals

Annual Salaries for Bruce and Sharon Johnston and The Crowne Inn's Net Income (Pre Tax) from 1997 to 2000

Year	Bruce	Sharon	Pre Tax	Totals
1997	53,500	20,000	(500)	73,000
1998	60,000	20,000	3,440	83,440
1999	62,000	22,000	6,450	90,450
2000	64,000	24,000	6,500	94,500

into the new location in 1959, renaming the bar, "The Crowne Inn."

The Crowne Inn was unique because it was patterned after the Old West. Old wooden barrels lined the front of the building. The building itself was made of wood boards, and signs that ranged from "Dance Girls Wanted" to "Whisky Served Here" to "Coldest Beer in Town" were placed all over the front of the building. On the top of the building was a 7-Up sign.

At the entrance of the smoke-filled bar there was a shiny, dark-stained, wooden bar with 10 swinging stools for customers. A pair of small swinging doors led to the back of the bar where a small cooler held mugs, cans, and bottles of beer and wine. There were five taps: one for Champagne, Cold Duck, and Miller High Life, and two for Budweiser (their best-selling beer). On the other side of the bar were a small grill, refrigerator, office, and cooler for kegs and cases of beer. A limited supply of hard alcohol and food items were also for sale behind the bar.

The Crowne Inn differentiated itself from other bars in a number of ways. First, the bar had a very homey atmosphere with approximately 15 tables and a total capacity of 70 people. This gave customers the ability to converse without all the hassles (e.g., fights, loud music) of a typical bar. The bar also served lunch (hamburgers, hot dogs, chili dogs, and chips) and snacks (slim jims, beef jerky, bags of peanuts). The bar initially had a pool table and color TV; however, they dropped the pool table due to fights.

The ambiance of the bar was enhanced by the shellacked, historic newspaper clippings on the walls. Actual articles on the Japanese surprise attack at Pearl Harbor, the sinking of the Lusitania, and the D-Day invasion were all exhibited on the wall. The bar was also full of historic relics, which included old menus, beer trays, political buttons, and beer cans. Jim Beam bottles (novelty bottles filled with whiskey) were also located all over the bar.

The Crowne Inn's busiest times were weekdays for lunch (11a.m.–1p.m.), happy hour (5–7p.m.), and weekend evenings (8p.m.–1a.m.). Business professionals made up the largest segment of customers at lunch. During the late afternoon and evenings, the customers were primarily local blue-collar workers.

Johnston and Smith worked alternating, two-week shifts: day (10a.m.–6p.m.) and evening (6p.m.–2a.m.). As their business slowly grew, so did their families. Smith eventually had four girls and moved into a beautiful four-bedroom house, while Johnston had five boys, moved into a small three-bedroom house, and struggled to pay his bills.

Transitional Years

In 1981, Harvey bought out Smith's stock in the company for $50,000 cash. At the age of 28, Karl joined the business full-time. Karl brought a new ambiance to the bar. He had a high level of energy, creativity, and numerous innovative ideas to enhance the sales of the bar. One of the first things that he did was add a large cooler that contained over 80 imported beers from all over the world. He also created an advertising campaign in the local entertainment papers, bought a popcorn machine, a stereo system, and a VCR to play movies. These ideas along with Karl's jovial personality bolstered sales and changed the culture of the bar from a primarily neighborhood blue-collar establishment to a younger, trendier 25- to 40-year-old crowd.

By late 1982, Karl had grown weary of the long hours, drunks, and low pay. Furthermore, he had recently been married and his wife, Jessica, wanted him to leave the bar business. Despite the rise in sales of the bar to $125,000, he was not making as much money as he had hoped. He quit the bar and moved to San Diego, California.

Turnaround

By late 1982, Johnston's middle son, Bruce, started working part-time for the bar; however, Harvey still worked the majority of the hours. In 1984, Karl returned from San Diego as a divorcee and started working at the bar again. Karl and Bruce came up with some innovative ideas to increase sales. They started selling warm, roasted peanuts at $.75 a bowl and ice-cold pints of imported beer on tap (e.g., Guinness, Heineken, Bass Ale). They also started selling pickles and added video games, a pinball machine, a jukebox CD player, and a big screen television.

After two years of working together, sales had increased to $185,000. Despite the increased success of the bar, Karl decided to quit. He had been robbed twice at gunpoint, including one time where the robbers took all of the money and jewelry from the customers. He also got remarried and his second wife, Judy, was pushing him to get out of the bar business. Karl and Judy moved to San Diego at the end of 1986.

By the end of 1986, Bruce was working full-time with his father. Bruce continued his entrepreneurial flair over the next 10 years. One of his most innovative moves was a strategic alliance with an Italian restaurant across the street, called Pappa's Pizza. This take-out or dine-in restaurant offered tasty Italian food. Because the bar did not serve food (besides snacks) in the evenings, it was an ideal strategy to allow people to order food from Pappa's Pizza and bring it into the bar. This strategy beefed up sales for both businesses.

Bruce also held promotional events where guest DJs would come in and play music. One of his most innovative special events was Crownewood. Crownewood was held every year on the night of the Oscars. Customers would vote on which stars would win. If they guessed correctly, they would win prizes. Other events focused on sporting events. For example, free chili was served during Monday Night Football.

These activities, combined with advertising in the local entertainment paper, *Rebel*, attracted two new market segments, the college crowd and young urban professionals. The Crowne Inn had transformed itself from a primarily blue-collar neighborhood bar into one of the most progressive bars in Kansas City. As a result, the Johnstons increased their prices and sales. Under Harvey and Bruce's tenure, the sales of the bar increased from $145,000 in 1984 to $200,000 in 1994 (4 percent increase in sales a year). See Exhibit 2.

One of the keys to Bruce's success in turning the bar around was his girlfriend, Sharon, whom he eventually married in 1985. Sharon was a very savvy businessperson with a very strict authoritarian management style with tight controls. This was in contrast to Harvey and Bruce's laid-back personalities, which led Sharon to take control the bar.

EXHIBIT 2	The Crowne Inn Sales from 1982 to 2000
Year	**Sales ($)**
1982	125,000
1983	135,000
1984	145,000
1985	165,000
1986	185,000
1987	170,000
1988	175,000
1989	180,000
1990	185,000
1991	190,000
1992	192,500
1993	197,500
1994	200,000
1995	225,000
1996	250,000
1997	295,000
1998	326,000
1999	346,000
2000	366,000

Failure of the Oral Agreement

In 1994, after 42 years of running the bar, Harvey was ready to retire. Harvey had emphysema, diabetes, and was obese. He approached his sons to see who wanted the bar. Bruce was the logical person to purchase the bar since he had been running it successfully for the past 11 years.

On the day of his father's retirement, Bruce entered into an oral agreement with his parents. In exchange for the future proceeds from the bar, Bruce agreed to pay off the $23,500 left on the second mortgage of his parents' house, give them $500 in cash per month, and pay for their health insurance and medical costs for the rest of their lives. Harvey refused to have a written contract.

Harvey remained president of the company and owned all of the stock. If he passed away, the stock would move into his wife's name. After they both passed away, the stock would then pass on to Bruce. The remainder of the estate's assets would then be divided among the other four siblings. The estimated amount of the remainder of the estate in 2001 was $50,000 (house), $80,000 (cash and securities), automobile ($10,000), and miscellaneous ($5,000).

Bruce had paid his parents' health care premiums with the most inexpensive policy up until his father's death in 1997. By 1998, when Barbara was eligible for Medicare, Bruce did not pay for any of her health care costs, which included Medicare ($46 per month) and medications ($300 per month). Cal ended up paying for the medications, which caused resentment from Cal and his wife. Barbara paid for her Medicare.

From 1994 to 1998, Bruce paid his mother $500 per month; however, he treated her as an employee. Therefore, taxes were deducted from her paycheck of $500, which resulted in a final sum of approximately $400. Bruce did pay $500 cash for one year, but in 2000 he treated his mother as an employee again. Furthermore, Barbara often complained that Bruce missed paying her on time (the 5th of the month). However, Barbara stated that after a phone call to Bruce, he always paid her by the end of the month. She insisted that he never missed a payment. To make matters worse, the bar's accountant was also Bruce and Barbara's personal accountant.

In April 2000, Bruce told his mother that she owed $10,000 in taxes for the tax year 1999. He stated that she owed this because she cashed in $15,000 in stock (initial cost basis of $1,352 in 1965) to refurbish parts of her house. Barbara's total income and taxes paid for 1999 can be seen in Exhibit 3.

Bruce and Sharon recommended that Barbara take out a $10,000 loan for the taxes that she owed. This was done within a 24-hour period of time. When Barbara informed her sons about this, they were suspicious. They decided to obtain a copy of the financial statements of the bar from 1997 to 1999. In October 2000, Danny requested a copy of the financial statements from Bruce. Bruce vehemently refused, stating that Danny was not a shareholder in the bar so he could not receive a copy of the financials. The next day Danny and Barbara visited Bruce's accountant and demanded a copy of the financial statements for the past three years. The accountant reluctantly gave copies to Barbara. See Exhibits 4, 5, and 6.

EXHIBIT 3 Barbara Johnston's Sources of Income and Tax Summary for the Tax Year 1999

Source of Income	Amount ($)
Taxable Interest	2,294
Dividends	2,752
Cashed-in Stock (Capital Gain)	13,648
Taxable Pension	5,778
Taxable S-Corp Income (Bar)	2,299
Total Income	26,771
Adjusted Gross Income	26,771
Standard Deduction	5,350
Personal Exemptions	2,750
Taxable Income	18,671
Total Federal Tax	2,576
Total State Tax	942
Total Tax	3,518

The next day the accountant called Barbara to tell her that she would be receiving a refund of approximately $6,482 from her taxes. Bruce and Sharon both went ballistic. They charged over to Barbara's house and threatened to disown her and the family:

> You have no right looking into our personal financial situation. You are trying to steal the bar away from us! You are taking away my kids' education money.

The following day Bruce and Sharon showed up unannounced at Barbara's house with an unsigned contract (see Exhibit 7). Under duress, they took Barbara to see their attorney and placed pressure on her to sign the contract. After this, they quickly went to see Barbara's attorney, Bobby Free. There was a sense of urgency on the part of Bruce and Sharon to get the contract signed immediately. Free could tell by the look on Barbara's face that she was under duress. Danny showed up at Free's office, and they stated that they needed time to examine the contract before they would allow her to sign anything.

Everyone left, but the turmoil continued. Danny updated the brothers and they determined that something had to be done about the situation. This had gone on for too long.

| EXHIBIT 4 | Income Statement for The Crowne Inn, 1997–1999 |

	1997		1998		1999	
	$	%Sales	$	%Sales	$	%Sales
Sales	$295,621	100.00%	$326,352	100.00%	$345,669	100.00%
Cost of Goods Sold	$156,100	52.80%	$157,231	48.18%	$174,139	50.38%
Gross Profit	$139,521	47.20%	$169,121	51.82%	$171,530	49.62%
Operational Expenses						
Advertising	$8,318	2.81%	$8,277	2.54%	$5,777	1.67%
Bank Charges	$892	0.30%	$1,094	0.34%	$1,592	0.46%
Insurance—General	$9,762	3.30%	$7,024	2.15%	$11,555	3.34%
Payroll—General	$94,951	32.12%	$96,027	29.42%	$98,383	28.46%
Professional Expense	$1,083	0.37%	$1,424	0.44%	$2,341	0.68%
Repairs and Maintenance	$2,096	0.71%	$9,211	2.82%	$1,687	0.49%
Taxes—Other	$7,813	2.64%	$23,312	7.14%	$27,308	7.90%
Utilities	$7,011	2.37%	$7,689	2.36%	$6,883	1.99%
Other	$5,678	1.92%	$7,882	2.42%	$6,369	1.84%
Total SG&A Expense	$137,604	46.54%	$161,940	49.63%	$161,895	46.83%
Operating Profit	$1,917	0.65%	$7,181	2.43%	$9,635	2.79%
Depreciation Expense	$1,753	0.59%	$2,353	0.72%	$2,086	0.60%
Interest Expense	$664	0.22%	$1,387	0.43%	$1,096	0.32%
Pretax Profit (Loss)	($500)	−0.17%	$3,441	1.05%	$6,451	1.87%

EXHIBIT 5		1997	1998	1999
The Crowne Inn Balance Sheet, 1997–1999 (in Thousands)	Current Assets			
	Cash & Marketable Securities	$ 6,280	$ 5,359	$ 8,118
	Inventory	$ 6,250	$ 7,325	$ 6,785
	Total Current Assets	$12,530	$12,684	$14,903
	Property, Plant, & Equipment	$80,790	$82,315	$86,467
	Less: Accumulated Depreciation	$60,791	$63,144	$69,384
	Total Net Fixed Assets	$19,999	$19,171	$17,083
	Total Assets	$32,529	$31,855	$31,986
	Current Liabilities			
	Accounts Payable	$ 5,146	$ 3,183	$ 3,456
	Sales & Income Tax Payable	$ 1,460	$ 1,481	$ 1,827
	Total Current Liabilities	$ 6,606	$ 4,664	$ 5,283
	Long-Term Liabilities	$14,045	$11,872	$ 9,085
	Total Liabilities	$20,651	$16,536	$14,368
	Common Stock or Owner's Equity	$ 6,000	$ 6,000	$ 6,000
	Retained Earnings	$ 5,878	$ 9,319	$11,618
	Total Equity	$11,878	$15,319	$17,618
	Total Liabilities and Owner's Equity	$32,529	$31,855	$31,986

EXHIBIT 6		1997	1998	1999
The Crowne Inn Cash Flow Summary, 1997–1999	Total Sales	$295,621	$326,352	$345,669
	Total Cash Available	$295,621	$326,352	$345,669
	Total Purchases	$156,100	$157,231	$174,139
	Increase (Decrease) in Inventory	$ 820	$ 1,075	($ 540)
	Cash Available After Purchase	$156,920	$158,306	$173,599
	Uses of Cash			
	Operating Expenses			
	Total per Income Statement	$137,604	$161,940	$161,896
	Financing Activities			
	Interest Expense	$ 664	$ 1,387	$ 1,096
	Principal Payments (Loan Additions)	($ 14,045)	$ 2,173	$ 2,787
	Assets Additions	$ 16,917	$ 1,525	
	Other Decreases (Increases)	$ 2,282	($ 1,942)	($ 3,532)
	Cash Flow	($ 157)	($ 921)	$ 2,759
	Beginning Cash	$ 6,437	$ 6,280	$ 5,359
	Ending Cash	$ 6,280	$ 5,359	$ 8,118
	Cash Flow Increase (Decrease)	($ 157)	($ 921)	$ 2,759

EXHIBIT 7   Contract Proposed by Bruce

AGREEMENT

This agreement made and entered into this 11th day of November 2000 by and between Barbara A. Johnston, hereinafter referred to as Seller, and Bruce S. Johnston, hereinafter referred to as Buyer:

WITNESSETH:

WHEREAS, Seller is the owner of a majority of the Stock in The Crowne Inn, Inc.; and

WHEREAS, Buyer desires to buy the Seller's stock, and to purchase all of the Seller's interest in the real and personal property where The Crowne Inn conducts business; and

WHEREAS, the parties had previously agreed to a monthly payment for the purchase of Seller's stock which agreement the parties wish to codify herein.

NOW THEREFORE, in consideration of the mutual promises and covenants contained herein, the parties agree as follows:

1. That seller shall sell to Buyer, and the Buyer shall buy from Seller, the real and personal property where The Crowne Inn, Inc., conducts its business. The parties agree that subsequent to this Agreement, all of the documents will be prepared, to effectuate said transfer, including a deed to the real property and bill of sale to all personal property and both parties shall execute such necessary documents. The consideration for this transfer shall be the sum of $50,000.00, which the Buyer shall pay forthwith even though the transfer documents shall not be prepared until after the date of this Agreement.

2. That Buyer shall continue to pay to Seller, the sum of $500.00 per month, for the remainder of her life, said payment being the consideration for the present transfer of all of the Seller's stock in The Crowne Inn, Inc. Seller shall, immediately upon receipt of said funds, execute any and all documents necessary to transfer all of Seller's interest in the stock in The Crowne Inn to Buyer.

IN WITNESS WHEREOF, the parties hereto have entered in this Agreement the day and date first above written.

_____

Barbara A. Johnston, Seller

_____

Bruce S. Johnston, Buyer

State of Missouri   :

                         : SS.

County of Jackson   :

(*continued*)

| EXHIBIT 7 | Contract Proposed by Bruce (*continued*) |

On this _____ day of _____, 2000, before me, the undersigned, a notary public, duly commissioned and qualified for said state, personally came Barbara A. Johnston, to me known to be the identical person whose name is subscribed to the foregoing instrument, and acknowledged the execution thereof to be her voluntary act and deed.

WITNESS my hand and notarial seal the day and year last above written.

_____

Notary Public
State of Missouri   :
                           : SS.
County of Jackson   :

On this _____ day of _____, 2000, before me, the undersigned, a notary public, duly commissioned and qualified for said state, personally came Bruce S. Johnston, to me known to be the identical person whose name is subscribed to the foregoing instrument, and acknowledged the execution thereof to be his voluntary act and deed.

WITNESS my hand and notarial seal the day and year last above written.

_____

Notary Public

The Bar Industry in 2001

In 2001, the bar industry was in the mature stage of the industry life cycle. The sales of alcoholic beverages in the United States had increased from $90.5 billion in 1998 to $96.1 billion in 1999. Packaged alcohol consumption increased from $44.7 to $48.7 billion, while alcoholic drinks increased from $45.8 to $47.4 billion during the same time period. A survey of 434 colleges polled by the Higher Education Research Institute found that beer drinking in 2000 had decreased from the previous year by a half percentage point (Dees, 2001).

Over the past few years, the industry has seen numerous changes. One of the more popular trends was the increasing amount of imported liquor and beer. Another trend was the increase in sales of micro-brewed beer. Many bars have also increased the number of movies/videos, video games, and billiards available to customers.

Technology was also having an effect on the bar industry. Leisure time had been reduced 25 percent over the past 10 years due to the introduction of the Internet, digital television, and game consoles. Sixty percent of the bars in the United States currently have access to the Internet. Finally, there was the increasing liability associated with owning a bar due to the implementation of the .08 alcohol intoxication limit in most states.

Local Environment and Competition in 2001

Kansas City was the home of pro baseball's Kansas City Royals and pro football's Kansas City Chiefs. The city was split in two by the Missouri River. There was a Kansas City, Kansas, and a Kansas City, Missouri. Two million people currently live in the metropolitan Kansas City area.

The cost of living index for Kansas City was 98.6 on a U.S. scale of 100. This was significantly lower that other high-cost areas like San Francisco, which had an index of 179.8. Wages for most occupations were close to the national average in the United States. Furthermore, out of 180 metropolitan areas surveyed by the National Association of Home Builders, Kansas City ranked fourteenth in housing affordability during the fourth quarter of 2000.

The Crowne Inn was located on the northeast side of Kansas City (Clay County) about five miles from downtown. The surrounding area was a combination of both residential and commercial properties.

The total number of households in the surrounding area with the same zip code was 12,800, with a population of 31,500. The median age, household income, and household size were 43, $37,786, and 2.3, respectively. Most of the people owned their homes; only 30 percent of the households had children.

The primary competitive advantage for The Crowne Inn was its location. Several businesses, two major universities, a medical school, and two major hospitals were located within a five-mile radius. In addition to the local residential market, this added an additional 30,000 people.

Five competitors were located within a one-mile radius. However, The Crowne Inn had its niche. Its reputation was a homey place where you could relax, get good food and drinks, and have quiet conversations.

The Decision

Barbara and her sons had to come to a final resolution with Bruce. It was quite evident that Bruce was unable to meet his oral obligations. Their attorney came up with three alternatives. First, they could sell the bar outright to Bruce and receive a lump sum. This would allow Bruce to pay off all of his future financial obligations to his mother in one lump sum. Second, they could have Bruce pay a smaller sum and continue with payments of $500 per month. Or third, they could sell the bar to a third party.

Karl and Bruce discussed an appropriate way to deal with the problem. Karl communicated to his family that Bruce wanted to pay a lump sum of not more than $60,000. Furthermore, it became increasingly evident that Karl was now on Bruce's side. He was not looking at the situation from an objective viewpoint. Karl insinuated that Bruce had done nothing wrong. Bruce stated to Karl:

> I am not willing to go above $60,000. If you want me to pay more than that, I will go into business with the owner of Pappa's Pizza. We have been talking about opening a new pizza/bar in one of the fastest growing segments of the city, the East. This area is dangerous. We have been robbed three times in the last three years. If we move, this would put The Crowne Inn out of business.

EXHIBIT 8   Money Bruce Spent on his Parents Since 1995

Type of Payment	Amount ($)
5 Years at 500/month	$25,000
Mortgage on House	23,500
Extra Money Given at X-Mas for 5 Years	4,000
Cost of Insurance	30,000
Lawn & Snow Care at House	3,000
Repair Bills Paid	2,000
New Furnace and Air Conditioner	4,800
Personal Tax CPA Costs	975
TOTALS	$93,275

The family, excluding Karl, Bruce, and Sharon, met over Christmas and discussed their next move. They were unsure whether or not the $60,000 was a fair offer. They were also uncertain as to how they would determine a fair lump sum. Bruce had previously sent Karl a letter outlining all of the money that he had spent on his parents over the years. In the letter he stated that he had given his parents $93,275 over the past five years. He insinuated that he had already paid for the bar. See Exhibit 8.

Danny asserted that $60,000 was a ridiculously low offer. In 1999, the bar had sales of $346,000, and Bruce and Sharon made $84,000 plus the profits from the bar. Danny stated that they should pay $175,000. Danny also had a great idea:

> We need to determine the average life expectancy for a person in Barbara's age group. Once we do this we can determine a fair offer.

According to the tables, Barbara had a life expectancy of 17.5 years; however, her history of past health problems (e.g., heart condition) reduced her life expectancy to 14.5 years. See Exhibit 9.

As the holidays came to an end, Karl, Cal, Tyler, and Danny had a number of questions. Was the lump sum method the best way to handle the problem? If so, was the $60,000 offer fair? If this was not a fair offer, what was fair? Furthermore, would Bruce be willing and/or able to pay a higher lump sum? He

EXHIBIT 9	Life Expectancy Table for Females
Age	**Life Expectancy (Years)**
10	68.6
20	59.8
30	50.2
40	40.6
50	31.4
60	22.9
65	19.0
66	18.2
67	17.5
68	16.8
69	16.0
70	15.4
80	9.1
90	4.7
100	2.5
110	1.3
120	.6

Source: Health Care Financing Administration (HCFA). *State Medical Manual 1999*, # 3258.9 (HCFA Transmittal No. 64).

had earlier told Karl that he was unwilling to pay $75,000. As they sat around pondering the situation, their mother was thinking,

> I do not want to lose my son and grandchildren over this bar. It is not worth it. However, Bruce made an oral agreement to take care of me.

Sources: Dees, J. (2001). "Fighting Back." http://www.nightclub.com/magazine/July01/fight.html; Health Care Financing Administration (HCFA). *State Medical Manual 1999*, # 3258.9 (HCFA Transmittal No. 64).

Discussion Questions

1. Describe the historical progression of The Crowne Inn. What has made the business successful?
2. What mistakes did Harvey make during the succession process? As a result of having no written succession plan, what happened?
3. Why were the brothers so mad? Were they justified?
4. Bruce attempted to get his mother to sign a contract. Do you think this was a fair contract? If not, what was wrong with the contract?
5. Bruce gave the brothers a detailed analysis of all of the money that he had given to their mother since 1995. What role should this play in determining your final recommendation to the family?
6. Based on the financial information in the case, place a value on the business using the following methodologies: (a) balance sheet method, (b) income statement method, and (c) discounted cash flow method.
7. Based on the financial and statistical information in the case, what would you recommend to the Johnston family? Why?
8. How do you think the culture of the family will change in the future?

LINKSYS: THE ESSENCE OF OPPORTUNITY RECOGNITION

Once upon a time, two immigrant entrepreneurs founded a company in the garage of their Orange County, California, home. After years of bootstrapping the company along, the founders had achieved a seven-year run on the Inc. 500 Fastest Growing Companies list, and in the spring of 2003 sold the company to a large technology company for $500 million. Sound like a fairytale? It's not. Victor and Janie Tsao represent the spirit of entrepreneurship; theirs is a story that inspires and teaches what it takes to survive and grow in the dynamic world of high technology.

The Opportunity

Victor and Janie Tsao met at Tamkang University in Taiwan. With the goal of becoming independent before the age of 40, they immigrated to the United States, where Janie worked in information technology at Carter Hawley Hale, and Victor did the same at Taco Bell while also earning an MBA from Pepperdine University. Both were known for their frugality (until the sale of the company, they drove a 12-year-old Mercedes), their drive, and their tireless ability to work day and night.

When Janie was 35 and Victor was 37, they decided to test their entrepreneurial skills by forming a consulting company they called DEW International that would match U.S. technology vendors with Taiwanese manufacturers who could do the work significantly more cheaply. From the garage of their Irvine, California, home, they worked and developed good relationships with Taiwanese manufacturers. One day one of the manufacturers brought a new product idea to the Tsaos. At that time, the cables that connected printers to computers could not exceed 15 feet in length because beyond that, the data would degrade. The manufacturer had invented a way to use telephone wire to extend that length to 100 feet, but he had no knowledge of markets and distribution and wanted the Tsaos to take this product to the U.S. market. The Tsaos agreed. Within a short period of time, the manufacturer also invented products that connected multiple PCs to multiple printers. The Tsaos immediately saw the opportunity to develop a new company, so they renamed their existing company Linksys and invested $7,000 in it. Over the next two years, Victor left his job, and the company moved twice, ending up in a 2,000-square-foot office. By means of technology catalogues, they were selling 8,000 units of their new device, which they dubbed Multishare, each month.

At the launch of Linksys, Victor began working 100 hours a week, surviving only with naps on the floor of his modest office because he felt the need to be involved in every part of the business. During the day, he immersed himself in the operations of the business; at night, he was on the phone to his Taiwanese manufacturers until the early hours of the morning. Janie's job was marketing and bringing in revenues, while Victor's was making sure they spent as little money as possible. By then their family had grown to four, and they lived on the $2,000-a-month salary that Janie drew from the company. Victor did not take a salary until the mid-1990s; even then, he wasn't the highest-paid employee, and he never took a raise.

The Linksys Culture

The Linksys culture is clearly one of frugality and making sure that everyone fits right in the organization. The Tsaos have been known to let great talent walk away if they didn't have the right mindset to fit into the culture at Linksys. The Tsaos run a lean and fast-moving operation with a pay scale that that is middling, at best. Because they don't have to pay top dollar for their talent, they tend to have young workers who are highly productive, producing about $1.8 million in revenue per full-time employee as compared with about $560,000 for Cisco. Their turnover rate is 5 percent, significantly below the industry average of 9 percent. Linksys saves money anywhere it can. It even produces its own graphics by photographing its products, scanning the photos, sending them to the printer, and even pasting the labels on the boxes.

Linksys also believes in fast product development. When one Taiwanese partner came to Victor with an idea for a product, they were able to move through product development in an astounding three weeks. Victor believes that he's not doing anything original—he just knows how to execute, and that's the secret to success in a fast-changing environment.

Linksys Grows

A key moment in Linksys' growth came when Microsoft introduced Windows 95 with built-in network functions. Now businesses and homes could network just like big business. To take advantage of the opportunity, Linksys had to get shelf space in the major retail chains. By 1995, Janie had pushed her way into Fry's Electronics and Linksys' revenue had doubled to $10.7 million, but Janie had her sights set on a national chain. It is rare that a company the size of Linksys wins a national account, but Janie was determined to get Linksys into Best Buy. In April 1996, she attended the RetailVision trade show, but was unable to secure an appointment with the buyer for Best Buy. Determined not to go home without a sale, she boldly tracked him to his hotel room and there presented their product line. The result was an order for $2 million.

From printer-to-PC connectors, Linksys expanded to Ethernet hubs, cards, and cords—everything small businesses and homeowners needed to connect their computers and share data and hardware. In 1994, this was a niche market and the company grew slowly and organically through internal cash flows until 2000, in part because the Tsaos refused to take on debt or investors. But getting into Best Buy helped to double their revenue to $21.5 million in 1996, $21.1 million in 1997, and $65.6 million in 1998. At that time, Linksys moved from its 2,000-square-foot office space to one with 20,000 square feet.

In the late 1990s, the home broadband Internet sector began to thrive despite the significantly higher costs to the user than that for dial-up connections. Victor again foresaw that people might want to link their home computers or small business computers to a single broadband line. To do this, they would need a router. Large corporations were already using routers to link computers and other hardware, but those routers were very expensive and difficult to configure. Victor saw this dilemma as an opportunity to solve a pain in the market. He developed a low-cost router for consumers and small businesses that ended up being a significant turning point for Linksys. It only cost $199 and had a wizard that walked people through the setup process. Linksys introduced the product in 1999 and succeeded in being the first low-cost router in the market. Curiously, the Tsaos' first big success occurred in Canada, which their competitors had avoided due to hardware compatibility problems. That success increased Linksys' market share from 10.8 percent to 18.6 percent in one year. Revenue increased from $107.6 million to $206.5 million. Victor attributes his ability to foresee a potential market to listening to manufacturers and customers rather than doing traditional market research.

Victor continued to introduce a stream of new products around his broadband router, such as cards that let laptops connect to routers. Then he discovered the next milestone in Linksys' growth—wireless networking. What could be better than giving customers a way to connect without wires? Again applying his strategy of being first with a low-cost version, he plunged into the 802.11g wireless standard. At that time, the industry, which was still arguing over aspects of the standard, expected the standard to be finalized in June 2003, but until then, changes in it were highly likely. Victor wanted to take advantage of Christmas sales and bring his new product out early, so the only way to avoid the possibility of the product being made obsolete because of a last-minute change in the standard was to allocate as many parameters as possible to the software. He calculated the risk and charged ahead. Fortunately for Linksys, Victor had covered all the bases, and the demand for the 802.11g access points was phenomenal. In the first quarter of 2003, Linksys had a half-million orders. Its market share increased to 34.2 percent. Victor's ability to spot an opportunity and quickly act on it is precisely what attracted the attention of networking giant, Cisco. See Figure 1 for Linksys' growth profile from 1988 to 2003.

The Cisco Opportunity

It was never the Tsaos' intention to sell their business. When the Cisco opportunity came along, it was a matter of what was best for the company. The Tsaos had wanted to expand globally, but they didn't have the cash to do it. They also knew that huge potential competitors—Dell, Microsoft, and HP—were all studying their market, and each of them had much deeper pockets than Linksys.

Cisco was interested in Linksys because it wanted to diversify into the small business and home office products sector. It saw Linksys as the premium-priced player with lean operating costs. Conversations with the Tsaos began in 2002 and by March 2003, they announced that Cisco would pay $500 million in stock for Linksys, and the Tsaos

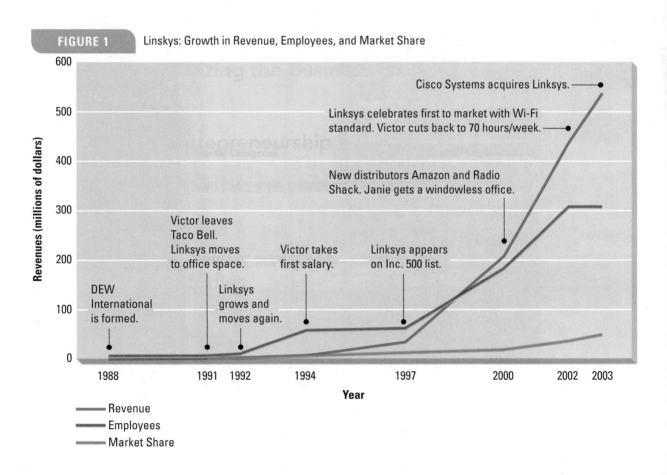

FIGURE 1 Linksys: Growth in Revenue, Employees, and Market Share

would stay on in their current positions for two years. This was the first time that Cisco had ever acquired a company and let it remain a separate company. At the time of the acquisition, the president of one of Linksys's main competitors, D-Link Systems, stated: "For Cisco to reach out to the consumer at large and come into the field of home networking in retail at this time means that it perceives the massive growth potential in the market, right where our market focus has been." After the acquisition, Victor positioned Linksys in the emerging multimedia-streaming and wireless-console-gaming market in addition to exploring the previously unsuccessful Internet telephony market. In 2006, Linksys introduced its iPhone® family of Voice over IP (VoIP) solutions to give consumers the ability to do more than simply talk on their phones—for example, to see when their friends are online and ready to receive a call. Victor and Janie moved from their shared position as senior vice president and general manager to focus on identifying new opportunities for Cisco in China.

Victor is happy with the way the company is operating, but if it ever stops being the Linksys he created and becomes more like Cisco, he will quit. Right now, things are moving as quickly and flexibly as they always did. The question is, how long will Cisco allow the company to operate independently? What will happen to the culture of Linksys if Cisco moves the offices to something more grand and plays a stronger role in how Linksys operates?

Sources: "Linksys Announces iPhone Family of Voice over IP Solutions." (December 18, 2006), http://www.linksys.com; Chai, W. (April 21, 2004). "Linksys Finds Its Voice." *CNET News.com,* http://www.news.com; "Early Wi-Fi Payoff for Linksys." *Goldsea Asian-American,* http://www.goldsea.com/Business, accessed July 9, 2004; Mount, I. (January, 2004). "Entrepreneurs of the Year." *Inc. Magazine,* http://www.inc.com.

Discussion Questions

1. Evaluate the Tsaos' financial strategy. Could they have done anything more effectively?
2. How did the acquisition of Linksys by Cisco benefit each of the companies? What new challenges did it create?

FINAGLE A BAGEL: MANAGING THE PACE OF RAPID GROWTH IN A FAMILY BUSINESS

Background

There are many paths to entrepreneurship. Sometimes starting from scratch is not the best way to own a business, especially one in an industry about which you know nothing, other than that you like the products. Laura Beth Trust and Alan Litchman loved bagels, but they had no idea how the bagel business worked. All they knew was that they wanted a business where they would be in direct contact with customers who would then help them decide which products to offer. As a husband and wife team, they also longed for an opportunity to start a family business.

Opportunity

Trust and Litchman, both MBA graduates of the Sloan School of Management at MIT, were well schooled in the art of recognizing a profitable opportunity. While in Hong Kong, they noticed a lot of American fast-food restaurants, including Starbucks, but what they did not see were bagel shops. It seemed to them that the sophisticated and multicultural Hong Kong would be enthusiastic about New York–style bagels, and so, with a great deal of optimism, they formed a corporation, found a partner, and then

began to do some research back in the United States.

Meanwhile thousands of miles to the east, Larry Smith was busy operating six very successful bagel stores in Boston. Smith was a serial entrepreneur, who in 1982 co-founded a cheesecake store, Julian's Cheesecakes, in historic Quincy Market. Faced with the problem of finding a use for leftover cream cheese, he decided to try his hand at making and selling bagels with cream cheese. The bagels were such a hit that Smith and his partners decided to refocus the store on bagels and even renamed it Finagle a Bagel. The demand at the first store led to the opening of several other stores in the Boston area, and sales rose to $10 million annually. In 1998 Smith was looking for capital to grow additional stores.

A Meeting of the Minds

Back from Hong Kong, Trust and Litchman met with Larry Smith to seek advice about the bagel business. They were attracted to Finagle a Bagel's strong brand recognition and loyal following in the Boston area. An added bonus was that both Trust and Litchman had family in the Boston area. In late 1998, after much research and many meetings with Smith, they purchased a majority stake in Finagle a Bagel and began to plan an aggressive growth strategy for the company. The plan worked so well that within just a few years, Trust and Litchman were able to buy out the original founder and become the sole owners.

This case was adapted from Pride, W. M., Robert J. Hughes, and Jack R. Kapoor, *Business,* 8th ed. (Boston: Houghton Mifflin, 2005), pp.100–101. Reprinted with permission.

Growing the Company

The foundation of the company's growth strategy was to model itself after the strategies of the Cheesecake Factory and In-and-Out Burger, two California-based successful chains that remained primarily in one state for many years before venturing beyond. In fact, to date In-and-Out Burger has never left California. Trust and Litchman wanted to dominate their geographic region before even considering geographic expansion.

One way for small companies to grow their current market is to diversify their product lines, so Trust and Litchman began introducing different kinds of bagels, sandwiches, and salads—all in one way or another linked to their core product, the bagel. The company is known for the freshness of everything it makes and also for customization, which requires a lot of interaction between employees and customers. To get ideas for new products, Finagle a Bagel does informal research with customers and employees in addition to exploring food magazines and cookbooks for new flavors. Once the staff comes up with a new idea, they begin developing a recipe and going through many iterations to find exactly the right combination of ingredients. They do a lot of taste-testing by giving the product (along with a coupon) away to customers, inviting them to come back and buy it. This is all part of one of Finagle a Bagel's fundamental tenets: Spend no money on advertising. Trust and Litchman believe that the best way to attract customers to a new product is to whet their appetites by giving them a sample. They have come up with a number of new products that give customers a reason to come back after breakfast and even lunch. One new offering that turned out to be a success was the bagel pizza.

Another way for small businesses to grow within their current market is find new customers for their current products. Finagle a Bagel began wholesaling bagels to universities, hospitals, and corporate cafeterias as well as selling packaged bagels under its brand name to the Shaw's Market grocery chain. This move into the Shaw supermarkets opened other opportunities for growth. If their bagels did well in a particular market, Trust and Litchman would open a store near the market to capture the supermarket customers who wanted to have a fresh bagel and coffee.

Another tenet of Trust and Litchman's philosophy about business is that they want to stay in control, so for them franchising was not an option because although the company would receive a large infusion of capital, the owners would not be able to control the people component of the business or the product and service quality. Raising money through an initial public offering (IPO) was also a possibility, but not very likely in the food business; again, the owners would not be able to control the timing of growth. It appeared that slow growth through internal cash flows might be the most appropriate strategy.

Building on the Brand

Having acquired a company with a loyal customer base and a good degree of brand recognition, it was Trust and Litchman's job to build on that base and give customers more opportunities to give input to the company. To reinforce the relationship with the customer, they began offering a Finagle a Bagel Frequent Finagler card, which gave cardholders one point for every dollar they spent at the store. The points could be redeemed for food items including a baker's dozen of bagels. They launched this concept on their website (http://www.finagleabagel.com) and gave customers the ability to check the status of their points and also receive free gifts by mail. Using the website was also a way to drive new traffic to their stores.

In Trust and Litchman's view, to build a successful brand, you must have consistency to reinforce the brand image. Their stores have a similar look and feel to assure customers that they won't be surprised at what they get. But they also recognize that the suburban stores serve a different clientele than the downtown stores. To recognize that, some of the suburban stores have furniture for children, free weekly concerts, and a family-friendly atmosphere. By contrast, the Harvard Square store, which services a large university crowd, has a trendier, more urban feel and even has a liquor license.

One thing Finagle a Bagel will never do, no matter what, is compromise quality. When they price a new product, they start by figuring in the cost of the finest ingredients. Then they calculate a retail price that they think the customer will pay and test it against competitors' pricing and what customers say is a great value for the price. The owners do not vary the pricing by store because they believe that it is important to treat every customer fairly.

Competition

Finagle a Bagel competes not only with other bagel shops in the Boston area but with other types of food establishments as well. Since people typically have limited disposable income when it comes to eating out, it is Finagle a Bagel's job to convince them that their money is best spent at their store. Much larger competitors, Bruegger's and Einstein, are expanding and revamping their bagel menus to include muffins and soups in addition to entrée salads and new sandwiches. Bruegger's is also looking at an upscale dining design with enhanced beverage options. The fast-food industry is a dynamic one where a company like Finagle a Bagel can survive if it innovates and capitalizes on its regional prominence.

The Company Culture

If you drew an organizational chart of the company, you would see the co-presidents, Trust and Litchman, at the top and then the middle management, store managers, and other employees beneath. But Heather Robertson, who wears many hats as Finagle a Bagel's director of marketing, human resources, and product development, enjoys turning that organizational chart upside down to point out that the co-presidents' role is to support everyone else, general managers support store managers, and so on down the chain. General managers are given the authority to do whatever it takes to alleviate problems in their stores or increase sales. Because Finagle a Bagel supports its employees, its turnover rate is very low compared to the rest of the industry, so they spend less time and money training new employees. In fact, a large number of employees have been with this 400-employee company for many years because they like the warm and caring atmosphere that the owners have fostered.

When choosing managers for their stores, Trust and Litchman have an easier time with the downtown stores because they are close enough to manage more carefully. For the suburban stores, they look for people who have an owner mentality and want to build a regional business. To encourage that, the company splits the profits with a store that has achieved more than a specified level of sales or profits. Historically, the best managers have come from the ranks of the company, working their way up.

Many of Finagle a Bagel's employees come from other regions of the world: Latin America, Europe, and Western Africa, among many others. The company often sponsors new Americans who need government-issued work permits to legally remain in the United States. There are many benefits to this multicultural workforce—new ideas and the ability to reach out to a broader customer base, to name two—but there are challenges as well. For example, to overcome the issue of language and avoid confusion, Finagle a Bagel requires that all its employees speak English when working with customers.

Technology

The company uses technology to create efficiencies, to interact with customers, and to learn which products should be kept and which should be dropped. Because every dollar counts, they only invest in technology that directly supports their business by making it more efficient or saving it money. For example, their new point-of-sale system makes it easier to track points on customer loyalty cards and determine which products are doing well and which are not. This new capability saves the company money by reducing inventory that doesn't turn over quickly and by focusing production on products that customers really want. Finagle a Bagel also believes in social responsibility. For example, no bagel ever gets thrown away at the end of the day. Leftover bagels are donated to schools, shelters, and other nonprofits. Bagels are also donated to fundraisers to feed the volunteers. The company also contributes to Children's Hospital, Boston; is the official bagel of the Boston Marathon; and four years running has been awarded the honor of one of the Top 100 Woman-Led Businesses in Massachusetts. In 2007, Finagle a

Bagel became the first bagel chain to eliminate the use of eggs from hens confined in abusive battery cages.

The Future

Today Finagle a Bagel is a 20-store chain with a corporate support center and a dough-making factory headquartered in Newton, Massachusetts. Nine of its stores are in downtown Boston and eleven in suburban areas. The company employs 320 people and has enough capacity in its current location to support 100 stores. Is franchising in their future? Their success so far has not gone unrecognized. They have twice been voted the best in Boston by *Boston Magazine*, and they have received the Best Small Business Award from the Massachusetts Chamber of Commerce in 1998, among several other awards.

The owners plan to continue opening new stores, but it is clear that one day they might receive an acquisition offer that they can't refuse because it will give them the ability to expand more rapidly. At that point, what will happen to the culture Trust and Litchman have built? Will the founders be able to give up control? Should they consider franchising?

Sources: "Finagle a Bagel Becomes First Bagel Chain to Hatch a Cage-free Egg Policy." *The Humane Society of the United States* (January 29, 2007), http://www.hsus.org/press_and_publications; Viser, M. (October 27, 2005). "Small, But Thinking Big." *The Boston Globe,* http://www.boston.com; "Finagle a Bagel to Move HQ to Newton." *Boston Business Journal* (January 13, 2005), http://www.bizjournals.com/boston.

Discussion Questions

1. As potential entrepreneurs, what did Trust and Litchman bring to the new venture they were considering? What were the factors that affected their decision about going into the bagel business?
2. Describe Finagle a Bagel's initial market strategy. What are their options for further growth?
3. Describe the culture of Finagle a Bagel. How does that culture affect their business strategy?
4. Should Trust and Litchman consider franchising as a growth strategy? Why or why not?

COMMAND AUDIO CASE STUDY: THREE START-UPS FOR THE PRICE OF ONE

Introduction

As Don Bogue, CEO of Command Audio, stood before the imposing assemblage of intellectual-property attorneys at the Marcus Evans November 2006 Conference in Washington, DC, he knew he was about to bring them a perspective of their field that only he, as an entrepreneur whose company developed and now licenses patents, could bring. He had facetiously titled his speech "Do Not Try This at Home: A Scarred Entrepreneur's View of Patent Licensing, Litigation, and Law." It was to be his version of how his company successfully developed a sustainable business model based on its intellectual-property assets.

> I am an entrepreneur, not a lawyer. Consequently, I see the world of patent law and litigation through a soda straw. My view of what is important out of the vast body of patent law is very narrowly focused: One company (mine), one technology, one portfolio of patents, and, at any given time, one lawsuit, one opponent, one set of facts, legal maneuvers, relevant law, prior art, etc., etc. While I may say things with which you disagree, just understand that they come from this tightly bounded perspective.

The attorneys listening to Bogue were about to hear an interesting and very unique case study of Bogue's company, Command Audio, which had been granted more than 60 U.S. and foreign patents and which had succeeded in leveraging its patent portfolio in each of the three principal ways that such a portfolio can be monetized: (1) attracting investment capital and protecting the technology position, (2) acquiring customers and strategic partners, and (3) licensing patent rights.

> We are unique (or nearly so) not only because we have had these three very intense, very high-risk business experiences, but also because we have lived to tell the story.

The Founding of a Company

Don Bogue grew up in a middle-class family with a father who worked in law enforcement; as a consequence, the family moved a lot. Nevertheless, Bogue, who was his high school's student body president, followed a reasonably straight path that took him to Harvard University, where he graduated *magna cum laude* with a bachelor's degree in economics. He then spent a decade at Ampex Corp, where he held a number of senior management positions.

In the early 1980s, while Bogue was at Ampex running its audio–video systems business, he met John Ryan, who was chief engineer for the camera group. John, it seems, was about to leave the company to start his own company, called Macrovision, which invented and patented anti-copying technology for VHS tapes, the popular mode of video storage at the time. While at Ampex, Ryan had learned the value of patents; so after filing his initial applications, he proceeded to file for patent protection on all the various ways that someone could defeat his original invention. Meanwhile, Bogue had moved on to join a small publicly held microwave test instrument company, Giga-tronics, as CEO. One day in June 1995, Ryan called Bogue to tell him about a new technology he had developed that didn't fit with the Macrovision portfolio. Bogue liked the technology and thought that he might have a good business model for commercializing it. The thought of leaving the relative security of a job in corporate America was a risk, but Bogue believed that as a founder and CEO of a start-up company, "If you're not scared, you're not paying attention. It's thrilling, which is the state between exciting and terrifying." Bogue had no personal start-up experience to follow—he had to learn it as he moved forward. "If you have any self-awareness at all, you realize you have been given a gift: great accountability, but you're in charge of building the entire company from the ground up. It's even more fun than just being CEO." Together Don and John decided in late 1995 to launch Command Audio.

> John Ryan invented the basic functionality of what has come to be known as the personal video recorder, or PVR; you may be more familiar with its best known branded version—TiVo. John's inventions—expressed in a series of patent applications he began filing in early 1993—cover the audio elements of devices that receive broadcast multimedia content, then store it as a database in some sort of random access memory for later replay at the convenience of the user. What you want, when you want it. (Don Bogue)

The technology that Ryan had invented would receive a broadcast signal and store all of it or only those parts that were of interest to the particular user. In other words, Command Audio would broadcast a variety of audio programming and the users could choose what they wanted to store and listen to. The receiver provided the users with an electronic program guide that let them select from the broadcast stream what they wanted to hear. A small hand-held device that was always on automatically captured the latest editions of the users' preferred programs for instantaneous access every time they got into their cars.

> I, for instance, had my receiver set up to give me, whenever I got in my car, instantaneously at a single press of a single button, the latest traffic report for my commute route, NPR's most recent top-of-the-hour newscast, a roundup of NFL action, today's "What's News Business and Finance Column" from the *Wall Street Journal* (in audio, of course), last night's Jay Leno monologue, and *News Hour with Jim Lehrer*. In short, with an RCA Audio-on-Demand receiver and a subscription to the Command Audio service, car commuters could listen to what they wanted whenever and wherever they were. (Don Bogue, Marcus Evans Conference, November 2006)

The receiver's interface was designed for "someone who is essentially blind and paralyzed, which, when you think about it, is a good analog for a person whose primary activity is driving a car at speed and only secondarily wants to access and listen to entertaining content: eyes on the road, not on a complex LCD display; hands on the wheel, not engaged in locating and pushing a dozen or more buttons." CA's research with consumers using driving simulators found, for example, that when people attempted to access content by navigating a three-level information hierarchy they invariably crashed. Two-level hierarchies in conjunction with distinctively shaped, tactile buttons and audio feedback were simple to use, at least as easy while driving as a conventional car radio. Who was the customer CA was trying to reach with its initial product and service? It wasn't the music listener, but rather car commuters who were looking for news and information in choices and amounts that fit their unique listening preferences during their morning and afternoon commute times. They already satisfied their on-demand music needs through conventional methods like tapes and CDs. The CA system would essentially do the same for non-music categories, and the content would be both local and national, although traffic, sports, and weather would have more detailed reports at a local level. The service would carry advertising, but the user would be able to opt out of listening to it. Bogue's market research determined that users actually wanted advertising if it was relevant to their interests and occurred at convenient times. CA placed advertising links at the end of program segments where they might logically occur according to the content presented. Users could also access advertising through a separate product information content menu. To provide such a service, CA had to acquire the content from broadcasters, acquire the rights to broadcast, and actually broadcast an interactive version. CA would receive an automated feed of broadcast material—for example, an NPR show. Then a technician would go through the broadcast and provide segment markers so the listener could choose the parts they wanted to listen to. This could actually be accomplished in a matter of seconds. CA broadcast 80 hours of content every day and, to this day, it believes it is the only company to which NPR has licensed broadcast rights to its "crown jewel" programs: *Morning Edition, Talk of the Nation,* and *All Things Considered.*

Audio content was ubiquitous, inexpensive, and provided by many companies. Moreover, in popular content areas like traffic, weather, news, sports, and business, users were indifferent to brand name, which further contributed to the low cost of the service. The CA system was most threatening to the AM band, which was the primary carrier of news, sports, and talk shows. And, to broadcast the signal, CA could use small pieces of idle spectrum in the FM band. In 1996, there were more than 7,000 licensed FM transmitters.[1] About 16 percent of those were in the top 100 metro areas that CA was targeting. Bogue figured that leasing the idle spectrum would provide the stations with incremental income at no cost. The amount of money involved might not be significant to leading stations, but to stations in smaller markets and to public radio, it would be enormously attractive.

The Command Audio system consisted of three main components:[2]

◗ A database of news and non-music entertainment material in audio form, which was then compressed, encrypted, and broadcast to hand-held receivers

◗ Receivers that sifted the incoming material and stored in memory those portions that were of interest to the user

◗ Specific items that, at the user's convenience, he or she could recall from memory for listening

Implementing the system required a program center where content was gathered, edited, formatted, and distributed by satellite link to local markets for transmission. CA then leased idle frequency spectrum from a network of local FM radio stations and pushed it to users' receivers.

The Industry

Just 30 years ago, most of what we rely on today for entertainment, networking, collaboration, and communication did not exist. With the advent of digital technology in the mid-1990s, the surge in new consumer electronics has been unprecedented. Digital TV (DTV) products emerged in 1998 after being adopted as the industry standard in 1996. As of 1998, one in four U.S. households had the basic equipment to put together a home theater system; VCRs were a commodity item, as were personal computers.[3] In 1996, digital cellular communications became available in the United States, and in June 1998, the first Internet-enabled phones appeared.

The consumer electronics industry actually began with radio, which was commercialized by Radio Corporation of America (RCA), a joint venture of General Electric, Westinghouse, and AT&T; and Telefunken, a joint venture of European companies Siemens and AEG.[4] RCA later led the commercialization of television worldwide, but failed in the 1970s from an ineffective effort to become a conglomerate. Meanwhile, by the late 1980s, Japanese companies Sony and Matsushita became the most important commercializers of electronics, in particular, the Walkman, Triton Color TV, the VCR, the CD, and the DVD, and succeeded in driving American companies out of their own domestic markets.

The personal video recorder industry grew rapidly when in 2001 the satellite and cable television companies began integrating the PVR function into their marketing packages in competition with existing PVR companies. In 1999, TiVo Inc. and ReplayTV Network Inc. were the industry leaders and the first to

---

[1]"By the Numbers." *Broadcasting & Cable* (March 4, 1996), p. 76.

[2]Command Audio Business Plan, 1996.

[3]J. Anderson. "Industry Focus: Consumer Electronics." *Raytheon* (1998). http://www.graduatingengineer.com/industryfocus/consumer.html.

[4]A. D. Chandler. "Gaps in the Historical Record: Development of the Electronics Industry." *Working Knowledge* (October 20, 2003), http://hbswk.hbs.edu/item/3738.html.

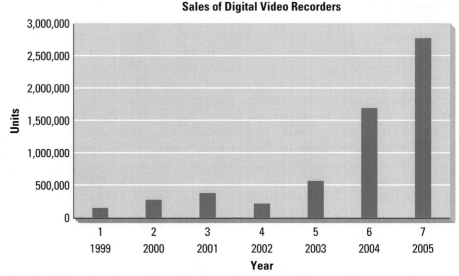

Sales of Digital Video Recorders

Source: Media Trends Track, Television Bureau of Advertising, Inc., http://www.tvb.org/nav/build_frameset.asp?url=
/rcentral/index.asp.

mass-market to consumers. Their technologies enabled consumers to pause and record live TV as well as enjoy instant replay. Because TiVo developed many strategic alliances with huge consumer product companies like Sony, Toshiba, GE, DirecTV, and Philips, it gained market share over ReplayTV, which struggled after being acquired by SONICblue. Unit sales of digital video recorders are depicted in Figure 1.

The Market and the Competition

In 1996, Bogue determined that approximately 120 million people in the United States commuted to work each day by car, and of those, 18 million spent 60 minutes or more commuting in their cars. His market research also indicated that more than 90 percent of those commuters were interested in CA's on-demand service. Bogue knew that a new consumer product might take years to be adopted by the mass market. Figure 2 depicts the comparative projected U.S. household penetration of radio-on-demand (ROD) against VCR and CD adoption patterns.

The "early adopters" of CA's service were defined as people who

▶ Resided in the 100 largest metropolitan areas[5]
▶ Spoke English as their primary language
▶ Commuted to work by car
▶ Spent an aggregate of 60 minutes per day commuting

Bogue believed that this target group represented the best chance for entering the market, and it consisted of 18 million people. Customers were disproportionately male, more inclined to purchase electronic devices, and had higher incomes. To validate his estimates and gauge demand, Bogue commissioned an independent market study. In a test in the San Francisco Bay area of 625 residents, respondents were favorably accepting of the concept. Figure 3 depicts the response pattern for this group.

As part of the follow-up to the telephone survey, the participants took part in focus groups where they were able to understand the CA concept more in-depth. Their response was similarly positive, with

[5]Top 100 Metropolitan Areas per "Metro Market Ranks." *Radio Advertising Source* (December 1995).

FIGURE 2

Overall Interest in Command
Audio Concept

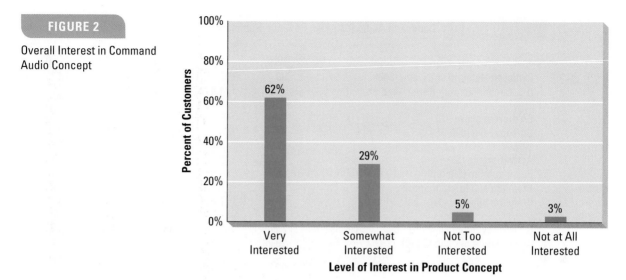

Source: Command Audio Business Plan, 2005, p. 33.

FIGURE 3

Comparative Projected U.S.
Household Penetration of
Radio-on-Demand (ROD)

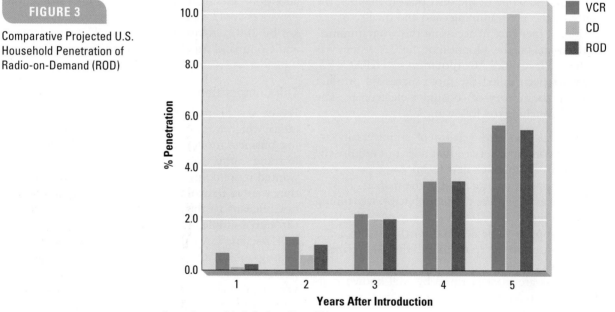

Source: Command Audio Business Plan, 1996.

their evaluation rising after they had viewed a demonstration of the system. Conjoint analysis, which asked participants to make explicit trade-offs between various product or service functions, features, and prices, further substantiated the conclusion relative to demand. With premium content, a free receiver, $30 per month subscription, and a Sony brand, the analysis was able to achieve gross penetration rates as high as 75 percent. Even with these positive results, however, Bogue knew that the actual penetration rate

FIGURE 4	Command Audio (CA) Plan Revenue Summary				
	1998	**1999**	**2000**	**2001**	**2002**
Radio-on-demand subs. avg (000)	98	596	1,501	2,778	4,589
U.S. household penetration, end (%)	0.2	1.0	2.0	3.5	5.5
CA market share (%)	100.0	90.0	88.0	70.0	60.0
CA subs, avg (000)	98	556	1,320	2,264	3,428
Activation fee ($)	10.00	10.00	10.00	10.00	10.00
Basic sub fee ($/month)	19.95	19.95	19.95	19.95	19.95
Premium sub fee ($/month)	9.95	9.95	9.95	9.95	9.95
Premium buy rate (%)	80.0	80.0	80.0	80.0	80.0
CA sub revenue ($ million)	38	209	487	835	1,265
Avg revenue per sub ($/mo)	29.28	28.71	28.28	28.17	28.12

of the CA service would depend on the marketing campaign, the scope of the distribution channel, the quality of the programming, and the quality of the individual experience in accessing the programming.

His model for the adoption of the CA system was Hughes Electronics Corporation's DIRECTV®, which has been called the most successful product launch in the history of consumer electronics. The similarities include the following:[6]

▶ CA is an advanced version of a universally accepted consumer service that does not require the mastery of a complex new technology.
▶ There appears to be a need in the market.
▶ The CA system gives the user control over timing and content.
▶ There appears to be demand for the system.
▶ Users purchase the receivers and then subscribe to the service.
▶ Receivers are manufactured by well-known consumer electronics firms.
▶ Service providers and hardware manufacturers conduct marketing campaigns to build consumer awareness.

Bogue understood the need to license to other radio-on-demand service providers and media and entertainment companies seeking new channels for

[6]Command Audio Business Plan, 1996, p. 38

content distribution if he was ever going to reach mass adoption. He figured that these additional service providers could capture about 40 percent of the market by 2002. Figure 4 displays total system demand and Command Audio's revenue projections.

The Competition

Bogue saw his primary competition as conventional radio, which was free to users because of its advertising business model and because it no longer had a learning curve. Nevertheless, he believed that users wanted more control over what they listened to and they wanted to avoid a clutter of advertising that was not relevant to their interests. For a low price and through a simple method, users could gain that control. Because CA's system could determine audience demographics, it would be easier for CA to convince prospective advertisers to use its medium over conventional radio in order to closely target ads to the interests of specific demographic groups.

One competitor was RBDS (Radio Broadcast Data System), a low data rate data broadcasting service that, in 1996, was being adopted by some FM stations. The service enabled "listeners with specially equipped car radios to receive supplementary program data and text messages that [could] be displayed on the receiver to show station call letters, programming format . . . title and artist of a current piece as well as playlists of the next several selections. In addition the radios could receive and display pager messages and low data rate information such as sports scores."[7] In 1995, approximately 5 percent of licensed stations were broadcasting some RBDS data, and fewer than 800,000 car radios were RBDS compatible.

In 1996, when Bogue wrote the Command Audio business plan, a few companies had announced intentions to bring satellite broadcast radio to market through point-to-multipoint systems that would transmit music and non-music programming to cars equipped with special receivers. These services promised better quality sound, the ability to select a station by format, a broader range of programming, and freedom from terrestrial-induced signal interference. However, satellite radio would not give the user control of what they listen to, how much, and when.

In 1996, wireless communication (cellular or PCS) was facing the same barriers to adoption, and their high cost to install or expand made them an unlikely delivery mechanism for on-demand radio because they could not match CA's pricing. Moreover, wireless did not have the bandwidth to deliver a program at a sufficient level of quality. The other potential competitor was Internet search engines and browsers, but they were not yet capable of providing simple and safe access to program material while driving. With this approach, users could not gain immediate access to current information and breaking events, and downloading would necessarily occur at a particular time when the user was connected to the Internet. So users would have to carry their receivers from the car to their computers and back. In addition, users would have to pay based on how much content they downloaded or they would be required to listen to advertisements. The biggest threat might come with the convergence of the Internet and wireless capability, which in 1996 was still several years away.

A significant advantage that Bogue saw for CA was its low infrastructure costs, which reduced its capital requirements significantly when compared to other information and entertainment service providers. "For example, in 1996 major direct-to-home satellite TV programmers spent between $0.5 billion and $1.5 billion each to purchase transmission licenses and launch satellites. Command Audio, by comparison, [spent] in total just $10 million on facilities and equipment in order to commence service . . . and only $23 million annually to lease the necessary FM subcarriers."[8]

Business Model #1: Raising Investment Capital and Protecting the Technology Position

In December 1999, just before CA launched its service, Audio on Demand, it raised $56 million in venture capital. Although this was a time of intense investment by the venture capital community, CA's funding was successful by any measure. It was designed to provide launch financing into four lead markets and to begin the exploration of another six markets.

The service was officially launched in January 2000, running 24 hours a day, 7 days a week. In March, CA began its media campaign to a lukewarm response; the customer acquisition rate was not nearly as fast as projected. To make matters worse, the service suffered a 25 percent churn because of the battery, which was too large and didn't have a long enough life span. Initially, CA charged $200 for the receiver and $9.99 per month for the service, but within three weeks they were forced to lower the price of the receiver to $99 and make adjustments to the service pricing and programming.

As the company also optimistically prepared for a potential initial public offering (IPO) of $150 million to roll out to the top 50 markets, April 2000 brought the crash of the public equity markets, especially for pre-profitability technology companies, and the investment banks CA had chosen to lead the IPO advised the company that the window of opportunity for companies like CA had closed but would likely open again in spring 2001. Although that was only a year away, if their predictions were correct, Bogue couldn't figure out how things would change fast enough to keep the company alive. They would be out of money by September 2000.

> Our senior management team realized very quickly that a seismic and very negative shift in our prospects had occurred. Though crushingly disappointed, we decided almost immediately to shut down our service

---

[7] Command Audio Business Plan, 1995, p. 48

[8] Command Audio Business Plan, 1996, p.14.

and downsize the company to conserve capital for a strategic redirection towards software development and licensing. In this new model, we generalized the tools and technologies we already had developed and licensed them to others who wanted to offer similar on-demand media services.

Business Model #2: Licensing Their Tools and Technologies

With a portfolio of valuable technologies and a determination not to give up, Bogue repositioned the company as a software development and licensing company that would license the systems and tools it had developed to companies that wanted to offer on-demand media services. Initial success with digital radio pioneers XM Satellite Radio and iBiquity encouraged Bogue that he had made the right decision. CA's growing patent portfolio was demonstrating to licensees, strategic investors, and partners that CA was the technology leader in broadcast on-demand media.

However, as optimistic as Bogue was, he soon discovered that his software licensees' plans had also been rather optimistic. Development delays resulted in these industry leaders deciding not to deploy CA's technology for three more years, which meant that CA would not be receiving any royalties for three years. Once again the company was faced with the possibility of a cash shortfall and once again Bogue downsized the company with a plan to reorganize yet again. In August 2002, Bogue sold CA's software development business to iBiquity Digital and licensed to that company all of CA's patents and software. iBiquity had the right to sublicense CA's patents in the terrestrial digital radio field, but CA retained the exclusive rights to license its intellectual property in every other field of use.

Business Model #3: Enforcing Existing Patents and Licensing Agreements

Still searching for a strategy that would enable CA to return its shareholders' capital, Bogue was about to undertake the most unconventional and risky business model of all: licensing and, where necessary, enforcing CA's patents. With digital and satellite radio already

under license, Bogue turned his attention to personal video recorders, the sort of device pioneered by TiVo and ReplayTV. This market was potentially very large, but it would prove extremely difficult to penetrate. For the next 15 months, Bogue and his team, now a very small company, worked hard to conserve CA's remaining cash and began to approach the major consumer electronics companies as well as manufacturers of cable and satellite television set-top boxes. Although these companies had an interest in personal video recorders and saw them as the next big thing, they were reluctant to accept the fundamental nature of CA's intellectual property and the need to acquire a license to use it. They figured that if they ignored CA, the company would eventually disappear.

Bogue had not gone into this effort without preparation. The response of the big consumer electronics companies was expected, and it was time to draw a line in the sand. It was clear that TiVo and Replay were using the audio time-shifting functionality embodied in John Ryan's inventions, even though they were focused on television. Their use of the technology could well have been inadvertent; they may simply have been unaware at the time they began developing their products that the same idea had occurred to Ryan a few years earlier. TiVo's founders came out of Silicon graphics and apparently, in their own way, had reached the same solution as John Ryan had. Bogue also foresaw that, down the road when video was delivered to cell phones, it would be delivered through broadcast rather than point-to-point technology and would be cached on the handset by users. That, too, would require manufacturers and service providers to obtain licenses to CA's patents. So now he had two choices: He could either shut down the company or he could fight the big boys. He chose the latter.

Bogue quickly realized that the key to his company's success was in having the money to go after the companies that were infringing his patents, and he had to have enough funding to outlast them. His current investors, as committed as they were, would not be supplying any more capital for this latest business model; in any case, the amount that Bogue needed was significantly higher than they might provide. An exhaustive search produced the answer: an insurance policy that covered the cost of offensive patent litigation and provided several million dollars of financing at a price the company could afford. CA would pay an up-front premium and, upon settlement of the lawsuit, would repay what had been put out plus a premium. This policy was the turning point because the company was now competing on a level playing field with the major electronics manufacturers.

With financing in place, Bogue began to study companies coming into the PVR market and selected a target to focus on for litigation: Sony Corporation. Bogue figured that if he could win this suit, the other companies infringing his patents would be more likely to fall in line and pay royalties rather than risk infringement litigation. On February 1, 2002, CA filed a patent infringement action against Sony Corporation. The litigation took four years, during which CA prevailed in multiple Markman rulings, summary judgment motions, and a bench trial on inequitable conduct. After the two companies had spent over $15 million, Sony decided to settle the lawsuit. It paid an up-front financial settlement and signed a royalty-bearing license for the use of CA's patents around the world.

This was a monumental win for Command Audio. The personal video recorder market, which consists of cable and satellite TV set-top boxes, DVD recorders, game consoles, and PCs, is perhaps twenty times as large as the digital and satellite radio market. And right behind that is television delivery to cell phones that incorporate broadcast tuners and PVR functionality, which is an order of magnitude larger than personal video recorders. Analysts estimate that in 2006 alone, more than 25 million PVRs were sold, and that number would grow by 30 percent in 2007.[9] In April 2007, CA signed a license agreement with Scientific Atlanta, a leader in cable television set-top boxes and a Cisco company. They intend to use CA's technology in all of their PVR set-top box products. Bogue knows that even with this pivotal win, the game is not over. Although he has aligned his patent and business strategies and prepared his company's financing, will every company infringing his patents agree to pay royalties? Is this a sustainable strategy?

Discussion Questions

1. What was the source of the opportunity for Command Audio?
2. What were the problems with the first business model: building and selling the CA box and service to consumers?
3. Why did the second business model fail? Could that failure have been avoided?
4. Was it necessary for the company to go through three business models before it found the right one to build a sustainable company?

---

[9]"Scientific Atlanta Purchases License to Use Command Audio's PVR Technology." Press release (April 24, 2007).

CliqUp

FEASIBILITY ANALYSIS

Prepared By

Chris Chen

Izu Matsuo

Winnie Peng

EXECUTIVE SUMMARY

Concept and Opportunity

Forrester recently estimated that $60 million is spent on social or user-generated media market research, with a potential market size of $489 million by year 2010. Several key factors drive the need for market research in this area:

- The emergence of the Internet is creating new markets to research, lower costs of entry, and new methodologies for acquiring data.

- Marketers continue to look for ways to reach the elusive and fragmented 18–34 user group that is connected online almost 24/7 and represents the majority of social media users.

- Social media usage is growing rapidly with the likes of MySpace and YouTube fueling this space.

- Marketers are more willing to experiment with new media as they become more comfortable with social media such as blogs, podcasts, and online videos.

- There are over 70 million blogs, doubling every 8 months. Given their nature, blogs are good sources to track market and consumer trends.

- Social media advertising is projected to grow 144.9% in 2006, with a 106.1% compound annual growth rate from 2005 to 2010.

The combination of these trends has created a demand that CliqUp will fulfill.

CliqUp is a consumer research company that tracks consumer behavior and trends in the social media space. CliqUp offers deeper customer insights and customizable reports that help corporate marketers identify opportunities and trends faster, which allows them to save time, set marketing strategies with more confidence, and ultimately achieve better results.

The Company is pursuing high-margin revenue streams through the following:

- Periodic Custom Research is sold on an annual contract basis offering bi-annual or quarterly reports for clients to have deeper understanding of their customers and markets so that they can set better marketing strategies.

- Periodic Syndicated Research is sold on a one-time or annual subscription basis offering generic reports to clients looking to identify opportunities and trends in their target customer markets.

- Ad-hoc Custom Research is sold on a one-time basis offering snapshots of a market for clients to identify the effectiveness of their marketing strategies.

- Advertising inventory on CliqUp's own website is sold to advertisers who are looking to tap the social media demographic audience.

These services offer a high degree of details about WHAT consumers do, and more importantly, WHY they do it. The results are delivered in flexible reports that are tailored to customer preferences, exceeding current industry expectations. The driving factor for CliqUp's ability to offer such deep consumer insights is its underlying technology for consumer behavior analysis.

Primary Research Results

CliqUp conducted in-depth interviews with five corporate marketers (Toyota, Honda, Intel, Frederick's of Hollywood, and FritoLay) who are known for experimenting with interactive social media. Through these interviews, the Company discovered some key findings regarding the needs that exist in the market:

- Increasing interest in exploring social media as a way to reach target consumers
- Lack of understanding of the new social media
- Lack of tools to track social media trends and changes
- Social media presents an enticing yet risky channel.
- Constant craving to have deeper understanding of target consumers
- Lack of customized and relevant market research reports
- The need is there and the interviewees have all expressed interest in paying for such services.

Management Team

CliqUp's management team possesses a diverse set of experience across languages and cultures to bring entrepreneurial, marketing, and engineering talent that is capable of executing vital tasks to take the business to success. To further complement the gaps that are not core to the business, CliqUp will form an Advisory Board consisting of executive managers and industry experts to further increase the chance of success for the business.

Financial Assessment

To successfully execute its plan, CliqUp requires about **$1 million in capital.** The capital needs are based on a cumulative negative cash flow of **$688,808** and a contingency factor of approximately **$330,000.** The Company plans to start in August 2007 and will incur a **start-up cost of $50,000.** The Company will be **profitable in January 2009 (month 19)** and will look for additional funding to continue its growth. The Company will reach **break-even in July 2009** for a **payback period of 25 months.**

	EOY 1 (June 2008)	EOY 2 (June 2009)	EOY 3 (June 2010)
Total Revenues	**$234K**	**$6.7MM**	**$25.1MM**
Gross Profit	$182K	$5.3MM	$19.9MM
Gross Margins	78%	79%	84%
EBITDA	($515K)	$851K	$6.4MM
EBIT	**($517K)**	**$847K**	**$6.4MM**
Net Profit After Tax	($517K)	$501K	$4.1MM
Net Profit Margin	-	7%	17%

Growth and Expansion

CliqUp's vision is to leverage its experience, customers, and technology to provide other services that require consumer behavior tracking, such as media measurement (i.e., measuring effectiveness of advertising) and the emerging $1.5 billion behavioral targeting field for targeted advertising.

Timeline to Launch

CliqUp is currently in the stage of testing its unique and proprietary technology that enables tracking of consumer tastes over time with high accuracy and precision without the use of traditional media. The Company is at a point where it needs additional funding to take its technology to market for further testing.

CliqUp will launch in August of 2007. Due to the nature of the business, CliqUp will spend the first six months of its operation collecting data necessary to launch its research services. Services will be introduced one at a time into the market beginning seven months after launch.

Feasibility Decision—GO!

After detailed research, target market interviews, and financial analysis, CliqUp recognizes a lucrative market to enter. The Company is moving forward with its decision to start this business.

TABLE OF CONTENTS

INDUSTRY ANALYSIS

The U.S. Market Research Services industry is a fairly stable industry that has undergone a few major changes due to the emergence of the Internet as a new channel to collect data and deliver reports. The Internet is lowering barriers to entry in this $6.9 billion industry and creating new opportunities for emerging companies to enter. CliqUp is prepared to capture these new markets and capitalize on these opportunities by entering into the largest sector, consumer research.

Industry Overview

The U.S. Market Research Services industry (Primary NAICS code 541910: Marketing Research and Public Opinion Polling, Primary SIC Code 8732: Commercial nonphysical research) involves data gathering and analysis activities primarily for measuring market share amongst competitors and consumer behavior. In this $6.9 billion industry,[6] data is gathered from consumers through touch points at retail outlets as well as through other forms of media including surveys, polls, focus groups, and online Internet-based channels. Market research companies generally own the data they acquire and revenue is primarily generated by selling access to data, generating analytical reports for their customers, and custom research projects.

Industry Characteristics

The following list provides a brief overview of industry characteristics:[7]

- The industry has reached a mature stage of growth. Market size is expected to grow by 58% (7–12% annually) from 2004 to 2009, reaching a total value of $10.9 billion in 2009 (Exhibit I.1, Figure 1). Economic performance is the primary factor in driving the market growth in the early periods of the forecast.

- Gross margins in traditional consumer research companies are roughly 55%, whereas Internet-based research companies are finding gross margins of 80% not atypical.[8]

- Consumer research takes up 40.5% of sales in 2004 and is the largest sector, with a growth of 13.8% from 2005–2009 (Exhibit I.1, Figure 2).

- Syndicated research takes up 30% of industry sales while custom research accounts for 70%.[9]

- Due to the nature of the services, majority of the work is done domestically.

- The industry is generally more resilient to economic fluctuations than the advertising industry.[10] This is partly due to the fact that clients still need constant research into media reach, brand equity measurements, consumer habits, etc., even in times of slow economic growth.

---

[6]"Market Research in the USA." *Euromonitor.* October 2005 [List information comes from source unless stated otherwise].

[7]"Market Research in the USA." *Euromonitor.* October 2005.

[8]"Research Services Industry." *Yahoo Finance.* [Accessed January 14, 2007]. http://biz.yahoo.com/ic/news/768.html.

[9]Syndicated researches are longer-term contracts or subscription based where companies usually must build up expertise over a period of many years. Custom research is typically contracted on a case-by-case basis by companies looking for specific information.

[10]"About GfK." *GfK Group.* [Accessed April 17, 2007]. http://www.gfk.com/group/company/sector/index.en.html.

Industry Trends and Drivers

Growth and changes are driven by trends that affect the industry life cycle and competitive landscape:

- Increase in niche players due to lower entry barriers driven by the emergence of the Internet as a new channel medium through which data can be acquired and reports can be delivered at lower costs.
- Technological advances in data analysis are improving market measurements and metrics monitoring.
- Increased investment in the Internet space is creating new opportunities for players to capture.
- The growing popularity of the Internet is creating new channels and methodologies for collecting data and delivering reports.

Competitive Landscape

The industry is fairly consolidated, with the largest four players (VNU, WPP Group plc, Information Resources Inc., and Taylor Nelson Sofres) taking up 52.6% of the market. All four firms are multinational firms with divisions and offices in multiple countries. They offer both syndicated reports and custom research. These firms maintain their revenue growth through acquisitions of smaller firms with innovative technologies and research methodologies.

With the emergence of the Internet as a cheaper way to acquire data and deliver reports, new competitors such as WebsideStory, BuzzMetrics, and Umbria are entering the market research space to capture new opportunities. CliqUp is prepared to fully take advantage of this new channel medium to grab a share of this lucrative market with high gross margins. See Exhibit I.2 for a list of industry players.

Critical Success Factors

Firms must have the following capabilities in order to succeed in this industry:

- **Quality, accurate, and reliable data.** Quality consumer data is what enables the buyers to identify opportunities and understand their markets better. Without quality data, there is no quality analysis.
- **High-quality analysis methodology and innovative technology.** A combination of both creates sustainable competitive advantages for firms who compete in an industry littered with small players.
- **Flexibility.** Market research comes in different flavors. Companies in this industry who are flexible so that it can customize their products to meet the changing demands of the customers.

MARKET ANALYSIS

The U.S. Consumer Research Market

The consumer research market offers research in consumer preferences, behavior, and spending habits. The sector is the largest sector in the market research industry. Figure 1 shows a 16.7% compound growth from 2000 to 2004. The market itself will continue to be the largest sector in 2009, accounting for 30.7% of the market in 2009. It is expected to continue at a similar growth rate, reaching $3.3 billion by the year 2009.[11] The stable growth indicates that the market is reaching maturity.

Market Trends

The Internet is a primary driver for a series of market changes. The Internet:

- Is driving demand for better and deeper understanding of online user behavior tracking and monitoring.[12]
- Demands new tracking and measuring innovations for new online markets for which current technologies for traditional media (i.e., TV, radio, etc.) are unable to satisfy.
- Creates new markets that demand new research services such as online advertising measurements and market adoption trends research.
- Shortens the time to collect and deliver reports. This is changing how fast companies can track shifting market conditions.
- Lowers the cost to enter the research market. Online focus groups, panels, and surveys are much lower in costs than their traditional counterparts.[13] Lower entry costs also place emphasis more on technological innovation rather than high capital resources.

FIGURE 1 Consumer Research Market Size

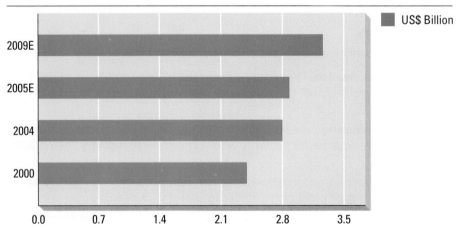

[11]"Market Research in the USA." *Euromonitor*. October 2005.

[12]Ann Palmer. Interview with Ann Palmer, Assistant Manager at Honda Interactive Marketing. February 26, 2007.

[13]Maryann Jones Thompson. "When Market Research Turns into Marketing." *The Industry Standard*. August 23, 1999. http://www.thestandard.com/article/0.1902.5995.00.html.

The Internet is creating new opportunities for smaller companies to compete directly with large players such as The Nielsen Company and TNS Media. CliqUp intends to enter the market by providing research services into new markets created by the emergence of the Internet.

Primary Research

Primary Research Methodology

In order to determine the existence of pain and needs of marketers as well as the existing market situation such as trends, competitor's reputation, and weaknesses, CliqUp conducted in-depth interviews with five corporate marketers. Interviews were conducted in person or via phone, lasting from 45 minutes to 2 hours for each marketer. The marketers were chosen based on those working in corporations known for using online advertisement and experimenting with interactive/social media. Each marketer interviewed had extensive experience in online advertising and initiating marketing efforts. Below is a list of companies, division, and titles of the marketers interviewed:

Corporation	Division	Title
Toyota	Scion Marketing	Interactive Marketer
Honda	Interactive Marketing	Assistant Manager
Intel	Integrated Marketing, Web Strategy	Manager
Frederick's of Hollywood	Corporate Brand Marketing	Senior VP
FritoLay	Doritos Marketing	Assistant Brand Manager

Terms

A set of technical terms is used throughout the section and is defined here to better understand the rest of the plan.

- **Interactive media:** Any media that is accessed through the Internet, such as online advertising, display banner ads, social media, etc.

- **Social media:** Social media describes technologies and channels that people use to share insights, experiences, perspectives, and opinions with each other. Social media channels include social networking sites, video and photo sharing sites, blogs, podcasts, wikis, and message boards. Another similar term to describe this is user/consumer-generated media.

Primary Research Key Findings

Through extensive interviews and analysis, CliqUp was able to discover a need and demand that exist in the market. Below is a list of key findings that the Company determined:

- **Increasing use of interactive media.** Interviewees indicated that the Internet is a lower-cost means to reach consumers as well as gather consumer data. This is mainly justified by how easy it is to track consumer behavior on websites.

- **Increasing interest in exploring social media as a way to reach target consumers.** Interviewees indicated that word-of-mouth is becoming more important as social media slowly becomes more prevalent on the Internet. Furthermore, interviewees are taking a more serious look at social media as their target customers, specifically from 18- to 25-year-olds, are moving rapidly into these media.

- **Lack of understanding of the new social media.** The social media is a new channel, and as such, interviewees are unable to find data to justify the value for their spending in such an emerging space. Interviewees are looking to have better understanding of the social media space and the ROI it can generate for their marketing dollars. Of course, interviewees are willing to experiment with these new media given enough budget and justification for value.
- **Lack of tools to track social media trends and changes.** The social media lacks tools to measure and accurately track marketing campaign effectiveness. For instance, with over 70 million blogs doubling every eight months, interviewees find it difficult to track who's saying what about whom.
- **Social media presents an enticing yet risky channel.** The social media is largely controlled, by definition, by the consumers themselves. Interviewees indicated lack of credibility, trust, and control as factors of great concern for using this channel, even though their target consumers are flocking into this space.
- **Constant craving to have deeper understanding of target consumers.** Interviewees are constantly craving to know more about their consumers' lifestyle attributes as well as their purchasing habits. Understanding their consumers' underlying behavior helps the interviewees to craft much more targeted campaigns to attract the consumers.
- **Lack of customized and relevant market research reports.** Interviewees voice their disappointment in current market research reports and how inadequate they can sometimes be. The interviewees complained how reports frequently show data and insights of what is, but never give a thorough reasoning behind why the consumers behave the way they do.

With the increasing prevalence of the social media, CliqUp is entering the right market offering market research services to the corporations. However, there are several obstacles that deter marketers from advertising in the alternative media. CliqUp intends to provide a set of services within the social media space to help marketers understand the emerging channel and its value in marketing campaigns. The need is there and the interviewees have all expressed interest in paying for such services.

Target Market

After extensive primary research (Exhibit M.2), CliqUp has identified a specific segment of the market that requires its services—corporations with the following characteristics:

- Their target customers are young people from ages 18 to 24. These people are rapidly increasing their use of social media into their lifestyles habits.
- They are looking to integrate social media into their marketing strategies in order to reach their target customers.

This need to understand the social media space creates a strategic opportunity that CliqUp will capture.

According to Forrester, the social media research sector is estimated at $60 million and growing rapidly.[14] Key drivers for research spending are increased willingness to experiment with new media, perception of ineffective traditional advertising, and desire to reach the coveted audience between the ages of 18 to 24 who are active social media users.

Market Entry Strategy

CliqUp will enter the consumer research sector through a niche market strategy by offering syndicated and custom research services in the social media space to corporations looking to integrate these media into their marketing strategy.

Our primary and secondary researches show that the social media is becoming one of the most influential channels on the Internet for branding, advertising, and PR. Marketers are actively evaluating this space to incorporate into their marketing strategies as a way to access highly targeted audience.[15] However, marketers spend time and effort equaling to about $8000 per campaign in locating appropriate and influential bloggers with the right audience.[16]

Although there is no available data that shows the growth rate of social media research due to its emerging state, it is comparable to the one of social media advertising spending market, which is projected to grow 144.9% in 2006 and a 106.1% compound annual growth rate from 2005 to 2010.[17]

Barriers to Entry

CliqUp faces challenges similar to new entrants in the consumer research market, including:

- **Trust and credibility.** New entrants must establish credibility within the market and prove that their analysis methodologies are accurate, objective, and insightful. Creating trust takes time.
- **Historical data availability.** New entrants start with little data to do comprehensive and accurate analysis. Increasing the rate of data collection will help mitigate this barrier.

Competition

CliqUp's innovative research process in capturing data, analyzing data, and generating reports is unique and reduces competition (see Exhibit M.1 for complete list). However, CliqUp faces competition including:

- **Direct competitors**—CliqUp has identified BuzzMetrics, Umbria, and Cymfony as the three most prominent direct competitors. Two of these companies have recently been acquired by large players in the market research industry, thus giving them more resources to work with.

---

[14]Abbey Klaassen. "Move Is Latest in Trend of Research Firms Nabbing Buzz-Measuring Experts." *Advertising Age (Midwest Region Edition)*. Chicago: February 26, 2007. Vol. 78, Iss. 9; pg. 3.

[15]Abbey Klaassen. "For Marketers Social Media Soars, Mobile and Gaming Lag." *Advertising Age.* March 27, 2007. http://adage.com/digital/article?article_id=115765.

[16]Interview with Nichole Taylor, Assistant Brand Manager of Doritos, who successfully executed the Crash SuperBowl campaign. March 27, 2007.

[17]Center for Media Research. "Blogs, Pods and Really Simple Stuff Deliver Advertising at an Increasing Rate." January 24, 2007. http://www.centerformediaresearch.com/cfmr_brief.cfm?fnl=060412.

Cymfony owns about 25% of the current social media research market.[18] In addition, these companies have their own technologies to solve similar problems existent in the market and gather data from the social media space. However, CliqUp believes that no competitor has found a good solution that can properly identify a consumer's true underlying values accurately and predictably online.

- **Traditional research companies**—CliqUp is concerned about large players entering into this market as the social media space continues its rapid growth. However, judging from current trends, it appears that these large players tend to enter new market through acquisitions as they do not seem willing to lose time rather than developing new technologies. Recently, The Nielsen Company acquired BuzzMetrics while TNS Media bought up Cymfony.[19] CliqUp believes that this trend will likely continue.

- **Online research companies**—Online research companies such as WebSideStory have the necessary capabilities to compete online with CliqUp. However, social media research requires a different technology to perform better research. Although online research firms can develop such technologies themselves, CliqUp believes that they will likely follow an acquisition strategy similar to traditional research companies as a way to enter the market that is rapidly growing.

CliqUp's Uniqueness

CliqUp's services help marketers identify opportunities and trends faster, have deeper insights into their consumers, and set marketing strategies to achieve better results. CliqUp differentiates itself from other competitors through its innovative data acquisition methodology and research process.

- **Data acquisition.** CliqUp uses its own website as the primary medium to gather its data, thus reducing its data acquisition costs and allowing ownership of the data. Furthermore, it collects data in a different way—from the social media space and without the user having to fill out surveys or join panels.

- **Data analysis.** CliqUp has a unique system to analyze data. CliqUp's Relationship Analyzer can analyze and produce highly precise consumer behavior changes and trends. The CliqUp Behavior Analyzer platform allows marketers to identify opportunities and trends sooner and gain deeper insights into their own customers compared to the services that other competitors offer.

- **Convenient tools.** Unlike other competitors where custom research reports are partly generic, CliqUp works with clients to offer customized reports that allow them to choose different sets of information for analysis. With access to different perspectives that they may not have observed if they were to go with competitors, marketers can have more confidence in setting their marketing strategies and achieving better results.

---

[18]Cymfony's sales is estimated at $10–$15 million. With current market size of $60 million, Cymfony should own at most 25% market share.

[19]Abbey Klaassen. "Move Is Latest in Trend of Research Firms Nabbing Buzz-Measuring Experts." *Advertising Age (Midwest Region Edition)*. Chicago: February 26, 2007. Vol. 78, Iss. 9; pg. 3.

SERVICE DEVELOPMENT PLAN

The goal for CliqUp's operations is to acquire data and provide market research services. CliqUp's business model is delivering high-quality custom research that is relevant and customized to customers' needs. Thus, CliqUp's key factors to production are user and data acquisition, data analysis, and client relationships. To achieve this goal, CliqUp has mapped out an innovative process flow to achieve excellence in each of these areas.

Process Flow

CliqUp's key factors to production are its data quality and data analysis methodology. The process flow shows how data is acquired, what technologies are used to analyze data, and how reports are delivered. Each process section is discussed in detail in Figure 2.

Technical Description of Products and Services

Figure 3 illustrates how the technical components interact with each other to gather data, analyze data, and deliver reports. Key parts to CliqUp's success and core differentiation are shown in color. The technical details of major components are discussed in further detail below.

CliqUp Rating System

CliqUp's innovative rating system is a hybrid rating/commenting system that serves as the main conduit for collecting the data used to analyze consumer preferences and values. Unlike current rating systems where users rate on interests/views with simple good/bad (+/–, thumbs up/down) or star (1–5) ratings, ClipUp's rating system enables users rating on any content based on what they feel and think without restriction (no defined set of attributes). In addition, the rating system serves as a simplified commenting mechanism that makes writing and sharing comments easy, useful, and engaging. The results generated from the ratings are also more detailed and precise than current personalization systems in the market when it comes to giving recommendations.

FIGURE 2 Process Flow Chart

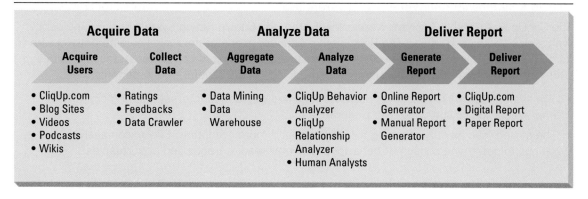

FIGURE 3

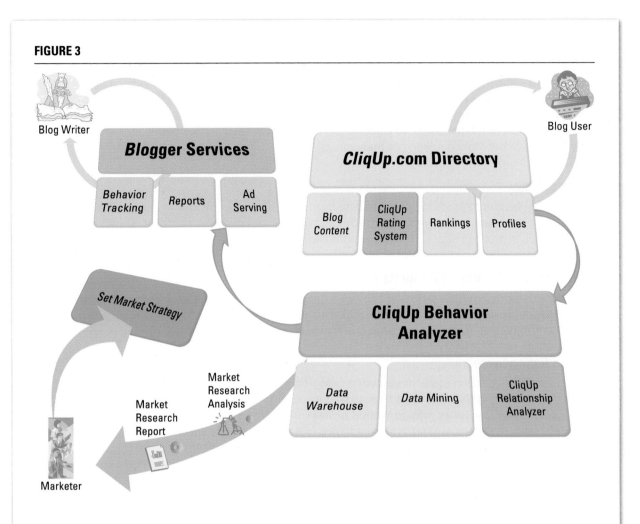

CliqUp Relationship Analyzer–Core Differentiator

The CliqUp Relationship Analyzer works closely with the CliqUp Rating System in grouping people with similar tastes and values. The Relationship Analyzer is one of the main key differentiators from its competitors. This revolutionary system offers precise tracking of consumer tastes and values over time. The information created by this methodology offers several unique benefits:

- The system can reliably discover user interests and degrees of interest, offering customers unprecedented insights into user preferences.

- The system can identify changing trends faster and more accurately. CliqUp can analyze the ratings to determine consumer behavior and overall market trends and opportunities.

- CliqUp can analyze the ratings to identify influential bloggers. Influential bloggers can be identified through general popularity or personalized influence factors.
- CliqUp can connect people with similar tastes to discover relevant content through others. The benefits for the user are higher relevancy, higher trust, time savings, and improved social interaction.

Complemented with current data mining and segmentation technology, CliqUp can tie additional information, such as demographics and Web traffic data, to deliver even more specific details about website visitors. Armed with this information, marketers are able to better identify trends and have deeper understanding of their target customers' behavioral dynamics. Advertisers can learn a great deal more about who is actually responding to ads. Lastly, bloggers can learn more about who is actually reading their articles and why.

Blogger Services

CliqUp offers a set of services and integration capabilities to bloggers that gives them valuable benefits when they partner up with the Company. These services are described in the table below.

Blogger Service	Features	Benefits for Bloggers
Profile and Ranking	• Maintain a blogger profile • Manage a blogger's reputation • Integrate and show rankings on blog sites • Find influential bloggers in the blog community • Find subject experts quickly and reliably	• Increase credibility and reputation • Increase reach to more users • Increase traffic through CliqUp's reference links • Deeper insights into tastes and interests of users who visit the blogger's website • Engage readers through more targeted content • Attract highly targeted traffic
Behavior Tracking	• Tracking of users' opinions and tastes on the blogger's own blog site • Easy integration with blog sites (similar to Google Analytics)	
Reports	• Detailed statistics of user behavior distribution • Understanding of overall user sentiments about the blog site • Discover similarities and differences of users • Identify user behavior trends	
Ad Serving	• Easily support advertising on blog sites • More targeted ads that match the users' behavior and interests • Higher payoffs for serving ads from CliqUp than from Google AdSense and other advertising networks	

Milestones and Development Status

CliqUp has finished its prototype design stage and is nearly finished with prototype testing. The Company has the following milestones to reach and timeframe to completion for each milestone. CliqUp is on schedule to achieve each of the milestones indicated in Figure 4.

FIGURE 4

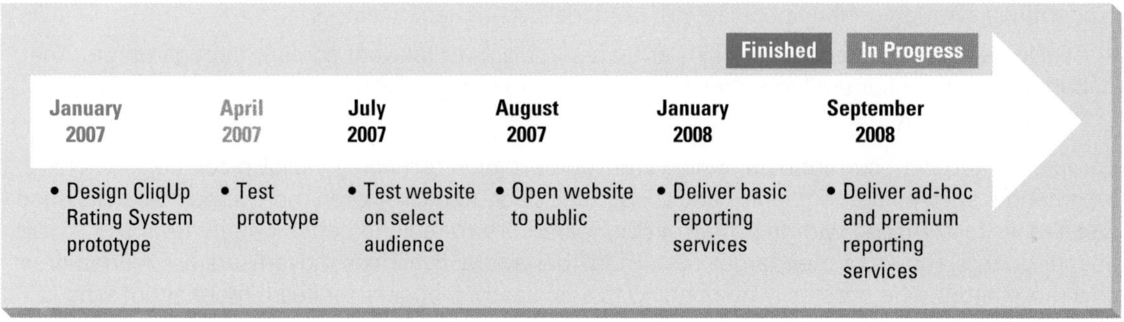

	January 2007	April 2007	July 2007	August 2007	January 2008	September 2008	Finished	In Progress
	• Design CliqUp Rating System prototype	• Test prototype	• Test website on select audience	• Open website to public	• Deliver basic reporting services	• Deliver ad-hoc and premium reporting services		

Intellectual Property

CliqUp deems the protection of its proprietary technology and information as important to its future success and ability to compete effectively in the market. As such, the Company plans to either keep its proprietary technology as a trade secret or patent it. However, the steps taken to protect its IP may not be sufficient. Initiating legal actions to enforce CliqUp's rights may be necessary.

MANAGEMENT TEAM

CliqUp's management team possesses a diverse set of experience across languages and cultures to bring entrepreneurial, marketing, and engineering talent that is capable of executing the vital tasks to take the business to success. To further complement the gaps that are not core to the business, CliqUp will form an Advisory Board consisting of executive managers and industry experts to further increase the chance of success for the business.

The Team

Chris Chen, Founder and President

Chris brings more than 12 years of entrepreneurial spirit and experience to CliqUp. He takes charge of day-to-day general operations. His insatiable thirst for disruptive technology has led him into the IT industry where he has extensive experience in IT management and software development. During college, he started his freelance IT consulting career and also his first company—a web design firm. After selling off the firm, Chris returned to consulting and teaching part-time for Learning Tree International. In 2001, he co-founded an online retail business that sold customized computer systems. He grew the business to $10 million in sales with 60 employees in three years. Chris received his BA from UCLA and MBA from USC Marshall School of Business in 2007.

Izu Matsuo, VP of Marketing

Izu oversees all marketing initiatives at CliqUp. She brings over 8 years of experience in the Internet industry. She has been involved in 3 start-ups, most recently an online gaming company where she headed strategic planning and directed all aspects of marketing and public relations. Additionally, she successfully raised capital from prominent venture capital and strategic partners. Izu received her BA in Law from Kyoto University and an MBA from USC Marshall School of Business in 2007.

Winnie Peng, VP of Information Systems

Winnie is responsible for information management, data mining, and technical engineering. Since her graduation in 1999, she has pursued a variety of career paths within the Information Technology arena including Webmaster, IT Consultant, Web Designer, and IT Project Manager. Her background also incorporates work experience in Healthcare, Financial, Consumer Products, and Insurance industries. She received her BS in Business Administration with a Computer Information Systems concentration and MBA from USC Marshall School of Business in 2007.

Additional Resources

CliqUp plans to bring in specialized talents on a consulting basis, particularly in the areas of finance. A CFO will initially be brought in on a part-time basis until full-time status is required. Additionally, CliqUp is actively searching for a VP in Market Research to manage research-related areas.

Advisory Board

To supplement the management team, CliqUp will recruit and form an Advisory Board. Members of the board will be selected based on their experience and industry knowledge. It will mainly consist of executive talents offering management advice and professionals from market research and advertising industries.

FINANCIAL PLAN

Summary of Key Financial Points and Capital Requirements

Based on sales and expense forecasting, CliqUp will require approximately **$1 million in capital**. The capital needs are based on a cumulative negative cash flow of **$688,808** and a safety factor of approximately $82,470 based on three months of cash expenses. Assuming a service start date of August 2007, the company will incur a **start-up cost of about $50,000**. The Company will be **profitable January 2009** (month 19) and will look for additional funding to continue its growth. The Company will reach **break-even in July 2009** for a **payback period of 25 months**. Refer to the exhibits for details and assumptions.

Business Model

CliqUp has several revenue streams, with its reporting services being the primary revenues:

- **Basic reporting** offers real-time do-it-yourself reports that are accessible through the Internet and sold on a monthly basis. Clients need to perform their own market research analysis from the data produced by CliqUp's reporting system.

- **Premium reporting** is an all-in-one product and service solution sold on an annual subscription basis where CliqUp offers quarterly or semi-annual reports of the consumer and market trends that clients wish to monitor. CliqUp uses its own market research analysts to produce data for clients.

- **Ah-hoc reporting** is sold on a one-time basis offering snapshots of a market for clients to identify the effectiveness of their marketing strategies.

- **Advertising** inventory on CliqUp's own website is sold to advertisers who are looking to tap the social media demographic audience.

Summary of Revenue Projections

The Company projects revenues of $234K in Year 1, $6.7MM in Year 2, $25.1MM in Year 3, with EBIT of ($517K), $847K, and $6.4MM respectively. These numbers are based on the results of industry analysis and market research with the customer.

	EOY 1 (June 2008)	EOY 2 (June 2009)	EOY 3 (June 2010)
Total Revenues	**$234K**	**$6.7MM**	**$25.1MM**
Gross Profit	$182K	$5.3MM	$19.9MM
Gross Margins	78%	79%	84%
EBITDA	($515K)	$851K	$6.4MM
EBIT	**($517K)**	**$847K**	**$6.4MM**
Net Profit After Tax	($517K)	$501K	$4.1MM
Net Profit Margin	–	7%	17%

The benefits of investing are high profit margins, large potential market, and extensibility of the software.

Cash Needs Assessment

The start-up costs before launch of the website in August 2007 involve marketing, office lease, office equipment, communication, legal, management, development, and server maintenance costs. The following table depicts the cash needs to launch and operate the business until a positive cash flow is achieved from the revenues generated by the business.

	Amount	Assumption
Start-Up Expenses		
Marketing	$1,000	
G&A	$10,835	
Human Resources	$30,200	
System Maintenance	$6,500	
Total Start-up	**$48,535**	
		Difference between highest negative CF and Start-up
Total Working Capital	**$615,273**	Expenses
Highest Cumulative Negative		
Cash Flow	$688,808	Occurs in month 18
		Based on three months of
Contingency Margin	$82,470	cash expenses
TOTAL CASH NEEDS	**$771,278**	

Financial Revenue Drivers, and Assumptions

There are three main products that will generate revenue—Basic Reporting, Ad-hoc Reporting, and Premium Reporting. In addition, there will be some advertising revenue on CliqUp's website in Year 3. Each of these products has a different release timeline and their own set of revenue drivers and associated assumptions as described in the appendix.

	EOY 1 (Year 6/2008)			EOY 2 (Year 6/2009)			EOY 3 (Year 6/2010)		
REVENUES	# Units sold	Total	% of Rev	# Units sold	Total	% of Rev	# Units sold	Total	% of Rev
Basic Reporting	31	234,075	100%	244	5,401,933	80%	555	15,037,126	60%
Ad-hoc Reporting	–	–	–	38	756,000	11%	100	1,982,880	8%
Premium Reporting	–	–	–	24	593,375	9%	125	7,911,226	31%
Advertisement	–	–	–	–	8,140	0%	–	191,481	1%
Total Revenues		**234,075**			**6,759,448**	100%		**25,122,713**	100%
Growth (%)					2788%			272%	

As depicted in the table on the previous page, CliqUp expects rapid growth and has multiple revenue sources. Most of its revenue will come from basic reporting in the first three years; however, premium reporting will scale as the technology for acquiring data for specific types of segments becomes extensible across multiple clients.

Pro-forma and Assumptions

Please refer to the Appendices for the Pro-forma and Assumptions.

TIMELINE TO LAUNCH

The following table shows the necessary tasks that need to be completed prior to launch of the business in chronological order. Due to the nature of the business, CliqUp must first collect data before it can launch its products. Thus, although the website opens to the public for acquiring data, the timeline also shows all the necessary tasks that need to be accomplished prior to the launch of the first product. Sales are primarily driven by the sales team, not the website.

CLIQUP TIMELINE TO LAUNCH AND SALES FORECAST

TIMELINE	Month 1	Month 2	Month 3	Month 4	Month 5	Month 6	Month 7	Month 8	Month 9	Month 10	Month 11	Month 12	EOY 1
	2007/07	2007/08	2007/09	2007/10	2007/11	2007/12	2008/01	2008/02	2008/03	2008/04	2008/05	2008/06	2008/06
Technology	Develop technology	Website opens					Basic reporting product release						
		System maintenance					Allocate 20% revenue for R&D						
Marketing		Advertisement of website starts					Target website user # 10,000						
Personnel (General)	Management (CEO, VP Marketing, VP Sales, VP Tech)					Hire sales personnel	Hire customer support						
Personnel (Tech)		Web programming and web designer (part time)			Start hiring full-time engineers		Start hiring full-time system maintenance, web programming, and design personnel						
Other	Office space & equipment set-up. Other misc. expected (legal, accounting, etc.)						COGS for credit card transaction and sales commission		First expected sales for basic reporting				
SALES FORECAST	Month 1	Month 2	Month 3	Month 4	Month 5	Month 6	Month 7	Month 8	Month 9	Month 10	Month 11	Month 12	EOY 1
	2007/07	2007/08	2007/09	2007/10	2007/11	2007/12	2008/01	2008/02	2008/03	2008/04	2008/05	2008/06	2008/06
TTL Revenue	$—	$—	$—	$—	$—	$—	$—	$—	$24,000	$47,400	$70,215	$92,460	$234,075

APPENDIX

EXHIBIT I.1 Market Size and Sector Sizes

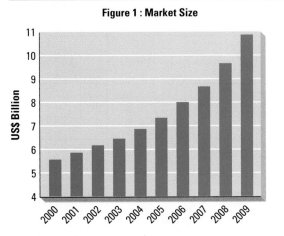

Figure 1 : Market Size

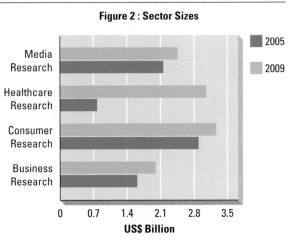

Figure 2 : Sector Sizes

Source: *Euromonitor,* October 2005.

EXHIBIT I.2 Abbreviated List of Industry Players

Player	Core Competency	Primary SIC Code	Revenues	Revenue Growth	Net Income
The Nielsen Company	General consumer research	8732: Commercial nonphysical research	$4.12B (2005)	−20.1% (2005)	$170MM (2005)
ACNielsen	Retail sales data collection through retail scanners and in-store audits.	8732: Commercial nonphysical research	N/A	N/A	N/A
Nielsen Media Research	Television	8732: Commercial nonphysical research	N/A	N/A	N/A
NetRatings (60% owned by Nielsen)	Web traffic data collection and analytics for more than 1500 clients	8732: Commercial nonphysical research	$68MM (2005)	14.7% (2005)	($8.4 MM) (2005)
Arbitron	Radio audience measurement	N/A	$310MM (2005)	4.1% (2005)	$67.3M
WebSideStory	Track and measure website activity for Internet-based clients; moving into building management for SEM.	8732: Commercial nonphysical research	$39MM	74.6% (2005)	$9.7MM (2005)

EXHIBIT M.1 Competitive Grid

Competitor	Service	Description/Features	Strength	Weakness	Key Statistics	Revenue Model	Other
BuzzMetrics	Trend discovery system	Search engine, buzz-tracking tools, trends (featured and search), blog stats (top, volume by topic, etc.), conversation tracker, blogger profiles (and ranking)	Research abilities Track record	Statistical	Headquarters: NYC CEO: Jonathan Carson Founded: 1999 Ttl identified blogs: 40,101,952 (1/28/07)	Research reports, tools Expertise in automotive, consumer electronics, nutrition, pharma-health and television	Part of The Nielsen Company
Cymfony	Social media research	Market research that uses specialized blog crawling technology to index blog posts and determine sentiments for different subjects and products.	Linguistic/ sentiment filtering, crawling technology	New, unproven technology and acceptance of data validity		Syndicated and custom research reports	Recently acquired by TNS Media. Estimated revenue at $10–15 million.
Technorati	Blog search/persona-lization	Ranks content according to favorites, search, tag, link	Social networking	Statistical	Headquarters: SF, CA Founder/CEO: David L. Sifry Reach: tracks 66.6 million blogs	Advertisement	
Blue Lithium	Behavioral targeting	Adds history of clicks in database or "clickstream" data, determines within 10 milliseconds which ad to serve up from the 1,000 handpicked sites.	Technology	Consumer privacy issues	Headquarters: San Jose, CA CEO: Gurbaksh Chahal Founded: 2004 Employees: 85 employees Revenue: Est $100M (2007) Impressions; 8B ad imp/mo	Online ad network, campaign/media planning	

(Continued)

EXHIBIT M.1 (*continued*)

Competitor	Service	Description/Features	Strength	Weakness	Key Statistics	Revenue Model	Other
Revenue Science	Behavioral targeting	Tracks behavior (recency and frequency of visits, articles consumed, or searches made), connects marketers to qualified audience	Technology, global, strong client list (WSJ .com, AOL, abc, Starbucks, etc.)	Consumer privacy issues	Headquarters: Bellevue, WA CEO: Bill Gossman Founded: 2000 Investment: $70M Impressions: 35B imp/mo; manages over 1B online behaviors/day	Online ad network, campaign/media planning	Certify audience quality (partnership with Nielsen/Netratings)
TACODA	Behavioral targeting	Advertise on TACODA Audience Networks (BT ad network)	Technology (patent pending), strong client list (BBC, NYTimes, etc.)	Consumer privacy issues	Headquarters: NYC Founder/Chairman: Dave Morgan Founded: 2001 Reach: 118M unique visitors/mo; 31 discrete audience networks	Online ad network, campaign/media planning	
Epinions	Reviews	Advice, personalized recommendations, shopping, rating of reviews	Social networking	Statistical		Advertisement, licensing, affiliate? Income share with writers (e-royalties)	Part of Shopping .com, an eBay company
Digg	Blog rating	Submit, rate, share content, popularity of content can be viewed visually (Stack, Swarm)	Social networking	Statistical	Headquarters: SF, CA CEO: Jay Adelson Founded: 2004 Impressions: 117,490,000 page views/mo	Advertisement	Advertising partners Federated Media
Yahoo	Internet services, behavioral targeting	Advertising on target customer segments	Large online user base	Different BT method (contextual)		Advertisement	

Microsoft	Internet services, behavioral targeting, contextual targeting	Detecting online commercial, intention, behavioral targeting tool (maps users' web-browsing habits, and allows advertisers to create their own segmentation, choosing what sort of web-goers they want to target with MSN search ads) "coming soon"	Large online user base	Different BT method (contextual)	Microsoft adCenter Incubation Lab formed (1/12/06)	Advertisement	
Google	Internet services, blog search, contextual targeting	Blogger, adSense	Large online user base	Not in personalization space		Advertisement	
Imagini	Behavioral targeting	Set of visual questions followed by a report on personality traits (mood, fun, habits, love), relative score, similar people, and gifts user may be interested in	Easy/fun way to take quiz	"Judgemental", Currently in UK only	Founder: Alex Willcock (former Conren Group marketing executive) Launched: June, 2005 130,000 have taken the quiz	Advertisement and affiliate?	UK
Wunderloop	Behavioral targeting	Integrated behavioral targeting, editorial targeting, search targeting, e-commerce targeting		Currently in Europe only (Luxembourg, Germany, England)	Headquarters: Luxembourg Founder: Ulrich Hegge Founded: 1999 Impressions: 18B imp/mo	ASP, licensing, consulting	

EXHIBIT M.2 Data from Primary Research—Interviews with Corporate Marketers

General Questions						
1.	Interviewee Information	Nichole Taylor Associate Brand Manager Doritos of FritoLay	Christina Liu Manager Sales and Marketing division, Integrated Marketing at Intel	Ann Palmer Assistant Manager Interactive Marketing Department at Honda/Acura	Yolanda Dunbar Senior Vice President Frederick's of Hollywood	Adrian Si Interactive Marketer Scion Marketing at Toyota Motor Sales
2.	How long have you been at your company/division?		- Prior experience in online advertising Online Ad Network, 5.5 years. Building products to building clients and delivering ads. Contextual advertising.	Since 1995 - Online Advertising	Launched in 1998, store on Amazon 1st, catalog online Started online advertising 2000, focused on affiliates/email blasts	
3.	Please describe your responsibilities and the decision process when evaluating an alternative marketing channel through the Internet.	Primary Customer Target Range: 16–24 age. Perfect age is about 19. Demographics and age to go and seek them out. It's good to buy media. But it's not really good about what's really important to them. So we'll have to research them more - Trend: They are connected 24/7 (Internet, mobile telephony, IM) - Trend: Authenticity, completely honest feedback. This is a group that's very savvy. "Give me the real deal." Very empowered group and a sense of entitlement.	Mainly to drive awareness. Banner campaigns. Search engine marketing. Better able to target who we want that drives us to increase our spending.			

General Questions					
		- We're very TV-based advertising. - We have a consumer insights group. Focus groups. 300–400 hours on consumer branding, ethnographies. - We have a brand team to go along on a lot of the research.			
Online Advertising					
4.	What type of online advertising do you do?	- Make sure we're meeting them where they are. - On YouTube, Yahoo, video, current TV to reach out to the producers. - Created interactive (rich media) banner ads. A ton of movement. Commercials. Some of them have music.		Affinity Sites, Brand Advertising (probably representative models), offer them tools. Campaign centers around rich media. Point-roll or eyeblaster, or pure video. Banners come along with it, but with clutter, so with banner advertising.	Banner, msn, search words, affiliate program	We are not interested in mass reach. Most of those we don't do. Mostly affinity marketing or "online marketing, integration."
5.	What is your motivation behind your online advertising efforts?		You are able to measure results and know exactly what your ROI is. They want to know exactly what they are getting with their marketing dollars. More and more ppl are on broadbands. • Direct response (sales) or branding?	We don't want to destroy our brands where people don't want to see them. We want to intrigue them without cluttering them. Like Acura, during election campaigns. We are now doing in-market advertising. We will occasionally buy spotlights. The in-market group does the make-model types of advertising. It's clickable. We don't usually throw in offers with a shopping message.	Drive traffic to site, to drive sales; priorities 1) e-mails (1–2 times a week), 2) search, 3) affiliates	

(continued)

EXHIBIT M.2 (*continued*)

	Online Advertising					
6.	How much ($) or % of your marketing budget do you spend on online advertising? Relative to traditional marketing?		We don't pull from one giant budget. Most of our budgets are aligned with vehicle launches. Budgets vary with product launches. 4–12% of what national is spending. It will continue to grow. Year on year.	Small % on advertising; 11% to net sales (up from 8%) for online. Catalog production is also advertising $s.	8% of total advertising media budget, which is about double other normal people's budget spending %. We plan to increase online spending in the near future. Team of analysts with an ASP style tool. They create metatags, keyword searches and what types of marketing they're doing. They have a team of analysts using the tool to pull monthly reports. - Ad-hoc reports (one time)—It is paid on an annual basis, which is less than 6 figures.
7	Is there a plan to increase (or decrease) your online advertisement efforts?				
8	How do you measure the effectiveness of online advertising?		Brand studies. Inside Express and Dynamic Logic (like Nielsen). After 3 exposures (frequency cap) or so they know the product is technologically advanced. I would like to know where they go before/ after they go to Consumer Reports, and the affinity.	ROI; $ to sales, 5 to 1 ROI	We work with sites about how much interest is there for particular pages.

Online Advertising					
9.	How would you rate your online advertising experience?				
10.	What are some advantages and disadvantages of online advertising?	- Disadvantages • Clickthrough rate on banners is about 1% (or closer to 3%). • When targeting a specific target group, you don't know who on that site is really in your target group.	TV viewership is down, with increasing interactive video. Inventory is low and price is up. Can't control the inventory issue.	+ cost effective, good ROI; efficient, flexible, timely; low production cost; reaching target market better - competition, more expensive	Overall awareness is a downside. AOL charges about $500,000 for one day on the front page.
		- There's definitely a metrics (People perceive that people who visit cnn.com don't visit other websites) - For the Super Bowl campaign, over 1 billion impressions and half of them are from nontraditional.	Upscale lifestyle sites - significant buy and look good on paper, but there are certain sites not being able to deliver. These sites' representatives are not supporting us enough. People forget there's more to be done after the sale. Timeliness is also a problem. The rate sheet—we're not interested in taking a section out of a magazine. Looking more for unique. Time spent and clicking through actually means something. Word of mouth is so important!		

(continued)

EXHIBIT M.2 (*continued*)

Blog						
11.	Do you advertise on blog sites?	- Maker and Watcher strategy (Super Bowl) - Maker Strategy: go to schools/film schools. Schools with communication degrees. Then I want you to go online and find folks on current TV (and Yahoo blog). And find me blogs that have certain keywords related to Doritos. Then we sent them letters/e-mails to join the programs. - Use it for word-of-mouth and grassroots, not banner advertising. - Went through hub-like blog sites that outlink to other blogs to find the bloggers that we are looking for. Many smaller blogs link to these articles so it's a good way to look for bloggers.	- Interested in services that provide data about the value of using alternative media. - SixApart—MovableType and offer services to help clients understand what's the value proposition to the blogs.	Advertise at their request. More of a backend sponsor. With smaller autoblogs, they need money, and they're willing to run between the line messages. The content of the blogs can be damaging but is a lot more helpful than the ads we place on blogs. Buzznet (civic tour). Autoblog.	Considered MySpace, blogs, phones. Dilemma = not enough funding to divert cash. Still exploiting search/affiliates. Not ready to test out alternative media, rather conservative	We advertise on community sites like MySpace, not exactly blog sites.
12.	What is your motivation behind your online advertising efforts?		• Direct response (sales) or branding. Building brand awareness and preference.			Research perspectives, 4 types of offerings—ASP model + training (you can pull them out yourself), Syndicated report (a quarterly or biannual report) of a report for a segment, Specific relationship with client where they do specific reports they have and customized for us, ad-hoc reporting (taking customization to the next level).

Blog				
13.	How much ($) do you spend on advertising on blogs?			Virtual communities is about 1%. Tool model—it's a supply vs. demand thing. With omniture, we pay over $100k Custom reports—$100k 2–3 times a year—Another $50–100k ad-hoc—much less expensive.
14.	How do you find the right blogger to advertise through? (What's the process? What sources do you use?)		Submit a request—background information, guidelines of what you can/can't write. Find industry experts. Unless it's focused around specific areas.	
15.	How much time do you spend to find the relevant blog sites to talk about them?	My boss, 2 people from our agencies, me, and one of our contacts at Yahoo Videos. We probably put in about 50 hours' worth per person. Yahoo Video will filter them to about 120. It was a couple weeks' worth of half-days going through them.	Most people volunteer them to do it. People do it because they're truly passionate about it and want to talk about it.	
16.	How do you measure the effectiveness of blog advertising?	We had about a 10–15% hit rate on the blogs that we identified as potential advocates for Crash the Super Bowl. The ones that ended up on the cutting room floor did not have significant membership, did not have regular posts, presented a liability.		Umbria (competitor)—their methodology for pulling in information. So linguistically they can determine positive/negative sentiments. They were too new to have infrastructure to provide us the reports nor human analysts.

(continued)

EXHIBIT M.2 (*continued*)

Blog					
17.	On a scale of 1–5 (1 = Very Dissatisfied, 5 = Very Satisfied), how would you rate your blog advertising experience?		Blog launched last year. Unless there is more credibility and we're talking to the right audience. You're truly engaging the customers. - New blog topics.		
18.	What are some reasons why you do not advertise on blog sites?	Problem—Credibility is also a problem. Double-edged sword. Less talk about demographics and more information and data analysis rooted in a psychographic target. Buzzmetrics has transparency issue—I would love to have a better understanding of the methodology for information retrieval—key words, webcrawlers, how particular sites were chosen as targets, etc. Customization— let's sit down and talk about how I want to use the data, so that I don't end up with stock report that I can't use. By the way, we paid Buzzmetrics $30,000 to conduct a one-time report for Crash the Super Bowl.	Challenges—don't really understand what's the value of this channel. Having content that's relevant and having content that interests people. It's not easy to have topic to attract ppl. No blog authors to contribute content to it.	A lot of companies doing tracking and measuring, i.e., Brand Dimensions. Track editorials and blogs. They rank credibility. Yahoo has a buzz meter. New Media Strategies. Not very well organized. They found a niche before they found a business model. Not really good digestable metrics.	10% is seeing 90% of the impressions. It's not good news if publishers can also target 10%. Tracking behavior. Privacy issues. We use Buzzmetrics but they cannot profile individuals. Using technology to track across websites will be really good. We are in the niche market. So the more niche, the better.
19.	Are you interested in advertising through bloggers? Why or why not?		Not too interested in advertising. But interested in participating.		

Blog					
20.	What would make you want to advertise through blogs?			The good—gives ppl a forum. Gives ppl the ability to bounce ideas off each other. The bad—the quality and reliability of the blogs. Very dangerous.	Hollywood insider destination type of place perhaps could be compelling Unique, lifestyle oriented, organic Watchful of organic growth to advertising in blogs.
Behavioral Targeting					
21.	Have you heard of behavioral targeting?		Yes	Yes	DB tracks behavior (i.e., purchase behavior) of Frederick's website	– not understanding what's the best way to advertise – blog authenticity – but this is mostly based on product and process
22.	Have you tried it?		Only when you are trying to drive the sale. – Profiling—online service where they write more about our website and tell us about ourselves. – Corporate Market Research budget.	Exhibit 1 ad twice, after behavior change, then I would serve something else.		
23.	What companies/ methods have you used for BT?	– Buzzmetrics . . . not sure, but about $20–25k for about a quarter. Sure. – I-trac—measure brand equity under regard and recognition, momentum, popularity, perception of how popular you are. They measure with every 6 months. – Ad-hoc is the effectiveness of a particular campaign.		– Advertising.com. Within 24 hours, it would serve them up an ad. They also pair 3 different actions. Advertisers use an ad-serving solution. The popular one is doubleclick's service. Brand Dimension— verbatims, charting and graphs. In the neighborhood of $15,000. If it's lower cost and more frequent, it's more useful.		Tagged.com Market Research Infrastructure— combination of tools and analysts. They work on an online media agency that deals with all this for us. Dynamic Logic— we don't like the way they present the data. They're survey-based. It's not very good.
24.	How much ($) do you spend on BT?	about $800k for Doritos				

(continued)

EXHIBIT M.2 (*continued*)

Behavioral Targeting			
25.	How do you measure the effectiveness of BT?	Equity Monitoring Frequency: every 6 months or a year. Comparison of a year before. Consumer Monitoring Frequency: For this target, once every month. But definitely every quarter, with a monthly newsletter. For FritoLay consumers, every year.	Effective. Customization is what customers want, respectful of marketer to hone into what their needs and interests are.
26.	How would you rate your BT advertising experience?		
27.	How effective do you think BT is compared to normal search-based advertising?	We look at programming, flavors, etc. Those trends are our filters and better understand the level of relevance that we are going to have for the consumers. Our goal is to gain more relevance with our consumers. Demographics tells us what websites to go on. It's mostly used for media buying. When shaping the marketing campaigns, the psychographics are extremely important and help anchor our brand's lifestyle.	Normal search-based advertising on portals: No strong brand attraction. Traffic but doesn't mean much. We can use what we learn from behavioral targeting to use on our keyword-based searches.

	Behavioral Targeting				
28.	How do you see BT working for you (on own website or on other systems)?			Work with data mining/purchase history. Work with cooperative DB already. Can identify best match profile (demo, psycho, purchase behavior), needs audience.	Advertising—If they get what they don't want, they will find it intrusive.
29.	Are you interested in advertising through BT? Why or why not?				
	Comments About CliqUp				
30.	Interested in CliqUp?	Interest is a big thing. Totally interested in a blog directory.	We are very interested in it, but it's a very small portion of the population. It's interesting for us to know what's going on. We would have to examine each site that has its own merit. Better for products that are higher end and very targeted. Go for affinity. Selling unique reports to unique marketers. Getting value beyond a specific value or brand, i.e., true blog meter expert with a different kind of chart. That makes it much easier to sell.	If faster and reliable, would be interested. Sponsorships? No Concerns = controlling brand image; controlling information that gets out there → need to be sure about trustworthy bloggers/content and followers	I will never consider any research or proposal more than a few hundred thousand dollars cuz we don't have enough sales. My caveat is that we're a very very small group, but if I have time, I am more than interested to help.

Chris C. Chen

5107 Halison Street, Torrance, CA 90503 • (310) 350-8503 • Chris.Chen.2007@.marshall.usc.edu

EDUCATION

University of Southern California, Marshall School of Business   Los Angeles, CA
Master of Business Administration. GPA: 3.65   May 2007

- Member of Beta Gamma Sigma Business Honor Society
- Winner of Venture Capital Investment Competition (8 teams total)
- Judge for 2007 Marshall MBA Strategy Case Competition

University of California, Los Angeles   Los Angeles, CA
Bachelor of Business Economics   June 1999

EXPERIENCE

XPCBox, Inc. (Customized computer systems online retailer)   City of Industry, CA
Co-Founder and VP of Operations & Information Systems   2001–2004
Co-founded a startup utilizing $50k initial capital and transformed it into a $10M company while managing 60 employees. Company became the 2nd largest computer system reseller on eBay averaging $7 million in sales.

- Analyzed and implemented an enterprise-wide business process, including policies, procedures, and an application system that integrated departments' processes. Increased business revenues by 1000% (from $100k to $1M) a month without a proportionate increase in labor.

- Created and merged a set of metrics measuring operation performance. Analyzed the data set and reallocated resources between divisions within the Fulfillment Department to optimize queue flows. Increased production efficiency by 15%.

- Analyzed inventory ($100k) and back order issues (200 orders) in order fulfillment. Designed and developed an inventory projection system that lowered inventory holding costs by 10% and decreased back orders by 30%.

- Analyzed order processing business workflow and enhanced application system to interface with external services (Authorize.NET, Fedex/UPS/USPS, eBay) to automate order management processes. Reduced average per order processing time of 4 minutes by 50%.

IdeaMAX Corp. (Online e-commerce retailer in entertainment industry)   Covina, CA
Director of IT Operations   1997–2001
Developed strategic technology platforms in conjunction with the President and VP of Operation in analyzing how information systems can improve business profits and efficiencies.

- Managed and supervised a staff of 10 programmers, systems/database administrators, and IT consultants.

- Negotiated with current and new vendors to reduce software licensing costs by 30%.

- Analyzed current market opportunities and recommended technology strategies to senior executives to capture a new video on-demand market. The new market increased overall sales by 20%.

IT Systems Consultant
Analyzed and researched business operations and presented recommendations to senior executives. Implemented IT solutions that increased staff efficiency by 40% and decreased operating costs by 30%.

Rhythm & Hues Studios (Post production facility in entertainment industry)   Marina Del Rey, CA
Senior Systems Administrator   1997–1999
Supervised and administered an enterprise network of 300+ servers and 500+ workstations across an organization of 600 employees.

- Analyzed software licensing costs and recommended a license consolidation strategy to management. Negotiated with the 5 largest software vendors to reduce licensing costs by 40%.

- Analyzed issue behind disorganized management of software and hardware assets. Programmed and deployed a web-based IT asset management system that kept records of software and hardware purchased by the company. Increased overall efficiency through an accurate accounting system of technology assets.

- Designed and implemented an enterprise-wide application allowing employees to personally manage internal mailing lists. Reduced the number of support requests for the IT department by 5%.

ADDITIONAL INFORMATION

- Computer knowledge: C/C++, Java, HTML, XML, Linux/Unix, Oracle, and Excel/Word/Access/Powerpoint.

- Languages: English (Fluent), Mandarin & Taiwanese (Fluent), Spanish (In Progress).

- Community service: Creator and maintainer of an open-source Instant Messenging software project.

- Interests: Photography, graphics design, snowboarding, sailing, violin, piano, traveling, and wushu.

Winnie Peng

2229 Cedar St. Unit C, Alhambra, CA 91801 • (626) 757–9157 • Winnie.peng.2007@marshall.usc.edu

EDUCATION

University of Southern California, Marshall School of Business   Los Angeles, CA
Master of Business Administration, Strategy and Management Consulting   August 2007

California State Polytechnic University, Pomona   Pomona, CA
Bachelor of Business Administration, Computer Information Systems   December 1999

EXPERIENCE

Transamerica Insurance & Investment Group (a division of AEGON   Los Angeles, CA
Financial Partners)   2003–2006
Web Site Manager
Facilitated and streamlined IT and operational solutions for agencies and customers.

- Directed a team of application developers in improving web-based automations that increased efficiency and accuracy for over 300 insurance agencies in North America and Pacific Rim.

- Researched and delivered strategic solutions that enhanced integration and collaboration in operational process between Customer Services and Underwriting team.

- Managed 8 web sites that generated a combination of about 1,500 hits daily and leveraged the sites to achieve seamless communication within departments and to deliver current product information to clients.

- Strategized with Marketing team in analyzing action plans in entering Pacific Rim market, presented and solicited strategic plans for implementation to senior management.

Philips Medical Systems (a division of Royal Philips Electronics)   Irvine, CA
Designer, Medical Facilities   2002–2003
Worked closely with senior management to synthesize web-based process automations for Site Planning department.

- Re-engineered key business processes by working with Sales, Customer Service, and eBusiness teams to leverage web-based technologies during customer acquisition and order fulfillment serving over 35,000 customers in North America and parts of Latin America.

- Spearheaded 4 operations projects encompassing job request submission, order tracking, internal project management, and knowledge database to increase overall departmental productivity over 25%.

- Designed and led training sessions to over 25 employees for newly deployed process automations and promoted cross training in software packages and up-to-date product knowledge within teams.

- Promoted from a Site Planner to a Designer within 7 months of employment.

Site Planner
Analyzed and provided recommendations for medical equipment planning in medical facilities.

Deloitte & Touche   Santa Ana, CA
Consultant   2000–2001
Reengineered and streamlined business transformation and technical solutions to several Fortune 500 companies.

- Consulted in all stages of project life cycle: researched problematic areas, assessed potential solutions, negotiated change management terms if need be, and implemented best practices within requested budgets.

- Built professional, long-term relationship and managed thorough communications with each client to ensure highest customer satisfaction and promote collateral sales. Client satisfaction resulted in a $30K project to deliver a second-phase implementation.

- Initiated cross-functional learning within teams for strategy formulation and technical expertise to promote higher utilization.

Nature's Flavors   Anaheim, CA
Webmaster   2000–2000
Formulated web-based marketing materials and engaged in customer services to promote product sales.

ADDITIONAL INFORMATION

- Fluent in English and Mandarin; intermediate level Japanese speaker.

- Member of Marshall Management Consulting Club, Marshall Strategy Group and Art Society of Marshall

- Selected and participated in a one-year international exchange program at Waseda University in Japan with substantial scholarship from Japanese government from summer of 2007 to summer of 2008.

Interests: Japanese Flower Arrangement, swimming, golfing, and traveling

Andy Chih-Yin Shih

1606 S. Edgewood Dr., Alhambra, CA 91803
(626) 695-4286
andycshih@gmail.com

Education	**B.S. Electrical Engineering** with Computer Engineering Option, *University of California, Los Angeles*	1999
Programming Languages	**C, C++, Java (J2EE), ColdFusion, ASP, JavaScript, SQL, Perl, HTML, XML, XSLT**	
Applications	**Eclipse, Visual Studio 6.0, Dreamweaver MX, Ant, JBoss, Adobe Acrobat, Microsoft Office Suite, OpenOffice, Microsoft SQL Server, Oracle 8i, Mozilla Firefox, Internet Explorer**	
Operating Systems	**UNIX (IRIX), Linux, Microsoft Windows (2000, 2003, and XP), DOS, Apple OS X**	
Work Experience	**Programmer Analyst** *AIG SunAmerica, Inc.*, Woodland Hills, CA	April 2001 to present

- Programmer and Analyst for Variable Annuity Product Development on Internet website (SunAmerica.com—website registration, account management, contract search, contract summary, fund transfer, future allocations, current and historical prices, and fund performance). Website coded in ASP and JavaScript. Website communicates with SQL Server (user registration and authentication, and general product information), Oracle (Enterprise Data Warehouse), Web Services (through MQSeries and J2EE policy application for policy information and transactions), and Vantage (mainframe system housing legacy policy information).

- Administrator for corporate Intranet website (maintain server, manage user access, assist in new user and developer training). Intranet website uses IIS 5.0 and is coded using ASP and JavaScript.

- Lead programmer for in house applications using JSP and Servlets (Content Management Tool, Rules Engine, Stock Ticker, automation of price upload).

- Created and maintained policies and procedures for access and development on both Internet and Intranet (Style guide, role definition, development procedures and documentation, training materials)

- Point of contact for business units and quality assurance (requirements gathering, prioritize feature implementations, resource management for quality testing, manage scheduling for testing and implementation, user training, documentation of development process)

- Created implementation plans for major website updates (SunAmerica .com Redesign, Intranet Redesign, Windows NT 4.0 to Windows 2000 migration, web server upgrade, SunAmerica Affordable Housing website launch, AIG Retirement Services portal launch)

Programmer   August 1999–March 2001

AppleOne, Inc., Glendale, CA

- Lead Analyst for web based application for staffing management
- Lead programmer for web based timecard system
- Lead programmer for timecard and staffing management application integration
- Administrator for web based applications and servers
- Timecard and staffing management application interface and business logic coded to J2EE standards using SilverStream Application Server. Sybase ASA 6.0 Suite used for database implementation

Hardware Operator

Rhythm and Hues Studios,   *Part time:* Oct. 1997 to Dec. 1998
Los Angeles, CA   *Internship:* June 1997 to Sept. 1997

- Maintenance of SGI workstations, PCs and Macintoshes
- Calibration of audio/visual equipment
- Network administrator of company Local Area Ethernet Network. Duties include, but not limited to management of IP's, setup of physical connections, general troubleshooting.
- Project: Windows 95 and Windows 98 upgrade to Windows NT 4.0
- Special Project: Creation of hardware inventory database with a web based interface using ColdFusion
- Special Project: Member of the team assigned to redesign and implement company LAN to increase throughput. Project included creation of DMZ for company LAN

Additional work experience available upon request

References

AIG SunAmerica, Inc.
Joseph Sowrimuthu
Senior Programming Analyst
(818) 673-4305

AIG SunAmerica, Inc.
Jose Lopez
Internet Marketing Analyst
(800) 820-9029 ×244

AIG SunAmerica, Inc.
Virginia Lang
Director of Internet Services
(619) 301–2073

AppleOne, Inc.
Kenneth Wong
Programmer
(626) 374–3680

Additional references available upon request

Misc.   Fluent in English, Mandarin, and Taiwanese

Naturalized US Citizen

Silver Medal at VICA Regional Competition for CAD (1994)

Acquiring Data—The Blog Community

With over 70 million blogs, CliqUp will use the blog community as the primary channel to gather consumer behavior and trends that are relevant to marketers. The blogger directory is the first service to be launched that allows the Company to gather ratings and ranking information about bloggers. The rating data can be analyzed to reliably discover and track people's tastes and values over time. To achieve this, the website will offer services such as blogger profiles and rankings as well as personalized content recommendations.

CliqUp will increase its data acquisition reach by collecting data not only on CliqUp.com, but also through other blog sites. To accomplish this, CliqUp will offer a set of *Blogger Services* to attract bloggers with benefits when they integrate their blog sites with CliqUp's system. These services are key to acquiring data as well as increasing CliqUp's credibility in the social media space. In exchange, the Company will offer improved reports and services to the bloggers themselves, thus creating mutually beneficial partnerships.

Analyzing Data—CliqUp Behavior Analyzer

Once data is collected, it is stored in the data warehouse and ready for analysis. CliqUp's experienced market analyst then uses data mining, human insights, and other statistical methods to perform a major portion of its data analyses and demographic clustering. Furthermore, the Company has created a new data analysis algorithm, called the *CliqUp Relationship Analyzer,* that can calculate "value and taste distances" between users. The technical description for the Relationship Analyzer is detailed in the "Technical Description of Products and Services."

Generating and Delivering Reports

Once the analysis is performed, report writers will begin writing the report. The report includes insights from market analysts as well as data used to derive that information. Basic reports are delivered online while ad-hoc and premium reports are delivered both online and in print. On average, basic reports are 10 pages long while premium and ad-hoc reports are 50–60 pages written. Basic reports cover mostly analysis results, trends, and drivers. Premium reports contain the data used to derive the results as well as more details into each analysis. Ah-hoc reports are similar to premium reports with additional analyses into differences between a before-and-after snapshot of the market.

APPENDIX F.1: FINANCIAL PLAN ASSUMPTIONS

Pricing Assumptions and Demand Calculations

1) Basic Reporting

Growth Drivers	Assumptions
Overall growth of the blogosphere	Dedicated direct sales team for Basic Reporting product
Number of salespersons	Closing percentage increases as reputation and brand evolve from 20% (year 1) to 27% (year 4)
Number of sales calls	
Percentage of sales closing	Product release: Jan 2008
Attrition rates	Monthly subscription fee of $3,000 per month—reference penetration pricing
	Product is directed to small- to medium-sized businesses 230% growth in blogosphere in 2006 and continued growth into 2011
	Source: http//www.masternewmedia.org/news/2006/11/08/blog_usage_statistics_and_trends.htm; Downloaded 3/31/2007
	http://www.cymfony.com/nws_pr_story.asp?docid=20051017_30140.html

2) Ad-Hoc Roporting

Growth Drivers	Assumptions
Overall growth of the market	Direct sales team
Number of salespersons	Dedicated sales team for both Ad-Hoc and Premium Reporting
Number of sales calls	Closing percentage increases as reputation and brand evolve
Percentage of sales closing	Product release: Sept 2008
Attrition rates	Ad-Hoc Reporting revenues average $20k per engagement
Strategic partnerships with advertising and professional services firms	Product is directed to large enterprises
	Each target client 1–2 major campaigns per year 230% growth in blogosphere in 2006 and continued growth into 2011
	Source:http://www.masternewmedia.org/news/2006/11/08/blog_usage_statistics_and_trends.htm; Downloaded 3/31/2007

3) Premium Reporting

Growth Drivers	Assumptions
Overall growth of the market	Direct sales team
Number of salespersons	Dedicated sales team for both Ad-Hoc and Premium Reporting
Number of sales calls	Closing percentage increases as reputation and brand evolve
Percentage of sales closing	Product release: Sept 2008
Attrition rates	Premium Reporting revenues average $100k per year—reference price determined through primary market research interviews with Toyota Scion and Doritos.
Referenceable clients	Product is directed to large enterprises
Strategic partnerships with advertising and professional services firms	Extensible economies of scale relating to customized client queries that can be syndicated to other similar clients.
	230% growth in blogosphere in 2006 and continued growth into 2011
	Source: http://www.masternewmedia.org/news/2006/11/08/blog_usage_statistics_and_trends.htm; Downloaded 3/31/2007

4) Advertisement

Growth Drivers	Assumptions
Number of users (growth through advertisement, marketing costs, and organic growth), page views, affiliate blog sites, advertisement price.	Number of users grows through organic growth (20%, based off previous Internet venture experience) and advertisement and marketing spending. Additionally, traffic will be generated through affiliate blog sites signing up on CliqUp's online directory services, with an estimated 5,000 users per blog site (see Reference: GuyKawasaki.com), increasing at 10% natural growth.
Extent of blog network	Based off of Google's ad words, cost of new users/ad cost is estimated at $0.50 ($0.10 position 4–6, conversion to user is 20%).
Extent of affiliate network of blog sites	Active users are calculated at 80%, attrition rate 20% (based off previous internet venture experience).

Page view per user is at 4.9, taking the 3-month average of comparable blog sites.

Page views per user	3 mos. Average
Stumbleupon.com	5.7
Technorati.com	3.7
Digg.com	5.3
Average	4.9

Advertisement revenue is calculated at $2 per CPM (1,000 impressions). Blog sites charge anywhere between $1–$15 per CPM.

Source: Google Adwords campaign management, Alexa.com

Reference: GuyKawasaki.com has 50,000 unique users per day

Cash Flow and Income Statement Assumptions

1) Revenues assumptions discussed as above.

2) Cost of Goods Sold is estimated based on the following:

Items	Percentage of sales	Description
Bloggers revenue share	50%	Advertisement revenue on CliqUp's affiliate blog sites will be shared with blog writers.
Credit card transaction costs	4%	Basic reports will involve credit card transactions, which will be paid to credit card companies.
Sales commission (ad hoc and premium)	18%	Sales commission will be paid to sales personnel based on closing deals for basic, ad-hoc, and premium reports.

3) Human resources expenses include salaries for general and administrative, sales and marketing, systems related, and part-time or project-based personnel.

The 2002 Economic Census date from the US Census Bureau for the Marketing research and public opinion polling industry was referenced for employees directly involved in market research report generation, however, CliqUp will pay higher and competitive-level salaries. The 2002 Economic Census data from the US Census Bureau for the Customer computer programming services Industry was referenced for employees directly involved in system development.

Industry	NAICS Code	Establishments	Receipts ($10)	Annual Payroll	Paid Employees	Average annual salary	Avg per month	CliqUp
Marketing research & public opinion polling	541910	5,460	10,890,323	4,080,844	122,359	33,351	2,779	3000–4000
Custom computer programming services	541511	48,953	60,125,952	30,082,100	439,395	68,463	5,705	4000–6000

Taxes and benefits, such as health insurance, pension, and sick leave, for employees were calculated at 30%.

Increase in salaries for management are calculated at 150% for Year 2 and Year 3. CliqUp may offer increase in salaries and bonuses for other employees in the future, but are not included in the financial plan at this point.

Source: US Census Bureau, 2002
http://www.census.gov/econ/census02/data/industry/E541.HTM

> Popkin, Joel. "Cost of Employee Benefits in Small and Large Businesses", US Small Business Administration, http://www.sba.gov/advo/research/rs262tot.pdf

4) Number of employees is estimated based on operational needs.

Number of employees directly involved in market research report generation is dependent on number of reports sold.

Marketing Account Executives and Senior Analyst are assumed to be able to handle 20 accounts per month, and report creators 10 accounts per month.

In the initial stages, web programming and design, as well as system and database administrators will be outsourced, but later will be done internally by the systems division.

Headcount	EOY 1	EOY 2	EOY 3
G&A	0	0	0
Management 1	1	2	2
Management 2	1	2	2
Management 3	1	2	2
Management 4	1	2	2
Admin	0	1	1
Total G&A	4	9	9
Sales & marketing			
Marketing Account Executive/20 accounts	0	2	7
Senior analyst/20 accounts	0	2	7
Report creator/10 accounts	0	4	16
Customer Support/100 basic accounts	1	3	6
Sales personnel—basic reports	1	2	3
Sales personnel—ad-hoc/premium reports	0	4	6
Total sales & marketing	2	17	45

(continued)

Systems	0	0	0
Engineer (Basic)	2	2	2
Engineer (Ad-hoc and Premium)	0	2	2
Web programming	1	1	1
Web design	1	1	1
Sys Admin & DB admin	0	1	1
Total systems personnel	4	7	7
Other personnel	0	0	0
Web programming, part time	0	0	0
Web design	0	0	0
Sys admin	1	0	0
DB admin	1	0	0
Total other personnel	2	0	0
Total headcount	12	31	62

5) Marketing expenses will be fixed at $1000 a month in the first year, and budgeted for 20% of sales in Year 2 and Year 3, based on industry comparables. Marketing will encompass both advertisement for CliqUp's website, as well as marketing and promotional expenses for the Company.

6) R&D expenses will be budgeted for 20% of sales, based on industry comparables.

7) Office rental expense was calculated based on the average rental price per square foot for potential office properties in Los Angeles, California, multiplied by the estimated amount of square footage needed per employee and number of forecasted employees in end of year 1, 2, and 3.

   a. Price per square foot = $21.80

Property name/Address	Area	Rental Rate (per square foot)	Space Available
N. Highland Avenue	Los Angeles, CA	$25.20	2,870 SF
National & Sepulveda	Los Angeles, CA	$24.00	400–1,000 SF
Figueroa Tower	Los Angeles, CA	$30.00	1,486–8,442 SF
Pacific Corporate Towers	Los Angeles, CA	$16.00	400–920 SF
Pacific Corporate Towers (Torrance)	Torrance, CA	$13.80	3,645 SF
Average square foot		$21.80	

   b. Square foot required per employee = 40 based off of cubicle size

   c. Number of employees

EOY 1 # employees	12
EOY 2 # employees	31
EOY 3 # employees	62

d. Rental expense includes required utilities (water and electricity)

e. Rental expense = a. x b. x c.

	Rental Expense (per Year)	Rental Expense (per Month)
Rental expense/employee	$872	$73
Year 1	$10,464	$872
Year 2	$27,032	$2,253
Year 3	$54,064	$4,505

Source: http://www.loopnet.com; as of 3/28/07

8) Other expenses including legal, communication, and accounting services are based on the 2002 Economic Census data from the US Census Bureau for the professional, scientific, and technical industry.

Industry	NAICS code	Establishments	Amount ($100)	Annual Costs	Monthly Costs
Professional, scientific, & technical services	541	771,305			
Cost of purchased legal services			6,028,254	7,816	651
Purchased communication services			8,833,739	11,453	954
Cost of purchased accounting, auditing, and bookkeeping services			3,317,164	4,301	358

9) One-time expense includes office equipment such as desks, chairs, and phones, assuming $500 per employee.

Per employee	$500	Total Expense	Expense per Year
EOY 1 # employees	12	$6,000	$6,000
EOY 2 # employees	31	$15,500	$9,500
EOY 3 # employees	62	$31,000	$15,500

10) Servers will be leased and hosted using GoDaddy's dedicated server services, assuming a cost of $500 per server per month. Number of servers are based on MySpace's user-to-server load calculations and CliqUp's milestones and user projections.

	Milestone 1	Milestone 2	Milestone 3
Webservers	1	2	3
DB servers	1	2	3
Mail/Other internal servers	1	2	2
Back-up servers			2

Source: MySpace   http://www.baselinemag.com/article2/0,1540,2082921,00.asp

GoDaddy   http://www.godaddy.com

10) Revenue collection and payments due are assumed on a 30-day cycle.

11) Corporate taxes are assumed at 35%

Source: "Small Business Taxes and Management," A/N Group.
http://www.smbiz.com/sbrl001.html#ci

APPENDIX F.2: BREAK-EVEN ANALYSIS

| | EOY 1 | | | EOY 2 | | | EOY 3 | | |
| | Year 6/2008 | | | Year 6/2009 | | | Year 6/2010 | | |
REVENUES	# Units Sold	Total Revenue	% of Rev	# Units Sold	Total Revenue	% of Rev	# Units Sold	Total Revenue	% of Rev
Basic Reporting Revenue	31	234,075	100%	244	5,401,933	80%	555	15,037,126	60%
Ad-Hoc Reporting Revenues	–	–	–	38	756,000	11%	100	1,982,880	8%
Premium Reporting Revenue	–	–	–	24	593,375	9%	125	7,911,226	31%
Advertisement Revenue	–	–	–	–	8,140	0%	–	191,481	1%
Total Revenues		**234,075**			**6,759,448**	**100%**		**25,122,713**	**100%**
Growth (%)					**2788%**			**272%**	

Basic	**Price**	**$3,000**	
Variable Costs	**Cost**	**Cost per Unit**	**%**
Customer support (1 per 100 units)	3,000	30	1%
COGS - credit card	% of sales		4%
Sales commission	% of sales		18%
Total Variable Costs		**690**	**23%**
Gross margin		2,310	77%
Fixed Costs	**Y 3**	**per month**	
Total SG&A	13,486,305	1,123,859	
Customer support	174,000	14,500	
SG&A less customer support	13,312,305	1,109,359	
Costs allocated by revenue ratio	7,968,041	664,003	
BEV		**287**	

Ad Hoc	Price	$20,000	
Variable	**Cost**	**Cost per Unit**	**%**
Marketing Account Executive/20 accounts	4,000	400	2%
Senior analyst/20 accounts	4,000	400	2%
Report creator/10 accounts	4,000	800	4%
COGS - credit card			4%
Sales commission			18%
Total Variable Costs		**6,000**	**30%**
Gross margin		14,000	70%
Fixed Costs	**Y 3**	**per month**	
Total SG&A	13,486,305	1,123,859	
Account exec, analyst, report creator	984,000	82,000	
SG&A less account exec etc.	12,502,305	1,041,859	
Costs allocated by revenue ratio	986,779	82,232	
BEV		**6**	

Premium	Price	$100,000	
Variable	**Cost**	**Cost per Unit**	**%**
Marketing Account Executive/20 accounts	4,000	400	0%
Senior analyst/20 accounts	4,000	400	0%
Report creator/10 accounts	4,000	800	1%
COGS - credit card			4%
Sales commission			18%
Total Variable Costs		**23,600**	**24%**
Gross margin		76,400	76%
Fixed Costs	**Y 3**	**per month**	
Total SG&A	13,486,305	1,123,859	
Account exec, analyst, report creator	984,000	82,000	
SG&A less account exec etc.	12,502,305	1,041,859	
Costs allocated by revenue ratio	3,937,017	328,085	
BEV		**4**	

APPENDIX F.4: REVENUE PROJECTION

REVENUE DRIVERS AND ASSUMPTIONS

Basic Reporting

Monthly cost per subscription	$3,000
Yr One—Number of direct sales personnel	1
Yr Two—Number of direct sales personnel	2
Yr Three—Number of direct sales personnel	3
Direct sales calls per person per month	40
Yr One—closing percentage	20%
Yr Two—closing percentage	25%
Yr Three—closing percentage	27%
Yr One—subscription attrition rate	30%
Yr Two—subscription attrition rate	20%
Yr Three/Four—attrition rate	20%

Ad-Hoc Reporting

Average revenue per report	$20,000
Yr One—Number of direct sales personnel	0
Yr Two—Number of direct sales personnel	4
Yr Three—Number of direct sales personnel	6
Yr Three/Four—Number of direct sales personnel	6
Direct sales calls per person per month	6
Yr One—closing percentage	20%
Yr Two—closing percentage	25%
Yr Three—closing percentage	27%
Yr One—subscription attrition	0%
Yr Two—subscription attrition rate	10%
Yr Three/Four—subscription attrition rate	15%

Premium Reporting

Monthly cost per subscription ($100,000 yearly)	$8,333
Yr One—Number of direct sales personnel	0
Yr Two—Number of direct sales personnel	4
Yr Three—Number of direct sales personnel	6
Yr Three/Four—Number of direct sales personnel	6
Direct sales calls per person per month	6
Yr One—closing percentage	15%
Yr Two—closing percentage	20%
Yr Three—closing percentage	25%
Yr One—subscription attrition	10%
Yr Two—subscription attrition rate	10%
Yr Three/Four—subscription attrition rate	10%

REVENUES	Param	Month 0 2007/06	Month 1 2007/07	Month 2 2007/08	Month 3 2007/09	Month 4 2007/10	Month 5 2007/11	Month 6 2007/12	Month 7 2008/01	Month 8 2008/02	Month 9 2008/03	Month 10 2008/04	Month 11 2008/05	Month 12 2008/06
Basic Reporting														
Number of subscriptions sold		0	0	0	0	0	0	0	0	0	8	8	8	8
Subscription attrition		—	—	—	—	—	—	—	—	—	—	0	0	1
Cumulative number of subscriptions		—	—	—	—	—	—	—	—	—	8	16	23	31
Basic Reporting Revenue		0	0	0	0	0	0	0	0	0	24,000	47,400	70,215	92,460
Ad-Hoc Reporting														
Number of reports sold		0	0	0	0	0	0	0	0	0	0	0	0	0
Subscription attrition		—	—	—	—	—	—	—	—	—	—	—	—	—
Ad-Hoc Reporting Revenues		0	0	0	0	0	0	0	0	0	0	0	0	0
Premium Reporting														
Number of subscriptions sold		—	—	—	—	—	—	—	—	—	—	—	—	—
Subscription attrition		—	—	—	—	—	—	—	—	—	—	—	—	—
Cumulative number of subscriptions		—	—	—	—	—	—	—	—	—	—	—	—	—
Premium Reporting Revenue		0	0	0	0	0	0	0	0	0	0	0	0	0
TTL Revenue from Reports		0	0	0	0	0	0	0	0	0	24,000	47,400	70,215	92,460
Ad Revenue														
Natural Growth	20%	0	0	280	336	347	349	350	350	350	350	350	350	350
Ad growth		0	1,400	1,400	1,400	1,400	1,400	1,400	1,400	1,400	1,400	1,400	1,400	1,400
Marketing cost		0	700	700	700	700	700	700	700	700	700	700	700	700
New users/ad cost		0	$0.50	$0.50	$0.50	$0.50	$0.50	$0.50	$0.50	$0.50	$0.50	$0.50	$0.50	$0.50
Ttl New Users		0	1,400	1,680	1,736	1,747	1,749	1,750	1,750	1,750	1,750	1,750	1,750	1,750
New users/day			47	56	58	58	58	58	58	58	58	58	58	58
Attrition rate	20%	0	0	280	616	963	1,050	1,330	1,610	1,890	2,170	2,450	2,730	3,010
Ttl Registered Users		0	1,400	3,080	4,816	6,563	8,313	10,063	11,813	13,563	15,313	17,063	18,813	20,563
Ttl Active Users	80%	0	1,400	3,080	4,816	5,251	6,650	8,050	9,450	10,850	12,250	13,650	15,050	16,450
Target Ttl Users									10,000					
Page view CliqUp	4.9	0	6,860	15,092	23,598	25,728	32,586	39,445	46,305	53,165	60,025	66,885	73,745	80,605
CliqUp Ad revenue (CPM)	0.002			30	47	51	65	79	93	106	120	134	147	161
# Affiliate blog sites	110%		20	20	22	24	27	29	32	35	39	43	47	52
Avg # users per blog site	5,000		100,000	100,000	110,000	121,000	133,100	146,410	161,051	177,156	194,872	214,359	235,795	259,374
Page view affiliate blogs	4.9		490,000	490,000	539,000	592,000	652,190	717,409	789,150	868,065	954,871	1,050,359	1,155,394	1,270,934
Blogger Ad revenue (CPM)	0.002		980	980	1,078	1,186	1,304	1,435	1,578	1,736	1,910	2,101	2,311	2,542
Ttl Ad Revenue		0	0	0	0	0	0	0	0	0	0	0	0	0
TOTAL REVENUE		0	0	0	0	0	0	0	0	0	24,000	47,400	70,215	92,460

APPENDIX F.4: (continued)

REVENUE DRIVERS AND ASSUMPTIONS

Basic Reporting

Monthly cost per subscription	$3,000
Yr One—Number of direct sales personnel	1
Yr Two—Number of direct sales personnel	2
Yr Three—Number of direct sales personnel	3
Direct sales calls per person per month	40
Yr One—closing percentage	20%
Yr Two—closing percentage	25%
Yr Three—closing percentage	27%
Yr One—subscription attrition rate	30%
Yr Two—subscription attrition rate	20%
Yr Three/Four—attrition rate	20%

Ad-Hoc Reporting

Average revenue per report	$20,000
Yr One—Number of direct sales personnel	0
Yr Two—Number of direct sales personnel	4
Yr Three—Number of direct sales personnel	6
Yr Three/Four—Number of direct sales personnel	6
Direct sales calls per person per month	6
Yr One—closing percentage	20%
Yr Two—closing percentage	25%
Yr Three—closing percentage	27%
Yr One—subscription attrition	0%
Yr Two—subscription attrition rate	10%
Yr Three/Four—subscription attrition rate	15%

Premium Reporting

Monthly cost per subscription ($100,000 yearly)	$8,333
Yr One—Number of direct sales personnel	0
Yr Two—Number of direct sales personnel	4
Yr Three—Number of direct sales personnel	6
Yr Three/Four—Number of direct sales personnel	6
Direct sales calls per person per month	6
Yr One—closing percentage	15%
Yr Two—closing percentage	20%
Yr Three—closing percentage	25%
Yr One—subscription attrition	10%
Yr Two—subscription attrition rate	10%
Yr Three/Four—subscription attrition rate	10%

REVENUES	Assm.	Month 13 2008/07	Month 14 2008/08	Month 15 2008/09	Month 16 2008/10	Month 17 2008/11	Month 18 2008/12	Month 19 2009/01	Month 20 2009/02	Month 21 2009/03	Month 22 2009/04	Month 23 2009/05	Month 24 2009/06
Basic Reporting													
Number of subscriptions sold		20	20	20	20	20	20	20	20	20	20	20	20
Subscription attrition		1	1	1	1	2	2	2	3	3	3	4	4
Cumulative number of subscriptions		50	69	88	107	125	143	161	178	195	212	228	244
Basic Reporting Revenue		150,919	208,403	264,930	320,514	375,173	428,920	481,771	533,741	584,846	635,098	684,513	733,105
Ad-Hoc Reporting													
Number of reports sold		—	—	—	—	—	6	6	6	6	6	6	6
Subscription attrition		—	—	—	—	—	1	1	1	1	1	1	1
Ad-Hoc Reporting Revenues		0	0	0	0	0	108,000	108,000	108,000	108,000	108,000	108,000	108,000
Premium Reporting													
Number of subscriptions sold		—	—	—	—	—	—	—	5	5	5	5	5
Subscription attrition		—	—	—	—	—	—	—	0	0	0	0	0
Cumulative number of subscriptions		—	—	—	—	—	—	—	5	10	14	19	24
Premium Reporting Revenue		0	0	0	0	0	0	0	40,000	79,667	119,003	158,011	196,694
TTL Revenue from Reports		150,919	208,403	264,930	320,514	375,173	536,920	589,771	681,741	772,512	862,101	950,524	1,037,799
Ad Revenue													
Natural Growth	20%	350											
Ad growth		30,184	41,681	52,986	64,103	75,035	107,384	117,954	136,348	154,502	172,420	190,105	209,188
Marketing cost		15,092	20,840	26,493	32,051	37,517	53,692	58,977	68,174	77,251	86,210	95,052	104,594
New users/ad cost		$0.50	$0.50	$0.50	$0.50	$0.50	$0.50	$0.50	$0.50	$0.50	$0.50	$0.50	$0.50
Ttl New Users		30,534	47,787	62,543	76,612	90,357	125,455	143,045	164,957	187,494	209,919	232,089	255,606
New users/day		1,018	1,593	2,085	2,554	3,012	4,182	4,768	5,499	6,250	6,997	7,736	8,520
Attrition rate	20%	3,290	8,175	15,821	25,828	38,086	52,543	72,616	95,503	121,897	151,896	185,483	222,617
Ttl Registered Users		51,096	98,884	161,427	238,039	328,396	453,851	596,896	761,853	949,347	1,159,266	1,391,355	1,646,961
Ttl Active Users	80%	40,877	79,107	129,142	190,431	262,716	363,081	477,517	609,483	759,478	927,413	1,113,084	1,317,569
Target Ttl Users		0	0	0	0	0	0	0	50,000	0	100,000	0	0
Page view CliqUp	4.9	200,297	387,624	632,794	933,112	1,287,310	1,779,095	2,339,833	2,986,465	3,721,442	4,544,324	5,454,112	6,456,086
CliqUp Ad revenue (CPM)	0.002	401	775	1,266	1,866	2,575	3,558	4,680	5,973	7,443	9,089	10,908	12,912
# Affiliate blog sites	110%	57	63	69	76	84	92	101	111	122	135	148	163
Avg # users per blog site	5,000	285,312	313,843	345,227	379,750	417,725	459,497	505,447	555,992	611,591	672,750	740,025	814,027
Page view affiliate blogs	4.9	1,398,027	1,537,830	1,691,613	1,860,774	2,046,852	2,251,537	2,476,690	2,724,359	2,996,795	3,296,475	3,626,122	3,988,735
Blogger Ad revenue (CPM)	0.002	2,796	3,076	3,383	3,722	4,094	4,503	4,953	5,449	5,994	6,593	7,252	7,977
Ttl Ad Revenue		0	0	0	0	0	0	0	0	0	0	0	8,140
TOTAL REVENUE		150,919	208,403	264,930	320,514	375,173	536,920	589,771	681,741	772,512	862,101	950,524	1,045,939

REVENUES		Month 25 2009/07	Month 26 2009/08	Month 27 2009/09	Month 28 2009/10	Month 29 2009/11	Month 30 2009/12	Month 31 2010/01	Month 32 2010/02	Month 33 2010/03	Month 34 2010/04	Month 35 2010/05	Month 36 2010/06
Basic Reporting													
Number of subscriptions sold	20%	32	32	32	32	32	32	32	32	32	32	32	32
Subscription attrition		4	5	5	5	6	6	7	7	8	8	8	9
Cumulative number of subscriptions		273	301	328	355	381	407	433	458	483	507	531	555
Basic Reporting Revenue		818,086	901,652	983,824	1,064,627	1,144,083	1,222,215	1,299,045	1,374,594	1,448,884	1,521,936	1,593,771	1,664,408
Ad-Hoc Reporting													
Number of reports sold		10	10	10	10	10	10	10	10	10	10	10	10
Subscription attrition		1	1	1	1	1	1	1	1	1	1	1	1
Ad-Hoc Reporting Revenues		165,240	165,240	165,240	165,240	165,240	165,240	165,240	165,240	165,240	165,240	165,240	165,240
Premium Reporting													
Number of subscriptions sold		9	9	9	9	9	9	9	9	9	9	9	9
Subscription attrition		0	0	0	0	0	1	1	1	1	1	1	1
Cumulative number of subscriptions		32	41	50	58	67	75	84	92	100	108	117	125
Premium Reporting Revenue		270,055	342,805	414,948	486,490	557,436	627,791	697,559	766,746	835,357	903,395	970,867	1,037,776
TTL Revenue from Reports		1,253,382	1,409,696	1,564,012	1,716,357	1,866,759	2,015,246	2,161,844	2,306,580	2,449,481	2,590,572	2,729,878	2,867,424
Ad Revenue		Month 25	Month 26	Month 27	Month 28	Month 29	Month 30	Month 31	Month 32	Month 33	Month 34	Month 35	Month 36
Natural Growth	20%	51,121	60,718	68,925	76,779	84,487	92,092	99,605	107,029	114,367	121,620	128,791	135,882
Ad growth		252,467	283,909	314,969	345,655	375,974	405,933	435,541	464,806	493,735	522,337	550,621	578,594
Marketing cost		126,234	141,955	157,485	172,828	187,987	202,967	217,771	232,403	246,868	261,169	275,310	289,297
New users/ad cost	$0.50	$0.50	$0.50	$0.50	$0.50	$0.50	$0.50	$0.50	$0.50	$0.50	$0.50	$0.50	$0.50
Ttl New Users		303,588	344,627	383,895	422,434	460,461	498,026	535,147	571,835	608,102	643,957	679,412	714,477
New users/day		10,120	11,488	12,796	14,081	15,349	16,601	17,838	19,061	20,270	21,465	22,647	23,816
Attrition rate	20%	263,514	312,088	367,228	428,651	496,241	569,914	649,599	735,222	826,716	924,012	1,027,045	1,135,751
Ttl Registered Users		1,950,549	2,295,176	2,679,071	3,101,505	3,561,965	4,059,991	4,595,137	5,166,973	5,775,075	6,419,032	7,098,444	7,812,921
Ttl Active Users	80%	1,560,439	1,836,141	2,143,257	2,481,204	2,849,572	3,247,993	3,676,110	4,133,578	4,620,080	5,135,226	5,678,755	6,250,337
Target Ttl Users		0	0	500,000	1,000,000	1,000,000	0	0	0	2,000,000	0	3,000,000	0
Page view CliqUp	4.9	7,646,152	8,997,090	10,501,957	12,157,898	13,962,904	15,915,164	18,012,939	20,254,533	22,638,293	25,162,606	27,825,902	30,626,651
CliqUp Ad revenue (CPM)	0.002	15,292	17,994	21,004	24,316	27,926	31,830	36,026	40,509	45,227	50,325	55,652	61,253
# Affiliate blog sites	110%	179	197	217	238	262	288	317	349	384	422	465	511
Avg # users per blog site	5,000	895,430	984,979	1,083,471	1,191,818	1,310,999	1,442,099	1,586,309	1,744,940	1,919,434	2,111,378	2,322,515	2,554,767
Page view affiliate blogs	4.9	4,387,608	4,826,369	5,309,006	5,839,907	6,428,897	7,066,287	7,772,916	8,550,207	9,405,228	10,345,751	11,380,326	12,518,358
Blogger Ad revenue (CPM)	0.002	8,775	9,653	10,618	11,680	12,848	14,133	15,546	17,100	18,810	20,692	22,761	25,037
Ttl Ad Revenue		8,954	9,850	10,835	11,918	13,110	14,421	15,863	17,449	19,194	21,114	23,225	25,548
TOTAL REVENUE		1,262,336	1,419,546	1,574,847	1,728,275	1,879,869	2,029,667	2,177,707	2,324,030	2,468,675	2,611,685	2,753,103	2,892,972

APPENDIX F.5: PRO FORMA CASH FLOW

	Month 0 2007/06	Month 1 2007/07	Month 2 2007/08	Month 3 2007/09	Month 4 2007/10	Month 5 2007/11	Month 6 2007/12	Month 7 2008/01	Month 8 2008/02	Month 9 2008/03	Month 10 2008/04	Month 11 2008/05	Month 12 2008/06
MONTHLY VARIABLES													
Basic Reporting													
Number of subscriptions sold	0	0	0	0	0	0	0	0	0	8	8	8	8
Subscription attrition	0	0	0	0	0	0	0	0	0	0	0	0	0
Cumulative number of subscriptions	0	0	0	0	0	0	0	0	0	8	16	23	31
Ad-Hoc Reporting													
Number of reports sold	0	0	0	0	0	0	0	0	0	0	0	0	0
Subscription attrition	0	0	0	0	0	0	0	0	0	0	0	0	0
Premium Reporting													
Number of subscriptions sold	0	0	0	0	0	0	0	0	0	0	0	0	0
Subscription attrition	0	0	0	0	0	0	0	0	0	0	0	0	0
Cumulative number of subscriptions	0	0	0	0	0	0	0	0	0	0	0	0	0
Advertisement													
Ttl New Users	0	1,400	1,680	1,736	1,747	1,749	1,750	1,750	1,750	1,750	1,750	1,750	1,750
Ttl Registered Users	0	1,400	3,080	4,816	6,563	8,313	10,063	11,813	13,563	15,313	17,063	18,813	20,563
Ttl Active Users	0	1,400	3,080	4,816	5,251	6,650	8,050	9,450	10,850	12,250	13,650	15,050	16,450
Page view CliqUp	0	6,860	15,092	23,598	25,728	32,586	39,445	46,305	53,165	60,025	66,885	73,745	80,605
# Affiliate blog sites	0	0	20	22	24	27	29	32	35	39	43	47	52
Avg # users per blog site	0	0	100,000	110,000	121,000	133,100	146,410	161,051	177,158	194,872	214,359	235,795	259,374
Page view affiliate blogs	0	0	490,000	539,000	592,900	652,190	717,409	789,150	868,065	954,871	1,050,359	1,155,394	1,270,934
Number of Employees	0	7	6	6	6	7	8	12	12	12	12	12	12
CASH INFLOW													
Basic Reporting Revenue	0	0	0	0	0	0	0	0	0	0	24,000	47,400	70,215
Ad-Hoc Reporting Revenues	0	0	0	0	0	0	0	0	0	0	0	0	0
Premium Reporting Revenue	0	0	0	0	0	0	0	0	0	0	0	0	0
Ad Revenue	0	0	0	0	0	0	0	0	0	0	0	0	0
Funding of Start-up													
TOTAL CASH INFLOW	0	0	0	0	0	0	0	0	0	0	24,000	47,400	70,215

	Month 0	Month 1	Month 2	Month 3	Month 4	Month 5	Month 6	Month 7	Month 8	Month 9	Month 10	Month 11	Month 12
	2007/06	2007/07	2007/08	2007/09	2007/10	2007/11	2007/12	2008/01	2008/02	2008/03	2008/04	2008/05	2008/06
CASH OUTFLOW													
Direct Costs													
COGS-Affiliate blogs revenue share (ad)	0	0	0	0	0	0	0	0	0	0	0	0	0
COGS-Credit card transaction costs (basic)	0	0	0	0	0	0	0	0	0	0	960	1,896	2,809
COGS-Sales commission	0	0	0	0	0	0	0	0	0	0	4,320	8,532	12,639
Total G&A	0	0	26,000	26,000	26,000	26,000	26,000	26,000	26,000	26,000	26,000	26,000	26,000
Total sales & marketing	0	0	0	0	0	0	0	5,200	9,100	9,100	9,100	9,100	9,100
Total systems personnel	0	0	0	0	0	0	11,700	16,900	23,400	23,400	23,400	23,400	23,400
Total other personnel	0	0	4,200	2,600	2,600	2,600	1,000	0	3,000	3,000	3,000	3,000	3,000
Systems Development/Maintenance	0	5,000	1,500	1,500	1,500	1,500	1,500	1,500	2,000	2,000	2,000	2,000	2,000
Total Direct Costs	0	5,000	31,700	30,100	30,100	30,100	40,200	49,600	63,500	63,500	68,780	73,928	78,947
Indirect Costs													
Marketing and Promotion	0	0	1,000	1,000	1,000	1,000	1,000	1,000	1,000	1,000	1,000	1,000	1,000
R&D	0	0	0	0	0	0	0	0	0	0	4,800	9,480	14,043
Office rent	0	0	872	872	872	872	872	872	872	872	872	872	872
Office equipment ($500 per employee)	0	0	3,500	-500	0	0	500	500	2,000	0	0	0	0
Comm. exp. & phone bills	0	0	954	954	954	954	954	954	954	954	954	954	954
Legal	0	2,000	651	651	651	651	651	651	651	651	651	651	651
Accounting	0	0	358	358	358	358	358	358	358	358	358	358	358
Misc	0	2,000	500	500	500	500	500	500	500	500	500	500	500
One-time expenses 1	0	0	0	0	0	0	0	0	0	0	0	0	0
Computers & software	0	0	7,000	0	0	0	0	0	4,000	0	0	0	0
Income Tax	0	0	0	0	0	0	0	1,000	0	0	0	0	0
Total Indirect Costs	0	4,000	14,835	3,835	4,335	4,335	4,835	5,835	10,335	4,335	9,135	13,815	18,378
TOTAL CASH OUTFLOW	0	9,000	46,535	33,935	34,435	34,435	45,035	55,435	73,835	67,835	77,915	87,743	97,325
Inflow-Outflow	0	-9,000	-46,535	-33,935	-34,435	-34,435	-45,035	-55,435	-73,835	-67,835	-53,915	-40,343	-27,110
Cumulative Inflow-Outflow	0	-9,000	-55,535	-89,470	-123,905	-158,340	-203,375	-258,810	-332,645	-400,480	-454,395	-494,738	-521,848

APPENDIX F.5: *(continued)*

	Month 13	Month 14	Month 15	Month 16	Month 17	Month 18	Month 19	Month 20	Month 21	Month 22	Month 23	Month 24
	2008/07	2008/08	2008/09	2008/10	2008/11	2008/12	2009/01	2009/02	2009/03	2009/04	2009/05	2009/06
MONTHLY VARIABLES												
Basic Reporting												
Number of subscriptions sold	20	20	20	20	20	20	20	20	20	20	20	20
Subscription attrition	1	1	1	1	2	2	2	3	3	3	4	4
Cumulative number of subscriptions	50	69	88	107	125	143	161	178	195	212	228	244
Ad-Hoc Reporting												
Number of reports sold	0	0	0	0	6	6	6	6	6	6	6	6
Subscription attrition	0	0	0	0	1	1	1	1	1	1	1	1
Premium Reporting												
Number of subscriptions sold	0	0	0	0	0	0	0	5	5	5	5	5
Subscription attrition	0	0	0	0	0	0	0	0	0	0	0	0
Cumulative number of subscriptions	0	0	0	0	0	0	0	5	10	14	19	24
Advertisement												
Ttl New Users	30,534	47,787	62,543	76,612	90,357	125,455	143,045	164,957	187,494	209,919	232,089	255,606
Ttl Registered Users	51,096	98,884	161,427	238,039	328,396	453,851	596,896	761,853	949,347	1,159,266	1,391,355	1,646,961
Ttl Active Users	40,877	79,107	129,142	190,431	262,716	363,081	477,517	609,483	759,478	927,413	1,113,084	1,317,569
Page view CliqUp	200,297	387,624	632,794	933,112	1,287,310	1,779,095	2,339,833	2,986,465	3,721,442	4,544,324	5,454,112	6,456,086
# Affiliate blog sites	57	63	69	76	84	92	101	111	122	135	148	163
Avg # users per blog site	285,312	313,843	345,227	379,750	417,725	459,497	505,447	555,992	611,591	672,750	740,025	814,027
Page view affiliate blogs	1,398,027	1,537,830	1,691,613	1,860,774	2,046,852	2,251,537	2,476,690	2,724,359	2,996,795	3,296,475	3,626,122	3,988,735
Number of Employees	18	22	21	22	25	25	25	26	26	30	30	31
CASH INFLOW												
Basic Reporting Revenue	92,460	150,919	208,403	264,930	320,514	375,173	428,920	481,771	533,741	584,846	635,098	684,513
Ad-Hoc Reporting Revenues	0	0	0	0	0	0	108,000	108,000	108,000	108,000	108,000	108,000
Premium Reporting Revenue	0	0	0	0	0	0	0	0	0	40,000	79,667	119,003
Ad Revenue	0	0	0	0	0	0	0	0	0	0	0	0
Funding of Start-up												
TOTAL CASH INFLOW	92,460	150,919	208,403	264,930	320,514	375,173	536,920	589,771	641,741	732,846	822,765	911,516

CASH OUTFLOW												
Direct Costs												
COGS – Affiliate blogs revenue share (ad)	0	0	0	0	0	0	0	0	0	0	0	4,070
COGS – Credit card transaction costs (basic)	3,698	6,037	8,336	10,597	12,821	15,007	17,157	19,271	21,350	23,394	25,404	27,381
COGS – Sales commission	16,643	27,165	37,513	47,687	57,693	67,531	96,646	106,159	122,713	139,052	155,178	171,094
Total G&A	26,000	41,600	41,600	41,600	41,600	41,600	41,600	41,600	41,600	41,600	41,600	41,600
Total sales & marketing	9,100	14,300	35,100	35,100	39,000	54,600	54,600	54,600	59,800	59,800	79,300	79,300
Total systems personnel	23,400	36,400	36,400	44,200	44,200	44,200	44,200	44,200	44,200	44,200	44,200	44,200
Total other personnel	3,000	3,000	3,000	0	0	0	0	0	0	0	0	0
Systems Development/Maintenance	2,000	2,500	2,500	2,500	2,500	2,500	2,500	2,500	2,500	2,500	2,500	2,500
Total Direct Costs	83,841	131,002	164,449	181,685	197,813	225,438	256,702	268,330	292,163	310,546	348,182	370,145
Indirect Costs												
Marketing and Promotion	1,000	30,184	41,681	52,986	64,103	75,035	107,384	117,954	136,348	154,502	172,420	190,105
R&D	18,492	30,184	41,681	52,986	64,103	75,035	107,384	117,954	138,348	154,502	172,420	190,105
Office rent	872	2,253	2,253	2,253	2,253	2,253	2,253	2,253	2,253	2,253	2,253	2,253
Office equipment ($500 per employee)	0	3,000	2,000	-500	500	1,500	0	0	500	0	2,000	0
Comm. exp. & phone bills	954	954	954	954	954	954	954	954	954	954	954	954
Legal	651	651	651	651	651	651	651	651	651	651	651	651
Accounting	358	358	358	358	358	358	358	358	358	358	358	358
Misc	500	750	750	750	750	750	750	750	750	750	750	750
One-time expenses 1	0	0	0	0	0	0	0	0	0	0	0	0
Computers & software	0	6,000	4,000	-1,000	1,000	3,000	0	0	1,000	0	4,000	0
Income Tax	0	0	0	0	0	0	21,075	28,104	38,901	51,704	56,645	69,652
Total Indirect Costs	22,827	74,333	94,327	109,438	134,671	159,535	240,809	268,978	318,064	365,675	412,451	454,827
TOTAL CASH OUTFLOW	106,668	205,335	258,776	291,122	332,485	384,973	497,511	537,308	610,227	676,221	760,833	824,972
Inflow-Outflow	-14,208	-54,417	-50,372	-26,192	-11,970	-9,800	39,409	52,463	31,515	56,625	62,132	86,544
Cumulative Inflow-Outflow	-536,057	-590,473	-640,846	-667,038	-679,008	-688,808	-649,399	-596,936	-565,422	-508,797	-446,665	-360,121

APPENDIX F.5: *(continued)*

	Month 25	Month 26	Month 27	Month 28	Month 29	Month 30	Month 31	Month 32	Month 33	Month 34	Month 35	Month 36
	2009/07	2009/08	2009/09	2009/10	2009/11	2009/12	2010/01	2010/02	2010/03	2010/04	2010/05	2010/06
MONTHLY VARIABLES												
Basic Reporting												
Number of subscriptions sold	32	32	32	32	32	32	32	32	32	32	32	32
Subscription attrition	4	5	5	5	6	6	7	7	8	8	8	9
Cumulative number of subscriptions	273	301	328	355	381	407	433	458	483	507	531	555
Ad-Hoc Reporting												
Number of reports sold	10	10	10	10	10	10	10	10	10	10	10	10
Subscription attrition	1	1	1	1	1	1	1	1	1	1	1	1
Premium Reporting												
Number of subscriptions sold	9	9	9	9	9	9	9	9	9	9	9	9
Subscription attrition	0	0	0	0	0	1	1	1	1	1	1	1
Cumulative number of subscriptions	32	41	50	58	67	75	84	92	100	108	117	125
Advertisement												
Ttl New Users	303,588	344,627	383,895	422,434	460,461	498,026	535,147	571,835	608,102	643,957	679,412	714,477
Ttl Registered Users	1,950,549	2,295,176	2,679,071	3,101,505	3,561,985	4,059,991	4,595,137	5,166,973	5,775,075	6,419,032	7,098,444	7,812,921
Ttl Active Users	1,560,439	1,836,141	2,143,257	2,481,204	2,849,572	3,247,993	3,676,110	4,133,578	4,620,060	5,135,226	5,678,755	6,250,337
Page view CliqUp	7,646,152	8,997,090	10,501,957	12,157,898	13,962,904	15,915,164	18,012,939	20,254,533	20,638,293	25,162,606	27,825,902	30,626,651
# Affiliate blog sites	179	197	217	238	262	288	317	349	384	422	465	511
Avg # users per blog site	895,430	984,973	1,083,471	1,191,818	1,310,999	1,442,099	1,586,309	1,744,940	1,919,434	2,111,378	2,322,515	2,554,767
Page view affiliate blogs	4,387,608	4,826,369	5,309,006	5,639,907	6,423,897	7,066,287	7,772,916	8,550,207	9,405,228	10,345,751	11,380,326	12,518,358
Number of Employees	40	42	45	46	47	51	52	55	57	58	61	62
CASH INFLOW												
Basic Reporting Revenue	733,105	818,086	901,652	983,824	1,064,627	1,144,083	1,222,215	1,299,045	1,374,594	1,448,884	1,521,936	1,593,771
Ad-Hoc Reporting Revenues	108,000	165,240	165,240	165,240	165,240	165,240	165,240	165,240	165,240	165,240	165,240	165,240
Premium Reporting Revenue	158,011	196,694	270,055	342,805	414,948	486,490	557,436	627,791	697,559	766,746	835,357	903,395
Ad Revenue	8,140	8,954	9,850	10,835	11,918	13,110	14,421	15,863	17,449	19,194	21,114	23,225
Funding of Start-up												
TOTAL CASH INFLOW	1,007,256	1,188,975	1,346,797	1,502,704	1,656,733	1,808,923	1,959,312	2,107,939	2,254,843	2,400,065	2,543,647	2,685,631

CASH OUTFLOW												
Direct Costs												
COGS – Affiliate blogs revenue share (ad)	4,477	4,925	5,417	5,959	6,555	7,210	7,932	8,725	9,597	10,557	11,613	12,774
COGS – Credit card transaction costs (basic)	29,324	32,723	36,066	39,353	42,585	45,763	48,889	51,962	54,984	57,955	60,877	63,751
COGS – Sales commission	186,804	225,609	253,745	281,522	308,944	336,017	362,744	389,132	415,184	440,907	466,303	491,378
Total G&A	41,600	61,100	61,100	61,100	61,100	61,100	61,100	61,100	61,100	61,100	61,100	61,100
Total sales & marketing	84,500	115,700	124,800	140,400	145,600	150,800	170,300	175,500	191,100	200,200	205,400	221,000
Total systems personnel	44,200	44,200	44,200	44,200	44,200	44,200	44,200	44,200	44,200	44,200	44,200	44,200
Total other personnel	0	0	0	0	0	0	0	0	0	0	0	0
Systems Development/Maintenance	2,500	3,000	3,000	3,000	3,000	4,500	4,500	4,500	4,500	5,500	5,500	6,500
Total Direct Costs	393,405	487,257	528,329	575,534	611,984	649,591	699,664	735,118	780,665	820,419	854,993	900,703
Indirect Costs												
Marketing and Promotion	209,188	252,467	283,909	314,969	345,655	375,974	405,933	435,541	464,806	493,735	522,337	550,621
R&D	209,188	252,467	283,909	314,969	345,655	375,974	405,933	435,541	464,806	493,735	522,337	550,621
Office rent	2,253	4,505	4,505	4,505	4,505	4,505	4,505	4,505	4,505	4,505	4,505	4,505
Office equipment ($500 per employee)	500	4,500	1,000	1,500	500	500	2,000	500	1,500	1,000	500	1,500
Comm. exp. & phone bills	954	954	954	954	954	954	954	954	954	954	954	954
Legal	661	651	651	651	651	651	651	651	651	651	651	651
Accounting	358	358	358	358	358	358	358	358	358	358	358	358
Misc	750	1,125	1,125	1,125	1,125	1,126	1,125	1,125	1,125	1,125	1,125	1,125
One-time expenses 1	0	0	0	0	0	0	0	0	0	0	0	0
Computers & software	1,000	9,000	2,000	3,000	1,000	1,000	4,000	1,000	3,000	2,000	1,000	3,000
Income Tax	80,091	90,380	110,260	126,193	146,025	164,718	178,148	197,378	211,842	228,509	246,649	260,035
Total Indirect Costs	504,932	616,408	688,672	768,226	846,428	926,759	1,003,608	1,077,554	1,153,547	1,226,573	1,300,416	1,373,370
TOTAL CASH OUTFLOW	898,337	1,103,685	1,217,001	1,343,760	1,458,413	1,575,350	1,703,272	1,812,672	1,934,212	2,046,991	2,155,409	2,274,072
Inflow-Outflow	108,919	85,310	129,796	158,944	198,321	233,574	256,040	295,266	320,630	353,073	388,237	411,559
Cumulative Inflow-Outflow	-251,202	-165,892	-36,096	122,848	321,168	554,742	810,782	1,106,048	1,426,679	1,779,752	2,167,989	2,579,548

APPENDIX F.6: THREE-YEAR INCOME STATEMENT

	Year 6/2008	Year 6/2009	Year 6/2010
REVENUES			
Basic Reporting Revenue	234,075	5,401,933	15,037,126
Ad-Hoc Reporting Revenues	—	756,000	1,982,880
Premium Reporting Revenue	—	593,375	7,911,226
Advertisement Revenue	—	8,140	191,481
Total Revenues	**234,075**	**6,759,448**	**25,122,713**
EXPENSES			
COGS			
Bloggers revenue share	—	4,070	21,697
Credit card transaction costs	9,363	216,077	146,614
Sales commission	42,133	1,215,235	1,087,893
Total COGS	51,496	1,436,383	4,099,138
Gross Margin	**78%**	**79%**	**84%**
OPERATING PROFIT	**182,578**	**5,324,065**	**19,937,865**
SG&A			
MARKETING			
Advertising (web)	8,400	675,945	2,512,271
Marketing General	3,600	675,945	2,512,271
Total Marketing and Promotions	12,000	1,351,690	5,024,543
OTHER EXPENSES			
Total other expenses	92,835	1,420,978	5,131,163
HUMAN RESOURCES			
Total G&A	312,000	499,200	733,200
Total sales & marketing	59,800	650,000	2,067,000
Total systems personnel	169,000	514,800	530,400
Total other personnel	31,000	6,000	—
Total human resources	571,800	1,670,000	3,330,600
TOTAL SG&A	676,635	4,442,867	13,486,305
System maintenance	21,000	30,000	54,000
EBITDA	**(515,057)**	**851,198**	**6,397,560**
Depreciation	2,751	3,234	3,234
Amortization	–	–	–
Total depreciation & amortization	2,751	3,234	3,234
EBIT	**(517,808)**	**847,954**	**6,394,326**
Total interest expense	–	–	–
PRE-TAX NET INCOME	**(517,808)**	**847,964**	**6,394,326**
Income tax	35%	346,172	2,238,014
NET INCOME AFTER TAX	**0%**	**(517,808)**	**501,792**	**4,156,312**

NOTES

Chapter 1

1. Lumpkin, G.T., and G.G. Dess (January 1996). "Clarifying the Entrepreneurial Orientation Construct and Linking It to Performance." *Academy of Management Review,* 21(1): 135.
2. Morris, M.H., P. Lewis, and D.L. Sexton (Winter 1994). "Reconceptualizing Entrepreneurship: An Input–Output Perspective." *SAM Advanced Management Journal,* 59(2): 21–31.
3. Ronstadt, R.C. (1984). *Entrepreneurship.* Dover, MA: Lord Publishing Co., p. 39.
4. Gartner, W.B. (1985). "A Conceptual Framework for Describing the Phenomenon of New Venture Creation." *Academy of Management Review,* 702.
5. Schumpeter, J. (1934). *The Theory of Economic Development.* Cambridge: Harvard University Press; Solow, R.M. (1970). *Growth Theory: An Exposition.* Oxford: Oxford University Press; and Grossman, G.M., and E. Helpman (Winter 1994). "Éndogenous Innovation in the Theory of Growth." *Journal of Economic Perspectives,* 8(1): 23–44.
6. Romer, Paul (1986). "Increasing Returns and Long-Run Growth." *Journal of Political Economy,* 94: 1002–1037.
7. Allen, K.R. (2003). *Bringing New Technology to Market.* Upper Saddle River: Prentice Hall.
8. Ibid.
9. Caballero, R., and M. Hammour (2000). "Creative Destruction and Development: Institutions, Crises, and Restructuring." Paper presented at the Annual World Bank Conference on Development Economics, Washington, DC.
10. *The Economist* (2002). "Self-Doomed to Failure." (July 6): 24–26; and Liao, D. and P. Sohmen (Spring 2001). "The Development of Modern Entrepreneurship in China." *Stanford Journal of East Asian Affairs,* 1: 31.
11. Jovanovic, B., and G. MacDonald (1994). "The Life-Cycle of a Competitive Industry." *Journal of Political Economy,* 102(2): 322–347.
12. Small Business Administration Office of Advocacy (October 25, 2006), http://www.sba.gov/advo.
13. Ibid.
14. Schumpeter, J. (1934). *The Theory of Economic Development.* Cambridge: Harvard University Press; Solow, R.M. (1970). *Growth Theory: An Exposition.* Oxford: Oxford University Press; and Grossman, G.M., and E. Helpman (Winter 1994). "Éndogenous Innovation in the Theory of Growth." *Journal of Economic Perspectives,* 8(1): 23–44.
15. Kirchhoff, B. (1994). *Entrepreneurship and Dynamic Capitalism.* Westport, CT: Praeger.
16. Reynolds, P.D. (July 1995). "Family Firms in the Start-up Process: Preliminary Explorations." Paper presented at the 1995 annual meetings of the International Family Business Program Association, Nashville, TN.
17. Shane, S., and S. Venkataraman (2000). "The Promise of Entrepreneurship as a Field of Research." *The Academy of Management Review,* 25(1): 217–226; and Begley, T., and D. Boyd (1987). "Psychological Characteristics Associated with Performance in Entrepreneurial Firms and Smaller Businesses." *Journal of Business Venturing,* 2: 79–93.
18. Bhave, M.P. (1994). "A Process Model of Entrepreneurial Venture Creation." *Journal of Business Venturing,* 9: 223–242; and Reynolds, P.D., and B. Miller (1992). "New Firm Gestation: Conception, Birth, and Implications for Research." *Journal of Business Venturing,* 7: 405–417.

19. Block, Z., and I.C. MacMillan (1985). "Milestones for Successful Venture Planning." *Harvard Business Review*, 85(5): 184–188.

20. Carter, N., W.B. Gartner, and P.D. Reynolds (1996). "Exploring Start-up Events Sequences." *Journal of Business Venturing*, 11: 151–166.

21. Reinertsen, Donald G. (1999). "Taking the Fuzziness Out of the Fuzzy Front End." *Industrial Research Institute, Inc.* (November/December): 25–31.

22. Op. cit., Small Business Administration Office of Advocacy.

23. Birley, S., and P. Westhead (1993). "A Comparison of New Businesses Established by Novice and Habitual Founders in Great Britain." *International Small Business Journal*, 12(1): 38–60.

24. Knaup, A.E. (May 2005). "Survival and Longevity in the Business Employment Dynamics Database." *Monthly Labor Review*, 128(5): 50–56; and Heald, B. (August 2003). "Redefining Business Success: Distinguishing Between Closure and Failure." *Small Business Economics*, 21(1): 51–61.

25. Headd, B. (January 2001). *Factors Leading to Surviving and Closing Successfully.* Center for Economic Studies, U.S. Bureau of the Census, Working Paper #CES-WP-01-01; advocacy-funded research by Richard J. Boden (Research Summary #204).

26. Cohen, W., and R. Levin (1989). "Empirical Studies of Innovation and Market Structure." In *Handbook of Industrial Organization*, 2nd ed., R. Schmalensee and R. Willig (eds). New York: Elsevier.

27. Case, J. (1992). *From the Ground Up.* New York: Belknap Press, p. 44.

28. Ibid., 46.

29. Ibid., 64.

30. Gupta, U. (1989). "Small Firms Aren't Waiting to Grow Up to Go Global." *Wall Street Journal* (December 5): B2.

31. McDougall, P.O., S. Shane, and B.M. Oviatt (1994). "Explaining the Formation of International New Ventures: The Limits of Theories from International Business Research." *Journal of Business Venturing*, 9: 469–487.

32. Reuber, A.R. and E. Fischer (1997). "The Influence of the Management Team's International Experience on the Internationalization Behaviors of SMEs." *Journal of International Business Studies*, 28: 807–825.

33. Audretsch, D., and R. Thurik (2005). "A Model of the Entrepreneurial Economy." *International Journal of Entrepreneurship Education*, 2(2): 143–166.

34. Drucker, P. (November 3, 2001). "The Next Society: A Survey of the Near Future." *The Economist*.

35. Thornton, P.H., and K.H. Flynne (2003). "Entrepreneurship, Networks and Geographies," in Z.J. Aes and D.B. Andretsch (eds), *Handbook of Entrepreneurship Research*. Boston: Dordrecht Kluwer Academic Publishers.

36. Op. cit., Audretsch and Thurik, 2005.

37. Minniti, M., I.E. Allen, and N. Langowitz (2005). "2005 Report on Women and Entrepreneurship." *Global Entrepreneurship Monitor.* Sponsored by Babson College and the London Business School.

38. Office of Advocacy (August 2006). "Women in Business: A Demographic Review of Women's Business Ownership." U.S. Small Business Administration, http://www.sba.gov/advo/research/women.html.

39. "Statistics on Women-Owned Businesses." National Women's Business Council, 2006, http://www.awib.org/content_frames/articles/womenstat07.html.

40. Buttner, H.E., and D.P. Moore (1997). "Women's Organizational Exodus to Entrepreneurship: Self-Reported Motivations and Correlates with Success." *Journal of Small Business Management*, 34–36.

41. *2000 Statistical Abstract of the United States.* Washington, DC: U.S. Department of Commerce, Bureau of the Census, http://www.census.gov/cds/mwb.

42. Lowrey, Y. (February 2005). "Dynamics of Minority-Owned Employer Establishments." *Small Business Research Summary*, No. 251.

43. Pitta, J. (1998). "Silicon Valley South." *Forbes* (November 16): 214–216.

44. Op. cit., Lowrey, 2005.

45. "Minority Vintners Call Attention to Growth Market." HispanicBusiness.com (August 15, 2003).

46. "Better Bosses." *Fortune Small Business* (October 2006): 91.

Chapter 2

1. Vogelstein, F. (2004). "14 Innovators." *Fortune* (November 15): 200.

2. Hofman, M. (October 2002). "Until You Get It Right." *Inc. Magazine*, http://www.inc.com; and http://www.idlabelinc.com.

3. Eng, S. (July 10, 2001). "Impress Investors with Your Firm's Endgame." *Wall Street Journal Startup Journal*, http://www.startupjournal.com.

4. Davidsson, P. (2005). "The Types and Contextual Fit of Entrepreneurial Processes." *International Journal of Entrepreneurship Education*, 2(4): 407–430.

5. Bird, B.J. (1989). *Entrepreneurial Behavior.* Glenview, IL: Scott, Foresman and Co.; and Volery, T., N. Doss, T. Mazzarol, and V. Thein (1997). "Triggers and Barriers Affecting Entrepreneurial Intentionality: The Case of Western Australian

Nascent Entrepreneurs." 42nd ICSB World Conference. June 21–24, San Francisco.

6. Barker, E. (July 2000). "Rambling for Gems." *Inc. Magazine,* http://www.inc.com.

7. Greco, S. (October 2002). "A Little Goes a Long Way." *Inc. Magazine,* http://www.inc.com/magazine/20021015/24779.html.

8. Aspelund, A., T. Berg-Utby, and R. Skejevdal (2005). "Initial Resources' Influence on New Venture Survival: A Longitudinal Study of New Technology-Based Firms." *Technovation,* 25(11): 1337.

9. Roberts, M.T., and L. Barley (December 2004). "How Venture Capitalists Evaluate Potential Venture Opportunities." *Harvard Business School Press.*

10. Breeden, R. (2002). "Older Can Be Better for Small Businesses." *Wall Street Journal Startup Journal,* http://www.startupjournal.com.

11. Drucker, P.E. (1985). *Innovation and Entrepreneurship.* New York: Harper & Row.

12. Gorman, G., D. Hanlon, and W. King (1997). "Some Research Perspectives on Entrepreneurship Education, Enterprise Education, and Education for Small Business Management: A Ten-Year literature Review." *International Small Business Journal,* 15: 56–77.

13. Beale, H.B.R. (2004). "Home-Based Business and Government Regulation." SBA Office of Advocacy, Contract # SBA-HQ-02-M-0464.

14. Westhead, P., D. UcBasaran, and M. Wright (2005). "Decisions, Actions, and Performance: Do Novice, Serial, and Portfolio Entrepreneurs Differ?" *Journal of Small Business Management,* 43(4): 393.

15. Rosa, P. (1998). "Entrepreneurial Processes of Business Cluster Formation and Growth by 'Habitual' Entrepreneurs." *Entrepreneurship Theory and Practice,* 22: 43–61.

16. Buchanan, L. (December 2002). "A Sharper Image." *Inc. Magazine,* http://www.inc.com; and http://premiumhg.com/PHG_Store/Premium_HG_About_Us.html.

17. Schmedel, S. "Making a Difference as a Social Entrepreneur." *Wall Street Journal Online,* http://www.wsj.com (accessed January 5, 2007).

18. Shane, S., and S. Venkataraman. (2000). "The Promise of Entrepreneurship as a Field of Research." *Academy of Management Review,* 25(1): 217–226; and Begley, T., and D. Boyd (1987). "Psychological Characteristics Associated with Performance in Entrepreneurial Firms and Smaller Businesses." *Journal of Business Venturing,* 2: 79–93.

19. Quinn, J.B. (1997). *Innovation Explosion.* New York: The Free Press.

20. Deutschman, A. (March 2005). "Building a Better Skunk Works, *Fast Company,* 92: 68.

21. Hawkins, J. (October 23, 2002) Stanford Thought Leader Lectures, Palo Alto, CA.

22. Barnett, William P., Henrich R. Greve, and Douglas Y. Park (1994). "An Evolutionary Model of Organizational Performance." *Strategic Management Journal,* 15 (Winter Special Issue): 11–28.

23. Baum, Joel A.C., and Christine Oliver (1991). "Institutional Linkages and Organizational Mortality." *Administrative Science Quarterly,* 36: 187–218.

24. Ramesh, G. (July–September 2005). "Entrepreneurial Traps: Autobiography of an Unknown Entrepreneur." *South Asian Journal of Management,* 12(3): 79.

25. Aldrich, H., and C. Zimmer (1986). "Entrepreneurship Through Social Networks," in D.L. Sexton and R.W. Smilor (eds), *The Art and Science of Entrepreneurship.* Cambridge, MA: Ballinger.

26. Granovetter, M. (1982). "The Strength of Weak Ties: A Network Theory Revisited," in P.V. Marsden and N. Lin (eds), *Social Structure and Network Analysis.* Beverly Hills, CA: Sage.

27. Grossman, E. (2005). *New Venture Creation and Network Tie Formation: A Longitudinal Study of Nascent Entrepreneurs' Efforts in Business Building,* Doctoral Dissertation, University of California at Los Angeles.

28. Burt. R.S. (2004). "Structural Holes and Good Ideas." *The American Journal of Sociology,* 110(2): 349.

29. Fisher, D., and S. Vilas (2000). *Power Networking: 59 Secrets for Personal and Professional Success.* Marietta, GA: Bard Press.

30. Hatala, J.P. (2005). "Identifying Barriers to Self-Employment: The Development and Validation of the Barriers to Entrepreneurship Success Tool." *Performance Improvement Quarterly,* 18(4): 50.

Chapter 3

1. Gryskiewicz, S.S. (September 2000). "Cashing In on Creativity at Work." *Psychology Today,* http://www.findarticles.com.

2. Drazin, R.D. (1999). "Multilevel Theorizing About Creativity in Organizations: A Sensemaking Perspective." *Academy of Management Review,* 24(2): 286; Drazin, R. (1990). "Professionals and Innovation: Structural–Functional Versus Radical–Structural Perspectives." *Journal of Management Studies,* 27(3): 245–263; and Amabile, T.M. (1988). "A Model of Creativity and Innovation in Organizations," in B.M. Staw and L.L. Cummings (eds), *Research in*

Organizational Behavior, Vol. 10. Greenwich, CT: JAI Press, pp. 123–167.

3. Op. cit., Drazin, 1999; and Woodman, R.W., J.E. Sawyer, and R.W. Griffin (1993). "Toward a Theory of Organizational Creativity." *Academy of Management Review,* 18(2): 293-321.

4. Singh, B. (1986). "Role of Personality Versus Biographical Factors in Creativity." *Psychological Studies,* 31: 90–92; Barron, F., and D.M. Harrington (1981). "Creativity, Intelligence, and Personality." *Annual Review of Psychology,* 32: 439–476; and Gardner, H. (1993). *Frames of Mind.* New York: Basic Books.

5. Amabile, T.M. (1988). "A Model of Creativity and Innovation in Organizations," in B.M. Staw and L.L. Cummings (eds), *Research in Organizational Behavior,* Vol. 10. Greenwich, CT: JAI Press, pp. 123–167; Oldham, G.R., and A. Cummings (1996). "Employee Creativity: Personal and Contextual Factors at Work." *Academy of Management Journal,* 39: 607–634; Mumford, M.D., and S.B. Gustafson (1988). "Creativity Syndrome: Integration, Application, and Innovation." *Psychological Bulletin,* 103: 27–43; and Payne, R. (1990). "The Effectiveness of Research Teams: A Review," in M.A. West and J.L. Farr (eds), *Innovation and Creativity at Work.* Chichester, England: Wiley, pp. 101–122.

6. Siler, T. (1999). *Think Like a Genius.* New York: Bantam Books.

7. Ibid.

8. Reuters. (February 23, 2006). "Work More, Do Less with Tech." *Wired News,* http://www.wired.com/news/wireservice/1,70274-0.html.

9. Henricks, M. (February, 2005). "Falling Behind: How Dependence on Tech Made Us Less Productive," *Entrepreneur,* http://findarticles.com/p/articles/mi_m0DTI/is_2_33/ai_n13470538.

10. Kanter, R.M. (Winter 2005). "How Leaders Gain (and Lose) Confidence." *Leader to Leader,* 35: 21.

11. Ibid.

12. Google Corporate Information, http://www.google.com/corporate/tenthings.html (accessed January 15, 2007).

13. Stewart, B. (2006). "A Butterfly Business Takes Flight." *Fortune Small Business* (November): 23.

14. Jones, M.D. (1998). *The Thinker's Toolkit.* New York: Three Rivers Press.

Chapter 4

1. Sloane, J. "Play Big." *Fortune Small Business* (November 2006): 28–29.

2. Thanks to Dr. Gerald Loeb, Nicholas Sachs, Hilton Kaplan, and the rest of the BION team for providing this example.

3. Magretta, J. (2002). "Why Business Models Matter." *Harvard Business Review,* Reprint R0205F, p. 4.

4. Downes L., and C. Mui (1998). *Unleashing the Killer App.* Boston: Harvard Business School Press.

5. Stern, L.W., and A.I. El-Ansary (1996). *Marketing Channels,* 5th ed. Englewood Cliffs, NJ: Prentice Hall.

6. Shafer, S.M., H.J. Smith, and J.C. Linder (2005). "The Power of Business Models." *Business Horizons,* 48: 199–207.

7. Hamel, G. (2000). *Leading the Revolution.* New York: Plume.

8. Tucker, R.B. (2001). "Strategy Innovation Takes Imagination." *Journal of Business Strategy,* 22(3): 23–27.

9. Op. cit., Shafer et al., 2005, 204.

10. Friedman, T.L. (2005). *The World Is Flat.* New York: Farrar, Straus & Giroux.

11. Hamermesh, R.G., P.W. Marshall, and T. Pirmohamed. "Note on Business Model Analysis for the Entrepreneur." *Harvard Business School* (January 22, 2002): 2.

12. "Building a Business Model and Strategy: How They Work Together" (October 30, 2004). Excerpted from *Entrepreneur's Toolkit: Tools and Techniques to Launch and Grow Your Business.* Cambridge, MA: Harvard Business School Press, p. 5.

13. Ibid.

14. Stuart, A. (December 2002). "This Year's Model." *Inc. Magazine,* http://www.inc.com.

15. Linder, J., and S. Cantrell (2001). "What Makes a Good Business Model Anyway? Can Yours Stand the Test of Change?" *Outlook: Point of View,* http://www.accenture.com.

16. Allen, L.H., and C.K. Prahalad (May/June 2004). "Selling to the Poor." *Foreign Policy,* 142: 30–37.

17. Chesbrough, H., S. Ahern, M. Finn, and S. Guerraz (2006). "Business Models for Technology in the Developing World: The Role of Non-Governmental Organizations." *California Management Review,* 48(3): 49.

Chapter 5

1. Helmer, H.W. (2005). "A Lecture on Integrating the Treatment of Uncertainty in Strategy." *Journal of Strategic Management Education,* 1(1): 94.

2. Knight, F. (1967). *Risk, Uncertainty, and Profit.* New York: Sentry Press, p. 233.

3. French, N., and L. Gabrielli (2005). "Uncertainty and Feasibility Studies: An Italian Case Study." *Journal of Property Investment & Finance,* 24(1): 49.

4. Savage, L. (1972). *The Foundations of Statistics.* New York: Dover Publications, Inc.

5. Op. cit., Helmer, 2005, 193–114.

6. Based on a feasibility study developed by David Dobkin, while a graduate student at the University of Southern California.

7. Merkle, R.C. (April 2001). "That's Impossible." *Foresight Nanotech Institute,* http://www.foresight.org/impact/impossible.html.

Chapter 6

1. Heller, R. "Stop the Life Cycle in Its Tracks." *Management Today* (January 1999): 17.

2. Anthony, S.D., and C.G. Gilbert (Spring 2006). "Can the Newspaper Industry Stare Disruption in the Face?" *Nieman Reports,* 60(1): 43.

3. Schrage, M. (2006). "The Myth of Commoditization." *MIT Sloan Management Review,* 48(2): 12.

4. Jin, J.Y., J. Perote-Pena, and M. Troege (2004). "Learning by Doing, Spillovers and Shakeouts." *Journal of Evolutionary Economics,* 14: 85–98.

5. McGahan, A.N. (2004). *How Industries Evolve.* Boston, MA: Harvard Business School Press.

6. Ibid., 10.

7. Ibid.

8. Porter, M.E. (1980). *Competitive Strategy: Techniques for Analyzing Industries and Competitors.* New York: The Free Press, p. 3.

9. Dees, J.G., J. Emerson, and P. Economy (2001). *Enterprising Nonprofits.* New York: Wiley; and "REDF Partners for Profit with San Francisco Ashbury Images." Press release, April 2, 2004.

10. Gray, R. (2000). "The Relentless Rise of Online Research." *Marketing* (May 18).

11. Norman, K.L., Z. Friedman, K.D. Norman, and R. Stevenson (2000). "Navigational Issues in the Design of Online Self-Administered Questionnaires." *Behaviour and Information Technology,* 20: 37–45.

12. Ulwick. A.W. (2002). "Turn Customer Input into Innovation." *Harvard Business Review,* product number 858X.

13. Chen, M.I. (1996). "Competitor Analysis and Intercompany Rivalry: Toward a Theoretical Integration." *Academy of Management Review,* 21(1): 100–134.

14. Bergen, M., and M.A. Peteraf (June–August 2002). "Competitor Identification and Competitor Analysis: A Broad-Based Managerial Approach." *Managerial Decision Economics* 23(4)5: 157–169.

Chapter 7

1. Wolff, M.F. (2003). "Innovation Is Top Priority Again." *Research Technology Management,* 46(4): 7.

2. Cooper, R.G., and S.J. Edgett (2003). "Overcoming the Crunch in Resources for New Product Development." *Research Technology Management,* 46(3): 48.

3. Cooper, R.G. (2001). *Winning at New Products: Accelerating the Process from Idea to Launch,* 3d ed. Boston: Perseus Publishing.

4. Crawford, C.M. (1992). "The Hidden Costs of Accelerated Product Development." *Journal of Product Innovation Management,* 9(3): 188–199.

5. Stevens, G.A., and J. Burley (2003). "Piloting the Rocket of Radical Innovation." *Research Technology Management,* 46(2): 16–26.

6. Ibid.

7. Mankin, E. (2004). "Is Your Product-Development Process Helping—or Hindering—Innovation?" *Strategy & Innovation.* Harvard Business School Press, p. 4.

8. Quinn, J.B. (2000). "Outsourcing Innovation: The New Engine of Growth." *Sloan Management Review,* 41(4): 13–29.

9. Reitzig, M. (Spring 2004). "Strategic Management of Intellectual Property," *Sloan Management Review,* 45(3): 35.

10. *Diamond v. Chakrabarty,* 447 U.S. 303 (1980).

11. Whitford, D. (2006). "Vision Quest." *Fortune Small Business* (April): 46.

12. "Qualifying for a Patent." NOLO Law for All, http://www.nolo.com/encyclopedia/articles/pts/pct3.html#FAQ-294.

13. Bonisteel, S. (2001). "Bounty Hunters Get Bonus for Effort on Amazon Patent." *Newsbytes* (March 14).

14. *Amazon.com, Inc. v. BarnesandNoble.com, Inc.,* 73 F. Supp. 2d 1228 (W.D. Wash. Dec. 1, 1999). Amazon's patent is U.S. Patent No. 5,960,411 (issued September 28, 1999).

15. *State Street Bank & Trust v. Signature Financial Group Inc.,* 149 F.3d 1368, 47 USPQ2d 1596 (Fed. Cir. 1998).

16. Love, J.J., and W.W. Coggins (2001). "Successfully Preparing and Prosecuting a Business Method Patent Application." Presented at AIPLA, Spring 2001, http://www.uspto.gov/web/menu/pbmethod/aiplapaper.rtf.

17. U.S. Patent and Trademark Office: Disclosure Document Program, http://www.uspto.gov/web/offices/com/pac/disdo.html, accessed March 2007.

18. Ibid.

19. Oddi, A.S. (1996). "Un-Unified Economic Theories of Patents: The Not-Quite-Holy Grail." *Notre Dame Law Review*, 71: 267–327.

20. Trademark Act of 1946, 15U.S.C. § 1127.

21. Brown, J.D., and J.E. Prescott (2000). "Product of the Mind: Assessment and Protection of Intellectual Property." *Competitive Intelligence Review*, 11(3): 60.

22. 2001 Duke L. & Tech. Rev. 0018, May 31, 2001.

23. *Whelan v. Jaslow*, 797 F.2d 1222; 21 Fed. R. Evid. Serv. (Callaghan) 571: U.S. Court of Appeals for the Third Circuit (1986).

24. Levine, R. (2006). "Unlocking the iPod," *Fortune* (October 30): 73–74.

25. Ibid., paragraph 22.

Chapter 8

1. Gartner, W.B., K.G. Shaver, E. Gatewood, and J.A. Katz (1994). "Finding the Entrepreneur in Entrepreneurship." *Entrepreneurship: Theory and Practice*, 18(3): 5–10.

2. Ruef, M. (2002). "Strong Ties, Weak Ties, and Islands: Structural and Cultural Predictors of Organizational Innovation." *Industrial and Corporate Change*, 11: 427–429.

3. Bird, B.J. (1989). *Entrepreneurial Behavior*. Glenview, IL: Scott, Foresman; and Kamm, J.B., J.C. Shuman, J.A. Seeger, and A.J. Nurick (1990). "Entrepreneurial Teams in New Venture Creation: A Research Agenda." *Entrepreneurship Theory and Practice*, 14(4): 7–17.

4. Ensley, M.D., J.W. Carland, and J.C. Carland (2000). "Investigating the Existence of the Lead Entrepreneur." *Journal of Small Business Management*, 38(4): 59–88.

5. Aldrich, H., and C. Zimmer (1986). "Entrepreneurship Through Social Networks," in D.L. Sexton and R. W. Smilor (eds), *The Art and Science of Entrepreneurship*. Cambridge, MA: Ballinger, pp. 3–23.

6. Moss Kanter, R. (2001). "A More Perfect Union." *Inc. Magazine* (February): 93–98, http://www.inc.com.

7. Dubini, P., and H. Aldrich (1991). "Personal and Extended Networks Are Central to the Entrepreneurial Process." *Journal of Business Venturing*, 6(5): 305–313.

8. Ibid.

9. Roure, J.B., and M.A. Madique (1986). "Linking Prefunding Factors and High-Technology Venture Success: An Exploratory Study." *Journal of Business Venturing*, 1(3): 295–306.

10. Murray, A.I. (1989). "Top Management Group Heterogeneity and Firm Performance." *Strategic Management Journal*, 10: 125–141.

11. Kamm, J.B., J.C. Shuman, J.A. Seeger, and A.J. Nurick (1990). "Entrepreneurial Teams in New Venture Creation: A Research Agenda." *Entrepreneurship Theory and Practice*, 14(4), 7–17.

12. Anonymous (2002). "Making Virtual Collaborations Work." *Research Technology Management*, 45(2): 6–7.

13. Gersick, C.J.G., and J.R. Hackman (1990). "Habitual Routines in Task-Performing Groups." *Organizational Behavior and Human Decision Processes*, 47: 65–97.

14. Kozlowski, S.W.J., S.M. Gully, P.P. McHugh, E. Salas, and J.A. Cannon-Bowers (1996). "A Dynamic Theory of Leadership and Team Effectiveness: Developmental and Task Contingent Leader Roles," in G.R. Ferris (ed), *Research in Personnel and Human Resource Management*. Greenwich, CT: JAI Press, pp. 253–305.

15. Friedman, M. (2002). "Create the Virtual Company." *Canadian Business and Current Affairs*, accessed via LexisNexis on September 30, 2003; Trialto Wine Group Ltd., http://www.trialto.com; and Winspeer International, Ltd., http://www.winspeer.com.

16. McDougall, P., S. Shane, and B. Oviatt (November 1994). "Explaining the Formation of International New Ventures: The Limits of Theories from International Business Research." *Journal of Business Venturing*, 9: 469–487.

17. Oviatt, B., and P. McDougall (1994). "Toward a Theory of International New Ventures." *Journal of International Business Studies*, 25(1): 45–64.

18. Miesenbock, K.J. (1988). "Small Business and Exporting: A Literature Review." *International Small Business Journal*, 6(2): 42–61.

19. Eisenhardt, K.M. and C.B. Schoonhoven (1996). "Resource-Based View of Strategic Alliance Formation: Strategic and Social Effects in Entrepreneurial Firms." *Organization Science*, 7(2): 136–150.

20. Fiegner, M., B. Brown, D. Dreux, and W. Dennis (2000). "CEO Stakes and Board Composition in Small Private Firms." *Entrepreneurship Theory and Practice*, 24: 5.

21. Kidwell, R.E., and N. Bennett (1993). "Employee Propensity to Withhold Effort: A Conceptual Model to Intersect Three Avenues of Research." *Academy of Management Review*, 18(3): 429–456.

22. Goodstein, J., K. Gautam, and W. Boeker (1994). "The Effects of Board Size and Diversity on Strategic Change." *Strategic Management Journal*, 15(3): 241–250.

23. Lavalle, L. (2002). "The Best and Worst Boards— How the Corporate Scandals Are Sparking a Revolution in Governance." *BusinessWeek* (October 7).

24. AICPA Center for Audit Quality, http://thecaq.aicpa .org/Resources/Sarbanes+Oxley/Sarbanes-Oxley+–+ The+Basics.htm (accessed March 10, 2007).
25. PricewaterhouseCoopers (2003). "The Message in Sarbanes-Oxley." *Growing Your Business,* (July/August).
26. PricewaterhouseCoopers (2007). "Finding the Silver Lining: How Private Companies Can Benefit from the New Governance and Disclosure Standards," http:// www.pwc.com/extweb/pwcpublications.nsf/docid/ 3B79ECB3FEFACFD085256F94005D5098 (accessed March 11, 2007).
27. Jonovic, D.J. "Professionalizing: The Key to Long-Term Shareholder Value, Part 1." Baylor University, http://hsb.baylor.edu/html/cel/ifb/legacies/ jonovic.htm.
28. Ibid.
29. Clifford, S. (2006). "The Worst-Case Scenario." *Inc. Magazine* (November): 111.
30. Lawton, J. (2000). "Mentors for Life." EntreWorld, http://www.entreworld.org.
31. Outsourcing Statistics, Bellsoft, http://www.bellsoftinc .com/outsourcing_s_method.asp (accessed March 10, 2007).
32. Barthelemy, J. (Spring 2001). "The Hidden Costs of Outsourcing." *Sloan Management Review,* 42(3): 60–69.
33. Sovereign, K.L. (1999). *Personnel Law,* 4th ed. Upper Saddle River, NJ: Prentice-Hall.
34. Arabe, K.C. (October 17, 2002). "Outsourcing Manufacturing Spreads." *ThomasNet.com Industrial Market Trends,* http://news.thomasnet.com/IMT/archives/ 2002/10/outsourcing_man.html?t=archive.

Chapter 9

1. McGrath, R.M. (1999). "Falling Forward: Real Options Reasoning and Entrepreneurial Failure." *Academy of Management Review,* 24: 1, 13–31.
2. Collis, D., and C. Montgomery (1995). "Competing on Resources: Strategy in the 1990s." *Harvard Business Review* (July–August): 118–128; and Wernerfelt, B. (1984). "A Resource-Based View of the Firm." *Strategic Management Journal,* 5: 171–180.
3. Covin, J., and D. Slevin (1990). "Content and Performance of Growth-Seeking Strategies: A Comparison of Small Firms in High and Low Technology Industries." *Journal of Business Venturing,* 5(6): 391–412.
4. Docters, R.G. (September/October 1997). "Price Strategy: Time to Choose Your Weapons," *The Journal of Business Strategy,* 18(5): 11–15.

5. Hogan, J.E., and J. Zale (February 15, 2005). "The Top 5 Myths of Strategic Pricing," MarketingProfs.com http://www.marketingprofs.com/5/ hoganzale1.asp.
6. Fishman, C. "Which Price Is Right?" *Fast Company* (February 2003): 68: 92.
7. Based on a feasibility study undertaken by Cassio Goldschmidt and Scott Webb, University of Southern California, 2006.

Chapter 10

1. Lawton, J. (March 1, 1999). "The Just-Right Business Plan." *Entrepreneur's Byline,* http://www.entreworld .org/Content/Entrebyline.cfm?ColumnID_75.
2. Gumpert, D.E. (2002). *Burn Your Business Plan! What Investors Really Want from Entrepreneurs.* Needham, MA: Lauson Publishing.
3. Kelly, P., and M. Hay (2000). "The Private Investor — Entrepreneur Contractual Relationship: Understanding the Influence of Context." in E. Autio et al. (eds), *Frontiers of Entrepreneurship Research.* Wellesley, MA: Babson College.
4. Ibid., 65.
5. Caggiano, C. (October 2002). "A Strategic Misalliance," *Inc. Magazine,* http://www.inc.com/magazine/ 20021015/24786_Printer_Friendly.html.
6. Hankin, R.N. (July 17, 2000). "Creating and Realizing the Value of a Business." *Entrepreneur's Byline,* EntreWorld.org, http://www.eventuring.org/eShip/ appmanager/eVenturing/eVenturingDesktop?_nfpb= true&_pageLabel=eShip_articleDetail&_nfls=false&id= Entrepreneurship/Resource/Resource_226.htm&_ fromSearch=true&_nfls=false.
7. Block, Z., and I.C. Macmillan (1992). "Milestones for Successful Venture Planning," in W.A. Sahlman and H.H. Stevenson (eds), *The Entrepreneurial Venture.* Boston: Harvard Business School Publishing, pp. 138–148.
8. Mason, C.M., and R.T. Harrison (2000). "Investing in Technology Ventures: What Do Business Angels Look for at the Initial Screening Stage?" in E. Autio et al., *Frontiers of Entrepreneurship Research.* Wellesley, MA: Babson College, p. 293.

Chapter 11

1. Curry, J., and J. Bryan (2007). *Statistics of Income Bulletin.* Internal Revenue Service SOI Program.
2. Greco, S. (2001). "Balancing Act." *Inc. Magazine* (January): 56–60, http://www.inc.com.

3. "Partnership Basics." NOLO Law for All, http://www.nolo.com/encyclopedia/articles/sb/partnerships.html.

4. "Partnership Basics." NOLO Law for All, http://www.nolo.com/encyclopedia/articles/sb/buy_sell.html.

Chapter 12

1. Barrier, M. (March 1998). "Doing the Right Thing." *Nation's Business,* http://www.findarticles.com/p/articles/mi_m1154/is_n3_v86/ai_20401415 (accessed April 2007).

2. Payne, D., and B.E. Joyner (2006). "Successful U.S. Entrepreneurs: Identifying Ethical Decision-Making and Social Responsibility Behaviors." *Journal of Business Ethics,* 65: 203–217.

3. Anderson, D., and K. Perine (March 6, 2000). "Marketing the DoubleClick Way." *The Industry Standard Magazine,* http://www.thestandard.com.

4. Brodsky, N. (October 2002). "Street Smarts: The Unkindest Cut of All." *Inc. Magazine.*

5. Evan, W., and R.E. Freeman (1996). "A Stakeholder Theory of the Modern Corporation: Kantian Capitalism," in T. Beauchamp and N. Bowie (eds), *Ethical Theory and Business.* Englewood Cliffs, NJ: Prentice Hall.

6. Banfe, C. (1991). *Entrepreneur—From Zero to Hero.* New York: Van Nostrand Reinhold.

7. Robinson, D.A., P. Davidsson, H. van der Mescht, and P. Court (2007). "How Entrepreneurs Deal with Ethical Challenges—An Application of the Business Ethics Synergy Star Technique." *Journal of Business Ethics,* 71: 411–423.

8. McDonald, G.M., and R.A. Zepp (1989). "Business Ethics: Practical Proposals." *Journal of Business Ethics,* 81: 55–56.

9. Josephson Institute for Ethics, http://www.charactercounts.org/defsix.htm.

10. Kant, I. (1964). *Groundwork of the Metaphysics of Morals.* New York: Harper & Row.

11. Cavanaugh, G.F., D.J. Moberg, and M. Valasquez (1981). "The Ethics of Organizational Politics." *Academy of Management Review,* 6(3): 363–374.

12. Dees, J.G., H.J. Emerson, and P. Economy (2001). *Enterprising Nonprofits: A Toolkit for Social Entrepreneurs.* New York: Wiley.

13. Rubicon Programs, Inc., http://www.rubiconprograms.org (accessed April 2007).

14. The Nature Conservancy, http://www.nature.org, (accessed April 2007).

15. Welles, E.O. (September 1998). "Ben's Big Flop." *Inc. Magazine,* http://www.inc.com/magazine/19980901/995.html.

16. Roper, J., and G. Cheney (2005). "Leadership, Learning, and Human Resource Management: The Meanings of Social Entrepreneurship Today." *Corporate Governance,* 5(3): 95.

17. Thompson, J.L. (2002). "The World of the Social Entrepreneur." *International Journal of Public Sector Management,* 15(4/5): 412–431.

18. Collins, J., and J. Porras (1997). *Built to Last: Successful Habits of Visionary Companies.* New York: HarperBusiness.

19. Ibid., 76.

20. Nash, L. (1988). "Mission Statements—Mirrors and Windows." *Harvard Business Review* (March–April): 155–156; and Schermerhorn Jr., J.R., and D.S. Chappell (2000). *Introducing Management.* New York: John Wiley.

21. "Drucker Foundation Self-Assessment Tool: Content—How to Develop a Mission Statement." Leader to Leader Institute, http://www.leadertoleader.org/knowledgecenter/sat/mission.html, (accessed April 7, 2007).

22. Boyd, D.P., and D.E. Gumpert (1983). "Coping with Entrepreneurial Stress." *Harvard Business Review* (March–April): 44–64.

Chapter 13

1. Barth, H. (2003). "Fit Among Competitive Strategy, Administrative Mechanisms, and Performance: A Comparative Study of Small Firms in Mature and New Industries." *Journal of Small Business Management,* 4(2): 133–148.

2. Hanks, S.H., and G.N. Chandler (1994). "Patterns of Functional Specialization in Emerging High Tech Firms." *Journal of Small Business Management,* 32(2): 22–37; and Jennings, P., and G. Beaver (1997). "The Performance and Competitive Advantage of Small Firms: A Management Perspective." *International Small Business Journal,* 15(2): 63–75.

3. Stone, M.M., and C.G. Brush (1996). "Planning in Ambiguous Contexts: The Dilemma of Meeting Needs for Commitment and Demands for Legitimacy." *Strategic Management Journal,* 17(8): 633–653.

4. Churchill, N., and V. Lewis (1983). "The Five States of Business Growth." *Harvard Business Review,* 61: 30–50.

5. Reed, M.I., and M. Hughes, eds (1996). *Rethinking Organizations: New Directions in Organization*

Theory and Analysis. London: Sage; Hassard, J., and M. Parker (1993). *Postmodernism and Organizations.* London: Sage; and Boje, D.M. (1996). *Postmodern Management and Organization Theory.* Thousand Oaks, CA: Sage.

6. Gumm, D.C. (2006). "Distribution Dimensions in Software Development Projects: A Taxonomy," *IEEE Software* (September/October): 45.

7. Bryne, J.A. (1993). "The Virtual Corporation." *Business Week* (February 8): 98–102.

8. Fitzpatrick, W.M., and D.R. Burke (2000). "Form, Functions, and Financial Performance Realities for the Virtual Organization." *S.A.M. Advanced Management Journal,* 65(3): 13–25.

9. Garaventa, E., and T. Tellefsen (2001). "Outsourcing: The Hidden Costs." *Review of Business,* 22(1/2): 28–32.

10. Watkins, M. (2004). "The First 90 Days." *Association Management,* 56(8): 44–54.

11. Sloane, J. (2007). "Cure Your HR Ills." *Fortune Small Business* (March): 65.

12. Osborne, R.L. (1992). "Minority Ownership for Key Employees: Dividend or Disaster?" *Business Horizons,* 35(1): 76.

Chapter 14

1. Hammer, M. (2004). "Deep Change." *Harvard Business Review* (April): 1.

2. Chang, M. (November 1995). "Turning Raw Materials into Finished Products." *Laser Focus World,* http://lfw.pennnet.com.

3. Anderson, E., and B. Weitz (February 1992). "The Use of Pledges to Build and Sustain Commitment in Distribution Channels." *Journal of Marketing Research,* 29: 18–34; and Doney, P.M., and J.P. Cannon (April 1997). "An Examination of the Nature of Trust in Buyer–Seller Relationships." *Journal of Marketing,* 61: 35–51.

4. Lusch, R.F., and J.R. Brown (October 1996). "Interdependency, Contracting, and Relational Behavior in Marketing Channels." *Journal of Marketing,* 60: 19–38; and Noordewier, T.G., G. John, and J.R. Nevin (October 1990). "Performance Outcomes of Purchasing Arrangements in Industrial Buyer–Vendor Relationships." *Journal of Marketing,* 54: 80–93.

5. "Play Big," *Fortune Small Business* (November 2006): 30.

6. "Feigenbaum's 40 Steps to Quality Improvement," in *Federal Quality Management Handbook,* Appendix

IA: "How to Get Started." (June 1990), http://deming.eng.clemson.edu/pub/tqmbbs/prin-pract/feig40.txt.

7. Ibid.

8. Bartholomew, D. (September 2001). "Cost v. Quality." *Industry Week,* http://www.industryweek.com.

9. Terry, R. (July 23, 2002). "Training Toys." *Washington Techway,* http://www.washtech.com.

10. "Basic Concepts: Process View of Work." *American Society for Quality,* http://www.asq.org/learn-about-quality/process-view-of-work/overview/overview.html (accessed April 22, 2007).

11. Challener, C. (July 16, 2001). "Six Sigma: Can the GE Model Work in the Chemical Industry?" *Chemical Market Reporter,* http://www.findarticles.com.

12. Boswell, C. (July 16, 2001). "Technically, Inc. Boosts Process Development with Six Sigma." *Chemical Market Reporter,* http://www.findarticles.com.

13. "You Can't Manage What You Can't Measure: Maximizing Supply Chain Value." *Knowledge@Wharton* (September 6, 2006), http://knowledge.wharton.upenn.edu/article.cfm?articleid=1546.

14. "Flexibility in the Face of Disaster: Managing the Risk of Supply Chain Disruption." *Knowledge@Wharton* (September 6, 2006), http://knowledge.wharton.upenn.edu/article.cfm?articleid=1102.

15. "The Future of Outsourcing." *BusinessWeek Online* (January 30, 2006), http://www.mhhe.com/omc/arts-frames.htm.

16. "As the BPO Business Grows, There's a Greater Focus on Metrics and Measurement." *Knowledge@Wharton* (January 14, 2005), http://knowledge.wharton.upenn.edu/article.cfm?articleid=1102.

17. "HSBC's Lessons in Outsourcing." *BusinessWeek Online* (January 30, 2006), http://www.businessweek.com/magazine/content/06_05/b3969426.htm (accessed April 22, 2007).

Chapter 15

1. Wind, J. (October 13, 1999). "Marketing Strategy in the Global Information Age." *Knowledge@Wharton,* http://knowledge.wharton.upenn.edu.

2. Cachon, G., C. Terwiesch, and Y. Xu (2006). "On the Effects of Consumer Search and Firm Entry on Multiproduct Competition." Working paper, University of Pennsylvania.

3. Anderson, C. (2006). *The Long Tail.* New York: Hyperion Books.

4. "The Diffusion Process." Ames: Agriculture Extension Service, Iowa State College, Special Report

No. 18, 1957; and Rogers, E. (1962). *Diffusion of Innovation*. New York: The Free Press.

5. Moore, G. (1999). *Crossing the Chasm: Marketing and Selling High-Tech Products to Mainstream Customers*. New York: HarperBusiness.

6. Woodruff, R. (1997). "Customer Value: The Next Source for Competitive Advantage." *Journal of the Academy of Marketing Science*, 25(2): 139–153.

7. Cooper, R.G. (2001). *Winning at New Products*, 3d ed. New York: Perseus.

8. Woodall, T. (2003). "Conceptualization 'Value for the Customer': An Attribution, Structural and Dispositional Analysis." *Academy of Marketing Science Review*, 12.

9. Op. cit., Woodruff, 1997, 141.

10. Smith, J.B., and M. Colgate (2007). "Customer Value Creation: A Practical Framework." *Journal of Marketing Theory and Practice*, 15(1): 7.

11. Frey, D. (February 19, 2002). "Your Seven-Step, One-Day Marketing Plan." http://MarketingProfs.com (accessed April 27, 2007).

12. MacInnis, D. (2006). "Just What Is a Brand, Anyway?" *Marketing Guides*, http://MarketingProfs.com (accessed April 29, 2007).

13. MacInnis, D., and C.W. Park. (2006). "Branding and Brand Equity: Clarifications on a Confusing Topic." *Marketing Guides*, http://MarketingProfs.com (accessed April 29, 2007).

14. Shipley, M. (March 13, 2007). "Keeping the Brand Health: The Annual Brand Checkup." http://MarketingProfs.com (accessed April 29, 2007).

15. "Want to Stand Out? Make a Splash with Mini Billboards," *Inc. Magazine* (December 2006): 35.

16. Levinson, J.C. (2005). *Guerrilla Marketing for the New Millennium: Lessons from the Father of Guerrilla Marketing*. Boston: Houghton Mifflin.

17. McConnell, B., and J. Huba (November 26, 2002). "Top 6 Tips to Understanding Customer Evangelism." http://MarketingProfs.com.

18. Singer, J.G. (Fall 2006). "Systems Marketing for the Information Age." *Sloan Management Review*, 48(1): 96.

19. Bartholomew, D. (September 2001). "Cost v. Quality." *Industry Week*, http://www.industryweek.com.

20. Gupta, S., and D.R. Lehmann (2002). "What Are Your Customers Worth?" *Optimize*, http://www.optimizemag.com/article/showArticle.jhtml?articleId_17700715&pgno_2.

21. Sciortino, J. (2006). "Sharing a Lobster," *Fortune Small Business* (October): 45.

Chapter 16

1. Venkataraman, S. (1997). "The Distinctive Domain of Entrepreneurship Research." *Advances in Entrepreneurship Research: Firm Emergence and Growth*, 3: 119–138; and Gompers, P. (1997). "An Examination of Convertible Securities in Venture Capital Investments." Working paper, Harvard University.

2. Barney, J. (1991). "Firm Resources and Sustained Competitive Advantage." *Journal of Management*, 17(2), 99–120.

3. Brush, C.G., P.G. Greene, M.M. Hart, and H.S. Haller (2001). "From Initial Idea to Unique Advantage: The Entrepreneurial Challenge of Constructing a Resource Base." *The Academy of Management Executive*, 15(1): 64–78.

4. Ibid.

5. Ibid.

6. Kirchhoff, B.A. (2003). "Entrepreneurship Economics," in W.D. Bygrave (ed), *The Portable MBA in Entrepreneurship*, 3d ed. New York: Wiley.

7. Global Entrepreneurship Monitor 2003, http://www.gemconsortium.org (accessed May, 2007).

8. Moore, G. (2002). *Crossing the Chasm*. New York: HarperBusiness.

9. Bhide, A. (1992). "Bootstrapping Finance: The Art of Start-Ups." *Harvard Business Review*, 70(6): 109–117.

10. Clifford, S. (February 2005). "Fast-Growth Firms Sidestep Bank Loans." *Inc. Magazine*, http://www.inc.com.

11. "Brief Profiles of 2004 Inc. 500 Companies." *Inc. Magazine* (October 2003), http://www.inc.com.

12. Ibid.

13. Aldrich, H.E., and E.R. Auster (1986). "Even Dwarfs Started Small: Liabilities of Size and Age and Their Strategic Implications." *Research in Organizational Behavior*, 8: 165–198; Carroll, G. R., and M. Hannan (2000). *The Demography of Corporations and Industries*. Princeton, NJ: Princeton University Press; and Jovanovic, B. (2001). "Fitness and Age: Review of Carroll and Hannan's Demography of Corporations and Industries." *Journal of Economic Literature*, 39: 105–119.

14. Wellner, A.S. (December 2003). "Blood Money." *Inc. Magazine*, http://www.inc.com.

15. Interview with Luis Villalobos, Tech Coast Angeles and ACA (December 1, 2004), http://www.socaltech.com; and Tech Coast Angels, http://www.techcoastangels.com.

16. Mayer, M. (2003). "Taking the Fear Out of Factoring." *Inc. Magazine* (December): 90–97.

Chapter 17

1. PricewaterhouseCoopers/National Venture Capital Association MoneyTree™ Report. Data: Thomson Financial, 2006.

2. Franke, N., M. Gruber, D. Harhoff, and J. Henkel (September 2006). "Venture Capitalists' Evaluations of Start-up Teams: Trade-offs, Knock-out Criteria, and the Impact of VC Experience." *Entrepreneurship Theory and Practice,* 12: 8–20.

3. Shepherd, D. (1999). "Venture Capitalists' Introspection: A Comparison of 'In Use' and 'Espoused' Decision Policies." *Journal of Small Business Management,* 27: 76–87.

4. Baker, M., and J. Wurgler (November 2000). "Market Timing and Capital Structure." Working paper, Harvard Business School, http://som.yale.edu/finance.center/pdf/CapitalStructure.pdf.

5. Reardon, M. (June 4, 2006). "Investors Sue Vonage over IPO." http://news.zdnet.com/2100-1035_22-6079765.html.

6. Renaissance Capital. http://IPOhome.com (accessed May 14, 2007).

7. Hamm, A.F. (February 11, 2005). "Small Start-ups Look to Foreign IPO Markets." *Silicon Valley/San Jose Business Journal,* http://sanjose.bizjournals.com/sanjose/stories/2005/02/14/story3.html.

8. Mikkelson, W.H., M. Partch, and K. Shah (1997). "Ownership and Operating Performance of Companies That Go Public." *Journal of Financial Economics,* 44: 281–308.

9. Peristiani, S., and G. Hong (2004). "Current Issues in Economics and Finance." *Federal Reserve Bank of New York,* 10(2), http://www.newyorkfed.org/research/current_issues (accessed September 2004).

10. Ibid.

11. Brokaw, L. (1992). "The First Day of the Rest of Your Life." *Inc. Magazine,* 15(5): 144.

12. Feldman, A. (September 2005). "Five Ways That Smart Companies Comply." *Inc. Magazine,* http://www.inc.com.

13. "SEC Member Dismayed That SOX Costs, Burdens Still High." *Gazette.net* (November 4, 2005).

14. "IPO Basics: Investment Bankers, Underwriters, and Other Key Players." *Inc. Magazine,* http://www.inc.com (accessed May 11, 2007).

15. Parsons, B. (August 8, 2006). "GoDaddy Pulls Its IPO Filing! Why I Decided to Pull It." http://www.bobparsons.com/WhyIPOPulled.html.

16. Hise, P. (2006). "Off-the-Grid IPOs: An Underused SEC Exemption That Deserves Another Look." *Inc. Magazine* (December): 40.

17. Spekman, R.E., L.A. Isabella, and T.C. MacAvoy (2000). *Alliance Competence: Maximizing the Value of Your Parnerships.* New York: John Wiley & Sons.

18. Anon. (2003). *Managing for Growth: Enabling Sustainable Success in Canadian SMEs.* http://www.business.queensu.ca/media (accessed May 11, 2007).

19. Ahuja, G. (2000). "The Duality of Collaboration: Inducements and Opportunities in the Formation of Interfirm Linkages." *Strategic Management Journal,* 21(3): 317–343.

20. Weaver, K.M., P.H. Dickson, and B. Gibson (1997). "SME-Based Alliance Use: A Three Country Comparison of Environmental Determinants and Individual Level Moderators." Paper presented at the International Council for Small Business Conference, San Francisco, California.

21. Birchard, B. (1999). "Intangible Assets Plus Hard Numbers Equals Soft Finance." *Fast Company* (28): 316, http://www.fastcompany.com (accessed September 2004).

22. "A Universe of Value." *Inc. Magazine* (January 2007): 100–101.

23. Lerner, J., and J. Willinge (April 8, 2002). "A Note on Valuation in Private Equity Settings," *Harvard Business School,* Reprint 9-297-050.

24. Ibid.

25. Ibid., 3.

26. Tuller, L.W. (1994). *Small Business Valuation Book.* Holbrook, MA: Bob Adams, p. 43.

27. Schilt, J.H. (1991). "Selection of Capitalization Rate—Revisited." *Business Valuation Review,* http://www.nacva.com/FTT_PDF/Chapter5+.pdf.

28. Boer, F.P. (2000). "Valuation of Technology Using 'Real Options.'" http://www.boer.org/files/RTMOptions2.doc (accessed September 2004).

Chapter 18

1. Kaplan, S., and R. Foster (2001). *Creative Destruction: Why Companies That Are Built to Last Underperform the Market—and How to Successfully Transform Them.* New York: Doubleday/Currency.

2. Mackey, J., and L. Valinkangas (2004). "The Myth of Unbounded Growth." *Sloan Management Review* (Winter): 89–92.

3. Stanley, M.H.R., L.A.N. Amaral, S.V. Buldyrev, S. Havlin, H. Leschhorn, P. Maass, M.A. Slainger, and H.E. Stanley (1996). "Scaling Behaviour

in the Growth of Companies." *Nature*, 379: 804–806.

4. Bishop, S. (1999). "The Strategic Power of Saying No." *Harvard Business Review* (November/December).

5. Gunther McGrath, R., and I.C. MacMillan (2005). "MarketBusting: Strategies for Exceptional Business Growth." *Harvard Business Review* (March): 4.

6. Ibid., 5.

7. Roberts, M.J. (1999). "Managing Growth." *New Business Venture and the Entrepreneurs*. New York: Irwin/McGraw-Hill.

8. Hannan, M., and J. Freeman (1984). "Structural Inertia and Organizational Change." *American Sociological Review*, 49: 149–164; and McKelvey, B., and H. Aldrich (1983). "Populations, Natural Selection, and Applied Organizational Science." *Administrative Science Quarterly*, 28(1): 101–128.

9. Terpstra, D.E., and P.D. Olson (1993). "Entrepreneurial Start-up and Growth: A Classification of Problems." *Entrepreneurship Theory & Practice* (Spring): 5–20.

10. Charitou, C.D., and C.C. Markides (2003). "Responses to Disruptive Strategic Innovation." *Sloan Management Review* (Winter): 55.

11. Strauss, S. (February 28, 2005). "Five Reasons Why Franchises Flop." *USA Today*.

12. Buchanan, L. (2007). "Find it. Use It." *Inc. Magazine* (May): 93.

13. Mannion, M.J. (July 2003). "Advice on Acquisition Advisors." *Inc. Magazine*, http://www.inc.com.

14. Ibid.

15. Kline, S.R. "Growth and Diversification Through Vertical Integration." *PF Online*, http://www.pfonline.com (accessed June 20, 2004).

16. Ibid., 52

17. Savitz, E. (April 13, 2007). "TiVo: JMP Starts Coverare with Market Outperform; Cites Pending Roll-Out with Comcast." *Tech Trader Daily*, Barrons Online.

18. Austin, N.K. (November 1999). "Sailor's Delight." *Inc. Magazine*, http://www.inc.com; and Charuk, R. "Boat Vendors of the Grenadines," http://www.usual-suspects-sailing.com/exp-grenadines-boat-vendors.htm (accessed September 8, 2007).

19. Karra, N., and N. Phillips (2004). "Entrepreneurship Goes Global." *Ivey Business Journal* (November/December): 1.

20. U.S. Department of Commerce (2000). *U.S. Export Statistics*, http://www.census.gov/foreign-trade/www (accessed September 2004).

21. Oviatt, B.M., and P. McDougall (1995). "Global Start-ups: Entrepreneurs on a Worldwide Stage." *The Academy of Management Executive*, 9(2): 30–44.

22. Ibid.

23. Owens, J.B. (2007). "Who You Need to Know and How to Find Them: Building a Global Network." *Inc. Magazine* (April): 116.

24. Chafkin, M., and N. Tiku (2005). "Twenty-First Century Interactive Treasure Map." *Inc Magazine*, http://www.inc.com/global/globalmap.html. Based on World Bank data.

Chapter 19

1. "Building a Better Blade: Knight & Carver." *EnergyBusiness* (August 2006), http://www.themanufacturer.com/us/energybusiness/article.html?article_id=97.

2. Thurow, L. (2004). "Help Wanted: A Chief Knowledge Officer." *Fast Company* (January): 78, 91.

3. Yates, J.F., and E.R. Stone (1992). "Risk Appraisal," in J.F. Yates (ed), *Risk-Taking Behavior*. New York: John Wiley & Sons.

4. Smeltzer, L.R., and S.P. Siferd (1998). "Proactive Supply Management: The Management of Risk." *International Journal of Purchasing and Materials Management*, 34(1): 38–45.

5. Krause, D.R. (1999). "The Antecedents of Buying Firms' Efforts to Improve Suppliers." *Journal of Operations Management*, 17(2): 205–224.

6. Lee, H.L., V. Padmanabhan, and S. Whang (1997). "The Bullwhip Effect in Supply Chains." *Sloan Management Review*, 43(4): 93–102.

7. Robertson, T.S., and H. Gatignon (1998). "Technology Development Mode: A Transaction Cost Conceptualization." *Strategic Management Journal*, 19(1): 515–531.

8. "Employer Costs for Employee Compensation Summary." U.S. Department of Labor (March 29, 2007), http://www.bls.gov/news.release/ecec.nr0.htm.

9. "Navigating Legal Challenges." *Fortune.com* (January 2007): S3.

10. Briody, D. (2007). "Full Coverage: How to Hedge Your Cyber Risk." *Inc. Magazine* (April): 47.

11. Bachrach, L. (January 22, 2007). "Global 500 CEO Departures at 15 Percent and Sweep All Regions." *Weber Shandwick Worldwide*, http://www.webershandwick.com/newsroom/newsrelease.cfm/contentid.14757.html.

12. Adler, C. (2007). "Find a CEO Who Can Do What You Can't." *Fortune Small Business* (May): 76.

13. Kahn, A.D. (1999). "Facing the Reality of Succession Planning." *The CPA Journal* 69(9): 66–67.

14. Matthews, C. (2001). "Planning for Succession." *Inc. Magazine* (October 17), http://www.inc.com.

15. Parker, P. (2006). "Racing Back." *Fortune Small Business* (March): 79.

16. Zsidisn, G.A., and A. Panelli (2000). "Purchasing Organization Involvement in Risk Assessments, Contingency Plans, and Risk Management: An Exploratory Study." *Supply Chain Management,* 5(4): 187.

17. Buchanan, L. (2003). "How to Take Risks in a Time of Anxiety." *Inc. Magazine* (May), http://www.inc.com.

18. Katz, J.A. (1995). "Which Track Are You On?" *Inc. Magazine* (October): 27.

INDEX

Note: *f* indicates *figure*, *p* indicates *profile*, and *t* indicates *table*.